P9-CSA-519

Anxiety and Its Disorders

ANXIETY
and Its Disorders

THE NATURE AND TREATMENT
OF ANXIETY AND PANIC

DAVID H. BARLOW

State University of New York at Albany

Foreword by Gerald L. Klerman

THE GUILFORD PRESS
New York   London

© 1988 The Guilford Press
A Division of Guilford Publications, Inc.
72 Spring Street, New York, NY 10012

All rights reserved

No part of this book may be reproduced, stored in a retrieval system, or transmitted, in any form or by any means, electronic, mechanical, photocopying, microfilming, recording, or otherwise, without written permission from the Publisher.

Printed in the United States of America

Last digit is print number: 9 8 7 6 5 4 3 2 1

Library of Congress Cataloging-in-Publication Data

Barlow, David H.
   Anxiety and its disorders.

   Includes bibliographies and index.
   1. Anxiety.   I. Title.   [DNLM: 1. Anxiety Disorders.
WM 172 B258a]
RC531.B28   1988   616.85′223   87-24842
ISBN 0-89862-720-6

For Deneige (at 16) and Jeremy (at 14).
May you retain your illusion of control.

FOREWORD

The field of anxiety and anxiety disorders is currently in a period of considerable activity and ferment. New ideas concerning the nature of anxiety have emerged; new modes for investigating the psychology and the biology of this important human emotion have gained widespread attention; and new treatments, psychopharmacological and psychological, have been developed and tested for their efficacy and utility.

Given these circumstances, the publication of this volume is doubly auspicious: first, because, in itself, it is a manifestation of the current activity, and second, because David Barlow has been one of the significant contributors to new knowledge and new thinking about anxiety.

A major feature of the renewed activity in the field of anxiety has involved a rediscovery and re-evaluation of the fundamental insights into anxiety—and, indeed, into all the emotions—that derive from Darwin. Darwin's *The Expression of the Emotions in Man and Animals*, published in 1872, was neglected for many years. After World War II, it was re-evaluated and now stands as the cornerstone for modern thinking about emotional states in general and anxiety states in particular.

Darwin's theory brought all emotional states, including anxiety, within an evolutionary framework. Within this framework, humans share with other mammalian species, particularly primates, emotional capacities. For the species, emotional capacities have played an evolutional adaptive function, comparable in importance to the evolutionary role of morphological structures, such as anatomical parts. Like morphological structures, emotional capacities facilitate the adaptation of the organism to the changing environment and promote the survival of the individual and of the species. With the increasing complexity of primate and other mammalian species, emotional expression has become more differentiated and elaborate. The unique combination of human emotional and linguistic capacities has further contributed to the adaptation of humans to their physical and social environment.

These aspects of the evolutionary significance of emotion have been the subject of intense animal behavior research and cross-species investigation by ethologists. Barlow draws heavily on this work, particularly its human application in the work of Izard and Ekman, in his efforts to relate clinical states to a generalized theory of emotion based on firm evolutionary theory and grounding.

Within these areas of broad agreement, differences still exist. The mental health field, including the area of emotions and anxiety, has long been the arena for various competing theories—competing "paradigms" in the view of Theodore Kuhn, the Princeton historian and philosopher of science. He has proposed that anxiety and anxiety research should be seen as within the outline of three large paradigms: the psychoanalytic paradigm, the biological paradigm, and the behavioral paradigm.

The *psychoanalytic paradigm* had been particularly prominent in the period between World Wars I and II. In this paradigm, anxiety was a signal of the threat of a breakdown of unconscious defenses. The "signal theory" of anxiety, enunciated by Freud in 1923, was the mainstay of psychoanalytic theory, not only of anxiety states, but of all neuroses. This mechanism was thought to be involved in the psychopathogenesis of all neurotic symptoms, including anxiety and phobia.

The *biological paradigm* regarded anxiety as one of the important emotional capacities of the organism within the Darwinian evolutionary view. The main focus of biological research has been to identify the specific mechanisms through which anxiety is mediated. Cannon's basic work enunciated the "fight or flight" reaction and identified the role of the adrenal medulla in the elaboration of adrenaline. Cannon's research was later supplemented by the work of Selye, who demonstrated the importance of the pituitary–adrenocortical system in regulating the secretion of adrenocortical hormone, which came to be regarded as another important response system along with the adrenomedullary system. Selye's concept of stress weighed heavily in military research exploring the precise relationship between anxiety and stress during combat. Research since World War II has focused on those specific brain mechanisms involving the brain monoamines that mediate various stress and anxiety responses—particularly those involving the locus ceruleus—and also on the benzodiazepines, which seem to block many of these reactions.

The *behavioral paradigm* emerged in North America in the period after World War II, although its theoretical bases go back to the writings of Pavlov and Watson in the first decades of the 20th century. A clinical theory of anxiety based on behavioral terms slowly emerged during the 1940s and 1950s. New techniques of behavior therapy were applied to anxiety states, particularly phobias. In this respect, the work of Barlow, in association with Agras, is highly important in demonstrating the power of behavioral techniques directed at sexual symptoms and against various forms of phobia.

By the 1960s, work in North America, South Africa, and the United Kingdom had established phobias as a major target of behavioral techniques. At first, the main sources of tension were between the psychoanalysts and the behavior therapists, as crystallized in the controversial articles on psychotherapy written by Eysenck. In the 1970s, however, the focus shifted. In the past decade, a major source of tension had been between the behavioral and biological theories of anxiety. The pure biological view, expressed by writers such as Sheehan and Klein, holds that panic anxiety is to be differentiated from generalized anxiety. According to this view, panic anxiety represents a specific, genetically determined, endogenous form of anxiety unrelated to situational or environmental stressors, with its predominant treatment found in drugs such as monoamine oxidase inhibitors, tricyclic antidepressants, and newly developed triazolobenzodiazepines, such as alprazolam. In this schema, behavior therapy is in a secondary, rehabilitative role, treating the social disability and phobic withdrawal that develops, according to the biological theory, as a secondary reaction to the biologically generated panic attack.

In contrast, the pure behaviorists, represented by Marks, emphasize the learned nature of anxiety and regard panic anxiety as an intense form of otherwise normal anxiety. They dispute the biologically internal nature of the spontaneous panic attack and claim therapeutic efficacy for behavior therapy, not only in the treatment of phobic avoidance, as seen in the agoraphobic syndrome, but also in the panic attack.

Barlow has played an important role in these intense professional and theoretical controversies. Although trained and most often identified as a behavioral psychologist, he has worked in a variety of settings, including medical psychiatric settings in Vermont, Mississippi, and Rhode Island, and is thoroughly familiar with the theories and rhetoric of medical thinking. Well versed in problems of differential diagnosis and clinical responsibility, he has established at Albany a Center for Stress and Anxiety Disorders, a highly specialized clinical research and teaching facility, within which he and his colleagues have developed the ADIS clinical interview.

Using this technique, Barlow has demonstrated the unique differentiation of the various diagnostic subtypes of anxiety disorder as codified in DSM-III and has produced valid evidence for the separation of panic anxiety from generalized anxiety. In this respect, he stands apart from many other behaviorists. On the other hand, his own research demonstrates the therapeutic value of behaviorally oriented techniques in treating panic anxiety and panic attacks and the relative therapeutic value of behavioral techniques in comparison with drug techniques for both panic anxiety and the phobic avoidance of the agoraphobic syndrome.

Gerald L. Klerman
Cornell University Medical College

PREFACE

"This tale grew in the telling," as J. R. R. Tolkien put it. After years of research and practice, it seemed a straightforward enough task to write a book on the nature and treatment of anxiety disorders. The surge of interest in these disorders during the past 5 years sparked rapid-fire advances in both psychological and pharmacological treatments, and I felt that such a book would be timely. After reviewing these advances, I planned to describe newly developed treatments for the anxiety disorders at our Center for Stress and Anxiety Disorders that take into account innovations from around the world. These treatments would be described in the framework of anxiety disorders as defined and described in the revisions to DSM-III. I told my publisher that I would have it for him in 12 to 18 months.

During this time, our own treatments changed dramatically as exciting new discoveries emerged from our research center and elsewhere on the nature and treatment of panic. These developments seemed to require, at the very least, a full explication of the nature of anxiety and panic based on these new developments. But these developments could not be described adequately without putting them in the framework of current theoretical conceptions of anxiety in general. I found that repeating tried and true theories of anxiety proved totally inadequate, since new conceptual approaches, ranging from neurobiological to social-constructivist, have appeared only in the past 2 years. These models are beginning to affect our view of anxiety. And then there is the mystery of panic!

This confusing combination of new and old perspectives on anxiety and panic led inexorably to a consideration of the nature of emotion. The book stood still for half a year while I absorbed once again the views of emotion theorists and attempted to integrate our rapidly emerging clinical knowledge of anxiety and panic with the old and distinguished tradition of emotion theory dating back to Darwin over 100 years ago. For anxiety disorders, in the last analysis, are emotional disorders. It became increasingly clear that it was impossible to say something fresh about emotional disorders without considering the traditions of emotion theory.

At this point, I started working backward, rewriting the book from the point of view of the accumulated wisdom of emotion theory. After the integration of relevant recent developments in cognitive science and neuroscience, what emerged was a new model of panic and anxiety with implications for treatment. This, in turn, prompted a chapter on the treatment of anxiety, panic, and emotional disorders in general, based on considerations of emotion theory. I have dubbed this approach, rather unoriginally, "affective therapy." These theories and concepts were then integrated with newly developed treatment protocols for the various anxiety disorders. Only then was I able to write the book I intended. After a chapter on the latest developments in classification, the last seven chapters are devoted to a detailed explication of the nature, assessment, and treatment of each anxiety disorder. Descriptions of assessment and treatment are taken from the newest treatment programs for each specific disorder developed in our center. By this time 3 years had passed, and my patient publisher finally received his manuscript. I learned at least as much writing this book as I brought to it. My hope is that others confronting the mysteries of panic and anxiety will find the subject matter in this book as exciting as I have.

This book owes much to interactions with colleagues over the years. I take full responsibility for the fact that their ideas and thoughts may not be represented exactly as they had intended. Nevertheless, in most cases, their contributions will be recognizable. In addition to these contributions, several of my students, colleagues, and friends contributed to this book in a more substantive way. These individuals took the time to read one or more chapters, or even to write brief inserts. In particular, I want to acknowledge with my deepest appreciation the contributions of Jack Maser and Kathy Shear. Each made detailed comments on several chapters. In addition, if they look closely, they will find that some of their own phrasings have crept into the book. The book is better for their attention. Michelle Craske and Ron Rapee read every word of earlier drafts of these chapters, and their comments did much to clarify my thinking at certain places. Janet Klosko and Baledon Coakely made important contributions to the more literary intiatives attempted in Chapter 1.

Beyond these individuals, a number of other friends and colleagues made important comments on one or more chapters. In my own department, Gordon Gallup, Bruce Dudek, Bob Rosellini, and Ed Blanchard updated me on the latest developments in genetics, neurobiology, learning, and stress. Other colleagues and friends who made important contributions by reading and commenting on one or more chapters are Tim Beck,

Tom Borkovec, Bob Cloninger, Carroll Izard, Jack Rachman, Philip Saigh, and Tom Uhde. My gratitude goes to all of them. To Chris Adler, Dave Williams, and Rhonda Salge, who spent many hours poring over hundreds of pages of texts and references to compile a complete and accurate index, I extend my deepest appreciation. Finally, to Mary Ann Beals, who put every word of this book on the word processor and then saw each word (along with a number of new words) three to five more times, as we made our way through seemingly endless revisions, I extend my admiration for her perseverance and her superior stress management abilities.

David H. Barlow
Nantucket Island
August 1987

CONTENTS

Anxiety and Its Disorders

One thing is certain, that the problem of anxiety is a nodal point, linking up all kinds of most important questions; a riddle, of which the solution must cast a flood of light upon our whole mental life.

—Freud (1917/1963, p. 401)

1

The Experience of Anxiety: Shadow of Intelligence or Specter of Death?

In our society, individuals spend billions of dollars yearly to rid themselves of anxiety. More people in the United States visit their physician for anxiety then for coughs or colds. (Marsland, Wood, & Mayo, 1976). Many take away prescriptions for tranquilizers, making these drugs among the most widely used in the world. For these individuals, anxiety is a curse—something they could live without. But could we all live without anxiety? Many of our most prominent philosophers, psychologists, and psychiatrists think not. Some think that it serves a protective function. For others, it is at the very root of what it means to be human. Still others believe that our very ability to adapt and plan for the future depends on anxiety. Consider the thoughts of the well-known early psychologist Howard Liddell:

> The planning function of the nervous system, in the course of evolution, has culminated in the appearance of ideas, values, and pleasures—the unique manifestations of man's social living. Man, alone, can plan for the distant future and can experience the retrospective pleasures of achievement. Man, alone, can be happy. But man, alone, can be worried and anxious. Sherrington once said that posture accompanies movement as a shadow. I have come to believe that anxiety accompanies intellectual activity as *its* shadow and that the more we know of the nature of anxiety, the more we will know of intellect. (Liddell, 1949, p. 185)

Is anxiety the shadow of intelligence? Or is anxiety the overwhelming specter of death and nothingness? The hypothetical advantages of being anxious are considered first.

1

THE SHADOW OF INTELLIGENCE

SURVIVAL

Since women reportedly suffer disproportionately from the pathological effects of anxiety, it is fitting that one of the most eloquent and lucid portrayals of the experience of anxiety comes from a woman. In a short story by M. F. K. Fisher entitled "The Wind Chill Factor,"[1] the character Mrs. Thayer is staying alone in a friend's cottage on the ocean during a brutal winter blizzard. The blizzard has been raging for days; nevertheless, Mrs. Thayer is warm, comfortable, and unconcerned with possible consequences of the storm as she drifts off to sleep.

> A little after four, an extraordinary thing happened to her. From deep and comfortable dreamings she was wrenched into the conscious world, as cruelly as if she had been grabbed by the long hairs of her head. Her heart had changed its slow, quiet beat and bumped in her rib cage like a rabbit's. Her breath was caught in a kind of net in her throat, not going in and down fast enough. She touched her body and it was hot, but her palms felt clammy and stuck to her.
>
> Within a few seconds she knew that she was in a state—perhaps dangerous—of pure panic. It had nothing to do with physical fear, as far as she could tell. She was not afraid of being alone, or of being on the dunes in a storm. She was not afraid of bodily attack, rape, all that. She was simply in panic, or what Frenchmen home from the Sahara used to call *le cafard affolé*. (p. 162)

At this point, Mrs. Thayer experiences an urge to flee that is among the most fundamental and ancient in the behavioral repertoire of living organisms.

> This is amazing, she said. This is indescribable. It is here. I shall survive it or else run out howling across the dunes and die soon in the waves and the wind. Such a choice seemed very close and sweet, for her feeling was almost intolerably wishful of escape from the noise. It was above and against and around her, and she felt that it was invading her spirit. This is dangerous indeed, she said, and I must try not to run outside. That is a suicide wish, and weak. I must try to breathe more slowly, and perhaps swallow something to get back my more familiar rhythms. She was speaking slowly to her whole self, with silent but precise enunciation. (p. 162)

---

1. Fisher, M. F. K. The wind chill factor or, a problem of mind and matter. In *As they were* by M. F. K. Fisher. Copyright 1982 by M. F. K. Fisher. Reprinted by permission of Alfred A. Knopf, Inc. Originally appeared in *The New Yorker*. Page numbers of excerpted passages refer to those in S. Cahill (Ed.), *Women and fiction 2: Short stories by and about women* (pp. 160–166). New York: New American Library, 1978.

Is this experience Liddell's shadow of intelligence? Is there anything intelligent or even useful in an unbearably strong urge to flee the warmth and security of a safe shelter to run headlong into a raging sea? Paradoxically, there probably is, and this tendency may well have been responsible for the survival of the species. But is it only humans who can experience "anxiety" in this way? According to the naturalist Charles Darwin, certainly not.

> With all or almost all animals, even with birds, Terror causes the body to tremble. The skin becomes pale, sweat breaks out, and hair bristles. The secretions of the alimentary canal and of the kidneys are increased, and they are involuntarily voided, owing to the relaxation of the sphincter muscles, as is known to be the case with man, and as I have seen with cattle, dogs, cats, and monkeys. The breathing is hurried. The heart beats quickly, wildly, and violently; but whether it pumps the blood more efficiently through the body may be doubted, for the surface seems bloodless and the strength of the muscles soon fails. . . . The mental faculties are much disturbed. Utter prostration soon follows, and even fainting. A terrified canary-bird has been seen not only to tremble and to turn white about the base of the bill, but to faint; and I once caught a robin in a room, which fainted so completely, that for a time I thought it was dead. (Darwin, 1872, p. 77)

How can this elemental response be useful? As every student in introductory psychology knows, this behavior and the overwhelming emotion associated with it represent the organism's alarm reaction to potentially life-threatening emergencies. The almost reflexive urge to escape or, alternatively, to stand and engage the threat ("flight or fight") seems clearly a behavioral tendency that has been selectively favored in an evolutionary sense. Organisms without this capacity undoubtedly were overwhelmed by the welter of emergencies when the species was young. Organisms able to respond quickly and efficiently to life-threatening situations survived and won the day.

On close inspection, the specific functional contributions of various components of this biological survival mechanism seem clear (Cannon, 1927). Activation of the cardiovascular system is one of the major components. Typically, peripheral blood vessels constrict, thereby raising arterial pressure and decreasing blood flow to the extremities. Excess blood is redirected to the skeletal muscles that can be used to defend oneself in a struggle. Blood pooled in the torso is more available to vital organs that may be needed in an emergency. Often people seem "white with fear"; that is, they blanch with fear as a result of decreased blood flow to the skin. Trembling with fear may be the result of shivering and perhaps piloerection, in which body hairs stand erect to conserve heat during periods of vasoconstriction. These defensive adjustments can also produce the commonly observed "hot" and "cold" spells. Breathing becomes more rapid and usually deeper to provide necessary oxygen to rapidly circulating blood. This increased blood circulation carries oxygen to the brain, where cognitive processes and sensory functions are stimulated. An increased amount of glucose (sugar) is also released from the liver into the bloodstream to further energize various crucial muscles and organs, including the brain. Pupils dilate, presumably to allow a better view of the situation. Hearing becomes more acute, and digestive activity is suspended, resulting in a reduced flow of saliva (the "dry mouth" of fear). There is often pressure to urinate, to defecate, and occasionally to vomit. In the short term, voiding will further prepare the organism for concentrated action and activity; in the longer term, vomiting and diarrhea may be reflexive reactions protecting against the danger of absorption of noxious substances (Beck & Emery, 1985).

Is this mobilization of the organism for fighting or escaping the only behavior associated with our ancient alarm system? It seems not. Consider the following case from our files: A young physician in radiology was attending an Ingemar Bergman movie one evening. The camera focused suddenly on massive bleeding from one character in an unexpected context. The physician slumped over. His companion thought he might be napping, although he had seemed quite interested in the movie to that point. When the physician came to, he was very shaken, realizing that he had fainted unexpectedly. Even more disconcerting was the fact that his faint was due to the sight of blood. In fact, throughout medical school, he had often noticed feeling uneasy in the presence of blood, but had "steeled" himself to the occasion. In all likelihood, he had employed various muscle-tensing strategies that maintain or increase blood pressure (Öst & Sterner, 1987; see Chapter 12). In any case, he remained sufficiently uncomfortable to choose a specialty where contact with blood was minimized. After the Bergman film, his discomfort escalated to a full phobic reaction, causing the avoidance of any situation where he might encounter blood.

Fainting, of course, requires a very different physiological response from that required by fighting or fleeing. Instead of the sustained sympathetically innervated surges in cardiovascular function that are associated with the usual alarm reaction, marked decreases in heart rate and blood pressure precede fainting. Could this also be an adaptive response? Very clearly it could, and it probably was such a response under conditions that existed in millenia past. When under attack, those who responded to injury and bleeding with a dramatic drop in blood pressure, thereby minimizing blood loss and the danger of shock, were far more likely to survive the attack than those who did not. Today, this behavioral action tendency is maladaptively present in the myriad of simple phobics with extreme fears of blood, injury, and injection (see Chapter 12).

4

But what of Darwin's robin, which presumably did not see blood, but nevertheless fainted so completely when caught that Darwin thought it was dead? Is this the same reaction as that described above? Probably not. In recent years, investigators have rediscovered an archaic response that seems to be yet another action tendency associated with alarm reactions in specific situations. When in the presence of an approaching predator, and particularly when in direct contact with a predator, most species will initially evidence the agitation associated with fight or flight. This reaction may be followed immediately by a very different response similar to paralysis, but characterized by waxy flexibility. These animals look as if they were dead, as did Darwin's robin. In fact, this is the "playing dead" or "freezing" response so often seen in animals in the wild under attack. Investigators in this area refer to the response as "tonic immobility" (Gallup, 1974) and differentiate it from the temporary motionless response exhibited by many animals preceding their attempts to flee from a predator seen at a distance (Woodruff & Lippincott, 1976). But investigators have determined that tonic immobility is not a volitional or strategic strategy on the part of the animal. Rather, this response represents another ancient behavioral reaction with obvious survival value. For the large number of predators for whom attack is triggered and maintained by movement, freezing is an effective antidote that prevents further attack and increases the victim's chances of survival.

This response may have important biological implications for human anxiety, as outlined in Chapter 5. But investigators concerned with human anxiety have showed little interest in tonic immobility, since it has not been thought to occur in humans. Now it seems we may have overlooked a tragic but obvious example of this reaction in humans. During brutal rapes, many women report feeling paralyzed. Comments such as "I felt trembling and cold—I went limp," or "My body felt paralyzed," or "My body went absolutely stiff" reflect this paralytic state. This may be analogous to the muscular rigidity and motor inhibition evidenced by animals during tonic immobility following manual restraint. Loss of consciousness does not occur, since the victim can later relate events that occurred during the attack. Some victims have reported feeling "freezing cold," which may reflect the characteristic decrease in body temperature of immobile animals. Many rape victims also report feeling completely numb or insensitive to pain during the ordeal; this may be similar to the analgesic effects of immobility observed in animals. Burgess and Holmstrom (1976) reported that 22 out of 34 rape victims demonstrated physical paralysis at some point during the encounter. The similarities between tonic immobility and rape-induced paralysis have been outlined by Suarez and Gallup (1979) and are found in Table 1.1.

It is not clear that the survival response of freezing obviates some of the dangers of rape. One could speculate that freezing decreases the risk

5

TABLE 1.1. Similarities between Tonic Immobility and
Rape-Induced Paralysis

Tonic immobility	Rape-induced paralysis
Profound motor inhibition	Inability to move
Parkinsonian-like tremors	Body shaking
Suppressed vocal behavior	Inability to call out or scream
No loss of consciousness	Recall for details of the attack
Apparent analgesia	Numbness and insensitivity to pain
Reduced core temperature	Sensation of feeling cold
Abrupt onset and termination	Sudden onset and remission of paralysis
Aggressive reactions at termination	Attempts to attack the rapist following recovery

Note. From Suarez, S. D., & Gallup, G. G., Jr. (1979). Tonic immobility as a response to rape in humans: A theoretical note. The Psychological Record, 29, 315–320. Copyright 1979 by The Psychological Record. Reprinted by permission.

of injury from physical aggression. Furthermore, restricted movement cues may reduce sexual arousal in the rapist (Suarez & Gallup, 1979). But recognizing that rape victims are paralyzed or tonically immobile could prevent a tragic interpretation by many authorities, who have assumed in the past that the victim is somehow acquiescing to the rape.

THE SOUND OF THE WIND

If these responses are termed "anxiety," and one considers it "intelligent" to avoid threats successfully, then anxiety may be the shadow of intelligence. But most would not consider this behavior to be "intelligent" in the sense of a complex rational response. Nevertheless, it shares something of Howard Liddell's conception, in that it is adaptive, useful, and indispensable.

But there is something very mysterious about the fictional Mrs. Thayer's experience that does not fit the Darwinian scenario. "It had nothing to do with physical fear, as far as she could tell. She was not afraid of being alone, or of being on the dunes in a storm. She was not afraid of bodily attack, rape, all that" (Fisher, 1978, p. 162). The threat in her own mind is not the storm or being alone, but the urge to flee itself: "This is dangerous indeed, she said, and I must try not to run outside. That is a suicide wish, and weak" (p. 162). But the "suicide wish" is more than a flirtation with death running through her head in the form of frightening thoughts. There are other components to this threat within her:

> The sound of the wind, for her, had been going sideways exactly on a line with the far horizon of the Atlantic for days, nights—too long. It was in her bowels and suddenly they were loosened, and later, again

to her surprise, she threw up. She told herself dizzily that the rhythm of the wind had bound her around, and that now she was defying it, but it kept on howling. (p. 165)

How does one cope with this human experience where the threat is internal and the consequence is death? With great difficulty, Mrs. Thayer struggles to walk to the kitchen, where she takes two aspirins and a mug of warm milk. Ritualistically, she remembers advice that during periods of deep stress one should drink the liquid in three slow sips, wait 5 minutes before taking three more sips, and so on. After the medicine and the rituals, she turns to other more psychological methods of coping:

> She pulled every trick out of the bagful she had collected during her long life with neurotics. She brushed her hair firmly, and all the while her heart kept ticking against her ribs and she felt so sick that she could scarcely lift her arm. She tried to say some nursery rhymes and the Twenty-third Psalm, but with no other result than an impatient titter. She sipped the dreadful sweet milk. She prayed to those two pills she had swallowed. (p. 163)

But at the last she turns to the great arbiter of all human difficulties, one's own reason.

> For a time, as the aspirin and the warm milk seemed to slow down her limitless dread (Dread of what? Not that the roof would fly off, that she was alone, that she might die. . .), she made herself talk reasonably to what was pulling and trembling and flickering in her spirit. She was a doctor—or, rather, an unwitting bystander caught in some kind of disaster, forced to be cool and wise with one of the victims, perhaps a child bleeding toward death or an old man pinned under a truck wheel. She talked quietly to this helpless, shocked soul fluttering in its poor body. She was strong and calm. All the while, she knew cynically that she was nonexistent except in the need thrust upon her, and that the victim would either die or recover and forget her dramatic saintliness before the ambulance had come.
> "Listen to your breathing," she said coolly. "You are not badly hurt. Soon you will feel all right. Sip this. It will make the pain go away. Lift your head now, and breathe slowly. You are not really in trouble." And so on. Whenever the other part of Mrs. Thayer, the threatened part, let her mind slip back to the horror of an imminent breaking with all reason—and then, so then, out the door it would be final—the kindly stranger seemed to sense it in the eyeballs and the pulse as she bent over the body and spoke more firmly: "Now hold the cup. You can. I know you can. You will be all right." (p. 164)

Mrs. Thayer perseveres and later decides that the pills, helped by the warm drink, have worked. She concludes that her mind has not failed her as she attempts to distract herself with the Twenty-third Psalm and convince herself that "she would never have run out like a beast, to die quickly on the dunes" (p. 165). Later she reflects on her experience.

> In another two hours everything was all right inwardly in her, except that she was languid, as if she had lain two weeks in a fever. The panic that had seized her bones and spirit faded fast, once routed. She was left wan and bemused. Never had she been afraid—that is, of tangibles like cold and sand and wind. She was not afraid, as far as she knew, of dying either fast or slowly. It was, she decided precisely, a question of sound. If the storm had not lasted so long, with its noise so much into her, into her brain and muscles . . . If this had been a kind of mating, it was without joy.
>
> . . . And during the late afternoon while she dozed with a deep, soft detachment, the sound abated and then died, and she was lost in the sweet dream life of a delivered woman. (p. 166)

TERMS AND MEANINGS

Mrs. Thayer's experience, and her methods of coping both during and after the experience, illustrate what is essential and mysterious about the human emotion we call anxiety. Is it really the wind that causes Mrs. Thayer's panic? Or is the search for causes necessitated by some fundamental human quality that cannot let events such as this go unexplained? Is it better that she find a cause, even if incorrect, than that she not search at all?

In fact, speculation concerning cues has played a pivotal role in theorizing about anxiety over the years. Many early theorists, among them Kierkegaard and Freud, based definitions and distinctions of "fear" and "anxiety" on the presence or absence of cues. For most, one important distinction became prominent: "Fear" was seen as a reaction to a specific, observable danger, while "anxiety" was seen as a diffuse, objectless apprehension. Theorizing about anxiety, then, involved a search for "hidden" cues that was not unlike Mrs. Thayer's speculations on the sound of the wind. This distinction between fear and anxiety produced the rich theoretical framework that still underlies much of our thinking on the development of psychopathology. Standard definitions of "fear" and "anxiety" in dictionaries and introductory psychology textbooks continue to refer to the presence or absence of identifiable cues as the essential distinction. The ascendance of direct behavioral approaches to treating fears and phobias began to change that, however (Wolpe, 1958). Behavior therapy assumed that all anxiety has clear identifiable cues, although some cues are more diffuse than others (e.g., patterns of light and dark, etc.). The distinction between "fear" and "anxiety" became blurred for many, and these terms increasingly are equated in psychology and psychiatry.

But terminology describing experiences such as Mrs. Thayer's is more varied and confusing than the hypothetical distinction between fear and anxiety. Among many terms in common use in the English language today are "anxiety, "fear," "dread," "phobia," "fright," "panic," and "apprehensiveness." Each of these terms often is qualified with such words as "acute," "morbid," "generalized," "diffuse," and so forth to provide different shades of meaning. In addition, no student of anxiety reflecting on terminology can omit the German word *angst*. Although difficult to translate, this word forms the basis for much of our thinking about the role of anxiety in psychopathology, since it was the word used by both Kierkegaard and Freud. For Kierkegaard, *angst* would be both "dread" and "anxiety"; however, sometimes one is used in English translations of Kierkegaard and sometimes the other. For Freud, *angst* came to reflect the notion of anxiety without an identifiable object. Rather, *angst* was a vague apprehension about the future (although the theoretical significance focused on the present and the past). When anxiety had an object, Freud also preferred the word *furcht* (fear). Although "anxiety" is the word with which we are now familiar, Sir Aubrey Lewis (1980) suggests that a more precise translation of *angst* would be "agony," "dread," "fright," "terror," "consternation," "alarm," or "apprehension." Essentially, the word *angst* signifies a far more shattering emotion than the English word "anxiety," which often is used as synonymous with "concern." As Lewis (1980) points out, the relevant root word passed down from Greek and Latin is *angh*, which refers literally in Latin to the concept of narrowness or constriction. Various derivatives of this root have evolved differently in different Western languages, as one can see by examining the number of words in English with the *angh* root. Among these are "anxiety," "anguish," and "anger."

The profusion of meanings and flavors surrounding the key words *angst*, "anxiety," and "dread"; the somewhat different usages in different languages; and the imprecision resulting from translations of seminal works have all resulted in an understandable vagueness surrounding the term "anxiety" in English. The short history of the usage of the term in psychopathology has produced even less precision. In recent years, "anxiety" has been used to refer to emotional states such as doubt, boredom, mental conflict, disappointment, bashfulness, and feelings of unreality. Various cognitive deficits, such as lack of concentration, are also labeled "anxiety." In addition, the term has been inextricably bound up with the variety of terms describing depressive emotional states. The emergence of theoretical and descriptive qualifiers (e.g., "unconscious," "conscious," "cognitive," "somatic," "free-floating," "bound," "signal") produces further confusion. For this reason, the difficulty in settling on precise distinctions among the anxiety-related terms in English is not surprising.

This state of confusion has caused some to propose that we drop the word altogether, since it is so imprecise as to be unscientific (Sarbin, 1964). In fact, Sarbin and modern-day social constructivists such as Hallam (1985) have proposed new ways of thinking about the concept. For example, Hallam suggests that anxiety is essentially a lay construct that can refer to vastly different cognitive and somatic points of reference from person to person (see Chapter 2). For social constructivists, anxiety is best considered a metaphor. For the moment, I forgo my own definitions of the crucial terms "anxiety," "fear," "panic," "apprehension," and so on; I elaborate on these terms at appropriate points in later chapters.

BEING AND PREPARING

Mrs. Thayer can find no reason for her panic until deciding, upon reflection, that the cause is the incessant sound of the storm. For this reason, many would say that her experience is one of anxiety rather than fear, although in the past 5 years many would employ the term "panic" as she herself does. But what could be the purpose of this experience? If Darwinian fear and panic facilitate survival, what is the purpose of "anxiety" in the traditional usage of the term, where there is nothing to fear? Philosophers preoccupied with a search for cues have often decided that there is something very valuable indeed in this experience, which may lead one, in an ironic way, to a greater sense of fulfillment and actualization.

Kierkegaard (1844/1944) was one of the first to make this suggestion when he decided that the source of anxiety is deep within the individual. Anxiety, thought Kierkegaard, is rooted not just in a fear of death, but in a fear of nonexistence, nonbeing, or nothingness. Only through recognizing and confronting this fear of becoming nothing—only through the threat of dissolution of the self—can one truly discover the essence of being. Only through this experience can one achieve a clear distinction of the self from other objects or from nonbeing.

More recent well-known theorists and clinicians have settled on a similar cause for diffuse and objectless anxiety. For example, Rollo May (1979) has proposed:

> [Anxiety is] the apprehension cued off by a threat to some value that the individual holds essential to his existence as a personality. The threat may be to physical life (a threat of death), or to psychological existence (the loss of freedom, meaninglessness). Or the threat may be to some other value which one identifies with one's existence (patriotism, the love of another person, "success," etc.). (p. 180)

In the sense that this confrontation results in a higher level of existence and a greater appreciation of what it is to be alive, this may represent the shadow of intelligence, and the purpose and meaning of anxiety.

As Freud saw it, *angst* can be cued by activation of elemental threats to the child, which are stored deep in memory and elicited in the adult by a variety of learned associations (Freud, 1926/1959; Michels, Frances, & Shear, 1985). In this sense, anxiety is related to the persistence of remembered danger situations that seemed real at an earlier stage of development. For example, the developmentally immature fears of castration or separation may be activated by the emergence of an associated wish or by the occurrence of a symbolically linked situation currently present in one's environment. Anxiety functions to warn of a potential danger situation and triggers the recruitment of internal psychological and/or external protective mechanisms. The institution of effective psychological defense mechanisms serves the adaptive purposes of protecting the integrity of the individual and allowing a higher and more mature level of functioning. Anxiety may also be adaptive in recruiting help from others when there is real danger. Sometimes defensive reactions are inadequate and lead to symptom formation. These may include phobic or compulsive symptoms that are symbolically related to the unconscious wishes or fears that have generated the anxiety. Self-defeating aspects of anxiety are further elaborated below.

Freud would view the raging storm and incessant noise of Mrs. Thayer's blizzard as providing sensory stimuli indicative of a real threat. Anxiety occurs in reaction to the possibility of being overwhelmed by this threat and rendered helpless. The sense of ultimate separation and isolation one can only experience alone in a blizzard may also elicit memories of childhood fears of separation. For Mrs. Thayer, this dual challenge leads to the emergence of unmanageable levels of anxiety and a strong primitive urge to find some human contact.

But even these popular and still current ideas probably do not capture Liddell's meaning when he talked of anxiety as the shadow of intelligence. Although Liddell was talking of human experience, his scientific explorations concerned the development of pathological anxiety in animals. In his most famous experiments, he produced what came to be called "experimental neurosis" (see Chapter 7). One consequence of experimental neurosis is that animals become more vigilant concerning future threats. Liddell theorized that vigilance has positive consequences in addition to simply helping the animal to notice more quickly the next threat to its well-being. He observed that vigilant animals seem to be conditioned or to learn more easily. Vigilance, therefore, which Liddell supposed to be the animal counterpart of anxiety, may produce more learning and therefore more intelligent animals. But it is the type of learning that is particularly important. The vigilant animal, occupied as it was with future threat, is concerned with what is going to happen in the immediate future. In a very elementary sense, the animal is planning for that future by taking an orientation to the future best characterized by the question

"What happens next?". The planning function is apparant. In humans, this is extremely adaptive. Liddell suggested that effective planning for the future and the retrospective enjoyment of past achievements are the means by which human beings construct culture. The capacity to experience anxiety and the capacity to plan are therefore two sides of the same coin. It is in this sense that anxiety accompanies intellectual activity as its shadow.

Anyone who has succeeded at any task, however small, has probably experienced some aspect of this fascinating and mysterious quality of anxiety. For we have known for 80 years that our physical and intellectual performance is driven and enhanced by the experience of anxiety, at least up to a point. In 1908, Yerkes and Dobson demonstrated this in the laboratory by showing that the performance of animals on a simple task was better if they were made "moderately anxious" than if they were experiencing no anxiety at all. Since that time, similar observations have been made concerning human performance in a wide variety of situations and contexts. Without anxiety, little would be accomplished. The performance of athletes, entertainers, executives, artisans, and students would suffer; creativity would diminish; crops might not be planted. And we would all achieve that idyllic state long sought after in our fast-paced society of whiling away our lives under a shade tree. This would be as deadly for the species as nuclear war.

In summary, several centuries of thought from very diverse sources have emphasized the importance of anxiety to creativity, intelligence, and survival itself. But it is unlikely that Mrs. Thayer, trapped in her cottage on the ocean at the height of a storm, comes to consider it a growth experience. For her in her fictional setting, as well as for countless millions of individuals in the course of their everyday existence, it is a dramatic life-and-death struggle with the ever-present possibility that death may win out. And there is evidence that death does win out on occasion, as a result of the cumulative consequences of anxiety.

THE SPECTER OF DEATH

THE NEUROTIC PARADOX

In 1950, O. Hobart Mowrer described a mystery:

> [It is] the absolutely central problem in neurosis and therapy. Most simply formulated, it is a paradox—the paradox of behavior which is at one and the same time self-perpetuating and self-defeating! . . . Common sense holds that a normal, sensible man, or even a beast to the limits of his intelligence, will weigh and balance the consequences of his acts: if the net effect is favorable, the action producing it will be perpet-

12

uated; and if the net effect is unfavorable, the action producing it will be inhibited, abandoned. In neurosis, however, one sees actions which have predominently unfavorable consequences; yet they persist over a period of months, years, or a lifetime. (p. 486)

This paradox is seen daily in clinics all over the world. Consider the case of John Madden, the well-known American sports announcer and former professional football coach, who has written widely about his anxiety and uses it in a humorous manner in several television commercials. While Madden has overcome the stigma and embarrassment that would be keenly felt by any 6'4", 260-pound former football player whose business is to be tough and courageous, he has not overcome the anxiety itself. Rather than taking a few hours to fly from New York to Los Angeles to announce the next football game, he must spend the better part of his week on a train going across the country. In fact, his fears are not limited to planes, but extend to all claustrophobic situations.

Although Madden was always tense in planes, he originally thought of his tension as a reaction to altitude, probably the symptoms of an inner ear infection. When he realized that his anxiety began before the plane took off, but after the stewardess closed the door, he questioned his previous diagnosis. One day while flying across the country, he experienced a particularly severe panic attack, left the plane at a stop halfway across the United States, and never flew again.

John Madden and countless millions of other individuals suffering from anxiety-based disorders are well aware that there is little or nothing to fear in the situations they find so difficult. Therefore, in Mowrer's terms, Madden should have long since weighed the consequences of his acts and decided that, since flying is the safest way to travel, it would be in his best interest to fly in order to save himself time and help maintain his lucrative career. And yet he does not and cannot abandon his self-defeating behavior. One might say that if Madden at least attempted to fly, he would learn something that does not seem amenable to the rational force of persuasion by either himself or others—namely, that flying is safe. But we know from years of clinical and scientific experience that even forced exposure to difficult situations does not always resolve the paradox.

The self-defeating nature of anxiety and its consequences is dramatically elaborated in psychoanalytic theory. Freud saw anxiety as the psychic reaction to danger. A situation can be defined as dangerous if it threatens a person with helplessness in the face of threat. Dangers regarding the external world lead to realistic anxiety, and dangers to conscience result in moral anxiety; however, dangers surrounding the strength of the passions lead to neurotic anxiety. Neurotic anxiety originates from an inner instinctual wish that is associated with a reactivation of an infantile fear situation. The generation of anxiety in any of these spheres leads to the institution of a defense mechanism. All forms of anxiety occur in normal individuals. In the process of development, individuals learn to modify and modulate the expression of anxiety from its most disruptive intense form to an unnoticeable form called "signal anxiety." Signal anxiety is imperceptible to the person experiencing it, and serves the sole purpose of rapidly and efficiently triggering a defensive reaction. Thus, normal anxiety is limited in intensity and duration and is associated with adaptive defenses. Anxiety is self-defeating or pathological when it is noticeable, intense, disruptive, and paralyzing, or when it triggers self-defeating defensive processes, also called "symptoms." Phobic and obsessive symptoms are especially common in reaction to anxiety. These symptoms represent an insufficient attempt at warding off a danger situation, and typically incorporate elements of the danger. For example, a dog phobia may develop in connection with the activation of an infantile fear of castration. The fear is displaced, but the aggressive component is retained.

In the world of Freud, we confront our infantile modes of psychological functioning. Pathological anxiety emerges in connection with some of our deepest and darkest instincts. Before Freud, the embodiment of good and evil and of urges and prohibitions was conceived of as external and spiritual, usually in the guise of demons confronting the forces of good. Since Freud, we ourselves have become the battleground of these forces, and we are inexorably caught up in the battle, sometimes for better and sometimes for worse.

MORTALITY

If anxiety, in the minds of some, is apprehension over confronting nothingness, consider the consequences of severe anxiety, which result occasionally in physical destruction or death. Consider the man with fears of choking so severe that he consumes only strained and blended food; the results may be malnourishment, loss of teeth, and eventually death. Or consider the obsessive–compulsive woman who ritualistically washes and disinfects her arms and legs for the better part of her waking day; the results may be massive abrasions, bleeding, and scabbing.

While self-defeating behavior associated with anxiety may occasionally produce death, the long-term consequences of anxiety itself may hasten the dreaded confrontation with nothingness. Long-term follow-up studies of both inpatients (Coryell, Noyes, & Clancy, 1982) and outpatients (Coryell, Noyes, & House, 1986) have found a greater-than-expected mortality rate in patients with original diagnoses of anxiety neurosis, particularly panic disorder. This excess mortality rate was attributed primarily to cardiovascular disease and suicide. In fact, suicide rates in anxious patients were equal to or slightly greater than those of a matched

14

group of patients suffering from depression at follow-up. Interestingly, excess mortality due to cardiovascular disease was limited to males with panic disorder. Expected death rates for females with panic disorder from cardiovascular disease were normal.

Death by suicide is an event most often associated with depression. The fact that preliminary studies find an equal frequency in patients with anxiety neurosis is a frightening discovery. Why would people who are anxious kill themselves? Coryell *et al.* (1986) speculate that patients diagnosed with anxiety disorders may subsequently develop major depression or alcoholism as a complication. It is possible that earlier studies overlooked the possibility of suicide in anxious patients because they noticed only the subsequent complication of alcoholism or depression. But if alcoholism or depression is a consequence of anxiety, then the long road to suicide may begin with anxiety.

ANXIETY AND SUBSTANCE ABUSE

Suicide may be an extreme consequence of the experience of anxiety, but evidence indicates that another self-destructive behavior is not. A series of investigations suggests that the relationship of substance abuse, particularly alcohol abuse, to anxiety disorders is startlingly high. For example, Quitkin, Rifkin, Kaplan, and Klein (1972) reported in some detail on 10 patients with anxiety disorders who also suffered severe complications from drug and alcohol abuse. The important suggestion by Quitkin *et al.* (1972) was that patients presenting with substance abuse problems may well be self-medicating an anxiety disorder. Thus, any treatment program for such alcoholics or drug abusers must target this anxiety if the program is to be successful, as well as if it is to prevent relapse.

While this has always been a common clinical observation, a study by Mullaney and Trippett (1979) attracted new attention to this potentially severe complication of anxiety. They discovered that 33% of 102 alcoholics also had severe, disabling agoraphobia and/or social phobia. In addition, another 35% had mild versions of the same phobias. Thus, over 60% of a large group of alcoholics admitted to an alcoholism treatment unit presented with identifiable anxiety disorders of varying severity. Smail, Stockwell, Canter, and Hodgson (1984) explored this same question in a particularly systematic and skillful way. They found similar although somewhat less dramatic results. Specifically, 18% of a group of 60 alcoholics also presented with severe agoraphobia and/or social phobia, with another 35% evidencing mild versions of the same phobias. Once again, over half (53%) of this group of alcoholics had identifiable anxiety disorders.

Other, more recent studies have come to similar conclusions. For example, Chambless, Cherney, Caputo, and Rheinstein (1987) carefully interviewed a group of 75 inpatient alcoholics and ascertained that 40% presented with a lifetime diagnosis of one or more anxiety disorders. The 40% figure in this case was conservative, referring only to anxiety disorders of a level of severity that would be seen in an anxiety disorders clinic. Studies using even more conservative criteria have also reported a rather high range from 25% to 45% of severe alcoholics presenting with one or more anxiety disorders (Bowen, Cipywnyk, D'Arcy, & Keegan, 1984; Mullan, Gurling, Oppenheim, & Murray, 1986; Powell, Penick, Othmer, Bingham, & Rice, 1982; Weiss & Rosenberg, 1985). Finally, Cox, Norton, Dorward, and Fergusson (in press) found that over 50% of a group of inpatient alcoholics reported at least one panic attack in the prior 3 weeks. Over 80% of these patients reported using alcohol to self-medicate their panic attacks.

The above-mentioned studies looked at the incidence of anxiety disorders in diagnosed alcoholics. Another approach involves examining the incidence of alcoholism in patients diagnosed as having an anxiety disorder. Thyer, Parrish, et al. (1986) found that 27 out of 156 anxiety disorder patients, or 17.3%, scored in the alcoholic range on the Michigan Alcoholism Screening Test. Bibb and Chambless (1986) also found from 10% to 20% of outpatient agoraphobics to be alcoholics. Anxiety patients who were also alcoholics generally presented with more severe anxiety. Woodruff, Guze, and Clayton (1972) found that 25% of their sample of anxiety neurotics were problem drinkers and that 15% of the total sample could be characterized as physically dependent on alcohol.

The obvious question is this: Which comes first, the anxiety or the substance abuse? Several investigators have looked at this issue, and the evidence emerging suggests that a complex relationship exists. Retrospective studies indicate that severe anxiety precedes the onset of drinking or substance abuse in most cases (Chambless et al., 1987; Mullaney & Trippett, 1979; Smail et al., 1984). Only one study suggests that alcoholism consistently predates the development of anxiety (Mullan et al., 1986). But this study, examining the onset of alcoholism and anxiety in twins from the Maudsley Twin Register, made the questionable assumption that identical twins also have similar anxiety disorders and underlying neuroticism; this is not true (see Chapter 5). Even in the remaining studies, however, there are some patients for whom the development of anxiety seems to follow serious substance abuse. Also, periods of abstinence seem to result in a general improvement in fear and anxiety in many patients (e.g., Stockwell, Smail, Hodgson, & Canter, 1984). Finally, there is now direct experimental evidence of a phenomenon reasonably well documented in the field of alcoholism: That is, contrary to myth, alcohol does not necessarily reduce anxiety and fear, and may in fact worsen it (Thyer & Curtis, 1984). As Stockwell et al. (1984) suggest, severe anxiety disorders may well precede substance abuse in many cases, and the alcohol (or drugs) may be used primarily for anxiolytic purposes by these patients. But once a patient is addicted, the alcohol (or drugs) may have a deleterious effect on mood, creating a vicious cycle. For this reason, patients with anxiety disorders who are also alcoholic may present with more severe anxiety (Chambless *et al.*, 1987) *because* of the use of alcohol. Thus, anxiety self-medicated with alcohol results in an ever-increasing downward self-destructive spiral—not only from the effects of alcohol (or drug) addiction, but also from the exacerbating effects of the drugs on the anxiety itself. It may be this complication, along with the development of helplessness and depression, that leads to the increased risk of suicide in patients with anxiety (Coryell *et al.*, 1986).

SURGERY

Substance abuse is usually a self-initiated attempt to cope with the unbearable experience of anxiety. In its most severe form, the paralysis and self-destruction associated with anxiety have led to equally dramatic attempts on the part of concerned health care practitioners to alleviate this suffering. Among the more dramatic efforts is psychosurgery (Marks, Birley, & Gelder, 1966; Smith & Kiloh, 1980). As with any major surgical procedure, death is a complication. Causes of death most often are cerebral hemorrhage or edema, although the use of stereotactic techniques and the trend toward more precise and limited lesions have greatly decreased the risk of serious side effects. Psychosurgical procedures as a treatment for anxiety disorders have been reported in the literature on thousands of patients (e.g., Smith & Kiloh, 1980). While rare in the United States and Great Britain, this therapeutic procedure is fairly standard in some countries. It is probably safe to conclude that hundreds of thousands of patients have consented to this surgical treatment, most often after all other treatments have failed. Positive effects, when they occur, are reportedly related to a decrease in emotionality. This, in turn, may make patients more amenable to therapy directed at behavioral components of anxiety disorders, such as phobic avoidance or rituals.

PREVALENCE

Anxiety kills relatively few people, but many more would welcome death as an alternative to the paralysis and suffering resulting from anxiety in its severe forms. Millions of individuals each year seek help for what is broadly construed as "anxiety" or "nervousness." Statistics compiled from the offices of front-line primary care practitioners startle even the most jaded experts in the area. In the state of Virginia, investigators surveying the reasons why patients sought out their local physicians found that hypertension, cuts and bruises, and sore throats ranked right behind a general medical checkup as the most common reasons motivating a visit. Close behind these common maladies was "anxiety," ranking well ahead of even bad colds or bronchitis (Marsland *et al.*, 1976). One poll, using reliable sampling methodology and conservative definitions, revealed that from 30% to 40% of the general population sufficiently suffered from the presence of anxiety that clinical intervention would have been useful (Shepherd, Cooper, Brown, & Kalton, 1966).

Is everyone who seeks out a local physician or health care practitioner complaining of "anxiety" or "nerves" really suffering from anxiety? Does everyone who takes minor tranquilizers have a clearly defined anxiety disorder? Most clinicians and investigators would guess that these millions of individuals do not present with clearly identifiable anxiety disorders, but rather with some vague combination of stress, adjustment to difficult family or work situations, or other temporary problems (e.g., difficulty sleeping, etc.). For years it was impossible actually to ascertain the number of these individuals presenting with anxiety disorders. Recently, epidemiologists have begun to undertake this arduous task, culminating in the most ambitious study of the prevalence of anxiety disorders ever undertaken.

Before this study is described, it is interesting to put the numbers in context. One of the first studies using sophisticated, up-to-date sampling techniques to estimate the distribution of fears and phobias in the general population was undertaken by Agras, Sylvester, and Oliveau (1969). They conducted a probability sample of the household population of a small city in the United States (Burlington, Vermont), and they interviewed the 325 individuals who made up the sample. From this study, the estimated total prevalence of phobia was 7.7%, but only 0.02% presented with phobia severe enough to result in an absence from work or the inability to manage common household tasks. The investigators diagnosed 0.06% of the sample, or 6 out of 1,000, as having agoraphobia. Many more individuals, approaching 50% of the population, presented with mild fears of objects or situations (snakes, heights, storms, etc.).

Another important finding from this study was that phobia ran a prolonged course: Most often an individual, once phobic, had that phobia in at least a mild form for a lifetime. Figure 1.1 shows the rates of incidence (the beginning of the phobia) and prevalence (the presence of the phobia) at various ages within the population. The findings on the prolonged course of phobia were confirmed in a later follow-up study: Agras, Chapin, and Oliveau (1972) found very little improvement in untreated phobics followed 5 years after the original study, particularly if they were 20 years old or older and if their phobias were more generalized. In fact,

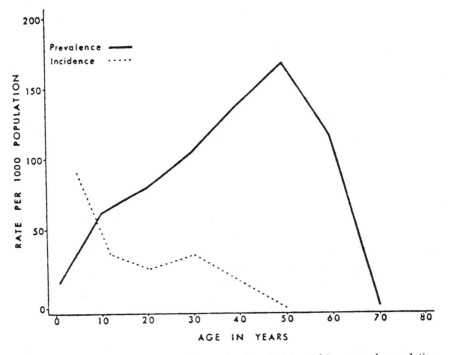

FIGURE 1.1. Incidence and prevalence rates for phobia within general population. From Agras, S., Sylvester, D., & Oliveau, D. (1969). The epidemiology of common fears and phobias. *Comprehensive Psychiatry, 10,* 151–156. Copyright 1969 by Grune & Stratton. Reprinted by permission.

a feature distinguishing between anxiety disorders and depression is that depression tends to remit whether treated or not, usually in a matter of months. Anxiety disorders, on the other hand, tend to be chronic and to remain present in somewhat less severe form even if successfully treated (Noyes & Clancy, 1976; Noyes, Clancy, Hoenk, & Slymen, 1980).

In 1973, Marks and Lader reviewed various studies from around the world estimating the prevalence of anxiety states in the population. The difficulty here was that vastly different diagnostic procedures and methods were used in these studies. Nevertheless, from this review Marks and Lader determined that anxiety states were fairly common, occurring in from 2% to 4.7% of the population, with a higher prevalence in women. For years, the studies by Agras *et al.* (1969) and Marks and Lader (1973) were cited as the best evidence we had on the frequency of various anxiety disorders.

Two very important developments made more sophisticated and wide-ranging efforts possible. First, diagnostic criteria for anxiety disorders have

now been specified in much more detail. This allows more certain identification of the various anxiety disorders. Second, structured interviews
have been devised; these insure that all investigators cover the same essential points when interviewing for the presence of anxiety (or other)
disorders (see Chapter 9). These developments permit a more standardized and objective approach to the question of the frequency of specific
clinical anxiety disorders in the population.

Preliminary data are now available from the Epidemiologic Catchment Area (ECA) study survey, sponsored by the National Institute of
Mental Health (NIMH); this survey has been ongoing in five different
sites around the country since 1980. The sample population size in each
site is approximately 300,000. Up to 5,000 or more individuals in each site
were interviewed. A structured interview that yields *Diagnostic and Statistical Manual of Mental Disorders,* third edition (DSM-III) anxiety disorder
diagnoses was employed by individuals trained to administer this interview. Some of the results from the first wave of interviews are presented
in Table 1.2. Now, from the second wave of the ECA study, we also have
an estimate of the prevalence of DSM-III generalized anxiety disorder of
4.0% (L. N. Robins, personal communication, May 29, 1986). Wittchen
(1986) found very similar prevalence rates for each case of DSM-III anxiety
disorder in Germany.

These are startling figures. Among many mysteries and paradoxes
present in these data, one will notice first that estimates of the prevalence
of agoraphobia in the population have risen from 0.6% in the Agras *et al.*
(1969) survey to between 2.7% and 5.8% in the ECA survey. Even if one
discounts the rather high estimate from Baltimore, this represents almost
a fivefold increase in prevalence. This would indicate, for example, that
in the United States alone between 7 and 12 million individuals suffer
from agoraphobia. What could account for these startling differences in
estimates of prevalence? Possibly it was the way the questions were asked.
For example, in the Agras *et al.* study, very conservative criteria were
used. But it seems unlikely that this could account for all of the difference. In the ECA study, as noted above, lengthy structured interviews
and specific, reliable, diagnostic definitions were employed; these factors,
when combined with the enormous numbers of people involved, tend to
make one more confident in these data. In the time between the two
studies, there has also been an enormous increase in awareness of the
problem of agoraphobia, although once again it is hard to see how this
could account for absolute increases in the prevalence of the problem. Is
the prevalence of agoraphobia increasing? For the time being, we do not
know. One remarkable discrepancy within the ECA study is the enormous difference in prevalence between Baltimore and the other sites. The
investigators themselves are uncertain about what could account for this

TABLE 1.2. Six-Month Prevalence of DSM-III Anxiety
Disorder Diagnoses in the First Wave of Interviews from the
ECA Survey

	New Haven	Baltimore	St. Louis
Panic (%)			
Male	0.3	0.8	0.7
Female	0.9	1.2	1.0
Total	0.6	1.0	0.9
Agoraphobia (%)			
Male	1.1	3.4	0.9
Female	4.2	7.8	4.3
Total	2.8	5.8	2.7
Social phobia (%)			
Male		1.7	0.9
Female		2.6	1.5
Total		2.2	1.2
Simple phobia (%)			
Male	3.2	7.3	2.3
Female	6.0	15.7	6.5
Total	4.7	11.8	4.5
Obsessive–compulsive disorder (%)			
Male	0.9	1.9	0.9
Female	1.7	2.2	1.7
Total	1.4	2.0	1.3

Note. Adapted from Myers, J. K., Weissman, M. M., Tischler, C. E.,
Holzer, C. E., III, Orvaschel, H., Anthony, J. C., Boyd, J. H., Burke,
J. D., Jr., Kramer, M., & Stoltzman, R. (1984). Six-month prevalence
of psychiatric disorders in three communities. *Archives of General Psychiatry, 41,* 959–967. Copyright 1984 by the American Medical Association. Reprinted by permission.

but will follow the results closely from additional waves of data, which
are forthcoming.

Another surprising finding is evident in the data on agoraphobia (and,
to a lesser extent, the data on other anxiety disorders). Almost 75% of all
agoraphobics are women! This has been a remarkably consistent finding
around the world; in some studies, it is even more dramatic. For example,
Burns and Thorpe (1977) interviewed 963 agoraphobics as part of a national survey throughout the British Isles. Fully 88% of these agoraphobics were women.

What could account for this difference? At least four different hypotheses have attracted varying amounts of attention. Some investigators

have assumed that there are just as many male agoraphobics, but that for
cultural reasons it is more acceptable for females to express fear and anxiety; thus, differences are due simply to more frequent reporting by women.
A related hypothesis suggests that the numbers with underlying panic
attacks are more nearly equal, but that females cope with their panic by
avoidance while males cope by other means, such as self-medication with
alcohol (see Chapter 10). A third hypothesis suggests that the differences
are real and are due to the fact that females experience marked endocrinological changes, which make them more susceptible to panic (see Chapter 5). A fourth hypothesis also suggests that the differences are real, but
once again culturally based, in that males are taught to "tough out" or
endure their fears; this leads to earlier and more complete elimination of
any avoidance behavior in males when compared to females. Answers are
beginning to emerge to this intriguing question and are taken up in some
detail in Chapter 10.

In any case, these startling statistics have established one overriding
fact: Anxiety disorders represent the single largest mental health problem
in the country, far outstripping depression, which was thought by many
to be the most common mental health problem before the ECA survey
proved otherwise. In fact, the prevalence of anxiety disorders surpasses
that of any other mental health disorder, including substance abuse, even
before one considers data for generalized anxiety disorder or posttraumatic stress disorder, which were not included in the first wave of ECA
interviews. Even the more limited category of phobia alone is the most
frequent mental health disorder in women and the second most frequent
in men, following only substance abuse. In view of the information reviewed above on the relationship of alcohol abuse and anxiety disorders,
it is very possible that a large proportion of individuals suffering from
substance abuse are continuing to medicate an underlying anxiety disorder. These findings will have a substantial impact on public health policy in the United States (Regier *et al.*, 1984). In addition, this information
has begun to direct more attention to the public health surveys (cited
above) on the enormous utilization of health care practitioners by individuals presenting with self-defined problems of "anxiety."

Using ECA data, Boyd (1986) has discovered that an individual with
panic disorder is more likely to seek professional help than an individual
with schizophrenia or any other mental disorder. Furthermore, the high
prevalence of panic attacks associated with other mental disorders may
be one of the primary reasons why many patients with other disorders
seek treatment. Boyd speculates that the overwhelming sensations of panic
and the associated thoughts of death and dying may be the motivating
factors in this enormous utilization of health resources. In addition, we
now know with some certainty that many of these patients end up in the
offices of cardiologists. For example, Beitman, Lamberti, *et al.* (1987) found

that a high proportion of cardiac patients who complained of chest pain but who had angiographically normal coronary arteries met criteria for panic disorder. Panic disorder patients have a long history of seeking out cardiologists (see Chapter 3).

Finally, patients with panic attacks do form a large part of the practice of primary care physicians. For example, Katon, Vitaliano, Russo, Jones, and Anderson (1987) found that 36% of a sample of primary care patients had had at least one panic attack in the past year and that many focused exclusively on the somatic symptoms of panic (rapid heartbeat, light-headedness, etc.), to the exclusion of more cognitive symptoms (feelings of extreme anxiety or impending doom). Nevertheless, thorough medical screening clarified that the symptoms were part of a panic attack (see Chapter 6 for implications of this perception).

ANXIETY ACROSS CULTURES

By all accounts, the shadow of intelligence or the specter of death that is the experience of anxiety should be universally present across cultures and species. For purposes of both survival in the Darwinian sense and effective planning for the future, as concluded by Liddell, evolution should favor members of a species who are anxious. But excesses of any valuable trait exist in certain individuals. Is anxiety in its pathological expression present in other cultures? If so, are the forms of the disorder the same as those found in Western culture? Consider the following case.

Several years ago a 31-year-old married Inuit (i.e., "Eskimo") male presented at the Alaska native health service complaining that he was "very nervous." Although Inuit was his native language, he spoke English well enough to communicate about his problem in that language. He reported that he had begun to feel nervous over 3 years earlier. Now he stayed at home most of the time, particularly in winter, when he felt worse. Since the men of his village were responsible for hunting, fishing, and carrying water or ice to the house with dog teams or snowmobiles, he was relying increasingly on other villagers, relatives, and public assistance for his contribution to these activities. Going out alone made him feel worse unless he went with his wife. Since she herself had a chronic physical illness, she seldom was able to venture away from home. However, since his condition had deteriorated substantially, both had decided that it was necessary to undertake the 50-mile journey to the hospital by snowmobile! He had no idea what caused his problem, but speculated that it might be connected with an episode of flu several years previously (Hudson, 1981).

It would seem that this Inuit suffered from the same disorder so frequently encountered in cities and suburbs of the Western world—namely, agoraphobia. That this occurred despite overwhelming differences between cultures is noteworthy. Nevertheless, preliminary conclusions from cross-cultural investigators suggest that what seems to be anxiety in one culture may take many different forms in other cultures. The expression of emotion in general is well known to be culturally determined. The intensity of emotion expressed by southern European and Mediterranean cultures compared to northern European cultures is legendary. Thus, it is not surprising that emotional disorders are expressed differently even if some common biological or etiological roots exist. What is surprising is how very differently anxiety presents in other cultures.

KORO

In 1967, a wave of severe anxiety swept Singapore. Numerous males, particularly among the large ethnic Chinese population, presented with anxiety so acute that they could be said to be in a state of panic (Ngui, 1969; Tan, 1969, 1980). Each expressed an overwhelming fear that his sexual organs were retracting into his abdomen. These individuals believed that when the organ totally retracted, death would result. Screams for help usually resulted in assistance from the family and the community. This assistance might take the form of the construction of various contraptions to prevent the genitals from retracting. Usually the anxiety subsided in a few hours (Tan, 1980). Recurrences also passed quickly, particularly if support was available in the community. These individuals were suffering from *koro*, a syndrome often encountered in that culture. This syndrome is less frequent in women, where it takes the form of fear of retraction of the nipples, the breasts, or occasionally the labia. Patients presenting with *koro* usually relate the onset of their condition to some sexual misdemeanor occurring in their past (Tan, 1980).

PA-LENG

Pa-leng, also found in Chinese cultures, is sometimes labeled "frigophobia" or "fear of the cold." Individuals with this problem present with cold, clammy hands; tachycardia; dry mouth; and other related somatic symptoms. Like *koro*, *pa-leng* can only be understood in the context of traditional ideas—in this case, the traditional Chinese notions of *yin* and *yang* (Tan, 1980). Chinese medicine holds that there must be a balance of the *yin* and *yang* forces within the human body for health to be maintained. *Yin* represents the cold, dark, windy, energy-sapping aspects of life; *yang* refers to the bright, warm, energy-producing aspect of life. In both *koro* and *pa-leng*, the presenting symptoms are associated with an excess of *yin*. In *pa-leng* individuals present with a morbid fear of the cold. They ruminate over further loss of body heat, which may be a threat to life. Closely associated with this fear of the cold is a fear of wind. Sufferers from *pa-leng* wear several layers of clothing even on a hot day to keep out wind and cold. Complaints of belching and flatulence may reflect the presence of too much wind, and therefore too much *yin* in the body.

HEART DISTRESS

In Iran, a frequently encountered disorder is referred to as "heart distress" (Good & Kleinman, 1985). Individuals experiencing palpitations or other sensations in their hearts interpret them within the framework of symbolic meanings peculiar to the culture of Iran. But the focus is almost always on somatic symptoms associated with the heart around which a disorder is constructed. Western observers studying this phenomenon find that in some instances patients with heart distress would fit into the Western category of depression, while other cases would more clearly be cases of anxiety, particularly panic disorder.

FRIGHT DISORDERS AND VOODOO DEATH

Heart distress contrasts with "fright disorders," which have their origins in observable fear reactions or exaggerated startle responses. Subsequent emotional disorders are ascribed to experiences of extreme fright. In fact, a wide variety of behavioral and emotional problems can be attributed to fright in these cultures, including hysterical conversion symptoms and temporary psychotic episodes. Nevertheless, the predominant expression seems to be similar to Western anxiety disorders. Many examples of fright disorders exist in different cultures. For example, *susto* in Latin American cultures is characterized by various anxiety-based symptoms (e.g., irritability, insomnia, phobias, the somatic symptoms of sweating and tachycardia, etc.). The causes of *susto* also lie in sudden fright, black magic, or witchcraft—in particular, the "evil eye," prominently mentioned in fright disorders around the world (Good & Kleinman, 1985; Tan, 1980). In Iranian culture, both "fright disorders" and "heart distress" are terms used to refer, for the most part, to symptoms of emotional disorders. But in fright disorders the cause is attributed to an event in the social environment. In heart distress, the particular symptom itself becomes the focus and cause of the disorder.

In what may be the ultimate specter of death, it seems that some individuals in certain cultures are scared to death. Black magic or the "evil eye" is associated with this event; this suggests that death may be an occasional complication of certain fright disorders in some cultures. Cannon (1942), examining the phenomenon of voodoo death, suggested that the sentence of death by a medicine man may create intolerable autonomic arousal with little opportunity for effective action. Ultimately, this results in damage to internal organs and death.

SHINKEISHITSU

The clinical presentation of what seem to be anxiety disorders in Japan is best summarized under the clinical label of shinkeishitsu. In general, the word shinkeishitsu refers to a broad category of people who might be referred to as neurotic in the West. For example, these individuals are perfectionistic, are extremely self-conscious, and become concerned quickly and easily over particular somatic or social issues. Shinkeishitsu was elaborated in some detail by the famous Japanese psychiatrist Shoma Morita, who subsequently formed his own school of psychotherapy. A good summary of the clinical presentation of shinkeishitsu is presented by Reynolds (1976):

> Morita therapists view the neurotic as a person with a particularly strong need to live a full life, perfectionistic tendencies, and extreme self-consciousness. . . . This person encounters some unpleasant event that focuses his attention on a particular problem; blushing, headaches, and constipation are typical examples. He becomes quite concerned about the problem and he becomes increasingly conscious of its effect on his life. He becomes caught in a spiral of attention and sensitivity which produces a sort of obsessive self consciousness. His efforts to overcome the problem directly by his will serve only to exacerbate his fixation. By the time he arrives at a Morita therapy clinic, such a person is generally very shy and sensitive; he is unable to function socially, preferring to spend his life in his room withdrawn from the world outside. He is immobilized by the storm of counterconflicts and pressures raging within his psyche. (pp. 9–10)

The crucial issue of self-focused attention or self-preoccupation, seemingly so much a part of shinkeishitsu, is taken up in some detail in Chapter 7.

There are three subcategories of shinkeishitsu. The first is described as the obsessive phobic form, which seems to account for about 50% of individuals with this disorder in Japan. This form would seem closely related to social phobia in Western culture. These people have a strong fear of looking people in the eye and are afraid that some aspect of their personal presentation (e.g., blushing, stuttering, body odor, etc.) will appear reprehensible. Individuals with the neurasthenic form display strong hypochondriacal symptoms, poor concentration, and feelings of shyness.

This category accounts for approximately 25% of individuals with *shin-keishitsu*. Finally, anxiety states, which seem descriptively very close to panic attacks, account for approximately 10% of these patients. This problem usually begins with some sort of heart palpitation or other somatic symptom. The remaining 15% do not fall neatly into one of these three categories.

ANXIETY ACROSS CULTURES: CONCLUSIONS

It is certainly not easy to map the symptoms and features of anxiety as we know them in the West onto other cultures. It seems clear that the experience of anxiety exists in nearly all cultures, but that this experience is articulated in culture-specific idioms. Various interpretations of the experience of anxiety from culture to culture affect its course, the specific aspects of its presentation (i.e., which symptoms are focused on), and various methods for resolving it. For example, attempts to treat various emotional disorders in China by Western pharmacological techniques have been quite unsuccessful, since patients believe that the causes of their emotional disorders are fully attributable to stresses at work, separation from their families or homes, or other environmental stressors. Thus, treatment with Western medicines does not produce a resolution of the experience of illness for these patients (Good & Kleinman, 1985).

The overwhelming finding from cross-cultural studies is that the somatic manifestation of emotional disorders is focused upon almost exclusively in Third World countries. Furthermore, this chronic somatization as a function of stress or other causes may take quite different forms from culture to culture. The preoccupation with sexual symptoms in Chinese cultures has been mentioned in the context of *koro*. Administering standardized checklists of anxiety symptoms to different cultures produces similar overall levels of "anxiety" from culture to culture, but the emphasis is on very different symptoms. Responses to a symptom checklist in a cross-national study were collected by Inkeles (1983) and are presented in Table 1.3. To take one example from this table, the overall percentage of symptoms endorsed is relatively similar in Israel and Nigeria, but awareness of rapid heart rate, shortness of breath, or complaints of "nervousness" are represented very differently in those two cultures.

In summary, some individuals in all cultures seem apprehensive, worried, fearful, and aroused, and make attributions concerning their worries and arousal. But the object of worry or apprehension, the source of fear, and the specific attributions these individuals make are culture-specific and have marked implications for classification, course, and treatment. One should not expect an anxious Chinese in Malaysia to be concerned over confronting nothingness, or to be amenable to attributing

TABLE 1.3. Responses to a Symptom Checklist in a Cross-National Study

	India	Chile	Israel	Nigeria
Average percentage of symptoms per country	24	29	22	28
Individual symptoms (%):				
Trouble sleeping	54	23	37	21
Nervousness	48	36	27	9
Heart beating	13	24	13	45
Shortness of breath	8	15	6	32
Disturbing dreams	21	22	35	48

Note. From Inkeles, A. (1983). *Exploring individual modernity* (pp. 262–263). New York: Columbia University Press. Copyright 1983 by Columbia University Press. Reprinted by permission.

anxiety either to unconscious instinctual wishes or to alterations in sensitivity of benzodiazepine receptors. The experience of anxiety seems to be culturally determined, even if the occurrence of basic negative affect is universal (see Chapter 2). With the enormous difficulties in defining "anxiety" even in our own culture, it is not surprising that problems increase across cultures. This makes an investigation into the basic nature of anxiety all the more compelling.

THE MYSTERIES OF ANXIETY

The mysteries of anxiety are legion. How can an emotion with which most of us are intimately familiar be at once so common and yet so diffuse and vague? Does the experience of fainting at the sight of blood or entering a seemingly involuntary state of paralysis when under attack really have anything in common with the forebodings concerning the welfare of our family, our occupation, or our finances, with which we are often preoccupied? Why are women strikingly more afflicted with anxiety in Western cultures, while males seek out treatment in equally remarkable numbers in Eastern cultures? Why do individuals around the world continue to engage in self-defeating, self-destructive behavior when they are perfectly able to verbalize a rational course of action and behavior that would be life-enhancing and rewarding? Finally, what is it in us that seems to necessitate an obsessive search for causes of our unpleasant and occasionally unbearable negative emotional experiences? Could this be the source of major cross-cultural differences? Does the sound of the wind in a cabin on the ocean or the terror of imagining one's genitals retracting result in the same experience, or is the experience itself somehow very different? Is anxiety really just a metaphor for such a heterogeneous human experience that the term no longer deserves to exist, as suggested by the social constructivists (Hallam, 1985)? Or is there really a universal experience that deserves a common name? Is it the specter of death that is universal about the experience of anxiety, whether it be separation from a loved one, confrontation with nothingness, voodoo death, or overwhelming *yin*? Or is it the shadow of intelligence, which drives individuals and cultures to higher levels of achievement? To answer these and all of the mysteries of anxiety, we must first explore what is basic about the nature of anxiety itself.

2

Emotions and Anxiety

THEORIES OF EMOTION

If the scientific study of human behavior has been characterized by mind–body dualism, the study of emotion has been the primary battlefield. In this way, studying emotion is much like experiencing emotion. One is continually buffeted by the variety of creative but conflicting ideas concerning this elusive phenomenon. For over 100 years, the development of biological and the development of psychological views of emotion have progressed—sometimes in tandem, but more often independently. Even in this age of astounding progress in the understanding of human behavior, entire books continue to appear concentrating on either the psychological or the biological view of emotion, without any reference whatsoever to the alternative intellectual tradition.

If the experience of emotion is Lewis Carroll's Wonderland, anxiety is the Red Queen. Always a future threat, often an unbearingly overwhelming present danger, the Red Queen dominates Wonderland in the same way the study of anxiety has dominated emotions. For this reason, it is difficult to consider the nature of anxiety without placing anxiety firmly in the context of what we know about emotion in general.

The intellectual tradition surrounding the study of emotion continues to be influenced by such intellectual giants as Darwin, James, and Cannon. Despite the attention that emotion has received from a number of points of view, no single generally accepted model of emotion has yet emerged. Rather, two traditions or models that concentrate on different aspects of emotion have generally coexisted over the last 75 years.

Most theorists agree that emotion consists of several components. Only one of these components is the actual subjective experience of affect, although the experience of affect defines emotion for most of us.

30

Affect is reported as a variety of rich and diverse feeling states (e.g., "happiness," "sadness," "anger," "surprise," "joy," "melancholy," etc.). Terms such as these are strongly represented in our common expressive and literary heritage. In our own experience, these terms have been elaborated into subtle variations that greatly enrich our appreciation of what it is to be human. But knowledge of affect relies on introspection, and an uncertain, qualitative type of introspection at that. As such, it is a slippery subject for science. Other components of the emotional system are more suitable for scientific inquiry, and therefore have been emphasized.

In addition to the subjective experience of affect, emotion is also considered to be a set of expressive behaviors; a function of the nervous system; and, more recently, a cognitive perception or appraisal. Of course, these three components of the emotional system are in no way mutually exclusive. For years, investigators have recognized three components as interacting in a meaningful way to comprise the richness of emotional response. Most investigators, following a particular tradition, have simply chosen to emphasize one aspect of emotion as being more salient or more fundamental to the emotional response. On the other hand, certain investigators concentrating on one component or another, such as the neurobiological or the cognitive aspects of emotion, will choose to ignore altogether additional components of the emotional response—usually to the marked detriment of their theory or program of research.

EMOTION AS BEHAVIOR

The Study of Behavior

The first great tradition in studying emotional behavior was initiated by Charles Darwin, in a book entitled *The Expression of Emotions in Man and Animals* (1872). Building on a tradition dating back to Aristotle, Darwin emphasized behavioral expression, particularly facial expression, as the fundamental aspect of emotion.

Darwin's legacy is not only alive and well today, but continues to lead the field in terms of its influence as well as the breadth and depth of supporting experimental evidence. Despite this long and glorious tradition, the implications of evidence emanating from the laboratories and literature of experimental and social psychology have been ignored for the most part by psychopathologists and clinicians investigating emotional disorders.

The intellectual legacy of Darwin is the study of expressive behavior and its function. The underlying premise is that emotions are innate, "hardwired" patterns of reaction and responding that have evolved in many life forms because of their functional significance. Although clearly modifiable by learning and maturation, these basic patterns of emotion are present in humans and animals at birth, and show a remarkable consistency both within and across species. In the best Darwinian tradition, the focus of study within this approach to emotions centers on (but is not limited to) expressive behavior and its function. Since the primary means of expressing oneself in both animals and humans is through nonverbal posture and facial expressions, these objective behaviors have become the focus of study. In humans, the study of facial expressions quickly assumed central importance—a state of affairs that continues to this day. A number of different lines of evidence have been used to support the centrality of expressive behavior (Izard, 1977; Plutchik, 1980). Among these are the above-mentioned consistencies in emotional expressions across many species of animals. In addition, Darwin pointed out that in humans, emotional expressions are similar at different ages. Infants express emotions in much the same way as adults, before the necessary learning required for this expression can possibly have taken place. Darwin also made the intriguing observation that subtle, emotional expressions as represented in facial expressions are the same in those born blind as in those who are normally sighted, and that many emotional expressions are present in a similar fashion across different cultures and races.

The primary function or adaptive value of emotional behavior is not only preparation for action, but also communication from one member of the species to another. For example, the function of the emotion of fear seems clearly to prepare the animal for immediate and decisive action— usually running away or fighting. But the expression of fear also communicates danger to other animals and therefore affects their chance for survival, enabling observers to respond more quickly to a threat they might not have anticipated. The expression of many emotions has the same communicative or signal value.

The underlying assumption of this expressive-behavioral approach is that basic patterns of emotion differ from one another in fundamental ways. But individual emotions can combine or blend, so that a somewhat different reaction may occur not only within individuals from time to time, but also between individuals. One of the foremost theorists of emotion, Carroll Izard (Izard, 1977; Izard & Blumberg, 1985), has proposed 10 basic emotions: fear, anger, disgust, surprise, shame, contempt, interest, joy, distress/sadness, and guilt. Since these emotions are considered fundamentally different innate responses, a further assumption is that they can be differentiated biologically as well as functionally.

In fact, there is some evidence for differentiation (e.g., Izard & Blumberg, 1985) at both the psychophysiological and neurobiological levels. Ax (1953) reported that fear and anger could be differentiated by psychophysiological measures. Unfortunately, succeeding years brought little confirmation that emotions could be differentiated on the basis of measures of

32

autonomic nervous system functioning. While this failure to replicate may have been due to methodological differences, the marked lack of evidence concerning differential autonomic patterns contributed to alternative traditions in the study of emotion, reviewed below. In recent years, however, the early findings of Ax have begun to receive important confirmation, with new, more creative methodology. For example, Schwartz, Weinburger, and Singer (1981) showed clear autonomic differentiation in measures of heart rate and blood pressure associated with emotional states of happiness, sadness, anger, and fear. In addition, each of these emotions differed from relaxation and a control condition. These conditions were instigated by intense, carefully contrived, affective imagery.

Ekman, Levenson, and Friesen (1983) also observed cardiovascular differentiation among professional actors who assumed different facial expressions by altering one muscle group at a time in response to instructions from the experimenter. In their entirety, these alternations in muscle groups recreated the facial expressions associated with one emotion or another, although the actors were not informed of this beforehand. The fact that these actors were presumably not feeling anything would seem to suggest a strong and innate association between facial expressions and biological aspects of the emotional response. In addition to these studies, a number of experiments have demonstrated subtle electromyographic (EMG) responses from facial muscles that were too small to be picked up by observers, but yet differentiated clearly among responses to different emotional sets induced by imagery (e.g., Rusalova, Izard, & Simonov, 1975; Schwartz, Fair, Salt, Mandel, & Klerman, 1976).

In terms of the process or temporal sequence of emotional components, theorists from the expressive-behavioral tradition assume that it is expressive behavior in general and facial expression in particular that leads to the subjective experience of affect through autonomic or central nervous system stimulation. Nevertheless, it is possible that too much emphasis has been put on facial expressions as perhaps the primary component of emotion. For example, some have suggested that cerebral vascular responses are more basic to emotions than are facial expressions (Zajonc, 1985), and that facial expressions exist to regulate blood flow in the brain. Since blood flow changes affect the temperature, and the quantity and quality of neurotransmitters released in the brain, it is this process that is responsible for subjectively felt emotion. But this theory which was originally developed by Israel Waynbaum (1907), specifies vascular changes as the primary mechanism of emotion and thereby shifts the focus away from behavior such as facial expression. Since the emphasis on expressed behavior and its evolutionary function rather than biology is central to any Darwinian or neo-Darwinian view of emotions, it is not surprising that this view has been controversial (e.g., Fridlund & Gilbert, 1985).

While the theoretical differences among these views are major, they share the scholarly tradition that emotions are innate complex responses to a variety of antecedents or stimuli that have adaptive value. Moreover, emotions are universal across cultures and often across species, and that the central component of this response is expressive behavior.

The Development of Emotions in Young Children

Another important line of evidence supporting the "innateness" of emotion comes from the study of the development of emotions in young children. Emotion theorists studying developmental processes have noted the emergence of seemingly innate emotional responses at very specific points in development. At 3 months, the facial expression of infants during certain emotional states begins to show a remarkable consistency with adult facial expressions reflecting the same emotion (Emde, 1980; Emde, Kligman, Reich, & Wade, 1978). These emotions and facial expressions in infants also seem to be cross-cultural (Bowlby, 1973; Izard, 1971). The functional value of the expression of emotion in infants is particularly evident, in that parents rely on these emotional expressions to guide their interaction with an infant and gauge the needs of the child. Since language is not available at this time, an understanding of nonverbal expressive behavior is really the sole means of communication, and its adaptive value is readily apparent.

The emergence of emotional expressions such as the smile and cry has been a focus of investigation by developmentalists (e.g., Emde, Gaensbauer, & Harmon, 1976). Particularly interesting for those concerned with adult anxiety is the emergence of what have been termed "stranger distress" and "separation distress" (Bowlby, 1973; Campbell, 1986).

Emde et al. (1976) suggest that these two forms of distress are separate phenomenon. Specifically, stranger distress appears in some infants between 7 and 9 months of age, with a mean age of onset at approximately 8 months and a peak at about 9 months of age. As suggested by the means, the onset is rapid (often within 1 month), decreasing rather rapidly after that. Stranger distress is characterized by fearful expressions, crying, and attempts to escape in the presence of a "stranger," who may in fact be a grandmother or other relative the infant has not seen for some time.

On the other hand, separation distress (specifically, distress at separation from the mother) seems to begin a bit earlier in some infants, at approximately 4 months, and increases gradually and sporadically; it reaches a peak at about 13–18 months and declines thereafter. Early theorists thought that stranger distress might reflect a fear of losing the mother, but careful observational studies suggest that this is not the case. To take just one example, many infants show stranger distress, although they have not yet developed separation distress and show no reaction to the mother's leaving. Because of these very different patterns of development and a variety of other evidence, separation distress and stranger distress seem very different and unrelated phenomena. Birds and mammals also seem to show stranger distress. Specifically, these species will begin to flee from strange species or certain visual configurations at very specific points in their development. It is likely that stranger distress represents the same response in humans, although the development of this response occurs somewhat later as one moves up the phylogenetic scale (or, more accurately, as neuronal organization becomes more complex). The approximate times of appearance of this flight reaction in different species have been organized by Emde *et al.* (1976) and are presented in Table 2.1 as adapted by Plutchik (1980).

In any case, Emde *et al.* (1976) suggest that the development of stranger distress indicates the emergence of a coherent fear system in humans between 7 and 9 months of age. Based on their observations of emotional development in infants, they conclude that this response has an innate basis; that it appears universally across cultures; that it has the same course in congenitally blind infants; and that it occurs in greater synchrony in monozygotic twins than in dizygotic twins. Furthermore, there is no evidence that learning has an effect on the emergence of this response. On the other hand, contextual factors, such as presence or absence of the mother, do seem to affect the expression of the response.

In addition, it seems that fear of strangers is but on example of specific fear that occurs to many stimuli at this point in time. If this is so, then stranger distress is the first and primary expression of pure fear and should be recognized as such by psychopathologists looking for devel-

TABLE 2.1. Approximate Time of Appearance of Flight Reactions in Different Species

Species	Time of appearance
Birds	24 hours
Cats	5 weeks
Dogs	5–7 weeks
Monkeys	2–3 months
Chimpanzees	4–6 months
Humans	7–9 months

Note. Adapted by Plutchik (1980) from Emde, R. N., Gaensbauer, T. J., & Harmon, R. J. (1976). *Emotional expressions in infancy.* New York: International Universities Press. Copyright 1976 by International Universities Press, Inc. Adapted by permission.

opmental precursors to adult anxiety disorders. This observation becomes important in the discussion of the etiology of panic in Chapter 6.

In contrast, Izard (C. E. Izard, personal communication, April 1986; Shiller, Izard, & Hembree, 1986), after further research into this area, has concluded that separation distress reflects the basic emotion of anger (along with distress/sadness) more than fear. This parallels naturalistic work by Bowlby (1973), who reported that anger and ultimately sadness follow separation.

Naturally, emotional reactions, both in infants and adults, are very rarely seen in pure forms. Not only are they greatly affected by maturational, learning, and other social variables, but they become more "complex" as time goes on, reflecting a blend of several basic innate emotions. Even stranger distress is affected strongly by developmental and contextual factors in its expression (Campbell, 1986; Sroufe, 1977).

The Primacy of Affect

The re-emergence of the expressive-behavioral tradition in basic psychology, if not psychopathology, is best represented by Zajonc's reiteration of the primacy of affect (Zajonc, 1980, 1984). Noting that affect is usually considered postcognitive by most contemporary theorists, he suggests the opposite. Specifically, he speculates that affect and cognition are under the control of separate and partially independent systems—a premise that is receiving increasing experimental support. For example, Derryberry and Rothbart (1984) summarize several lines of research indicating that information can be encoded affectively without conscious cognitive evaluation. This information, in turn, influences ongoing perceptual and evaluative processes. Zajonc also suggests that affective responses are "effortless, inescapable, irrevocable, holistic, more difficult to verbalize yet easy to communicate and to understand" (1980, p. 169). While this article has sparked healthy controversy in the literature over the primacy of affect versus the primacy of cognition (Lazarus, 1984; Zajonc, 1984), more importantly, it has served to reawaken the sleeping giant of innate emotions.

EMOTION AS THE SENSATION OF BODILY CHANGES: THE JAMES–LANGE THEORY

A related approach to emotions, one familiar to everyone who has read an introductory psychology textbook, was first proposed by William James (1890). Subsequent work by a Danish physiologist named G. Carl Lange suggesting a similar idea resulted in the conceptualization known as the "James–Lange theory." The basic premise of their ideas was that bodily changes, which differ from emotion to emotion, occur as a response to some antecedent event, but that the sensation or "feeling" of these bodily changes constitutes the emotion. James pointed out that this sequence is contrary to the more common-sense view, in which an emotion occurs because the perception of a situation gives rise to a "feeling" of emotion, which is then followed by various bodily changes. "Bodily changes," for the most part, refer to visceral or psychophysiological changes (heart rate increases, temperature changes, etc.) of which the person can be aware.

In fact, this approach is similar to and compatible with evolutionary behavioral conceptions of emotions, although a slightly different emphasis appears (see below). Within the James–Lange conception, the idea that basic emotions exist that differ from each other and have functional adaptive value is consistent with behavioral theories. What James did was to emphasize visceral reactions as one of the primary components of emotion, while at the same time noting the importance of the subjective experience of affect—a combination largely ignored by early evolutionary theorists.

Unfortunately, evidence quickly accumulated that emotions can be experienced, expressed, and felt, without the types of visceral physiological changes thought so important by James. Most of the evidence for this observation revolved around examples where autonomic reactivity was disconnected, sometimes surgically, from the remainder of the nervous system; nevertheless, emotional experience and behavior were not diminished. For example, in 1929 Walter Cannon reported that when no visceral sensory impulses whatsoever were available to animals after surgical disconnection, they were still able to show typical emotion-related behavior. A variety of additional arguments have been mustered against this conception of emotion (Plutchik, 1980). But neoevolutionary theorists have handled this objection easily by noting that the whole variety of sensory experience, including feedback from the motor components of expressive behavior in addition to any visceral changes, contributes to the affective component of emotion.

In any case, these arguments are concerned more with the process of emotion than with theories of the nature of emotion. In other words, what is the exact sequence of events that results in the experience of emotion? A more difficult contradiction for proponents of discrete, hard-wired emotions is the concept of discordance or lack of correlation among components of emotion. This evidence, to which I refer repeatedly throughout this book, concerns the lack of correlation or the loose correlation between and among behavioral, cognitive/experiential, and somatic and visceral physiological components of emotion. Beginning with Lang (1968), investigators have continuously observed emotional responding in one response system such as self-report, without correlated responding in other systems, such as behavioral or physiological. These observations are particularly well known to clinicians working with anxiety disorders (the emotional construct within which Lang first made his observations). But these findings raise questions about the existence of coherent, discrete emotional states that are consistent across individuals, cultures, and even species. This is just one of many contradictions existing in the study of emotions.

EMOTION AS BIOLOGY

A truly different tradition in the study of emotion was initiated by Walter Cannon (1929), who viewed emotion as primarily a brain function. After dismissing the James–Lange theory, Cannon's creative and influential research centered on the process of "extirpation of parts," or surgical removal of various areas of the brain in animals. Cannon found, among other things, that removal of part or all of the cerebral cortex seemed to release emotions. Therefore, the cortex, by and large, was not directly involved in emotion except to serve a controlling function. Rather, the site of emotion was thought to be the hypothalamus, which, when destroyed, resulted in a dramatic elimination of most of the components of emotion. Essentially, Cannon reasoned that the subjective experience of affect, as well as expressive behavior and any associated bodily changes, was a function of activity in the hypothalamus.

A long and distinguished series of investigators have attempted to understand emotion in terms of brain processes that are active during emotional states. Much of this activity has centered on the limbic system (e.g., MacLean, 1963), although other areas of the brain have also been involved. For years, the primary research methodology continued to be extirpation of various sections of the brain, with changes in emotional responses subsequently observed. In later years, more precise electrical stimulation of various areas of the brain was correlated with emotional behavior. The goal of brain ablation and stimulation studies was to locate specific neuroanatomical areas associated with each emotion. This has been a fruitful and useful line of research, although many questions remain unanswered. This research suggests that areas of the brain associated with emotional expression are generally more phylogenetically ancient and primitive, and that there may be direct neurobiological connections between these ancient areas and the retina, which allow emotional activation without intermediation of the higher cognitive processes (Moore, 1973; Zajonc, 1984). These brain areas are shared to a great extent with other, more primitive species. Many of these species do not possess cortical areas associated with higher cognitive processes. This fact may well account for observations from the behavioral evolutionary tradition of the universality of emotions across species.

38

Nevertheless, no easy answers have been forthcoming on the precise site of various emotions, since stimulation of the same area under somewhat different conditions may produce different emotional (and nonemotional) responses. Conversely, stimulating somewhat different areas may produce similar emotional responses at different points of time (Izard, 1977; Panksepp, 1982; Plutchik, 1980). More recently, advances in neuroscience have focused attention on specific neurotransmitter receptor systems and their relationship to emotions. With this new emphasis has come the realization that fine-grained neuroanatomical exploration will never offer a full explanation, even at a basic neurobiological level, of the workings of emotions.

Within the biological tradition of study, the notion that emotional responses are distinct and separate remains largely intact. Although Cannon (1929) assumed that emotional "arousal" is a unitary phenomenon, with different levels of arousal accounting for the different emotions, most modern neurobiologists seek different neurotransmitter systems involving multiple areas of the brain as possibly underlying the variety of emotions. While no firm evidence is yet available, there are some promising leads. (A review of research relevant to anxiety within this context is presented in Chapter 5.) Of course, neurobiological theorists concentrate on biological processes and tend to ignore issues involving the antecedents to emotions and the perception that begins the emotional process. This tendency, along with the ever-present danger of reducing a complex human response such as emotion to its cellular components, has kept many biological theorists less than fully aware of advances in alternative approaches to emotions—a state of affairs that, unfortunately, characterizes the study of emotion in general. As Lazarus (1984) points out, no less an authority on the neurobiology of emotion and behavior than Sperry (1982) despairs of finding specific anatomical sites or neurobiological systems exclusively associated with one or another emotion.

EMOTION AS COGNITION

The most recent and, in a way, the most radical approach to emotion can be characterized as cognitive. While many investigators and theorists have proposed explanations of emotions emphasizing cognitive factors, two approaches stand out.

Appraisal Theory

The first approach, which came to be known as "appraisal theory," can be said to have originated in 1962 with publication of the well-known experiment by Schachter and Singer. Concluding that there is little evidence that emotions are associated with differential patterns of arousal as suggested by Cannon, Schachter and Singer concluded that generalized arousal may be reported differently, depending on the context. That is, noticing arousal, individuals may appraise the context to determine an appropriate label for the arousal. If one were aroused while jumping out of a plane without a parachute, the arousal would be described as fear, while the same level of arousal during sexual relations would be described as love. The essential step in understanding emotion is, then, the process of appraising the context and attributing a causal relationship following the perception of a generalized, undifferentiated arousal state.

This hypothesized sequence of events has proved to be an exciting and thought-provoking theory that has generated considerable discussion and experimentation. Nevertheless, there is little evidence to support this theory in its entirety (e.g., Reisenzein, 1983), and evidence is accumulating that it does not account for the facts. One of the most cogent criticisms has been provided by Maslach (1979a, 1979b), who concluded that any differences found in the original Schachter and Singer experiment were very weak and that even those differences were experimentally confounded. In addition, several attempts have been made to replicate the original experiment, without success (Marshall, 1976; Marshall & Zimbardo, 1979). These replication attempts found that unexplained arousal is perceived negatively, irrespective of the environmental cues. For example, arousal will not be attributed to happiness or love simply because that is the context. While this variability does not support an attribution theory of emotion in general, it is a finding that becomes important when models of psychopathological anxiety are considered in Chapter 7. Ever since the early experiments by Walter Cannon, investigators have demonstrated time and again that emotional behavior and reports of emotion can occur in the absence of arousal. What is probably the best-known restatement of this old fact was made by Peter Lang (1968), who observed (as noted above) that the three response systems comprising anxiety—behavior, verbal report, and physiological arousal—are only loosely correlated. The implication of this restatement, since confirmed, is that reports and behavior associated with anxiety can occur in the absence of arousal (Barlow & Mavissakalian, 1981).

Richard S. Lazarus (Lazarus, 1968; Lazarus, Averill, & Opton, 1970) has also developed a theory of emotions involving cognitive appraisal. Specifically, changes in the environment are appraised in terms of their potential impact on the individual. For example, one may appraise a gun as dangerous and thus experience fear. Although this approach is rich and complex, and considers emotion as an adaptive behavior, the emphasis is clearly on cognitive appraisal of events as the primary determinant of the type and quality of an emotional response. This work has put a necessary emphasis on an aspect of emotion often ignored by other theories—the initial perception, as well as cognitive elaborations of that perception.

Nevertheless, several problems arise with Lazarus's formulation. For example, one difficulty encountered by appraisal models is the phenomenon of irrational emotions. It is common for an individual either to report an emotional experience that is recognized as irrational ("There was no reason for me to feel that way"), or at least to be unable to verbalize any rational appraisal preceding the emotional response, despite careful inquiry. Appraisal theorists have some difficulty handling this event, usually resorting to an "out-of-awareness" or unconscious process, which is difficult to test.

Of course, depending on how broadly "appraisal" is defined, it is possible that a very basic type of appraisal, closely connected with an initial perception, does precede emotion. For example, as noted above (Derryberry & Rothbart, 1984) and reviewed below (e.g., MacLeod, Mathews, & Tata, 1986), it appears that information *is* appraised (or perceived) and processed out of awareness. Furthermore, cognitive sets or expectancies can markedly alter the expression of even the most intense of emotions (see Chapter 4). Therefore, as Hollandsworth (1986) eloquently points out, cognitive-appraisal theories may be much closer to biobehavioral theories citing the primacy of affect (e.g., Zajonc, 1984) than one might think. Differences may simply revolve around definitional elaborations of "appraisal." For example, does any perception qualify as a basic form of appraisal, or do appraisals have to involve conscious rational elaboration of settings and consequences? In any case, cognitive-appraisal approaches have generated a proportionately large amount of interest among clinical investigators and clinicians working with emotional disorders, particularly those interested in cognitive therapy for emotional disorders.

Lang's Bioinformational Approach

A second cognitive theory of emotion is currently in formation and seems likely to have a substantial impact on emotion theory. Termed a "bioinformational approach" and originated by Peter Lang (e.g., Lang, 1978, 1979, 1984, 1985), this cognitive theory conceptualizes emotion as action tendencies stored in memory and accessed in a variety of ways, all of which involve the processing of information.

Lang recognizes that all emotional expression exists along several dimensions. One dimension is low arousal–high arousal; a second involves valence from pleasant to unpleasant; and the third is control (or lack of it). (A dimensional approach to emotion and anxiety is fully considered below.) Despite the importance of considering the dimensional aspects of emotion, Lang considers the essential core to be behavioral acts or broad response dispositions that occur in specific stimulus contexts. These stimulus contexts define the function and direction of the act (e.g., approach–avoidance, etc.). These emotional dispositions or acts are likened to software in a computer. The "data file" of these acts includes not only stimulus information, which prompts action, but also response propositions that are appropriate, such as avoidance and underlying physiological reactivity. "Response propositions" are data in the form of statements relevant to response components of the emotion stored in long-term memory. "Meaning propositions," wherein the stimulus information and response propositions are interpreted, are also part of the data file and essentially define the event's significance. For example, in a phobic situation, stimulus information would refer to recognition of the frightening object. Response propositions would be relevant responses, such as avoidance and elevated physiological responding to prepare for the emergency. But meaning propositions would tie these two together. For example, meaning propositions might include the following statement: "In this situation, that thing is unpredictable and dangerous, and my responding indicates that I'm afraid."

Since data structures are stored in memory as propositions more or less strongly associated, the entire network is conceptual and accessed by information-processing mechanisms. The likelihood of accessing an emotion is increased by presenting information that maximizes the number of propositions matched. For example, if one hears mention of a fearful object (or sexual object or anger-producing object), this may or may not be sufficient to activate the entire emotional prototype. But if one is face to face with the object and the context is correct, *and* one is already physically aroused from exercise, *and* the appropriate emotional (fear, anger, or sex) meaning propositions have been primed (perhaps through unrelated conversation), then the chance of accessing the full emotional response is maximal.

This creative and carefully thought-out theory avoids the difficulty of discordance that confronts the theory of discrete emotions, since weak or incomplete matching of propositions may only access part of the response. The evolutionary behavioral theorists, on the other hand, would suggest that a fundamental, innate discrete emotion is always present in its entirety, albeit at varying levels of intensity.

Lang does not elaborate on the origin of emotions, but presumably emotional prototypes are, by and large, learned, He does admit to the possibility that some stimulus propositions are innate, and therefore more likely to evoke a strong emotional response. Examples would be "prepared" fear stimuli such as snakes and spiders, or perhaps various sexual postures. But most emotional responding is thought to be the product of experience and conditioning rather than of innate neurocircuitry. This approach also bypasses the requirement of an intervening cognitive appraisal, which produces difficulty for appraisal theorists. That is, emotional responses are directly accessed without intervening appraisal if enough propositions are matched. Of course, meaning propositions, which are basically interpretations, come very close to the concept of attributions as elaborated by Schachter (1964), but attributions are seen as simply one type of propositions among many, not as necessary antecedents.

Perhaps most significant from the point of view of cognitive science, the scientific exploration of this process does not depend on self-report of experiential thought or feeling. Self-reports can be influenced by conditions that distort the underlying information-processing sequence. Bioelectric recording, conversely, is seen as a more direct, contemporaneous method of examining bioinformational processing without the distortions of self-report. It is direct because emotion is considered an action set that generates efferent output, whether the behavior is actually expressed or not. That is, experiencing fear will produce physiology associated with avoidance responding, whether one actually avoids the feared object or not.

This conceptually rich theory will have a significant impact and will generate an increasing body of research over the years. Nevertheless, it is still a theory in construction, and the data in support are very limited at this point. What data do exist have been collected on small numbers of volunteers for the most part, and the data have been relatively weak and inconsistent in terms of statistical significance (e.g., Lang, Levin, Miller, & Kozak, 1983). Also, reliance on psychophysiological recording as the primary dependent variable, despite the enormous advance this method promises for cognitive science, may prove problematic in view of the relative unreliability of this measure (e.g., Arena, Blanchard, Andrasik, Cotch, & Myers, 1983). And this theory places an enormous burden on psychophysiological measures. As Lang (1984) observes,

> From the perspective of the psychophysiological investigator, the difficulties in assessing non-exposure response codes are considerable. He must often sort through three different but coincident physiologies. For example, when a socially anxious person imagines performing in a public speaking context there is, first, the physiological code of speech presentation (efferent representations of the motor task of speaking and the cognitive demands of generating or reading the required text); for the anxious subject there is a second coded physiology of alertness and preparation for disapproval and to repel attack (usually the target physiology of the emotion researcher); finally, there is a third physiology of the imaginal act itself, i.e., the immediate biological cost of memory retrieval, regeneration of the relevant conceptual network, and its central processing. (p. 223)

Interestingly, this theory requires an ultimate concordance of the various response systems constituting an emotion (at least the strongly coherent emotions) somewhere deep in memory structure, even if this concordance is not always apparent upon expression—or, more accurately, even if all components of the emotion are not accessed. In view of the existing data on discordance and Lang's own pioneering conceptualization of these data, this requirement demands a leap of faith for the time being. On the other hand, as Lang (1985) argues, some emotions may be more coherent and "tighter" in their structures; once such emotions are accessed, an "all-or-none" type of response occurs, including all response components. Other emotions may be much more diffuse, with a great deal of fluidity among affective response structures. Thus, many stimuli may partially access these more fluid structures, although not as intensely and with greater discordance. Lang considers "generalized" anxiety as one possible example of this more fluid, diffuse affective state.

THEORIES OF ANXIETY

Now that major theories and approaches to the study of emotion have been presented, theories of anxiety need only be briefly reviewed, since they map approaches to emotion closely. Theories of anxiety are also elaborated in theories of personality where anxiety is conceptualized as a personality trait. "Trait," in this context, refers to a disposition to behave anxiously with some consistency over time or across situations. For example, the most popular measure of trait anxiety, the State–Trait Anxiety Inventory (Spielberger, Gorsuch, & Lushene 1970), simply asks subjects whether they feel anxious much of the time ("trait") as opposed to at that moment ("state"). Therefore, the present review of models of anxiety integrates state and trait approaches.

ANXIETY AS EXPRESSED BEHAVIOR

I have highlighted the neoevolutionary approach, where fear is considered a basic, fundamental, discrete emotion that is universally present across ages, cultures, races, and species. Few would disagree that this emotion, whether innate or not, is universal and has a clear functional value in the evolutionary sense. But for all the clarity with which discrete-emotion theorists conceptualize fear as a basic, individual emotion, "anxiety" is considered both different from discrete emotions and at the same time something very vague, imprecise, and muddled.

For example, Izard (1977) views anxiety as a hybrid or blend of a

44

number of emotions, although fear, admittedly, is dominant in the blend. The basic emotions most commonly considered to combine with fear to make up anxiety include distress/sadness, anger, shame, guilt, and interest/excitement. Furthermore, anxiety, according to Izard's view, may assume a different blend across time and situations. For example, in one instance, fear, distress, and anger may be the blend referred to as "anxiety" by the individual; in another instance, shame and guilt may be combined with fear. Naturally, such combinations make it difficult indeed to talk of anxiety in a precise way. Nevertheless, anxiety is considered to be a blend of fundamental, innate emotions, each of which is modified by learning and experience. Individuals may learn to associate discrete emotions such as fear with a large number of cognitive and situational factors including the evocation of other, related emotions.

According to Izard (Izard, 1977; Izard & Blumberg, 1985), the development of an anxious personality results from the interaction of learning with basic emotions, resulting in stable affective–cognitive structures that are trait-like. These "traits" result from the repeated occurrence of particular patterns of affective–cognitive interactions. Izard and other neoevolutionary theorists allow for biologically determined "emotion thresholds," which contribute to the frequency or intensity of an emotion or a blend of emotions and to its perception as a personality trait. In keeping with Izard's differential-emotion theory, however, biological emotion thresholds are specific to one emotion or another, rather than contributing to a general trait of emotionality. This combination of factors, then, is thought to account for the development of an "anxious" personality. Although fear is a basic innate emotion, an anxious personality for the most part is learned. But Izard (1977) concludes that anxiety, because of this vagueness, "can never obtain the requisite precision to guide definitive scientific investigation" (p. 378). As noted in Chapter 1, many clinicians have been unaccustomed to making distinctions between fear and anxiety, and generally have paid little attention to fear and anxiety as conceptualized by the emotion theorists.

ANXIETY AS BIOLOGY

While all theorists admit to the role of neurobiology in both anxiety and emotion, some consider it primary and causal. Although the focus on research has shifted from a solely neuroanatomical perspective to one combining neuroanatomy with receptor physiology and biochemistry, the emphasis, dating back to Cannon, on emotion (and therefore anxiety) as a neurobiological event remains. Genetic, psychophysiological, and neurobiological views of anxiety are presented in some detail in Chapter 5. However, at this point it is useful to consider briefly several trait models of anxiety that are based on biological theorizing, since these personality theories have played a significant role in our thinking about anxiety.

Eysenck's Introverted Neurotics

What is undoubtedly the most widely known biological theory of personality was originated and elaborated by Hans Eysenck (1967, 1981). Eysenck's theory is based on different levels or intensities of cortical arousal. He suggests that positive or pleasant emotions are associated with moderate levels of arousal; negative or unpleasant emotions are associated with arousal that is either too high or too low. This state of affairs motivates individuals to seek moderate levels of arousal and avoid the extremes. However, since individuals differ markedly in their resting level of arousal, which is biologically determined, consistent and lasting differences in behavior appear as a direct result of levels of arousability. Specifically, individuals with relatively low levels of cortical arousal (due to a chronic low level of reactivity of the ascending reticular activating system) tend to seek out higher optimal levels of cortical arousal and greater amounts of stimulation. People in this group are "extraverts." "Introverts," on the other hand, find their optimal levels of arousal at much lower levels of stimulation.

The other well-known axis in Eysenck's theory has a construct called "neuroticism" at one end and one termed "stability" at the other end. The underlying biological factor associated with this dimension of personality is thought to be autonomic nervous system reactivity, which would feed back to influence limbic system activity. Neurotic individuals would possess the characteristic of intense autonomic nervous system activity and very slow rates of habituation. These axes, presented in Figure 2.1, have appeared for decades in textbooks on psychopathology. Eysenck's theory has had a profound influence. In a sense, all other theories, including those reviewed below, are based on Eysenck's work.

While Eysenck's theory is a modern personality theory that attempts to encompass the full range of behavior, the close relationship of this approach to biological theorizing on emotion, and its direct relationship to Cannon's (1929) views on emotion, are apparent. Thus, emotion in general and anxiety in partiuclar are seen as resulting largely from the interaction of individual traits of cortical arousal and autonomic nervous system reactivity with the influence of the limbic system. Anxious individuals tend to have both high resting levels of cortical arousal and high autonomic nervous system reactivity. Unlike Cannon, of course, Eysenck was a pioneer in advocating the interacting role of learning and conditioning in the formation and expression of these personality traits, as well as in the alleviation of psychopathology arising from extremes of these biological traits. In propagating these notions, Eysenck (1960) became one of the founders of behavior therapy.

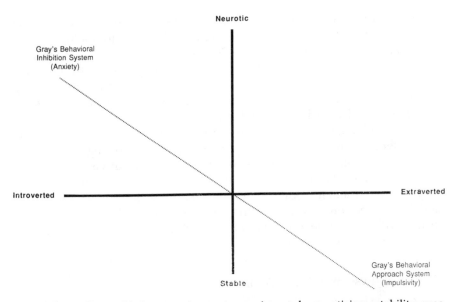

FIGURE 2.1. Eysenck's introversion–extraversion and neuroticism–stability axes, with Gray's anxiety–impulsivity axis superimposed. Adapted from Eysenck, H. J. (Ed.). (1967). *The biological basis of personality*. Springfield, IL: Charles C Thomas. Copyright 1967 by Charles C Thomas. Adapted by permission.

Gray's Behavioral Inhibition System

One of the foremost theorists of the neurobiological basis of anxiety is Jeffrey Gray, whose careful experimentation in his animal laboratories and subsequent creative theorizing is mentioned frequently in this book. Rather than relying on the increasingly untenable concept of differential intensity of arousal (see Chapter 5), Gray (1982) has proposed that personality and emotions are determined by two affective–motivational systems. The primary system in his model is the behavioral inhibition system, which consists of the septal–hippocampal system, its monoamine afferents, and the frontal cortex. After specific stimulus input (particularly signals of punishment, nonreward, and novelty), the behavioral inhibition system suppresses ongoing behavior and redirects attention toward the relevant stimuli. In Gray's view, an active and sensitive behavioral inhibition system that reacts to novelty or punishment with exaggerated inhibition is the biological basis of anxiety. A complementary system involving the medial forebrain bundle responds to signals of rewards and nonpunishment (safety signals) by facilitating approach. These two systems, then, regulate much of the organism's behavior. As Gray (1982, 1985) points out, what he has done is to emphasize a new dimension or axis, one end of which falls between Eysenck's introversion and neuroticism (see Figure

2.1). Thus, the trait of "anxiety" falls 45 degrees from either introversion or neuroticism. Individuals with an active behavioral inhibition system (i.e., anxious individuals) would reflect a combination of Eysenck's introversion and neuroticism. On the other hand, people with an active approach system, which is sometimes referred to as "impulsivity," would reflect a combination of extraversion and stability. Gray's new axis is superimposed on Eysenck's axes in Figure 2.1.

Gray's biological theorizing has the advantage of being relatively comprehensive, involving as it does a variety of neurobiological systems. Many theories restrict themselves to the brain stem, but Gray's formulation encompasses both "old" and "new" cortex. Although an increasing body of experimental evidence supports many of the predictions of this model, in some important ways the model is already dated. The reasons for this will become clear in Chapter 5, which examines biological theorizing in greater detail.

Cloninger's System of Harm Avoidance

Another biologically based theory emphasizing anxiety as a personality trait has recently been proposed by Cloninger (1986). Since this is a comprehensive theory by a well-known clinical investigator, it is likely to have some impact, and it is thus considered briefly here. Cloninger (1986) begins by accepting the evidence supporting Gray's two-system model (specifically, the behavioral inhibition system and the behavioral activation system). But he alters the labeling of these traits to "harm avoidance" rather than "anxiety" (highly active behavioral inhibition system) and "high novelty seeking" rather than "impulsivity" (strong behavioral activation system). Gray's two axes with Cloninger's new labels are presented in Figure 2.2.

To these, Cloninger adds a third trait previously identified by personality theorists such as Eysenck through factor analysis, but usually accorded a less important position in most personality theories. This trait was originally labeled by Eysenck as "psychoticism" or "tough-mindedness" —labels that have been criticized in the past as being particularly undescriptive of the items comprising the cluster. Cloninger labels this trait "reward dependence" and defines it as a heritable tendency to respond intensely to reward and succorance and to learn to maintain rewarded behavior. All three traits are considered to be orthogonal, but may combine to produce a variety of personalities—or, in the extreme, psychopathological states.

What is particularly interesting about Cloninger's model is his next step. He proposes that each of the three heritable personality traits is strongly related to variations in specific monoaminergic neurotransmitter pathways. Specifically, high harm avoidance (or anxiety) is associated with

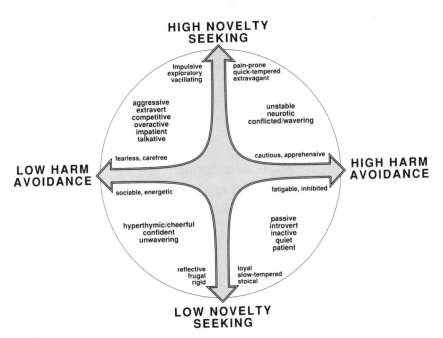

FIGURE 2.2. Interaction of two of Cloninger's proposed personality dimensions: harm avoidance and novelty seeking. From Cloninger, C. R. (1986). A unified biosocial theory of personality and its role in the development of anxiety states. *Psychiatric Developments*, 3, 167–226. Copyright 1986 by Oxford University Press. Reprinted by permission.

high serotonergic activity; high novelty seeking is associated with low basal dopaminergic activity; and high reward dependence is associated with low basal noradrenergic activity. These relationships are presented in Figure 2.3. Cloninger marshals biological and psychological evidence to support his model. For example, the trait of high harm avoidance is associated with the cognitive disposition of hypervigilance, as well as with reduced biological habituation to potentially dangerous situations. Cloninger suggests that when high harm avoidance is combined with low reward dependence and low novelty seeking, individuals develop a very strong pattern of recognizing hidden threats and contingent relationships, and therefore overestimate potential risks in ordinary circumstances. These individuals then become sensitized over time and develop "chronic anxiety," complete with strong patterns of anticipatory anxiety, ruminative worrying, and social introversion.

This theory is important for several reasons. First, it offers an interesting distinction between the anxiety and somatoform disorders. For example, Cloninger suggests that individuals with somatoform disorders (with

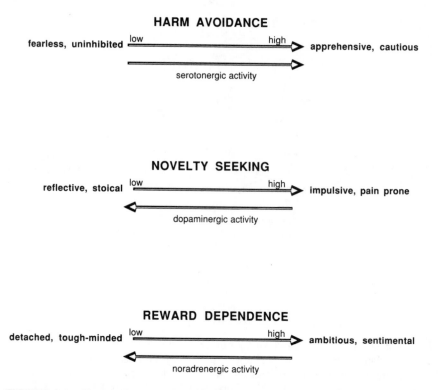

FIGURE 2.3. Cloninger's three heritable personality traits and their underlying neurobiolgoical systems. Adapted from Cloninger, C. R. (1986). A united biosocial theory of personality and its role in the development of anxiety states. *Psychiatric Developments, 3,* 167–226. Copyright 1986 by Oxford University Press. Adapted by permission.

a strong component of what he calls "somatic anxiety") differ markedly on several personality dimensions from individuals with "cognitive anxiety," which he equates broadly with the anxiety disorders. To take one example, individuals with somatoform disorders are very high on novelty seeking. In addition, this model presents what is probably the first good example of the integration of modern neuroscience into theories of personality and psychopathology. Current biological theorizing within general theories of personality results in a subcategorization of what used to be termed as "general arousal" into different neurotransmitter systems. The theory then outlines an intriguing web of data connecting these specific "arousal" systems with fundamentally different personality traits.

Cloninger's theory clearly belongs to the new generation of biological theories of personality. This approach also recognizes the interaction of biological and cognitive systems, as well as the role of learning in the full expression of personality. Nevertheless, it is difficult to believe that complex behavioral traits can be mapped quite so neatly onto specific neurotransmitter systems. Because Cloninger's 1986 paper is only the first statement of the theory, it will most likely undergo modification as our knowledge of neurobiology increases.

One difficulty with neurobiological theories of emotion and anxiety (as well as some cognitive theories) is the linear nature of the presumed causal sequence. This difficulty is particularly true of theories where the seat of emotion is in the "old" brain or the brain stem. Many theories, including some cognitive theories, assume that all emotion begins with biological activation, such as arousal. What these theorists ignore is the evidence that behavioral, perceptual, and emotional changes produce marked alterations in basic neurobiological systems. These alterations may be specific, depending on the "meaning" of the stimulus. Some of this evidence has been reviewed above in terms of somatic and autonomic (cardiovascular, electrodermal) changes that are specific to perceptual and emotional activation. But even basic neurotransmitter systems will vary systematically, depending on perceptual input and the motivational significance or "meaning" of a stimulus (Derryberry & Rothbart, 1984; Foote, Ashton-Jones, & Bloom, 1980; Rolls, Burton, & Mora, 1980). This evidence is discussed more fully in Chapter 5. Suffice it to say that linear models of causation usually fare poorly when compared with more complex but conceptually satisfactory models involving systemic feedback loops.

ANXIETY AS COGNITION

Attribution and appraisal theories, with their intuitively appealing description of the relationship of cognitive processing to emotion, have achieved enormous popularity among clinicians working with anxiety disorders. Cognitive or cognitive–behavioral therapies widely used with emotional disorders are based largely on the premise that irrational emotions are a function of inappropriate attributions or appraisals. Therapy is thus a process of directly attacking these maladaptive appraisals and attributions. A variety of individuals have considered creatively the role of cognition in anxiety, but the primary theorists in this area are Richard S. Lazarus, George Mandler (e.g., 1975), Charles D. Spielberger (1985), Irwin G. Sarason (1985), Aaron T. Beck (e.g., Beck & Emery, 1985), and, more recently, Richard Hallam.

Mandler's Interruption Theory

Mandler (1975) highlights a process whereby ongoing cognitive activity is interrupted. This interruption produces a diffuse autonomic discharge.

The autonomic discharge results in detailed appraisal of the source of the interruption, which is then evaluated either positively or negatively, depending on the results of the appraisal and the relationship of this appraisal to the intensity of the autonomic arousal. Naturally, if the arousal is very high, and the deduction as a result of the appraisal is that some sort of a threat to the individual is involved, then the resulting emotions will be fear and anxiety. The assumption of this approach is that arousal is relatively undifferentiated and that the burden of emotional formation is on the cognitive process of appraisal following the interruption.

Spielberger's State–Trait Model

A different model has been proposed and elaborated by Spielberger (1966, 1972, 1979, 1985). This model is presented in Figure 2.4. Spielberger is

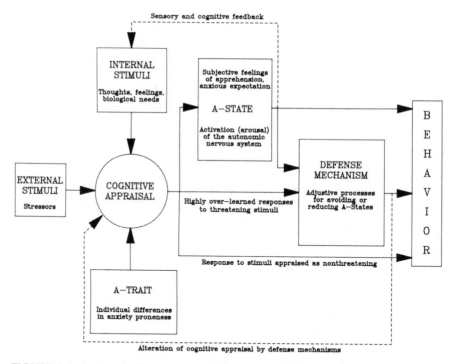

FIGURE 2.4. A state–trait–process model of anxiety. The model posits two anxiety constructs, state anxiety (A-State) and trait anxiety (A-Trait), and specifies the relationships between these constructs, external and internal stressors, cognitive appraisal of threat, and psychological defense mechanisms. From Spielberger, C. D. (1972). Anxiety as an emotional state. In C. D. Spielberger (Ed.), *Anxiety: Current trends in theory and research* (Vol. 1, p. 43). New York: Academic Press. Copyright 1972 by Academic Press. Reprinted by permission.

one of the few cognitive theorists who, as evidenced in his state–trait conceptualization, considers anxiety as a personality trait. State anxiety is considered to be a transitory emotional state, whereas the disposition to experience state anxiety frequently or to be "anxiety-prone" is considered a personality trait (trait anxiety). In the model presented in Figure 2.4, external stressors as well as internal stimuli will be appraised in such a way as either to produce anxiety or not. In part, this appraisal will be a function of one's level of trait anxiety. As one can see, the most critical point of this process is, once again, the act of appraisal. State–trait notions have proved useful in distinguishing common anxiety reactions from more frequent, intense, and consistent anxiety, although the causes of these individual differences in trait anxiety are unknown. As with all appraisal theories, there is some difficulty in handling irrational anxiety.

Beck's Cognitive Schemata

A cognitive approach with a different emphasis from that of appraisal theory is advocated in the pioneering work of Beck (e.g., Beck & Emery, 1985). Beck recognizes emotions in general and anxiety in particular as complex biopsychosocial responses with important evolutionary, biological, affective, and cognitive components. Beck fully appreciates the fact that most basic emotions are innate, survival-oriented responses to an environment that has changed greatly over the course of evolution. For example, he suggests that the behavioral expression and action set associated with fear, which was adaptive during the millenia when human beings were hunter–gatherers, may no longer be appropriate when threats and danger are primarily psychological rather than physical. It is under conditions where emotions are inappropriate, exaggerated, or disordered that Beck begins to emphasize the importance of cognitive factors. Thus, Beck's theorizing is confined largely to instances where danger is misperceived or exaggerated.

More specifically (Beck, 1985; Beck & Emery, 1985), the locus of the problem in the anxiety disorders is not in the affective system, but in hypervalent cognitive schemata where reality is continually interpreted as dangerous. Information about one's self, the world, and the future (the "cognitive triad") is continually processed in a distorted way as dangerous. Consequently, states of anxiety are associated with (automatic) thoughts and images relevant to danger. For Beck, these automatic thoughts and images, resulting from distorted information processing, trigger inappropriate motor, physiological, and affective components of the anxiety response. Therapy is directed at altering these automatic thoughts and the underlying schemata responsible for distorted processing of information. This approach is not really a theory of anxiety, but rather a theory of anxiety *disorders*, since Beck would agree that anxiety and fear continue to be adaptive under some circumstances.

Unlike previous models, this approach does not depend on conscious rational appraisal, but is closer to a "verbal-mediational" model of learning. The cause of anxiety lies in faulty processing of information, rather than a clear, on-the-spot, rational perception of threat. This twist begins to circumvent the difficulties that other cognitive approaches have with irrational anxiety, since the automatic thoughts present within the irrational hypervalent schemata are not always obvious to the individual. It is not at all unusual for anxious patients to report that their fears are irrational, but this knowledge does not stop continuous thoughts of threat and impending doom. Of course, if "not obvious" comes to mean "not open to scientific scrutiny of any kind," then the theory will be incapable of disconfirmation and will die the slow death of other theories with this fault. Fortunately for the theory, this does not seem to be the case.

There is evidence (reviewed below) that anxious patients do selectively perceive threat more often than nonanxious patients, and that automatic thoughts of threat are present if the antecedents of anxiety are systematically monitored. Nevertheless, there is little or no evidence that inappropriate habitual cognitive schemata actually precede emotional disorders—an issue that is important to the integrity of this model. Of course, it is possible that pre-existing cognitive schemata may yet be discovered or that they are difficult to detect (see Chapter 7). It is also possible that automatic thoughts and cognitive schemata are simply by-products of the disordered emotional response, with the cause of both phenomena lying elsewhere Beidel & Turner, 1986; Hallam, 1985).

Some have assumed that the proven success of cognitive therapy with depression lends support to Beck's theory. But, to anticipate the discussion of therapeutic approaches to emotional disorders, there is little if any evidence that cognitive interventions alone, as derived from these theories, are responsible for this success. All cognitive therapies contain enactive behavioral components, which may be responsible for their success (e.g., Bandura, 1977b; Beidel & Turner, 1986). In fact, experimental attempts to isolate the contribution of cognitive procedures have often been unable to ascertain any added therapeutic effect from the direct modification of cognitions or cognitive schemata (see Chapter 8), although some exceptions are now appearing (see Chapters 14 and 15). Nevertheless, Beck's thinking and his early attempts at integrating the vast diversity of information concerning anxiety from different points of view are extremely valuable. These efforts have already guided a new generation of research and clinical practice, and it seems certain that this influence will grow.

Hallam's Theory of Anxiety as a Personal Construct

An approach differing substantially from other theoretical views of emotion has appeared recently and deserves careful consideration. While this approach emanates from a somewhat different tradition than do other theories of anxiety, it remains cognitive in its epistemological underpinings; it is also relevant in the context of definitional problems with anxiety discussed in Chapter 1. Basing his thinking on the work of the social constructivists, Hallam concludes that anxiety can never have scientific status, since it is essentially a multireferential lay construct. Hallam's conclusion about the nature of anxiety comes surprisingly close to Izard's neoevolutionary view.

In the great tradition of constructivist thinking, Hallam suggests that anxiety (and panic) is basically a metaphor based on a construing of certain combinations of events by an individual. These events may include, but may not be limited to, a client's beliefs, linguistic skills, purposes, and concurrent identity problems. The important question for constructivists is what causes the individual to report anxiety. As Hallam (1985) points out, "the most positive contribution a social constructivist position has to offer is to dissuade researchers from regarding these real life problems as reflecting an underlying *emotion* of anxiety or, even less helpful, an anxiety disorder" (p. xiv).

Constructivist positions have always seemed very extreme to clinicians and clinical researchers accustomed to dealing daily with people suffering from anxiety (Barlow, 1986a). However, by emphasizing how the individual construes his or her world in the context of situations where anxiety is often reported, Hallam is introducing an additional theoretical issue that may prove to be important in elucidating the basis of anxiety complaints. To paraphrase Hallam, one of the most important errors preventing us from advancing our knowledge about anxiety and panic (or any emotion, for that matter) is our inability to consider it as a multireferential lay construct. Based on the evolution of convenient but vague terms from everyday conversation, our conception of anxiety has changed from anxiety as a metaphor to anxiety as an actual entity encapsulated within the organism. For accurate reports on its nature, this entity needs only to be carefully observed and reported by the individual (since it is not observable by others). These reports of anxiety are treated as if they are (imperfect) observations of this entity. In fact, according to Hallam (1985), a number of antecedents and internal (e.g., somatic) and external consequences are functionally related to reports of anxiety, but always in a complex way. Among these referents are specific and contextual environmental events, sensory feedback from autonomic and other somatic processes, overt and covert behavior (e.g., escape, facial expressions), and combinations of these classes of referents, as well as cognitive schemata representing beliefs and attributions of causality. The undeniable point that Hallam hammers home is that any or all of these referents may be present without an individual's reporting panic (or anxiety), and certainly without an individual's requesting treatment for the same. Rather, the individual, as an agent, construes these referents in such a way that anxiety is reported. Only by untangling the functional relationship of these many referents in a given individual, in the context of how he or she construes them, can we say anything about the nature of anxiety.

Hallam's ideas are not nearly as radical as they might seem; furthermore, as noted above, they have an intriguing similarity to Izard's (1977, 1985) conception of anxiety. Any approach based on cognitive appraisal is, in some sense, constructivist, but Hallam elegantly takes it to a logical extreme. Hallam is certainly not saying that anxiety and anxiety disorders do not exist, but rather that a variety of biological and cognitive factors may be functionally related to reports of anxiety in a given individual, and that these factors differ across individuals and within individuals over time. Once again, the important questions for Hallam are the following: What factors are functionally related to reports of anxiety in an individual? What would be the critical processes involved in changing the individual's construction of those events that are associated with considerable suffering and are reported as anxiety?

EMOTION–COGNITION INTERACTIONS

Any theorectical analysis of emotion and anxiety is incomplete without consideration of the burgeoning field of emotion–cognition interactions (e.g., Izard, Kagan, & Zajonc, 1984). While some persevere in holding a linear view of cognition–emotion relationships, most experimentalists analyzing these phenomena are adopting systems or views consistent with the complex interactions that are unfolding as research progresses. Several of these issues, such as differential cognitive content associated with specific emotional states and selective processing of information among emotionally disordered patients, have implications for the etiology of anxiety disorders and are taken up below. But two emotion–cognition phenomena are more relevant to theories of emotion and anxiety and are receiving increasing attention in the laboratories of experimental psychology. The first of these is the relationship of mood and memory, and the second is the relationship of emotion to attention.

MOOD, MEMORY, AND INFORMATION PROCESSING

In 1981, Bower (see also Gilligan & Bower, 1984) reviewed a series of studies demonstrating that subjects' free associations, interpretations of social behavior, and impressions of persons they may be viewing for the first time are congruent with their ongoing (state) moods. That is, if one's mood is positive, then one's associations, interpretations, and impressions will also tend to be positive. Conversely, more negative moods will negatively bias the same cognitive processes. Most of Bower's experiments were accomplished through the hypnotic induction of various mood states, followed by subsequent assessment of selective memory and perception.

Bower's research has already had a marked impact on the study of depression. For example, Teasdale and his associates have conducted a series of studies (Teasdale, 1983; Teasdale & Fogarty, 1979) examining the effects of mood, particularly sadness, on recall of pleasant and unpleasant cognitions. Subjects took longer to recall pleasant memories when they were in a depressed mood than when they were in an elated mood, suggesting that depression reduces the ability to process or recall positive cognitions. Conversely, the probability of recalling unhappy memories increased, while depressed and the likelihood of recalling happy memories decreased. Similar results were observed using a somewhat different paradigm by Bower (1981). Bradley and Mathews (1983) have also demonstrated a similar phenomenon with clinically depressed patients.

The important implication of this work is that mood-congruent memories are a function of mood-dependent (or state-dependent) learning. That is, negative cognitions and judgments are more readily retrieved when one is depressed, because they were originally learned and encoded in memory in this mood state. Therefore, the recurrence of a depressed mood cues or disinhibits this cognitive material. These findings are very consistent with Lang's view of emotion as a series of associated propositions stored in memory. Therefore, the recurrence of depressed mood will also cue other propositions related to this emotion, such as recall of specific cognitive content. As Gilligan and Bower (1984) point out, this concept finds ready validation in our common experience, where the cheerful optimist sees the world through rose-colored glasses and the bottle as half full. Anyone who has been depressed, on the other hand, knows that the bottle is half empty. The parameters of the relationship of mood and memory are currently in the process of elaboration (e.g., Clark & Teasdale, in press); such findings as possible sex differences are emerging, with important implications for psychopathology.

Interestingly, there seem to be no studies that establish mood-congruent recall of threat-related or anxiety-related memories in people who are anxious. In fact, one study designed to examine this issue did not find this recall bias in clinically anxious patients (Mogg, Mathews, & Weinman, 1987). However, a corollary to Bower's network model of memory is that individuals should also display bias in *perceiving* mood-congruent material. Words or concepts that are mood-congruent should have more perceptual salience then noncongruent materials, and therefore should be recognized more quickly. A number of investigators have looked at this phenomenon (e.g., Burgess *et al.*, 1981; Parkinson & Rachman, 1981b). MacLeod *et al.* (1986), using the most sophisticated methodology yet employed to examine this particular question, determined that clinically anxious subjects carrying a diagnosis of generalized anxiety disorder consistently shifted attention toward threat words, compared to normal control subjects, who actually tended to shift attention away from threat words. Once again, parametric research is continuing on this interesting and important cognitive–affective relationship.

The encoding and recall bias reviewed above in the context of mood-congruent cognitive activity also relates to the issue of narrowed attention during emotional states. For example, although it was not directly tested, the tendency to perceive and encode threat-related material (MacLeod *et al.*, 1986) should also reduce attention and encoding of alternative non-threat-related material.

EMOTION AND ATTENTION

A second and related phenomenon observed in numerous experiments with different purposes and methodologies over the past 25 years involves what has been called "narrowing of attention" during emotional arousal. Easterbrook (1959) was one of the first to describe this process. He suggested that narrowing of attention is a preoccupation with mood-congruent material during emotional reactivity that varies as a function of the intensity of the emotion: The more intense the emotion, the narrower the attention. Specifically, the number of cues utilized decreases as emotional intensity increases. One becomes preoccupied with the central mood-congruent cues as intensity of mood increases, at the expense of concurrent attention to external stimuli. Stimuli relevant to the emotion become more salient, whereas mood-incongruent or irrelevant stimuli are allocated less and less attention.

This phenomenon has been verified in a number of different experiments (e.g., Callaway & Stone, 1960; McNamara & Fisch, 1964). Some investigators suggest that extreme cue restriction results in decreased processing efficacy and impaired performance. For example, Korchin (1964) suggested that at the most intense levels of arousal, attention is characterized by distractibility and disarray. That is, since the individual loses the broader perspective, he or she is unable to respond adaptively. This seems similar to, and may account for, the Yerkes–Dobson law (Yerkes & Dobson, 1908), where performance relates to arousal in an inverted U-shaped function. According to this law, performance initially increases and then decreases as arousal reaches maximal levels. Thus, narrowing of attention and its consequence may explain the Yerkes–Dobson law. Derryberry and Rothbart (1984) suggest specific neurobiological processes by which affective–motivational systems control sensory modulation and attention.

The relationship between intensity of emotion and cognition is only beginning to be studied. It is not entirely clear what impact this relationship has on emotional disorders. For example, it is a well-established clinical phenomenon that severe-intensity anxiety and panic seem to eliminate competing rational cognitive activity. Also, while studying male erectile dysfunction (which appears to be very similar to a social phobia), my colleagues and I have discovered that direction of attention during arousal may be the key factor in determining whether an individual is sexually functional or dysfunctional (Barlow, 1986c). I elaborate on this theme when I discuss the etiology of anxiety in Chapter 7.

As with most phenomena in the study of emotion, the relationship between intensity of emotion and attention or performance is not simple. In an intriguing experiment, Gilligan and Bower (1984) tested recall of either happy or sad material that was learned while subjects were experiencing either happy or sad moods of different intensity. Data are presented in Figure 2.5. The usual mood-congruent effect was noticed; that

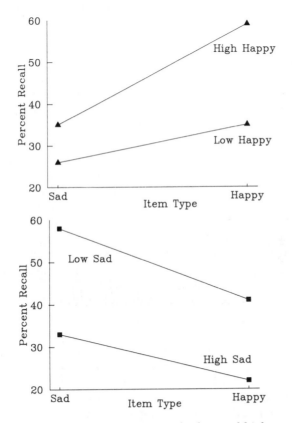

FIGURE 2.5. Top: Recall by happy subjects under low and high mood intensities. Bottom: Recall by sad subjects under low and high mood intensities. From Gilligan, S. G., & Bower, G. H. (1984). Cognitive consequences of emotional arousal. In C. E. Izard, J. Kagan, & R. B. Zajonc (Eds.), *Emotions, cognition, and behavior* (p. 564). New York: Cambridge University Press. Copyright 1984 by Cambridge University Press. Reprinted by permission.

is, those who learned happy and sad material while experiencing a happy mood showed greater recall of happy material. A similar result was evident for those who learned the material while in a sad mood. What is important is the amount of retention or recall that was observed as a function of different intensities of mood. People who were more intensely happy actually remembered more of *both* the happy and sad material than people who were only mildly happy. But the reverse occurred for the sad group. People who were more intensely sad remembered generally *less* of the material than people who were only mildly sad. Thus, it appears that there are specific relationships between mood and memory as a function of the mood. High-intensity sadness interferes with the cognitive function of retention and recall, even for mood-congruent material. Since fear and anxiety are also negative affects, it is possible that a similar finding might be associated with these moods. If so, this will have important implications for psychopathology.

THE COMPONENTS OF EMOTION

It is fair to say that the three approaches to emotion—biological, cognitive, and expressive-behavioral—have progressed in remarkable isolation. This statement is particularly true of cognitive and neurobiological approaches, with the possible exception of Lang's bioinformational approach. Although dealing with the same phenomena, these approaches behave as ships passing in the night on the sea of emotion. Occasionally, one approach will vaguely acknowledge the other: For example, the neurobiological tradition may observe that some elaboration and processing of basic biological events occur in higher cortical centers. But it is most often left at that. Similarly, cognitive theorists may admit that emotions are associated with neurobiological processes, but content themselves with referring to some vague, unidimensional biological activation or arousal. It is perhaps the behavioral approach, with its long tradition, that has advanced the furthest in attempts to integrate different aspects of the study of emotion, although these investigators would be the first to admit that current attempts are preliminary (e.g., Izard & Blumberg, 1985).

In any case, most emotion theorists would agree that there are three principal components to emotion, even if an individual investigator emphasizes only one. This is also true for any one emotion, such as fear or anxiety. These components are the neurophysiological/biochemical, the expressive-behavioral, and the feeling/experiential.

THE NEUROBIOLOGICAL COMPONENT

The neurobiological component, as noted above, began with an emphasis on anatomical studies of brain structures. Early on (Papez, 1937), the limbic system and structures within the system, such as the hippocampus, hypothalamus, and amygdala, were thought to be heavily involved in emotion. Included within this system would be research on central autonomic nervous system function and the long tradition of psychophysiological measurement of emotion, usually in the peripheral autonomic nervous system. Once again, the evidence suggests that the neuroanatomy and neurophsiology of emotions are complex, with multiple pathways among various structures associated with changes in emotional processes. A newer area of inquiry, as described above, includes sophisticated studies of neurotransmitters and hormones that might be implicated in emotions. As reviewed in Chapter 5, norepinephrine and serotonin, as well as gamma-aminobutyric acid (GABA), have been implicated in anxiety research.

THE BEHAVIORAL COMPONENT

In recent years, the study of expressive behavior associated with emotions—particularly facial expressions, but also other action tendencies—has received renewed attention. Creative clinical investigators have also speculated on and studied the possible functional adaptive value of emotional behavior (e.g., Beck, 1985). While many investigators do not emphasize this aspect of emotion, few now ignore its functional value. Within fear and anxiety, the old adage "fight or flight" (Cannon, 1929) continues to capture best the action tendencies associated with fear, with an occasional reference to immobility (being frozen with fear) (Gallup, 1974).

THE EXPERIENCE/FEELING COMPONENT

Since the work of William James, self-reports of affect and emotional sensation have been a primary arena of investigation. For the lay public, subjective experience defines emotion. For these reasons, studies of the subjective experience of emotion have a long and interesting history, particularly in terms of efforts to specify basic dimensions of emotions. Nevertheless, it is important to note that this component of emotion cannot be equated with cognitive theories of emotion. Lang's (1985) bioinformational approach uses psychophysiological variables as primary measures of cognitive processes, eschewing self-report of affect. Also, the study of experience and feeling is an inherently difficult area, because one is relying on imprecise linguistic symbols to represent private internal feeling states. Language itself is a multidetermined system, with its own distortions and individual variability. Any science of self-report is bound to be imprecise, at least at the level of one individual. To take one small example, Swinson and Kirby (1986) make the common observation that patients often present at the clinic reporting that they are terribly anxious because they are chronically tired and distressed or sad. Similarly, patients report depression because they are on edge and apprehensive. Nevertheless, aggregated across large groups, self-reports acquire more consistency and reliability (Tellegen, 1985) and make a substantial contribution to our understanding of the nature of emotion.

These components of emotion cannot be equated with measures of emotion (Barlow, 1985). As stated, Lang finds it important to measure "cognition" with physiological measures, but introspective reports of affect can also be used. Similarly, the expressive-behavioral or action tendencies of emotion, such as avoidance in fear, can be measured directly, by report ("I feel like running away"), or physiologically (as Lang does with action tendencies and Schwartz *et al.* [1981] have done with facial expressions). For this reason, the chapters in this volume on assessment and treatment of specific clinical disorders present a judicious mix of measures based on current evidence.

THE DIMENSIONS OF EMOTION

A survey of different theoretical traditions illuminates the variety of approaches one can take in attempting to understand emotion in general or specific emotions, such as fear, in particular. The development of a consensus on the basic components of emotion permits the coordinated study and measurement of emotion. But only a thorough analysis of the basic dimensions shared by all emotions allows a complete theoretical elaboration of the nature of emotion. For that reason, careful consideration of the dimensions of emotion finds its way into leading theoretical analyses from several different traditions (e.g., Izard, 1977; Lang, 1984).

An important consequence of a dimensional analysis is a greater specification of the nature of individual emotions, such as fear and perhaps anxiety. By contrasting these emotions or mood states with affective states that are often closely related, such as depression, one can begin to see what is essential about anxiety. Finally, specifying the critical dimensions of anxiety has important implications for the etiology and treatment of anxiety disorders.

DIMENSIONAL MODELS OF EMOTION

The primary method of studying the subjective experience of emotion is through self-report, using the variety of affect-laden adjectives available from the richness of language. As noted above, self-report, particularly retrospective report, is subject to a variety of distortions resulting from inadequacies of memory, contrast effects, and repression. Nevertheless, in everyday life, one of the most common personal interactions is to ask someone "How are you?" or "How are you feeling?" and receive a similar question in return. This common question has become an important part of the self-monitoring of disordered emotional states. Patients with affective disorders are asked while in specific situations or at specific times to rate a particular affect, such as depression, anxiety, or anger, along levels of intensity (Barlow, 1981). Using this approach, some investigators have attempted a semantic mapping of the world of emotions. The purpose of this semantic mapping is to ascertain basic emotional expressions based on self-report, and to examine the dimensions of affect shared by all emotions. Similarities or differences in discretely described emotions can then be determined by their relationship to one another in the context of the major dimensions of emotion.

The primary measurement tools in this type of research are adjective checklists. Subjects check adjectives that are judged to describe their current emotional state or their long-term emotional dispositions. Major instruments include the Multiple Affect Adjective Checklist (Zuckerman & Lubin, 1965), the Profile of Mood States (McNair, Lorr, & Droppleman, 1971), and the Mood Adjective Checklist (Nowlis & Nowlis, 1956). The primary analytic tools for determining relevant discrete as well as overall dimensions of affect have been sophisticated correlational procedures, such as factor analysis and related cluster-analytic techniques. When stable emotional dispositions are the subject of inquiry or measurement, rather than moment-to-moment emotional states, the study of mood becomes the study of personality.

Despite the identification of discrete emotions through factor-analytic work, over the years researchers investigating dimensions of personality and emotion have consistently narrowed down the possibilities to two or three major bipolar dimensions (e.g., Eysenck, 1961; Russell, 1980; Wundt, 1896). Eysenck has put most of the emphasis on two discrete, orthogonal axes. Most investigators have concluded that this arrangement puts an undue burden on the specification of one axis that comprises emotion or personality. For that reason, a consensus has developed that the best way to represent the factors emerging from these factor-analytic studies is a circumplex model (Plutchik, 1980).

In a circumplex model, various emotions are placed circularly in order to reflect their relationship to other dimensions of affect, as well as their opposites to be found on the other side of the circle. Emotions that are highly positively correlated will be found close to each other, while negatively correlated emotions will be found on opposite sides of the circle (e.g., see Figure 2.6, below). One of the best-known early examples, of a circumplex model was proposed by Freedman, Leary, Ossorio, and Coffey (1951) and later elaborated for its clinical relevance by Timothy

Leary (1957). For example, distributed along one side of the circle are "critical," "punitive," and "rejecting," while on the opposite side are "loving," "cooperative," and "trustful," and so on around the circumplex. Circumplex models are perfectly amenable to identification, description, and "plotting" of discrete emotions through factor-analytic techniques. Indeed, Izard and his colleagues, using adjective checklists, identified (and therefore validated, in Izard's view) the 10 fundamental discrete emotions emerging from expressive-behavioral studies (Izard *et al.*, 1984). Furthermore, facial expressions can be arranged in a circumplex model corresponding to descriptive adjectives.

RUSSELL'S CIRCUMPLEX

Nevertheless, analyses of the dimensions of affect such as Russell's (1980) have identified two axes within the circumplex that account for the major proportion of the variance in attempts to ascertain dimensions of emotion. The first of these axes can be termed "activation," with high activity or arousal at one end and low activity or calmness at the other. Russell also includes "valence," which refers to a bipolar dimension of pleasure–displeasure. Russell and Mehrabian (1977) have identified a third dimension that accounts for somewhat less of the variance, but would seem to be important in making certain discriminations among emotions. This dimension is termed "dominance–submission." But they put it more descriptively as feelings of total lack of control versus feelings of influence or being in control. After studying this dimension further, Russell (1980) has concluded that dominance–submission is not really an affect, but a strong cognitive correlate of emotion. Control is a perceived *consequence* of an emotion, rather than an emotion per se. Nevertheless, the perception of control may be particularly important within the emotion of anxiety, since perceptions of control under high arousal and negative valence (unpleasurably high arousal) may discriminate, for example, between anger and anxiety. People who are angry may feel unpleasantly aroused but in control of the situation or dominant, while anxious people may feel not in control and submissive, helpless, or vulnerable.

TELLEGEN'S CIRCUMPLEX

One of the most creative and sophisticated researchers in the area of personality has proposed yet another circumplex of emotion, which organizes the data somewhat differently from previous models but seems to fit the (self-report) data best. Starting with a long representative list of adjectives from current self-rating inventories for mood, Auke Tellegen (1985) replicated the primary discrete emotion factors found by Izard and others, but also demonstrated, as did Russell (1980) before him, that the item intercorrelations were dominated by two large dimensions. These dimensions repeatedly emerged from studies of different groups of subjects tested on the same occasion, or of the same group of subjects tested periodically over periods of time ranging up to 3 months (e.g., Zevon & Tellegen, 1982). This latter method is particularly convincing, since it avoids the problem of retrospective distortion.

Tellegen (1985) has also found that arranging the emotional descriptors emerging from these two major factors in a circumplex proves most satisfactory in terms of describing their relationship. Thus, the circle is divided into eight sections, since correlations have yielded consistent descriptors that fit into these eight sections. The two major factors are labeled in a straightforward manner: "positive affect" and "negative affect." The full circumplex model is presented in Figure 2.6. This emphasis differs from earlier descriptions, where "arousal" and "valence" axes have

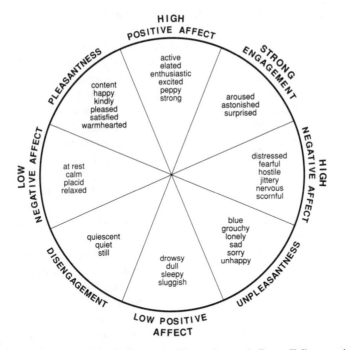

FIGURE 2.6. The two-factor structure of self-rated mood. From Tellegen, A. (1985). Structures of mood and personality and their relevance to assessing anxiety, with an emphasis on self-report. In A. H. Tuma & J. D. Maser (Eds.), *Anxiety and the anxiety disorders* (p. 691). Hillsdale NJ: Erlbaum. Copyright 1985 by Lawrence Erlbaum Associates. Reprinted by permission.

been highlighted (e.g., Russell, 1980). But the term "engagement," appearing in the upper right quadrant, is preferred by Tellegen over the term "arousal," resulting in an engagement–disengagement axis. "Engagement" refers to the same clustering of adjectives previously called "arousal." The "valence" dimension, also identified by others, is termed "pleasantness–unpleasantness" in this circumplex. Arousal (or engagement) and valence (or pleasantness–unpleasantness) are, therefore, found as diagonal axes in this circumplex. However, Tellegen notes that he prefers emphasizing the axes of positive and negative affect, for several reasons. He suggests that they conform more closely to the factor-analytic data, as well as to major personality factors discussed below. In addition—and more importantly, from our point of view stressing emotional disorders—this configuration seems to identify more clearly those features that distinguish anxiety from depression.

WHAT IS ANXIETY?

THE DIMENSIONS OF ANXIETY AND DEPRESSION

With the foregoing overview of the dimensions of emotion, it is now possible to approach this question: What is anxiety? More specifically, how does what we call "anxiety" relate to discrete emotions, as well as to more general dimensions of affect? Since all theorists (and therapists) agree that anxiety and depression are closely related, a more specific version of this question is as follows: How does anxiety differ from depression?

This is a particularly good way to begin an examination of the nature of anxiety, since this question has been extremely troublesome to basic emotion theorists and clinical practitioners. Clinicians and clinical researchers often assume that anxiety and depression overlap to such an extent that it is not useful to consider them as distinct (Barlow, Di Nardo, Vermilyea, Vermilyea, & Blanchard, 1986; Foa & Foa, 1982). Nowhere is this overlap more evident than in measures of anxiety and depression based on rating scales. One good example is provided by the Hamilton Anxiety Rating Scale and the Hamilton Rating Scale for Depression, where the overlap among specific questions exceed 70% (Barlow, 1985). It is not surprising that these scales are highly correlated, share considerable variance, and demonstrate poor discriminant validity (although discrimination or diagnosis is not the purpose of these scales).

Even more telling is evidence presented by Dobson (1985), who calculated correlations between a number of anxiety and depression self-rating scales, such as the State–Trait Anxiety Inventory (Spielberger et al., 1970) and the Zung Self-Rating Depression Scale (Zung, 1965). The correlation among anxiety scales was .66; among depression scales, it was

.69; and between anxiety and depression scales, it was .61. The amount of shared variance for each correlation was very high, ranging from .37 to .47. This degree of shared variance suggests that these questionnaires are not useful in measuring the intensity of two different affective states, anxiety and depression; rather, they are measuring the same or very similar affective states. Breslau (1985) found a similar lack of discriminability in the Center for Epidemiological Studies Depression Scale, which is a widely used depression rating scale.

On the other hand, pure cases of anxiety and pure cases of depression certainly seem to exist (Klerman, 1980; Prusoff & Klerman, 1974), and common clinical experience validates differences between these states. Basic research from an expressive-behavioral point of view (e.g., Izard, 1977) and factor-analytic studies identify discrete emotions commonly labeled "fear" and "sadness/distress." What is clearly needed is an understanding of the essence of anxiety and depression, not only to differentiate them for clinical purposes, but to better answer the basic question: What is anxiety?

Measuring self-report of affect, Tellegen (1985) has begun to provide some interesting answers to this question. To accomplish this analysis, he assembled five scales. The first scale consisted of items that were clearly high or low on negative affect. A second scale consisted of items that were high or low on positive affect. The remaining scales tapped anxiety and depression items and items depicting pleasant and unpleasant mood (valence). Anxiety and depression items were those typically used in anxiety and depression scales. Data on these scales were then collected from 284 college students. Analyses revealed that depression and anxiety scales were highly correlated ($r = .83$) and that both were strongly related to unpleasant mood (see Figure 2.7). But Tellegen's data do suggest that these two emotional states can be distinguished and that their core features can be enhanced.

What seem to distinguish these mood states most clearly are the independent dimensions of positive and negative affect. Anxious mood can be best (and most essentially) characterized as high negative affect with a fear component, which Tellegen also describes as "unpleasant engagement" in his circumplex. Some of the descriptors of high negative affect are "distressed," "fearful," "hostile," "jittery," "nervous," and "scornful." Depressed mood, on the other hand, can be described as low positive affect ("unpleasant disengagement"). This arrangement has a great deal of face validity and seems to come closest to capturing the essence of these mood states. Furthermore, Blumberg and Izard (1986), using methods derived from discrete-emotion theory, have arrived at a similar point of view. Future clinical assessment techniques should be developed that identify what is unique in these mood states, rather than what they have in common. Assessment of the core concepts should allow more

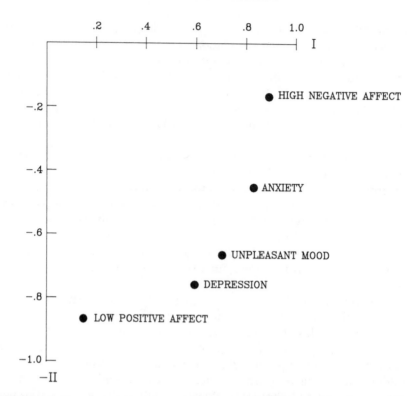

FIGURE 2.7. Two-factor structure of five mood scales. "I" identifies the positive pole of negative affect; "−II" identifies the negative pole of positive affect. From Tellegan, A. (1985). Structures of mood and personality and their relevance to assessing anxiety, with an emphasis on self-report. In A. H. Tuma & J. D. Maser (Eds.), *Anxiety and the anxiety disorders* (p. 693). Hillsdale, NJ: Erlbaum. Copyright 1985 by Lawrence Erlbaum Associates. Reprinted by permission.

careful inquiry into issues regarding course of illness and treatment outcome in patients who might have varying blends of these two affective states. Of course, positive and negative affect are overriding dimensions of mood that do not necessarily map neatly onto the more clinical concepts of anxiety and depression. As Tellegen (1985) notes, it will be important to determine what is essential and discriminable about anxiety and depression at a more discrete level of analysis, in addition to his own global two-dimensional analysis.

Efforts along these lines are now under way (e.g., Dobson, 1985; Lipman, 1982). For example, in our own clinic, motor retardation, hopelessness, and several related variables have proved discriminating (Barlow, 1983). Riskind and Beck (1983) also found the cognitive variable of hopelessness to be somewhat discriminating between depression and anxiety.

Riskind, Beck, Brown, and Steer (1987) have revised the two Hamilton scales to clearly discriminate more between major depressive disorder and generalized anxiety disorder. This successful revision is one of the first attempts to construct scales based on what is essential and important about anxiety and depression when compared to each other, as opposed to scale construction based simply on descriptors of unpleasant mood or dysphoria that are common to both anxiety and depression. As such, it becomes important to identify the discriminators between anxiety and depression. Replicating the data just reviewed, the depressive items most strongly correlated with a diagnosis of major depressive disorder (after depressed mood) were suicidal thoughts, feelings of hopelessness and helplessness, and motor retardation. For anxiety, the item that correlated most strongly with the diagnosis of generalized anxiety disorder was the item relating to complaints of "psychic" anxiety (i.e., to apprehension and worry). This was followed by the item covering somatic and visceral symptoms (e.g., cardiovascular and gastrointestinal activity, muscle twitching, pain and stiffness, and agitation during the interview) (Riskind et al., 1987). Beck reports a similar discrimination between general anxiety and minor depression or dysphoria (A. T. Beck, personal communication, 1986).

From this point of view, fundamental differences between clearly defined anxiety and depression may be found in action tendencies and underlying associated physiology. Anxiety suggests engagement and activation; depression suggests disengagement and inactivity. Anxiety implies an effort to cope with difficult situations, and the physiology is there to support active attempts at coping. Depression is characterized by behavioral retardation and an associated lack of physiology. If emotional states, as in Lang's view, are fundamentally behavioral acts, then anxiety and depression are fundamentally different, despite the vagueness associated with these terms.

METAPHORS AND CONSTRUCTS: ANXIETY AND FEAR

But this hypothetical discriminability does not mask the fact that anxiety and depression, particularly dysthymia or "neurotic" depression, are closely related constructs devised by clinicians and investigators. These constructs overlap considerably in definition and concept, since they are both subjectively unpleasant affective states. For example, even analyses emphasizing the discriminability of anxiety and depression find strong similarities between these two unpleasant affects on many dimensions, such as feelings of "vulnerability or helplessness" (Beck, 1988). The major cognitive and somatic features mentioned above that characterize anxiety are only vague referents to a construct that presents differently from in-

69

dividual to individual and certainly presents differently across cultures (see Chapter 1).

This view of anxiety as a construct requires consideration of potentially important difference between fear and anxiety, alluded to above. Neoevolutionary emotion theorists inform us that fear (and sadness) are distinct and basic emotions, and human experience in general would validate this. Fear is a primitive alarm in response to present danger, characterized by high negative affect and arousal; there is no mistaking it for sadness. But what, then, is anxiety? Again, the emotion theorists help us by suggesting that anxiety is a diffuse blend of emotions reflecting interest, anger, and excitement mixed with a primary component of fear. As will become evident below, perceptions of unpredictability and lack of control over potentially aversive events contribute to a marked apprehension surrounding the future ("It could happen again and I might not be able to deal with it"). For this reason, the term "anxious apprehension" may reflect this diffuse, future-oriented mood state more precisely.

Interestingly, depression (particularly "neurotic" depression) is considered a blend of similar emotions, which always seem to include fear and distress. Izard (1972) suggests that "anxiety" and "depression" are very imprecise terms and for this reason are not amenable to careful scientific analyses. At one time they may refer to one specific blend of emotions, and at another time a different blend. At a neurophysiological level, Tompkins (1981) has pointed out that anger, interest/excitement, surprise, and fear are closely related, since all share a relatively sudden increase in the density of neural firing; this strengthens the notion that these are common components of the blend. Modern neurobiological theorizing considers the similtaneous activation of several neurotransmitter-mediated arousal systems (Cloninger, 1986; Gray, 1982). Bull (1951), from the perspective of examining basic emotions, found that fear and a tendency to escape are often combined with interest and a tendency to explore.

Other emotion theorists also underline the "diffuseness" of anxiety. Lang (1984, 1985), for example, considers generalized anxiety a pervasive, diffuse emotion comprised of a loose but widespread affective network in memory. This is in contrast to "focal" emotions such as specific fears, which are seen as tightly organized, coherent affective structures. Any state of arousal, according to Lang, may be sufficient to facilitate transfer of "anxiety," since the elicitation of very different emotions (anger, sexual arousal, or interest and excitement) may be sufficient to activate somatic or visceral elements held in common with "anxiety." This activation insures that the negative memories associated with perceptions of unpredictability of events or lack of control will continually become associated with new contexts and situations. Lang does not make a fundamental distinction between anxiety and fear, but places them at opposite ends of a continuum such that marked differences are readily apparent.

70

Hallam's (1985) view of anxiety as a personal construct is also consistent with this conception, since any number of internal or external stimuli or events can be construed in such a way that an individual will report anxiety (or depression). And, with the "diffuseness" of this concept, these stimuli (both internal and external) may differ considerably across individuals or within individuals over time. Thus, there is wide theoretical agreement that what we call "anxiety" differs from fear.

To return to dimensional analyses, Russell's (1980) findings and conclusions regarding control become important. Control, or lack of control, assumes a position of sufficient strength to appear in factor analyses of self-report ratings of affect adjectives. Since the variety of negative emotional states that share high engagement or activation are close together in any circumplex, it is possible that what characterizes and distinguishes a report of anxiety from a report of anger or even interest is a sense of lack of control. In this sense, anger and hostility are closer to anxiety than to depression, since both are negative affects in any dimensional scheme of emotional states that share action tendencies of engagement with supporting physiology. This fact may have important implications for differentiating anxiety and stress disorders, as outlined in Chapter 7.

In any case, this sense of uncontrollability has a number of effects, according to this view. Among these are a decrease in valence or pleasure associated with the emotion or emotion blend. Another effect is a marked shift in attention from the object of interest to salient material or events congruent with apprehensiveness and anxiety, as well as to one's own affective response to these events (see Chapter 7), for the sense of control (or the lack of it) is a construct with primarily internal referents. As noted above, this interruption and shift in attention constitute an integral part of many theories of anxiety, including biological and cognitive theories (Gray, 1982; Mandler, 1975). The anticipated uncontrollability is future-oriented rather than something that actually happens. In other words, it is not present danger, but a vague sense of future danger, which is due to a sense of impending uncontrollability combined with distorted and unadaptive shifts in allocation of attention. While these perceptions may also characterize depression, the action tendencies should be very different in clearly defined cases.

These views converge on a single theme: Anxiety and depression are not "emotions" in any basic, focal, or innate sense. As the behavioral emotion theorists point out, anxiety and depression cannot really be analyzed as emotions from a scientific point of view. To comprehend anxiety (as opposed to fear), one must consider a variety of cognitive and behavioral operations not generally considered to be within the purview of emotion theory. In my view, anxiety is a diffuse cognitive–affective structure consisting of a negative feedback cycle characterized to varying degrees by components of high negative affect; a sense of both internal and

71

external events proceeding in an unpredictable, uncontrollable fashion; and maladaptive shifts in attention. In this view, it does not make sense to say that anxiety "begins" with activation of the limbic system, perceptions of threat or uncontrollability, or attentional shifts. Each individual component contributes to the cycle in a manner that in turn affects other components of the structure. The nature and origin of anxiety, according to this view, are fully explicated in Chapter 7.

If anxiety is a clinical manifestation of a diffuse cognitive–affective structure spanning a variety of emotional cognitive and behavioral operations, then what is the clinical manifestation of fear? In my view, fear is panic, and panic is the unadulterated, ancient, possibly innate alarm system human beings call "fear."

3

The Phenomenon of Panic

I was 25 when I had my first attack. It was a few weeks after I'd come home from the hospital. I had had my appendix out. The surgery had gone well, and I wasn't in any danger, which is why I don't understand what happened. But one night I went to sleep and I woke up a few hours later—I'm not sure how long—but I woke up with this vague feeling of apprehension. Mostly I remember how my heart started pounding. And my chest hurt; it felt like someone was standing on my chest. I was so scared. I was sure that I was dying—that I was having a heart attack. And I felt kind of queer, as if I were detached from the experience. It seemed like my bedroom was covered with a haze. I ran to my sister's room, but I felt like I was a puppet or a robot who was under the control of somebody else while I was running. I think I scared her almost as much as I was frightened myself. She called an ambulance.

This description was offered by a recent patient in our clinic. Compare this to an earlier account of an anxiety attack that "erupts into consciousness without being called forth by any train of thought":

An anxiety attack may consist of a feeling of anxiety alone, without any associated ideas, or accompanied by the interpretation that is nearest to hand such as ideas of the extinction of life, or a stroke, or the threat of madness . . . or the feeling of anxiety may have linked to it a disturbance of one or more of the bodily functions—such as respiration, heart action, vasomotor innervation or glandular activity. From this combination the patient picks out in particular now one, now another, factor. He complains of "spasms of the heart," difficulty in breathing," "outbreaks of sweating" . . . and such like; and in his description, the feeling of anxiety often recedes into the background. (Freud, 1895/1940, p. 86)

The roots of the experience of panic are deeply embedded in our cultural myths. The Greek god Pan, the god of nature, resided in the

73

countryside, presiding over rivers, woods, streams, and the various grazing animals. But Pan did not fit the popular image of a god: He was very short, with legs resembling those of a goat, and he was very ugly. Unfortunately for ancient Greeks traveling through the countryside, Pan had a habit of napping in a small cave or thicket near the road. When disturbed from his nap by a passer-by, he would let out a blood-curdling scream that was said to make one's hair stand on end. Pan's scream was so intense that many a terrified traveler died. This sudden, overwhelming terror or fright came to be known as "panic," and on occasion Pan would use his unique talent to vanquish his foes. Even the other gods were subject to his terror and at his mercy.

While Pan has faded deep into myth, his power is experienced daily by millions. In fact, panic may be so common, so widespread, and so much a part of our experience that we have managed to overlook its importance. In lay terms, "panicking" is a part of our lives, usually occurring before some deadline that seems impossible to make or at points when one is suddenly faced with danger. But the importance of the phenomenon of panic may be such that increasing our understanding is essential if we are to solve the many puzzles surrounding anxiety disorders. In addition, we now know that a full understanding of other major psychological disorders, such as depression, somatoform disorders (e.g., hypochondriasis), and stress disorders, may be difficult without first understanding panic. And yet we know very little about the phenomenon of panic.

WHAT IS PANIC?

THE PRESENTATION OF PANIC

Much of our recent increased attention to the concept of panic has resulted from the description of panic in DSM-III (America Psychiatric Association, 1980), where it was defined as "the sudden onset of intense apprehension, fear or terror, often associated with feelings of impending doom" (p. 230). "Sudden onset" has come to mean 10 minutes during which panic will reach a peak, and this temporal criterion is included in the revision of DSM-III (DSM-III-R; American Psychiatric Association, 1987).

A second important part of the definition is the list of symptoms comprising a panic attack. Most of these symptoms are physical or somatic expressions of panic, such as palpitations or dizziness. DSM-III listed 12 symptoms and specified that at least 4 must be present to label the event a true or "full-blown" panic attack. In DSM-III-R, 14 symptoms are listed. This has been accomplished by adding 1 (nausea or abdominal distress) and by breaking down the 12th symptom listed in DSM-III (fear of dying, going crazy, or doing something uncontrolled during an attack) into two symptoms: fear of dying, and fear of going crazy or doing something uncontrolled. This allows a bit more precision in identifying the characteristic physical symptoms as well as the cognitive expression of dread (going crazy or dying) with which an individual may present during a panic attack. The 14 symptoms from DSM-III-R are listed in Table 3.1. Once again, the individual must report having a panic characterized by "the sudden onset of intense apprehension" and so on, *and* must report at least 4 of these symptoms.

These symptoms have been arrived at largely through the clinical experience of investigators working with the anxiety disorders. Clinical experience also tells us that different individuals may experience different combinations of the symptoms, and that the same person may report a slightly different mix of symptoms from one panic attack to another. Typically, patients who are experiencing panic attacks report far more than the minimum number of four symptoms specified in DSM-III or DSM-III-R. My colleagues and I asked a large group of patients to indicate symptoms each of them experienced during their typical or most recent panic. Table 3.2 illustrates the number and percentage of a group of 41 DSM-III agoraphobics with panic who endorsed each of the 12 DSM-III symptoms. For purposes of comparison, the same data from a more recent group of 55 patients with the new DSM-III-R diagnosis of panic disorder with agoraphobia are also presented. Some patients in the latter group may have had very little agoraphobic avoidance, due to the new DSM-III-R criteria (see Chapters 9 and 10). In fact, 25 of these patients would have met

TABLE 3.1. List of DSM-III-R Panic Symptoms

1. Shortness of breath (dyspnea) or smothering sensations
2. Choking
3. Palpitations or accelerated heart rate (tachycardia)
4. Chest pain or discomfort
5. Sweating
6. Faintness
7. Dizziness, lightheadedness, or unsteady feelings
8. Nausea or abdominal distress
9. Depersonalization or derealization
10. Numbness or tingling sensations (paresthesias)
11. Flushes (hot flashes) or chills
12. Trembling or shaking
13. Fear of dying
14. Fear of going crazy or doing something uncontrolled

Note. From American Psychiatric Association. (1987). *Diagnostic and statistical manual of mental disorders* (3rd ed., rev.). Washington, DC: Author. Copyright 1987 by the American Psychiatric Association. Reprinted by permission.

DSM-III criteria for panic disorder, while 30 would have met the criteria for agoraphobia with panic. But the definition of a panic attack is very similar, as described above.

As one can see from the table, most of these patients reported the physical symptoms of palpitations, dizziness, and trembling. Shortness of breath (dyspnea), sweating, faintness, and hot and cold flashes were also common. Choking, paresthesias, feelings of unreality, and chest pain were somewhat less common, although the percentage endorsing the last symptom was quite different between groups. No fewer than 90% of the first group reported a fear of dying, going crazy or losing control. When these cognitive symptoms were broken down according to DSM-III-R, more patients endorsed the fear of losing control, although the percentage endorsing one or the other was close to 100%. It should be noted that since these descriptions were taken mostly from the patients' "typical" panics, the specific number of symptoms associated with any one discrete panic may have been somewhat less.

Another approach to this issue is to examine relative intensity of symptoms. Ley (1985b) also interviewed a group of agoraphobics with panic and chronicled their symptom reports by ranking the symptoms on

TABLE 3.2. Number and Percentage of 41 DSM-III Agoraphobia with Panic Patients and 55 DSM-III-R Panic Disorder with Agoraphobia Patients Reporting Each of the Panic Symptoms

Symptom	DSM-III agoraphobia with panic ($n = 41$)		DSM-III-R panic disorder with agoraphobia ($n = 55$)	
	Number	%	Number	%
Dyspnea	37	90	41	75
Palpitations	40	98	48	87
Chest pain	31	76	21	38
Choking	30	73	28	50
Dizziness	39	95	48	87
Unreality	28	68	31	57
Paresthesias	26	63	32	58
Hot or cold flashes	35	85	40	74
Sweating	35	93	38	70
Faintness	31	76	37	68
Trembling	36	88	47	86
Fear of dying, going crazy, losing control	37	90		
(DSM-III-R:)				
Abdominal distress			30	56
Fear of dying			29	52
Fear of going crazy, losing control			42	76

TABLE 3.3. Rank Orders of the Intensity of Symptoms
Experienced by Agoraphobics during Panic Attacks

Symptoms	Ley's rank	Barlow's rank	Composite rank
Fear of dying, etc.	1	2	1
Palpitations	3	1	2
Trembling	2	4	3
Dyspnea	4	5.5	4
Dizziness	7	3	5
Hot or cold flashes	6	5.5	6
Faintness	8.5	7	7
Unreality	5	11	8
Sweating	8.5	8	9
Chest pain	10	10	10.5
Choking	11	9	10.5
Paresthesias	12	12	12

Note. From Ley, R. (1985). Blood, breath, and fears: A hyperventilation theory of panic attacks and agoraphobia. *Clinical Psychology Review, 5,* 271–285. Copyright 1985 by Pergamon Journals, Ltd. Reprinted by permission.

the basis of intensity. He then compared his group with rankings from the 41 DSM-III agoraphobics described above. This list, appearing in Table 3.3, demonstrates a strikingly similar patterning of the intensity with which these symptoms were reported.

LIMITED SYMPTOM ATTACKS

Clinicians have identified what seems to be another variety of panic attack, which meets all the criteria for panic mentioned above with one exception: Fewer than four symptoms are reported. In DSM-III-R, these experiences are called "limited symptom attacks." In other sources, such as the Upjohn Cross-National Collaborative Panic Study mentioned in Chapter 11, they are referred to as "minor" attacks. There is now evidence that these "minor" attacks are aptly named, since on the whole they are rated by patients as less intense than major attacks (Taylor *et al.*, 1986), although this is not always the case. For example, my colleagues and I interviewed a woman who reported that her initial panic episode consisted of two specific symptoms: diarrhea and excessive perspiration. Following that first episode, a typical agoraphobic pattern emerged in which she would avoid going out as much as possible. Her greatest fear was that the diarrhea and sweating would suddenly recur (which would occasionally happen). Thus, when she did go out, she would always check for the availability of bathrooms, and would only begin to feel more comfortable when she had easy access to a bathroom. She was also particularly conscientious about applying antiperspirants and so forth. This woman soon learned the location of every bathroom along her frequented routes in the small city in which she lived.

Functionally, the limited symptom attack seems to serve the same purpose as a full panic attack. That is, it has the same consequences (see Chapter 10). However, in our clinical experience this type of attack is relatively rare *in the absence of major panic attacks*. For example, in the series of 41 agoraphobics mentioned above, only one person reported having had these limited attacks without ever having experienced a major attack.

On the other hand, patients who experience a major panic may have a number of these minor attacks. For example, while self-monitoring panics for 6 days in a group of 12 patients with panic disorder, Taylor *et al.* (1986) noted that 8 out of 33 panic attacks would be classified as minor or limited symptom attacks. However, criteria from the Upjohn Cross-National Panic Study were used in this report, in that only three rather than four symptoms were required to qualify an attack as "major." This left only reports of one or two symptoms eligible for the "minor" category. If DSM-III criteria were used, and attacks with three symptoms were also counted as "minor" attacks, the percentage of minor attacks might have been higher. Nevertheless, these limited attacks were rated by patients at an average intensity of 2.5 (compared to 3.9 for major attacks) on a scale of 0–10, and they were associated with an average heart rate increase of 17.3 beats per minute (BPM), as compared to an increase of 49.2 BPM for major attacks.

In summary, panic attacks are described as sudden bursts of emotion consisting of a large number of somatic symptoms and feelings of dying and/or losing control. The symptoms are relatively consistent on the average across people experiencing panic; however, individual panic attacks may present with a different "mix" or number of symptoms and may vary in intensity. The reports clearly resemble the primitive alarm of fear described in Chapter 1 (Cannon, 1927; Darwin, 1872). While these reports seem to describe a unique event, do more objective measurement procedures support these reports?

THE PSYCHOPHYSIOLOGY OF PANIC

Recently, my colleagues and I recorded detailed physiological changes preceding and accompanying "spontaneous" panic attacks in two patients who happened to be undergoing physiological assessments at the time (Cohen, Barlow, & Blanchard, 1985). These panic attacks were unexpected by the patients and certainly unexpected by us. Interestingly, both attacks occurred while the patients were engaging in relaxation—one during a psychophysiological assessment, and the other during a biofeedback-assisted relaxation training session. Why relaxation might provoke a panic is a fascinating issue taken up later in this volume (see Chapter 4). Because these serendipitous data provide part of the answer to the question "What is panic?," the two patients and their data are presented in some detail here.

The first patient was a 33-year-old female who, interestingly, was diagnosed as having generalized anxiety disorder (see Chapter 15). She is referred to here as "Mary." She presented to our Phobia and Anxiety Disorders Clinic with primary complaints of chronic tension, irritability, palpitations, faintness, and an inability to relax. Prior to her seeking treatment at our clinic, she had been treated by her family physician for irritable bowel syndrome. She reported experiencing occasional panic attacks, but not of sufficient frequency to meet the DSM-III criteria for panic disorder. (She was seen in 1984, before revisions were made to DSM-III; see Chapters 9 and 10.)

The panic attack presented here occurred while Mary was undergoing a pretreatment psychophysiological assessment. After a 10-minute period of adaptation to the laboratory, a 4-minute baseline was recorded. Next, Mary was instructed to relax first her whole body, and then her face and forehead. The panic attack occurred during this relaxation period. Following the attack, after a few minutes of reassurance by the experimenter, she was able to resume the assessment. In later phases of the assessment she was required to perform a series of stressor tasks, including mental arithmetic, stressful imagery, and the cold pressor test, which involved submerging her hand in a bucket of ice-cold water for as long as she could; she completed these tasks with little difficulty. At the end of the session, when asked to rate her anxiety levels during each phase of the assessment, she reported having felt the most relaxed during the relaxation phase, just prior to her panic attack. She also reported slight nausea associated with the relaxation, however.

The second subject was a 34-year-old female, "Jill," who was being treated for panic disorder. She reported experiencing many of her panic attacks in stressful situations. On occasion, however, they would occur at times when she felt carefree and relaxed, although usually shortly following a period of increased stress. For example, she recalled a recent panic attack that had occurred in a restaurant. She had been very tense and pressured, attempting to dress her children and see to it that her family arrived at the restaurant in time for their reservation. She was fearful that her increased tension would precipitate an attack in the restaurant, but after finally settling down and ordering her meal, she remembered thinking, "Everything is all right now, I made it." As she began to relax and enjoy her meal, she experienced an intense panic attack.

The panic presented here occurred during Jill's third biofeedback treatment session, in which she was being taught to relax her muscles.

Prior to beginning biofeedback training, she had practiced progressive relaxation for several weeks. She had made good progress, although on several occasions she had experienced slight dizziness during her practice. In this particular session, a 4-minute baseline was recorded, after which she was instructed to begin relaxation.

Physiological changes for both subjects from the start of the recording session through the onset and peak of the panic attacks are presented in Figure 3.1 for Mary and in Figure 3.2 for Jill. In each case, physiological recording ceased at the time the therapist entered the room to comfort and reassure the patient. Since the panics occurred during relaxation, and thus do not represent a separate phase of the procedure, their onset is indicated by the broken line on the figures.

The figures show remarkably similar changes for Mary and Jill. During the relaxation phase, up to the onset of the panic attacks, both Mary and Jill were relaxing nicely as indicated by decreases in heart rate and frontalis EMG. Mary showed a mean heart rate decrease of 4 BPM and a mean EMG decrease of 2.4 μV. Jill's heart rate dropped 2 BPM, while her EMG level declined 5.5 μV. These heart rate decreases were followed by abrupt increases during the panic, reaching a level of tachycardia within 1 minute for Mary and 2 minutes for Jill. EMG measures during the panics also showed increases for both patients. Hand surface temperature showed minimal changes, but the pattern was consistent for both Mary and Jill (i.e., decreases during relaxation were followed by increases during panics). Particularly striking are the magnitude of the increases and the abruptness with which they occurred. Mary's heart rate increased about 40 BPM within 1 minute and Jill's increased over 50 BPM within 2 minutes, *while both of them were relaxing!*

Lader and Mathews (1970) observed a similar pattern of physiological responses from three patients who were also undergoing physiological assessment but panicked part way through. In each case these panics were unexpected, although patients were experiencing various levels of anxiety during the assessment. In at least one case, however, the patient reported that she was "coming to" from a state of mild drowsiness when the panic occurred. This may be similar to Jill's and Mary's situation. The attacks were also over in several minutes for Lader and Mathews's patients, prompting them to speculate on innate inhibitory physiological mechanisms that must have been present to cause such a rapid decrease in the panic.

More recently, clinicians and clinical investigators have begun to monitor patients who are vulnerable to panic attacks as they go about their day-to-day affairs. This is made possible by advances in technology allowing relatively unobtrusive physiological monitoring on a 24-hour basis. Furthermore, this allows the investigators to see whether naturally occurring panic attacks look the same as those captured in the laborato-

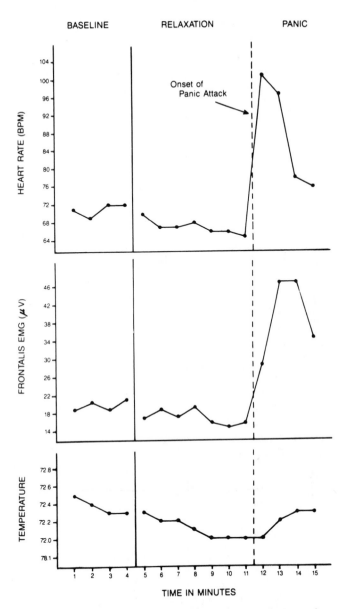

FIGURE 3.1. Physiological changes for Subject 1 ("Mary") from the start of the recording session through the onset and peak of the panic attack. From Cohen, A. S., Barlow, D. H., & Blanchard, E. B. (1985). The psychophysiology of relaxation-associated panic attacks. *Journal of Abnormal Psychology, 94,* 96–101. Copyright 1985 by the American Psychological Association. Reprinted by permission.

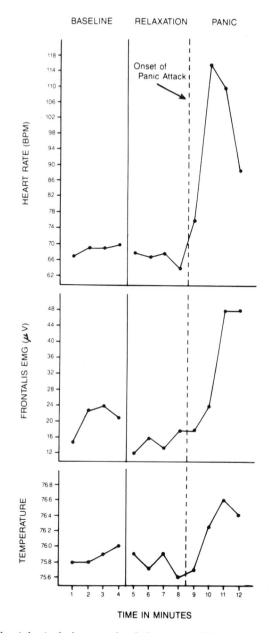

FIGURE 3.2. Physiological changes for Subject 2 ("Jill") from the start of the re-cording session through the onset and peak of the panic attack. From Cohen, A. S., Barlow, D. H., & Blanchard, E. B. (1985). The psychophysiology of relaxa-tion-associated panic attacks. *Journal of Abnormal Psychology, 94,* 96–101. Copyright 1985 by the American Psychological Association. Reprinted by permission.

ries. For example, Robert Freedman and his colleagues in Detroit (Freedman, Ianni, Ettedgui, & Puthezhath, 1985) monitored patients with panic disorder over a period of 2 days, and "caught" five patients having one or more panic attacks. Increases in heart rate and changes in other physiological indicators were substantial, but the attacks were essentially over in 5 minutes, as were the laboratory attacks described above.

One of the difficulties in identifying naturally occurring panic attacks is that people wearing ambulatory physiological monitors are engaging in their usual and customary routines, most of which involve some sort of physical activity. Distinguishing the proportion of a sudden physiological change that is due to a sudden increase in physical activity or exercise from the proportion that may be due to panic is a sophisticated task that C. Barr Taylor and his associates at Stanford have recently attempted (Taylor et al., 1986; Taylor, Telch, & Haavek, 1983). In an early study (Taylor et al., 1983), they observed that the high heart rate noted from several patients during a self-reported panic attack was confounded by the fact that the patients were physically very active at the time. They devised a statistical program to separate out heart rate increases that are due to panic attacks rather than to physical activity. Essentially, this procedure specifies heart rate increases over and above what may be expected from the physical activity ongoing at the time.

In a landmark study, Taylor et al. (1986) then monitored 12 patients with panic disorder and 12 matched normals for 6 days, 24 hours a day. They proved that naturally occurring panic attacks could be identified on the basis of abrupt elevations in heart rate that could not be attributed to physical activity. Data from one of their patients, for whom both heart rate and activity levels were monitored concurrently, are presented in Figure 3.3. The physiological signature was very similar to that observed previously in the laboratories. Average heart rate increase from the start of the panic to the peak was 38.6 BPM. Heart rate reached its peak in an average of 4 minutes. Patients reported that the entire episode lasted an average of 15.8 minutes. But according to the criteria developed by Taylor et al., the panic, as measured by heart rate, lasted a mean of 20.2 minutes from beginning to end. While these values were slightly longer than durations reported in the laboratory, the reassurance of an experienced therapist was not present during these naturally occurring panics. Finally, the time of day associated with the greatest frequency of "spontaneous" panic attack was 1:30 to 3:30 A.M., while the patients were in bed and presumably relaxed! Typically, patients who panic during the night awaken briefly before panicking, as was the case in the description of a typical panic at the beginning of this chapter. The fascinating phenomenon of nocturnal panic is examined below.

At least two features of this important study raise perplexing questions. First, approximately 40% of the major panic attacks reported by

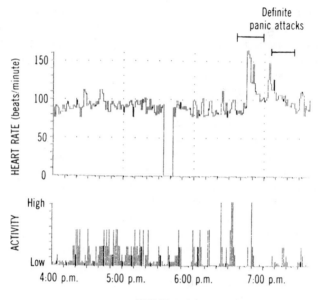

FIGURE 3.3 Heart rate and activity level during two definite panic attacks. From Taylor, C. B., Sheikh, J., Agras, W. S., Roth, W. T., Margraf, J., Ehlers, A., Maddock, R. J., & Gossard, D. (1986). Self-report of panic attacks: Agreement with heart rate changes. *American Journal of Psychiatry, 143*, 478–482. Copyright 1986 by the American Psychiatric Association. Reprinted by permission.

these patients *were not* accompanied by heart rate changes that were different from what would be expected during normal activity. Nevertheless, patients reported an adequate number of panic symptoms to meet criteria. Since heart rate elevations during "typical" panic are very marked (see Figures 3.1 and 3.2), and since these patients were not necessarily exercising vigorously, there appeared to be a phenomenon that was identified by these patients as "panic" but that was not accompanied by characteristic physiological responding. On the other hand, panic attacks that *were* accompanied by heart rate increases were rated as more intense (a mean of 4.7 on a scale of 0–7) then those not not accompanied by heart rate increases (a mean of 3.3 on the same scale).

Second, when Taylor *et al.* (1986) examined the 24-hour physiological records, they found a large number of otherwise unexplainable heart rate elevations (not due to activity) that would have met the criteria for the most severe panic attack, but were not in any way labeled "panic" by the patients. What this indicates is that marked heart rate elevations alone are not a good indicator of panic in the absence of the subjective experience of the symptoms. What is needed, in addition to 24-hour physiological monitoring, is 24-hour similtaneous monitoring of cognitive processes possibly associated with panic.

The Taylor *et al.* (1986) results reinforce a growing awareness of the importance of determining how patients construe somatic symptoms, as suggested by Hallam (1985; see Chapter 2). For example, panic may be a unique event. But once a panic disorder develops, patients may become extremely sensitive to all somatic sensations originally associated with panic. They may then overreport these symptoms and exaggerate their significance. These issues become very important as the nature of panic is elaborated on below.

Finally, this study provides a fascinating look at what happens to normal people who find themselves in situations that are very stressful—situations that many of us have experienced. In one case, one of Taylor *et al.*'s normal subjects had been working on a suicide prevention line for the first time and received her first call. On examination, her heart rate pattern met the criteria for a severe panic, but she reported only one symptom (feeling anxious and tense), rather than the three required in this study to meet the criteria for panic attack. Another woman reported two situations in which she reported that she "panicked." In the first, her young child suddenly ran out into the middle of the street. In the second situation, she was driving to the shopping mall when another car came speeding along and appeared to be about to crash into her. There were *no* heart rate change during either of these episodes that could be attributed to anxiety, and she reported only one instead of three or more symptoms in each instance. Not one of Taylor's 12 normal subjects ever met the criteria for a panic attack combining both required heart rate elevations and reports of three or more symptoms. What happened to the alarm reaction described in Chapter 1? Is this reaction representative of individuals suddenly experiencing the emotion of fear? A variety of evidence suggests that it is not (see Chapter 2). But this limited sampling of three events in two individuals clearly underlines the need for larger-scale investigations into this issue utilizing new technological advances. Now an expanded analysis with 19 normal control subjects (Margraf, Taylor, Ehlers, Roth, & Agras, 1987) suggest that panic and anxiety episodes do appear very similar in presenting symptoms to those of patients. Differences occur only in frequency and intensity of the events.

NOCTURNAL PANIC

As noted above, Taylor *et al.* (1986) found that the greatest frequency of panic attacks occurred between 1:30 and 3:30 A.M. Perhaps no experience is more terrifying than panicking while sleeping, as illustrated by the report of the patient at the beginning of the chapter. Approximately 25% of all panickers and agoraphobics with panic attacks who present at our Phobia and Anxiety Disorders Clinic reported the experience of at least one nocturnal panic attack. Recently, we assessed a group of 41 individuals who had experienced nocturnal panic (Barlow & Craske, 1988). These people gave affirmative answers to the question, "Are there times when you awake from sleep in a panic?" They were then questioned specifically about the duration of such panics, amount of sleep before onset of panics, symptom intensity, and differences between nocturnal and day panics. The majority of nocturnal panics occurred within 1–4 hours of sleep onset (especially between the second and third hours), the time during which slow-wave sleep is most prevalent. This is the same time frame reported by Taylor et al. (1986). Slow-wave sleep tends to be associated with reduced eye movements, lowered blood pressure, and reduced heart rate and respiration. These are also the common characteristics of wakeful relaxation. It is therefore tempting to make a connection between nocturnal panic and the relaxation-associated panic described above (Cohen et al., 1985). Relaxation is known to be associated with cognitive, physiological, or sensory side effects that may be perceived as unpleasant (Heide & Borkovec, 1984). For example, a patient may become alarmed by a decreasing heart rate that occurs during relaxation—a cue to which the panic-prone patient is very sensitive, and which may therefore trigger a panic attack (see Chapter 4). Similarly, a sleeping individual may be oblivious to his or her environment, but may remain attuned to personally significant stimuli. For example, a mother may be undisturbed by the noise of a loud truck driving past her house, but may awaken to the sound of her baby crying. Hauri, Friedman, Ravaris, and Fisher (1985) were able to record five night panics in their sleep laboratory from a group of agoraphobics with panic attacks. They noted that the panics tended to occur in non-rapid-eye-movement (non-REM) sleep, although occasionally an attack would occur during REM sleep. Non-REM sleep is associated with occasional violent muscular twitches. The agoraphobics were found to spend a greater number of minutes in delta or slow-wave sleep and to exhibit more large movements during sleep than either a normal group or a group of psychophysiological insomniacs. It is possible that muscular movements served as cues precipitating the elevation in physiological activation that preceded awakening in this group of patients.

Of the 41 nocturnal panickers we assessed (Barlow & Craske, 1988), 43% reported that their first symptom upon awakening was cognitive (e.g., fear of losing control, dying, or going crazy), whereas 57% reported that their first symptom upon awakening was somatic (e.g., a racing heart). In regard to symptom severity, 54% reported that their nocturnal panics were more severe than their day panics, 25% said that they were less severe, and 21% said that they were of equal severity. In regard to symptom frequency, 46% reported that they experienced more symptoms during nocturnal panic than during the day, 21% reported fewer symptoms at night, and 33% said that there was an equal number of symptoms. Nocturnal panic lasted, on average, 24.6 minutes, with a range of 1–180 minutes.

Eighteen subjects were questioned in detail concerning the occurrence and severity of each DSM-III panic symptom during their most recent nocturnal panic. The frequency with which each symptom was cited by the sample is shown in Table 3.4 (percentages are shown in parentheses). The symptoms reported with the greatest frequency were strong, rapid, or irregular heart beat; shortness of breath; hot and cold flashes; choking or smothering sensations; trembling; and fear of dying. Also listed in Table 3.4 are mean severity ratings. Difficulty breathing, fear of dying, heart palpitations, and nausea were the most intensely experienced symptoms. Of interest is the finding that shortness of breath was also one of the most frequently and intensely experienced symptoms during this sample's daytime panics—a pattern that differentiated them somewhat from a representative sample of typical panickers who did not report the experience of nocturnal panic. In general, fewer symptoms were reported during nocturnal panics, but the overall severity of symptoms was comparable across daytime and nocturnal panics (see Table 3.4).

Clinicians often assume that nocturnal panic attacks may result from sleep apnea. Sleep apnea refers to a pause or complete cessation of breathing: "People with such apneas typically go through a repeating cycle of sleep apnea, arousal, resumption of breathing, and sleep once again" (Van Oot, Lane, & Borkovec, 1984, p. 711). The consideration of sleep apnea is logical, given the prominence of the reported shortness-of-breath symptom. However, two factors suggest otherwise. First, there was no evidence of obesity in our sample of nocturnal panickers (a characteristic associated very frequently with sleep apnea). Second, the concentration of nocturnal panic during the first 4 hours of the sleep cycle is not consistent with the repeating pattern of sleep apnea. Of interest will be a determination of the number of people with sleep apnea who experience panic attacks.

Several changes in internal state that occur during different phases of the sleep cycle may serve as triggers for a panic-prone person: reduced heart rate and respiration during show-wave and deep sleep, as would occur in the case of deep relaxation; erratic breathing patterns that occur during REM sleep; and major muscular twitches that occur during delta or slow-wave sleep. The issue of cues for panic is considered in more detail below.

In summary, the typical panic attack seems to be a unique psychological event characterized by feelings of apprehension, terror, or impending doom, and a report of three or four (or more) somatic symptoms or fears

TABLE 3.4. Frequency (Percentage) and Average Severity for Those Subjects Reporting Each Symptom

| | Nocturnal panickers (n = 18) | | | | | | Panickers without nocturnal panic (n = 46) | | |
| | Nocturnal | | | Day | | | | | |
	Number	%	Mean severity	Number	%	Mean severity	Number	%	Mean severity
Dyspnea	12	67	2.42	13	72	2.15	23	50	2.09
Palpitations	17	94	2.29	13	72	2.06	37	80	2.54
Chest pain	6	33	1.33	9	50	1.56	15	33	1.73
Choking/smothering	11	61	1.90	11	61	2.00	15	33	1.73
Nausea	3	17	2.33	10	56	2.00	20	43	2.10
Dizziness	6	33	1.67	13	72	2.15	35	76	2.20
Feeling of unreality	10	56	1.33	11	61	1.73	30	65	2.20
Paresthesias	5	28	1.60	10	56	2.00	21	46	1.91
Hot/cold flashes	12	67	1.67	14	78	1.64	35	76	2.09
Sweating	10	56	2.00	13	72	1.62	26	57	2.08
Faintness	4	22	2.00	11	61	1.55	24	52	2.13
Trembling	11	61	1.73	14	78	1.93	29	63	2.28
Fear of dying	11	61	2.45	11	61	2.09	21	46	2.48
Fear of going crazy or losing control	7	39	1.98	12	67	2.17	23	50	2.52

Note. From Barlow, D. H., & Craske, M. G. (1988). The phenomenology of panic. In S. Rachman & J. D. Maser (Eds.), *Panic: Psychological perspectives* (p. 31). Hillsdale, NJ: Erlbaum. Copyright 1988 by Lawrence Erlbaum Associates. Reprinted by permission.

of losing control or dying. Often, these attacks are also accompanied by heart rate elevations of approximately 40 BPM that cannot be accounted for by physical exercise. In these cases, panic seems a clear example of the ancient alarm reaction of fear (Darwin, 1872). Occasionally, these attacks may be "limited," in that fewer than three or four symptoms are reported and/or they are not accompanied by marked elevation in physiological measures. These "limited" attacks are often but not always rated as less intense. Finally, some patients report panic in the absence of any clear biological markers, such as rapid elevation in physiological responding. It is possible that these patients have become sensitized to any number of somatic and cognitive events formerly associated with panic, and that these events are now "construed" as panic by the patients. In any case, with the dramatic presentation of this terrifying event, it is surprising that we have recognized its significance only recently.

CONCEPTIONS OF PANIC IN TIMES PAST

In view of the nature and significance of panic, why was it not recognized earlier? The answer is that it *was* recognized and given a variety of names, many of which depicted hypothetical causes of this sudden burst of emotion. In fact, attacks have been observed and reported for hundreds of years, but the significance of panic was overlooked. Instead, the phenomenon was integrated into various theories of pathology, both psychological and physical.

As indicated at the beginning of the chapter, one does not have to look beyond Freud for a cogent description of panic. Freud accomplished the unique and singular task of integrating almost every facet of human behavior and emotion into an all-encompassing theory. Whatever one thinks of his theoretical constructs, his extraordinary intellectual achievement rests in his ability to integrate, on a conceptual level, so much of our experience. The experience of anxiety is no exception, and, in view of their prominence within psychoanalytic theory, Freud's views on anxiety and panic are particularly interesting from a historical point of view.

Freud actually distinguished three types of anxiety. In 1917 he noted differences among free-floating or generalized anxiety, which he referred to as "expectant anxiety"; "phobic anxiety," or anxiety that only occurs in specific situations; and "anxiety attacks." On the basis of his descriptions, these "anxiety attacks" would be called panic today (Freud, 1917/1963). In fact, even earlier in 1895, he seemed to describe very clearly the process of the development of agoraphobia when he stated, "In the case of agoraphobia, etc., we often find *the recollection of an anxiety attack;* and what the patient actually fears is the occurrence of such an attack under the special conditions in which he believes he cannot escape it" (1895/

1962, p. 81; Freud's italics). Unfortunately, as Klein (1983) points out, Freud's clear observations eventually became blurred by the heavy theoretical baggage that his constructs of anxiety carried, and by 1932 these distinctions had been largely lost.

A more interesting but completely different view of the phenomenon arose over the years within the field of medicine and the subspecialty of cardiology in particular. For example, in 1871, DaCosta described a syndrome he encountered in a series of 300 patients that he saw during the Civil War in the United States. This syndrome was characterized by palpitations, dizziness, and so on, and originated without any clear cause. DaCosta called it "irritable heart." In England during World War I, Lewis (1917) described a condition he referred to as "effort syndrome," which in fact seemed to be a collection of the same symptoms observed by DaCosta during the American Civil War. Lewis called it "effort syndrome" because he observed this problem in a large series of soldiers who developed the syndrome during physical exertion associated with their combat activities. He noted that this problem seemed to occur in those soldiers with "constitutional weaknesses," either nervous or physical, or in those "played out" by exposure and strain. His early reference to stress as a precipitant is still interesting (see Chapter 6). It is also interesting, in light of recent theories, that he suspected blood acidosis produced by changes in CO_2 or lactate acid levels as playing a role in the genesis of these attacks (see Chapter 4).

From somewhat different points of view, Oppenheim (1918) and Cohen and White, conducting epidemiological work in the 1940s and 1950s (Cohen, Badal, Kilpatrick, Reid, & White, 1951; Cohen & White, 1950), referred to seemingly the same syndrome as "neurocirculatory asthenia." This is the old term for anxiety states with marked cardiovascular features.

In the meantime, Roth (1959, 1960) identified a separate syndrome, which he and his colleagues termed the "phobic anxiety–depersonalization syndrome." In a particularly perceptive analysis of 135 patients with this syndrome, Roth (1959) suggested that the phenomenon of depersonalization and the underlying psychophysiology of the regulation of awareness associated with depersonalization might be important keys to the disorder. But his major contribution was to set off this group of patients, who presented very clearly with panic attacks, in a nosological way from "those with anxiety neurosis," who are not fully described in his papers but most probably presented with generalized anxiety. The distinction between panic and generalized anxiety has since become a subject of intense study.

A variety of other labels have been used over the decades to refer to what seems to be the same disorder. These include "vasoregulatory asthenia," "nervous tachycardia," "vasomotor neurosis," and "nervous exhaustion" (Cohen & White, 1950).

THE "UNIQUENESS" OF PANIC

Is the psychological experience of panic a truly unique event? To be unique, it should be qualitatively different from the more usual generalized anxiety with which we are all so familiar. As we observed above, panic has always attracted attention in the clinical literature, but usually these experiences were described as "anxiety attacks"; the implication was that these experiences were simply manifestations of intense generalized anxiety.

DONALD KLEIN AND PHARMACOLOGICAL DISSECTION

As is so often the case in science, the initial suggestion that panic might be qualitatively different was based on an insightful clinical hunch. This clinical hunch was then bolstered by a line of research that came to be called "pharmacological dissection." In fact, this approach provided only weak evidence supporting panic as a qualitatively different experience. Nevertheless, this clinical hunch and the subsequent research generated opened up other more direct and powerful lines of investigation, from which we have learned much about the nature of panic.

In 1959, when agoraphobics were still called "schizophrenics" by most clinicians because of their severe symptoms and marked social impairment, Donald Klein began studying the then new and unmarketed drug imipramine. Although expecting a stimulant effect, he found, much to his surprise, that imipramine first caused sedation in depressed patients, followed after several weeks by marked improvement in mood. At this time, Klein had a number of patients on his unit who, in retrospect, were panicking. Since these patients were not responding to other forms of psychotherapy or drug therapy, Klein decided to try imipramine—not because of any prior scientific findings indicating that it would be effective, but rather, "it was more a case of our not knowing what else to do for them, and thinking that perhaps this strange new safe agent with peculiar tranquilizing powers might work" (Klein, 1981, p. 237). Initially, patients, ward staff, nurses, and therapists noted no improvement whatsoever from these drugs. But after several weeks nurses observed that patients had stopped running to the nurses' station with protests of dying or losing control. When asked, the patients said that they stopped running to the nurses' station because they had learned that the nurses couldn't do anything for them.

Klein published these clinical results in 1962 (Klein & Fink, 1962), and reported on a small double-blind study in 1964 (Klein, 1964). In this double-blind study, which was part of a larger study, 14 patients who had been described as having affective disorders were reclassified as having phobic anxiety reactions, based on a retrospective diagnostic review. Of these, 6 received placebo, 7 received imipramine, and 1 received chlorpromazine. The patient on chlorpromazine had the poorest response of any of the 14 and actually deteriorated somewhat. However, based on global clinical ratings by two psychiatrists, the 7 on imipramine improved more than the 6 receiving placebo.

While panic was not specifically measured in this very early study, Klein's clinical observations were that the drug reduced or eliminated panic attacks, but did nothing for the chronic anticipatory anxiety continuously present, which seemed to keep the patients from leaving a safe place or a safe person. As Klein concluded,

> [T]he panic attack was much more severe than the chronic anxiety, but one could hardly believe that the panic attack was simply the quantitative extreme of chronic anxiety since imipramine could dispel the apparently worse anxiety, but had little effect on the chronic minor form. Again, this implied a qualitative discontinuity between these two distressing affects that had initially seemed so similar. (1981, p. 239).

Thus, Klein noted that imipramine had a very specific effect on panic attacks, and therefore he "dissected" panic attacks from generalized chronic or anticipatory anxiety as a qualitatively different state.

Unfortunately, inferring something about the nature of a psychopathological state by observing treatment effects is a very weak experimental approach, subject to a logical fallacy (*post hoc ergo propter hoc*, or "the result implies the cause"). The weakness of this experimental approach becomes an issue again when the nature of panic is explored further below. But, nevertheless, this type of evidence was suggestive and was found again in the following experiment, conducted from a somewhat different vantage point.

PSYCHOLOGICAL DISSECTION

The purpose of one preliminary experiment in our clinic was to evaluate the effects of psychosocial treatments on intense anxiety that included but was not limited to panic episodes (Waddell, Barlow, & O'Brien, 1984). Three patients with panic disorder were treated with a combination treatment, consisting of a cognitive therapy phase followed by a phase combining cognitive therapy and relaxation training. The phases were introduced in a staggered fashion, so that each therapeutic phase was started for different patients at different times in a multiple-baseline-across-subjects experimental design format (Barlow & Hersen, 1984). This allowed us to observe specific effects of therapeutic procedures as they were introduced to each patient. The patients recorded both number and duration of episodes of "heightened or intense" anxiety and panic, using detailed self-monitoring forms devised for this purpose. In addition, they recorded ratings of chronic background anxiety (not necessarily associated with periods of intense anxiety and panic) four times a day. All patients demonstrated a marked decrease in the number and duration of episodes of intense anxiety and panic—an improvement that was maintained at a 3-month follow-up. However, two patients showed a clear increase in background anxiety at the same time that episodes of intense anxiety were lessening during the combined treatment phase. For the third patient, chronic background anxiety decreased in synchrony with episodes of panic.

This experiment suffered from the same logical flaws as the early work in pharmacological dissection, since it would be tempting to conclude from these results that there are two different types of anxiety. In addition, results from only three subjects were reported, and only two of them showed the "split" in their recordings of panic versus chronic background anxiety. In fact, most treatment outcome data for patients with panic disorder show clear reductions in *both* panic attacks and generalized anxiety. It is possible that certain treatments (both psychological and pharmacological) are effective for anxiety in some patients only when anxiety is "intense," but that this intense anxiety or panic does not differ in any real qualitative way from less intense anxiety. Despite their weaknesses, these results were also suggestive, and paved the way for more direct comparisons of panic and generalized anxiety.

DIRECT COMPARISONS OF PANIC
AND GENERALIZED ANXIETY

Further supporting evidence for differences between generalized anxiety and panic has come from some of the studies described earlier in the chapter, where both generalized anxiety and panic were monitored during day-to-day activities. For example, Taylor et al. (1986) had patients record both anticipatory anxiety and panic in the manner described earlier over a period of 6 days. In each of eight periods of intense anticipatory anxiety, heart rate remained relatively stable, and was significantly lower than heart rate recorded during panic attacks. Heart rate averaged 89.2 BPM during anticipatory anxiety, as compared to 108.2 BPM during spontaneous panic attacks. These differences in heart rate occurred in spite of the fact that subjective ratings of intensity during the two types of anxiety were virtually identical.

In a similar vein, Freedman et al. (1985) measured heart rate during self-reported panic attacks and also observed heart rate during "control periods," in which anxiety was reported as equally intense, but was not labeled as panic. For example, if a panic attack was rated at an intensity of 80 on a scale of 0–100, the investigators examined heart rate at another time when the patient also reported anxiety to be at an intensity of 80, but did not report a panic attack. Presumably, these control periods represented anticipatory or generalized anxiety. Abrupt heart rate elevations did not occur during these control periods. This is illustrated for several patients in Figure 3.4.

These studies are useful, since a direct comparison of panic and generalized anxiety in the same patients is possible. Another line of evidence comes from studies that compare groups of patients with diagnoses of generalized anxiety disorder or panic disorder, most usually on various questionnaire measures. This is a weaker approach, since patients with panic disorder also experience marked anticipatory or generalized anxiety. Nevertheless, some interesting information is available from these sources.

In our clinic, an early series of patients with panic disorder evidenced a stronger somatic component to their anxiety than did patients with generalized anxiety disorder on questionnaire measures of anxiety (Barlow, Cohen, *et al.*, 1984). Subjects with panic disorder scored significantly higher on the Somatic scale of the Cognitive and Somatic Anxiety Questionnaire (panic disorder mean = 23.9; generalized anxiety disorder mean = 15.50; $t = 2.91$, $p < .02$). Scores on the Cognitive scale, on the other hand, did not differ, although the mean score was slightly higher for subjects with generalized anxiety disorder (panic disorder mean = 17.55; generalized anxiety disorder mean = 18.38). Hoehn-Saric (1981) compared 15 patients with generalized anxiety disorder to 36 mixed anxiety disorder patients suffering from panic attacks. Scores on a variety of questionnaires, including the Somatic Symptom Scale, the Eysenck Personality Inventory, and the State–Trait Anxiety Inventory, were compared. Essentially no differences emerged between the groups, with the exception of scores on the Somatic Symptom Scale. Patients with panic attacks scored significantly higher on this scale, indicating more intense and more severe somatic signs of anxiety (e.g., muscle tension, respiratory symptoms, palpitations, etc.).

Other studies have replicated this finding by demonstrating a stronger somatic presentation in panic patients than in patients with generalized anxiety disorder (Anderson, Noyes, & Crowe, 1984; Rapee, 1985b). The

---

FIGURE 3.4. Heart rates during panic attacks and high-anxiety control periods. Anxiety ratings are shown in parentheses after case numbers. Solid lines represent first attack; dotted lines, second attack. From Freedman, R. R., Ianni, P., Ettedgui, E., & Puthezhath, N. (1985). Ambulatory monitoring of panic disorder. *Archives of General Psychiatry, 42,* 244–250. Copyright 1985 by the American Medical Association. Reprinted by permission.

Panic Attacks   High-Anxiety Control Periods

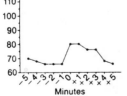

lack of differences observed on measures of "general" anxiety such as the State–Trait Anxiety Inventory in these studies is interesting, since patients suffering primarily from panic do not score *higher* on these scales, as might be the case if panic disorder were simply a more intense version of generalized anxiety disorder. In fact, Rapee (1985b) reported that patients with panic disorder in Australia scored *lower* than patients with generalized anxiety disorder on the Taylor Manifest Anxiety Scale. Finally, patients with panic present with a different pattern of cognitions than do anxiety patients without panic. For example, both Hibbert (1984) and Rapee (1985b) observed more intense cognitions centering on physical, psychological, or social disaster in panic patients than in patients without panic. Recently, Beck and Emery (1985) have elaborated on specific cognitive processes in panic patients. This pattern of catastrophic thoughts concerning present danger (dying, losing control, etc.) certainly fits with the notion of panic as the ancient emotion of fear. Of course, these differences may be epiphenomenal, reflecting defining characteristics of patients falling into this category rather than something fundamental about panic. For example, the tendency for patients with panic disorder to overreport and exaggerate somatic symptoms has been mentioned above.

In summary, there are hints that panic is a unique event distinguishable from generalized anxiety on the basis of presenting characteristics. But it is not possible to infer a fundamental, qualitative difference. I return to this issue when I consider the biology of panic and anxiety in Chapter 5.

THE UBIQUITY OF PANIC

In view of the distinctive presentation of panic, it is important to determine the prevalence of panic across different diagnostic categories. Panic attacks were first observed, of course, in the context of what we now call "panic disorder" or "agoraphobia with panic" where attacks occurred in an unexpected fashion without identifiable cues; thus the term "spontaneous." To determine the prevalence of DSM-III definitions of panic across various diagnostic categories, we examined for panic attacks in 108 consecutive patients meeting DSM-III anxiety or affective disorder diagnoses (Barlow *et al.*, 1985). These patients were carefully diagnosed using a new structured interview devised in our clinic, the Anxiety Disorders Interview Schedule (ADIS; Di Nardo, O'Brien, Barlow, Waddell, & Blanchard, 1983) (see Chapter 9).

During each interview, patients were asked about the occurrence of any panic attacks and about their onset and frequency. Specifically, each patient was asked, "Have you had times when you felt a sudden rush of intense fear or anxiety or feelings of impending doom?" If the patient admitted to having had a panic attack, he or she was then asked about each of the 12 symptoms of panic attacks listed in DSM-III. Questions centered on presence or absence and degree of intensity of each symptom, using a typical or the most recent attack as a point of reference. Each symptom was rated by the interviewer on a 5-point scale of severity (0 = "absent," 4 = "very severe"). "Spontaneity" of the panic attack was ascertained by careful questioning regarding the circumstances surrounding the panic, as well as whether the panic was expected or not.

Table 3.5 lists the frequencies of primary diagnoses represented by the sample, along with the mean age and sex distribution for each diagnostic category. Also included in this table are the percentages of each subgroup who reported having had a panic attack and the percentage who met the DSM-III criteria for panic disorder. A "report of panic" meant that the patients answered "yes" to the question "Have you ever had times when you felt a sudden rush of intense fear or anxiety or feelings of impending doom?" "Diagnosis met except for panic frequency" meant that the patients reported panic and also reported at least 4 of the 12 symptoms listed as associated with panic in DSM-III. "Diagnosis on DSM-III panic criteria" meant that the patients reported panic, met the 4 symptom criteria, and reported at least three panics in a 3-week period.

Six patients eventually received a consensus diagnosis of major depressive disorder. Of course, these patients did not represent a random sample of major depression, since they were referred to our clinic for problems with anxiety. Nevertheless, their data are included for comparison purposes.

From Table 3.5, it is clear that panic is a ubiquitous problem among patients with anxiety disorders: At least 83% of patients in each diagnostic category reported at least one panic attack. Furthermore, almost all patients reporting a panic attack (a sudden rush of intense fear) also endorsed at least 4 of the 12 symptoms necessary to meet the DSM-III definition of panic. Only in regard to the frequency criteria did differences among diagnostic groups emerge: The percentages of patients with social phobia, simple phobia, and generalized anxiety disorder who met the frequency criteria were markedly lower than the percentage with panic disorder.

The apparent anomaly in Table 3.5, whereby only 82% of patients with a diagnosis of panic disorder met the full DSM-III criteria, was an artifact of the methods used (see Barlow et al., 1985).

PANIC SEVERITY ACROSS DIAGNOSTIC GROUPS

Although patients in all diagnostic categories in Table 3.5 reported DSM-III panic attacks, perhaps there were some differences in severity or number of symptoms reported across groups. In Table 3.6 are listed, for those

TABLE 3.5. Sample Descriptors and Incidence of Panic across Diagnostic Categories

Variable	Agoraphobia with panic	Social phobia	Simple phobia	Panic disorder	GAD	Obsessive-compulsive	Major depressive episode	Statistical comparison
Men (n)	2	10	2	6	8	2	1	
Women (n)	39	9	5	11	4	4	5	
Mean age (in years)	36.2_{ab}	28.8_a	44.6_{bc}	34.8_a	36.1_{ab}	28.5_a	46.3_c	$F(6, 101) = 4.64$**
Reports of panic (%)	98	89	100	100	83	83	83	$\chi^2(6, n = 108) = 7.27$
Diagnosis met except for panic frequency (%)	98	84	85	100	75	83	83	$\chi^2(6, n = 108) = 9.50$
Diagnosis on DSM-III panic criteria (%)	74	50	33	82	29	t	t	$\chi^2(6, n = 108) = 14.67$*

Note. Categories sharing subscripts are not significantly different by Duncan's multiple-range test. t, *n*'s were too low to analyze because of missing data on panic frequency. However, for the 3 obsessive–compulsives and 3 depressed patients for whom we had complete data, 100% met the criteria. GAD, generalized anxiety disorder. From Barlow, D. H., Vermilyea, J. A., Blanchard, E. B., Vermilyea, B. B., Di Nardo, P. A., & Cerny, J. A. (1985). The phenomenon of panic. *Journal of Abnormal Psychology, 94,* 320–328. Copyright 1985 by the American Psychological Association. Reprinted by permission.

*$p < .03$.
**$p < .001$.

TABLE 3.6. Average Severity Ratings of Specific Panic Symptoms across Diagnostic Categories

Symptoms	Agoraphobia with panic	Social phobia	Simple phobia	Panic disorder	GAD	Obsessive-compulsive	Major depressive episode	df	F
Dyspnea (0–4)	1.71	1.33	1.33	1.29	1.67	1.80	1.10	6, 90	0.66
Palpitations (0–4)	2.35	2.03	1.67	2.21	1.67	2.10	0.96	6, 91	2.05
Chest pain (0–4)	1.31	0.31	0.92	1.29	1.00	1.00	0.90	6, 91	2.30
Choking (0–4)	1.35	0.90	1.17	1.06	0.83	1.50	0.70	6, 91	0.74
Dizziness (0–4)	2.04_b	0.91_a	0.58_a	1.76_b	1.39_{ab}	1.70_{ab}	0.70_a	6, 91	5.04*
Unreality (0–4)	1.28	0.88	0.83	1.83	0.78	1.80	0.90	6, 91	1.86
Paresthesias (0–4)	0.76	0.22	0.92	1.00	0.78	1.10	0.80	6, 91	1.72
Hot or cold flashes (0–4)	1.71	0.94	1.50	1.41	1.11	2.10	1.70	6, 91	2.12
Sweating (0–4)	1.51	1.38	1.33	1.44	0.78	1.60	1.60	6, 91	0.76
Fainting (0–4)	1.61	0.66	0.67	1.15	0.94	1.10	0.10	6, 91	3.02
Shaking (0–4)	1.74	1.19	1.42	1.71	1.11	2.00	1.10	6, 91	1.33
Fear of going crazy, losing control (0–4)	2.11_{bc}	0.97_a	1.58_{abc}	2.50_c	0.89_a	1.50_{abc}	1.10_{ab}	6, 90	5.53*
Average percentage of symptoms endorsed	85.6_b	61.3_a	68.0_{ab}	83.3_b	58.3_a	90.2_b	61.6_a	6, 91	6.21*

Note. Means sharing subscripts are not significantly different by Duncan's multiple-range test. Severity ratings were made on the following scale: 0 = "none," 1 = "mild," 2 = "moderate," 3 = "severe," and 4 = "very severe." GAD, generalized anxiety disorder. From Barlow, D. H., Vermilyea, J. A., Blanchard, E. B., Vermilyea, B. B., Di Nardo, P. A., & Cerny, J. A. (1985). The phenomenon of panic. *Journal of Abnormal Psychology, 94,* 320–328. Copyright 1985 by the American Psychological Association. Reprinted by permission.
*$p < .001$.

individuals who admitted to having had a panic attack, the severity ratings of the DSM-III symptoms of panic.

On two symptoms, there were significant differences in the severity ratings: dizziness, and fear of going crazy or losing control. Patients with panic disorder and agoraphobia with panic reported more severe dizziness than did patients with social phobia, simple phobia, or major depression. Those with generalized anxiety disorder or obsessive-compulsive disorder did not differ from either of these two groups. For the symptom of fear of going crazy or of losing control, patients with panic disorder had the highest average severity rating, midway between moderate and severe. This rating was significantly higher than for patients with social phobia, generalized anxiety disorder, or major depressive disorder. The average rating for those patients with agoraphobia with panic on this symptom also exceeded the scores of those with social phobia and generalized anxiety disorder. The overall severity scores were somewhat low, due to the fact that many patients who *reported* panic and at least 4 of the 12 symptoms did not *have* all the symptoms. Therefore, a number of zeros on each particular symptom lowered the average severity rating.

The average percentages of symptoms endorsed by those patients reporting panic in the different diagnostic groups are given in the last row of Table 3.6. Patients with agoraphobia with panic, panic disorder, and obsessive–compulsive disorder reported high percentages of the 12 symptoms (85.6%, 83.3%, and 90.2%, respectively). These were significantly higher percentages than those of all other diagnostic groups except simple phobia.

In general, few differences in panic phenomenology emerged among diagnostic categories. On only 2 out of 12 symptoms, as well as the average percentage of symptoms endorsed, were there any differences. When differences existed, patients with agoraphobia with panic, panic disorder, and obsessive–compulsive disorder tended to score slightly higher on symptom severity and percentage of symptoms reported, while social phobics scored lower.

PANIC ASSOCIATED WITH NON-ANXIETY-RELATED DISORDERS AND WITH PHYSICAL DISORDERS

Reports are now flowing in from around the world confirming the ubiquity of panic in a variety of diagnostic categories. Early studies ascertained that many patients presenting with panic would meet older definitions for hysteria (Sheehan & Sheehan, 1982). Using the Feighner criteria, Feighner *et al.* (1972) determined that all patients with panic met the criteria for hysteria. Perley and Guze (1962) also noticed a high frequency of panic attacks (64%) in a group of patients meeting their criteria for hysteria. However, this may reflect the lack of specification of older diagnostic categories, which were so broad as to convey very little information.

Most of these patients would now be diagnosed as having panic disorder.

More frequent and precise observations have been made of the prevalance of panic within the affective disorders, particularly major depression. For example, in a small survey by Pariser, Jones, Pinta, Young, and Fontana (1979), 5 out of 17 patients presenting with panic earned the diagnosis of major depression, while 2 patients presenting with panic had no psychiatric diagnosis. The remainder were diagnosed as having panic disorder. In a very important series of studies, Leckman and his colleagues (Leckman, Weissman, Merikangas, Pauls, & Prusoff, 1983), using DSM-III criteria, reanalyzed a large group of 133 patients with major depression and found that nearly 25% met the criteria for panic disorder or agoraphobia with panic. Since the criterion for panic disorder was a very strict one of six panics in a 6-week period, this is a very high percentage. Breier, Charney, and Heninger (1984) noted that over 80% of their depressed patients reported panic. In a study from our clinic designed to answer this question, the percentage of patients with affective disorders who presented with panic was approximately 50% (Benshoof, 1987). Whether patients with depression panic or not may have important implications for classification (see Chapters 5 and 9).

Now we have evidence on the ubiquity of panic in psychiatric disorders other than anxiety and affective disorders, as well as in nonpsychiatric medical disorders. Boyd (1986) extracted information from the large NIMH-sponsored ECA study (reviewed in Chapter 1) on percentage of patients with different diagnoses who reported at least one panic attack in the last 6 months. The results are presented in Table 3.7. The results

TABLE 3.7. Prevalence of Panic Attacks among Subjects with Other Diagnoses in Five Sites: Weighted Data (in Percents)

Diagnostic Interview Schedule	New Haven 1980–1981 ($n = 5,034$)	Baltimore 1981–1982 ($n = 3,481$)	St. Louis 1981–1982 ($n = 3,004$)	Durham, NC 1982–1983 ($n = 3,921$)	Los Angeles 1983–1984 ($n = 3,132$)
Somatization	44	—[a]	34	49	—[a]
Schizophrenia	28	35	62	33	63
Major depressive episode	39	25	42	24	25
Mania	41	18	53	31	19
Dysthymia	21	19	8	8	15
Obsessive–compulsive	35	25	32	24	23
Antisocial personality	30	27	13	6	9
Phobia	26	13	28	12	23
Alcohol abuse or dependence	6	12	10	6	7
Drug abuse or dependence	17	12	9	6	6
Cognitive impairment (severe)	2	6	5	1	2

Note. From Boyd, J. H. (1986). Use of mental health services for the treatment of panic disorder. American Journal of Psychiatry, 143, 1569–1574. Copyright 1986 by the American Psychiatric Association. Reprinted by permission.

[a] There were too few cases to make a stable estimate.

vary widely across sites, but the rates are very high for a number of disorders.

Finally, panic is astonishingly prevalent in the offices of nonpsychiatric medical specialists. Beitman, DeRosear, Basha, Flaker, and Corcoran (1987) discovered that 40% of a group of cardiology patients with nonanginal chest pain evidenced clear panic attacks. Katon *et al.* (1987) reported that 36% of 195 primary care patients were diagnosed with panic disorder. Klonoff, Polefrone, Dambrocia, and Nochomovitz (1986) report that the problem is sufficiently pervasive among patients with chronic obstructive pulmonary disease that the American Lung Association has published a self-help book for these patients on managing panic.

PANIC IN THE GENERAL POPULATION

Studies from around the world are converging to suggest that occasional panic attacks are also relatively frequent in the general population. The first study to suggest this was reported by Norton, Harrison, Hauch, and Rhodes (1985), who administered questionnaires to 186 presumably normal young adults. Fully 34.4% of these subjects reported having had one or more panic attacks in the past year. The percentage reporting more frequent attacks during the past year decreased markedly. For example, of this 34.4%, 17.2% reported two or more attacks in the past year; 11.3% reported three to four panic attacks; and 6% reported five or more attacks in the past year. In the past 3 weeks, 17.2% reported experiencing one panic attack, while 4.8% (nine subjects) reported two panic attacks in the past week, a frequency that would meet DSM-III criteria for panic disorder. In addition, 2.1% (four subjects) reported avoiding some activities or situations because of panic attacks.

One interesting facet of these data is that the number reporting panic attacks that would meet clinical criteria is very close to (and even a little bit less than) what we might expect, given recent epidemiological investigations reviewed in Chapter 1 (Myers *et al.*, 1984) This fact, as well as subsequent replication, lends credence to these data. These nonclinical panickers also reported significantly more depression, anxiety, and phobic anxiety on the well-known and often used Hopkins Symptom Checklist—90 (Derogatis, Lipman, & Covi, 1973) than those who had never panicked.

It is also interesting to observe that these nonclinical panickers seemed to experience fewer symptoms and less severe symptoms during their panics than patients. For example, two-thirds of the infrequent panickers experienced six symptoms or less, whereas two-thirds of the patients in Table 3.2 reported 10 or more symptoms. In addition, patients reported average symptom severity ratings of 5.5 on a scale of 0–8, while the nonclinical panickers' average symptom severity score was 3.0. Of course, as Norton, Harrison, *et al.* (1985) suggest, some of these people might progress later into full-blown panic disorder and increase the number of symptoms they would report, as well as their ratings of symptom severity.

While assessment of the presence or absence of panic attacks by questionnaire can be justifiably criticized, more careful assessment of 24 of these nonclinical subjects who reported panic by structured interview revealed that 22 met DSM-III criteria for panic attacks (but not necessarily panic disorder). The remaining two subjects actually reported experiencing intense nonpanic anxiety (Harrison, 1985). This finding also supports the validity of these data.

In a cross-validation study reported by Norton, Dorward, and Cox (1986), 256 subjects completed a variety of questionnaires, including a more sophisticated questionnaire than was utilized in the first study. This questionnaire assessed not only the presence or absence of panic attacks, but severity, temporal factors associated with the attacks, whether the attacks were predictable or unpredictable, and so on. Once again, panickers scored significantly higher than non-panickers on general anxiety and depression as measured by a number of scales, such as the State–Trait Anxiety Inventory, the Beck Depression Inventory, and the Anxiety and Depression subscales of the Profile of Mood States. Closely replicating the first study, 35.9% (or 92 subjects) reported experiencing one or more panic attacks in the past year, with 22.6% experiencing one or more panic attacks within the past 3 weeks. Other data were also comparable to those of the first report, and both sets of data are presented in Table 3.8.

This replication provided new information regarding the situations in which nonclinical panickers reported experiencing panic attacks. Situa-

TABLE 3.8. Panic in the Normal Population

	Norton, Harrison, Hauch, & Rhodes (1985)($n = 186$)	Norton, Dorward, & Cox (1986)($n = 256$)
One or more panics in last year	34.4%	35.9%
Panic frequency last year		
1–2	17.2%	
3–4	11.3%	
5+	6.0%	
Panic frequency last 3 weeks		
1	17.2%	12.5%
2	4.8%	7.0%
3+	2.1%	3.1%

tions most frequently associated with panic attacks were as follows: public speaking, mentioned by 55.2% of all panickers; interpersonal conflict, mentioned by 46.6%; periods of high stress, mentioned by 54.5%; and tests and exams, mentioned by 77.3%. In addition, 27.6% of the subjects reported experiencing panic attacks totally out of the blue, or, in other words, without any identifiable precipitant whatsoever. Smaller percentages reported panics during sleep (13.8%) and during relaxation (8.6%). Number and severity of symptoms were similar to those found in the earlier study.

Similar data on the prevalence of panic in the general population have recently been reported by Craske, Rachman, and Tallman (1986). Survey data from our clinic (Rapee, Ancis, & Barlow, 1987) suggest that approximately 14% of the population has experienced uncued, unexpected, "spontaneous" panic. This figure is in close agreement with data collected by Wittchen (1986) in West Germany for this type of panic, although survey data reported by Von Korff, Eaton, and Keyl (1985) reflect somewhat lower figures.

Another factor that builds confidence in the validity of these findings concerning the high rates of panic in the general population is evidence on the aggregation of panic and other psychopathology in the families of nonclinical infrequent panickers. For example, Norton *et al.* (1986) found that a significantly greater proportion of panickers than nonpanickers reported fathers, mothers, brothers, and sisters who had had panic attacks. These findings are particularly strong, since the results were statistically significant for each class of relatives, rather than just in the aggregate. These data resemble results demonstrating a high familial aggregation of panic in the families of patients with panic disorder (see Chapter 5). For example, Crowe, Noyes, Pauls, and Slymen (1983) found that 25% of first-order relatives of panic disorder patients also met DSM-III criteria for panic disorder. An additional 30% experienced infrequent panic attacks. In Norton *et al.* (1986), approximately 30% of first-order relatives were reported to experience panic. The data from Crowe *et al.* also attest to the seemingly high prevalence of panic in the population at large.

In summary, it seems clear that panic attacks are not limited to panic disorder. Rather, panic ranges far and wide across a number of mental and physical disorders and in the normal population. This fact has substantial implications for classification and treatment. More importantly, it underlines the necessity of acquiring a deeper understanding of the nature of panic.

DSM-III implicitly recognized the ubiquity of panic by noting that panic attacks may accompany withdrawal from substances such as barbiturates, intoxication due to caffeine or amphetamines, and so on. More importantly, DSM-III pointed out the now well-known fact that panic attacks occur in the context of simple or social phobias, although only in the specific phobic situation. That is, there are clear "cues" for the panic attacks. These panic attacks are referred to as "situational" by some clinical investigators, as in, for example, the Upjohn Cross-National Panic Study. Usually such attacks are contrasted to "spontaneous" attacks, such as those that occur occasionally in panic disorder where clear cues or triggers are not readily identifiable.

DESCRIPTORS OF PANIC

CUED VERSUS UNCUED AND EXPECTED
VERSUS UNEXPECTED PANIC

In fact, the phenomenon of panic has accumulated many descriptors and qualifiers. Among the terms often utilized are "spontaneous," "situational," "predicted," "major," "minor," and so on. In my view, the current evidence suggests that panic can be best categorized by the use of the terms "expected" and "cued" and their antonyms, as illustrated in Table 3.9.

For example, claustrophobics report panicking in small enclosed places. This, then is their reported "cue" for panic, a cue readily understood by the patients. However, as Rachman and Levitt (1985) have clearly demonstrated in a study to be described more fully in Chapter 4, claustrophobics may either expect or not expect to have a panic at a given time when entering a small enclosed place. Similarly, agoraphobics may identify a variety of "cues" for their panics, including shopping malls and crowded spaces, but may also have panics in the absence of any of these cues—for example, when they are in a safe place or with a safe person. Since identifiable cues preceding panic are in many cases cognitive (Barlow *et al.*, 1985), the term "cued" seems preferable to the term "situational."

Clinicians are also well aware that many patients with panic disorder with or without agoraphobia report expectations of panic in the absence of any identifiable cues. Most often this occurs when agoraphobics awaken and report that they are going to have a "bad day," which means that

TABLE 3.9. Panic Descriptors

	Expected	Unexpected
Cued		
Uncued		

they expect to experience a number of panics. Most likely, they are responding to increased tonic arousal (see Chapter 6). Thus, cued panics can be either expected or unexpected, and uncued panics can also be expected or unexpected. Naturally, the term "cued" is phenomenological, in that it refers only to the patient's perception of the presence of a discriminated cue and not to the actual presence of a cue. As Margraf *et al.* (1987) point out, even when cues are obvious (as in common panic situations), panic patients may fail to discriminate the cues and report panic as "spontaneous." All clinical investigators at this time believe that there are clear antecedents, either biological or psychological, for all panic attacks. Nevertheless, whether a patient perceives a cue or not (regardless of the actual existence of the cue) has important implications for symptom development, particularly in terms of the development of avoidance behavior. That is, patients will tend to avoid a cue perceived to be associated with panic. This is an important issue to be taken up in subsequent chapters. For these reasons, the terms "cued" and "expected" and their antonyms are used from this point on to describe panic.

IS THERE A DIFFERENCE BETWEEN CUED AND UNCUED (SPONTANEOUS) PANIC?

The impression has grown that "uncued" panics differ in ways other than lack of identifiable antecedents from "cued" panics. Apart from various speculations, this is due largely to one study (Zitrin, Klein, & Woerner, 1980; Zitrin, Klein, Woerner, & Ross, 1983). In this study, a differential response to treatment with imipramine was reported in agoraphobics with panic and mixed phobics (phobics with spontaneous panic but lacking a broad pattern of avoidance) versus simple phobics. That is, agoraphobics and mixed phobics with uncued panic who were treated with a variety of structured and unstructured exposure-based procedures improved somewhat more if they also received imipramine instead of placebo (see Chapter 11). This was not true for the simple phobics. Thus, the differential drug response suggested qualitative differences between cued and uncued panic. However, a close look at the results indicates no drug–diagnosis interactions for uncued panic across these three groups. That is, according to the major statistical analysis (an analysis of covariance), there was no differential improvement from imipramine between patients with cued panic and patients with uncued panic, although, as the authors point out, the error variance was large. More fine-grained analyses of drug effects within the diagnostic categories (despite the lack of an interaction) revealed that some measures of panic within the agoraphobia and mixed phobia categories showed a drug effect (most often at the .10 level of significance) and others did not. Similar analyses of drug effects in simple phobics either do not show this effect or, more often, are not reported. One other study also reported differences in drug effects between agoraphobics and simple phobics (Sheehan, Ballenger, & Jacobson, 1980), but panic was not directly measured and only nine specific phobics were treated. Overall, these results provide only modest support for a differential drug response in cued versus uncued panic.

As noted above, inferring the nature of psychopathological states by observing treatment effects is, of course, a very weak experimental approach, subject to a logical fallacy. A more straightforward approach is to examine directly the phenomenon of both cued and uncued panic across various diagnostic categories.

While patients with panic disorder suffer from uncued ("spontaneous") panic by diagnostic definition, other patients, who do not meet DSM-III criteria for those two diagnostic categories, also experience uncued panic occasionally (Barlow, Di Nardo, et al., 1986; Zitrin et al., 1980). Typically, these are simple or social phobics who, if they experience panic, report that it occurs in their feared situations, but also report recurring and unexpected panic in the absence of their phobic cues. Some patients with obsessive–compulsive disorder, generalized anxiety disorder, and major depressive disorder also report uncued panic.

To contrast cued and uncued panic more directly, patients who had never reported uncued panic were compared to three groups of patients who did report uncued panic (Barlow et al., 1985). Patients with a diagnosis of depression were not included, in order to restrict the analyses to the anxiety disorders. Group 1 consisted of patients who reported never having experienced an uncued panic. Simple and social phobics, as well as patients with generalized anxiety disorder who reported experiencing at least one uncued panic during their lifetimes, comprised Group 2. This group has been referred to as "mixed" by previous investigators (e.g., Zitrin et al., 1983). Group 3 consisted of DSM-III agoraphobics with panic, while DSM-III panic disorder patients made up Group 4. These data are presented in Table 3.10, which lists the severity ratings of the 12 DSM-III symptoms of panic for those individuals in the four groups who admitted having had a panic attack.

As one can see, patients in Groups 3 and 4 endorsed significantly more of the 12 symptoms than did those in groups 1 and 2. Patients in both Group 3 and Group 4 endorsed over 80% of the 12 symptoms. In this analysis, patients with uncued panic also rated most of the symptoms as more severe. This was particularly true for Groups 3 and 4, with Group 2 occupying a somewhat intermediate position.

However, when average severity ratings were recalculated on the basis of only those patients who actually reported having each symptom, a different picture emerged. In this analysis, no differences among symptoms emerged, and in no case did the severity of symptoms in Group 4

TABLE 3.10. Average Percentage of Symptoms Endorsed and Average Severity Ratings of Four Groups of Patients Reporting Cued or Uncued Panics

	Group 1: Cued panic ($n=27$)	Group 2: Mixed ($n=11$)	Group 3: Agoraphobia with panic ($n=41$)	Group 4: Panic disorder ($n=17$)	df	F
Average percentage of symptoms endorsed	58.23_a	66.50_a	85.60_b	83.29_b	3, 85	11.63**
Dyspnea	1.04	1.29	1.67	1.75	3, 91	2.31
Palpitations	1.46	1.77	2.29	2.21	3, 92	3.77
Chest pain	0.37_a	0.86_{ab}	1.28_b	1.29_b	3, 92	5.31*
Choking	0.74	0.95	1.32	1.06	3, 92	1.60
Dizziness	0.72_a	1.00_a	1.99_b	1.76_b	3, 92	10.82**
Unreality	0.65_a	0.77_{ab}	1.24_{bc}	1.82_c	3, 92	4.76**
Paresthesias	0.30	0.73	0.74	1.00	3, 92	3.47
Hot or cold flashes	0.70_a	1.36_b	1.67_b	1.41_b	3, 92	6.23**
Sweating	0.98	0.95	1.48	1.44	3, 92	1.85
Faintness	0.56_a	0.73_a	1.57_b	1.15_{ab}	3, 92	5.64**
Shaking	0.93	1.14	1.70	1.71	3, 92	4.02
Fear of going crazy, losing control	0.63_a	1.41_b	2.06_{bc}	2.50_c	3, 91	15.19**

Note. Means sharing subscripts are not significantly different by Duncan's multiple-range test. From Barlow, D. H., Vermilyea, J. A., Blanchard, E. B., Vermilyea, B. B., Di Nardo, P. A., & Cerny, J. A. (1985). The phenomenon of panic. *Journal of Abnormal Psychology, 94,* 320–328. Copyright 1985 by the American Psychological Association. Reprinted by permission.
*$p<.004$.
**$p<.001$.

exceed the severity in Group 1. This result indicated that almost all of the differences found in Table 3.10 were due to the tendency for those experiencing uncued panic to endorse a larger number (a greater percentage) of the 12 symptoms, thereby inflating some of the severity scores.

Because differences emerged in the number of symptoms endorsed, Table 3.11 examines the patterning of symptoms across cued and uncued panic with chi-square analyses. The pattern of chi-square tests matches the pattern of results shown in Table 3.10, which again suggests that patients with uncued panic endorsed more symptoms than did patients with cued or predictable panic. Because of the highly conservative nature of the statistical test used (see Barlow et al., 1985), significant differences among groups emerged only on the symptoms of dizziness and fear of going crazy or losing control.

It seems, then, that there are some differences between cued and uncued panic. Specifically, patients with spontaneous panic were more aware of the somatic symptoms associated with panic. That is, they endorsed more symptoms than did patients with cued panic. This was par-

TABLE 3.11. Number of Patients and Percentage of Group Endorsing Each Symptom across Groups Having Cued or Uncued Panic

Symptom	Group 1: Cued panic (n = 27)		Group 2: Mixed (n = 11)		Group 3: Agoraphobia with panic (n = 41)		Group 4: Panic disorder (n = 17)		df	χ^2
	n	%	n	%	n	%	n	%		
Dyspnea	17	63	8	80	37	90	14	82	3	0.93
Palpitations	21	78	8	80	40	98	15	88	3	8.33
Chest pain	9	33	6	55	31	76	12	71	3	13.13
Choking	12	44	7	64	30	73	10	54	3	1.43
Dizziness	12	44_a	7	64_a	39	95_b	17	100_b	3	30.96*
Unreality	12	44	5	45	28	68	16	94	3	13.06
Paresthesias	6	22	5	45	26	63	12	71	3	14.22
Hot or cold flashes	15	56	9	82	35	85	14	82	3	8.75
Sweating	16	63	9	82	35	93	14	94	3	0.95
Faintness	11	41	7	64	31	76	11	65	3	8.50
Shaking	15	56	8	73	36	88	16	94	3	13.03
Fear of going crazy, losing control	9	35_a	10	91_{bc}	37	90_c	17	100_c	3	38.26*

Note. Categories sharing subscripts are not significantly different, based on orthogonal planned comparison. From Barlow, D. H., Vermilyea, J. A., Blanchard, E. B., Vermilyea, B. B., Di Nardo, P. A., & Cerny, J. A. (1985). The phenomenon of panic. *Journal of Abnormal Psychology, 94,* 320–328. Copyright 1985 by the American Psychological Association. Reprinted by permission.
*$p < .001$.

ticularly apparent for the symptom of dizziness. In addition, the major cognitive manifestation of panic—fear of going crazy and losing control—was endorsed more frequently. Norton *et al.* (1986) also compared non-clinical subjects with predictable (cued, expected) versus unpredictable (uncued, unexpected) panics. As with data for clinical panickers (Barlow *et al.*, 1985), those with uncued, unexpected attacks experienced more panic attacks and rated two symptoms (tachycardia and unreality) as being somewhat more severe than did those with cued and expected attacks.

If these findings are replicated and prove reliable, several explanations are possible. For example, these data may suggest a qualitative difference among these types of panic, due, perhaps, to differential underlying biological processes (e.g., Klein, 1981; see Chapter 5). But another possibility is that these differences have more to do with the perception of cues or attributions about causes of panic than with any more basic biological difference in types of panic.

Cues, of course, serve as the major defining characteristic of panic. That is, the cues or antecedents for panic in simple and social phobias are obvious and readily reported by the patients. Cues in obsessive–compulsive disorder are also usually obvious and are tied to identifiable, aversive intrusive thoughts or to dangerous or contaminating external situations that are not readily escapable. But cues in panic disorder are not obvious to a patient by definition, although panic attacks in the context of agoraphobia often become associated with leaving a safe place or a safe person, or with large crowded areas.

I have noted above that patients with panic disorder seem sensitized to somatic symptoms and overreport and exaggerate these events (e.g., King, Margraf, Ehlers, & Maddock, 1986; see Chapter 9). Evidence is presented in Chapter 6 suggesting that a variety of subtle somatic (or cognitive) sensations become cues for panic attacks in patients with panic disorder. Since they do not discriminate or recognize these cues, panic attacks then seem unexpected and unpredictable. Thus, all panics may be cued, but patients not recognizing these cues perceive panic as unpredictable.

But we are only beginning to examine possible differences in types of panic. For example, Margraf *et al.*'s (1987) agoraphobic patients reported that cued (situational) attacks were much more severe in terms of intensity and number of symptoms reported than were uncued (spontaneous) attacks, although the two types of attacks were otherwise quite alike. But this observation was *within* a group of agoraphobics, as opposed to the Barlow *et al.* (1985) observations, which compared agoraphobics to simple and social phobics and so on. In addition, Margraf *et al.* used the greatly preferred method of prospective self-monitoring (see Chapter 10), rather than retrospective recall, which is subject to more distortion within cued panics. Rachman and Levitt (1985) have begun to study the phenomenon of expected versus unexpected panic and have found unexpected panics to be a more devastating experience. On the other hand, preliminary data from our clinic suggest that panic disorder patients rate expected panic as slightly more severe (Street, Craske, & Barlow, 1987).

Examination of possible differences in types of panic is just beginning. But it is safe to say that if any differences exist among cued, uncued, expected, and unexpected panics, they are very small in terms of the presenting characteristics of the panic attacks themselves. Nevertheless, whether a cue is perceived or not by the patient may have important functional implications.

But the causes or maintaining factors of panic attacks, whether cued or uncued, are only speculations based on the descriptive data provided in this chapter. All we can say for certain at this point is that panic itself seems a distinctive event based on presenting characteristics, with clear topographical differences from generalized anxiety. One important way to learn more about the nature and cause of panic is to produce it experimentally in the laboratory. It is to this rich area of clinical investigation that I now turn.

4

Provoking Panic in the Laboratory

If one can produce a psychological or biological phenomenon in the laboratory, one can begin to talk about the cause of that phenomenon. On the other hand, what appears at first blush to be the immediate cause may be misleading. From all available evidence, it seems that we can produce panic in the laboratory. Furthermore, investigators have been provoking panic in the laboratory for over 65 years. A report of a patient's reactions during an early well-done study (Lindemann & Finesinger, 1938) illustrates a typical panic provocation session. In fact, this patient was administered two antagonistic substances approximately 1 month apart: adrenaline, with marked sympathetic effects, and mecholyl (i.e., acetylcholine), with primarily parasympathetic effects. An account of both sessions provides an interesting contrast that has renewed importance for current theorizing on the nature of panic.[1]

[The subject was a] 42-year-old white, American, college graduate who was treated in the [outpatient department] because of attacks of anxiety which [have] troubled him frequently during the last ten years. The atttacks occurred whenever he tried to walk long distances alone, when he attempted to use a bus or train alone, [and] when he attempted to drive the car alone. He then was seized by a sensation of panic, intense fear that his heart might stop, that he might drop dead the next moment, or that he might disintegrate in some way. He felt weak in his knees, dizzy, and had a feeling of fullness and oppression in his upper abdomen. He was keenly aware of his heart, which seemed to pound but not to race. Occasionally he broke out in perspiration. The first of these attacks occurred suddenly when he was sitting in a movie, watching a vaudeville act in which a box containing a living woman was supposedly sawed into pieces, the woman ap-

---

1. From Lindemann, E., & Finesinger, J. E. (1938). The effect of adrenaline and mecholyl in states of anxiety in psychoneurotic patients. *American Journal of Psychiatry, 95,* 353–370. Copyright 1938 by the American Psychiatric Association. Reprinted by permission.

pearing without injury afterwards. At that time the patient, for a moment, thought he was going to become blind, left the theatre in a panic and for the next few weeks was in a state of almost continuous fear which gradually changed into a state of greater calm except for the siituations described above. He had to give up his job, as a successful business man, and is now working on a [Works Progress Administration] project.

The physical examination showed no abnormal findings. The neurological examination was negative. The pulse rate was at about 70, blood pressure 140/80. The vasomotor reactions were not abnormal. The hands were usually warm and slightly moist. On March 7, 1936, this patient was observed under the influence of adrenaline. At 11:33 he received a preliminary injection of 1 cc. of saline before the injection of adrenaline at 11:40. Two minutes later he asked what made the heart beat differently, "If I put the diaphragm out it seems to stop the palpitation." After 4 minutes he noticed that his hands were sweaty. "I suppose that is nervousness but there is no real difference." After 6 minutes he still insisted there was no difference in his feelings but reported that he was quivery all over as though he were shivering when cold, "Shivering as if I were waiting for a street car on a cold night." After 7 minutes one noticed a gross tremor of his hands. After 9 minutes the patient stated that his heart was pounding and he still felt a quivering in his thighs. He had a slight feeling of insecurity in his legs. The patient did not seem anxious at all. He reminisced about former attacks of anxiety. After 17 minutes he seemed thirsty and asked for a glass of milk. Standing up he still had the sensation of shivering in the knees. From then on one noticed that the patient was rather self-absorbed and did not talk much. After 37 minutes he became impatient, "How much longer is it going to last, Doctor? I am getting hungry. The shivering is wearing off. The pounding is still there but not so bad." From then on he became more talkative again.

It must be noted that under the influence of adrenaline the patient reported about the typical sensations of shivering and about heart pounding, but that he had no attack of anxiety.

On April 11 he received mecholyl. During the preliminary period he stated that he felt good, noticed no difference in his feelings. At 11:32 the injection was started. 15 mgs. were injected in the course of 5 minutes. After 2 minutes the patient appeared alarmed, frightened, was restless and wanted to get up. He rose from the bed, held on to the examiner as if in a state of panic, "I feel terrible. Don't you see that I have cold perspiration all over? Must you go on?" Then he continued, "Am I going to die? I feel very uncomfortable, really very weak. Sweat is pouring all over me." The patient had a flushed face and was perspiring. Patient laughed in a curious manner several times. After 5 minutes he began to feel chilly, "I'm awfully afraid," and began to cry, "I'm soaking wet all over. My nose is running. I feel as if I had gotten a cold in a couple of minutes." After 9 minutes he continued, "This is the most powerful stuff you ever gave me. I don't want to have anything like that ever again." Turning directly toward the experimenter, he addressed him, "Why should you have inflicted this upon me? I have manifested kindness and for all the kindness I seem to get an illness and have to suffer. Look at the water coming off my body. I have a headache too." After 12 minutes the patient's panic reaction seemed to abate and he became very talkative. He kept in close contact with the examiner and continued, "Let me explain to you. When you put that needle in I don't know what happened. I worked myself up to a pitch of fear. That is the way the fear comes on me. I start thinking about it and it manifests itself. It works itself to a panicky feeling. Suddenly the fear came. All that fear came to my mind, as if something was working itself to a climax. You don't know when it is going to stop. Just panicky." The patient appeared like a person who was greatly perturbed and eagerly trying to figure out something that puzzled him. He continued, "My heart did not pound at all, yet I had that panic. Standing up I was not dizzy but weak. It was working up somehow to a peak. I wasn't going to faint. It was just a cross between panic and calm, as if you were gradually going to rise right up. This seems to be leading . . . losing my integrity." During these words the patient seemed somewhat hostile, "I thought you were cruel and punishing me. You are cruel. You just kept on." After 25 minutes he appeared more relieved. He began to joke, remained very talkative, reported the story of how he came to see a doctor. After 33 minutes he was somewhat more silent, complained about a chill going up and down his legs. He continued, "I think I have had all the sensations that I have had in my condition in that one medicine. There was a fear of fainting, a feeling that the heart was going to stop, a terrible panic, the feeling of alarm, the sensation of losing my equilibrium. I lost the sense of control, of contact with the world, as if something was radically wrong and it came so naturally, it came so suddenly." "I'm laboring under the idea that there wasn't any medicine in there at all. You were waiting so long. You said, 'This won't hurt.' Perhaps the response came entirely through my concentration on the needle. I was more alarmed than anything else, just like a man being blindfolded and being told he is going to be branded. Then he is touched with a piece of ice and he thinks he is branded. I think it is just because it took so long. If there was really . . . it washes out of my argument, and then the medicine did what you expected anyway." After 60 minutes the patient was more quiet. He said, "It's all over now, I guess." (pp. 357–362)

Since this experiment, thousands of patients have experienced the terror of panic in the laboratory. (The fact that this patient reacted unexpectedly to mecholyl rather than adrenaline is just one of many puzzles taken up in this chapter.) But determination of the cause of panic remains elusive. A variety of procedures have been used to produce panic or panic-like symptoms. The panicogenic qualities of many of these operations were discovered quite by accident, opening up new avenues of investigation into the nature of panic. Some of these techniques involve biochemical infusions; others implicate respiratory systems in a direct way. Panic can also be elicited by a number of behavioral procedures.

The experimental provocation of panic by whatever means deepens our understanding of the nature of panic. At the same time, these procedures undermine many current assumptions and raise important new questions. In this chapter, the major procedures for provoking panic are described. Putative mechanisms of action associated with each procedure, according to current thinking, are reviewed and integrated. Commonalities among seemingly diverse provocation procedures suggest factors that might maintain panic attacks in susceptible individuals. This, in turn, contributes to a comprehensive theory of panic and anxiety disorders, which is outlined in Chapters 6 and 7.

PHARMACOLOGICAL PROVOCATION

SUBSTANCES USED IN PHARMACOLOGICAL PROVOCATION STUDIES

The laboratory provocation of panic by pharmacological agents has aroused considerable interest of late. Experiments on lactate infusion are receiving intensive investigation. But pharmacological infusion procedures for provoking panic and anxiety have a lengthy and extensive history (Shear, 1986; Wamboldt & Insel, 1988). Among the variety of substances utilized over the years are adrenaline, isoproterenol, yohimbine, caffeine, and lactate.

Adrenaline and Epinephrine

One of the earliest studies in which an attempt was made to provoke panic in the laboratory is noteworthy since the methods employed are nearly identical to those employed today in studies of this type. In 1919, Wearn and Sturgis injected 5 mg of adrenaline into army recruits suffering from "the irritable heart syndrome." As noted in Chapter 3, this seems to have been one of the terms for panic disorder during World War I. What makes this study important is that Wearn and Sturgis injected control subjects in a similar fashion, making this one of the few early studies to use a control group. In the "irritable heart" patients, symptoms characteristic of their acute anxiety reactions occurred and were reported. These included the typical panic symptoms of palpitations, dizziness, and tachycardia. Control subjects also manifested some physiological symptoms, although less pronounced, but reported little or no "anxiety."

In fact, Breggin in 1964 reviewed what was by then a very extensive literature on adrenaline infusions, consisting of at least 24 separate studies over the intervening 45 years. Naturally, not all were controlled studies, and most suffered from a lack of clear definitions of patients and reactions. Furthermore, the "adrenaline" used in the early studies was a poorly defined mixture of epinephrine and norepinephrine (Wamboldt & Insel, 1988). But Breggin (1964) reported consistent support for the early Wearn and Sturgis (1919) results. In study after study, subjects who developed acute anxiety during the infusions had a past history of recurrent anxiety reactions characterized by sudden high levels of arousal and anxiety. On the other hand, subjects without this history did not experience intense anxiety during infusions, according to their own reports as well as observations by the experimenters. These subjects would report, on occasion, that they were feeling "as if" they might be anxious, in that they would experience physiological reactions without subjective feelings of fear or dread. In his lengthy and perceptive review, Breggin (1964) noted another factor that seemed to influence the extent of the anxiety (panic) reation during the infusions. He referred to this variable as "environmental cues." By this, he meant cues in the situation that made it possible or likely for subjects to attribute their strong emotional reaction to one emotion or another, such as fear, anger, or elation. For example, if a situation was made to seem more "dangerous" through the use of "awe inspiring monitoring apparatus and a large number of observers including psychiatrists" (p. 560), then more marked fear or anxiety responses could be expected. This observation, of course, was motivated by the then relatively new findings on the possible importance of attributing an emotional state to the context of the situation one happens to be in (Schachter & Singer, 1962). As noted in Chapter 2, this particular theory has not survived intact, but Breggin's general impressions are receiving substantial experimental support, as described in some detail below.

The biological effects of epinephrine are relatively well mapped out. Epinephrine is, of course, an endogenous catecholamine secreted through the adrenal medulla that produces wide-ranging peripheral arousal. It stimulates both alpha- and beta-adrenergic receptors.

Naturally, there is some question whether these early studies with adrenaline or epinephrine were actually provoking panic. Since current diagnostic conventions were not available, it is not possible to know for certain; however, from descriptions provided in many of these early studies (including the Lindemann & Finesinger [1938] study, quoted above), it would seem that major panic attacks were occurring. For example, in the first study (Wearn & Sturgis, 1919), the soliders with "irritable heart" suffered the "acute anxiety reaction" that brought them to the clinic in the first place. These attacks were characterized by cardiovascular instability, dizziness, and fatigue, as well as by the subjective psychological symptoms of anxiety and dread. This pattern of symptoms, along with the observation of the similarity of these laboratory "panics" to naturally occurring anxiety attacks, largely fulfills even the more stringent current definitions of laboratory panic. In view of the possible relevance of this work, it is surprising that few if any studies on adrenaline or epinephrine have been reported since 1965.

Isoproterenol

Frohlich, Tarazi, and Duston (1969) infused isoproterenol into 15 patients who were complaining of panic-like symptoms. Reactions in this group were compared to those of groups of hypertensives and normotensives who were also infused. In 9 out of the 14 patients with panic-like symptoms, "isoproterenol evoked an hysterical outburst, almost uncontrollable" (p. 4). Once again, subjects in the control groups experienced some increases in physiological measures, but no subjective feelings of anxiety. Consistent with previous patients, they reported feeling "as if" they were anxious. Easton and Sherman (1976) also produced what seemed to be clear panic attacks with isoproterenol infusions in five patients suffering from panic-like symptoms.

Rainey *et al.* (1984) compared the effects of isoproterenol with those of sodium lactate in patients with established diagnoses of panic disorder. This is one of the few studies that has directly compared two panicogenic substances. Eleven patients with panic disorder and 10 control subjects received lactate and isoproterenol, as well as a placebo consisting of a 5% glucose solution. The authors reported that 10 of the 11 panic disorder patients and 3 of the 10 control subjects experienced a panic attack during lactate. During isoproterenol infusion, 8 of the 11 panic disorder patients and 2 of the 10 control subjects experienced panic. Four of the panic patients and none of the control subjects panicked during the glucose placebo infusion. The patients rated their panic attacks during both lactate and isoproterenol as very much like their naturally occurring panic attacks. Overall, lactate panics were rated as somewhat more intense than isoproterenol panics.

There is some question about the overall "severity" of these attacks. In all instances, patients rated their panics at relatively low severities on a scale put together for this experiment. In addition, the Research Diagnostic Criteria definition of panic was used rather than the DSM-III definition; the former allows for a less severe burst of emotion. In contrast to the studies described above, Nesse, Cameron, Curtis, McCann, and Hubber-Smith (1984) did not observe any panic attacks in a group of eight patients and six controls infused with isoproterenol. However, the isoproterenol infusions were part of a long 4-hour protocol that also included a variety of exercise and rest conditions.

Isoproterenol is particularly interesting, since it selectively stimulates only beta-adrenergic receptor sites. As such, it acts more specifically than epinephrine, although still at a peripheral level. This becomes important when the effects of drugs that block beta-adrenergic receptor sites (beta-blockers) on panic are reviewed.

Yohimbine

Yohimbine, an alpha-adrenergic antagonist, has also been used to provoke panic. Yohimbine is one of the few biochemical agents of its type capable of crossing the blood–brain barrier and acting centrally, probably in an area of the midbrain called the locus ceruleus. The locus ceruleus is increasingly implicated in studies of anxiety. This makes investigation of yohimbine important from the perspective of mechanisms of action of panic provocation (see below).

In 1961, Holmberg and Gershon injected patients carrying a variety of diagnoses with yohimbine and compared their reactions to those of control subjects similarly injected. The reactions they noted in this early study included perspiration, pupillary dilation, flushing, a rise in heart rate and blood pressure, trembling, and "irritableness." In a later study, Garfield, Gershon, Sletten, Sundland, and Ballows (1967) injected yohimbine as well as epinephrine into "schizophrenic" and "nonschizophrenic" patients. they concluded that the presentation of symptoms, particularly in terms of the combination of physiological and psychological aspects of anxiety, indicated that yohimbine produced more intense and realistic clinical anxiety than did epinephrine.

While these early studies suffered from a rather global definition of "anxiety" and marked heterogeneity in the patient populations, a more recent study has corrected these flaws. Charney, Heninger, and Breier (1984) compared the reactions of 39 patients with clear diagnoses of either agoraphobia with panic or panic disorder to those of 20 healthy subjects. All subjects were injected not only with yohimbine, but also with placebo. Both physiological and psychological reactions were examined. During yohimbine injections, patients rated themselves significantly more anxious and nervous, and reported that their reaction was similar in quality to that experienced during naturally occurring panic attacks. Patients also experienced marked increases in somatic symptoms, such as palpitations, hot and cold flashes, tremors, blood pressure, and pulse rate. Consistent with the results of other infusion studies, control subjects reported mild increases in somatic symptoms that were not accompanied by psychological symptoms such as subjective reports of nervousness or anxiety. Uhde, Boulenger, Vittone, Siever, and Post (1985) also reported that five out of seven patients reported panic attacks after oral ingestion of a low dosage of yohimbine.

Lactate

Despite the long history of research on infusions of various types with anxious patients, one of the more important studies in terms of its impact was not reported until 1967. At that time, Pitts and McClure (1967) observed that standard exercise had produced characteristic anxiety symptoms in several previous studies (Cohen & White, 1950; Holmgren & Strom, 1959; Jones & Mellersh, 1946; Linko, 1950. They hypothesized, as had other investigators, that the anxiety symptoms found in these studies might have been due to an extremely rapid rise of blood lactate acid occurring as a consequence of the exercise. Pitts and McClure concluded that the lactate ion itself may produce anxiety attacks in susceptible persons. Pilot work revealed that all nine patients with "anxiety neurosis" who were tested developed typical anxiety attacks during lactate infusion. In a subsequent double-blind study, 14 patients and 10 normal controls were infused with lactate, as well as with a modified lactate infusion containing a calcium ion, and a third infusion consisting of only glucose. Of the 14 patients, 13 reported an anxiety attack similar to their naturally occurring attacks during the lactate infusion; 2 of the 10 control subjects also reported panic attacks. Less intense anxiety was experienced during the modified lactate infusion. Neither patients nor controls reported any particular response to the glucose. The investigators hypothesized that the lactate ion may cause panic attacks through alkalinization of the blood. They also noted that the effects observed could have been due to "nonspecific stress."

This study, more than any other, generated interest in the possibility of uncovering the nature of panic attacks through this methodology. Since that time, no fewer than 20 studies describing lactate infusion with anxious patients have been reported. For example, similar results were reported by Fink, Taylor, and Volavka (1970); Bonn, Harrison, and Rees (1971); and Kelly, Mitchel-Heggs, and Sherman (1971). More recent studies of lactate infusion include those of Liebowitz, Fyer, et al. (1984), as well as an important study by Ehlers, Margraf, Roth, Taylor, Maddock, et al. (1986). In view of the significance and sophistication of these latter two studies, some of their findings are reviewed in more detail when the possible mechanisms of action of biochemically provoked panics are discussed below.

Even monkeys have not escaped the effects of lactate. Friedman, Paully, and Rosenblum (in press) administered lactate to primates. According to blind behavioral ratings, lactate, compared to a placebo, produced intense circumscribed emotions in monkeys that differed from a generalized arousal response. The emotional response most closely resembled fear!

To summarize studies on lactate infusion, 54–90% of patients with anxiety or panic attacks, as compared to 0–25% of nonpsychiatric control subjects, respond with "panic attacks" to lactate infusions. The figure of 54% comes from one of the most experienced laboratories (Gorman et al., 1985). Similarly, between 5% and 36% of patients respond with panic attacks to placebo infusions, such as glucose.

Caffeine

It is no secret to millions of people throughout the world who drink coffee that caffeine results in increased alertness and attention. Nevertheless, surveys of caffeine consumption and the effects of caffeine suggest marked individual differences in response to this drug. For example, the personality characteristics of neuroticism or introversion as described by Eysenck (see Chapter 2) seem to relate to caffeine consumption. Neurotic introverts drink less coffee, particularly under stressful conditions (Bartol, 1975). These findings with normals have raised questions about the effects of caffeine in patients with anxiety disorders.

Boulenger, Uhde, Wolff, and Post (1984) surveyed caffeine consumption as well as self-rated anxiety and depression in a series of patients with clear diagnoses of panic disorder or major depressive disorder. These patients were compared to well-matched control groups. They found that patients with panic disorder (but not depressed patients or normal controls) reported levels of self-rated anxiety and depression that correlated with their degree of caffeine consumption: The more caffeine, the more anxiety. In fact, patients with panic disorder had a marked sensitivity to the effects of even one cup of coffee. The experience of drinking coffee was judged to be aversive by the panic patients. Of the 30 panic patients, 20 had stopped drinking coffee, compared to only 5 of the 23 depressed patients. Of the 20 panic patients who had given up coffee, 11 mentioned central nervous system stimulation as the reason for stopping, and 2 more mentioned gastrointestional symptoms. Similar results were reported by Lee, Cameron, and Greden (1985).

Of course, survey research differs markedly from the infusion studies discussed above. Recently, two studies have compared ingestion of caffeine in panic disorder patient versus controls. In a preliminary study, Uhde, Boulenger, Vittone, et al. (1985) found that two patients with panic experienced severe anxiety, including panic attacks, after ingestion of small amounts of caffeine. Eight normal control subjects also experienced acute anxiety, and two evidenced major panic attacks.

Charney, Heninger, and Jatlow (1985) administered 10 mg/kg of caffeine orally to 21 patients meeting DSM-III criteria for agoraphobia with panic or panic disorder, as well as 17 healthy subjects. Of the patients, 71% "panicked" in that they reported marked increases in subjective anxiety, as well as somatic signs of anxiety. They also judged that these attacks were similar to panic experienced in the natural situation. Smaller numbers of control subjects reported increases in subjective anxiety (approximately 25%). Similarly, control subjects evidenced smaller increases in somatic symptoms when compared to patients. Higher baseline ratings were also evident on somatic symptoms for patients before ingestion of caffeine.

In view of the relative consistency with which lactate, caffeine, isoproterenol, yohimbine, and epinephrine provoke panic, speculation has increased on the underlying neurobiological mechanisms associated with panic attacks. This speculation has been confounded by hints that the various pharmacological agents may be associated with fundamentally different neurobiological processes. This raises difficult questions about the causes of panic.

THE CAUSES OF PHARMACOLOGICALLY PROVOKED PANIC

Hypocalcemia

In 1967, Pitts and McClure put forth a new conception of the "cause" of panic, as noted above. They suggested that anxiety symptoms may be related to hypocalcemia produced by excess lactate. They suggested that one may find in these patients "a defect in aerobic or anerobic metabolism resulting in excess lactate production, a defect in calcium metabolism or some combination of these" (p. 1335). Grosz and Farmer (1969) criticized these notions on several grounds. First, they pointed out that anxiety can occur without high blood lactate concentrations and, conversely, that high blood lactate levels may be present without accompanying anxiety. In addition, lactate infusions produce metabolic alkalosis, but lactate produced by exercise shifts the acid-based balance of the body to metabolic acidosis. Finally, they noted that the rise in lactate produced by infusions should cause only a very small change in ionized calcium. In fact, Pitts and Alan (1979) themselves confirmed this notion in a later experiment when they demonstrated that infusions of a powerful calcium chelator, strong enough to produce symptoms of tetany in panic patients, did not induce panic attacks.

As an alternative hypothesis, Grosz and Farmer (1969) suggested that sodium bicarbonate levels rise with lactate infusions and that the accompanying state of hyperventilation may cause feelings of discomfort. In a subsequent study, Grosz and Farmer (1972) repeated the Pitts and McClure (1967) experiment with the addition of an infusion of sodium bicarbonate. Both infusions produced marked anxiety, but neither was associated with a rise in blood lactate. Unfortunately, Grosz and Farmer (1972) infused only normals and not patients suffering from anxiety disorders. With these experiments, the hypocalcemia hypothesis suffered on early demise, although the role of breathing irregularities is continuing to receive increased attention as a panicogenic mechanism.

With the fate of the hypocalcemia hypothesis sealed, a number of other specific biological mechanisms underlying laboratory-provoked panic have been suggested. Table 4.1 presents several of these hypotheses as enumerated by Levin, Liebowitz, Fyer, Gorman, and Klein (1984). While these hypotheses were formulated in the context of lactate-provoked panic, they also cover, in large part, suggested mechanisms of action for other substances capable of provoking panic. Two of the most intriguing pos-

TABLE 4.1. Potential Mechanisms for
Lactate's Induction of Panic

1. Lowering of ionized calcium
2. Metabolic alkalosis
3. Beta-adrenergic hypersensitivity
4. Peripheral catecholamine release
5. Central noradrenergic stimulation
6. Hyperventilation
7. Endogenous opioid dysregulation
8. Alteration of NAD^+-to-NADH ratio[a]
9. Nonspecific stress

Note. From Levin, A., Liebowitz, M., Fyer,
A., Gorman, J., & Klein, D. F. (1984). Lac-
tate induction of panic: Hypothesized
mechanisms and recent findings. In J. C.
Ballenger (Ed.), *Biology of agoraphobia* (p. 83).
Washington, DC: American Psychiatric
Press. Reprinted by permission of the pub-
lisher and authors.

[a]The ratio of the oxidized form of nicotin-
amide–adenine dinucleotide to the reduced form.

sibilities center on beta-adrenergic hypersensitivity and central noradrenergic stimulation.

Beta-Adrenergic Hypersensitivity

Beta-adrenergic hypersensitivity as a biological mediator of panic has attracted considerable attention. For example, epinephrine is an endogenous catecholamine that stimulates both alpha- and beta-adrenergic receptors. Isoproterenol infusions, on the other hand, are thought to
selectively stimulate beta-adrenergic receptors. Both of these infusions
seemingly have produced panic in some subjects but not in others. One
obvious experiment is to block beta-adrenergic receptors during infusion
with panicogenic substances and ascertain whether patients panic or not.
Gorman *et al.* (1983) administered propranolol, which lowers beta-adrenergic sensitivity (i.e., it is a beta-blocker), to six patients who previously
had panicked when infused with sodium lactate. In all six cases, panic
attacks occurred during lactate infusion, despite pretreatment infusion with
propranolol. Examination of the data in Figure 4.1 shows that heart rate
was, in fact, reduced by preinfusion with propranolol in the group receiving it, as one would expect from this beta-blocker, although heart rate did
increase during the lactate infusion. But because heart rate had dropped
initially, there was little or no heart rate increase over baseline values in
the group receiving propranolol. And yet all patients reported panic. The

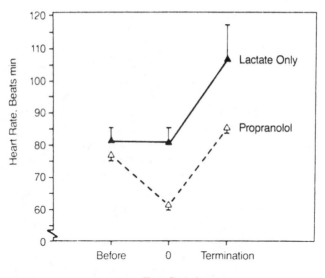

FIGURE 4.1. Comparison of effect on mean heart rate of 5% dextrose–sodium lactate and propranolol hydrochloride–sodium lactate in six subjects. Vertical lines indicate plus or minus the *SEM*. From Gorman, J. M., Levy, G. F., Liebowitz, M. R., McGrath, P., Appleby, I. L., Dillon, D. J., Davies, S. O., & Klein, D. F. (1983). Effect of acute β-adrenergic blockage on lactate-induced panic. *Archives of General Psychiatry, 40,* 1079–1082. Copyright 1983 by the American Medical Association. Reprinted by permission.

fact that reports of panic can occur *without* absolute increases in heart rate has been described in Chapter 3 (e.g., Taylor *et al.*, 1986).

On the basis of these data, both Rainey, Ettedgui, Pohl, and Bridges (1985) and Gorman and Klein (1985) have suggested that lactate and iso-proterenol infusions must produce panic by different biological mecha-nisms. That is, in view of the ineffectiveness of propranolol in blocking lactate-induced panic, lactate must not operate by the mechanism of beta-adrenergic hypersensitivity. Of course, this conclusion has been arrived at by logical inference rather than direct experimentation. For example, the assumption is made that propranolol or other beta-blockers will block isoproterenol-provoked panic, since isoproterenol does selectively stimu-late beta-adrenergic receptors. But this has not been tested. This issue may now be moot. Liebowitz, Gorman, Fyer, Levitt, *et al.* (1985) strongly suggest that no peripheral biochemical or physiological change serves as a trigger for lactate panic. Rather, lactate-induced panic attacks appear to be primarily a central nervous system phenomenon with inconsistent pe-ripheral sequelae.

Central Noradrenergic Stimulation

In view of these conclusions, a somewhat more interesting hypothesis addresses the role of central noradrenergic stimulation as the neurobiological bases for biochemically provoked panic. Central noradrenergic discharge centering around the region of the locus ceruleus has long been suggested as an important mediator of fear or alarm responses (Gray, 1982, 1985; Redmond, 1985) (see Chapter 5). This "pathway" for panic immediately comes to mind in relation to the literature on yohimbine infusion summarized above, but also may be interesting from the point of view of lactate. In their review of the biochemical and physiological correlates of lactate provocation, Liebowitz, Gorman, Fyer, Levitt, et al. (1985) point out that lactate metabolism produces CO_2 which freely crosses the blood–brain barrier. Thus, lactate infusion may produce transient cerebral CO_2 elevation, even though peripheral partial pressure of CO_2 (pCO_2) falls because of the hyperventilation that occurs during lactate infusions. Since CO_2 is a locus ceruleus stimulant (Elam, Yoa, Thoren, & Svensson, 1981; Wamboldt & Insel, 1988), increases in CNS CO_2 produced by lactate infusion may also stimulate locus ceruleus activity in the same manner as yohimbine. Thus, lactate and yohimbine may be provoking panic in fundamentally the same manner, both acting centrally rather than peripherally.

On the other hand, locus ceruleus activity seems to be enhanced by a variety of nonanxiogenic sensory stimuli and may operate in a global, orienting manner, rather than as a specific pathway for anxiety-related stimulation alone (Gray, 1982). In other words, locus ceruleus stimulation in and of itself may not be sufficient to produce panic, since many stimuli affect the locus ceruleus without producing panic or even mild anxiety. Also, as Liebowitz, Gorman, Fyer, Levitt, et al. (1985) point out in a particularly cogent observation, increased central nervous system CO_2 drives respiration, which may give panic patients the feeling of being "out of control." It is this feeling of being out of control that may be the common denominator in the provocation of panic (more on this below). In addition, there is no evidence that the central nervous system CO_2 hypothesis would accommodate isoproterenol-, caffeine-, or epinephrine-provoked panics.

For example, Charney, Heninger, and Jatlow (1985) note that caffeine does not seem to alter plasma 3-methoxy-4-hydroxyphenylethylene glycol (MHPG) levels. MHPG is a common concomitant of peripheral catecholamine increases present in most other infusion studies, and is thought to reflect central noradrenergic activity (Redmond, 1985). These results suggest that caffeine may not operate through central noradrenergic stimulation. The consensus at the present time is that caffeine acts on the adenosine receptor system (Wamboldt & Insel, 1988). In fact, even lactate infusions produce inconsistent noradrenergic effects (Liebowitz, Gorman, et *al.*, 1986). On occasion, *drops* in MHPG have been observed during lactate panics (Carr *et al.*, 1986).

Finally, the locus-ceruleus-stimulatory effects of yohimbine are enhanced by one very interesting pharmacological agent. This agent is imipramine, which is widely thought to block panic attacks (Zitrin *et al.*, 1983) (see Chapter 11). In one of the early studies mentioned above, pretreatment with imipramine was found to *augment* rather than to block the yohimbine response (Holmberg & Gershon, 1961). Charney and Heninger (1985) found similar although weaker effects in patients. This raises questions about the similarity of lactate and yohimbine panics (e.g., Levin *et al.*, 1984), although this particular evidence concerning imipramine has some weaknesses, as noted below. Also, as Charney and Heninger (1985) point out, yohimbine and imipramine may interact with the noradrenergic system in basically different ways. Therefore, imipramine may not necessarily block yohimbine effects.

Multiple Pathways to Panic

In fact, the very different pathways to panic have never been better illustrated than in the early and largely overlooked study by Lindemann and Finesinger (1938) comparing the effects of adrenaline with one of its antagonists, mecholyl (i.e., acetylcholine). Lindemann and Finesinger's report was one of the long series of studies investigating the effects of adrenaline on individuals with "anxiety attacks." Consistent with most of these reports, adrenaline provoked "anxiety attacks" in 11 of 20 patients. That these patients clearly seemed to be suffering from what we would now call "panic disorder" is also evidenced in the case report from this study presented at the beginning of this chapter. However, in a very elegant methodological twist, the investigators also administered acetylcholine in a counterbalanced fashion to these patients. Acetylcholine is antagonistic to adrenaline, with primary parasympathetic rather than sympathetic activation. The investigators were very careful to record not only physiological responses such as heart rate, but also detailed cognitive and somatic reactions to the injection. In addition, they encouraged simultaneous verbalization about the experience, as is evident in the case report. Despite the limited apparatus available at the time, this methodology still ranks among the most sophisticated laboratory provocation studies.

Adrenaline, of course, produced the usual sympathetic constellation of physiological responses. Acetylcholine, on the other hand, produced quite a different effect, including vasodilation of the face and excessive perspiration. The results indicated that, out of 20 patients, 6 panicked with adrenaline but not with acetylcholine; 5 patients panicked with acetylcholine but not adrenaline; both drugs activated a panic attack in 5 patients; and neither of the drugs activated panic in 4 patients.

A final issue concerns whether differences between patients and controls in response to pharmacological provocation are quantitative or qualitative. Some of the studies reported above noted little or no subjective reactions from normals (e.g., Charney et al., 1984). Other studies observed somatic and subjective reaction in normals at a less intense level (e.g., Charney, Heninger, & Jatlow, 1985; Rainey et al., 1984. And a few studies observed outright panic in normals (Uhde, Boulenger, Vittone, et al., 1985). The Ehlers, Margraf, Roth, Taylor, Maddock, et al. (1986) lactate infusion study is important in this regard.

In this study, where subjective anxiety and heart rate were monitored at baseline and throughout the infusion process, the major difference between patients and controls was a constantly elevated report of anxiety and heart rate in panic patients _throughout the procedure_. The rather startling conclusion from this study was that all differences, including elevations in subjective anxiety and heart rate during infusion, could be accounted for by these pre-existing baseline differences. That is, while most patients reported these elevations to be panic and controls did not, the only difference was in the labeling, since both groups reacted identically to the lactate infusions. Because most other studies have not administered baseline measures as systematically, this finding may have been overlooked. These intriguing findings are discussed further in the section on provocation by CO_2 inhalation.

In summary, the best evidence at the present time is that the variety of pharmacological agents utilized thus far to provoke panic are associated with several different neurobiological processes. Some of these processes seem mutually exclusive. Of course, it is possible that a common underlying neurobiological mechanism of action may yet be discovered, reflecting a more fundamental dysfunction in the regulation of neuronal excitability. Wamboldt and Insel (1988) review a number of these possibilities in a particularly lucid manner. Alternatively, panic may be associated with a psychological process (e.g., induced feelings of loss of control) that may be common to these procedures. These feelings of loss of control may be associated (learned) with specific patterns of somatic symptoms (e.g., Lindemann & Finesinger, 1938) and may also be present in normals at less severe levels (Ehlers, Margraf, Roth, Taylor, Maddock, et al., 1986). More likely, the answer will be found in a complex psychobiological interaction.

ISSUES IN PHARMACOLOGICAL PROVOCATION STUDIES

Before I proceed to provocation studies utilizing other procedures, several issues that arise in pharmacological provocation studies require comment and clarification.

126

Pharmacological Blockade of Laboratory Panic: Implications for Neurobiological Mechanisms of Action

Data from attempted pharmacological blockade of laboratory panic are often weighed heavily when possible neurobiological processes in panic are discussed. For example, much has been made of the fact that imipramine seems to block lactate-induced panic in patients *after long-term treatment*, despite the fact that these patients panicked previously when infused with lactate before treatment (e.g., Fyer, Liebowitz, Gorman, Davies, & Klein, 1983; Rifkin, Klein, Dillon, & Levitt, 1981). Similar reports have appeared suggesting the effectiveness of phenelzine or alprazolam in blocking panic after long-term treatment (e.g., Charney & Heninger, 1986b; Kelly *et al.*, 1971; Woods *et al.*, 1986). These reports should be contrasted with other experiments, such as that by Gorman *et al.* (1983; summarized above), where a drug (propranolol) was infused *immediately preceding* lactate provocation. In that case, the question of the interaction of the drug and the provocation procedure can be answered somewhat more clearly. But in the former cases, interpretation is very difficult, since much more goes on during long-term treatment than simply administration of the drug. For example, patients with panic disorder with agoraphobia who are receiving drugs such as imipramine are often treated in the context of a phobia program, where activist strategies for facing feared situations associated with panic are encouraged. But these exposure-based treatments alone are successful in reducing panic attacks (see Chapter 11). Furthermore, a well-controlled double-blind experiment involving a single subject now exists demonstrating that *in vivo* exposure blocked lactate-induced panic in a patient who had previously panicked with lactate (Guttmacher & Nelles, 1984). Other studies in progress report similar findings (M. K. Shear, personal communication, 1987). To make inferences about neurobiological processes from long-term pharmacological effects, one would have to insure the absence of other potential therapeutic operations. For example, one could administer counterexposure instructions to prevent patients from carrying out their own therapeutic program while on a certain drug.

The Definition of Panic

One of the major difficulties precluding clear interpretations in early studies involves the definition of panic. At first blush this would not seem to be a problem, in view of the distinctive appearance of a panic attack. But this issue forces investigators to confront the problem of deciding what is essential to the experience of panic and what are nonessential by-products. These are the same difficult issues one confronts in defining an emotion (see Chapter 2).

One danger from a theoretical point of view is that panic will be mistaken for mild to moderate anxiety. Based on the definitions offered in Chapter 2 and elaborated below, this would greatly complicate our quest to understand the nature of panic. While this problem is often ignored in provocation studies, sophisticated investigators such as Liebowitz and colleagues (Liebowitz, Fyer, *et al.*, 1984; Liebowitz, Gorman, Fyer, Levitt, *et al.*, 1985) have expressed concern about definitional problems—specifically, the lack of objective indices for panic. In their procedure, determining the primary criteria for panic, in addition to the patient's report of panic, requires clinicians to rate the patient at various points in time during the infusion process on a variety of panic-related symptoms. Clinicians are not blind to the procedure, nor have the reliability of these ratings been reported. But it is not surprising that the investigators themselves report that these judgments are sometimes very difficult.

In other studies, such as that of Rainey *et al.* (1984), the investigators determined whether the minimum number of symptoms was present by means of a rating scale. If so, patients were then asked whether the experience was like their naturally occurring panic. There is no indication that patients' reports of experiencing fear or terror were part of the definition. In other words, ratings of somatic symptoms, without a subjective sense of "panic" and without objective verification of the reports, seemed to comprise the criteria. In fact, many "panics" were rated as quite mild subjectively. To correct for definitions of panic based on "judgment" or other inconsistent criteria, Liebowitz, Gorman, Fyer, Levitt, *et al.* (1985) suggest more objective criteria, such as specific increases in heart rate or hyperventilation. But data from Taylor *et al.* (1986; described in Chapter 3) indicate that the heart rate criterion is problematic, since clear reports of panic occur in the abbsence of elevated heart rate. Similarly, Gorman *et al.* (1983) blocked absolute increases in heart rate with beta-blockers but noted the occurrence of panic attacks.

The complexity of this definitional problem is also encountered in the other extremely well-done report on lactate provocation, by Ehlers, Margraf, Roth, Taylor, Maddock, *et al.* (1986). In this study, a variety of well-worked-out questionnaires assessing panic symptoms were completed by patients before and after infusions. Since these patients had been self-monitoring panic for a week or more prior to the procedure, they were well accustomed to filling out these scales. Patient ratings eliminate judgmental difficulties on the part of the clinician, but also open the procedure to subjective distortion. However, the scales used in this study were psychometrically sound and went well beyond simply asking the patient whether a symptom occurred. In addition, objective physiological measures were taken.

Thus far, investigators have tried several different combinations of criteria for capturing the essentials of panic, relying on two components of emotion, physiological and subjective (experimental). But behavioral criteria are also possible. For example, a request that the infusion be stopped is a relevant behavior. In the Ehlers, Margraf, Roth, Taylor, Maddock, *et al.* (1986) study, 4 out of the 10 patients and none of the controls requested termination of the procedure. Interestingly, the 4 patients who made the request were also those carrying an agoraphobia diagnosis. By definition, these patients were in the practice of attempting to avoid panic in their daily lives. Thus, this definition of panic may reflect the ability or inclination to tolerate panic and anxiety rather than the occurrence of panic itself.

Another possible definitional criterion is simply to compare and equate laboratory panic during infusions with naturally occurring panic, and most investigators have done this to some extent. Patients in the report by Ehlers and colleagues had participated in extensive monitoring of panic for several weeks. Therefore, these patients were presumably familiar with definitions of panic in use. In this study, reports were almost identical for laboratory versus natural attacks. Also, patient ratings of specific DSM-III symptoms were not different for lactate versus natural panics for patients, although heart rate increases were somewhat lower for laboratory attacks. Overall, 7 out of 10 patients in this study reported laboratory attacks to be essentially similar to natural attacks, while 3 reported that they were somewhat dissimilar.

The final possibility for defining panic, employed by all investigators, is to examine directly the number of symptoms that occur, including both somatic symptoms and cognitive symptoms relating to subjective reports of panic. A close look at these data in studies reported thus far point out the difficulties of relying on only one of these symptoms (e.g., increases in heart rate) as the major definition of panic. For example, the two patients who reported the greatest "surge" of subjective anxiety in the Ehlers, Margraf, Roth, Taylor, Maddock, *et al.* (1986) study did not necessarily show the highest heart rates. In fact, the heart rate in one of these patients rose gradually from 72 to only 85 BPM. This underlines the necessity of incorporating both subjective and physiological measures, if not behavioral measures, into any definition of panic. Studies reviewed in Chapter 2 on emotion theory suggest that expressive-behavioral measures such as facial expressions, and other behavioral correlates of fear, may be useful.

One intriguing definitional possibility that could be examined more closely involves latency to maximum heart rate increase. Ehlers, Margraf, Roth, Taylor, Maddock, *et al.* (1986) found that increases in heart rate and subjective anxiety in most of their patients were gradual and smooth over the 20-minute infusion period. But two patients showed the abrupt surge in heart rate that seems to have been evidenced by Mary and Jill as described in Chapter 3. Liebowitz, Gorman, Fyer, Levitt, *et al.* (1985) also found markedly different latencies in reaching panic among their patients, ranging from 5 to 20 minutes. But no physiological or biochemical differences seemed to be evident in those panicking within 5 minutes of an infusion versus those going the full 20 minutes. They do note that these heart rate increases "usually occurred abruptly," but no further information is provided. "Abruptness" may be one way to discriminate panic (fear) from anxiety. This would be consistent with the conception of panic as an "alarm" requiring immediate action (fight or flight). If this is true, then it may be inappropriate to plot average values of surges of anxiety, as is now done in most provocation studies. It may be that only those subjects showing an instantaneous alarm reaction peaking within a minute or two can be said to be experiencing panic. (Good examples would be Jill and Mary in Figures 3.1 and 3.2.) Subjects displaying more gradual increases may be experiencing anxious apprehension.

In view of our lack of knowledge of the nature of panic and the seeming discordance between self-reports of panic and physiological or behavioral measures that commonly occurs, the best way to define panic either in the laboratory or in the natural situation is not yet clear. For the time being, it would seem important in the laboratory both to record subjective surges of anxiety in a psychometrically sound fashion and to record increases in physiological measures, particularly abrupt increases. At the same time, investigators should ascertain the similarity of this experience to panic attacks occurring in the natural environment, not only in terms of the patterning of symptoms but also in terms of intensity. Only the most recent studies meet these criteria (e.g., Ehler, Margraf, Roth, Taylor, Maddock, *et al.*, 1986; Margraf *et al.*, 1987; Woods *et al.*, 1986; Woods, Charney, Goodman, & Heninger, 1987).

RESPIRATION-RELATED PROVOCATION PROCEDURES

Although biochemical provocation of panic has received the lion's share of attention, a number of diverse studies have provoked intense anxiety and/or panic through procedures that directly affect respiration or through behavioral methods. While these procedures have been organized under different headings, we should not lose sight of the fact that all provocation procedures may have similar mechanisms of action—biological, psychological, or, most likely, some combination of the two. Thus, one has to rely on operational definitions to categorize procedures. The three procedures grouped in this section are superficially quite diverse; however, each technique markedly affects respiration. Alterations in respiration are heavily implicated in at least some panic attacks.

EXERCISE

Recently a patient, referred to here as "Jack," arrived at our clinic and presented with a severe case of agoraphobia. Jack was an office manager in his late 40s who had transferred from a higher-paying blue-collar job within his company to his current position. Although industrious and hard-working, he was also impulsive, irritable, and given to angry outbursts. This had led to a stormy relationship with his wife and children, and occasional brief physical altercations with his sons. He reported that in years past his agoraphobia had been so severe that he had spent many days confined to his bed, unable to move for fear of provoking a panic attack. Further questioning revealed that Jack had requested the transfer to the lower-paying desk job, thinking it would be less stressful than his previous job, which had involved a great deal of hard physical labor. Jack had done reasonably well at this desk job for a number of years, but an incident several months ago had precipitated a relapse and resulted in his eventual referral to our clinic.

As Jack described the incident,

> I was feeling pretty good. I really hadn't had any nervous problems to speak of for about a year, and I was able to go places and do things in pretty much of a normal way. [This included taking walks and doing other things around the house.] It was a Saturday morning and we'd just had a cord of wood delivered for the woodstove. Usually I order the wood cut and split, but this time I was feeling pretty good, so I thought I'd split it myself. Also, I can really use the exercise, since I'm sitting at a desk all day. I got out there fairly early in the morning and started splitting the wood, and worked up a good sweat. Then all of a sudden I felt it coming on. It was the same old problem. I got dizzy and started to tremble, and now the sweat was really starting to pour off my forehead. My legs were so weak I didn't think I was going to be able to make it to the house. I had the same old feeling that it wasn't really me struggling to get to the house and that it wasn't really my house, but some kind of nightmare. I managed to crawl into bed and stayed there all weekend. My wife brought me cold towels to put on my forehead, which always seems to help a little bit. Since that time I've been able to struggle in to work, but that's about it.

Jack's story is typical of many patients with panic disorder. In Jack's case, it is interesting that he did not make a tight connection between physical exercise and panic, because, as he put it, "there is nothing scary about chopping wood." But he had managed to arrange his life so that he engaged in as little physical exercise as possible over the years, despite his strength and stature. For example, it seemed that his job transfer was motivated by avoidance of physical exercise rather than by stress or job pressure. Cases like Jack's were undoubtedly responsible for one of the most popular names for panic disorder in the 1940s, "effort syndrome." As noted in Chapter 3, this term, originated by Lewis (1917), came out of World War I to describe soldiers who had great difficulty tolerating the physical exertion connected with army duty. An inability to do hard work, or to engage in strenuous physical exercise or any activity that required an "effort," then became the most prominent sign of what we would now call "panic disorder" during the period between the two World Wars.

At the time, the term "effort syndrome" implied an etiology associated with cardiac problems. However, Jones and Mellersh (1946) reported that during World War II a change occurred. Gradually, effort syndrome came to be considered as more of a psychological than a cardiological problem. As a result, the number of cases diagnosed as "effort syndrome" began to drop, and various diagnoses connected with "anxiety" were utilized instead. Nevertheless, a number of studies continued to examine the response of these patients to exercise in contrast to some comparison group. These studies, it will be recalled, originally suggested the lactate hypothesis (Pitts & McClure, 1967). In 1969, Grosz and Farmer pointed out the very different biological consequences of lactate produced by exercise as opposed to infusions of lactate (exercise produces metabolic acidosis, but lactate infusions produce metabolic alkalosis). After this observation, the early literature on exercise and effort tests was largely ignored. Nevertheless, the fact that increases in blood lactate cannot account for panic during exercise still leaves us with the finding that physical exercise seems capable of provoking anxiety attacks or panic in susceptible patients. For that reason, it is interesting to examine briefly some of these early studies.

Typical of these early experiments are reports by Linko (1950) and Holmgren and Strom (1959). In these reports, it was simply noted that blood lactate levels were somewhat higher in "anxiety" (panic?) patients during and after exercise, compared to a variety of control groups. Exercise was typically defined as a certain amount of effort on a stationary bicycle. Nothing was mentioned about the psychological responses to exercise in patients with effort syndrome.

In a more complete and sophisticated series of studies carried out by Mandel Cohen and his associates, the response of these patients to exercise was examined more comprehensively (Cohen & White, 1947, 1950). In these studies, walking or running on a treadmill was the exercise. In addition to blood lactate concentration, measures of pulse and respiration, as well as of oxygen consumption during work, were collected. During rest periods, Cohen and White reported that pulse and respiration rates were somewhat higher in patients with "neurocirculatory asthenia" (the term they used), but that measures of oxygen consumption and blood lactate concentration were normal. However, during moderate or exhausting exercise, marked differences emerged between patients and controls. Generally, patients evidenced higher blood lactate concentrations and lower oxygen consumption and ventilatory efficiency. As Cohen and White noted, the more strenuous the exercise, the more clearly these differences emerged. Patients tended to resemble other groups with low work capacity who were in relatively poor physical shape or who exercised infrequently.

Patients in the Cohen and White studies also terminated the treadmill exercise earlier than control subjects and complained of numerous symptoms (e.g., dizziness, weakness, chest pain, trembling, etc.) as reasons for terminating the test. Controls, on the other hand, when they did terminate, almost always stated only that their legs gave out or they ran out of wind.

In fact, these studies of respiration rate and oxygen uptake during exercise showed a very consistent finding: Patients ventilated more rapidly than healthy controls to meet optimal conditions for oxygen assimilation. In other words, patients with effort syndrome demonstrated a low ventilation efficiency (Cohen & White, 1950; Jones & Mellersh, 1946). Furthermore, both Jones and Mellersh (1946), and Cohen and White (1950) found higher rates of respiration at rest in effort syndrome patients than in controls. Jones and Mellersh reported a very large difference, with effort syndrome patients breathing approximately twice as fast and half as deeply as normal controls at rest. Cohen and White reported a much smaller difference—a respiratory rate of 15.8 breaths per minute for patients, compared to 13.2 breaths per minute for controls. These differences in patterns of breathing suggest that chronic hyperventilation might be responsible for symptoms. But Jones and Mellersh (1946) reported no evidence of hyperventilatory alkalosis in effort syndrome patients, and also reported adequate oxygen saturation of the blood. Jones and Mellersh concluded that these patients were hyperventilating, but not to the point of markedly altering pH levels.

Low ventilation efficiency does not seem to have been the whole story in these early exercise studies. Cohen and White (1950) also reported that for the same amount of work and at the same rate of ventilation, there was a substantially greater awareness of shortness of breath among patients than among control subjects. Dyspnea, of course, is one of the most prominent and frequent symptoms associated with panic attacks (see Chapter 3). Heightened sensitivity to dyspnea and other somatic events is also a hallmark of panic patients.

While the Cohen and White (1947, 1950) studies only hinted at the patients' subjective response to exercise, the earlier study by Jones and Mellersh (1946) provided what may be more useful information. In this study, 10 patients with effort syndrome were compared to 10 patients with "anxiety states" and "somatic anxiety symptoms," but with no evidence of effort syndrome. Both groups of anxious patients were compared with 20 control subjects. The patients with effort syndrome showed symptoms typical of descriptions of this syndrome in the 1940s. In addition to difficulties associated with putting forth "effort," they evidenced excessive emotional response to any excitement. When described in detail, they sound very much like patients with panic disorder. The remaining patients in this study with "anxiety states" seem to have resembled patients with generalized anxiety disorder, although there is no way to confirm this.

Response to pedaling a stationary bicycle revealed patterns similar to the studies described previously with effort syndrome patients. But a new finding emerged from this study: *Both* effort syndrome and anxiety state patients showed some deficiencies in oxygen uptake. Blood lactate concentrations were also higher, along with pulse rate, for both patient groups at baseline as well as during exercise. Jones and Mellersh concluded that the patients with anxiety states were not really different from the effort syndrome patients in their response to these tests on physiological measures. However, they were very different in terms of their subjective response to exercise. As the authors put it,

> In the one group the patient is conscious of this poor exercise response and tends to associate his symptoms with physical effort (in fact develops an effort phobia); in the other group no such awareness is present and the somatic anxiety symptoms are not correlated with exercise. This conforms to the clinical impression that most ES [effort syndrome] patients are indistinguishable from anxiety states, except for the fact that they do have an effort phobia. (Jones & Mellersh, 1946, pp. 185–186)

This is an intriguing hypothesis that was not pursued by these investigators. However, 40 years later, similar hypotheses are now receiving increased attention—a topic to which I return below.

Finally, an observation was made in these early studies that would be confirmed repeatedly in the decades to follow. Anxiety patients, with or without effort syndrome, evidenced elevated pulse and respiration rates and other indices of chronic hyperarousal *while at rest* (see Chapter 5).

Nevertheless, this early work can provide only the barest hints of important relationships. Among the many problems is the necessity of equating old diagnostic categories with new diagnostic categories, as well as the lack of definition of panic in these early experiments. In light of our current knowledge, it would be useful to replicate these experiments using more up-to-date definitions and procedures to determine the panicogenic qualities of exercise in susceptible patients. Until these experiments are repeated with up-to-date procedures, these findings are of historical interest only.

In a more recent study, Crowe *et al.* (1979) exercised 20 anxiety neurotics on a treadmill and also found differences in heart rate and oxygen consumption, compared to a control group. Although DSM-III diagnoses were not used, it would seem that these 20 patients would fit the DSM-III category of panic disorder. Upon closer examination, Crowe *et al.* (1979) observed that differences in heart rate and oxygen consumption could be attributed to a subsample of the anxiety group with evidence of mitral valve prolapse (MVP). Nothing was reported about the psychological responses to the exercise regimen. This result also needs replication, in view of the seeming independence of MVP and panic reported in recent studies (see Chapter 10).

Studies on the effects of exercise are now few and far between. However, despite the lack of evidence that hyperventilation mediates exercise provoked anxiety or panic, there is renewed interest in the effects of hyperventilation and clear evidence that instructions to hyperventilate can provoke panic attacks.

HYPERVENTILATION

Hyperventilation is a common human experience familiar to many of us at one time or another. The basis of hyperventilation is very straightforward. Any time one overbreathes or blows off an excess of CO_2, a hyperventilation syndrome may develop. In its more severe form, sustained overbreathing leads to dramatic symptoms, such as unconsciousness or tetany. However, the more common signs and symptoms of hyperventilation include chronic sighing, as well as a variety of physical symptoms such as dizziness, paresthesias, palpitations, and dyspnea (Huey & West, 1983; Ley, 1985a; Lum, 1975, 1976). These symptoms are also common during panic attacks. For that reason, there is renewed interest in the possibility that hyperventilation under certain circumstances causes panic. A natural step is to attempt provocation of panic attacks through hyperventilation.

The physiological basis of the hyperventilation syndrome is well known, although not fully worked out. Increased breathing blows off CO_2 from the lungs faster than it can be manufactured by the body. This decreases the pCO_2 in the lungs and blood. This in turn raises the blood pH (increases blood alkalosis). The rise in blood alkalosis directly or indirectly leads to the physiological symptoms mentioned above.

It now seems that there are individual differences in resting pCO_2 levels that result in a greater sensitivity to increased ventilation. In other words, only small increases in rates of breathing will result in the beginnings of hyperventilation symptoms for some people, whereas more rapid breathing is required to produce the same symptoms in others (Lum, 1975,

1976). It is not clear why some people maintain this lower resting pCO_2 level. One possibility is that they have developed a habit of rapid ventilation. For example, Huey and West (1983) used a screening questionnaire containing hyperventilation-related symptoms to choose either likely hyperventilators or unlikely hyperventilators from an otherwise normal student population. They found that likely hyperventilators ventilated more rapidly during baseline conditions and developed more somatic symptoms after a period of overbreathing then did unlikely hyperventilators. This was one of the few experiments on hyperventilation to provide adequate controls for demand characteristics. It is possible, then, that panickers may be likely hyperventilators who have developed a "habit" of rapid breathing.

Another possible explanation for low resting pCO_2 in some individuals is that it is but one component of chronic hyperarousal in "anxious" subjects. In one experiment testing the relationship of hyperventilation and panic, Garssen, VanVeenendaal, and Bloemink (1983) asked 28 patients with agoraphobia with panic to hyperventilate. Specifically, they were asked to breathe as deeply and rapidly as possible until pCO_2 was decreased to approximately half of its resting value and maintained at this level for a period of at least 90 seconds. After hyperventilating, the patients reported on the similarity of this experience to their panic atttacks. If hyperventilatory symptoms were mild or the symptoms were not similar to panic attacks as reported by a patient, hyperventilation was not scored as panicogenic for that patient. If some of the symptoms of a typical panic attack were produced in a robust fashion, but not others, the data were scored as "questionable." In this procedure, 17 or 61% of the 28 patients experienced panic symptoms while hyperventilating. Although number and type of symptoms were not recorded, it can be presumed that at least four DSM-III symptoms of panic were produced, in view of the well-known physiological effects of hyperventilation in both patients and normals (Ley, 1985a). However, it is not clear whether any subject reported an actual panic attack, since this was not part of the procedure. The patients simply reported that the somatic symptoms were similar or identical to those experienced during a panic attack.

More recently, Rapee (1986) carefully selected 20 patients with panic disorder, as well as 13 subjects with DSM-III generalized anxiety disorder who had never experienced a panic attack. In this study, patients with panic disorder evidenced lower resting pCO_2 and higher resting heart rate then those with generalized anxiety disorder. Since patients with generalized anxiety disorder who had experienced any panic attacks were excluded, it is possible that these patients were less severely anxious than the panic disorder patients.

After 90 seconds of voluntary hyperventilation, patients were administered a questionnaire on which they indicated the number of symptoms they experienced and the amount of distress caused by each symptom on a rating scale. Patients with panic disorder reported a significantly greater number of symptoms, as well as greater mean distress associated with each symptom, than did patients with generalized anxiety disorder. Furthermore, when asked about the similarity of their experience to naturally occurring anxiety, 80% of the panic disorder group reported a marked similarity of symptoms, while 20% reported no resemblance. This compares to 25% of the patients with generalized anxiety disorder who reported the experience to be similar and 75% who said that the hyperventilatory symptoms were quite dissimilar from their (generalized) anxiety. No subject reported an actual panic attack. All patients indicated that they did not "panic" because they knew what was causing the symptoms and felt that they were in a safe environment.

One additional experiment explored the panic-provoking qualities of voluntary hyperventilation. Gorman, Askanazi, et al. (1984) compared hyperventilation with two other panicogenic procedures in a small group of patients. Twelve patients with panic disorder or agoraphobia were first infused with lactate. Eight of these 12 patients panicked, as defined by the criteria used in this laboratory (see below; Liebowitz, Gorman, Fyer, Levitt, et al., 1985). Approximately 1 week later, these patients were fitted with a clear plastic canopy box that was sealed around their heads. An indwelling catheter was also placed in a radial artery in order to sample arterial pH values. After 15 minutes of normal breathing, 5% CO_2 was added to the air until a panic attack occurred or a maximum of 20 minutes passed. After another baseline phase, subjects were instructed to hyperventilate for 15 minutes until they became too fatigued to continue or until a panic attack occurred. In this later hyperventilation phase, 3 out of 12 subjects reported a panic attack.

Of course, the hyperventilation procedure in this experiment differed considerably from those of the previous experiments. First, patients were instructed to hyperventilate for the very long period of 15 minutes. The mean time until panic for the three patients who reported panics was 6.7 minutes. Furthermore, this was the third panic-provoking procedure within a 1-week period and the second within one laboratory session for those patients. All three patients who reported panic during hyperventilation also panicked during the other procedures. Curiously, the "panic attacks" were described by these patients as dissimilar to their natural panics (or to lactate-induced or CO_2-induced panics). Furthermore, although marked physical discomfort was reported, Gorman, Askanazi, et al. (1984) note that these patients reported little anxiety during hyperventilation. The report of panic, but relatively little anxiety, once again raises the definitional problems involved in studying panic in the laboratory.

It is not clear how data from this study relate to those from the previous studies. At the very least, the demand characteristic would have been very different in a study such as this, where patients had undergone several procedures prior to the hyperventilation episode. Controlling for the sequential confounding of provocation procedures present in this experiment might have led to a different pattern of results.

Hyperventilation and its physiological consequences may play a role in other panicogenic procedures, both biochemical and behavioral. For example, as noted above, Liebowitz, Gorman, Fyer, Levitt, et al. (1985) found that lactate infusions produced hyperventilation and alkalosis. But they have gone on to suggest a different underlying mechanism summarized above, wherein the metabolism of lactate would produce increases in central nervous system CO_2. This change would seem to occur independently of the drop of peripheral CO_2 produced by the hyperventilation. Central nervous system CO_2 would then stimulate the locus ceruleus, and so forth. On the other hand, Ley (1985a) suggests that infusions of lactate may somehow directly raise the pH level of the blood (i.e., may increase blood alkalosis). In view of the lower resting pCO_2 in panic disorder patients, this increment in pH as a result of the lactate infusion would bring about a greater number of intense symptoms. Ley goes on to speculate that those few control subjects who panic in response to lactate infusion may also be chronic hyperventilators.

Now, J. M. Gorman et al. (1986) have examined alkalosis during lactate provocation more carefully in patients with panic disorder and normal controls. Consistent with previous studies, panic patients as a group evidenced lower resting pCO_2, although only 20% could be classified as acute hyperventilators. Once again, this could have been just one additional sign of chronic overarousal in these patients. But during lactate infusions, panicking patients did not demonstrate higher metabolic alkalosis or pH than nonpanicking patients. In fact, panicking patients kept their pH very close to that of nonpanicking patients. This indicates that metabolic alkalosis is not the proximate cause of panic during lactate infusion. Based on ambulatory monitoring of pCO_2 levels, Gelder (1986) also concludes that hyperventilation is not likely to be the cause of panic in the majority of patients. In addition, exercise did not markedly alter pH levels in patients in the early exercise studies, despite more rapid breathing at rest in those patients (Jones & Mellersh, 1946). van den Hout (1988) points out a number of additional reasons why hyperventilation cannot account for lactate panic, and Weiner (1985) describes more fundamental dissimilarities between physiological effects of anxiety and hyperventilation. Finally, it is not clear how mechanisms associated with hyperventilation can be extended to cover the effects of other panicogenic substances, such as yohimbine, caffeine, or isoproterentol, with their seemingly very different neurobiological actions. Nevertheless, it is clear that hyperventilation plays a role in at least some panic attacks. Case reports clearly illustrate the tight relationshihp between panic and hyperventilation in some cases (e.g., Salkovskis, Warwick, Clark, & Wessels, 1986). The possible importance of respiratory control procedures in treating panic, at least in those panickers with hyperventilatory symptoms, is described in Chapter 11 (e.g., Clark, Salkovskis, & Chalkley, 1985).

CO_2 INHALATION

The third provocation procedure in which respiratory symptoms are strongly implicated involves inhaling various amounts of CO_2. It is particularly interesting to compare and contrast the panicogenic qualities of voluntary hyperventilation with those of CO_2 inhalation.

Testifying once again to the long historical tradition of provocation studies, the inhalation of CO_2 was demonstrated very early to provoke panic-like symptoms in susceptible patients. In 1919, Drury found that patients with "irritable heart syndrome" displayed an exquisite sensitivity to the inspiration of even low percentages of CO_2. This sensitivity included symptoms that would now be described as panic.

Cohen and White (1950) reported an experiment in which 43 patients and 27 control subjects first breathed oxygen for 12 minutes, and then inhaled air containing 4% CO_2 for 12 minutes. Of the 43 patients, 47% developed symptoms rated as identical to their anxiety attacks, while another 37% developed symptoms described as similar to their attacks. Thus, a substantial proportion of 84% of the patients found that inhaling CO_2 was anxiogenic and possibly panicogenic. These findings were overlooked until recently, although it is not clear why. One possibility is that for a period of years, inhalations of CO_2 were used to *reduce* anxiety in anxious patients. Beginning with Wolpe (1958), who first popularized the method, a number of clinical reports suggested that inhalations of CO_2 were effective in reducing anxiety in patients with a variety of anxiety problems, including what we would now call panic (Latimer, 1977; Ley & Walker, 1973; van den Hout & Griez, 1982; Wolpe, 1973). In fact, some investigators (e.g., Thyer, Papsdorf, & Wright, 1984) use the apparent anxiolytic effects of CO_2 inhalations to further support the possibility of a hyperventilatory etiology of panic where CO_2 is rapidly blown off! van den Hout and Griez (1982), who have both increased and decreased anxiety with CO_2 inhalations, conclude that CO_2-induced sensations are either pleasant or unpleasant, depending upon prior expectations. For example, Ley and Walker (1973) instructed their patients to expect less anxiety, and this is what they found. The issue of expectations and demand in panic provocation studies is taken up again below.

A number of reports have confirmed the panic-provoking qualities of inhalations of CO_2. van den Hout and his colleagues have administered single-breath 35% CO_2 in a number of experimental and clinical contexts, with important results. For example, van den Hout and Griez (1982) instructed a group of healthy normal subjects to inhale 35% CO_2. DSM-III somatic panic symptoms occurred in a large proportion of these subjects. Furthermore, the administration of propranolol prior to this inhalation reduced these symptoms by about 20% in a well-controlled double-blind experiment. Even in this normal group, approximately 20% reported the cognitive symptoms of panic such as fear of dying or losing control. Minna Fyer and her colleagues also used a 35% CO_2 inhalation with eight panic patients. Six of the patients responded with panic, compared to none of five control subjects (Fyer et al., 1986).

From the point of view of mechanisms of action, 35% CO_2 initially produces respiratory acidosis. This would seem to make it incompatible with hyperventilation and possibly lactate infusion, which produce respiratory (and metabolic) alkalosis. But, as van den Hout (1988) points out, the intense stimulation of a breath of 35% CO_2 produces a hypocapnic undershoot. This results very quickly in a rebound to a state of alkalosis. Therefore, 35% CO_2 seems to produce the same effects as hyperventilation, despite the process of blowing off CO_2 on the one hand and inhaling it on the other. For this reason, among others, there has been more interest from a theoretical point of view in procedures where (approximately) 5% CO_2 is inhaled. The 5% CO_2 produces a clear acidosis with no rebound. This provides a clear contrast to effects of hyperventilation or lactate. And yet, beginning with the Cohen and White (1950) study described above, the evidence is as firm on the panicogenic effects of inhaling 5% CO_2 as it is for any other provocation procedure, including lactate.

Gorman, Askanazi, et al. (1984), in the experiment described above, had the same 12 patients who had previously undergone lactate infusions inhale air containing 5% CO_2. Of these patients, 7 panicked and reported the attacks as being very much like both lactate panics and their naturally occurring attacks. These patients reported being particularly uncomfortable with having their respiration increased or "driven" in an out-of-control manner. Cohen and White (1950) also reported that rapid, out-of-control breathing was particularly discomforting to their patients.

In our laboratory, we compared the severity of the DSM-III panic symptoms provoked by inhaling 5% CO_2 to the severity of symptoms of a natural attack recorded by one patient during self-monitoring. This comparison is valuable, because the patient rated the severity of each DSM-III-R symptom of panic at the time it occurred, thus precluding retrospective distortion. The severity ratings are presented in Table 4.2 (Sanderson, Rapee, & Barlow, 1987b). As one can see, the ratings are very similar, although symptoms in the natural attack were somewhat more intense. Furthermore, the patient demonstrated marked elevation in physiological responding and subjective reports of anxiety during the 6th minute of the inhalation procedure. At that time, she reported panicking and requested

TABLE 4.2. Severity of DSM-III Panic Symptoms Reported by the Subject during a "Natural" Panic Attack and during the Panic Attack Induced by Inhaling CO_2

Symptom	Natural panic	CO_2 panic
Numbness or tingling in extremities	6	1
Trembling or shaking	4	3
Dizziness, lightheadedness	7	5
Pounding or racing heart	6	5
Breathlessness/smothering sensation	8	6
Faintness	4	3
Chest tightness or pain	5	6
Choking	5	2
Sweating	0	0
Hot flushes or cold chills	2	1
Feeling of unreality	7	3
Nausea or abdominal distress	2	4
Fear of dying	8	4
Fear of going crazy	0	3
Fear of losing control	8	7
Sensation of panic or fear	8	7

Note. Severity was rated on an 9-point scale: 0 = "none," 2 = "slight," 4 = "moderate," 6 = "strong," 8 = "very strong." From Sanderson, W. C., Rapee, R. M., & Barlow, D. H. (1987, November). *Panic induction via inhalation of 5% CO_2 enriched air: A single subject analysis of psychological and physiological effects.* Paper presented at the annual meeting of the Association for Advancement of Behavior Therapy, Boston.

that the procedure be terminated. Therefore, this panic attack not only was reported as similar to her naturally occurring attack, but looked very similar on every objective measure.

Several other well-controlled studies point to the panicogenic effects of 5% CO_2. In one study, 7 out of 10 medication-free patients with agoraphobia and panic attacks who inhaled a 5% CO_2 mixture experienced panic attacks. These 7 (along with another patient who had a strong reaction but did not actually report panic) indicated that the experiences were very similar to naturally occurring panics. This compares to 4 out of 22 control subjects who reported panic (Woods *et al.*, 1986). The investigators specifically tested the hypothesis that panic patients might have abnormally high central medullary chemoreceptor sensitivity. However, no differences in ventilatory responses to CO_2 emerged between patient and control groups. These investigators have conducted a second, more intensive study in which a wide range of physiological, biochemical, and behavioral measures were collected over a period of 3 hours surrounding the provocation procedure. In addition, healthy control subjects breathed two different mixtures of CO_2 (one containing 5% and another containing

7.5%. Of 14 patients, 8 experienced panic attacks while breathing 5% CO_2, compared to 3 out of 11 control subjects. In an interesting development, 7 out of 8 healthy control subjects experienced panic attacks at the higher 7.5% level of CO_2 (Woods, Charney, Goodman, & Heninger, 1987).

This last study is important for three reasons. First, this study was placebo-controlled. Despite the long history of investigation in this area, well-controlled placebo studies are only beginning to appear. Second, this is the first report of a substantial majority of normal healthy subjects reporting clear panic attacks defined not only by somatic symptoms but also by cognitive symptoms (marked subjective anxiety, fear of losing control, etc.). In this regard, normal control subjects differed from patients only in requiring a stronger concentration of CO_2 before panicking. Third, no differences emerged on physiological or biological measures between patients and controls at any point in the experiment. This included the 5% CO_2 inhalation comparison, where patients reported significantly more anxiety and panic attacks than did controls. Once again this raises questions about the basic mechanisms of action of panic.

Another well-done study yielded similar results. Ehlers, Margraf, and Roth (1987) administered a 5.5% CO_2 mixture to 16 panic patients and 18 control subjects. These investigators also observed a similar response to the provocation procedure on the part of patients and controls. Patients reported significantly more anxiety as well as more panic attacks (depending on the criteria used) only because of differences in baseline anxiety prior to the CO_2 inhalation. That is, panic patients were more anxious to begin with, but there were no differences in absolute increases in subjective or physiological measures of anxiety over and above those demonstrated by control subjects. All differences could be accounted for by baseline levels.

These findings do not agree entirely with those of Woods, Charney, Goodman, and Heninger (1987), since the patients in the Woods et al. study did show greater increases in anxiety and some phsyiological measures over baseline values, compared to controls. Nevertheless, the marked response from control subjects after inhaling 7.5% CO_2 in the Woods, Charney, Goodman, and Heninger (1987) study does support the contention of Ehlers et al. (1987) that perhaps differences are quantitative rather than qualitative, with panic patients reacting to a less intense mixture. If this is true, then biological surges associated with panic, whatever their origins, are not sufficient to account for panic. Rather, one must incorporate psychological factors to fully explain panic attacks. Even in the Fyer et al. (1986) study, where no control subjects reported panic, nearly parallel increases in measures of anxiety occurred in patient and control groups after one breath of 35% CO_2. Once again, the major difference between groups can be accounted for by pre-existing baseline levels of anxiety. Repeated ratings of anxiety during CO_2 inhalations from both the

Woods, Charney, Goodman, and Heninger (1987) and Ehlers *et al.* (1987) experiments are presented in Figures 4.2 and 4.3, respectively. Physiological measures showed similar patterns.

The responding of normal subjects to panic provocation procedures, albeit at less intense levels, has interesting parallels with the survey research described in Chapter 3 on the experience of panic in the general population. In those studies, the experience of panic also resembled panic attacks in patients with panic disorder in most respects. The one consistent finding was that panic attacks were rated as less severe by nonclinical panickers than they were by patients.

The fact that normal subjects responded with negative affect as well as somatic symptoms to panic provocation procedures is not surprising. A variety of experiments from the laboratories of experimental and social psychology have demonstrated that unexplained arousal is aversive (see

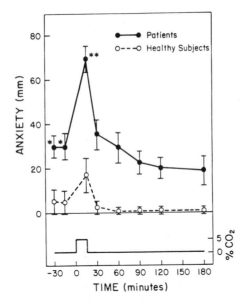

FIGURE 4.2. Anxiety visual analogue scale ratings and inspired CO_2 concentrations on the 5% CO_2 day in panic disorder patients and healthy subjects. *$p <$ .001, baseline values, patients versus healthy subjects, unpaired t test, two tailed. **$p <$ .001, time point versus baseline, paired t test, two-tailed, *and* $p <$ .05, change from baseline, patients versus healthy subjects, unpaired t test, two-tailed. From Woods, S. W., Charney, D. S., Goodman, W. K., & Heninger, G. R. (1987). Carbon dioxide-induced anxiety: Behavioral, physiologic, and biochemical effects of 5% CO_2 in panic disorder patients and 5 and 7.5% CO_2 in healthy subjects. *Archives of General Psychiatry, 44* 365–375. Copyright 1987 by the American Medical Association. Reprinted by permission.

143

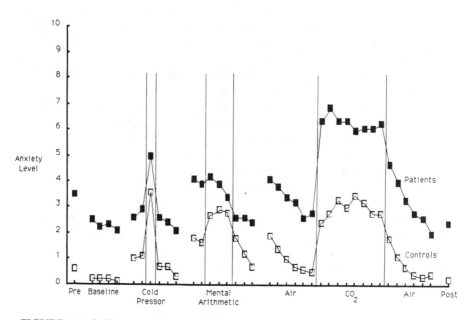

FIGURE 4.3. Self-reported anxiety for patients and controls during baseline, cold pressor, mental arithmetic, and CO_2 paradigms. From Ehlers, A., Margraf, J., & Roth,W. T. (1987). Interaction of expectancy and physiological stressors in a laboratory model of panic. In D. Hellhammer & I. Florin (Eds.), *Neuronal control of bodily function—basic and clinical aspects: Vol. II. Psychological and biological approaches to the understanding of human disease* (p. 60). Göttingen: Hogrefe. Copyright 1987 by Hans Huber Publishers. Reprinted by permission.

Chapters 2 and 7). It may be more surprising that some of the studies reviewed above reported no subjective reaction on the part of control subjects to somatic symptoms associated with panic provocation procedures such as lactate. This may well reflect instructional sets that affected subjects' expectancies about the procedure. For example, in the Woods, Charney, Goodman, and Heninger (1987) study, which was conducted with appropriate placebo control conditions, normal subjects were subjected to three different inhalation procedures in a blind fashion. Presumably, these subjects were less certain about the effects of any one condition than subjects in other experiments, who were experiencing only one experimental procedure. This may account, perhaps, for the negative affect experienced by the control subjects in this study.

Finally, these studies reinforce findings from pharmacological provocation studies concerning multiple underlying biological processes associated with provocation of panic. The inhalation of 5% CO_2 is incompatible with respiratory alkalosis, which is the physiological consequence of hyperventilation. Similarly, exercise, to the extent that it is panicogenic, would also seem incompatible with respiratory alkalosis, since increased oxygen consumption is necessary to meet increased metabolic demands. What all three procedures have in common, of course, are the discomfort and distress associated with suddenly increased rates of ventilation. This is the out-of-control, "driven" respiration mentioned by Liebowitz, Gorman, Fyer, Levitt, et al. (1985) as a possible panic trigger in lactate infusion.

BEHAVIORAL PROCEDURES

CONFRONTATION WITH A PHOBIC SITUATION

For decades, therapists have been exposing patients to their phobic objects or situations for therapeutic purposes. Beginning with the rise of behavior therapy in the late 1950s (Wolpe, 1958), the principles of systematically exposing patients to their feared situation has become the backbone of the behavioral treatment of phobia (Mavissakalian & Barlow, 1981b). Since that time, behavior therapists treating phobic patients, (particularly agoraphobics) are accustomed to seeing full-blown panic attacks occur in this context. Only recently has it occurred to investigators to use these procedures to study the nature of panic. A large part of the credit for this goes to George Curtis and his colleagues, who first proposed this idea.

In Curtis and colleagues' typical experimental paradigm (Curtis, Nesse, Buxton, Wright, & Lippman, 1976), they select simple phobics whose phobic object is readily available and portable, such as a small animal or insect. The patient is seated in a chair, and the phobic object is moved rapidly closer to the patient until he or she either refuses to have it brought closer or is judged to be on the verge of running away. As Curtis, Nesse, et al. (1976) describe their procedure, they are unwilling to take "no" for an answer, always considering it a "maybe." This procedure is far more direct and intense than even therapeutic flooding, and results in anxiety that is usually "quite pronounced and frequently truly dramatic during the course of the treatment. Manifestations include screaming, weeping, running from the room, goose flesh, gross tremors, tachycardia and hyperventilation" (p. 156). In other words, a DSM-III panic attack occurs. Curtis and colleagues (Nesse et al., 1985) generally find a variety of physiological and endocrinological changes correlated with these attacks. Increased pulse, blood pressure, and catecholamines, specifically norepinephrine and epinephrine, as well as increased adrenocortical responses such as insulin, cortisol, and growth hormone have been observed. But they report that these responses are not reliable, sustained, and coordinated in the way that a simple theory of stress might predict. Instead, they consist of relatively inconsistent, brief, and seemingly uncoordinated changes. In fact, in their early studies (Curtis, Nesse, Buxton, & Lipp-man, 1978, 1979; Nesse, Curtis, & Brown, 1982; Nesse, Curtis, Brown, & Rubin, 1980), they failed to find increases in these measures, particularly adrenocortical responses. Only through carefully controlling for a variety of potentially confounding variables (including time of day of administration of the test), as well as transforming the data in such a way as to eliminate the enormous intersubject variability, were they able to observe these responses (Nesse *et al.*, 1985). Patterns of endocrine and cardiovascular response during panic are discussed again in Chapter 5.

Ko *et al.* (1983) elicited panic in six agoraphobic subjects in order to investigate biological correlates of panic. In their procedure, patients journeyed to a nearby shopping mall or some other equally panic-provoking setting. They returned to the laboratory 30 minutes after panicking to have blood samples taken. Plasma levels of MHPG (the object of this study) increased markedly following panic attacks. Since MHPG is thought to reflect central noradrenergic activity, this lends some support to noradrenergic associations with naturally occurring panic. However, in a more extensive and thorough analysis of naturally occurring panic in agoraphobics, these findings were not replicated. Woods, Charney, McPherson, Gradman, and Heninger (1987) studied 18 drug-free agoraphobics and 13 matched healthy controls. Of the 18 patients, 15 experienced "situational" panic attacks. But the key to this experiment was requiring control subjects to engage in the same behavior (go walking through malls, etc.) as patients. Patients differed from controls only in evidencing somewhat higher heart rate during panic attacks. No differences were observed in MHPG or other endocrinological measures. This lack of differences in biochemical measures replicates results found in laboratory provocation work (e.g., Woods, Charney, Goodman, & Heninger, 1987).

More extensive analysis of panic provoked by confrontations with phobic situations from a number of perspectives will undoubtedly be forthcoming. One such study has now appeared that concentrates on psychological rather than biological aspects of panic. As mentioned briefly in Chapter 3, this study explicates an interesting functional relationship between panic and generalized (anticipatory) anxiety. Rachman and Levitt (1985) exposed 17 severe claustrophobics recruited from a student population to a small dark room. They were required to stay in this room for a period of 2 minutes, although subjects were free to leave the room if they wished before the 2-minute period was over. Before entering the room, subjects were asked to indicate in a psychometrically sound manner whether they expected to panic or not, as well as how long they expected to remain in the room and how fearful they thought they would become. After leaving the room, subjects were asked not only how fearful they had become, but also whether they had panicked. In addition, subjects were given the DSM-III-R 14-item checklist of panic symptoms to complete. Each subject experienced two of these trials before undergoing up to 20 exposure-based treatment sessions. After treatment, six different 2-minute posttest trials were administered to each subject under a variety of different experimental conditions.

Of the subjects, 75% reported experiencing a panic on at least one of the occasions and 66% panicked on at least two occasions, according to the Upjohn modifications of the DSM-III definitions of panic (Taylor *et al.*, 1986). Panic occurred on 67 out of 258 trials. Since two-thirds of these trials were posttreatment trials, after many of the subjects had improved considerably, the proportion of panic is probably lower than it would have otherwise been. Of the total of 67 panic attacks, 50 were correctly predicted and 17 were unexpected. In addition, there were 39 errors of overprediction, in which a panic was expected but did not occur.

The pattern of analyses in this experiment led to some particularly interesting findings on the consequences of laboratory-provoked panic. For example, the occurrence of panic was followed by a significant increase in anticipatory anxiety scores on subsequent trials. However, there was an actual decrease in reported fear scores on the trial following the panic. In other words, panic attacks led to greater expectations of subsequent fear, but the expectations were not necessarily confirmed. Figure 4.4 shows the consequences of having a panic for both predicted and reported fear. When unexpected panics were compared to expected pan-

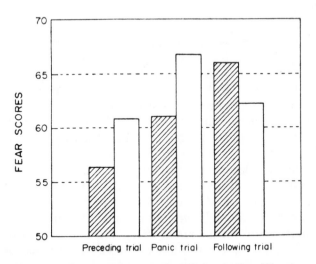

FIGURE 4.4. Effects of panic on fear scores. While predicted fear scores (hatched bars) rose following a panic ($p = .015$), reported fear scores (open bars) decreased following a panic ($p = .098$). From Rachman, S., & Levitt, K. (1985). Panics and their consequences. *Behaviour Research and Therapy, 21*, 585–600. Copyright 1985 by Pergamon Journals, Ltd. Reprinted by permission.

ics, unexpected panics resulted in a much larger increase in anticipatory anxiety on subsequent trials. Neither expected nor unexpected panics had any significant effect on reported fear.

Subjects who improved during exposure-based treatment were also compared with those who did not improve. Subjects who improved experienced an average of 2.3 panics during treatment trials, while those who did not improve experienced an average of 6 panics. In other words, the more frequent occurrence of panic seemed to prevent overall reduction in claustrophobic symptoms.

The Rachman and Levitt (1985) study is one of the first, but undoubtedly not the last, of many studies whose purpose is to provoke panic systematically and directly by means of confrontational techniques. If this study is any indication, we will learn much about the nature of panic and its relationship to generalized and anticipatory anxiety and phobic behavior. Furthermore, the results of this study, taken together with the work from Curtis's laboratory (e.g., Nesse *et al.*, 1985) as well as the Woods, Charney, McPherson, *et al.* (1987) study, indicate that panic attacks produced in this way are on the whole quite similar to panic provoked pharmacologically or through respiratory procedures. The same patterning of physiological, endocrinological, and symptomalogical expression of panic seems to occur across various provocational procedures.

RELAXATION

In Chapter 3, the panic attacks of Jill and Mary have been described in some detail. Seemingly, these were "spontaneous" or uncued attacks that just happened to occur while these patients were relaxing. Another possibility is that the process of relaxation itself is panicogenic for susceptible patients. In theory, relaxation was suggested several years ago as a potentially important trigger for anxiety (Denny, 1975). In fact, there is increasing evidence for this phenomenon. Clinical reports abound describing what seems to be a relatively common problem during the early stages of relaxation or meditation. Jacobson and Edinger (1982) observed rapid exacerbation in anxiety during relaxation at a sufficient frequency to term it a "side effect" of relaxation. Kennedy (1976) reported depersonalization occurring as a consequence of some meditational techniques. Others have reported similar problems (Fewtrell, 1984).

One of the leading investigators of the effects of relaxation, Thomas Borkovec, observed this phenomenon frequently; as a result, he began a systematic attempt to examine anxiety and panic provoked by relaxation and meditation techniques (Heide & Borkovec, 1983, 1984). In the preliminary study (Heide & Borkovec, 1983), 14 subjects meeting the DSM-III criteria for generalized anxiety disorder were recruited. Each subject experienced one session of training in each of two relaxation methods: progressive relaxation or mantra meditation. Prior to the session, subjects briefly practiced the specific procedure to be used. During this practice period, 4 subjects reported increases in anxiety, such as restlessness, feeling uptight, and fear of losing control. An additional subject reported what seemed to be a full-blown panic attack, characterized by crying and reports of intense anxiety. She chose to terminate the experience immediately. Posttreatment questionnaires, as well as results from the physiological measures, revealed that 31% of the subjects reported feeling increased tension during progressive relaxation on either subjective or physiological measures of anxiety or both. Moreover, 54% reported increased anxiety during the meditation procedure. From a number of psychological scales, the investigators attempted to determine what factors mediated these increases in anxiety. Generally, fear of losing control and the experience of sensory side effects of relaxation were strongly associated with poor outcome on the relaxation measures. Norton, Rhodes, Hauch, and Kaprowy (1985) have reported similar results.

These preliminary experiments would seem to establish the phenomenon of relaxation-induced anxiety. Nevertheless, these studies really say very little about the possibility of relaxation-provoked panics, since panic was not the object of the investigation, nor was it systematically measured. Now a preliminary study from our clinic has examined the panicogenic properties of relaxation in a group of 15 panic disorder patients with or without agoraphobia (Adler, Craske, & Barlow, 1987a, 1987b). Each patient listened to three 15-minute audiotapes in random order: a relaxation tape, a tape with instructions on muscle tension, and a neutral tape containing a passage from a popular novel. Significant differences emerges among the three tapes on number of severity of DSM-III-R panic symptoms reported. The greatest symptomatology was associated with the relaxation tape. The number of patients reporting symptoms at a moderate severity or more (4 or more on a scale of 0–8) are presented in Figure 4.5. The response to the relaxation tape was associated with a significantly greater similarity to natural panic and with less self-control than were the responses to the other tapes. Abrupt, if modest, elevations in heart rate were associated with these symptoms in some patients. Two of the patients reported panicking; both reported panics occurred during the relaxation condition. Based on the more liberal Upjohn criterion of three symptoms (cf. Taylor et al., 1986), fully 67% of the patients panicked during the relaxation tape, compared to 24% during the neutral tape. But none of these experiences was nearly as severe as the panics experienced by Jill and Mary and described in Chapter 3.

Relaxation is surely the strangest of panic provocation procedures. If these preliminary reports are replicated, we will have the phenomenon of abrupt surges of anxiety (panic) occurring without the type of neurobio-

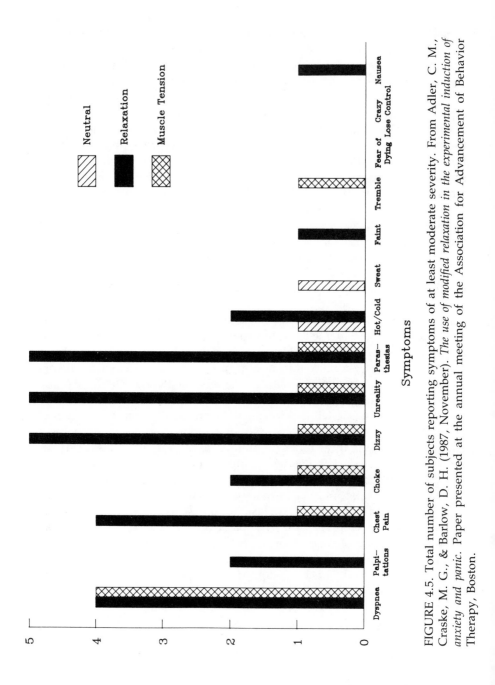

FIGURE 4.5. Total number of subjects reporting symptoms of at least moderate severity. From Adler, C. M., Craske, M. G., & Barlow, D. H. (1987, November). *The use of modified relaxation in the experimental induction of anxiety and panic.* Paper presented at the annual meeting of the Association for Advancement of Behavior Therapy, Boston.

logical "push" associated with pharmacological or respiratory provocators, or the intense phobic stimuli of the behavioral confrontation procedures.

A common thread running through all provocation studies is the possibility that panic is provoked by specific sensitivity to certain somatic sensations or events. These somatic sensations may have come to be associated with a sense of loss of control. During relaxation, subjects are often instructed to give up control of specific somatic responses (e.g., "Let go totally of your muscles; make no attempt to control them"), as they were in the relaxation tape in the Adler *et al.* (1987a) study. Both in Borkovec's work and in our study, fear of losing control and a seeming sensitivity to sensory side effects of relaxation mediated anxiety and panic when these occurred. These findings suggest a psychological contribution to the provocation of panic. They thus underline the importance of determining the contribution of psychological factors to more biological methods of panic provocation—a topic to which I now turn.

COGNITIVE MECHANISMS IN LABORATORY-PROVOKED PANIC

Prior to 1967, the prevailing view of the data produced from the myriad of infusion studies suggested a complex interaction of biological and psychological processes in the production of anxiety attacks and panic. For example, Breggin (1964), in reviewing the early studies on adrenaline and epinephrine, specified four separate factors interacting to produce panic: (1) the elicitation of physiological sensations; (2) the strength of the subject's previously learned association between physiological sensations and psychological feelings of acute anxiety; (3) the degree of current (baseline) anxiety; and (4) the degree of anxiety elicited by the experimental setting (in other words, the "experimental demand" in the situation). Essentially, Breggin suggested that for patients who have already experienced an anxiety attack, any physiological sensations resembling the attack may further increase anxiety or apprehension. This anxiety is then exacerbated by the experimental demand in the situation. This process is most likely to occur if the patient comes into the situation already anxious. As Breggin put it,

> When the past conditioning of internal cues is taken into account, some differences in the results of various experiments still remain unexplained. Most of these differences can be accounted for by a second variable: the degree to which the experimental environment or external cues reinforce anxiety. This second variable must be separated out by inference since there are very few studies which attempt to control the environment. For example, the presence or absence of a psychiatric interviewer is an important variable which has not been controlled but which seems significant in several studies. (1964, p. 560)

151

Despite the surge of interest in provoking panic in the laboratory, only a few experiments have attempted to parcel out the effects of demand. Even Liebowitz, Fyer, *et al.* (1984) and Ehlers, Margraf, Roth, Taylor, Maddock, *et al.* (1986) did not institute the double-blind procedure that is widely accepted as a minimal methodological requirement in pharmacological research. This issue is highlighted in the Liebowitz, Fyer, *et al.* study, since the experimenter was the one who recorded the ratings that comprised one of the major dependent variables. Ehlers and colleagues did at least absent the experimenter from the infusion room (the experimenter communicated with each subject via an intercom) and the experimenter was not aware whether the subject was a patient or a control. However, the procedure itself was only single-blind.

The importance of controlling for expectancies or demand is hard to overestimate. As Liebowitz, Gorman, Fyer, Levitt, *et al.* (1985) pointed out, panic cannot occur without subjective feelings of apprehension, dread, and loss of control. As noted above, those investigators suggested that the crucial factor in CO_2- and lactate-induced panic may be the fact that both procedures drive respiration. Thus, the possibility exists that panic is secondary to the feeling that one's breathing is out of control—an experience that panic patients, but not control subjects, would find intolerable. This suggestion is relevant to the last hypothesis among those suggested by Levin *et al.* (1984; see Table 4.1) as a mechanism of action for lactate-induced panic: namely, nonspecific stress. With this suggestion, Levin *et al.* have returned full circle to Breggin's (1964) early suggestion: Sudden physiological changes that panic patients have *previously learned to fear* as a signal of possible loss of control are what provoke panic in the laboratory. Subjective feelings of apprehension and loss of control are psychological phenomena that are particularly subject to the effects of expectancies and demands. A frequent occurrence in laboratory provocation studies is a report by the patient during an infusion that "I would have panicked if you weren't here, but I know you wouldn't let things get out of control" (e.g., Liebowitz, Gorman, Fyer, Levitt, *et al.*, 1985).

Now several studies have demonstrated the importance of this factor. For example, Rapee, Mattick, and Murrell (1986) arranged for panic disorder patients or social phobics without "spontaneous" panic to inhale a very strong 50% CO_2 mixture. Half of each group received instructions on exactly what somatic symptoms to expect, while routine instructions that did not specify the somatic symptoms were administered to the other half (the no-explanation condition). Subjects with panic attacks who were given no explanation reported significantly more intense somatic symptoms, more catastrophic thoughts, and significantly greater similarity of the experience to naturally occurring panics than did panic disorder patients who were told what symptoms to expect in some detail. Social phobics, on the other hand, evidenced no difference as a function of the instructions.

van der Molen, van den Hout, Vromen, Lousberg, and Griez (1987) administered lactate under two different instructional sets. One of two small groups of normal subjects was told that lactate would produce unpleasant bodily sensations, similar to those experienced during periods of anxiety, as well as anxious affect. The other group was told that the infusions would invoke feelings of pleasant tension, such as those experienced during sports. Consistent with predictions of the investigators, lactate with anxiety instructions produced considerable anxiety. One normal subject even panicked. "Pleasant" instructions resulted in little or no change in ratings of anxiety during lactate. It is interesting that suggestions that anxious symptoms would occur seems to have *increased* anxious responding in these normal subjects, whereas it *decreased* anxiety in the patients in the Rapee *et al.* (1986) study. Obviously, the van der Molen *et al.* study needs to be repeated with patients.

Finally, there is some evidence that panic patients respond with more anxiety and physiological arousal to false feedback concerning abrupt heart rate increases when compared to control subjects receiving the same false feedback (Ehlers, Margraf, Roth, Taylor, & Birbaumer, 1988). These data support the suggestion that subjects who have previously panicked are more sensitive to interoceptive cues.

As noted above, a theme running through all provocation studies is the potential importance of a sense of loss of control. In fact, this is one of the defining features of panic, and it is also the major cognitive symptom in the DSM-III-R panic attack symptom list. Experiments manipulating expectancies and demand may be affecting this sense of control. For example, in the Rapee *et al.* (1986) experiment, a full explanation of symptoms on the part of the experimenter communicated that the experimenter was in control. In our laboratory, we have now directly manipulated perceptions of control on the part of patients with panic disorder during inhalations of 5% CO_2 mixtures.

We (Sanderson, Rapee, & Barlow, 1988) administered 5.5% CO_2 to two groups of 10 patients with panic disorder under two different conditions. Both groups were told that manipulating a dial would regulate the inflow of CO_2 when a light on a panel in front of them was illuminated. For one group, the light was always illuminated during the 15-minute CO_2 administration period. For the other group, the light was never illuminated. In other words, one group assumed they were in control of the CO_2; in fact, they were not. The second group was not under this "illusion of control." The group who *did not* think they were in control experienced significantly more anxiety and panic, and rated their panics as more similar to naturally occurring panic. Results are presented in Table 4.3.

153

TABLE 4.3. Panic Symptoms for Groups of Subjects Differing in "Illusion of Control" over CO_2 Administration

	Control (n = 10)	No control (n = 10)	F	p
DSM-III-R panic[a]*	2 (20%)	8 (80%)	—	—
Similarity[b]	1.8	4.5	9.64	.006
Subjective units of disturbance (SUDs)[c]				
Pre	3.1	2.9	0.10	.754
Post	2.3	4.8	4.76	.043
Highest	4.1	5.9	4.08	.083
Symptoms				
Number of symptoms reported	4.3	9.2	11.76	.003
Mean intensity[d]	2.7	4.0	6.01	.023
Mean fear/panic[d]	3.6	5.3	3.83	.091
Cognitions				
Catastrophic	0.9	2.4	3.95	.062
Noncatastrophic	2.1	1.5	1.18	.291

Note. From Sanderson, W. C., Rapee, R. M., & Barlow, D. H. (1988). *The influence of an illusion of control on panic attacks induced via inhalation of 5.5% CO_2 enriched air.* Manuscript submitted for publication.

[a]Defined as a sensation of panic/fear accompanied by at least four physical symptoms plus one cognitive symptom (fear of dying, fear of losing control or going crazy) from the DSM-III-R.

[b]Rating of similarity of CO_2 effects to "natural" panic (scale ranging from 0 = "not at all similar" to 8 = "identical").

[c]Scale ranging from 0 = "no anxiety" to 8 = "as anxious as can be."

[d]Scale ranging from 1 = "slightly felt" to 8 = "very strongly felt."

*$\chi^2 = 8.32$, $p < .01$.

CONCLUSIONS

It seems safe to say that a number of widely varying procedures are capable of provoking major panic attacks in the laboratory. In fact, the variety of methods used to provoke panic in a long and rich experimental tradition have been limited only by the imaginations of clinical investigators, or, more accurately, by their ability to take advantage of serendipitous observations. It also seems safe to say at this time that there is no single underlying biological mechanism of action that can account for these diverse provocation procedures. On the contrary, there is direct evidence of the incompatibility of hypothetical mediating factors in many of these procedures. It is also important to reiterate that definitions of panic in the laboratory are probably inadequate in most studies. If panic is an "alarm," then only the most abrupt surges of emotion would qualify as panic. More gradual rises over 15 or 20 minutes would be better characterized as anxiety. One cannot determine whether panic has occurred from a plot of the average response of a large number of subjects. This issue notwithstanding, several important facts can be derived from panic provocation studies.

Thus far, two factors emerge as common across all panic provocation procedures. First, a high level of apprehension or high baseline anxiety seems a consistent predictor of panic in the laboratory across different procedures (Ehlers, Margraf, Roth, Taylor, Maddock, *et al.*, 1986; Liebowitz, Fyer, *et al.*, 1984). For example, Liebowitz, Fyer, *et al.* (1984) reported that patients who panicked had a greater sense of anxiety *prior to infusion* than patients who did not panic. Also, heart rate, as reported in Liebowitz, Gorman, Fyer, Levitt, *et al.* (1985) averaged 83.98 BPM during baseline for patients who went on to panic, as opposed to 75.30 BPM during baseline for nonpanic patients. Heart rate in control subjects was 62.79. This finding of greater subjective reports of anxiety, as well as of higher baseline autonomic levels in patients who go on to panic is fully consistent with reports in Ehlers, Margraf, Roth, Taylor, Maddock, *et al.* (1986). Baseline differences in the levels of anxiety between patients and controls before panic provocation have been reported by almost all studies dating back to the 1940s (e.g., Cohen & White, 1950).

The finding that subjective apprehension as well as higher autonomic lability may serve as a "platform" for panic, whatever the provocation process, may be extremely important. For example, high baseline anxiety may contribute to the origins of initial panic attacks in both clinical and nonclinical panickers. Similarly, lowering levels of anxiety may remove the "platform" from which most panic attacks emerge. This suggests a potentially important relationship between panic and anxiety, which is taken up in subsequent chapters. Ehlers, Margraf, and Roth (1986), in an interesting twist, found suggestive evidence on one possible cause of high baseline anxiety in their study. Panickers who knew they were about to breathe CO_2 evidenced significantly higher physiological responding than on a previous day when they knew they were about to breathe room air in the same experimental chamber. Thus, expectancy may also serve to increase baseline anxiety in some patients, leading to an increased likelihood that panic will occur during provocation. In all likelihood, however, the primary causes of high baseline anxiety predate knowledge of infusion procedures (see Chapter 5).

The one possible exception to findings on high baseline anxiety leading to panic comes from studies of relaxation-associated panic. In these studies, patients seem to have entered a somewhat relaxed state as indicated by self-report and physiological ratings prior to panicking (Adler *et al.*, 1987a, 1987b; Cohen *et al.*, 1985). But it is possible that even these subjects were relatively more anxious before beginning the procedure.

The second factor common across provocation studies is the elicitation of a specific somatic response that is associated with a sense of loss of control. Procedures with very different physiological consequences, such as exercise, hyperventilation, CO_2 inhalations, and lactate infusions, have in common somatic signs and symptoms such as rapid breathing, which are often perceived by vulnerable patients as indications of being "out of control". This sense of loss of control is vividly illustrated in the case report at the beginning of this chapter and plays an important role in the conceptions of emotion reviewed in Chapter 2. Klein has suggested that perhaps some panic provocation procedures trigger a suffocation alarm mechanism (Liebowitz, Gorman, et al., 1986). In fact, all successful provocation procedures have in common the elicitation of an alarm reaction associated with a sense of being out of control. This symptom is one important factor differentiating patients who panic during provocation procedures from patients (or normals) who do not, all of whom may experience similar somatic "rumblings" of different intensities.

Of course, it is not clear from these studies what causes a sense of loss of control, since it could be a by-product of the alarm reaction itself. But the fact that a sense of control can be manipulated in the context of provocation studies was highlighted in a preliminary way in the Sanderson et al. (1988) and Rapee et al. (1986) experiments described above. These manipulations dramatically affected whether the experiences were reported as panic or not. Thus, the elicitation of intense somatic symptoms, particularly respiratory symptoms, may be an important but not sufficient cause of panic in the laboratory. These somatic symptoms may have to interact with psychological factors to result in panic.

This interaction differs in one important respect from the "nonspecific stress mechanism of action mentioned by Levin et al. (1984) as one possible unifying explanation for the genesis of panic. The implication of the nonspecific stress hypothesis is that any "stressor" (somatic disruption) will be panicogenic. But we see time and again that only very specific stimuli are panicogenic in the laboratory and that these vary from individual to individual. This has never been better illustrated than in the data reported long ago by Lindemann and Finesinger (1938), where individual patients responded differently to adrenaline or acetylcholine. But it is also evident in numerous recent studies reviewed above that individuals are specifically sensitive to widely varying and dissimilar provocation procedures. This implies that individuals may have learned a specific association between panic and certain discrete somatic sensations, possibly associated with an earlier major alarm reaction. This explanation is more parsimonious at the present time than postulating an entirely different set of causal mechanisms for each individual pattern of panic would be. Of course, if somatic sensations are sufficiently intense, such as the feelings of suffocation induced by 7.5% CO_2 in the Woods, Charney, Goodman, and Heninger (1987) study, even normal subjects will panic if psychological conditions are appropriate (i.e., if the sensations are unexpected). This may be the purest example of the innate emotion of fear.

156

This reaction in normals also suggests that panic patients and normal controls respond in a similar fashion (at least to CO_2), but that panic patients are far more sensitive and respond to less intense levels of the stimulus, perhaps because they have "learned" to associate the physical symptoms with loss-of-control sensations.

Once again, these are not new ideas. Breggin's (1964) suggestion of four factors that seem to interact to produce panic in the laboratory are worth reiterating: (1) the elicitation of physiological sensations; (2) the strength of the subject's previously learned association between physiological sensations and fear; (3) the degree of current (baseline) anxiety; and (4) the degree of anxiety elicited by the experimental setting (demands, a sense of control, etc.). Of course, we know much more about panic then we did when Breggin wrote his review. Therefore, Breggin's model is accurate in only a general sense and is incomplete as far as it goes. In addition, any model of panic provocation in the laboratory cannot account for the appearance of an initial panic or the development of panic disorder (see Chapters 6 and 10). But this psychobiological model, now over 20 years old, still accommodates the laboratory provocation data to a degree that no unidimensional psychological or biological model can attain.

5

Biological Aspects of Anxiety and Panic

As our science becomes more complex and more specific, the overriding relationship between biology and behavior is often forgotten. For centuries scientists, approaching behavior from an evolutionary point of view, have argued persuasively that biology serves behavior. In this view, all biological processes have a purpose or a function in behavioral or emotional expression that enhances adaptation and survival. Anxiety in its various manifestations is no exception.

Anxiety has been thought to serve several functions, as noted in Chapter 1. The most usual and common function of anxiety or "stress" is to prepare the organism both biologically and psychologically to meet the challenges and conflicts of day-to-day life. Contemporary human challenges are numerous and include such usual and customary activities as meeting a deadline, taking an examination, or introducing oneself to new people. As long ago as 1908, Yerkes and Dodson demonstrated that "anxiety" does in fact facilitate performance up to a point, usually termed "moderate" anxiety. However, beyond this point, further increases lead to deterioration of performance.

Another important function long subsumed under the term "anxiety" is the massive alarm reaction experienced in response to imminent threat or danger. This is the well-known "fight or flight" response first described by Cannon (1929) and mentioned in all theories of emotion since that time.

Traditionally, these two functions of anxiety, preparation and alarm, have been assumed to be on a continuum, with the alarm reaction clearly at one extreme. Alternatively, these functions may be distinct to a certain extent. That is, while a degree of overlap obviously exists both behaviorally and biologically, there are system characteristics that are not shared. It is possible that the biological and behavioral dimensions of the alarm reaction gone awry represent panic, while the pathological expression of the organizing function of anxiety is "generalized" anxiety. My suggestion that panic is the basic emotion of fear, while anxiety is a loose cognitive–affective structure, also implies possibly different biological underpinnings.

In Chapter 4, evidence relating to neurobiological (and other) correlates of panic attacks provoked in the laboratory has been reviewed. But this is a very narrow perspective, fraught with a number of conceptual and methodological difficulties, not the least of which concerns adequate definitions of "panic." The purpose of this chapter is to examine biological aspects of panic and anxiety within a more comprehensive biopsychosocial framework. Information from genetic, physiological, endocrinological, and neurobiological studies is reviewed and integrated. This information plays a necessary and important role in a new theory of panic and anxiety, described in Chapters 6 and 7.

The biological basis of anxiety and panic can be examined from a number of different perspectives. One of the more intriguing perspectives addresses the strong evidence concerning a genetic basis for anxiety and panic. Preliminary evidence that anxiety and panic may have different genetic bases is also examined here.

FAMILY AND GENETIC STUDIES

PANIC, PANIC DISORDER, AND AGORAPHOBIA WITH PANIC

A variety of studies (e.g., Raskin, Peeke, Dickman, & Pinkster, 1982; Terhune, 1949; Webster, 1953) have looked at anxious patients' reports of developmental antecedents such as parenting characteristics, using questionnaires or brief interviews. These studies were conducted on patients with panic disorder or agoraphobia with panic. On occasion control groups were included, and some brief questions referred to the existence of panic or other symptomatology in relatives. These studies on developmental antecedents are reviewed in Chapter 10 in the discussion of panic disorder and agoraphobia. But the difficulty with trying to determine in this manner whether differences exist among families of different patient groups is that such reports are subject to considerable distortion. The person who is asked must *know* the information about a specific family member; he or she must also *remember* it. For this reason, ascertaining relevant factors about psychological problems in the families of patients by asking the patients usually requires lengthy, carefully constructed interviews. This strategy is called the "family history method."

An even better method is to interview the family members of patients directly. Although the personnel and effort required by such interviews are considerable, there are many reasons to undertake them. For example, if a disorder aggregates in families, then it is possible that some genetic contribution to the disorder exists. Of course, the fact that a problem aggregates in families is neither a necessary nor a sufficient proof that a genetic link exists. In simple phobia, for example, we know that social influence or modeling is sufficient to instill severe fears in some cases (see Chapter 12). However, a lack of familial aggregation for a specific disorder would all but rule out any genetic link. For this reason, family studies are very important from the point of view of etiology. A series of studies on the incidence of panic disorder in families of patients with panic, compared to other types of anxiety, has recently been reported by a research group very competent in this area.

Family Studies

In 1983, Crowe et al. reported data collected from 278 first-degree relatives of 41 hospitalized patients with panic disorder. In addition, they collected data on 262 first-degree relatives of a group of control subjects who were either surgical patients or employees of the hospital. Over 60% of these relatives were interviewed directly. Data from the remainder were collected by interviewing the patients using the family history method. Members of the control group were matched with the patient group for age and sex, and did not have panic disorder, according to the diagnostic interview.

After completing the large amount of work involved in interviewing these first-degree relatives over a number of years, the investigators established diagnoses in a blind fashion. The diagnoses in which they were particularly interested were panic disorder (including "probable panic disorder," which refers to the presence of limited symptom attacks or very mild panic attacks) and generalized anxiety disorder. Because these patients were diagnosed before DSM-III criteria were available, the 41 patients with panic disorder were not distinguished into subtypes. Retrospectively, the authors reported that 11 of the 41 patients could be diagnosed as having agoraphobia with panic, while an additional 11 had limited but distinct avoidance behavior, which would probably classify them in DSM-III-R as having panic disorder with mild agoraphobia (see Chapter 10). This left 19 subjects who had panic attacks with no appreciable avoidance.

Based on these data, the risk of a relative in the patient group having panic characterized by either major attacks or limited symptom attacks or both was 24.7%, as opposed to a risk of 2.3% for a relative in the control group. These data are presented in Table 5.1. To put it another way, 20 of the 41 families of patients had at least one member with a definite panic disorder, and 13 families had one member with "probable panic

TABLE 5.1. Anxiety Disorders in Patients' and Control Families

	Patients' families	Control families
Morbidity risk (%)[a]		
Definite panic disorder	17.3 ± 2.5	1.8 ± 0.9
Probable panic disorder	7.4 ± 1.7	0.5 ± 0.5
Generalized anxiety disorder (definite and probable)	4.8 ± 1.4	3.6 ± 1.4
Families with familial disorder (no.)[b]		
Definite panic disorder	20	4**
Probable panic disorder	13	1*
Generalized anxiety disorder (definite and probable)	10	8

Note. From Crowe, R. R., Noyes, R., Pauls, D. L., & Slymen, D. (1983). A family study of panic disorder. *Archives of General Psychiatry, 40,* 1065–1069. Copyright 1983 by the American Medical Association. Reprinted by permission.

[a] Risks are given as means ± *SE*s.

[b] These families had the specified disorder diagnosed in one or more of the proband's first-degree relatives.

*$p = .0007$ (Fisher's exact test).

**$p = .0002$ (Fisher's exact test).

disorder" (limited symptom attacks). Altogether, 25 of the 41 families (51%) had a relative with either diagnosis.

Importantly, there was no difference in the incidence of generalized anxiety disorder among first-degree relatives of the two groups. That is, a family member of a patient with panic disorder did not stand a greater risk of having generalized anxiety disorder than a family member of a control subject. The finding of no differences in incidence indicates a lack of association between the syndromes of generalized anxiety disorder and panic disorder, and suggests a qualitative difference between panic and generalized anxiety. However, following DSM-III conventions (which have been dropped in DSM-III-R), the investigators did not diagnosis generalized anxiety disorder if panic disorder was present. Since the prevalence of generalized anxiety disorder in relatives reflects only those cases where panic disorder was not found, it is possible that many more cases of generalized anxiety disorder would appear in relatives with panic disorder as a coexisting diagnosis. This tricky question is discussed at some length in Chapters 9 and 15. But this possibility weakens the conclusion that panic and generalized anxiety associated with these two disorders are qualitatively different, due to different aggregations in the families of these two groups of patients. That is, the finding may be an artifact of a now-discarded diagnostic convention (see below).

In a study that overlapped somewhat with the study just described, Harris, Noyes, Crowe, and Chaudhry (1983) separated out 20 patients with agoraphobia with panic from 20 patients with panic disorder and compared both groups to a control group of 20 patients. (The Crowe *et al.* [1983] study did not separate out agoraphobics specifically.) The panic disorder and control patients were the same subjects described above, as were some of the agoraphobics. Additional agoraphobics were recruited from a local self-help group. The risk for all anxiety disorders was similar in the agoraphobia with panic and panic disorder families: 32% of the first-degree relatives of patients with agoraphobia with panic and 33% of the relatives of patients with panic disorder showed a risk of having one or more of the anxiety disorders. These percentages were far greater than the risk found in the control group. First-degree relatives of patients with panic disorder or agoraphobia with panic also showed essentially similar risks for having one of these two disorders: The relatives of agoraphobics showeed a 16.3% risk, and those of panic disorder patients showed a 22.4% risk. Again, these rates were far higher than that found in the control group. This finding is consistent with other evidence presented throughout this book suggesting that panic disorder and agoraphobia with panic (at least as they present to the clinic) are the same disorder, differing only in the amount of avoidance behavior that is present and associated complications. In fact, the investigators had some difficulty discriminating panic disorder from agoraphobia with panic among first-degree relatives in this study, due to ambiguous levels of avoidance in many patients. This same difficulty has occurred in most anxiety clinics around the world. This difficulty accounts in part for the revision of these categories in DSM-III-R, where avoidance behavior associated with panic attacks is now described on a continuum from "none" through "severe" (see Chapter 10).

However, In a puzzling finding from this study, avoidance behavior severe enough to warrant a diagnosis of agoraphobia with panic was found more frequently in the first-degree relatives of agoraphobics than in the relatives of those with panic disorder alone (8.6% vs. 1.9%). Extending the patient group to 40 subjects, as illustrated in a later report (Noyes *et al.*, 1986), did not change this pattern of results (or any other result reported above). It is not clear whether this finding is simply an artifact or whether the avoidance component of panic disorder truly aggregates differently in families. If it does, one strong possibility is that cultural or social factors present in families mediate the types of strategies used to cope with panic. This possibility would be consistent with evidence presented in Chapter 10 on cultural determinants of agoraphobic avoidance. This explanation seems more likely than the alternative hypothesis that somehow the avoidance component within agoraphobia is genetically transmitted and presents a biologically more severe variant of the disorder. On the other hand, there are isolated examples of identical twins raised apart, both of whom develop very similar agoraphobic avoidance (Carey, 1982). Additional research may clarify this issue.

In a particularly well-done study, Moran and Andrews (1985) concentrated on agoraphobia with panic to the exclusion of panic disorder. Using the family history method, they interviewed 60 patients with agoraphobia with panic, and observed a lifetime prevalence of agoraphobia with panic (conservatively diagnosed) in 12.5% of first-degree relatives. They note that 12.5% is considerably above the estimates of the prevalence of agoraphobia in the population (4.14%), based on the ECA data (Robins *et al.*, 1984). While a prevalence of 12.5% is not as high as figures obtained in studies reviewed above, for both panic disorder and agoraphobia the figure of 12.5% refers only to agoraphobic relatives of agoraphobic patients. Panic disorder, as noted above, was not included.

Moran and Andrews (1985), in analyzing the possible modes of transmission, echo a theme on which most evidence converges: Both simple genetic transmission and purely cultural transmission are ruled out. Their tentative conclusion, which is consistent with that of most other investigators (e.g., Slater & Shields, 1969), is that a diathesis or vulnerability for panic (and agoraphobia) may be inherited, but the expression of the disorder is a function of environmental factors (e.g., stress).

Another family study yielding similar results strengthens conclusions regarding a familial link for panic disorder (and agoraphobia), and also raises the issue once again of a possible lack of familial aggregation for generalized anxiety disorder. Cloninger, Martin, Clayton, and Guze (1981) reanalyzed an extensive data set in which 500 outpatients were carefully interviewed in St. Louis in the late 1960s. Over 1,200 of their first-degree relatives were also interviewed. Cloninger and his colleagues followed up these patients 5–10 years later and found 54 cases who received a diagnosis of an anxiety disorder both originally and at the follow-up. Applying DSM-III criteria, the investigators attempted to categorize these patients as either having or not having a primary panic component (panic disorder or agoraphobia with panic). Patients lacking such a component would presumably fit the classification of generalized anxiety disorder, although this was not specified. In any case, only 10 patients fell into this category. Nevertheless, the relatives of patients who had panic disorder or agoraphobia with panic showed a slightly greater risk for having panic attacks or some other anxiety disorders themselves; this was not true for the relatives of those patients with probable generalized anxiety disorder. Once again, the results are preliminary, but they do agree with the data described above.

Two additional early studies are also relevant to the familial aggregation of panic disorder and agoraphobia. Buglass, Clarke, Henderson, Kreitman, and Presley (1977) investigated the tendency for this disorder to aggregate in families and found only weak support for this notion among the relatives of 30 agoraphobics and 30 well-matched controls. Although a few more parents and siblings of agoraphobic patients also had a phobic disorder, this finding was not statistically significant. Solyom, Beck, Solyom, and Hugel (1974), on the other hand, observed that the relatives of agoraphobics seemed to have agoraphobia at a higher frequency than the relatives of control subjects. Since almost all of these agoraphobics presumably would be classified as having agoraphobia with panic, according to DSM-III criteria, then this study provides some further evidence for the tendency of panic (and associated avoidance behavior) to aggregate in families.

Twin Studies

Of course, even family studies with the strongest results provide only suggestive evidence of genetic transmission. An equally likely interpretation is that something in the environment facilitates the acquisition of various emotional disorders or disordered behaviors in families. To explore a possible genetic link, it is necessary to find individuals who have identical gene pools but who do not necessarily share the same environmental influences. Only the study of twins fulfills this qualification. For this reason, twin study methodology is at the heart of human behavioral genetics, and we are fortunate to have several studies of this type dealing with panic.

Torgersen (1983a) was able to locate 32 monozygotic and 53 dizygotic adult, same-sex twins, at least one of whom had an anxiety disorder. As anyone familiar with research in genetics knows, this is a difficult type of study to complete, because of the problems in locating a large number of twins in whom one member has a certain diagnosis. Most of these studies come from Scandinavia, where excellent demographic records are available. For this reason, along with the fact that the Scandinavian countries are relatively small, it becomes easier to locate and keep track of twins. Torgersen completed his study in his native Norway.

Even with the relatively large number of twins in Torgerson's study, in which at least one member was found to have an anxiety disorder, the numbers were quite small and many comparisons did not reach statistical significance. However, for our purposes, one analysis is very important. Torgersen created a category termed "anxiety disorder with panic attack." Into this category fell twins who met the diagnoses of panic disorder and agoraphobia with panic, as well as a diagnosis termed "possible panic disorder." (Rather than the limited symptom attacks discussed above, "possible panic disorder" referred only to frequency of panic attacks, and included twins having between one and four panic attacks a month.) The minimum criterion for inclusion in the "anxiety disorder with panic attack" category was one panic attack in a 1-month period at any time during the patient's life. This is a very liberal criterion but it is tempered somewhat by the fact that all of these probands (the identified twins with the anxiety disorder) sought treatment for their problem at some point.

Thus, the anxiety problem was severe enough to motivate a visit to a therapist.

When this group was compared with a group of probands diagnosed as having generalized anxiety disorder, some significant differences emerged (Torgersen, 1983a). If the probands (patients) had either panic disorder or agoraphobia with panic, then the frequency of Torgersen's category of "anxiety disorder with panic attack" was 31% in monozygotic twins but 0% in dizygotic twins. The 31% figure represented 4 out of 13 possible monozygotic twins, while the 0% figure was based on 16 dizygotic twins. These data are presented in Table 5.2. This difference was statistically significant. On the other hand, only two dizygotic and no monozygotic cotwins of probands with generalized anxiety disorder had "anxiety disorder with panic attack." This suggests a genetic component for panic. In fact, when all anxiety disorders with the exception of generalized anxiety disorder were lumped together, the concordance for anxiety disorders in the proband group was 45% in monozygotic pairs against 15% in dizygotic pairs. This difference was also statistically significant.

It is possible that identical twins raised in the same family are treated more nearly alike and experience more similar environmental influences then fraternal twins. Therefore, the difference could be explained by environmental rather than genetic factors. In fact, this is unlikely. Torgersen found no relationship between similarity in environment and the likelihood of a cotwin's having an anxiety disorder or not. Therefore, this study strongly supports the family studies demonstrating familial aggregation of panic disorder (and agoraphobia), but it takes the evidence a step fur-

TABLE 5.2. Disorders in Cotwins of Probands with Panic Disorder, Agoraphobia with Panic Attacks, and Generalized Anxiety Disorder

Proband diagnosis[a]	Cotwin diagnosis			
	Anxiety disorder with panic attacks, no. (%)	Anxiety disorder without panic attacks, no. (%)	Other psychiatric disorders, no. (%)	Total cotwins
Panic disorder and agoraphobia with panic attacks				
MZ	4 (31)	2 (15)	1 (8)	13
DZ	0 (0)	4 (25)	1 (6)	16
Generalized anxiety disorder				
MZ	0 (0)	2 (17)	3 (25)	12
DZ	2 (10)	2 (10)	5 (25)	20

Note. From Torgersen, S. (1983). Genetic factors in anxiety disorders. *Archives of General Psychiatry, 40,* 1085–1089. Copyright 1983 by the American Medical Association. Reprinted by permission.
[a]MZ indicates monozygotic cotwin; DZ, dizygotic.

ther by indicating a genetic basis for this aggregation. It also raises once again the puzzling finding of a lack of heritability for generalized anxiety disorder.

The report by Torgersen is just a recent study in a long line of twin studies suggesting a genetic component in the anxiety disorders. For example, Slater and Shields (1969) reported strong concordance in a group of monozygotic compared to dizygotic twins for anxiety disorders (not further differentiated). Similarly, Carey (Carey, 1982; Carey & Gottesman, 1981) followed a number of phobic twins, where most of the probands were agoraphobic with panic. Fully 88% or 7 out of 8 monozygotic co-twins had at least mild phobic features, but only 38% of 13 dizygotic twins presented with these features. Of course, these latter two studies did not separate out panic or panic disorder specifically.

Doubts and Difficulties

These studies seem to provide strong evidence for the heritability of panic disorder, and weaker evidence for the nonheritability of generalized anxiety disorder. But behavioral geneticists are known for careful scientific work and close reasoning, and they themselves point out numerous problems that prevent us from being as certain of either of these facts as it would seem we could be. One major problem, for example, is the different risk rates that seem to emerge across different studies. Cloninger *et al.* (1981) and Carey and Gottesman (1981) point out that when one compares twin studies with family studies, the risk rates for dizygotic twins should be the same as those for first-degree relatives in general, since they share the same genetic relationship to the probands (the patients under study). But the risk rates are not the same. The risk rates for dizygotic twins in the twin studies of anxiety disorders, notably those of Slater and Shields (1969) and Torgersen (1983a), are considerably lower than those found in the family studies. For example, the risk rate in first-degree relatives in the Crowe *et al.* (1983) study was 24.7%, but for dizygotic twins in Slater and Shields (1969) the rate was 4%, and in Torgersen (1983a) it was 15%.

Carey and Gottesman (1981) suggest a number of possibilities for these discrepancies. For example, the probands from Crowe *et al.* (1983) may have had more severe cases of anxiety disorders, and there is some evidence that family risk rates are much higher when the probands are more severely disordered (Carey & Gottesman, 1981). We also know that diagnostic methods used for probands and their relatives can yield different diagnoses, depending on the type of method used. For example, carefully structured interviews are much more systematic than nonstructured methods, but the structured interviews have only been in use for a few years; this makes it difficult to compare newer studies with older ones.

Finally, diagnostic standards have changed over the years, and these changes alone may account for discrepancies in studies using one standard or another.

Nevertheless, the bulk of the evidence provides a strong suggestion that panic and panic disorder runs in families and probably has a genetic component. But, as Torgersen has pointed out, the number of discordant monozygotic twins in his study was very high. In fact, as one can see in Table 5.2, only 31% of the monozygotic twins were concordant for an anxiety disorder including panic, leaving nearly 70% of the monozygotic cotwins without a panic-based anxiety disorder. This indicates the importance of environmental factors in the development of this disorder, and also raises the question of what is inherited.

As noted above, the most widely accepted premise is that one inherits a vulnerability to panic, which may or may not manifest itself as a result of particular experiences one may confront. The notion of "vulnerability" seems to be the most productive and useful way to conceptualize the role of genes across all emotional or behavioral disorders. Two people with exactly the same vulnerability to panic may have different life experiences, such as periods of intense stress, that would cause one person to develop panic disorder while the other never experiences it. This issue comes up again below in the discussion of the origins of panic.

One final mystery is the marked difference in the familial aggregation of panic disorder versus generalized anxiety disorder found in family studies, and also in Torgersen's (1983a) twin study. These findings suggest a possible genetic difference between the two types of anxiety associated with these disorders. In fact, the findings are at odds with other evidence as well as with the broader view of the heritability of anxiety, often referred to as "nervousness" or "emotionality." This issue is explored in some detail below.

Do Children Inherit Panic?

A common question of interest to families concerns the degree to which panic or other anxiety symptoms may be passed on to their children. Crowe *et al.* (1983) parceled out first-degree relatives into categories that yielded numbers too small for statistical analyses. However, a diagnosis of definite or probable panic disorder was observed in 50% of the daughters of patients with panic disorder. On the other hand, only 10% of the sons showed a similar diagnosis. In this case, the percentages were more strongly in favor of female children than other female relatives, but it is impossible to separate out the factor of learning via the route of family influence. Other studies have noted a strong tendency for children of patients with anxiety disorders (which may or may not involve panic) to develop anxiety disorders. For example, Berg (1976) noticed a 15% increase in the risk of school phobia among children of agoraphobics in the age range of 7–15. School phobia is a condition that some think resembles agoraphobia. Similarly, in an older study Wheeler, White, Reed, and Cohen (1948), using the global category of "anxiety neurosis," noted that as many as 50% of the children of patients with an anxiety neurosis also carried that diagnosis. This compared to approximately 6% among the children of controls. On the other hand, Buglass *et al.* (1977) did not notice any increased risk for phobic disorder in the children of agoraphobics when compared to a well-matched control group. In fact, the children in the control group had more phobias!

Recently, Turner, Beidel, and Costello (1987) examined the incidence of anxiety and anxiety disorders in 16 children of patients with anxiety disorders. These children, who were between the ages of 7 and 12, were compared to 14 children of dysthymic patients as well as to children of healthy parents. Both sets of children of patients had more anxiety disorders than children of control parents. Of the children of anxious patients, 44% (7 of 16) evidenced either an anxiety disorder or dysthymia, compared to 21% (3 out of 14) of the children of dysthymic patients. Only 8% (1 out of 13) of the children of normals presented with an anxiety disorder.

Data collected by Wendy Silverman and her colleagues in our clinic also indicate a strong association between anxiety disorders in parents and children (Silverman, Cerny, & Nelles, in press). Forty-two children from 28 families in which at least one parent had an anxiety disorder were assessed by structured interview and relevant questionnaires. Of these children, 24, or 57%, received a clinical anxiety disorder diagnosis or scored in the clinical range on the Child Behavior Checklist (Achenbach & Edelbrock, 1983).

But these data do not directly address the question of the inheritance of panic. Only the Crowe *et al.* (1983) data demonstrate an association with panic disorder specifically, and the children in that study were *adult* children. Rather, the strong association is between any anxiety-related problem in a child and an anxiety disorder in a parent. In fact, there is evidence that children under 12 do not experience panic attacks as we know them in adults. There may be interesting developmental reasons for this fact that illuminate the nature of panic (Nelles & Barlow, 1987). Nevertheless, most evidence indicates that children of parents with anxiety disorders, particularly an anxiety disorder that includes panic, seem to be at risk for anxiety disorders of their own. Their risk is as great as or greater than that of more distant relatives.

GENERALIZED ANXIETY

Clinical manifestations of anxiety seem to run in families and probably have a genetic component. The studies reviewed above attempted to analyze familial aggregation of and genetic contributions to panic and panic disorder specifically, but early studies did not distinguish between panic and generalized anxiety. These studies usually looked at clinical anxiety under a broad term, such as "anxiety neurosis." It is possible that some of these anxiety neurotics also suffered from panic attacks, but since frequent panickers often ended up in the offices of cardiologists with diagnostic labels such as "neurocirculatory asthenia" or "effort syndrome," it is not clear how many "anxiety neurotics" might have suffered from panic disorder. It is clear from the criteria for "anxiety neurosis" that the diagnosis encompasses what is now referred to as "generalized anxiety," regardless of whether DSM-III or DSM-III-R definitions of "generalized anxiety disorder" are met. This section briefly examines the evidence from these early studies bearing on the heritability of generalized anxiety and possible differences between this and the heritability of panic.

Whether investigators have used the family history method or have interviewed family members directly, a consistent finding has been that "anxiety neurosis" aggregates in families. For example, Cohen et al. (1951) found that approximately 15% of first-degree relatives also manifested an anxiety disorder. Other early studies (e.g., Brown, 1942) found a similar percentage affected. A study mentioned above (Wheeler et al., 1948) found that 49% of the children of anxiety neurotics also presented with clinical anxiety, compared to only 6% of a group of control children whose parents were not anxious. The rather higher figures in this study may be accounted for by the fact that only children, not parents, were surveyed. Also, the children were directly interviewed, as opposed to the more indirect method of asking the parents about anxiety in their children. A much higher percentage was also found by Crowe, Pauls, Slymen, and Noyes (1980), in an earlier report of the Crowe et al. (1983) study mentioned above. In this report, 41% of all *interviewed* relatives were diagnosed as having an anxiety disorder, which would be roughly equivalent to "anxiety neurosis." Crowe et al. (1983), with a larger number of subjects, showed that the percentage of relatives who had a definite or probably panic disorder was 29.7%; however, if generalized anxiety is added, the percentage rises to approximately 35%. Therefore, studies in which relatives have actually been interviewed have yielded consistently higher percentages with clinical anxiety. Only twin studies can begin to separate out genetic contributions from the social influence variables inherit in family studies, but even twin studies suggest a genetic contribution to the development of anxiety disorders. The most famous study was the Slater and Shields (1969) investigation mentioned briefly above. Slater and Shields found that 41% of monozygotic cotwins also could be diagnosed as having an anxiety disorder, while 4% of dizygotic twins carried this diagnosis. Torgersen (1983a) found similar results in his study.

While these results, taken together, suggest a strong genetic influence on clinical anxiety in general, there are marked discrepancies among the data; these are probably due to different diagnostic standards and to different methods of ascertaining the prevalence of neurotic conditions in the relatives. As one illustration of the difficulties in making useful estimates from these early studies, Carey, Gottesman, and Robins (1980) surveyed population prevalence rates for different types of neurotic disorders. Their goal was to determine the utility of prevalence rates for family and genetic research. They found that rates varied widely among studies for all neurotic conditions combined, as well as for specific subtypes. This variability was true even among those studies using similar methods to examine supposedly similar populations. Carey et al. (1980) suggest that methods for identifying affected cases, and careful definitions of the threshold for identifying a case, may be among the most important factors accounting for the unacceptably wide variations. But the conclusion they draw is that all of the early studies are probably not helpful, since it is difficult to interpret these studies meaningfully. As further evidence for the wide divergence among data attained from study to study, Torgersen (1983b) found a higher concordance for monozygotic twins only among inpatient "neurotic" probands compared to outpatients, and only among male twins rather than female twins. In other words, if Torgersen had restricted the sample in this study to females (who, in fact, present with the majority of anxiety disorders) or to outpatient clinics (where most anxiety disorders are found), he would have found no genetic contribution to neurotic disorders! These results differ substantially from those of earlier studies; Torgersen attributes this difference to sampling variation.

Even among current studies (many of which have been reviewed above), there are wide differences. For example, the premiere investigations in this area are the twin studies reported by Slater and Shields (1969) and Torgersen (1983a), as well as the family studies by Crowe and colleagues (Crowe et al., 1983; Harris et al., 1983; Noyes et al., 1986). But the fact is that the first-degree relatives in the family interview studies and the dizygotic twins in the twin studies should yield about the same percentage of anxiety disorders, since they show the same degree of "relatedness" to the patient with the anxiety disorder. And yet they do not.

DIFFERENTIAL HERITABILITY OF PANIC AND GENERALIZED ANXIETY

The Confound of DSM-III

One of the major advances distinguishing the newer studies, such as those of Torgersen (1983a) and Crowe et al. (1983), is the use of objective, precise DSM-III criteria to distinguish between diagnoses. These two studies produced the surprising finding that any genetic contribution to the anxiety disorders might be accounted for entirely by the heritability of panic disorder, since generalized anxiety disorder did not aggregate differently in "anxious" families compared to control families, or in monozygotic twins compared to dizygotic twins. But there are several problems with this conclusion. First, a diagnostic convention in DSM-III introduces an artifact into these data. According to DSM-III, generalized anxiety disorder is a residual category to be diagnosed only in the absence of any other anxiety-based symptoms, such as panic, phobic avoidance, or obsessive thoughts. In fact, almost all patients with panic disorder also present with marked "generalized anxiety" (Barlow, Blanchard, Vermilyea, Vermilyea, & Di Nardo, 1986). Most of these patients are severely anxious, whether they have panicked recently or not (see Chapter 11). This reflects the distinction between generalized anxiety and generalized anxiety disorder alluded to above. Therefore, the only patients included in the DSM-III category "generalized anxiety disorder" in the Crowe et al. (1983) study were those who were not panicking at all. It is likely that these patients were less severely anxious than the panic patients. Torgersen (1983b) found a genetic contribution to neurotic disorders only among those probands who were inpatients and not those who were outpatients, possibly suggesting, once again, the influence of severity of heritability. Cloninger et al. (1981), in sketching out the natural history of panic disorder, note that one of the first symptoms recalled by the patients in late childhood was "nervousness," with panic not appearing until early adulthood. Since it is difficult to find panickers who do not have generalized anxiety, establishing different heritability rates for panic and generalized anxiety would require at least matching the two groups on severity.

There are other problems within the studies themselves that would make a conclusion that generalized anxiety does not have a genetic component premature. For example, much is made of Slater and Shields's (1969) finding of the low concordance (4%) in dizygotic twins for "anxiety neurosis." However, when Slater and Shields took a broader view of anxiety and included such diagnoses as "anxious personality" or noted a "clear presence" of anxiety (which might, however, be within normal limits), the concordance increased to 65% in monozygotic twins and 13% in dizygotic twins. The fact that twin concordance was raised by including these anxiety "traits," which almost certainly did not include panic, raises some question about the hypothesized differential genetic components of panic and generalized anxiety mentioned above. Furthermore, as Carey and Gottesman (1981) point out, Shields (1962) reported that three pairs of monozygotic twins raised apart were all concordant for anxiety symptoms; however, judging from their case histories, none of them exhibited panic disorder. Studying twins raised apart is the most rigorous test of the genetic hypothesis, and in these cases what seemed to be "genetic" was anxiety and not panic.

The Trait of "Nervousness"

Another line of evidence may provide an even stronger suggestion of a genetic component to "generalized" anxiety. In the difficult field of genetic determinants of behavior and emotion in humans, we are quite confident that being "high-strung," "nervous," or "emotional" runs in families and has a genetic component. This conclusion is supported by several different lines of evidence. Animal behaviorists have demonstrated that it is possible to breed emotionality in rats and dogs (Bignami, 1965; Broadhurst, 1975; Fuller & Thompson, 1978; Gray, 1971, 1982). By all estimates, this "emotionality" is the analogue of anxiety in humans. In at least one experiment, rats bred for emotionality were found to have a greater number of benzodiazepine receptor sites in the brain (Robertson, Martin, & Candy, 1978). The benzodiazepine receptor system is heavily implicated in anxiety (see below).

In addition, studies of normal personality almost always isolate a factor that is termed "anxiety" or "neuroticism." Usually this factor is measured by structured questionnaires, such as the Eysenck Personality Inventory (e.g., Eysenck, 1970), but also by the Minnesota Multiphasic Personality Inventory (MMPI) or the California Psychological Inventory. There is even stronger evidence that this personality dimension is heritable than the evidence for the clinical anxiety disorders. For example, Shields (1962) has found that this personality trait correlates as highly in twins raised apart as it does in twins raised together. Eaves and Eysenck (1976) have found that even specific aspects of the manisfestation of anxiety as a personality trait can be accounted for in part by genetic contributions. Also, Young, Fenton, and Lader (1971) administered the Middlesex Hospital Questionnaire and a modified version of the Eysenck Personality Inventory to 17 pairs of identical twins and 14 pairs of fraternal twins. The Middlesex Hospital Questionnaire covers symptoms of traits relevant to anxiety, depression, and personality disorders that one might look for in a clinical interview. The Eysenck instrument taps the personality characteristics of "neuroticism" and "extraversion." That these twins were "normal" was verified by demonstrating that their total scores matched scores from other "normal" samples. The results clearly demonstrated that anxiety was highly correlated in identical twins but not fraternal twins, whether measured by clinical items on the Middlesex Hospital Questionnaire or indicated by the personality trait termed "neuroticism" (or emotionality). Now an impressive study involving over 3,500 pairs of twins confirms a strong genetic contribution to anxiety symptoms and suggests a genetic contribution to depression symptoms as well (Kendler, Heath, Martin, & Eaves, 1986). Even symptoms reflecting social anxiety such as "shyness" seem clearly heritable (Plomin & Daniels, 1985).

In fact, most personality traits do not show evidence of heritability based on questionnaire measures. This lack of evidence makes it all the more striking that anxiety or emotionality consistently demonstrates heritability (Fuller & Thompson, 1978; McGuffin & Reich, 1984).

It seems inconsistent to conclude that mild generalized anxiety manifested as a personality trait, whether determined by interview (Slater & Shields, 1969) or questionnaire (Eysenck, 1970; Young et al., 1971), is heritable, but that the more severe pathological expression of this trait, generalized anxiety, is not. It also makes no difference whether the questionnaire measuring the personality trait taps standard personality descriptions of emotionality or more clinical items (Young et al., 1971). One might question whether there is continuity between clinical manifestations of generalized anxiety and anxiety as a personality trait. But only a brief examination of the behaviors that make up each, including excessive worry, autonomic nervous system activity, and muscle tension, persuades one that only quantitative differences distinguish the two. For this reason, almost all investigators have recognized and accepted the relationship between personality traits of anxiety and "neurosis" (Lader, 1980a; 1980b; McGuffin & Reich, 1984; Slater, 1943; Tyrer, 1976).

In summary, there is no firm evidence for the differential heritability of panic and anxiety (or panic disorder and generalized anxiety disorder). Studies reporting this difference have not controlled for the fact that all panic disorder patients are generally anxious or for different levels of severity artifactually imposed by the hierarchical arrangement of DSM-III. Nor have these differences been replicated. For example, Gavin Andrews (personal communication, December 1986), studying a large number of Australian twins, did not find differential heritability for panic disorder or generalized anxiety disorder. Severity of intensity of a trait always affects its heritability (see below). Furthermore, the strongest tradition of evidence suggests that the trait of anxiety, emotionality, or nervousness is clearly and consistently heritable. When one takes this evidence into account, it would seem that the more severe and pathological expression of anxiety should be at least equally heritable. Panic may ultimately prove to have a specific differential hereditary component, but it has not yet been demonstrated.

On the other hand, circumstantial evidence from other sources does suggest that the tendency to panic may be differentially heritable. Chapter 1 discussed the ancient, seemingly innate defensive reactions of freezing when under attack by a predator and fainting at signs of blood and injury. While remnants of the freezing or tonic immobility response seem to occur seldom, if ever, in humans, fainting at the sight of blood is fairly common (see Chapter 12 for a review and discussion). The interesting fact is that both of these reactions seem to have a very strong genetic component. For example, Gallup (1974) reported that extreme tonic immobility reactions could be bred quickly in chickens. While this has not been observed in humans, a phobic reaction to blood seems to aggregate more strongly in families than does any specific anxiety disorder (Marks, 1986). For example, fully 67% of blood phobics reported biological relatives with the same reaction (Öst, Lindahl, Sterner, & Jerremalm, 1984). Blood phobics experience a very specific and unusual response at the sight of blood. As noted above, they develop extreme bradycardia and hypotension, and occasionally they faint. As Marks (1986) suggests, it is most likely this reaction that is genetically transmitted. The phobia develops over the possibility of having another reaction (see Chapter 6).

But what about panic? It has been suggested in Chapter 2 that panic may also be a manifestation of an ancient, hard-wired alarm reaction. It is possible that this mode of responding to stressful situations has a strong genetic component, much as fainting and freezing are strongly genetically determined responses in certain similar situations. In this manner one may inherit a tendency to be "nervous" or "emotional," or, more precisely, to be very reactive biologically to environmental changes. One may also be disposed to experience an alarm (panic), much as people are more or less disposed to faint at the sight of blood. This may reflect a differential, biologically based threshold for emotion, as posited by some emotion theorists. In each case the response is unexpected (at least at first) and may lead to the development of a phobia concerning possible recurrences of the response in the future. This process is described more fully in Chapters 6 and 7. Thus, tendencies to be "nervous" and to panic may both be genetically transmitted independently. Alternatively, genetically determined emotional reactivity may, when activated by stress, lower the threshold for the expression of a specific emotion such as fear and its strong escapist action tendencies through a psychological process. This explanation receives some support from evidence in Chapter 4 that successful panic provocation can be predicted by high levels of anxiety prior to the provocation. In this way, anxiety may serve as a "platform" for panic. What is inherited may be a proneness to anxiety associated with a biologically labile response to stress, but this anxiety proneness may interact with specific psychological and environmental triggers (internal and external) in a complex way to determine emotions.

If these speculations are correct concerning the heritability of panic, where would we find the evidence? Probably not in the clinic, where the presenting picture is very complex. Patients with panic disorder not only panic, but also evidence intense anxiety and, perhaps, depression and addictive behavior. They seem to "construe" many somatic reactions as panic. A clearer picture might be forthcoming from the study of nonclinical panickers, in whom panic presents more purely (see Chapter 3).

SPECIFIC FEARS AND OBSESSIVE–COMPULSIVE DISORDER

There is also some rather limited evidence for a genetic contribution to specific fears and phobias and to obsessive–compulsive disorder that might not be part of the panic syndrome. For example, Torgersen (1979) studied specific fears in a large groups of twins. Eleven pairs of twins were specifically selected because one of the twins in each pair had been hospitalized for a neurotic disorder; the remaining pairs consisted of a relatively unselected sample. Scores on a fear questionnaire indicated that monozygotic twins were more strongly concordant than dizygotic twins for specific fears of animals, mutilation, and social situations, but, interestingly, not for separation fears. Nevertheless, Torgersen points out that the most likely reasons for this discrepancy between monozygotic twins and dizygotic twins were differences in personality development (e.g., learning) due largely to psychosocial, not genetic, influences. Using a similar approach, Rose and Ditto (1983) found greater concordance among monozygotic than among dizygotic twins for a variety of fears, such as fears of small animals and social fears; however, these data are subject to the same interpretive problems mentioned by Torgersen. In addition, all of these data describe "normal" fears rather than clinical phobias. Carey (Carey, 1982; Carey & Gottesman, 1981) demonstrated that phobias of all types aggregated in families of volunteer probands with agoraphobic symptoms, but specific types of fears did not seem connected.

A few studies have also looked at genetic contributions to obsessive–compulsive disorder or obsessive–compulsive traits (see McGuffin & Reich, 1984, for a review). While the evidence is limited, one of the most thorough analyses was reported by Carey and Gottesman (1981), who found that obsessive–compulsive disorder, as well as mild obsessive traits or features that were not clinically significant, aggregated in families. In addition, obsessional behaviors were found approximately twice as often in monozygotic twins as in dizygotic twins. Once again, this need not imply that obsessive traits are specifically heritable. Rather, it could be a reflection of differential socialization of monozygotic twins living together compared to dizygotic twins, or of underlying emotionality.

If specific phobias are found to have a genetic component, however small, it is possible that the inherited trait of "emotionality" or "arousability" makes one more vulnerable to the development of fears, perhaps through a process of classical conditioning as has been suggested for years by Eysenck (e.g., 1980). However, many problems have arisen with conditioning theory as an etiological explanation for the development of specific fears (Rachman, 1978). Conditioning may play a somewhat different role in the etiology of phobia than previously assumed, as outlined in Chapter 6.

Another potential genetic influence on the development of specific fears has been proposed by Seligman (1971). He suggests that evolution has favored some fears, and that we are more "prepared" to learn these fears. Over the course of our evolution these objects or situations threatened our survival, although this may no longer be the case in our civilized world. This may explain why many of us still fear spiders, heights, and snakes, but not guns, hammers, and other more dangerous modern inventions. These interesting issues are examined in the discussion of the etiology of phobia in Chapter 6.

SUMMARY OF FAMILY AND GENETIC STUDIES

Behavioral geneticists have a great deal of exciting work in front of them before firm and specific conclusions can be drawn. It does seem safe to conclude that some aspects of anxiety run in families and are almost certainly heritable. However, the safest bet is that what seems to be inherited is a "vulnerability" to develop an anxiety disorder, rather than a specific clinical syndrome itself. This interpretation is supported by the fact that even in studies suggesting a strong genetic contribution, no simple or clear mode of genetic transmission is apparent, and more of the variance seems to be accounted for by environmental influences than by genetic influences (Crowe et al., 1983; Torgersen, 1983a). But what exactly is this vulnerability?

Eysenck (1967) makes a strong case for a labile or "overly responsive" autonomic nervous system as the underlying biological vulnerability predisposing the development of a clinical anxiety syndrome under the right combination of environmental or psychological conditions. Supportive evidence is provided by twin studies on the heritability of specific autonomic nervous system traits. For example, Hume (1973) and Lader and Wing (1964) both showed that habituation of the galvanic skin response (GSR), as well as pulse rate and number of spontaneous fluctuation in GSR, seems to be genetically determined. As McGuffin and Reich (1984) suggest, these psychophysiological characteristics may well reflect the substrate on which both the personality trait of "emotionality" and the clinical anxiety disorders are based. What is this substrate? Evidence reviewed in the next section suggests that it may be a diffuse biological reactivity, arising, perhaps, from labile neurotransmitter systems. This liability, in turn, may be related to Eysenck's notion of a reactive limbic system. This tendency may only become apparent under stress (see Selye, 1976), demonstrating even at this level that biological–environmental interactions are important.

Furthermore, this vulnerability in and of itself may not be "anxiety." This same vulnerability may also underlie Type A personalities or stress disorders such as essential hypertension where little or no "anxiety" is present. Evidence now exists supporting the heritability of stress reactions of this type (Rose & Chesney, 1986). The subsequent development of anxiety, stress, anger, or even depression may depend on psychological elaboration (see Chapter 7).

An exception to this nonspecific vulnerability may occur in strong alarm reactions or in specific action tendencies, such as fainting or freezing. That is, specific emotional reactions, such as fear and its associated action tendencies, may be independently transmitted as suggested above. There is good, if selective, evidence for the heritability of these behavioral action tendencies and their associated physiology in both animals and humans. Indeed, the intensity of the first expression of a coherent fear response, stranger distress, seems to have a genetic component, as reviewed in Chapter 2.

Even if these processes are independently transmitted, they may be related. Genetically determined stress-produced biologial reactivity, possibly elaborated psychologically into anxiety (see Chapter 7), could in turn trigger off basic emotions or defensive reactions as a function of differential inherited thresholds for these action tendencies. This model depicts a dual genetic vulnerability, which, nevertheless, would still not account for the full expression of a clinical disorder. Alternatively, and perhaps more parsimoniously, the nonspecific biological vulnerability may simply lower the threshold for the expression of specific emotions and associated action tendencies, the form of which may be determined, for the most part, by psychological and environmental factors. In this way, panic (or other emotions—e.g., depression, anger; see Chapter 7) may "spike off" a baseline of stress-related reactivity or "anxiety." Lang's bioinformational emotion theory would account nicely for this model. Activation of various neurobiological systems may present a sufficient number of response or stimulus propositions to trigger specific emotional action tendencies stored deep in memory. The increased arousal itself may provide sufficient stimulus and response propositions under the right circumstances. In this way, a specific action tendency associated with a discrete emotion may occasionally "fire" out of situational context. In other words, under stress-produced biologial reactivity, perhaps elaborated into anxiety (see Chapter 7), one may experience specific action tendencies such as panic in the absence of any external danger. This hypothetical organization is depicted in Figure 5.1.

In fact, with our present knowledge, it is illogical to assume that a specific clinical anxiety disorder, even a simple phobia, can be directly inherited as one intact behavioral and emotional response set in some sort of simple Mendelian mode, much as hair and eye color are inherited. The demonstrated psychosocial influence on the formation of these behavioral and emotional patterns almost surely points to a complex, interactive,

177

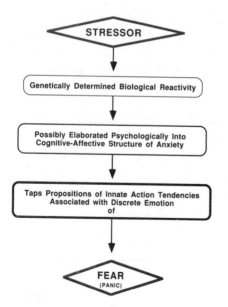

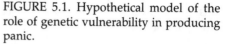

FIGURE 5.1. Hypothetical model of the role of genetic vulnerability in producing panic.

biopsychosocial model of the development of anxiety disorders. Strong evidence for a nonspecific genetic vulnerability interacting with psychosocial factors to form anxiety continues to appear (e.g., Kendler, Heath, Martin, & Eaves, 1987).

At present, there is no behavioral or emotional disorder for which a classical Mendelian model of single-gene heredity seems applicable. Even for the major psychotic disorders, where genetic links have long been suspected, almost all investigators (including geneticists) seem to think that an underlying vulnerability exists that interacts with a variety of psychological and social factors to produce the disorder (Falconer, 1965; McGuffin & Reich, 1984; Radouco-Thomas et al., 1984; Tsaung & Vandermey, 1980). At most, geneticists suggest that a polygenic–multifactorial model may be appropriate, in which the underlying genetically determined vulnerability is normally distributed across the population through the additive effect of many genes ("polygenic"), but environmental factors also account for a necessary contribution ("multifactorial"). In the case of psychosis, it is even possible that there are different types of genetic vulnerability for the same disorder (Gershon, Targum, Matthysse, & Bunney, 1983). The recent discovery of genetic markers for bipolar affective disorder in Amish families (Egeland et al., 1987) has not changed this view (e.g, Koshland, 1987).

Strong evidence for an inherited vulnerability that interacts with environmental factors have also been put forth for other disorders, such as alcoholism and psychopathic personality (Cloninger, 1987; McGuffin &

Reich, 1984). Interestingly, Cloninger believes that his conception of anxiety proneness constitutes the genetically determined vulnerability for a substantial proportion of alcoholics. This view of the role of the genetic contributions to anxiety disorders is in keeping with the biopsychosocial approach advocated here. In conclusion, the evidence is clear that genetic factors are implicated in anxiety. Discovering the precise nature of the inherited vulnerability, as well as the nature of the interaction of specific emotional alarm reactions and action tendencies, is a task ahead of us. But hints of promising future directions may be found in other areas of the biological investigation of anxiety.

PSYCHOPHYSIOLOGICAL AND NEUROENDOCRINOLOGICAL ASPECTS OF ANXIETY

THE PSYCHOPHYSIOLOGY OF ANXIETY AND PANIC

One of the more exciting areas of biological research is that of the psychophysiological measurement and assessment of anxiety. This extensive body of research has contributed a new perspective on the nature of anxiety that must play a major role in current theorizing. A variety of methods have been employed in this research. This section reviews studies that compare physiological measures in anxious patients and controls, both while at rest and in response to a stressful task. Finally, recent evidence on possible psychophysiological differences between patients with panic disorder and generalized anxiety disorder is reviewed.

Resting Differences between Patients and Normals

One of the most robust findings to emerge from the study of anxiety is that anxious subjects from both normal and patient populations are highly aroused and alert, and generally in a state of "overpreparedness" as indicated by physiological measures. Hyperarousal has been demonstrated in normal subjects made anxious in the laboratory by means of such procedures as the threat of painful electric shock while performing a task. With anxious patients, an anxiety-producing situation is not necessary to produce hyperarousal; it is chronic (Lader, 1975, 1980a, 1980b).

This feature of anxious patients continues to show up in unexpected places. Recently, this happened in our clinic. For almost 20 years investigators around the world, including ourselves, have used heart rate as a convenient measure of therapeutic change when treating agoraphobics, along with more direct behavioral and self-report measures (Barlow & Mavissakalian, 1981). In this experiment (Holden & Barlow, 1986), 10 agoraphobic women and 10 control subjects were carefully matched on age,

179

physical condition, and other factors that might influence physiological responding. They were then tested in a variety of ways. The major assessment was a behavioral test in which the subjects would walk a specified course away from the clinic toward a downtown area. Since agoraphobics find it difficult to leave a safe place, this test has been standard since at least 1966 (Agras, Leitenberg, & Barlow, 1968). In addition, the course typically leads the agoraphobic into a busy downtown area, which makes it increasingly anxiety-provoking. Agoraphobics carry a small map of the mile-long course, which is divided into 20 approximately equidistant stations. When they reach a station, they are instructed to tell us how anxious they feel at that station on a self-report scale of 0–100 (subjective units of disturbance, or SUDs). Each subject makes this report into a lapel microphone connected to a small tape recorder carried in a purse or pocket. Subjects are also fitted with a portable and rather unobtrusive device for measuring heart rate directly as they walk. This small device fits conveniently into pocket or purse, and is one of a number of instruments available to assess physiological measures in natural circumstances (Leelarthaepin, Gray, & Chesworth, 1980; see Chapter 10).

Patients customarily take this test before treatment, halfway through treatment, and immediately following treatment. For purposes of this experiment, however, both patients and control subjects actually walked this course three times before the patient began treatment. The walks were separated by at least several days and occurred over approximately 2 weeks. Whenever an agoraphobic patient took the walk, her matched control subject was also ready to take the walk within the hour. This helped control for the myraid factors that could influence heart rate, such as temperature, time of day, and traffic conditions on the course. Our patients then received 12 weeks of treatment, taking the walk once again halfway through, or after 6 sessions. The control subjects also walked at this time. After treatment was over, the patients again took three walks over approximately a 2-week interval, and the control subjects continued to walk at nearly identical times. Thus, each subject took a total of seven walks.

We also administered baseline measures of heart rate after each walk. In one baseline condition, the patients and control subjects rested comfortably in a chair in a quiet room. This was termed a "resting" baseline. In another baseline condition, they walked the hallways of the clinic for approximately 6 minutes but did not leave the safety of the clinic. Thus patients experienced the same type of "exercise" as they did during the behavioral test, but were not anxious. This was termed a "walking" baseline. Both of these baseline procedures were administered *after* the patients had taken their walks around town, in order to insure that the patients were not experiencing anticipatory anxiety about the upcoming walk.

Heart rate was calculated in five different ways to control for various factors, such as how far patients walked. But the primary data of interest are presented in Figure 5.2. As one can see, the mean heart rate for the agoraphobics was consistently higher at each walk than that of the control subjects. However, much to our surprise, heart rate decreased or habituated in both groups over the seven walks. The only difference in the slope of this change was in the very last walk, when agoraphobics showed a marked increase in heart rate that was significantly different from the continuing habituation showed by the control subjects. Perhaps the agoraphobics knew it was the last walk and reacted with what Grey, Sartory, and Rachman (1979) have termed a "final exam" effect. This is an often-noted phenomenon, which seems to reflect a greater effort as one at-

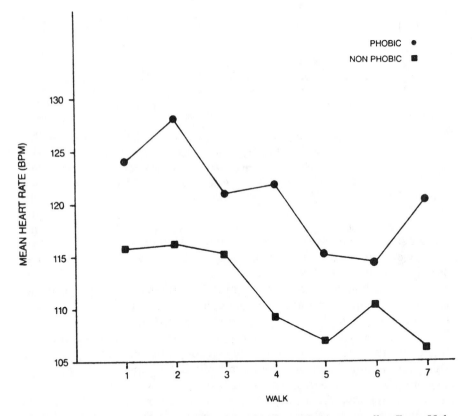

FIGURE 5.2. Mean heart rate of both groups during the seven walks. From Holden, A. E., & Barlow, D. H. (1986). Heart rate and heart rate variability recorded in vivo in agoraphobics and nonphobics. *Behavior Therapy, 17,* 26–42. Copyright 1986 by the Association for Advancement of Behavior Therapy. Reprinted by permission.

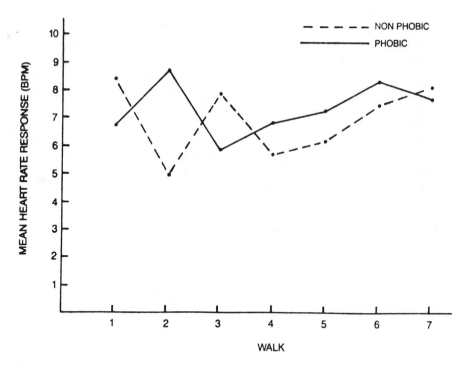

FIGURE 5.3. Mean heart rate response (increase over baseline) of both groups during the seven walks. From Holden, A. E., & Barlow, D. H. (1986). Heart rate and heart rate variability recorded in vivo in agoraphobics and nonphobics. *Behavior Therapy, 17,* 26–42. Copyright 1986 by the Association for Advancement of Behavior Therapy. Reprinted by permission.

tempts to "do well" on a final assessment. Naturally, the control subjects (who were not treated for anything) did not perceive this as a test, but simply another walk.

The fact that there were no significant differences in rates of habituations raises questions about the usefulness of heart rate as a measure of change for agoraphobia. This issue is discussed further in Chapter 10. For present purposes, the fact remains that heart rate was significantly higher for the phobic group than the control group. However, when one subtracts baseline heart rate from heart rate during the walk, another interesting finding emerges. This measure, which we termed "heart rate response" (Holden & Barlow, 1986), is presented in Figure 5.3. The data indicate no difference between the two groups in their heart rate during the supposedly frightening (for the patients) walk, relative to what their heart rate happened to be on that day as measured during resting baseline procedures. This indicates that higher heart rate during the walk for agoraphobics was due entirely to the fact that the patients came in that day with higher heart rate as reflected in their baseline measures. This was confirmed in a later series of comparisons. In other words, our test does not seem to be specific for changes in the agoraphobic syndrome as measured by a physiological response. Rather, it seems to reflect simply the finding that agoraphobics are chronically overaroused.

One other finding from this study is of interest in an examination of the psychophysiology of anxiety. A measure of variability in heart rate was taken as the subjects proceeded along the course. This variability, called "lability," simply reflected the amount of absolute change from one station to the next. As one can see in Figure 5.4, heart rate in the patient group was more labile during the walks than in the control group.

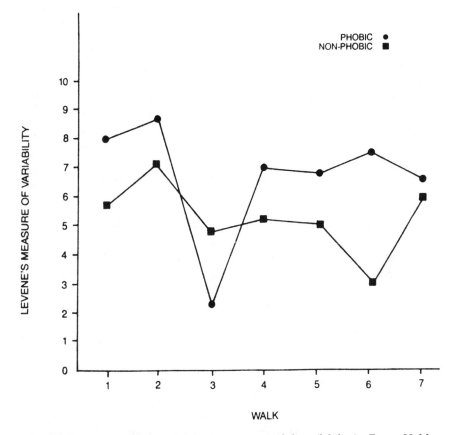

FIGURE 5.4. Levene's test—between-state variability (lability). From Holden, A. E., & Barlow, D. H. (1986). Heart rate and heart rate variability recorded in vivo in agoraphobics and nonphobics. *Behavior Therapy, 17,* 26–42. Copyright 1986 by the Association for Advancement of Behavior Therapy. Reprinted by permission.

In summary, then, agoraphobics presented with a chronically high and labile heart rate compared to controls, whether they were engaged in a fear-provoking task or not. These findings echo a well-done but seldom-cited early study by White and Gildea (1937), who also reported that heart rate was higher and more variable in patients with "anxiety states" than in normal controls, both at rest (baseline) and during the cold pressor test (a common stress test in which subjects submerge their hands in a bucket of cold water for as long as they can tolerate it). A number of studies described in Chapter 4 (e.g., Nesse et al., 1984) have also reported that panic and agoraphobic patients come to the laboratory with clearly higher heart rates than those of controls, and that this difference persists through a variety of experimental tasks.

Our experiment (Holden & Barlow, 1986) was separated from that of White and Gildea (1937) by almost 50 years, and yet the common finding is that patients with anxiety disorders are more aroused than normals and that this arousal carries over into various experimental tasks whether these tasks are stressful or not. Although studies of lability in anxious patients seem to be limited to these two studies (see also Burdick, 1978), the central finding of chronic overarousal has been demonstrated many times in the intervening 50 years with a variety of psychophysiological measures, both peripheral and central. For example, in studies reviewed in the last chapter, Cohen and White (1947, 1950) reported chronic overarousal in patients with effort syndrome or neurocirculatory asthenia as compared to normals. Excellent reviews of this work are published periodically by Malcolm Lader (e.g., Lader, 1975, 1980a, 1980b). Among various physiological measures showing resting differences between anxiety patients and controls, in addition to heart rate, are forearm blood flow (Kelly, 1966), EMG activity (Goldstein, 1964), and GSR (Lader & Wing, 1966; Raskin, 1975). Differences in GSR are evident, whether measured as levels of conductance or as spontaneous fluctuations. Robust differences in colonic motility, a process thought to underlie irritable bowel syndrome, are also found in anxious patients when compared to normals (Neff & Blanchard, 1987).

Equally interesting are comparisons made between patients and normals using more central physiological measures. For example, early studies using electroencephalographic (EEG) procedures have consistently shown less alpha and more beta activity in anxious patients than in normals (Lindsley, 1951). This type of activity, of course, is correlated with subjective reports of tension or relaxation and indicates that anxious patients are less relaxed. Other central measures that differentiate anxious patients from controls include various aspects of the contingent negative variation (McCallum & Walter, 1968; Walter, 1964), as well as harmonic driving in the EEG induced by photic stimulation. "Harmonic driving" refers to alpha responses that mimic certain frequencies of a rapidly flickering light in a laboratory procedure. Shagass (1955) demonstrated that harmonic driving was much higher in anxious patients than in normals or depressed patients. Ulett, Gleser, Winokur, and Lawler (1953) illustrated how this response increased with increasing anxiety in patients. As Lader (1980a) points out, these results fit in with the findings of elevated beta activity in the resting EEG of anxious patients.

Findings of chronic overarousal are not limited to humans. Monkeys bred for anxiety-like behavior also demonstrate chronic hyperarousal and greater physiological reaction to stress than non-"anxious" monkeys (Suomi, 1986).

Another important paradigm for studying physiological responses involves examining the rate at which subjects habituate to various stimuli. For example, Lader and Wing (1964) devised a paradigm in which, following a 10-minute rest period, 20 identical auditory stimuli of 100-dB intensity and 1-second duration were administered at intervals varying randomly between 45 and 80 seconds. GSRs to the stimuli, as well as spontaneous fluctuations, were calculated. Lader and Wing (1964) demonstrated that habituation of GSR was much slower in patients when compared to controls. Patients also had a higher frequency of spontaneous skin conductance fluctuations and heart rates 15 BPM higher than those of controls. Furthermore, the more anxious the patient (according to ratings and direct observations), the slower the habituation and the more rapid the fluctuations. While all control subjects had fully habituated after 20 repetitions of the auditory stimuli, only 6 of the anxious patients had done so at that time. This finding of slower habituation has been repeated often (Johnstone et al., 1981; Maple, Bradshaw, & Szabadi, 1982), and also has been replicated using other physiological measures, both peripheral and central, (e.g., contingent negative variation; Walter, 1964).

Of course, there are difficulties with these studies that make interpretation problematic under certain circumstances. Most of these difficulties are due to the fact that many date back 30 years or more, when diagnostic standards were different (or, more often, nonexistent). Most usually, patients in these studies were lumped together under the general heading of "anxiety neuroses." However, in a landmark study that changed thinking on the classification of anxiety disorders, Lader (1967) examined physiological responsiveness among a number of well-defined groups of patients. Lader applied the habituation procedure to the following groups of subjects: (1) patients with both anxiety and depression; (2) patients whose main complaint was pervasive anxiety; (3) agoraphobics; (4) social phobics; (5) specific phobics; and (6) normal subjects. These groups are arrayed on the basis of habituation rate and spontaneous skin conductance fluctuations in Figure 5.5 (Lader, 1980b).

In this study, normals and specific phobics were indistinguishable,

185

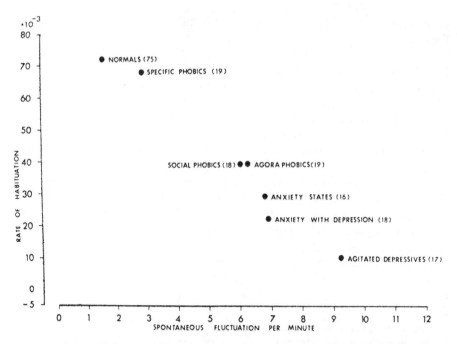

FIGURE 5.5. Relationship between habituation rate and spontaneous skin conductance fluctuations in various groups of subjects. The figures in parentheses are the numbers in each group. From Lader, M. H. (1980). The psychophysiology of anxiety. In H. van Praag, M. Lader, O. Rafaelsen, & E. Sachar (Eds.), *Handbook of biological psychiatry* (p. 229). New York: Marcel Dekker. Copyright 1980 by Marcel Dekker, Inc. Reprinted by permission.

in that they both habituated quickly and had fewer spontaneous fluctuations. They were also rated clinically as less overtly anxious. On a discriminant-function analysis, all other patients with anxiety disorders clustered together and were quite different from the normals and the specific phobics (Lader, 1967). Only 3 out of 19 specific phobics and 8 out of 71 other patients were misclassified using the author's cutoff score.

This study demonstrated that patients with simple phobias are not in the same state of overarousal or overpreparedness that characterizes the other anxiety disorders. Nevertheless, the anxiety states, as well as social phobia and agoraphobia, clearly demonstrate chronic overarousal. This finding has been demonstrated repeatedly in studies of anxiety disorders, including obsessive–compulsive disorder, which was not one of the groups in the Lader study (Turner, Beidel, & Nathan, 1985).

One study has specifically compared the psychophysiological responses of patients carrying the DSM-III diagnoses of generalized anxiety disorder or panic disorder, both at rest and during a variety of stressful tasks. Physiological assessment was carried out before treatment for both

186

groups of patients (Barlow, Cohen, *et al.*, 1984). Physiological data were recorded on a polygraph during both relaxation and stressor tasks. During relaxation tasks, each subject was asked to relax the whole body, and then to relax the face and forehead specifically. Stressor tasks included mental arithmetic, imagery of personally stressful scenes, and a cold pressor test. As one can see in Figure 5.6, subjects with panic disorder manifested a greater intensity of muscle tension. Panic disorder subjects were also higher at every assessment point on mean heart rate, but this difference did not reach statistical significance. However, Rapee (1985b) recently reported that 20 patients with panic disorder did manifest significantly higher resting heart rate (mean = 92.4 BPM) than 13 patients with generalized anxiety disorder (mean = 76.4 BPM); this finding supports and strengthens the Barlow, Cohen, *et al.* (1984) data.

Once again, it is likely that these were simply quantitative differ-

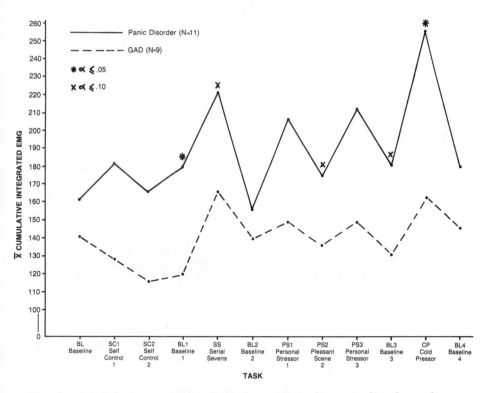

FIGURE 5.6. Pretreatment physiological assessment for panic disorder and generalized anxiety disorder: EMG values. From Barlow, D. H., Cohen, A. S., Waddell, M. T., Vermilyea, B. B., Klosko, J. S., Blanchard, E. B., & Di Nardo, P. A. (1984). Panic and generalized anxiety disorders: Nature and treatment. *Behavior Therapy, 15,* 431–449. Copyright 1984 by the Association for Advancement of Behavior Therapy. Reprinted by permission.

ences, reflecting a greater severity of arousal in the panic disorder patients than in the generalized anxiety disorder. Some evidence for greater severity is found on global clinical ratings of severity at pretest (Barlow, Cohen et al., 1984). Panic disorder patients averaged 5.10 on a severity scale of 0–8, but generalized anxiety disorder patients averaged 4.67. It is also important to remember that at the time of these evaluations the patients with panic disorder were not panicking. Therefore, there is no reason to believe that their arousal would reflect qualitatively different patterns, since the phenomenon of panic was not measured. Evidently, the measures were reflecting general anxiety. As Lader (1967) demonstrated, all patients with anxiety disorders except simple phobics are chronically overaroused, but some may be more overaroused than others.

Comparisons of Anxious Patients and Normals during Stressful Tasks

The finding that anxious patients are generally overaroused and overalert is robust when measures are taken at rest or during baseline procedures. But the finding is surprisingly less robust, and often disappears, when patients are compared to normals when performing a mildly to moderately stressful laboratory task. This discrepancy has been overlooked by most investigators, but may have marked implications for studies into the nature of anxiety. For example, in the Holden and Barlow (1986) study, the supposedly difficult test of walking away from the safe clinic was reported as frightening by the agoraphobic patients, but provoked an equally strong heart rate response from the normal control subjects, despite the fact that this was not a bit frightening for the controls (according to their reports). Differences in heart rate, once again, were accounted for totally by levels of heart rate at rest.

A careful examination of studies in which patients and controls were compared during a variety of contrived "stressful" situations reveals similar findings. Kelly (1966), in a study mentioned above, compared anxiety patients with normal controls, not only at rest but while attempting to calculate a series of figures in their heads as they were harassed by an experimenter. Patients were clearly higher on forearm blood flow than normals at rest. But under the stress condition, both controls and patients showed clear increases in forearm blood flow to comparably high levels, such that differences were no longer apparent.

Early studies also show evidence for this comparability. For example, Malmo, Shagass, and Heslam (1951) looked at blood pressure in patients and controls during a cold pressor test. Patients displayed higher blood pressure levels before the test and habituated much more slowly to the task. However, both patients and controls showed blood pressure increases during the task itself.

This similarity also shows up in central measures of arousal. For example, in a study measuring contingent negative variation during which subjects were instructed to respond to a series of flashes, patients differed from controls during acquisition procedures. When a distracting stimuli was introduced, making it more difficult to concentrate on the task at hand, both groups showed marked and similar changes in contingent negative variation. Once again, the normals habituated much more quickly to this distracting task, leaving the anxiety patients different at the end of the task (McCallum & Walter, 1968).

Of course, there is the occasional study where seeming differences arose between anxiety patients and normals during various tasks. For example, Goldstein (1964) found that patients not only had significantly higher EMG levels than patients during baseline procedures, but also showed stronger EMG responses to a white-noise stimulus than controls. Nevertheless, the more striking findings were chronically elevated heart rate, respiration rate, and blood pressure both at rest and during tasks for patients.

How can we account for the lack of differences between anxious and control subjects during performance? There are several possibilities. First, one must consider the nature of the task. The tasks used in psychophysiological studies most often involve mild stress or conflict. In fact, Malmo et al. (1948) stipulated that the requirements of an anxiety-provoking task include the criterion that it be relatively mild as well as being uniform and controllable. The number of tasks meeting these criteria have been limited only by the ingenuity of investigators. The task most widely adopted for humans has involved anticipating painful but harmless electric shock. However, other tasks include anticipating or actually undergoing thermal pain, as in the cold pressor task; watching stressful movies (e.g., a movie in which a victim is about to be attacked by a chainsaw); or threatening subjects with a variety of negative evaluations if they do not perform some task at a certain level. While some of these tasks might have face validity as "anxiety"-producing, many of the tasks simply require performance of some kind under time limits or some other "stress."

What all of these test situations have in common is their novelty. Very few experiments of this type repeatedly test subjects over time. In addition, investigators often present the subject with the necessity of meeting a challenge, such as performing under pressure. These tasks elicit the increased alertness and preparation for responding that most people bring to any new task they undertake. While there may be some minor individual differences, the primary responses common to both anxious patients and normals include increased vigilance, muscle tension, autonomic and central nervous system activity, and a variety of endocrinological responses. These tasks, no matter how carefully devised, are not tapping a clinically significant anxiety response, but rather the general response of preparation or mobilization for a task.

What seems to differentiate patients from controls, at least on a physiological level, is that they come to these tasks with a higher state of arousal and they habituate more slowly from levels of arousal reached during the task itself. These differences, of course, could be due to any number of factors. For example, it is possible that anxious patients are chronically "ready" or prepared to meet life's challenges. This "vigilance" in turn could be due to chronic, exaggerated, negative cognitive activity regarding upcoming challenges or tasks; to basic biological hyperreactivity; or to a combination of the two, as suggested in Chapter 7.

The fact that reactions are basically the same is also supported by examining the *patterning* of physiological responding, in addition to the absolute level of responding, in anxious patients and normals in various stressful or mildly anxiety-producing situations. As Lader points out (1980a, 1980b), the specific pattern of arousal is the same in normals made mildly anxious as it is in anxious patients in their chronic state. The only difference, once again, is in the consistency or chronicity of arousal in the patients, along with the slower rate of habituation.

Another possibility is that the lack of differences may be accounted for by the law of initial values. Since anxiety patients manifest an initially high response, one can hypothesize that they reach a "ceiling" more quickly and with less additional response, resulting in an equality between anxious and normal groups. But this hypothesis is not supported, because almost all studies show clear differences during performance of a task. Only when baseline values are considered is it apparent that all differences are accounted for by baseline levels (e.g., Holden & Barlow, 1986).

Cerebral Blood Flow Studies

Another intriguing life of research that forms a bridge to neurobiological studies (taken up below) comes from an investigation of cerebral blood flow. A preliminary report has suggested differences in blood flow between patients with panic disorder and normals. Specifically, when positron emission tomography was used, panic patients evidenced a relative reduction in cerebral blood flow in the left compared to the right parahippocampal gyrus in the resting state. The same patients panicked when infused with sodium lactate (Reiman, Raichle, Butler, Herscovitch, & Robins, 1984). In a methodologically rigorous and intriguing extension of this study (Reiman *et al.*, 1986), similar results were found. Specifically, eight panic patients who later panicked during lactate provocation differed in several ways from eight panic disorder patients who did not panic, as well as from 25 controls. It is important to note that all tomographic scans were taken in a nonpanic, resting state. Patients who panicked demonstrated the parahippocampal asymmetry, as well as an abnormally high whole-brain oxygen metabolism. They also evidenced acute respiratory alkalosis, as reflected in low pCO_2. Since projections to this region arise from several areas, including the locus ceruleus and the septo-hippocampal region, it is possible that this finding is another manifestation of Gray's (1982) behavioral inhibition system (see Chapter 2). As such, it may be another biological process associated with the chronic overarousal of anxiety rather than with panic.

Reiman et al. (1986) suggest that the majority of previous evidence indicates that these changes are reversible markers of anticipatory anxiety. This explanation is made more compelling by the evidence reviewed in Chapter 4 that the strongest (and only) predictor of panic during lactate provocation is high anticipatory anxiety. In view of the acute respiratory alkalosis, it is also possible that Reiman et al.'s patients were simply hyperventilating and that this behavior produced temporary blood flow changes, as suggested by Turner, Beidel, and Jacob (1988). Although the use of brain-imaging techniques is certain to lead to additional important research, there is no evidence here of basic biological differences between anxiety and panic. These findings are reminiscent of previous studies such as that by Mathew, Weinman, and Claghorn (1982) using xenon inhalation techniques; Mathew et al. also reported a reduction in blood flow to various brain areas in anxious patients compared to normals, although Kety (1950) had reported *increases* in cerebral blood flow in anxious patients. Of course, these experiments utilized very different experimental procedures and methods of assessment.

ENDOCRINOLOGICAL STUDIES

Catecholamine Levels

Catecholamines are reliably increased in normals in response to stress. The types of "stress" that produce these normal increases are wide-ranging and include exercise, concentration, temperature changes, and even postural changes (Dimsdale & Moss, 1980; Kopin, 1984). In fact, almost any change in stimulation seems to increase catecholamine excretion (Weiner, 1985). This reaction to stimulation seems to be true not only for epinephrine and norepinephrine, but for their major metabolites (Uhde, Siever, Post, 1984; Uhde et al., 1982). In view of this evidence, it has been assumed that catecholamine levels may be chronically higher in anxious patients than in controls. Nevertheless, the evidence for this is mixed. For example, Mathew, Ho, Kralik, Taylor, and Claghorn (1981) found increased catecholamines in anxious patients compared to controls. However, in a later, more sophisticated study (Mathew, Ho, Francis, Taylor, & Weinman, 1982), they found no differences in catecholamine excretion, either during baseline procedures or 20 minutes after a small injection of epinephrine in a group of patients diagnosed with generalized anxiety disorder. This lack of difference occurred because the control subjects also showed increased catecholamine excretion and increased anxiety scores on the State form of the State–Trait Anxiety Inventory (Spielberger et al., 1970).

Other studies with patients have also failed to find differences in catecholamine levels between patients and control subjects. Although some elevations in catecholamines are found in all subjects with increased states of affect, particularly after stress testing, most usually patients present with normal catecholamine levels (Lader, 1980)—a finding reported once again by Liebowitz, Gorman, Fyer, Levitt, et al. (1985). Ballenger et al. (1984), on the other hand, observed higher circulating levels of norepinephrine (as well as MHPG) in agoraphobics at pretreatment than in normals. These differences in many cases were small, but nevertheless statistically significant.

In a well-done study, Nesse et al. (1984) also reported elevated epinephrine and norepinephrine levels in patients with panic disorder and in agoraphobics, compared to controls. These differences seemed "chronic" in that they were present at baseline and maintained throughout a series of tasks. Differences between the two last-mentioned studies and Mathew, Ho, et al. (1982) may have been due to diagnoses. The patients in Mathew, Ho, et al. were diagnosed as having generalized anxiety disorder, while the patients in Ballenger et al. and Nesse et al. with higher plasma catecholamines were panickers or agoraphobics. On the other hand, Liebowitz, Gorman, Fyer, Levitt, et al.'s (1985) patients were also panickers, and yet no differences were found.

Elevated catecholamines also seem nonspecific and have been reported in tests of a variety of other emotional and behavioral disorders, including depression, mania, and schizophrenia (Kemali, Del Vecchio, & Maj, 1971; Lake et al., 1982). In view of these inconsistencies, the findings of Ballenger et al. (1984) and Nesse et al. (1984) will need replication, but they are consistent with the conception of chronic overarousal in these patients.

Thus, for the most part, anxious patients do not seem to respond differently in a physiological sense to conflict or stressful tasks, either quantitatively or qualitatively. Only in the persistence of their responding do they differ. But how does this preparatory and anticipatory arousal relate to the phenomenon of panic on a physiological level? Is panic simply an exaggerated version of anticipatory arousal physiologically? From data reviewed thus far, it is not possible to make this determination, since very few direct comparisons exist. But some interesting inferences can be drawn from data that do exist, some of which pertain to adrenocortical responses.

Adrenocortical Function

In a well-done early study that continues to be cited today, Bliss, Migeon, Branch, and Samuels (1956) examined adrenocortical responses, primarily 17-hydroxycorticosteroids (17-OHCS), in both normals and a heterogeneous group of psychiatric patients. These subjects were tested under two types of conditions. The first condition was described as "naturally occurring stressful events." For psychiatric patients, these included events such as admission to the hospital or preparation for eletroconvulsive therapy. For normals, naturally occurring stressful events included an injury to a relative or a major exam. The second condition consisted of experimentally contrived laboratory stressors.

A variety of comparisons both between groups and within individuals over time revealed a relatively consistent finding. During naturally occurring stressful events, small but reliable, increases in 17-OHCS occurred for both patients and normals; however, responses were weak or nonexistent during mild laboratory stress. Although many patients were psychotic, one individual case study was carried out with a severe "neurotic" who seemed quite clearly to be panicking. Although variability was great, 17-OHCS values averaged approximately 10 mg higher during intense anxiety (which might have been panic) than during less intense anxiety in this one subject. Could this be a marker of panic? In light of evidence presented in Chapter 4, it is unlikely.

Despite the promise of the Bliss *et al.* (1956) study, there have been few further attempts to compare neuroendocrine differences between anxious patients and normals, either at rest or while performing a task (Stokes, 1985). Almost all evidence bearing on neuroendocrine responsiveness comes from studies of otherwise normal subjects exposed to typical conflict or stressful situations described above, such as watching dramatic movies, undergoing stressful interviews, or engaging in varying timed motor tasks. The general finding once again is a brief increase in neuroendocrine responses to these tasks, measured most usually by plasma cortisol, 17-OHCS, and related hormones.

Research with patients yields a similar finding. But even this weak initial response is elusive. This is highlighted in work by Curtis and colleagues, reviewed in Chapter 4. When these investigators (Curtis, Buxton, Lippman, Nesse, & Wright, 1976) provoked panic in simple phobics by confronting them with their feared object (usually a small animal), they noted, much to their surprise, no response in the adrenocortical system as reflected by measures of prolactin, thyroid-stimulating hormone, and plasma cortisol. This lack of response occurred despite the fact that by all other criteria the subjects seemed clearly to be panicking. On the other hand, there were slight increases in growth hormone response. Stokes

(1985) points out that, contrary to most studies with normal subjects, there was no uncertainty or novelty in this situation. That is, phobic subjects were clearly informed of what was to occur and experienced repeated flooding sessions with the phobic object. Furthermore, Curtis, Buxton, *et al.* (1976) did report some increase in adrenocortical responding at the first session, when patients came in for initial measurements, perhaps again reflecting novelty or anticipation. This, of course, would be consistent with other physiological responses.

In a more recent and particularly well-done study from the same laboratory, Nesse *et al.* (1985) were able to observe weak and inconsistent increases in cortisol, growth hormone, and insulin in response to phobic panic. However, even this weak response decreased by the second trial. Of course, all physiological and catecholamine responses (with the exception of blood pressure), as well as subjective anxiety, also decreased at the second trial, raising the possibility that the results reflected therapeutic changes rather than just habituation to novelty. Nesse *et al.* (1985) reversed their earlier lack of results only by exercising extreme care in the timing of their measurements as well as other experimental control procedures. Returning to the most usual pattern of findings, Liebowitz, Gorman, Fyer, Levitt, *et al.* (1985) report little or no catecholamine surge and inconsistent trends in cortisol and prolactin during lactate-induced panic—a finding echoed by Woods, Charney, Goodman, and Heninger (1987) with CO_2-induced panic. What is interesting here is that adrenocortical measures during panic provoked in the laboratory, either biochemically (Liebowitz, Gorman, Fyer, Levitt, *et al.*, 1985) or behaviorally (Nesse *et al.*, 1985), do not seem to reflect any unique pattern. Rather, what we seem to see is the same response that we see from both patients and normals in a mildly anxiety-provoking situation: that is, a brief, inconsistent elevation associated with novelty or preparedness.

SUMMARY OF PSYCHOPHYSIOLOGICAL AND NEUROENDOCRINOLOGICAL STUDIES

Studies of the physiology and endocrinology of anxiety yield surprisingly few firm conclusions. Physiological and endocrinological responses to mildly stressful events do not differentiate anxious patients from normals. Surprisingly, no specific pattern emerges even during intense laboratory-provoked panic using either biochemical or behavioral procedures, as reviewed in Chapter 4. The results reflect either no change or a transient elevation similar to that found during the generalized anxiety or arousal occurring during mildly stressful tasks. The one robust finding is that anxious patients are chronically hyperaroused and slow to habituate. They are continually vigilant and ready for action. As suggested above, this may reflect a genetically determined neurobiological hyperactivity; a chronic cognitive state of relative helplessness, associated with chronic apprehension over future events; or a combination of the two.

The psychophysiological profile of panic, as captured in studies reviewed in Chapter 3, shows a topography different from that of generalized anxiety. That is, panic seems to be a short-lived but intense event. The argument can be made that panic is simply a more intense version of generalized anxiety, with the patterning of the responses and the direction of various measures similar to what is noted in laboratory-provoked generalized anxiety. On the other hand, it becomes important to observe once again the fingertip vasodilation during panic attacks experienced by Mary and Jill (see Figures 3.1 and 3.2). The commonly observed psychophysiological correlate of anxiety is not a peripheral vasodilation, but vasoconstriction (Bloom, Houston, & Burish, 1976; Lader, 1980a). But this response has almost always been noticed in the context of anticipatory or preparatory arousal. Ballenger et al. (1984) also reported the interesting observation of significant drops in fingertip temperature during successful treatment of agoraphobics with imipramine. None of their patients had cold extremities as a significant complaint before treatment, which might otherwise have been expected in patients experiencing significant and repeated anxiety attacks. Of course, the Ballenger et al. patients evidenced an increase in heart rate during treatment as a result of imipramine medication, and the drug obviously interacted with the psychophysiological measures. Since measures in the Ballenger et al. study were not taken while patients were panicking, it is not clear whether these results support the physiological profile of vasodilation during panic or not.

Does this peripheral vasoconstriction versus vasodilation reflect a fundamental difference between panic and anxiety? It is too early to tell, since this profile needs to be replicated across laboratories. But it is an intriguing finding. Even more intriguing are recent observations of a patient in our clinic experiencing several severe, naturally occurring panics during exposure treatment. During one panic, his extremities were clearly warm, as verified by touch. Not 30 minutes later, a second panic occurred, and (speaking figuratively) his hands were as cold as ice.

THE NEUROBIOLOGY OF ANXIETY AND PANIC

The evidence reviewed in Chapter 4 and above has not revealed any biological marker for panic, either central or peripheral (Ballenger, 1986; Liebowitz, Gorman, et al., 1986; Margraf, Ehlers, & Roth, 1986a). Among mechanisms ruled out, at least on the basis of lactate-induced panics, are peripheral catecholamine surges; lowered calcium levels; metabolic alkalosis; hypothalamic–pituitary–adrenocortical axis activation; abnormalities of pyruvate lactate phosphate and blood acidity; and abnormalities in the opoid system or the autocoids thromborane B_2 and platelet factor 4 (Ballenger, 1986). In fact, the surprising finding is that very few biological reactions of any kind are associated with panic, other than markedly elevated physiological responding. Even the most recent promising hypothesis, CO_2 sensitivity in the central nervous system, has been the subject of conflicting evidence.

For example, studies reviewed in Chapter 4 demonstrate unequivocally the panicogenic effects of CO_2 inhalation. Fyer et al. (1986) suggest that brain stem CO_2 receptors are abnormally sensitive, resulting in an extreme ventilatory response. But this response may also be mediated reflexively via the peripheral chemoreceptors located in the carotid and aortic bodies. Fyer et al. hypothesize that panic patients have both peripheral and central CO_2 sensitivity. Studies of differential ventilatory responses of patients and controls under a variety of conditions such as exercise date back over 40 years (see Chapter 4). But Woods et al. (1986), using a rebreathing technique to measure ventilatory response to CO_2, specifically found no differences between patients and controls. A number of alternative hypotheses have been offered to account for differential ventilatory responses when these occur (e.g., Jones & Mellersh, 1946).

Nevertheless, some exciting research, particularly research with animal models, suggests that specific neurotransmitter systems may be differentially associated with panic. The system receiving the most attention is the noradrenergic system.

THE NORADRENERGIC CONNECTION

In the late 1970s, Gene Redmond and his colleagues began an interesting series of experiments in which they electrically or pharmacologically stimulated noradrenergic neurons in stump-tailed monkeys. A major nucleus in this noradrenergic system is an area of the brain called the locus ceruleus. The locus ceruleus is situated in the pons with projections to the cerebral cortex and limbic system, as well as the brain stem, the reticular system, and the pain-sensitive neurons in the dorsal horn of the spinal cord (Redmond, 1977, 1979; Redmond & Huang, 1979). Redmond and his colleagues noted that the reaction induced by stimulation appeared very similar in these monkeys to what happens in the wild when the animals are exposed to an overwhelming natural threat. The implication is that this reaction may be analogous to intense fear or panic.

The most direct biological test of the noradrenergic connection in humans has occurred in the context of the infusion of yohimbine. Yohimbine is a specific alpha$_2$-adrenergic receptor antagonist that increases locus ceruleus activity (Charney et al., 1984; Uhde, Boulenger, et al., 1984;

Uhde, Roy-Byrne, Vittone, Boulenger, & Post, 1985). Conversely, cloni-dine, an alpha$_2$-adrenergic receptor agonist, is a potent inhibitor of locus ceruleus activity. As reviewed in Chapter 4, yohimbine is one method among many used to provoke panic, and there is some evidence that clonidine may be capable of blocking panic (Hoehn-Saric, Merchant, Key-ser, & Smith, 1981; Liebowitz, Fyer, McGrath, & Klein, 1981; Siever & Uhde, 1984). This evidence is inconclusive, since there seem to be many paths (both biochemical and behavioral) to provoking panic, at least some of which do not seem to involve noradrenergic functioning specifically. To take just one example from the same group of investigators, Woods *et al.* (1987) found no evidence of heightened noradrenergic activity during naturally occurring situational panics in a group of panic patients. In fact, responses connected with noradrenergic functioning did not differ from those of healthy controls, although heart rate in patients was considerably higher.

Another strategy for investigating this hypothesis is to identify spe-cific markers of central noradrenergic activity and to look for these mark-ers while subjects are anxious. An interesting possibility is MHPG, a nor-epinephrine metabolite. MHPG is thought to specifically reflect central noradrenergic functioning rather than peripheral catecholaminergic activ-ity. Following behaviorally induced panics in agoraphobics, Ko *et al.* (1983) observed marked increases in MHPG. However, Maas, Hattox, Greene, and Landis (1979) suggest that peripheral and central MHPG levels are closely correlated (Kopin, 1984). Furthermore, the preponderance of evi-dence suggests that MHPG behaves much like other catecholamines (or, for that matter, like other adrenocortical or physiological responses) in displaying a transient elevation both in normals and anxious patients after confrontation with a general stressor (e.g., Ko *et al.*, 1983; Uhde *et al.*, 1982; Uhde, Siever, & Post, 1984). In addition, there is little evidence of any differences in MHPG between patients and normals at rest. It is pos-sible that differences may be discovered in view of recent findings of dif-ferent catecholamine levels in panic patients versus controls (Ballenger *et al.*, 1984; Nesse *et al.*, 1984). But Charney *et al.* (1984) did not report dif-ferences in MHPG levels at baseline or after infusions of yohimbine in panickers compared to normals, although a subset of patients with partic-ularly high frequencies of panic did differ from normals. Finally, Woods *et al.* (1987), in the interesting study reported above, found no elevations in MHPG during naturally occurring situational panics. As Ko *et al.* (1983) point out, it will be difficult to sort out MHPG from other physiological and neuroendocrine responses to anxiety specifically, or from responses to stress in general.

Despite the seeming lack of biochemical markers, there is other indi-rect evidence for the noradrenergic connection as a potential biological substrate for panic. For example, in data from biochemical provocation studies of panic, no peripheral biochemical or physiological changes could be found that might trigger lactate panics. Rather, lactate-induced panic appeared to be primarily a central nervous system phenomenon, with noradrenergic functioning one strong possibility.

What makes this biological hypothesis interesting is that some supporting and converging evidence has been provided by Jeffrey Gray (1982, 1985). Gray also suggests, from a different point of view, a critical role for the ascending noradrenergic fibers originating in the locus ceruleus. Working with animal models, as does Redmond, Gray bases his observation in part on the fact that lesions of the dorsal ascending noradrenergic bundle (which carries locus ceruleus efferents destined for the limbic system in the neocortex) partially mimic the behavioral effects of certain antianxiety drugs. This neuroanatomical arrangement does not necessarily imply a specific role for this system in panic, since no separation of panic or generalized anxiety was attempted in Gray's experiments.

But, to return to Redmond's work, it is interesting that Redmond accomplishes his pharmacological activation of the locus ceruleus by withdrawing the animals from opiates. For anyone who has observed these symptoms, the acute bursts of emotion do resemble panic states. Furthermore, this particular reaction to opiate withdrawal also seems to be blocked by clonidine and enhanced by yohimbine. It follows that opiates should reduce this reaction in animals as well as panic in humans.

While one would not consider using addiction-producing opiates clinically to treat panic, there has been some interesting animal work. In a prototypical animal laboratory paradigm, reactions to a painful stimulus (e.g., a shock), as well as reactions to a signal threatening that stimulus (e.g., a light), are measured. Reactions during the signal provide one of the most common paradigms for examining anticipatory or general anxiety in animals and humans. This paradigm has been used to test many anxiolytic drugs, such as the benzodiazepines. These experiments suggest that these antianxiety drugs seem to reduce responses to stimuli or signals associated with unconditioned painful stimuli, but not responses to pain itself (Gray, 1977).

Conversely, the opiates are known to reduce pain reactions, but have few effects on responses to stimuli associated with pain in this animal paradigm. It is possible, as Gray points out, that there are diverse symptoms of anxiety and that not all are mediated by identical mechanisms (although there may be some overlap). Specifically, anxiety produced by opiate withdrawal and mediated by the noradrenergic system in the locus ceruleus may be more closely akin to panic, while more traditional animal models of anxiety, involving conflict, challenge, or anticipation of an aversive event, reflect generalized anxiety. In an interesting bit of theorizing, which also has the necessary feature of being testable, Gray (1985) suggests that opiate receptors involved in the panic-like opiate withdrawal syndrome are situated mainly on locus ceruleus cells that send their efferents to the spinal cord. Few of these receptors are on cells that contribute to the dorsal ascending noradrenergic bundle. Conversely, benzodiazepine receptors may be found in larger numbers at the latter site. This hypothesis suggests that opiates and withdrawal from opiates are involved primarily with somatic symptoms of anxiety. In fact, one of the phenomenological marks of panic is its heavy somatic component, as noted in Chapter 3. Needless to say, there is far more in the way of speculation than of facts in this account.

Much remains to be understood regarding the adequacy of the noradrenergic connection as a neurosubstrate for panic. Our knowledge of this system, particularly in its relationship to other biological systems, is far from perfect. At present there are many results that seem to undermine the noradrenergic hypothesis and few that directly support it, as noted above (Carr & Sheehan, 1984; Uhde, Boulenger, et al., 1984; Uhde, Roy-Byrne, et al., 1985). In fact, some investigators believe for a variety of reasons that there are too many disconfirming facts to allow continued support for the specificity of the noradrenergic system, and they hypothesize alternative regulatory mechanisms underlying panic (Carr & Sheehan, 1984). However, two recent studies converge to cast a somewhat different light on the role of the noradrenergic system.

Both Charney and Heninger (1986a) and Nutt (1986) have produced preliminary data suggesting that the noradrenergic system may have a greater dynamic range (more lability) in panic patients, due possibly to a regulatory problem with alpha$_2$-adrenergic receptors or greater lability of noradrenergic cardiovascular mechanisms. Of course, these results are preliminary and seem to apply only to a subgroup of patients at this time. Nevertheless, further research is clearly indicated.

One major question will involve the state versus trait nature of the observed lability of alpha$_2$-adrenergic receptors if it holds up. For example, is this lability associated with panic specifically, or is it simply another marker of chronic hyperarousal? In this regard, this response should be evaluated in anxious or stressed patients without panic, or in normals made anxious in laboratory settings. It may develop that this lability is one important source of increased neurobiological activity in anxious patients that may even be (partially) genetically determined. But it may be nonspecific in relation to panic.

A SEROTONERGIC CONNECTION?: TONIC IMMOBILITY

Redmond's animal model for studying panic centers around the contrived pharmacological state of opiate withdrawal. Another animal model exists that may be relevant to panic and anxiety. I have taken the position that panic is the discrete emotion of fear and that emotions are fundamentally behavioral action tendencies. In Chapter 1 and above, I have referred to the closely related action tendency of tonic immobility in animals. Tonic immobility is interesting here because it seems also to be associated with the emotion of fear in animals, but may be programmed to occur only after the primary action tendency (escape) has failed, and then only under the specific stimulus condition of contact with a predator. In between attempts to escape and the response of freezing are aggressive action tendencies directed at the predator. Freezing has obvious survival value in animals, since movement cues often trigger predation.

It would seem that panic in humans has little to do with tonic immobility, since we seldom see panickers freezing, although there are occasional reports of people being "scared stiff" or "frozen with fear." People experiencing panic attacks are seldom aggressive, either. But it is possible that we may see vestiges of this response in humans on the far edge of terror during rape and on the battlefield. The personally tragic but theoretically intriguing phenomenon of rape-induced paralysis has been described in Chapter 1.

In view of this potential connection, the biology of tonic immobility and other parameters affecting the response are of interest. For example, hyperventilation occurs during the response, and the duration of tonic immobility in animals is greatly influenced by baseline anxiety levels. Any manipulations that increase anxiety prior to tonic immobility, such as conditioned aversive stimuli, loud noises, injections of adrenaline, or suspension over a visual cliff, will prolong the response. On the other hand, most procedures that reduce baseline anxiety, such as safety signals and handling, antagonize the reaction. These findings are similar to data from laboratory provocation studies of panic.

The neurobiological process that underlies tonic immobility is well worked out and involves the serotonergic system (Boren, Gallup, Suarez, Wallnau, & Gagliardi, 1979; Wallnau & Gallup, 1977). The evidence for this comes from several sources. Manipulations of tryptophan, the essential amino acid precursor to serotonin, results in the expected increases or decreases in the duration of tonic immobility. Also, drugs that systematically affect serotonin concentration in turn systematically affect tonic immobility (Boren et al., 1979). Among the more interesting of these drugs is imipramine, which, when administered peripherally, clearly blocks tonic immobility (Maser & Gallup, 1974).

Several other investigators have considered the potential role of serotonin. For example, Cloninger's new neurobiological theory, described in Chapter 2, posits serotonergic action as the basis for panic. Mavissakalian, Perel, and Michelson (1984) have suggested that the beneficial effect of imipramine may be mediated through serotonergic action. Two preliminary studies have directly examined serotonin levels or function in panic patients. Evans *et al.* (1986) found lower levels of circulatory serotonin in patients than in controls. Charney and Heninger (1986b), on the other hand, found no differences between panic patients and controls in the ability of the serotonin precursor tryptophan to increase prolactin levels, suggesting that serotonin function in patients is normal.

THE BENZODIAZEPINE SYSTEM

One of the most exciting neurobiological developments in recent years is the discovery of the benzodiazepine receptor system. If speculation has centered on noradrenergic (and serotonergic) neurotransmitter systems as neurobiological substrates of panic, equally interesting speculations suggest that the benzodiazepine system may be a specific neurobiological substrate for more generalized anxiety. Of course, the benzodiazepine class of minor tranquilizers has been used for years in the treatment of clinical anxiety, but it was only in 1977 that the discovery of the benzodiazepine receptor was reported (Mohler & Okada, 1977; Squires & Braestrup, 1977). Since that time, evidence has accumulated that this brain receptor has a specific affinity for benzodiazepines. Subsequent work showed that the inhibitory neurotransmitter GABA potentiates the binding of benzodiazepines to the receptor sites (e.g., Skolnick & Paul, 1982). One interesting consequence of these discoveries is the realization that there must be naturally occurring clinical substances in the brain that are specific for benzodiazepine receptors. These substances, which may be anxiolytic, have yet to be isolated, although recently a peptide has been discovered that does bind to these receptors (Alho *et al.*, 1985). Surprisingly, this peptide is anxiogenic (i.e., it increases rather than decreases anxiety).

Evidence supporting the benzodiazepine model has come largely from investigating the effects of anxiolytic drugs, specifically the benzodiazepines, on various paradigms for provoking "anxiety" in animals. Many such paradigms exist, most of which have been utilized for almost a century to produce what some have termed "experimental neuroses." The nature of experimental neuroses is explored more thoroughly in Chapter 7. For now, suffice it to say that these situations typically produce mild anxiety through threat of shock, the omission of expected reward ("frustrative nonreward"), or the punishment of previously reinforced behavior. The prototypical paradigm is the Geller–Seifter conflict test (Geller & Seifter, 1960), where liquid reinforcers are paired with foot shock, setting up a conflict over pressing the bar for the liquid. These paradigms are thought to be analogous to anxiety rather than panic, since there is little evidence of an overwhelming alarm response. Rather, a state of relatively "chronic" anxiety is assumed, since an animal's behavior is characterized by increased attention and vigilance, arousal, and the interruption of ongoing behavior.

Evidence for the specific anxiolytic involvement of the benzodiazepine system comes from several sources. First, a variety of GABA antagonists seem to be anxiogenic. That is, anxiety in the context of various animal models is increased by GABA antagonists (Gray, 1985; Insel, 1986). Second, neurons that release GABA at the synaptic junction are termed "GABA-ergic," and most often the release of this neurotransmitter serves to inhibit firing from the postsynaptic neuron. The apparent behavioral effect is reduced anxiety. When this inhibitory function is facilitated pharmacologically, anxiety is reduced even further. Thus, the benzodiazepines may exert anxiolytic effects by virtue of the enhanced GABA-ergic inhibition they produce. But the benzodiazepines have other well-known actions, including sedation, anticonvulsant effects, and muscle relaxation. This diversity of functions makes it difficult to conclude that the GABA system is specifically anxiolytic.

However, to return to the animal experimental neurosis or conflict studies, there are several important pieces of supporting information. For example, there is a high correlation between receptor occupancy and anticonflict effects in rats (Braestrup, Nielsen, Honore, Jensen, & Petersen, 1983). "Anticonflict" in this context means that under the influence of some drugs, a rat will continue bar pressing for milk despite the "conflict" of shock. Also, as mentioned above, studies in which rats were selectively bred for emotionality suggest a reduction of brain benzodiazepine receptor sites in these animals (Robertson et al., 1978), although other evidence indicates that it is difficult to replicate this work (Braestrup & Nielsen, 1981). Even more interesting are experiments that show acute modification in number of benzodiazepine receptors as a function of stress or anxiety. For example, exposing animals to stress, such as immersion in ice water or convulsions, can increase cortical benzodiazepine receptors by 20% within 15 minutes. This level returns to normal after 60 minutes (Paul & Skolnick, 1978, 1981). Other evidence includes the induction of anxiety-like states in monkeys using inverse agonists, which have powerful effects on the benzodiazepine system in a direction opposite to that of the benzodiazepines (Insel et al., 1984).

Even this evidence, however, does not identify the GABA system as specifically anxiolytic. It is possible that the reduction in generalized arousal associated with sedative and anticonvulsant effects is also the mechanism of action for any anxiolytic effects observed, although arousal reduction need not be as great as for sedative effects. This, in fact, is the assumption of a leading psychopharmacologist, Malcolm Lader (1985). In addition to sedative and muscle relaxant effects, Bond and Lader (1979) have found that benzodiazepines reduce anger, hostility, and aggression. Even more interesting is the finding of reduction in reports of positive emotional states, such as "eager anticipation" and pleasure (Lader, 1975). Benzodiazepines may act to reduce emotion in general, or, more likely, the arousal associated with many emotional or affective states (Lader, 1985).

On the other hand, it is possible that the discovery of different varieties of benzodiazepine receptors, and specific varieties of benzodiazepines with more selective effects, may lead to a more focused anxiolytic agent (Hoehn-Saric, 1982; Paul & Skolnick, 1981). In addition, the evidence accumulated thus far does not entirely answer the question regarding the source of the anxiolytic effects of this system. Suffice it to say, the discovery of the system is relatively new, and the neurobiological implications are far from worked out. For example, it now seems that there are several different types of GABA receptors that act in different ways, with only one of them having an affinity for the benzodiazepine compound (Gray, 1985; Hoehn-Saric, 1982). Furthermore, the GABA system seems to interact in an unspecified way with the septo-hippocampal system, which has a specific neuropsychological function in regard to the behavioral expression of anxiety in mammals (Gray, 1982).

SUMMARY OF NEUROBIOLOGICAL STUDIES

There is little question that the neurobiology of anxiety and panic is among the most exciting research frontiers today. But it is hard to underemphasize the preliminary state of our knowledge and the need for additional research. For that reason, the various inferences described below are particularly speculative. For example, there is a critical assumption on which all work on the benzodiazepine system is partly based: that the benzodiazepines are strongly anxiolytic in humans. In fact, the benzodiazepines seem to have rather weak and short-lived effects that are subject to rapid habituation in humans, at least as the drugs are normally prescribed (Lader, 1985; see Chapter 15). Thus, understanding the neurobiology of the benzodiazepine system may be only a small contribution to the complex biopsychosocial construct of anxiety.

Are Panic and Anxiety Neurobiologically Distinct?

The emerging work on distinct neurotransmitter systems invites attempts to compare and contrast the hypothetical neurobiological substrates of panic and generalized anxiety. This exercise is valuable if we keep in mind that it is for heuristic purposes only. Insel (1986) has accomplished this task in a particularly thought-provoking way, and his comparison of these two systems on various dimensions is displayed in Table 5.3.

While the pharmacological agonists and antagonists must be studied

TABLE 5.3. Neuropharmacologic Systems Involved in Anxiety

Receptor	Agonist	Antagonist	Phylogeny	Anatomical highest density	Animal behavior paradigm	Possible clinical correlate
BZD-GABA-Cl[a]	Diazepam	β-CCE[b]	Recent	Telencephalon	Conflict	Generalized anxiety disorder
Adrenergic (α₂)	Clonidine	Yohimbine	Ancient	Brain stem	Alarm	Panic disorder

Note. From Insel, T. R. (1986). The neurobiology of anxiety: A tale of two systems. In B. F. Shaw, Z. V. Segal, T. M. Vallis, & F. E. Cashman (Eds.), *Anxiety disorders: Psychological and biological perspectives* (p. 46). New York: Plenum Press. Copyright 1986 by Plenum Publishing Corp. Reprinted by permission.
[a]BZD-GABA-Cl, benzodiazepine–gamma-aminobutyric acid–chlorine channel receptor complex.
[b]β-CCE, beta-carboline–3-carboxylic acid ethyl ester.

more thoroughly, Insel's speculations echo themes on possible functions of anxiety in an evolutionary sense. We must remember that biology always serves behavior. Comparing functions of a behavioral or emotional state, even though those functions no longer have survival value, is probably a useful strategy in determining which biological systems are distinct. The all-important issue of a functional analysis of panic and anxiety is discussed again below.

Unfortunately for the symmetry of our observations and speculations, there are also strong indications that the systems are related as we always thought they were. As Insel (1986) points out, lesioning noradrenergic pathways in the forebrain leads to as much as a 30% reduction in benzodiazepine receptors. In addition, benzodiazepines decrease the firing by locus ceruleus neurons. The facts strongly suggest overlapping systems.

Other evidence comes from pharmacological studies, which provided the original impetus for separating these systems. For example, it has been assumed that benzodiazepines have no effect on panic. This assumption was derived from the "pharmacological dissection" work reviewed earlier. But the best evidence at a clinical level is that benzodiazepines *do* have a clinically beneficial effect on panic if the dosage is strong enough (e.g., Noyes *et al.*, 1984; see Chapter 11). In fact, a wide variety of drug and psychological treatments seem effective for panic. Many of these drugs, such as the new triazolobenzodiazepine alprazolam (Xanax), may have relatively nonspecific actions on a variety of neurotransmitter systems (e.g., Charney & Heninger, 1985). Futhermore, Chapter 11 presents evidence that all drugs, whether they are thought to affect primarily one or the other neurotransmitter system, do not seem to block panic directly. Rather, any effectiveness seems due to a general anxiolytic action.

Nevertheless, some clear differences are apparent. For example, tricyclic antidepressants seem to demonstrate anxiolytic effects for very different reasons than benzodiazepines do. Specifically, the hypothetical direct effect of tricyclics on the noradrenergic system at first produces some increase in anxiety (which may account for initial high dropout rates when panic disorder is treated by imipramine), followed by a down-regulation of beta-adrenergic receptors. Interestingly, psychological exposure-based treatments may work in the same way, through a process described as "toughening up" (reviewed in Chapter 8). But benzodiazepine and perhaps drugs that block beta-adrenergic receptors (e.g., beta-blockers) interfere with this toughening-up process (Gray, 1985)—a factor that may account for extremely high relapse rates following withdrawal from benzodiazepines (see Chapter 11).

In any case, the exploration of biological systems will be relatively barren without a full integration of the functioning of the cortex into any system. As Uhde, Boulenger, et al. (1984) point out, anxiety, and perhaps panic specifically, are most likely multiply loaded in the brain because of their important survival value. Both the noradrenergic system and the serotonergic system, organized with cell bodies in the brain stem and having diffuse projections throughout the brain, are capable of the global function of alerting and alarming the organism.

Several ambitious biological theorists have attempted this Herculean feat of integration, most notably Gray (1982). In Gray's theory, the biological bases of feedback systems are integrated with the more basic systems of arousal discussed above. Specifically, Gray suggests that noradrenergic (as well as serotonergic) afferents are anxiogenic to the extent that they innervate the septo-hippocampal system under conditions of stress. These areas in turn receive input from neocortical projections that pass through a variety of regions of the brain. Gray suggests that the central task of this overall system is to compare actual with expected stimuli. If there is discordance between actual and expected stimuli, or if the predicted stimulus is aversive, then this system, which Gray terms the "behavioral inhibition system" (see Chapter 2), takes control of the organism and produces the increased attention, vigilance, scanning, and interruption of ongoing motor behavior that are characteristic of anxiety. The fact that language and meaning structures are the most common stimuli for anxiety in humans requires a complex neurobiological system.

Implicit in Gray's theory is a relatively integrated and interdependent neurobiological system, necessarily involving not only all discrete neurotransmitter systems, but also higher cortical functions. Among other things,

[Cortical areas] afford a route by which language functions of the neocortex can control the activities of the limbic structures which are the chief neural substrate of anxiety. In turn, limbic structures, via subicular and hippocampal projections to the entorhinal cortex, are able to scan verbally coded stores of information when performing the functions allotted to them in the theory outlined above. In this way, it is possible for human anxiety to be triggered by verbal stimuli (relatively independently of ascending monoaminergic influences) and to utilize verbally coded strategies to cope with perceived threats. It is for this reason, if the theory is correct, that lesions to the prefrontal and cingulate cortices are effective in cases of anxiety that are resistant to drug therapy (Powell, 1979). (Gray, 1985, p. 10)

Issues raised by Gray's theory are discussed further in Chapter 7.

Yet another possibility exists. From a functional and phenomenological point of view, panic does seem different from generalized anxiety. To echo a theme running throughout this book, panic seems clearly to be the pathological experience of an alarm reaction associated with clear action tendencies of immediate escape. Generalized anxiety, on the other hand, seems to be the pathological expression of our motivational and operational system for dealing with day-to-day conflicts. The function here is to organize and enhance performance to deal better with the task or conflict at hand. This would explain why novelty has effects similar to those of conflict in animal paradigms for studying anxiety. Panic is intense, but of short duration; it is accompanied by a variety of marked somatic symptoms that are at once more varied and more intense than those found in generalized anxiety. Generalized anxiety is more chronic than panic and usually has a more gradual onset and offset. Finally, generalized anxiety occurs in the absence of panic, and panic seems to occur in the absence of generalized anxiety (i.e., when one is relatively relaxed; Cohen et al., 1985), although these results are only preliminary at present.

If panic is fear, as I am suggesting, the emotion theorists would remind us that fear is fundamentally a behavioral act (Izard, 1977; Izard & Blumberg, 1985). As such, panic may not have a specific neurobiology separate from that of "anxiety" or "stress," since it is a coherent action tendency most likely stored (programmed) deep in memory. In the same way, any number of purposeful acts may have similar neurobiology but different functions. The only distinctive biological characteristic may be the marked physiological changes. And all of these changes serve one purpose: to support instant action such as escape. This purpose can explain many facts. For example, the tendency to hyperventilate often present during laboratory-provoked panic (e.g., J. M. Gorman et al., 1986) is there to support the programmed action tendency of escape by providing the heart and muscles with adequate oxygen. If escape were to take place, the "problem" of hyperventilation would not occur, since the exercise

206

would compensate for the respiratory alkalosis. Thus, hyperventilation would not be a *cause* of panic, but simply another aspect of the action tendency.

The only neurobiology associated with panic, in this view, would be the activation of a diffuse stress response or (perhaps) Gray's behavioral inhibition system, which has a strong genetic component. The increase in vigilance associated with the behavioral inhibition system would then lower the threshold for panic action tendencies, as suggested in Figure 5.1.

The Reciprocal Relationship of Neurobiology and Psychology

There is strong evidence, some of it reviewed above, that neurotransmitter system functions in isolation are insufficient to account for anxiety, even in animal models. Rather, one must superimpose psychological constructs, such as meaning and interpretations or attributions, as well as conditioning and learned coping responses. For example, Segal and Bloom (1976) stimulated the locus ceruleus in awake rats. They found that electrical activity or firing rate of hippocampal neurons was either increased or decreased, depending on prior learned associations the animal had made with specific stimuli. Furthermore, there is good evidence that noradrenergic alterations can be conditioned in such a way that merely returning the animal to a cage where it has been previously shocked is sufficient to produce substantial noradrenergic activity. These observations are consistent with the seeming ease with which emotional states are quickly conditioned (see Chapter 6). Noradrenergic functioning also seems strongly influenced by the adequacy of coping responses, as in a learned helplessness paradigm (Anisman, 1984). This has been demonstrated for serotonergic functioning, as noted above (Maser & Gallup, 1974). Similar observations can be made concerning animal paradigms involving conflict, which may underlie more generalized anxiety. As we have known for a long time, catecholamine secretion is strongly affected by psychological factors. For example, Cassens, Roffman, Kuruc, Orsulak, and Schildkraut (1980) demonstrated clear increases in MHPG in rats after exposure to previously neutral stimuli that had been paired with stress (conditioned stimuli). Most recently, Bandura, Taylor, Williams, Mefford, and Barchas (1985) demonstrated that changes in perceived self-efficacy alter catecholamine secretion.

As Gray (1985) observes, one cannot get away from attributing complex interactions between feeling and cognition to the rat if one is attempting to make sense of many experimental observations. "The animal's brain must detect nonreward centrally, send signals to the autonomic nervous system, receive efferents informing it of the consequent peripheral autonomic disturbance, and alter behavior accordingly" (Gray, 1985,

p. 24), much as postulated long ago in the James–Lange theory of emotion.

From another perspective, other scientists such as Kandel (1983) are working out the molecular and neurobiological basis of the development of anxiety in organisms low on the phylogenetic scale, such as sea snails (*Aplysia*). Using classical fear conditioning paradigms, Kandel has observed profound changes in synaptic strength and number of receptors as a function of learning and experience. These results recall the work mentioned above on alteration of the number of benzodiazepine receptors as a function of learning and experience (Paul & Skolnick, 1978, 1981).

One fact noted earlier is that chronic arousal may be a biological marker for most anxiety disorders. However, it is not entirely clear whether chronic overarousal is directly inherited, as some evidence would suggest, or whether it is the product of a complex psychobiological interaction. The work of Kandel (1983) and others on the biology of learning indicates that at the level of individual cells, increases in both receptors and neurotransmitters involved in fear conditioning seem to be permanent as a result of learning. Kandel (1983) speculates that the very genetic structure of cells within the central nervous system is changed as a result of learning. Specific inactivated genes become active during learning, leading to such changes in structure as the increase in receptors. If the behavior is extinguished, the change is reversed. Perhaps some biological disposition that is even more basic interacts with learning at a cellular level to produce the kind of chronic hyperarousal that occurs in individuals with anxiety disorders.

Whatever the eventual model, it is clear that our science cannot proceed without a full consideration and integration of both biological and psychological factors. With these principles in mind, I now begin to outline models of the etiology of panic and anxiety.

6

The Origins of Panic: True Alarms, False Alarms, and Learned Alarms

We have only just begun to collect information on the nature of panic. Much of what is known has been presented in the preceding chapters. But the accumulating evidence points to a complex biopsychosocial process. This process involves the interaction of an ancient alarm system, crucial for survival, with inappropriate and maladaptive learning and subsequent cognitive and affective complications. Some of the thinking on the origins of pathological panic presented in theoretical form below is speculative, but there should be enough coherence within the theory to enable investigators to design research protocols that result in confirmation or disconfirmation. This chapter beings with a brief analysis of the alarm system most commonly known as fear.

TRUE ALARMS

There is general agreement that fear occurs when we are directly threatened with a dangerous, perhaps life-threatening, event. An impending attack from wild animals is something few of us experience today, but our ancestors knew this threat well in millenia past. This history may account for our somewhat greater susceptibility to becoming "alarmed" in the presence of snakes and mountain lions (Cook, Hodes, & Lang, 1986; Seligman, 1971). Relevant threats today include speeding vehicles, guns, drowning, or seeing the safety of our children threatened. Under these conditions, the emotion of fear mobilizes us physically and cognitively for quick action and sometimes "superhuman" efforts. Most typically, running away or escaping is the behavioral manifestation of fear. Occasionally, directed action to counter the threat is apparent, such as attacking a predator or single-handedly lifting an automobile so that a child trapped underneath can escape. These reactions represent Cannon's emergency reaction characterized by the compelling action tendencies of "fight or flight." Sometimes these actions are counterproductive, as in the the case of a drowning victim vainly struggling when the rational response would be to lie still and attempt to float. The ancient response of "freezing" (tonic immobility) may be called forth if other action tendencies such as escape or aggression are ineffective or not available and one is under direct attack by a predator, as mentioned in Chapters 1 and 5. Most theorists would agree that these basic responses are primative alarm reactions observed far down the phylogenetic scale. As such, they have profound evolutionary significance.

FALSE ALARMS

Only recently have we noticed the phenomenon of false alarms. What I have earlier termed "spontaneous" or "uncued" panic seems nearly identical in all respects to fear phenomenologically, except for the ability to specify an antecedent. The evidence for this has been reviewed in Chapters 3 and 4. The very definition of panic, specifying as it does sudden feelings of marked apprehension and impending doom that are associated with a wide range of distressing physical sensations, would certainly qualify as a definition for fear in other contexts. While few would disagree that panic seems to be intense fear, a goal for future research is to compare directly the expressive-behavioral, neurobiological, and cognitive aspects of intense fear and uncued panic.

In any case, if fear is an alarm, then we seem to be faced with the phenomenon of false alarms, where marked fear or panic occurs in the absence of any life-threatening stimulus, learned or unlearned. How common are false alarms, and why do they occur?

False alarms or panic attacks seem to be far more prevalent in the general population than was assumed previously. In fact, studies from around the world are converging to suggest that occasional panic attacks occur relatively frequently in the general population.

Detailed evidence on the frequency of panic has been reviewed in Chapter 3. For example, data from Norton and colleagues (Norton et al., 1986; Norton, Harrison, et al., 1985) suggest that over 30% of a large group of individuals reported at least one panic attack in the past year (see Table 3.8). Typically, attacks were less intense and less frequent in these nonclinical panickers than in patients. Panic attacks also occurred during sleep in nonclinical panickers and aggregated more strongly in the families of these individuals than in families of subjects who did not panic (Norton et al., 1986). As noted in Chapter 3, more and more studies are confirming these results. The frequency of panic in the general population plays an important role in the models of anxiety disorders outlined below.

Although false alarms seem remarkably prevalent, relatively few people seek treatment for this problem—an issue that is discussed further below. Nevertheless, it is important to determine the "causes" of false alarms, since they may represent the beginning of panic disorder, although false alarms alone clearly are not sufficient to account for panic disorder. Unfortunately, we are not very far along in our search for the causes of false alarms. Ongoing lines of investigation are targeting several areas, among which are biological dysregulation, a history of separation anxiety, and stress. The strongest web of evidence implicates life events and resulting stress in the genesis of initial false alarms (panic).

BIOLOGICAL DYSREGULATION

It would certainly seem logical that a biological dysregulation underlies false alarms. After all, the very nature of false alarms specifies that there is no readibly identifiable external or internal antecedent or cue. For this reason, investigators have attempted to identify a biological marker in patients with panic disorder that would be associated with an underlying biological dysregulation, or that at least would point in the direction of a biological dysregulation. This research has been reviewed in Chapters 4 and 5. As I conclude in those chapters, at the present time there is no evidence for any specific biological marker; nor, for that matter, is there evidence for any important neurobiological differences between patients with panic disorder and nonpanickers. The exception, of course, is chronic hyperarousal, which seems a biological and/or psychological marker of sorts. But chronic hyperarousal and its (as yet undiscovered) biological underpinnings characterize almost all anxiety disorders, as noted in Chapter 5, and would not constitute a specific biological marker for panic. However, hyperarousal may interact with other variables and contribute to the genesis of false alarms in a manner suggested below.

As noted in Chapter 3, there is always the possibility that we are looking in the wrong place. Patients with panic disorder present with a number of emotional complications. It may be that their panic attacks are no longer purely false alarms, but rather learned alarms that are contaminated by substantial emotional interference in the form of generalized anxiety and depression, and therefore present somewhat differently than does a pure false alarm (e.g., Taylor *et al.*, 1986). If this is so, investigators in their search for crucial biological markers may be better off studying people with infrequent panic attacks who have not yet presented for treatment.

SEPARATION ANXIETY

A second intriguing hypothesis concerns the relationship of separation anxiety in children to the later development of false alarms (and panic disorder). Separation anxiety has occupied a prominent place in many theories of child development and psychopathology.

Early clinical reports (Klein & Fink, 1962) suggested that the panic attacks seen in agoraphobic patients may well be a "mature" expression of the type of distress and panic some children evidence upon separation, particularly from their mothers. Rachel Gittelman has written most extensively on this topic and has evaluated evidence, both pro and con, concerning the relationship of separation anxiety to the development of panic disorder and agoraphobia (e.g., Gittelman & Klein, 1985). Generally, there are three lines of evidence supporting this relationship: similarity of drug treatment effects for separation anxiety and adult agoraphobia; family concordance for separation anxiety and agoraphobia; and history of childhood separation anxiety in agoraphobic adults.

Gittelman-Klein and Klein (1973) treated 44 severely school-phobic children with imipramine and found that, when compared to a group receiving placebo, most of the children reported feeling better, had fewer complaints on school days, and showed less distress at separation as reported by the mothers. Since some studies indicate that imipramine is effective for panic disorder (see Chapter 11), these investigators suggest that panic and separation anxiety may be similar.

Weissman, Leckman, Merikangas, Gammon, and Prusoff (1984), in a well-designed study, examined the family concordance of separation anxiety and adult anxiety. They determined the prevalence of separation anxiety in the 6- to 18-year-old children of depressed and normal adults identified in community surveys. These adult patients, diagnosed by direct structured clinical interview, were classified into four groups: (1) depressed with no anxiety disorder, (2) depressed with agoraphobia, (3) depressed with panic disorder, and (4) depressed with generalized anxiety disorder at any time in their adult life. Separation anxiety was diagnosed in 24% of the children whose parents had a diagnosis of both depression and agoraphobia or panic. In contrast, none of the children of adults with pure depression and only 6% of the children of parents with depression and generalized anxiety disorder reported separation anxiety. This suggests a connection between separation anxiety and panic disorder, with or without agoraphobic avoidance.

Finally, in some recently analyzed data, Gittelman and Klein (1985) report on the incidence of separation anxiety in agoraphobic adults. These data were collected from clinical interviews with adult agoraphobics who were asked to recall separation anxiety in their childhood. This method suffers from the weaknesses of any retrospective study, but it is one of the few studies of its type to employ a control group consisting of simple phobics. Nevertheless, in both childhood and adolescence (the periods examined), agoraphobic patients recalled significantly more separation anxiety than the comparison group of patients with simple phobia who were also asked about these recollections. Intriguingly, this group difference was due entirely to a high prevalence of separation anxiety disorder in female agoraphobics. No differences were found between male agoraphobics and simple phobics. The data for female agoraphobics are presented in Table 6.1; it can be seen that fully 48% of female agoraphobics reported separation anxiety, compared to only 20% of females with simple phobia.

Unfortunately for the separation anxiety model, considerable evidence exists contradicting these positive results. For example, Thyer, Nesse, Curtis, and Cameron (1986) administered carefully structured questionnaires to 23 panic disorder patients and 28 small-animal phobics and found essentially no differences in reports of childhood separation anxiety. This research group (Thyer, Nesse, Cameron, & Curtis, 1985) had also found no differences in reports of separation anxiety when comparing agoraphobics to simple phobics. Other studies have also failed to find an increased incidence of reports of separation anxiety during the childhood of agoraphobics (Buglass et al., 1977; Parker, 1979). Examining it from another perspective, Tennant, Hurry, and Bebbington (1982) found no association between forced childhood separations due to illnesses or other family circumstances and the later development of anxiety and depression. Similarly, Gittelman-Klein (1975) failed to find any incidence of agoraphobia or panic disorder in the parents of 45 school-phobic children.

One cannot say that the connection between separation anxiety and panic disorder is convincing at this time, although there are some intrigu-

TABLE 6.1. Separation Anxiety in Childhood in Women Patients ($n = 95$)

	Diagnosis			
	Agoraphobia		Simple phobia	
Separation anxiety	n	(%)	n	(%)
Absent	17	(37)	34	(69)
Present	22	(48)	10	(20)
Never separated	7	(15)	5	(10)
Total	46	(100)	49	(100)

Note. $\chi^2 = 10.42$, 2 df, $p < .01$, two-tailed. Adapted from Gittelman, R., & Klein, D. F. (1985). Childhood separation anxiety and adult agoraphobia. In A. H. Tuma & J. D. Maser (Eds.), *Anxiety and the anxiety disorders* (p. 398). Hillsdale, NJ: Erlbaum. Copyright 1985 by Lawrence Erlbaum Associates. Adapted by permission.

ing hints of a possible relationship. While one can probably dismiss the one study on the equivalence of drug effects, the family concordance data (Weissman *et al.*, 1984) and the history of separation anxiety in female agoraphobics as documented by clinical interview (Gittelman & Klein, 1985) are the strongest threads of evidence. Of course, the children were not interviewed directly in the family concordance study, and it is possible that this represents selective perception on the part of depressed parents with panic and agoraphobia. But the Gittelman and Klein (1985) data on reported history of separation anxiety seem to converge with other information to be reported below.

Specifically, Gittelman and Klein reported a history of separation anxiety only in women with current agoraphobia. Chambless and Mason (1986) found that sex-role inventory measures of masculinity were inversely related to severity of avoidance behavior in agoraphobia. That is, the less "masculine" the scores on these inventories, the more the subjects tended to use avoidance as a coping mechanism, regardless of biological sex. What these data suggest (the suggestion is taken up in detail in Chapter 10) is that the incidence of panic in men and women is actually nearly equal, but that women cope with panic by avoiding, whereas men tend to cope with panic in other ways, such as consuming alcohol. This difference in coping strategies may account for the high percentage of agoraphobics who are females. What Gittelman and Klein may have discovered is that separation anxiety reflects an early expression of a greater tendency toward avoidance, which in females is culturally acceptable in our society. Therefore, reports of separation anxiety in the history of female agoraphobics, if they are borne out by subsequent research, may simply reflect the early expression of a generalized method of coping with stress and anxiety. If this is true, then the relationship between separation anxiety and subsequent panic may be only incidental to the stronger relationship between separation anxiety and the use of avoidance as a coping mechanism for stress or anxiety in general. In other words, if one sees children, particularly females, avoiding (and/or refusing to separate) in childhood, one can predict that they will continue to cope with any stress or anxiety as adults by avoiding. While interesting, this observation tells us very little about the causes of false alarms.

It is also possible that females are more inclined to *report* separation anxiety because of the same cultural factors that seem to determine the use of avoidance as a method of coping with panic. That is, any differences may be an artifact of selective reporting. It is difficult to get around these issues in retrospective studies.

In addition, it is not entirely clear how the phenomenon of separation distress, as studied intensively by the developmentalists and reviewed in Chapter 2, relates to clinical manifestations of childhood separation anxiety on the one hand, or to the occurrence of forced separations during childhood as studied by Tennant *et al.* (1982) on the other. Evidence reviewed in Chapter 2 indicates that separation distress may begin as early as 4 months, reaching a peak at 13–18 months, and thereafter diminishing in the 3rd year of life (Emde *et al.*, 1976). Shiller *et al.* (1986) suggests that separation distress in infants more closely reflects the basic emotion of anger rather than fear, as noted in Chapter 2. These investigators (Emde *et al.*, 1976; Shiller *et al.*, 1986) consider stranger distress rather than separation distress to be the innate precursor of a fear or panic response in humans and the first sign of the emergence of a coherent fear system. As concluded in Chapter 2, variations in the intensity of stranger distress may have a stronger relationship to the later adult phenomenon of false alarms than separation distress may have.

The relationship of forced separations as studied by Tennant *et al.* (1982) in later childhood to separation distress during this early crucial period is also not clear. It would seem from this research that many children undergo forced separations of one type or another during childhood after the age of 3 and during adolescence without any ill effects whatsoever.

To enable us to determine that the clinical presentation of separation anxiety is an important precursor to panic rather than a learned method of coping with stress or anxiety, several lines of evidence would have to converge. First, a relationship needs to be established between separation distress during the crucial biological period peaking at about 18 months and later separation anxiety in childhood or adolescence. With this evidence, we might begin to talk of a specific connection linking the seemingly hard-wired response of separation distress to the clinical syndrome of separation anxiety and the subsequent development of panic. Without this evidence, there would be little reason to assume that separation anxiety is anything more than a learned and culturally acceptable method for coping in families that are anxiety-prone—a trait for which we already have good evidence of familial aggregation and perhaps genetic transmission (see Chapter 5). In other words, the behavior of avoiding separation in children would have no direct connection with later false alarms. Rather, both would be consequences of the underlying biological trait of anxiety proneness.

STRESS

A remarkably consistent observation of biological and psychological clinicians and investigators has been the evidence of negative life events preceding the first panic attack in patients who later present with panic disorder and agoraphobia. What makes this observation interesting is that few of these patients can identify a precipitating event when asked a question such as "what caused your first panic attack?" As noted above, the defining characteristic of false alarms is that, at least initially, they are uncued and unexpected (spontaneous). However, systematic questioning about life events reveals that approximately 80% of these patients describe clearly one or more negative life events preceding their first panic (Buglass et al., 1977; Doctor, 1982; Finlay-Jones & Brown, 1981; Mathews, Gelder, & Johnston, 1981; Roth, 1959; Snaith, 1968; Solyom et al., 1974; Uhde, Boulenger, Roy-Byrne, Geraci, Vittone, & Post, 1985). For example, Shafar (1976) reported precipitating stressors in 83% of her sample, and Sheehan, Sheehan, and Minichiello (1981) reported such stressors in 91% of their large sample. The largest series of its type has been reported by Doctor (1982), who interviewed 404 agoraphobics and found separation and loss (31%), relationship problems (30%), and new responsibility (20%) to be the most common precipitants of panic and agoraphobia. Sometimes these questions are answered by the patient without any awareness that there may be a connection between the two phenomena.

Typical of these studies and the types of negative life events reported are results from an early series of 58 agoraphobics (53 females and 5 males) from our clinic (Last, Barlow, & O'Brien, 1984c). The occurrence of negative life events was assessed by a structured clinical interview. Categories of life events and the frequencies with which they were reported are presented in Table 6.2. Of the 58 agoraphobics, 81% reported one or more of

TABLE 6.2. Life Events Occurring Prior to Onset of Agoraphobia

Precipitating events	Frequency ($n = 58$)	%
Interpersonal conflict situations		
Marital/familial	20	34.5
Death/illness of significant other	9	15.5
Total	29	50.0
Endocrine/physiological reactions		
Birth/miscarriage/hysterectomy	17	29.3
Drug reaction	7	12.1
Total	24	41.4
Other		
Major surgery/illness (other than gynecological)	2	3.4
Stress at work/school	2	3.4
Move	2	3.4

Note. Frequencies exceed the number of patients interviewed because many patients reported more than one significant life event occurring prior to their first panic attack. From Last, C. G., Barlow, D. H., & O'Brien, G. T. (1984). Precipitants of agoraphobia: Role of stressful life events. Psychological Reports, 54, 567–570. Copyright 1984 by Psychological Reports. Reprinted by permission.

these stressful life events, while 19% reported no significant life events prior to the development of agoraphobia. For heuristic purposes, we collapsed life events reported by our patients into conflict events versus endocrine/physiological reactions, and the results are presented in Table 6.2. These two major categories accounted for approximately 91% of the life events reported. Liebowitz and Klein (1979) also reported a large proportion of individuals developing panic attacks after experiencing endocrinological changes, and Klein (1964), in an early survey, noted "endocrine fluctuations" (e.g., those associated with birth, menopause, and gynecological surgery) as events immediately preceding panic in a subgroup of patients.

Perhaps the best study in this group was also one of the earliest. Roth (1959) found that 96% of a sample of 135 agoraphobics reported some type of background stress preceding the development of their disorder. The stressors of 83% of these patients were categorized as follows: bereavement or a suddenly developing serious illness in a close relative or friend (37%); illness or acute danger to the patient (31%); and severance of family ties or acute domestic stress (15%). In an additional 13% of the women, panic began during pregnancy or after childbirth and was characterized by an abrupt onset shortly after delivery. What makes this study important is that Roth was the only investigator to employ a control group. He found that the incidence of identifiable stressors in his agoraphobic patients was significantly greater than that found in 50 control patients suffering from some other form of "neurosis," as well as in 50 additional individuals who had recently recovered from a physical illness but had never suffered a psychiatric disorder. Roy-Byrne, Geraci, and Uhde (1986) and Faravelli (1985) have also found a greater occurrence of negative and more impactful life events in panic patients compared to healthy controls in the year prior to the first panic.

These data, consistent as they are, have led many to assume that stress plays a major role in the etiology of panic (Margraf, Ehlers, & Roth, 1986b; Mathews *et al.*, 1981; Tearnan, Telch, & Keefe, 1984). But what can we conclude from these intriguing observations? While the consistency of these observations attests to the reliability of reports of this relationship, one cannot escape the fact that these are retrospective reports. Patients suffering from panic may be predisposed to recall negative and threatening life events. Although there is no evidence that anxious patients selectively recall mood-congruent material (as opposed to recognizing threatening or mood-congruent stimuli), it would not be surprising if some evidence supporting mood-congruent anxious recall were to turn up (see Chapter 2). Finally, only the Roth (1959) and Roy-Byrne *et al.* (1986) studies employed control groups. Of these two, only the Roth study utilized an appropriate control group, consisting of patients with other "neurotic" disorders not including panic. However, the nature of these other "neurotic" disorders is not clear, since a different nomenclature was in use at that time. By any reasonable assessment, we have hardly begun to analyze the relationship of stressful life events to panic. This area of study is fraught with methodological difficulties and logical pitfalls (Depue & Monroe, 1986). Only prospective studies with carefully devised frequent measurement in clearly defined, well-diagnosed clinical populations will begin to provide definitive answers on this relationship.

It is also becoming increasingly apparent that stress, as defined by negative life events, seems to be associated with the onset or exacerbation of any number of physical and psychological disorders. For example, relationships have been demonstrated between stress and cardiovascular disease, complications associated with pregnancy and birth, tuberculosis, multiple sclerosis, diabetes, arthritis and even chronic back pain (Flor, Turk, & Birbaumer, 1985), to name only a few disorders. Of particular interest is the demonstrated association between stressful life events and depression (e.g., Depue, 1979; Hammen, Mayol, deMayo, & Marks, 1986; Lewinsohn, Hoberman, & Rosenbaum, in press; Lloyd, 1980).

The most common explanation for the effects of stress is the well-known stress–diathesis model. In this model, stress precipitates and facilitates a particular physical or emotional disorder to which the individual is already predisposed. In the case of psychophysiological stress responses such as hypertension and ulcers, the "weak organ" model best expresses this hypothesis. Essentially (and simplistically), the effect of stress is to overactivate one's (physiological) system until the weakest part of the system breaks down. This weakness may be constitutional or a result of earlier traumatic processes (Selye, 1956, 1976).

Within psychological disorders, the hypothetical process is a little less clear because of the methodological difficulties mentioned above, particularly in operationalizing the psychological disorder. In the area of depression, methodologically rigorous studies are just beginning to appear (e.g., Hammen et al., 1986; Lewinsohn et al., in press), although the relationship of stressful life events to depression has been hypothesized for years. Many of these recent studies have not adequately sampled the general population, and those that have often produced weak or confusing patterns of results (e.g., Breslau & Davis, 1986). The best-designed studies are explored in the next chapter, which compares and contrasts the etiology of anxiety and depression.

A common finding across all disorders studied is that even acute stress, usually defined as a negative life event, correlates only modestly with psychopathology. That is, while there may be a clear association (as it seems there is between stress and panic), a large number of people, even if "prone" to a disorder, experience similar life events without developing panic or some alternative disorder.

In this regard, an increasing body of evidence clearly demonstrating the existence of variables that moderate the effects of stress, as well as the biological reactions associated with stress (noted in Chapter 5), is worth mentioning briefly. These moderating variables account for some of the individual variability in response to stress (e.g., Depue & Monroe, 1986; Sarason & Sarason, 1981). Since stress, both chronic and acute, is so much a part of our lives, how is it that some of us survive it without ill effects even if we are "prone" to a specific stress-related disorder, while others come down with any of the variety of problems or disorders mentioned above? The primary factors that seem capable of moderating effects of stress are (1) individual cognitive and personality characteristics and (2) social support. For example, Johnson and Sarason (1978) have reported that subjects will respond differentially to stress, depending on their perceptions of control that they have over their environment and the stressful events within that environment. Using the Internal–External Locus of Control Scale, Johnson and Sarason found that individuals with an external locus of control (reflecting their own perception of a relative lack of control over events in their environment) experienced higher levels of anxiety and depression under high life stress than did those with an internal locus of control. Bandura *et al.* (1985), in a study described in Chapter 5, found that a biological consequence of stress, catecholamine secretion, was modified as a function of changes in self-efficacy. The important issue of perceptions of control is discussed further below. The moderating effect of social support is also an area receiving increased attention and is considered repeatedly in subsequent chapters.

It is very possible that other, as yet unspecified individual moderator variables exist. For example, neurobiological activity may increase susceptibility to negative life events because of summative effect on autonomic responding occasioned by stress. These complex relationships are only beginning to be understood, and little research on variables that moderate stress is available with patients suffering from anxiety disorders (although see Chapter 13 on post-traumatic stress disorder). For this reason, conclusions are tentative.

CONCLUSIONS

The circumstantial evidence supporting a crucial role for stress—not only in the genesis of false alarms, but also in the etiology of all anxiety and affective disorders—is strong. This requires detailed examination of the nature of stress and why some vulnerable individuals become either anxious or depressed or both when subjected to negative life events. This evidence, in turn, leads to an exploration of the essential differences between anxiety and depression and the place of panic in this broader perspective. These complex issues are addressed in the next chapter.

Suffice it to suggest for now that a variety of evidence indicates that certain individuals are susceptible to stress produced by negative life events because of constitutional factors, relatively low social support, and/or some combination of personality and cognitive dispositions; these individuals react to negative life events in much the same way they might react to physical threats from wild animals or snakes. That is, they evidence a fear response much as they would when confronted with any other threat to their well-being. As suggested in Chapter 5 and outlined in the next chapter, it is likely that false alarms are not a direct response to stress. Rather, these alarms are mediated initially by neurobiological responses to stress. The idea that initial panic attacks "spike off" a stress response will bring to mind the robust finding (reviewed in Chapter 4) that high baseline anxiety predicts successful provocation of panic in the laboratory. In any case, because the fear response is not temporally associated (within hours) with the negative life event, the individual is unable to specify an antecedent to or a "cause" of the fear. Indeed, there is no antecedent that would require an immediate alarm reaction, with all of its associated action tendencies of fight or flight. For that reason, the alarm is false.

If the stress–diathesis model of false alarms and panic is correct, then one would predict that infrequent nonclinical panickers would continue having occasional false alarms of varying severity, depending on their biological reactivity, their threshold for action tendencies associated with alarms, the intensity and frequency of negative life events, and the presence of moderating variables such as adequate coping responses. But even when circumstances line up correctly, the relationship does not stay as simple as this. The overwhelming experience of panic in some individuals seems to insure that learning will take place that markedly affects the subsequent course of false alarms.

LEARNED ALARMS

Before the critical issue of learned alarms is discussed, it is necessary to consider briefly what we now know about how one learns to be afraid. Although many emotions theorists consider fear to be innate and universally present across cultures and species, none would suggest that all objects or situations that elicit fear are also innate. Indeed, it is crucial for the survival of any species to be flexible. "Flexibility," in this context, implies a capacity to learn quickly to fear new threatening objects or situations. Although a far more complex issue than previously assumed, one of the fundamental laws of learning, discovered and elaborated in the laboratories of experimental psychology, is that fear can be learned by a process of association. In fact, this universally acknowledged process is central to many theoretical approaches to anxiety and psychopathology. For example, both psychoanalytic and behavioral approaches posit that fear and anxiety can be associated with neutral objects (signal anxiety) or conditional stimuli (CSs), although there may be disagreements on the source of the original anxiety and the degree to which symbolic processes might be involved. The importance of this associational process, whether one is "aware" of it or not, cannot be underestimated. While it is a very normal psychological process, it also seems a crucial step in the development of psychopathology under certain conditions. Echoing the discussion of fundamental ancient emotions in Chapter 2, this form of learning is also primitive, heavily biological, and subject to evolutionary pressures. It occurs across cultures and species and far down the phylogenetic scale. Researchers have isolated the process underlying the learning of fear at the level of the single cell in the earthworm, as described in Chapter 5 (Kandel, 1983). Although this is not the only way one learns to be afraid, it is important, in the context of the present discussion, to describe this process, most commonly called "classical" or "Pavlovian" conditioning, in some detail. It is also important to note at the outset that this process cannot account for either panic attacks or panic disorder; however, conditioning plays a role in a more comprehensive theory of panic and panic disorder, outlined below.

FEAR CONDITIONING

The paradigm (or operation) of classical fear conditioning, familar to everyone who has read elementary psychology, is that neutral stimuli that are present during a fear-arousing experience acquire the capacity to elicit fear. This fear is termed "conditional" or "conditioned," because only under certain conditions (the symbolic or actual reappearance of the neutral stimulus) will fear (the conditioned response, or CR) occur. Typically, the strength of the fear response depends on a number of factors. These factors, which include, but are not limited to, the number of pairings of the new CS with the unconditioned stimulus (UCS; the original source of the fear) and the intensity of fear evoked by the UCS. Stimuli that are similar to the CS also come to elicit fear as a direct function of their similarity; the more similarity, the more fear. This relationship between the CR and similarity of the evoking stimulus to the CS is called a "generalization gradient." Watson and Raynor (1920) conducted some of the earliest research demonstrating these principles in humans. In this well-known study, a young child, Albert, was exposed to a loud noice (the USC) while viewing a rat (the CS) on several occasions. Albert subsequently developed a conditioned fear to rats that spread or "generalized" to other objects that resembled rats, such as rabbits and other furry animals. Most of the principles of classical fear conditioning have been well worked out in the laboratories of experimental psychology over the ensuing decades (cf. Eysenck, 1979). This is one of the most widely researched forms of affective learning.

Conditioning is also well established as a method of learning emotional responses in humans. One of the most dramatic examples, occurring daily in our major hospitals, involves the widespread acquisition of conditioned nausea in oncology patients undergoing chemotherapy (e.g., Redd & Andrykowski, 1982). Typically, these patients develop moderate to severe nausea reactions to any "neutral stimuli" associated with the administration of chemotherapy. Most usually, the stimuli are associated with nursing staff administering the therapy and can include sights, sounds, and often smell, such as a particular perfume or cologne. This effect is very strong. For example, 60–80% of a recent series of patients with Hodgkin disease clearly evidenced conditioning (Cella, Pratt, & Holland, 1986). Estimates from a review of a larger series of studies suggest that a variable but somewhat lower percentage of patients undergoing chemotherapy develop this response (Burish & Carey, 1986). Among factors that seem to account for conditionability (or lack of it) in these patients is the strength of the nausea-producing properties of the drug (the UCS) and the intensity of the initial nausea reaction.

To deal with this problem therapeutically, oncologists and psychologists working in cancer units have come up with a number of methods to counter and minimize the effects of classical conditioning. These methods are also derived from basic knowledge of classical conditioning elaborated in the animal laboratories (e.g., Cella *et al.*, 1986).

What is particularly interesting for our purposes is that this type of conditioning can be very rapid in both humans and animals. For example, in a theoretically interesting experiment that may have some bearing on the discussion of etiology below, Campbell, Sanderson, and Laverty (1964) produced an intense fear CR to neutral tones in just one trial. Ordinarily, this would be very unusual during classical fear conditioning, since a number of trials are usually required to condition fear successfully. However, one variable accounting for the speed of this response clearly stands out: Campbell *et al.* used succinylcholine as the UCS. This drug, once injected, produces respiratory paralysis in a matter of seconds. As a result, subjects cannot breathe and feel that they are suffocating and dying.

The results are seldom as dramatic in terms of clear conditioning effects as those reported in the experiments above, or those seen daily on the oncology ward (Barlow, 1978). One probable reason is that seldom is a UCS as powerful as succinylcholine or chemotherapy ever used in these paradigms. But there are other reasons as well.

MODIFICATIONS TO CONDITIONING THEORY

In the 1950s, with the rise of behavior therapy, it was widely assumed that all phobias were learned through simple traumatic conditioning (e.g.,

Wolpe, 1958) and that therapy involved extinction of these traumatically learned fears. The success of behavior therapy with phobias strengthened this assumption about etiology. By the late 1960s, however, it was becoming clear that traumatic conditioning alone could not account for the genesis of phobic reactions, since conditioning could not accommodate several facts about clinical phobias. Among other objections, it was noted that conditioning theory can not explain the selectivity of phobias (Marks, 1969). Specifically, why do we learn to fear some objects or situations more than other? Another objection specified the failure of phobias to extinguish despite repeated exposure to the CS—a phenomenon that is almost always seen in the animal laboratories (Rachman, 1977). Finally, it became clear that fears and phobias can be acquired through simple provision of information (instructions), as well as vicariously (Bandura, 1969; Rachman, 1977, 1978). The clinical implications of observational or instructional acquisition of phobias are discussed below and in subsequent chapters. At this point, it is important to turn our attention to recent developments in our knowledge of classical fear conditioning itself.

An early modification to classical fear conditioning theory was the avoidance learning model (Mowrer, 1947), which hypothesized that fears or phobias will fail to extinguish if one successfully learns to avoid the feared stimulus. The idea here was that substantial avoidance prevents the individual from "reality testing" or learning that there is no longer any reason to be afraid. This notion, known as the "two-factor theory," was popular for decades, since it seemed to explain why phobias do not extinguish: Fear is originally learned through classical conditioning and is subsequently maintained due to avoidance.

But various difficulties also arose with a strict transfer of this paradigm from animal laboratories to clinical phobia. Among these difficulties were obvious differences in the amount of fear or distress produced by avoidance conditioning paradigms when compared to that observed in clinical phobias. Animals seem to display no subjective distress after they learn to avoid the feared stimulus successfully, presumably because they do not encounter it. But the avoidance response itself is highly resistant to extinction. Clinical phobics, on the other hand, can often overcome their avoidance behavior, but they continue to experience marked distress in the feared situation. This "distress" does not always seem to extinguish. In fact, enduring these situations with dread is a defining characteristic of clinical phobia in DSM-III-R. This failure to extinguish is part of the "neurotic paradox" referred to in Chapter 1.

Modifications to this theory, specifying the importance of "cognitive" variables, seem necessary to account for the data (Seligman & Johnston, 1973). In fact, modern learning theorists have long since abandoned a mechanistic behavioral framework in studying animals. The new integrative approach employs a wide range of cognitive concepts, including, but not limited to, concepts of probability learning, information processing, and attention (e.g., Martin, 1983; Martin & Levey, 1985). The principles of conditioning or emotional learning have not been abandoned; the evidence is far too strong for that. But it is also clear that people will utilize their rational powers to analyze their irrational feelings. Thus are cognitive and emotional processes inextricably intermixed. In fact, this interaction and occasional conflict between rational and emotional (sometimes irrational) processes become the battleground on which emotional disorders are played out. While this notion will not be new to many clinicians (Freud, 1926/1959), the scientific developments specifying these interactions are new.

The two-factor theory has not fared particularly well, although it undoubtedly makes a contribution to understanding anxiety disorders, particularly when modified. What may be a more important modification to conditioning theory is why we seem to learn fears and phobias selectively (Seligman, 1971). One possibility is that certain types of objects or situations have become highly prepared for learning over the course of evolution, because this learning facilitates survival of the species. This explanation is the theory of evolutionary "preparedness," which integrates biological points of view with classical conditioning. Öhman and his colleagues performed the initial important work in this area (e.g., Öhman, Erixon, & Lofburg, 1975). Although this notion is still undergoing elaboration and has some weaknesses (see McNally, 1987, for a review), it is receiving increasing support (Cook *et al.*, 1986; Mineka, 1985b: Öhman, Dimberg, & Öst, 1985). The implication, then (as noted in Chapter 2), is that some aspect of what we learn to fear, in addition to the fear response itself, may be innate.

At this time, it is not entirely clear what makes a stimulus prepared for conditioning. For example, several investigators (e.g., Bennett-Levy & Marteau, 1984) have hypothesized that in humans certain stimulus configurations, such as rapid or abrupt movement in stimuli or objects that are discrepant from the human form, are significantly correlated with fear ratings. In other words, what are "prepared" are certain perceptual configurations, rather than complete objects such as snakes and spiders.

However, Pitman and Orr (1986) demonstrated that both anxiety patients and matched controls developed an emotional CR to pictures of angry faces but *not* pictures of neutral faces. The next finding in this study is particularly important: The CR in patients failed to extinguish, even though the electrodes were removed and they were *told* that no further mild shocks (the UCS) would occur. Normals, on the other hand demonstrated CR extinction. This difference in the process of extinction reflects the common finding reviewed in Chapter 2 that anxious or "neurotic" people condition more easily and extinguish more slowly. But this apparent biological vulnerability interacts with the type of object or situation with which one is faced. It is not hard to imagine how survival

224

might be associated with a propensity to respond fearfully to angry faces, much in the same way that it seems selectively associated with snakes and spiders. Of course, other explanations of these preliminary findings are still possible.

Another development is the demonstration by Cook *et al.* (1986) that certain UCSs "belong" with certain CSs in humans. These findings hark back to the work of Garcia and his colleagues, who observed very rapid (one-trial) development of aversion in animals to the taste of certain foods that had previously resulted in nausea or illness (e.g., Garcia, McGowan, & Green, 1972). It is easy to see how survival might be associated with the capacity to learn quickly to avoid poison food. Pairing another UCS, such as shock, with food would not produce learning as quickly or intensely, since this association is presumably not as important from an evolutionary point of view.

Another selective association to account for the prevalence of certain CSs among phobic disorders is proposed below. Specifically, situations or circumstances that prevent strong action tendencies of some emotional responses, such as alarms, are more likely to become CSs (phobic situations). Thus, situations that prevent, even partially, the powerful action tendency of escape during a false alarm (the unconditioned response, or UCR) most likely intensify the alarm further, resulting in strong emotional learning. Hence the prevalent feelings of being "trapped" in many phobias. More is said about this below.

In any case, discovery of these modifications or contradictions to a direct traumatic conditioning theory of the etiology of phobias led some to abandon conditioning theory altogether as a viable explanation for how one learns fear. But the majority of investigators working directly in the area (e.g., Rachman, 1977) concluded that conditioning in general and fear conditioning in particular clearly occurs in a variety of individuals (e.g., Pitman & Orr, 1986), although fear can also be learned in other ways, and the process of fear conditioning is subject to a variety of qualifications.

THE ETIOLOGY OF PHOBIA

With this in mind, we can now consider ways in which false alarms may be learned and implications of these for the etiology of phobia. For years, investigators have searched the histories of phobic individuals for signs of traumatic conditioning. This line of inquiry has all of the weaknesses inherent in asking any patient with a disorder to recall situations or facts that may have occurred many years ago. Nevertheless, the research has produced interesting information. The primary finding is that most phobics cannot recall a traumatic conditioning event to account for the development of their fear or phobia. For example, Rimm, Janda, Lancaster, Nahl, and Dittmar (1977) found that 36% of their phobic subjects could not account for their fears in terms of past learning experiences of any kind. This finding is even more apparent for minor fears. For example, Murray and Foote (1979) found that most college students who were afraid of snakes could not recall a bad experience with snakes. Rather, they had acquired their fears through verbal or vicarious means. Usually they reported hearing about the dangers of snakes from a parent or observing a parent behave fearfully in the presence of snakes. In fact, casting further doubt on the importance of traumatic conditioning, Murray and Foote reported on three individuals in their large sample who had actually been bitten by snakes but reported no fear whatsoever!

One of the strongest demonstrations of vicarious learning of fear as opposed to direct traumatic conditioning has been reported, paradoxically, with laboratory monkeys. Mineka and her colleagues (e.g., Cook, Mineka, Wolkenstein, & Laitsch, 1985; Mineka, Davidson, Cook, & Keir, 1984) introduced laboratory-reared adolescent monkeys to their wild-reared parents. Prior to the reunion, the lab-reared animals had displayed no avoidance behavior to snakes whatsoever. They observed their parents reacting fearfully in the presence of real, toy, and model snakes for short periods of time. After only brief periods of observation, Mineka and colleagues found that the offspring demonstrated behavioral avoidance and disturbances that were not significantly different from the parents' behaviors. The intensity of these fear responses did not change at a period extending up to 3 months.

The overwhelming evidence is that many phobias and the majority of fears are not learned through a traumatic experience. (More is said about the phenomenon below.) On the other hand, Öst and Hugdahl (1981, 1983) reported that a large number of their patients with simple phobias and agoraphobia recalled a traumatic conditioning experience, and few remembered acquiring their fear through vicarious means. For example, Öst and Hugdahl (1983) found the 48% of animal phobics, 58% of social phobics, 61% of blood and dental phobics, 69% of claustrophobics, and 91% of agoraphobics identified direct conditioning histories. The remainder identified vicarious or informational transmission as crucial events responsible for the acquisition of their fears. Between 10% and 20% of all groups could not remember any incident that might account for their fears.

The Öst and Hugdahl (1983) information seems totally at odds with our clinical understanding of the etiology of panic and agoraphobia. Clearly, agoraphobics are very seldom, if ever, run down by a car in the parking lot of a shopping mall. Nor are they assaulted in church, or a movie theater, or some other crowded location. What is the traumatic experience Öst and Hugdahl are talking about that leads to "conditioning"? Before the answer to this is considered, it is interesting and useful to refer to other retrospective information concerning simple phobics.

McNally and Steketee (1985) interviewed 22 outpatients presenting for treatment with animal phobias. When questioned about etiology, most (15) of these patients could not remember what had happened. Of the remaining 7 cases, 5 had had a frightening encounter with an animal, whereas 2 seemed to have acquired their fear through instructional or vicarious modes. Nevertheless, what they all dreaded now was not attack from their feared animal; rather, they were afraid they would panic and suffer the consequences of panic following an unavoidable encounter with the animal. Munjack (1984), in an interesting retrospective analysis, questioned individuals with a more common type of simple phobia about the etiology of their fear of driving. Of his 30 subjects, a few (20%) reported some traumatic incident while driving that seemed to lead to their fears, such as a collision. Almost half (40%) reported no such incident. Rather, they noted that suddenly, for no apparent reason, they had "panicked" while driving and since then had been unable to drive on freeways. While these patients presented with a fear of driving, what actually seemed to make them anxious, much as with McNally and Steketee's patients, was the possibility of having unexpected panic attacks. It also seems possible that where the etiology was less clear, experiences similar to panic or possibly limited symptom attacks played a role.

Clinicians are familiar with one of the most common types of simple phobias, fear of flying. It is the rare individual who reports developing a fear of flying after crashing in an airplane, or even after reading about a crash in the newspaper. The more common situation is that an individual who may have flown successfully for years suddenly develops an incapacitating fear of flying. The example of John Madden, a well-known sports announcer in the United States, has been described in some detail in Chapter 1. Often such people will report, when pressed, that they are afraid of some catastrophe occurring or of the plane crashing. What they really seem to fear is the possibility of having another panic attack.

In this context, the Öst and Hugdahl findings mentioned above become clear. The majority of these simple phobics, social phobics, and agoraphobics reported experiencing an intense, overwhelming false alarm in situations or contexts that subsequently became "phobic" for these individuals. It was the false alarm, rather than a realistic traumatic event, that seemed implicated in their "conditioning."

It is entirely possible that some simple phobics experience an alarm reaction in response to a realistic threat to their well-being, which then becomes associated with the same or similar objects or situations. Being attacked by a dog may be an example. A larger number of simple phobics experience a false alarm, which is of such intensity that learning occurs. Specifically, false alarms become strongly associated with the object or situation that set the occasion for the first false alarm. In this model, the phobic individual evidences anxiety in the presence of the object or situation (or similar objects or situations) that have set the occasion for the first false alarm, but anxiety occurs primarily over the possibility of having another (unpredictable) false alarm in the presence of the cues that signal the possibility of this alarm.

As noted above, this association is not a random event. Conditioning is more likely to occur to some evolutionary prepared stimuli than to others. Similarly, some CSs and UCSs are more likely to "belong" to each other, as in taste and illness reactions surrounding food. But another possible association may account for much of the nonrandom quality of phobic reactions. A common theme is the danger of being trapped. This theme is obvious in agoraphobics. Fears of sitting too far from the door in a church or movie theater, or of being trapped in a crowded mall, are prototypic agoraphobic situations. One early name of agoraphobia, the "barber's chair syndrome," reflects the difficulty that many of these individuals have with confinement to dentists' or beauticians' chairs. But the feeling of being "trapped" is also strongly present in phobias of driving, flying, or other forms of transportation. It is also present in fears of crossing bridges. What these situations have in common is that the context prevents easy escape in the event of a false alarm. That is, the overwhelmingly powerful and ethologically ancient action tendency of escape is blocked. At the very least, this intensifies and prolongs the alarms and potentiates learning. It is probably interference or conflict with this survival-based behavior that is the most important factor in "convincing" the organism not to let this happen again at any cost. And the cost is often high. If emotions are fundamentally behavioral acts (Lang, 1985), anything that interferes with the execution of this most important of all emotional acts (escape) should have profound significance.

The implications of this model for simple phobics are clear. An actual traumatic event (true alarm) involving the phobic object or situation may not be necessary. Only a false alarm may be required in the presence of a previously benign object or situation, particularly where escape is difficult, or where the context is "prepared" in some other way. These conditions may insure that a learned alarm occurs the next time the object or situation is encountered. These ideas concerning the etiology of simple phobias are elaborated in Chapter 12.

The occurrence of a false alarm may be one of the "missing links" in a traumatic conditioning etiology of some phobias. This missing link—identifying as it does an intense UCS, capable of providing strong emotional learning in as little as one trial—fulfills a theoretical prediction made years ago by Wolpe (1952, 1954).

In "vicarious" learning, a similar phenomenon is present. Mineka (1987) has demonstrated in monkeys that what is crucial for vicarious acquisition of a phobic response is the *intensity* of the fear reaction of the model. Fear intensity correlates almost perfectly with the intensity of the alarm from the subject and with the subsequent strength of the phobic reaction. Thus, the well-known principle of "emotion contagion" from the emotion theory literature may underlie observational etiology of phobia. Emotion contagion, in turn, reflects the social communication function of emotional behavior.

Thus, the occurrence of a false alarm may be one crucial element heretofore overlooked in etiological accounts of phobia. But there is another link (described below) that, in my view, is required for a satisfactory etiological account.

FALSE ALARMS AND PANIC DISORDER

What of patients with panic disorder, with or without agoraphobia? The majority of these individuals are unable to report a clearly demarcated cue for their alarms, although agoraphobics often report a series of diffuse situations of which they are wary, many of which revolve around being "trapped" away from a safe place. But agoraphobic avoidance is often limited in panic disorder. It is possible that the major difference between panic disorder and other phobic disorders may be in the association (or lack thereof) between a false alarm and a specific cue, as suggested in Chapter 3. What is learned then in this case? To understand this more fully, consider an important but little-known line of research conducted by Russian investigators.

For years Russian investigators conducted a series of experiments demonstrating that fear could be conditioned to internal physiological stimuli. These stimuli came to be known as "interoceptive" (Razran, 1961). To take a typical example, the colon of a dog was slightly stimulated (the CS) at the same time that an electric shock was administered. As a result of this procedure, the dog began to evidence signs of intense conditioned anxiety during the natural passage of feces. The Russians demonstrated that this type of learning was particularly resistant to extinction. That is, it would persist indefinitely, despite repeated physiological sensations in the absence of the original UCS (shock). These findings are robust (e.g., Martin, 1983).

The clear implication is that it is possible to learn an association between internal cues and false alarms, and that these internal cues serve the same function for patients with panic disorder (with or without agoraphobia) that external cues do for simple phobics. That is, they signal the possibility of another false alarm.

The association of false alarms with internal or external cues results in the phenomenon of learned alarms. Furthermore, a characteristic of any learned response is that it need not fully replicate its unlearned counterpart. For example, the limited fear propositions present in a given context may elicit only part of the emotional response (Lang, 1985; see Chapter 2). Thus, learned alarms may be only partial responses, such as cognitive representations without the marked physiological component of alarms or limited symptom attacks. Ambulatory monitoring of learned alarms supports this contention (Taylor et al., 1986; see Chapter 3). Escapist action tendencies are probably present most of the time.

One clear consequence of this learning in individuals who develop anxiety and become phobic is the rapid development of acute sensitivity and vigilance concerning the newly acquired phobic cues. Someone recently bitten by a dog will quickly become acutely sensitive to any sign of dogs. This vigilance will extend to unfamiliar areas where dogs may be roaming free. Someone experiencing a false alarm in a elevator will become acutely aware of any plans in the immediate future that may require entry into an elevator. And someone who has learned to associate interoceptive cues with false alarms will become acutely sensitive to the vigilant of specific somatic cues that may signal the beginning of another alarm.

Evidence that people presenting with panic disorder are apprehensively anxious about interoceptive cues is accumulating along several fronts. Much of this evidence has been reviewed in Chapter 3 (Rapee, 1986). van den Hout, van der Molen, Griez, and Lousberg (1987) isolated a sensitivity to interoceptive cues as specific to panic disorders. They assessed 29 patients with panic disorder (with or without agoraphobia) and compared them to 28 nonpanicking "neurotic" and 29 normal control subjects on a questionnaire designed to measure fears of interoceptive sensations. The panic patients scored considerably higher than both control groups, which did not differ significantly from each other. Tyrer and Lader (1974) also found significantly greater cardiac awareness in agoraphobics than in simple phobics. Using a newly developed questionnaire to measure sensitivity to the consequences of anxiety, Reiss, Peterson, Gursky, and McNally (1986; see Chapter 10) found that agoraphobics scored higher than other anxiety disorder patients, who in turn were more "anxiety-sensitive" than normals.

A variety of additional evidence supports the contention that patients with panic disorder have learned to fear interoceptive cues. Chapter 4 has reviewed the substantial body of evidence, dating back 60 years, on the provocation of panic using both pharmacological and behavioral methods. As suggested there, the weight of the evidence indicates that fear can be learned to a variety of somatic cues, particularly respiratory, cardiovascular, and vestibular. The preliminary report on the response of panic patients, but not controls, to a false increase in heart rate feedback is another indication of this relationship (Ehlers et al., 1988). Evidence reviewed in Chapter 4 (e.g., Lindemann & Finesinger, 1938) also suggests that alarms become associated with specific cues rather than with the general physiological activation of nonspecific stress.

The interesting phenomenon of nocturnal panic, reviewed in Chapter

3, suggests that panic or false alarms may be associated with sudden changes in physiological homeostasis, even when these changes are ordinarily anxiolytic. A case in point involves relaxation and the closely associated state that occurs during the beginning of delta sleep. Clinical evidence (also reviewed in Chapter 3) from self-monitoring of patients with panic suggests that specific interoceptive cues may precede unexpected panic. A final indication that panic patients fear interoceptive cues is that direct exposure to interoceptive cues is an effective treatment for panic. Treatment of panic disorder in this manner, along with other evidence pointing to fear and anxiety concerning interoceptive cues in panic disorder patients, is taken up in some detail in Chapters 10 and 11.

From this perspective, it is tempting to speculate on the origins of seemingly vastly different "anxiety" disorders found in other cultures, as reviewed in Chapter 1. Could *koro* result from a false alarm that is then attributed to a culturally popular cue or cause? Is "heart distress" in Iran similar to what was called "irritable heart syndrome" in the early part of the century in the United States? If so, perhaps both heart distress and irritable heart syndrome are precipitated by a false alarm attributed to a cardiovascular disease process.

INTERNAL VERSUS EXTERNAL CUES

If this account is correct, what accounts (1) for the development of fear associated with external or internal cues, and (2) for the variety of anxious propositions (including types of causal attributions) present during the alarm? One factor would seem to involve the particular situation in which the individual finds himself or herself during a false alarm. In the case of a true alarm, where one's welfare is threatened, the location of the first alarm is not an issue, at least initially, since all attention is focused on the source of the threat (e.g., a car careening out of control). When one experiences a false alarm, however, attention may be allocated in many different ways, since there is no obvious cause for alarm. If one is "trapped" in a situation where no exit is possible while experiencing the full effects of a false alarm, with its associated sense of death, dying, and loss of control, then it is intuitively likely that the largest share of attention will be directed to the "trapped" situation, which prevents the powerful action tendency of escape. Common examples mentioned above include planes or other means of public transportation; dentists' or hairdressers' chairs, where it is difficult to suddenly get up and leave; or public places such as churches, where a quick exit may prove embarrassing.

When one is alone at home, one's attention may be focused more fully on internal cues associated with the false alarm. Preliminary evidence from our clinic indicates that the location of the individual during the first panic is important in this respect, since panic patients without agoraphobic avoidance tend to have more of their first panics at home while accompanied; panic patients with agoraphobia tend to have their first panics out of the house, alone.

It is unlikely, however, that one's attention will be as neatly divided in the event of a false alarm as is implied by this description. Clinical experience indicates that patients present with a varying mixture of apprehension to internal and external cues, with only a minority fearing one or the other exclusively. Examples in the latter category include the plane phobic who experiences a false alarm while flying but has associated this alarm exclusively with planes, or the panic disorder patient with no avoidance whatsoever (a very rare occurrence indeed; see Chapter 10), whose concern is focused exclusively on somatic sensations. But most patients who have experienced false alarms fall somewhere in between and are apprehensive about a varying mixture of internal and external cues.

It is also interesting to consider the minority (approximately 30%) of panic disorder patients who can clearly cite an unfavorable experience with drugs such as anesthesia, cocaine or, marijuana as the setting event for their first panic (e.g., see Table 6.3) (Aronson & Craig, 1986). Here the "cause" in terms of a temporally associated event seems clear, and the anesthesia or the recreational drug is subsequently avoided. But a full panic disorder syndrome also develops, including marked sensitivity to a variety of somatic cues and repeated panic attacks in the absence of external cues. This division of attention between internal and external cues may be more typical of clinical phobia. But whether a drug is involved in the etiology or not, aversive unexplained arousal clearly becomes the major focus of concern and the stimulus component of the anxious propositions. Internal or external cues that happen to be associated with an initial false alarm, even if prepotent in some way as in "trapped" situations), cannot fully account for the development of all anxiety disorders. In subsequent chapters devoted to each clinical disorder, I suggest factors in addition to the location of the first alarm that determine the focus of anxious apprehension.

Finally, the avoidance behavior that develops (whether the initial reaction is a true or a false alarm) in simple or social phobics seems to differ somewhat from the avoidance behavior that develops subsequent to a false alarm in panic disorder with agoraphobia. As described in more detail in Chapter 10, much of the extensive avoidance behavior sometimes seen in panic disorder with agoraphobia, resulting in eventual housebound status, seems secondary to a learned alarm. For example, if these people are home alone during the first false alarm and then begin experiencing an increasing number of learned alarms associated with various internal cues, they will come to avoid a variety of situations where they do not feel "safe" in the event of an unexpected panic attack (if cultural, social, and environmental contingencies allow such avoidance). This type of secondary avoidance then becomes a method of coping with learned alarms and is more readily understood from the point of view of a safety signal analysis (e.g., Rachman, 1984). That is, where and with whom is it safe to be if one has a panic attack? For this reason, the avoidance in agoraphobia is more diffuse and variable than that in simple or social phobias. It is also more clearly related to the presence or absence of a "safe" person (Craske *et al.*, 1986). This issue is discussed further in Chapter 10.

ALARMS AND ANXIETY

Thus far, I have highlighted the role of stress and associated neurobiological reactions in the genesis of an initial false alarm. The fact that at least some of these alarms are associated with a variety of internal and external cues also receives substantial support. One final link in the etiological chain derives from the fascinating issue of who develops clinical disorders associated with false or learned alarms and who does not. As noted above (Norton *et al.*, 1986; Norton, Harrison, *et al.*, 1985), many more people seem to experience alarms (false and learned) than those who actually present with clinical disorders. In fact, nonclinical panickers form a substantial minority of the population. At present, the difference between those who develop full-blown clinical syndromes and those who do not is largely speculative, since we know so little about infrequent panickers. For example, nonclinical panickers with occasional alarms seem to experience them less frequently, although a small minority may be experiencing as many as three in a 3-week period and yet have evidently not considered seeking help. These subjects also seem to experience their alarms less intensely.

It is possible, of course, particularly among those who are experiencing more frequent panics, that a full-blown panic disorder will develop. But another possibility is that they simply do not "fear" these alarms, or, more accurately, that they are not apprehensively anxious about them. What could account for this? One possibility is that the alarms simply are not of sufficient intensity to result in clinical complication. But another, more likely possibility is that people who develop full-blown panic or phobic disorders are specifically susceptible to developing anxiety over their alarms because of a combination of individual biological and psychological factors or a combination of the two. Among these factors may be biologically based stress reactivity, perceptions of unpredictability and uncontrollability of the alarms or other negative events, and poor coping skills or social support. In other words, if an alarm calls forth a variety of anxious propositions (in Lang's sense) concerning perceptions of unpredictability–uncontrollability, increased arousal surrounding the alarm, and a shift of attention to internal self-evaluative modes, then it is possible that the conditions will be ripe for the development of an emotional disorder. If, on the other hand, one does not experience unpredictability or loss of control as a result of this event, one may simply attribute it to benign events of the moment ("something I ate," "a fight with my boss"). In this case, one will not experience an internal self-evaluative shift in attention (see below), and the false alarm will be just that. Life will then go on as before, with perhaps an occasional rather mild false alarm reappearing from time to time under stressful conditions.

Somewhere between these nonclinical panickers and panic disorder patients are a minority of patients who seek help from nonpsychiatric physicians such as cardiologists. Studies on the ubiquity of panic in these settings have been reviewed in Chapter 3. For example, Beitman, Basha, *et al.* (1987) found that 12 out of 38 cardiology patients who otherwise met the criteria for panic disorder did not report apprehension or a sense of loss of control accompanying their attacks. (The other 26 cardiology patients did report these symptoms.) Obviously, these alarms were distressing, or the 12 patients would not have sought help. Therefore, anxiety and distress may have been equivalent between the 12 patients who did not report apprehension and the 26 who did (as seemed to be the case on questionnaire scores), with differences in reporting styles accounting for the lack of subjective reports of apprehension during interviews. For example, Beitman, Basha, *et al.* (1987) suggest that these patients may have been "less likely to report emotions" (p. 491).

In any case, the lack of distress or anxiety over the possibility of having another alarm, found in a large percentage of the general population and perhaps a few nonpsychiatric medical patients, suggests a fundamental distinction between these individuals and patients with anxiety disorders. To develop an anxiety disorder, one must be susceptible to developing anxiety or apprehension over the possibility of subsequent alarms or other negative events. Obviously, this notion requires a further elaboration of the hypothetical distinction between alarms (panic, fear) and anxiety (anxious apprehension).

7

The Process and Origins of Anxiety

THE PROCESS OF ANXIOUS APPREHENSION

In Chapter 2, I have concluded that anxiety can best be characterized as a diffuse cognitive–affective structure. At the heart of this structure is high negative affect, composed of various levels and combinations of activation or arousal, perceptions of lack of control over future events, and shifts in attention to self-evaluative concerns. This structure is described as "diffuse" because it can become associated with any number of situations or events and may be expressed somewhat differently from individual to individual, or even within a given individual across time. In Lang's (1985) conceptualization, all elements of the affective core of this structure (negative affect) are stored deep in memory in the form of stimulus and response propositions, as well as "meaning" propositions triggered by various cues in the environment. For example, mention of an upcoming event where the individual will be required to "perform" in some way (defined very broadly) may be sufficient to evoke an anxious mood. Similarly, response characteristics, particularly those associated with arousal, may also bring forth anxious apprehension. Of course, as pointed out in some detail in Chapter 2, different theoretical conceptualizations point to the implicit appraisal of threat in upcoming situations or misattribution of unexpected arousal as triggers for "anxiety." Biological theorists, on the other hand, may look to abnormal GABA-ergic activity as a trigger. But I take the more integrated Langian perspective here before speculating on the specific cognitive–affective interactions that characterized anxiety. I refer to this structure as "anxiety" or anxious apprehension," since evidence suggests that its essence is _arousal-driven apprehension_. Thus, this definition of anxiety refers only to the cognitive–affective structure elaborated below. Another term often paired with anxiety is "anticipatory."

But in the present definition, all anxiety is anticipatory, so this qualifying adjective does not appear again. "Anxiety" or anxious apprehension" also allows a clear discrimination from "panic" or "fear"—terms that have often been categorized under the general rubric of "anxiety" in the past.

Preliminary evidence from an unexpected source now indicates that the components of anxiety may be organized in a negative feedback cycle in such a way as to maintain the process of "anxious apprehension" indefinitely. The unexpected source of this evidence is research on male sexual dysfunction. Several years of systematic research into the factors that maintain this disorder have helped to reveal the roles of affect, cognition, and their interactions, with implications for the way anxiety works (e.g., Barlow, 1986c). Before these new developments on the relationship of cognitive and affective elements within anxiety are discussed, it may be helpful to describe the context from which these data emerged.

ANXIOUS APPREHENSION IN SEXUAL DYSFUNCTION

ANXIETY AND SEXUAL AROUSAL

For years, writers of virtually every theoretical persuasion believed that "anxiety" played a substantial role in the development and maintenance of sexual dysfunction for both men and women. For example, Fenichel (1945) considered anxiety to be a contributing factor to the development of the various types of sexual dysfunctions in both men and women. More recently, Masters and Johnson (1970) underlined the importance of performance fears and fears of inadequacy as major factors in individuals and couples experiencing sexual dysfunctions. Kaplan (1974) has also given fear of failure to perform adequately a primary role in the development of sexual anxieties, and has added other fears (e.g., demands for performance on the part of the partner and excessive need to please partners) to the list of sexual anxieties. Sexual anxieties are seen as preventing an individual from experiencing sexual arousal, and, in fact, as inhibiting autonomic nervous system functioning to such an extent that physiological arousal is inhibited (Kaplan, 1974). In both Masters and Johnson's and Kaplan's conceptualizations, a major task of therapy is overcoming performance fears and feelings of sexual inadequacy, as well as treating other sources of sexual anxiety.

In a similar vein, as early as 1958 Wolpe suggested the use of systematic desensitization in the treatment of sexual dysfunctions, with the elimination of anxiety as the goal of treatment. This is familiar ground for most clinicians, particularly those who have ever dealt with sexual dysfunctions. People with these problems report the signs and symptoms of anxiety, and most treatments are aimed at reducing this anxiety (or determining the cause of it).

In fact, this state of affairs is an example of a situation common to our clinical science, in which facts that have been available for years simply do not support these assumptions. As early as 1943 Ramsey surveyed adolescent boys and reported that approximately 50% of the boys noted erections from some type of nonerotic stimulus. These nonerotic responses usually involved elements of fear, excitement, or other nonsexual emotional situations. They included events such as accidents, near-accidents, being chased by the police, fear of being punished, and so forth.

More recently, Sarrel and Masters (1982) reported a series of startling and gruesome events that are difficult to believe if one assumes that anxiety inhibits sexual arousal. These gruesome events involved rape, but not the unfortunately familiar scenario of men raping women. Rather, gangs of women accosted a number of men and demanded that they have sexual relations, threatening them at knifepoint or with other weapons if they failed. Under these circumstances the men reported not only achieving erection, but the ability to perform repeatedly (although they did suffer severe emotional consequences, forcing them to seek clinical assistance).

For anyone who has worked with patients suffering from paraphilias or sexual deviations, particularly exhibitionsts or voyeurs, the association between fear and sexual arousal is evident. Many of these individuals are unable to become sexually aroused without first experiencing fear or anxiety over the possibility of being apprehended or otherwise threatened in some way (Beck & Barlow, 1984). Nor is the relationship of fear and sexual arousal limited to humans. Barfield and Sachs (1968) have observed similar phenomena in rats.

Some of the more interesting experiments on the relationship between anxiety and sexual arousal (or attraction) come from the social psychologists. In one of the best examples, Dutton and Aron (1974) arranged to interview male students who had just crossed a rickety suspension bridge, thereby evoking some mild fear or anxiety, and compared them to students who had not crossed the bridge. Both groups of male students were then interviewed by an attractive female student. Students who had crossed the bridge, and therefore had become mildly "anxious," reported more sexual material in a projective test designed to assess this issue without the subjects being aware of it than students who had not crossed the bridge. In addition, they called the female student (who had provided them with her telephone number on a pretext) and asked for a date significantly more times than the comparison group! The conclusion of Dutton and Aron (1974), and other social psychologists approaching the issue from a somewhat different perspective (e.g., Berscheid & Walster, 1974; Brehm, Gatz, Goethals, McCrimmon, & Ward, 1978; Riordan, 1979), was that experimentally induced anxiety can *increase* interpersonal or sexual attraction.

Following some preliminary laboratory experiments (Hoon, Wincze,

& Hoon, 1977), this notion was tested more rigorously with sexual arousal in normal male volunteers (Barlow, Sakheim, & Beck, 1983). The purpose of this experiment was to find out, under controlled laboratory conditions, the effects of inducing "anxiety" simultaneous with sexual arousal. Anxiety was manipulated by shock threat during an explicit erotic film. Before the actual experiment was begun, the tolerance level of all subjects to a painful but harmless electric shock to the forearm was determined, and the subjects were told that this would be used in the experiment. Each subject experienced three different experimental conditions administered in a counterbalanced fashion. Each condition was signaled by a different light above the video screen the subject was watching.

In the first condition, a light signaled that no shock would occur. This was the control condition. In the second condition, subjects were told that there was a 60% chance that they would receive a shock while they watched the erotic film. This condition was termed "noncontingent shock threat," since there was no indication that the shock threat would have anything to do whatsoever with the subjects' behavior. In the third condition, however, subjects were told that there was a 60% chance they would receive a shock if they did not achieve at least as large an erection as the average male in our laboratory. This condition was termed, quite appropriately, "contingent shock threat." In fact, subjects were never actually shocked during the experiment, but postexperimental assessment indicated that they thought they would be and were appropriately "anxious."

Rather than decreasing sexual arousal, the results indicated that the noncontingent shock threat increased sexual arousal when compared to no shock threat. But, in an unexpected development, the contingent shock threat also increased sexual arousal when compared to no shock threat. In fact, this condition produced the highest overall sexual arousal! The data are presented in Figure 7.1. These data have specific implications for the clinical issue of sexual dysfunction (Barlow, 1986c). But interest here is in the fact that the clinically important condition of performance demand not only did not interfere with sexual arousal, but actually increased it. This revelation made an investigation of the reaction of sexually dysfunctional men to this same paradigm all the more important.

We now have ongoing studies on any differences that exist between sexual functional and dysfunctional groups when exposed to this paradigm. In fact, sexually dysfunctional subjects have shown significantly *less* sexual arousal during shock threat conditions than during the no-shock condition (Barlow, 1986c; Beck, Barlow, Sakheim, & Abrahamson, 1984, 1987). Thus, shock threat, which is a typical manipulation to produce "anxiety" in the laboratory, increases sexual arousal in sexually functional males, but decreases in sexually dysfunctional males.

Together with the information reviewed above from the social-psy-

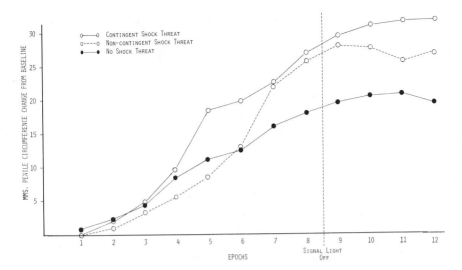

FIGURE 7.1. Average penile circumference change for each 15-second epoch during each of three conditions: no-shock threat, noncontingent-shock threat, and contingent-shock threat. From Barlow, D. H., Sakheim, D. K., & Beck, J. G. (1983). Anxiety increases sexual arousal. *Journal of Abnormal Psychology, 92,* 49–54. Copyright 1983 by the American Psychological Association. Reprinted by permission.

chological and developmental literature, it seems that emotions can "transfer," such that eliciting one emotion simultaneously with a second makes the second more "intense" (Zillmann, 1983b). Another possibility is that shock threat "motivated" our normal subjects to higher levels of performance. Postexperimental inquiry seemed to support this interpretation, since several subjects made comments such as "I didn't want any part of that shock, so I really concentrated on the film." Nevertheless, sexual arousal increased almost as much in the noncontingent condition, where presumably no motivational factors were present. Thus it would seem that <u>emotion transfer</u> accounts for the majority of the effect.

Emotion transfer is a relatively common theme in theories of emotion, particularly in more cognitive theories (see Chapter 2), where appraisal of physiological arousal and the context in which this arousal occurs plays an important role in emotional expression. One can also rely on a Langian analysis, also supported by Zillmann (1983b), by suggesting that the experimental conditions gave a "boost" to the response propositions involved in sexual arousal, thereby producing more successful accessing of sexual arousal. For present purposes, though, it is probably not necessary to consider whether an elementary type of appraisal occurred. It is enough to note that arousal transferred and increased in an additive way, but only for functional subjects, not for those who were already sexually dysfunctional. What could have caused such marked differences in the way these people responded to the same experimental conditions?

COGNITIVE INTERFERENCE

Since emotion seems to have transferred between anxiety and sexual arousal very nicely in sexually functional subjects, what was happening to our sexually dysfunctional patients? It would seem that something was interfering with the transfer of emotion, but it is difficult to conceive of the nature of this interference. A close examination of ongoing cognitive processes, particularly in the manner in which they might interfere with sexual activity, seemed an obvious place to start.

In fact, we know with some certainty that cognitive factors can interfere with sexual arousal, and some of these cognitive factors have been isolated. For example, Briddell *et al.* (1978) and Lansky and Wilson (1981) have reported that inducing various expectancy sets in a systematic way seems to influence arousal. Another body of research has indicated that males are capable of suppressing their arousal during erotic stimulation if asked to do so (e.g., Abel, Blanchard, & Barlow, 1981). When suppression occurs, presumably the mechanism by which subjects suppress erections is self-distraction or a shift in attention. Geer and Fuhr (1976) tested this idea directly in normal volunteers, using a dichotic listening device. While listening to erotic audiotapes in one ear, subjects were required to listen to increasingly distracting cognitive tasks in the other ear. Sexual arousal decreased as the complexity of the distracting task increased.

To examine the effects of distraction more closely, we tested the effects of neutral distraction (listening to audiotapes portraying a nonsexual passage from a popular novel) on both our sexually dysfunctional patients and age-matched normal volunteers (Abrahamson, Barlow, Sakheim, Beck, & Athanasiou, 1985). Subjects viewed an erotic film while listening to the distracting audiotapes and were told they would be questioned on material from the audiotapes after the experiment. This was contrasted to a condition where distraction was not present. Both groups achieved adequate and equivalent levels of penile responding under the no-distraction condition. The normal volunteers evidenced significant detumescence during distraction. But, in a surprising development, our sexually dysfunctional patients were not affected by distraction and maintained tumescence; if anything, their arousal increased a bit during the distracting condition. The data are presented in Figure 7.2. Although dysfunctional patients usually show slightly less sexual arousal than functional subjects in our laboratory, it is not unusual for subjects with psychogenic erectile dysfunction (who have been carefully screened to exclude any

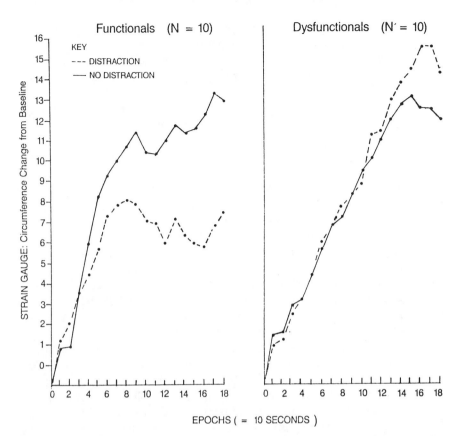

FIGURE 7.2. Mean strain gauge responding across subjects by epoch during distraction and no distraction: Sexually functional (left) versus sexually dysfunctional (right) subjects. From Abrahamson, D. J., Barlow, D. H., Sakheim, D. K., Beck, J. G., & Athanasiou, R. (1985). Effects of distraction on sexual responding in functional and dysfunctional men. *Behavior Therapy, 16,* 503–515. Copyright 1985 by the Association for Advancement of Behavior Therapy. Reprinted by permission.

individuals with organic components, such as vascular problems) to demonstrate substantial arousal under these benign laboratory conditions. What is surprising is the marked difference in the response of these two groups to distraction; it is particularly puzzling because clinicians working with these patients have long observed that distraction while trying to perform sexually seems to be a major difficulty that dysfunctional people encounter. This paradox is discussed further below.

There is also evidence that a variety of alternative experimental conditions are capable of decreasing arousal. For example, when sexually dysfunctional patients and normal volunteers both watched an erotic film of a woman who was obviously highly aroused, compared to an erotic film where the woman did not appear sexually aroused, interesting differences emerged. Normal volunteers showed substantial arousal to the erotic film where the woman was not aroused, but this arousal increased significantly when they perceived the woman as aroused. On the other hand, sexually dysfunctional patients showed *less* arousal if they perceived that the woman was highly aroused, compared to a film where she was not aroused (Abrahamson, Barlow, Beck, Sakheim, & Kelly, 1985; Beck, Barlow, & Sakheim, 1983). What seemed to be happening was that the highly responsive woman elicited performance-related concerns, which were "distracting" to our patients. Normal volunteers, on the other hand, attended to and concentrated on the erotic cues under either condition.

Preliminary conclusions from these and related experiments (cf. Barlow, 1986c) suggest that our dysfunctional patients are also subject to the strong influence of distraction, but that the distracting influences differ in terms of their effects on patients and normal volunteers. The normal volunteers show marked decrements in their arousal under the influence of neutral off-task types of distracting influences, but demonstrate marked increases in arousal under conditions of performance demand. Our patients, on the other hand can accommodate the neutral distraction quite easily, even showing some disinhibition, but are markedly affected by the influence of performance demand. This performance demand condition seems to cue a variety of self-evaluative thoughts concerning internal physiology, as well as the strong possibility of failure to perform and subsequent humiliation. Such thoughts are strong salient or "hot" cognitions with an intense negative affective tone; they seem impervious to rational intervention or the simple effects of persuasion. In other words, they seem to be an integral part of a basic, automatic, instantaneous, affective response.

Confirmation of differential responding to neutral versus performance-related distracting stimuli was present in a subsequent experiment when the two types of distraction were compared directly (Abrahamson, Barlow, & Abrahamson, in press). Specifically, dysfunctionals were distracted only by performance-related cues and not by neutral cues. Normal volunteers were distracted by neutral cues but not performance-related cues. One reason for the strength of this cognitive process may emerge, at least partially, from the next series of experiments, which targeted the relationship of cognition and affect in this group of patients.

In one experiment, our normal volunteers were presented with erotic audiotapes simultaneous with four levels of shock threat: no shock, half tolerance, tolerance, and twice tolerance (Beck *et al.*, 1987). As a further check on their level of attention to the audiotapes, a sentence recognition task administered with signal detection methodology was carried out immediately following presentation of the stimuli. Essentially, the results indicated that shock threat lowered sexual responding, particularly during half tolerance and tolerance shock; however, during the twice-tolerance condition, sexual responding returned somewhat and approached responding under the no-shock condition. Performance on the sentence recognition task improved during half tolerance and tolerance shock, and then deteriorated somewhat during the twice-tolerance condition. Thus, performance on the sentence recognition task formed an inverted U-shaped function under increasing intensities of shock threat, as one can see in Figure 7.3.

This finding, of course, is as old as the Yerkes–Dobson law (Yerkes & Dobson, 1908) referred to in Chapter 2: That is, efficiency of perfor-

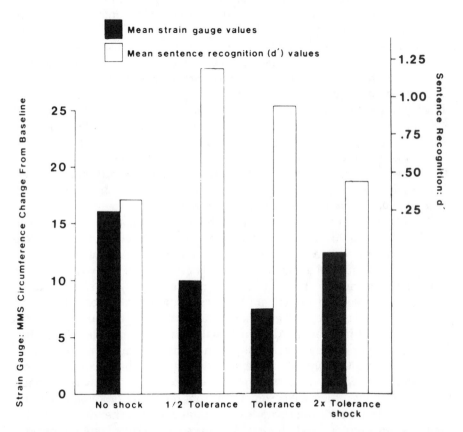

FIGURE 7.3. Mean strain gauge responding averaged across stimulus duration, and mean sentence recognition values during four shock threat conditions. From Beck, J. G., Barlow, D. H., Sakheim, D. K., & Abrahamson, D. J. (1987). Shock threat and sexual arousal: The role of selective attention, thought content, and affective states. *Psychophysiology, 24,* 165–172. Copyright 1987 by the Society for Psychophysiological Research, Inc. Reprinted by permission.

mance (in this case, on the sentence recognition task) will increase, up to a point, under conditions of arousal (in this case, shock threat). What is particularly interesting, however, is the effect of this experimental condition on the process of sexual arousal. As one can see in Figure 7.3, sexual arousal essentially mirrored this inverted U. The better that subjects did on the sentence recognition task (presumably as a function of greater attention to the sentences), the less sexual arousal they demonstrated. In our previous shock threat experiments we did not have this type of task, and therefore these effects were not observed. The initial conclusion is that "anxiety" induced by shock threat will improve performance or concentration in an inverted U-shaped function; however, if the focus of attention is nonsexual, sexual arousal will suffer proportionally. What is the implication of this finding for our dysfunctional patients? In these patients, as the reader will remember, anxiety or shock threat seems to interfere with sexual arousal even when no overt alternative focus of attention is available. Therefore, it is possible that the dysfunctional patients are already focusing on or attending to something other than erotic cues. Increasing levels of "anxiety" then evidently sharpen and increase the efficiency of their focus of attention. Unfortunately, this other-directed focus occurs at the expense of sexual arousal. Evidence that this is happening is present in the distraction studies described above and in some subsequent, rather complex experiments (Beck & Barlow, 1986a, 1986b).

Now an experiment from our laboratory seems to confirm this differential focus of attention between groups (Jones, Bruce, & Barlow, 1986). Sexually dysfunctional and age-matched normal volunteers both viewed erotic films under the four levels of shock threat described above. The primary finding to emerge was that normals showed increased sexual arousal in an inverted U-shaped function as intensity of shock threat increased (up to full tolerance level), but dysfunctionals showed decreased arousal in a normal U-shaped function. In other words, the sexual arousal pattern of these two groups under these experimental conditions mirrored each other. The data are shown in Figure 7.4. This outcome seems to confirm that normal and dysfunctional individuals are attending to different cues. For our dysfunctional patients, the cues are non sexual.

Therefore, the preliminary evidence suggests that sexually normal volunteers do worse (i.e., evidence lower sexual arousal) when given a task that removes their focus somewhat from the direct processing of erotic cues. But, to return to the paradox mentioned above, the intriguing finding not yet discussed fully here is that our sexually dysfunctional patients either show no effect or do slightly better when distracted from processing erotic cues by a neutral, off-task distraction, such as readings from popular novels. On the other hand, performance-related sexual demands seem to "distract" our patients, and the presence of increasing levels of anxiety during performance demand further decreases sexual arousal,

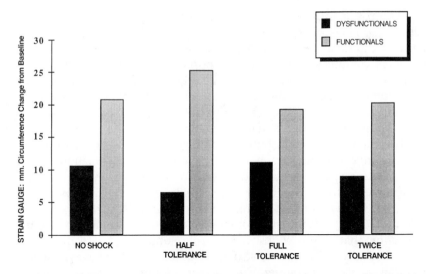

FIGURE 7.4. Mean strain gauge responding, averaged across stimulus duration, during four shock threat conditions. From Jones, J. C., Bruce, T. J., & Barlow, D. H. (1986, November). *The effects of four levels of "anxiety" on sexual arousal in sexually functional and dysfunctional men.* Poster presented at the annual convention of the Association for Advancement of Behavior Therapy, Chicago.

probably by enhancing concentration on the nonerotic content of their attentional focus. Presumably, as suggested above, this focus centers on internal physiology (including erectile response); on performance-related concerns; and on apprehension of scrutiny, failure, and ridicule.

But introducing a competing nonerotic task for dysfunctional subjects, such as counting numbers or listing to neutral stories, does not reduce sexual arousal and in some cases disinhibits it slightly. It is possible that the shift in allocation of attention produced by counting numbers or listening to stories while watching an erotic film has the effect of taking the patients' minds off the performance-related concerns ("hot cognitions") that so occupy their attention. Of course, it is unclear that this reallocation of attention will ever lead to functional levels of performance, since the allocation of attention still remains relatively split, but it is an interesting possibility.

COGNITIVE AND AFFECTIVE DIFFERENCES

Several other differences between our dysfunctional patients and age-matched normal volunteers have emerged that bear on our emerging conception of the specifics of the diffuse cognitive–affective structure now called "anxious apprehension." First, these two groups have different affective responses in a sexual context. As might be expected, patients evidence substantial negative affect in a sexual context, whereas the dysfunctional volunteers report generally positive affective responses (according to affect adjective checklist items). For these patients, negative affect is situationally specific to the sexual context, and may well be a result of expectancies of inadequate responding or inability to control responding. An intriguing possibility is that these negative affective responses predate the dysfunction and contribute to its etiology. For example, Donn Byrne has been investigating personality variables that are dispositional in terms of adequate responding to erotic cues. The trait that emerges falls along the dimension he has termed "erotophilia–erotophobia" (Byrne, 1977, 1983a, 1983b). The negative affective responses of sexually dysfunctional men place them within the erotophobic end of the dimension, and it is interesting that Byrne chooses the term "-phobic." These men may be psychologically vulnerable to sexual dysfunction in some way. I speculate on the nature of this vulnerability below. In any case, these negative affective responses may contribute to an avoidance of erotic cues, and thereby may facilitate the cognitive interference produced by focusing on nonerotic cues.

Also, our psychogenically dysfunctional patients consistently underreport their actual levels of sexual arousal. That is, at the same level of erectile response, psychogenically dysfunctional men report far less sexual arousal than do sexually functional or organogenically dysfunctional men (Sakheim, Barlow, Abrahamson, & Beck, in press). This also seems true for dysfunctional women (Morokoff & Heiman, 1980).

In an interesting preliminary report, this inaccurate perception of arousal seems to have extended to estimates of personal control over arousal. That is, when patients and normal volunteers were asked to suppress their arousal, both groups did so, but the normal volunteers reported success, whereas the patients seemed unaware that they were successfully suppressing arousal and were unable to report any means by which they were or might be able to control their sexual arousal. In the minds of these patients, then, a sexual context, particularly one in which performance might be required, brought forth strong negative affective responding and perceptions of lack of control over their sexual responding (Barlow, 1986c).

A MODEL OF ANXIOUS APPREHENSION IN SEXUAL DYSFUNCTION

While experiments dealing with sexual dysfunction may seem far afield from anxiety, they are extremely relevant. All evidence suggests that sexual dysfunction falls quite neatly into the category of social phobia, as implied by Byrne's "erotophobic" trait. Sarason, in a rigorous and systematic series of studies on test anxiety, has isolated what seems to be a similar process (Sarason, 1982, 1984, 1985). Specifically, level of autonomic arousal seems unrelated to eventual performance on tests; rather, the amount of distracting cognitive activity regarding the possibility and the consequences of failure seems directly related to poor test performance. Furthermore, highly test-anxious students do worse under conditions that increase distracting cognitive activity, such as shifts in focus of attention to self-evaluative concerns (Carver, Peterson, Folansbee, & Scheier, 1983; see below), while students low in anxiety do better under these conditions. Other parallels are outlined elsewhere (Beck & Barlow, 1986b).

Of course, test anxiety and sexual dysfunction are only two small examples of contexts where the process of anxiety is operative. But they are particularly suitable for experimental analysis, because the responses or behavioral outputs directly affected by anxiety are quantifiable (test scores and erections). Therefore, one can "input" any one of the hypothetical elements of the cognitive–affective structure of anxiety, either singly or in combination, and examine carefully the effects on subsequent behavior.

In the field of sexual dysfunction, it therefore becomes possible to construct a "minimodel" of the processes operating in this disorder. This model is presented in Figure 7.5. Basically, the perception of a sexual context—particularly the possibility of having to perform—elicits negative affective responding, including perceptions of lack of control or inability to obtain desired results. At this point a critical shift of attention occurs from an external focus (on erotic material, in this instance) to a more internal self-evaluative focus. The increasing arousal associated with this affective structure narrows attention in the manner described by basic research on attention narrowing (see Chapter 2). But the focus of attention is on negatively affective self-evaluative statements and/or the autonomic signs and symptoms of arousal itself. Since increasing arousal insures an increasingly efficient focus or "narrowing of attention," the negative affective content (in this case, aspects of the sexual response and the consequences of failure during sexual performance) becomes even more salient or "hot." At this point, these patients may actually become distracted from what they are doing, which, in the worst instance, interferes with performance. This narrow, intense focus on negative affective material is what has been called "worry" (Borkovec, 1985; Sarason, 1985); if worry is driven strongly enough by underlying arousal, disruptions in performance will occur, as is the case with sexual dysfunction and test anxiety.

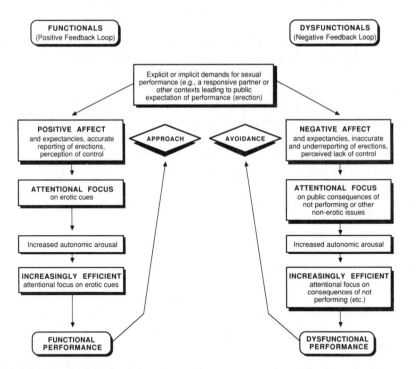

FIGURE 7.5. Model of inhibited sexual excitement. From Barlow, D. H. (1986). Causes of sexual dysfunction: The role of anxiety and cognitive interference. *Journal of Consulting and Clinical Psychology, 54,* 140–148. Copyright 1986 by the American Psychological Association. Reprinted by permission.

A MODEL OF ANXIOUS APPREHENSION

Adapting this minimodel of the process of anxious apprehension in sexual dysfunction to anxious apprehension in general yields a similar negative feedback cycle. Before elaborating on important aspects of the model, I briefly summarize the major points.

Certain situational contexts, or the presence of arousal from other sources capable of tapping the propositions of anxiety, will elicit negative affect. Negative affect is associated with a perceived inability to predict, control, or obtain desired results in upcoming situations or events. This cognitive set, which can be categorized as an apprehensive "hypervalent cognitive schema," leads to (1) a shift in focus of attention from external to internal self-evaluative content, (2) further increases in arousal, (3) narrowing of attention, and (4) hypervigilance regarding sources of apprehension. At sufficient intensity, this process results in disruptions in concentration and performance, and ultimately in avoidance of *sources* of apprehension if this method of coping is available.

Arousal-driven worry or anxious apprehension will, of course, only interfere with performance is some performance is required. In situations where performance may not be called for immediately, but where perceptions of loss of control or other negative affective content have become associated with a number of important life events (e.g., health, finances, and family concerns), then the process of "worry" will emerge. The intensity of worry will become more or less, depending on situational context, the amount of underlying autonomic arousal that is available at the time for transfer (Zillmann, 1983b; see below), and/or presence of other "propositions" capable of calling forth this diffuse cognitive–affective structure. Ongoing concentration will be disrupted in direct relationship to the intensity of the worry process.

Naturally, a tendency to avoid entering a negative affective state is always present. This tendency becomes more pronounced, depending on the severity or intensity of the negative affective structure and the specificity of the contextual cues that set the occasion for anxious apprehension. Thus, test-anxious individuals will avoid tests to the extent that this is possible, and sexually dysfunctional individuals will eventually avoid sex. But this rather maladaptive coping skill may not be available to individuals whose anxious apprehension has diffused itself to many different situational contexts (or, more accurately in Langian terms, across many different "networks in memory"). These individuals become chronic worriers. Worry, or concern over future events, is not problematic until it is so driven by arousal to narrow attention to the exclusion of other more important ongoing activities. It is in this sense that chronic worry is disrupting to performance. This negative feedback cycle is represented in Figure 7.6.

The reader may have noticed that this is not a discussion of the etiology of anxiety, but rather a description of the process of anxious apprehension. The origins of anxiety are mysterious and difficult to elucidate, but there are some intriguing hints on how this state may come about. These hints relate to the discussion of false alarms in Chapter 6 and suggest ways in which false alarms may be connected with anxious apprehension. However, before etiology is discussed, it is important to elaborate on several more components of the cognitive–affective structure termed "anxious apprehension." Prominent among these components are attention shifting and worry.

SELF-FOCUSED ATTENTION

In Chapter 2 I have considered the cognitive–affective process of attention narrowing, mood-congruent recall and recognition, and the theoretical issue of what triggers emotion (e.g., propositions, appraisals). Not

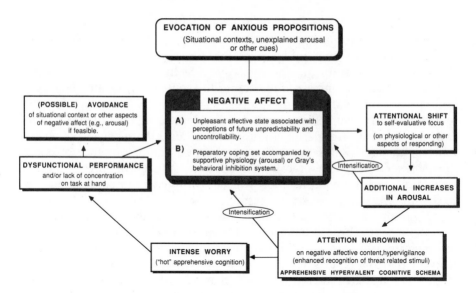

FIGURE 7.6. The process of anxious apprehension.

yet discussed is a process represented in the present diagrammatic structure of anxiety, to which my colleagues and I accord major significance on the basis of our research. This process is the shift from an external to an internal, self-evaluative focus of attention during anxious apprehension, strongly implied in data collected from our sexually dysfunctional patients. This tendency toward self-focus may well be an important, although largely overlooked, component of the cognitive–affective structure of anxious apprehension. Fortunately, basic social-psychological research with normal volunteers has begun to explore some of the issues involved in this process.

Since the advent of biofeedback, we have been aware that it is possible for individuals to discriminate changes in autonomic activity with an unexpected degree of accuracy (Blanchard & Epstein, 1977; Schwartz, 1976). Why, then, are people usually so poor at ascertaining their internal state? Zillmann (1983a, 1983b) suggests, on the basis of the biofeedback literature, that it has nothing to do with abilities to perceive internal changes, which obviously are highly developed. Rather, people do not use these capacities at anywhere near their full potential. As Shapiro (1974) points out, there may well be a very good reason for this. Specifically, the relative lack of attention to (or limitations in awareness of) internal events may have been functionally adaptive in an evolutionary sense. Placing a limit on awareness of internal events reduced an important source of distraction to ongoing external activity. In other words, human functioning in past millennia as hunter–gatherers, or today in the home or the office, would be far less efficient if people were distracted continually by a welter of internal stimuli to which they fully attended. Consider how quickly external efficiency breaks down when internal events force themselves into awareness: (1) angina and other pain; (2) the sensations arising from the urge to eliminate waste products; (3) hunger; (4) triggering of the cough or sneeze reflex; (5) fever. Nevertheless, people's abilities to monitor their own functioning closely at all times remain, and the way in which this capacity is exercised may play a role in the development and maintenance of emotional disorders.

Basic research (e.g., Kahneman, 1973) has demonstrated that attention has several properties. It can be concentrated or diffused over a number of contexts. It can also be characterized by more or less vigilance, alertness, or effort (Scheier, Carver, & Matthews, 1983). Some of these qualities undoubtedly are related to the amount of arousal associated with attention. For example, arousal seems to result in attention narrowing, as described in Chapter 2. Social psychologists (e.g., Duval & Wicklund, 1972; Scheier, Carver, & Matthews, 1983) have determined that there is a limited amount of attention to allocate, and that although attentional capacity may vary somewhat over time, a mutual antagonism exists between a focus on the self and a focus on the environment. In other words, the amount of attention directed to external events or tasks limits proportionately the amount of attention directed to internal events. Furthermore, shifts of attention from external focus to self-focus can be reliably manipulated or cued. In the laboratories of social psychologists, mirrors have been used to turn attention inward, but any environmental cue may prompt a shift to self-focused attention through learning. Duval and Wicklund (1972) first systematized these observations into a theory of objective self-awareness.

One of the major cues resulting in a shift to self-focused attention is the perception of physiological sensations. For example, in an interesting basic experiment. Wegner and Giuliano (1980) manipulated general arousal in their subjects by having them either lie down and relax, sit in a chair, or run in place; they then presented the subjects with a form containing a series of sentences with words missing. The results indicated that subjects who had experienced and noted marked arousal (after running in place) chose more self-relevant words to complete the sentences, while those who relaxed chose fewer self-relevant words. Fenigstein and Carver (1978) came to a similar conclusion in an experiment on false heart rate feedback. It seems that making physiological sensations salient causes individuals to reflect more intensely about themselves in general, drawing their attention to affective qualities, values, standards of behavior, and self-critical judgments (Duval & Wicklund, 1972). In view of these results with rather weak manipulations, one can only wonder about the effect of attention of the dramatic, intense physiological sensations associated with false alarms.

Several results of this important work on self-focused attention are relevant to present purposes. First, as with any human trait, individuals seem to vary in their disposition to be self-attentive, as measured by psychometically sound questionnaires (e.g., Carver & Scheier, 1981; Scheier & Carver, 1983). Examining the effects of self-attention (either measured as a disposition at any one time or experimentally manipulated in the laboratory through mirrors or other devices), investigators have demonstrated that self-focused attention greatly increases sensitivity to bodily sensations and other aspects of internal experience. Furthermore, this sensitivity to bodily sensations quickly spreads to other aspects of the self, such as self-evaluative concerns. In basic research, "self-focused attention" refers to matching one's behavior to pre-ordained standards and often coming up short. In normal subjects, attention to the self can have some potentially positive consequences. For example, subjects high in a disposition to be self-attentive or subjects experimentally manipulated to be high in self-attentiveness will be much less susceptible to the suggestibility inherent in placebo manipulations. If given a placebo and told that it will make them aroused, alert, and excitable, self-attentive subjects will be less susceptible to the suggestion than will more externally directed subjects.

But the most important consequences of direction of attention in the context of emotional disorders concern its effect on emotion. Experimental provocation of various emotions in the laboratory is experienced as more intense by individuals with a greater disposition to self-focus than by those with a greater disposition to external focus. This does not, of course, imply support for the James–Lange notion that perception of physiological or other internal sensations is the trigger for emotional experience. Rather, this notion is consistent with most emotion theories, including expressive-behavioral formulations. That is, a self-directed focus and the resulting increased sensitivity to physiological of proprioceptive sensations are likely to result in greater subjective intensity of emotional experience after the emotion has been elicited. Evidence that the attentional shift to a self-focus follows initial arousal or affect comes from several experiments (e.g., Carver, Blaney, & Scheier, 1976; Wegner & Guiliano, 1980). Of course, a small negative feedback loop within the larger loop is created by the intensifying of arousal and negative affect that follows the shift in attention to self-focus. This small feedback loop is also represented in Figure 7.6.

One additional important consequence of self-focused attention is a failure to habituate to external stimuli while in this attentional mode (Scheier et al., 1983). This aspect of self-focused attention has substantial implications for the theories of anxiety reduction described in the next chapter.

A final step in the process of self-focused attention relevant to emotional disorders concerns different aspects of internal experience to which attention can be allocated in concentrated, selective ways. Two important aspects attracting attention are the stimulus sensations associated with the experience and the emotional or affective components of the experience. In an interesting experiment, Leventhal, Brown, Shachan, and Engquist (1979) instructed normal volunteers to immerse their hands in cold water (the cold pressor test) while periodically assessing their emotional distress. Subjects also reported on strength of physical sensations during the test. Among the number of instructional sets administered to these subjects before they immersed their hands were two that emphasized either the precise stimulus qualities to expect (e.g., cold, tingling, numbness) or the emotional distress they would experience (e.g., apprehension, "butterflies," tension, weakness). Subjects concentrating on the rather mechancial aspects of physical stimulus and response sensation reported less distress and less intense emotional aspects of the experience. As Scheier *et al.* (1983) point out, it is likely that concentration on the emotional aspect of an experience also leads to further sympathetic discharge. This finding is consistent with earlier work on intensification of the emotional state through self-focused attention.

In summary, self-focused attention seems to increase the accuracy and sensitivity of the perception of internal states. If one experiences an affective state, this state can be intensified by subsequent self-focused attention. However, in a more ambiguous situation, the direction of self-attention can be allocated either to the stimulus configurations (as well as other operational aspects of the context) or to the affective qualities of the experience. This latter focus seems particularly salient if the affective qualities involve distress of some sort (Scheier *et al.*, 1983).

The implications for clinical anxiety disorders are suggested in two analogue studies (Scheier, Carver, & Gibbons, 1981). In one experiment, snake-phobic subjects approached a snake either in the presence of a mirror or with no mirror. In a second experiment, subjects high and low in self-consciousness were threatened with electric shock on a pretext. In both experiments, self-directed attention intensified fear and resulted in stronger and more rapid avoidance behavior. Similar findings are apparent in other analogue studies. For example, individuals who are high in self-consciousness react more negatively in terms of affect to negative events such as failure (e.g., Hull & Young, 1983). But since high self-consciousness correlates with depression (e.g., Ingram & Smith, 1984), and probably also with anxiety, these early studies could not attribute the negative emotional reaction solely to a disposition to be highly self-conscious. It could have been due to the depression. In a preliminary analogue study,

Ingram (1986) equated levels of depression in subjects high and low in self-consciousness and *still* found a greater exacerbation of negative affect after a negative event in highly self-conscious subjects.

This basic work in the laboratory has striking parallels in clinical research, which are discussed at greater length below. For example, Rapee *et al.* (1986), in an experiment described in Chapter 4, found that panic was all but eliminated during a laboratory provocation experiment if the panic patients were told in great detail about the specific sensory experiences associated with CO_2 inhalation. During the trial, presumably, the patients focused attention on these sensations at the expense of the affective or distress components of the experience.

To return to my colleagues' and my work on sexual dysfunction, there are some more interesting parallels (Beck & Barlow, 1986a, 1986b). In one experiment, sexually dysfunctional patients and age-matched functional controls were instructed either to focus on their sensations or feelings of arousal while watching an erotic film, or to focus more objectively on how much genital response they were achieving "as if from an outsider's perspective." The latter instructional set was meant to reproduce as closely as possible the concept of "spectatoring," mentioned so often in the sexual dysfunction literature as a possible maintaining factor. These instructional sets were delivered under either the threat of contingent shock described above ("There is a 60% chance you'll be shocked if you are not as aroused as the average subject") or no threat. Normal subjects were distracted by these "spectatoring" instructions, and shock threat seemed to intensify the effects of the distracting instructions for the normal subjects by reducing arousal. Once again, this was not the case for dysfunctional patients, who surprised us by showing their highest levels of arousal when the "spectatoring" instructions were accompanied by shock threat. Thus, whether normal subjects are told to focus on the content of a neutral story while watching an erotic film (see Figure 7.2) or to attend to the mechanical stimulus aspects of the size of their erection, attention to erotic cues and resulting sexual arousal will suffer. But for dysfunctionals, attending to a neutral story does not reduce arousal, and may actually disinhibit it slightly (see Figure 7.2); attending to mechanical aspects of the size of their erection seems to have the same effect. Here is the paradox once again. But when subjects in the experiment just described were asked to attend to affect and feelings, different results were observed. Dysfunctionals evidenced some negative affect and generally seemed to distance themselves slightly from the situation. Normals, on the other hand, were subjectively involved and interested (Beck & Barlow, 1986b).

In view of these findings, it is possible once again, that the mechanical spectator focus for the dysfunctionals in this experiment took their minds off the negative, self-evaluative aspects of their affect or distress associated with sexual functioning, and thus facilitated sexual responding! In fact, careful examination of their focus of attention suggested that dys-functionals tended to drift back to the erotic film significantly more than functionals during the "spectatoring" condition. It was almost as if having something else to focus on during the film allowed them somehow to bypass their negative affect regarding this situation. Thus, a shift to self-focused attention seems critical; however, after this shift occurs, focusing on negative affect or distress rather than mechanical stimulus contexts seems implicated in emotional disorders.

To return to Figure 7.6 one can now suggest that situational cues associated with negative affect result in a shift from an external to an internal focus of attention, directed to the affective and self-evaluative components of the context, which results in further increases in arousal, and so on.

Normal and Pathological Anxiety

These findings suggest a crucial distinction between "normal" and pathological anxiety. Before any type of performance, including most of the challenges we confront daily, an adaptive human response includes physical and mental preparation. The essence of this response consists of arousal and preparation to cope, which, as shown in Chapter 1 and above, improve performance.

Sometimes this response is termed a "stress response" (see Chapter 5). This is also Liddell's (1949) "shadow of intelligence," described in Chapter 1. According to our data, as well as this experimental tradition, preparatory increases in arousal are not pathological. What *is* pathological is the associated shift in attention to an off-task focus that seems to be an integral part of the cognitive–affective structure of anxiety. This disruption of attention is in large part responsible for decreases in performance. This attentional shift in turn contributes to a vicious cycle of anxious apprehension, in which increasing anxiety leads to further attentional shifts, increased performance deficits, and subsequent spiraling of arousal.

But how do nonanxious individuals experience arousal, particularly the arousal that accompanies important challenges, such as major speeches or other critical events in one's life? There are few data available from normal volunteers in our laboratory situation, but a television conversation between two well-known former major league baseball players, while announcing a game for the New York Yankees, provides a clue. Discussing their preparation for a big game, Phil Rizzuto commented, "I used to get very nervous!" Bill White replied, "I don't think it was nerves, it was just excitement. We were getting 'up' for the game!" Rizzuto thought about it before replying, "No way, it was nerves." But when Rizzuto and White took the field as players, this preparatory arousal (however it was construed) was translated into effective action, as is the case with almost all professional athletes and performers. For this to happen, attention has to be focused fully and completely on the task at hand. Without this attentional shift to external events, professional performers would be like our sexually dysfunctional patients, unable to concentrate and ultimately unable to perform. Other factors contributing to the process of anxious apprehension are discussed further below.

Implications for Stress Disorders

The importance of self-focused attention is highlighted by considering the possible consequences of an exaggerated, exclusively external focus of attention. Scheier *et al.* (1983) make some particularly interesting observations in this regard on the association between focus of attention and stress, using Type A personalities as an example. They speculate, with some supporting evidence, that Type A personalities are characterized by a very strong external focus of attention. They exert control over their world and the stressors in it by concentrating fully on the task at hand. This results in a marked decrease in the amount of attention available for internal focus and a subsequent lack of sensitivity to internal bodily events.

One consequence of this focused attention is that Type A personalities seek out medical assistance less often for real physical problems, including pain associated with myocardial infarction or other stress-related physical conditions. These conditions would be noticed and attended to by individuals with a greater facility for shifting to an internal focus. Suls and Fletcher (1985b) confirmed that individuals lower in self-consciousness become ill more often, probably as a result of internal insensitivity. This suggests that either predominantly internal or predominantly external direction of attention may be pathological under certain circumstances. Suls and Fletcher (1985a) have characterized these operations as "avoidant" and "nonavoidant" strategies for coping with stress. The differential adaptiveness of these strategies in specific circumstances is discussed further in Chapter 8.

In any case, a very interesting and perhaps essential difference between stress and anxiety disorders is suggested—a difference that has perplexed clinical investigators for years. It is possible, that individuals with some specific stress disorders are characterized by an external focus of attention and a perception of control over events in the environment. Therefore, they experience few if any of the affective qualities that accompany anxious self-preoccupation in connection with stressful experiences. On the other hand, stress-prone individuals evidence physical breakdowns based on organ or system vulnerability because of their relative insensitivity to the beginnings of symptoms associated with these physical conditions. Patients with chronic anxious apprehension have learned to attend very early to internal sensations in general, and have become preoccupied with the affective qualities of these sensations. Thus, otherwise normal life events evoke self-focused attention and a cycle of anxious apprehension. This difference in focus may also account for the observation (Barlow, 1985) that stress disorder patients present with somatic symptoms of anxiety, but few of the "cognitive" symptoms. Anxious patients, on the other hand, clearly have cognitive symptoms, but also have the somatic symptoms of anxiety because of the spiraling of sympathetic arousal.

This self-evaluative focus most likely becomes integrated with the response propositions of anxiety as time goes on. It may not be conceptually correct to separate evaluative self-focus from the cognitive representations of negative affect, as implied in Figure 7.6, despite the evidence that a shift to self-focus initially follows arousal or affect. But I continue to consider it separately here, since this particular feature of anxious apprehension has implications for therapy.

WORRY

While investigating the nature and treatment of insomnia several years ago, Thomas Borkovec observed that psychologically based insomnia was associated with uncontrollable cognitive intrusions. In severe cases, these intrusions would interfere with the ability to go to sleep or remain sleeping. While the content might be logical and related to ongoing activities of the day, such as problems at home or at the office, the setting for considering these issues was entirely inappropriate. To Borkovec and his colleagues (e.g., Borkovec, 1979), these cognitions seemed to have the quality of being "driven" by some process totally out of the control of the individual suffering from insomnia. On the basis of these important observations, Borkovec began studying chronic "worriers" (Borkovec, 1985; Borkovec, Robinson, Pruzinsky, & DePree, 1983). Most likely these individuals, if their symptoms were severe enough would fit neatly into the DSM-III-R category of generalized anxiety disorder, with its emphasis on apprehension as its defining feature (see Chapter 9). Borkovec and his colleagues observed a driven, unending process as in generalized anxiety disorder: Chronic worriers entertained a stream of thoughts and images regarding possible negative or traumatic events in their future and ways in which they might deal with them. They also noted that no solutions were ever reached in terms of possible methods of dealing with these future "what-if" possibilities, but that the process continued in any case.

More structured empirical studies comparing worriers and nonworriers revealed that distraction and difficulty in "shutting off" worry activity were among the most noticeable discriminators. Pruzinsky and Borkovec (1983) also found that worriers were significantly more depressed and anxious than nonworriers on general affect questionnaires. This finding is interesting, since these subjects were chosen strictly on the basis of frequent worrying, rather than on criteria of depression or anxiety. They also demonstrated significantly more negative imagery and had more difficulty with attentional control on the Imaginal Process Inventory (Singer & Antrobus, 1972). More recently, these investigators have demonstrated that worry can and does interfere with performance (Borkovec, in press).

At this point in the hypothetical process of anxious apprehension, then, worry is the point at which "hot" cognitions driven by spiraling arousal attain a life of their own, traveling beyond the volitional control of individuals. Worry may seem, on the face of it, a perfectly reasonable activity in view of one or another ongoing situation that may need attention. Worry may even provide the illusion of taking some action in regard to a foreboding future. This would be consistent with the strong preparatory set and supportive physiology that seem to be essential components of anxiety. For this reason, there seems to be a reinforcing and therefore self-perpetuating quality to worry (Borkovec, in press), which relates to attempts to cope and regain control. But, in fact, it is a totally nonfunctional consequence of negative affect and the subsequent spiraling of arousal, followed by extreme narrowing of attention. Eventually, concentration and ongoing activities are disrupted. The logical antidote, the refocusing of attention of external tasks, is usually out of the individual's reach.

SUMMARY OF THE MODEL

The complex negative feedback cycle sketched out in the preceding pages is supported by diverse bodies of basic research that require further conceptual and experimental "fitting" to the process of clinical anxiety. Nevertheless, my colleagues' and my research on sexual dysfunction, as well as other related research, converges to support the broad outlines of a model of anxious apprehension as it would be operative in a clinical context (see Figure 7.6).

At the heart of this process is a negative affective state that can be characterized roughly as a state of "helplessness" because of perceived inabilities to predict, control, or obtain desired results in certain upcoming situations or context. This state is associated with arousal, which may underlie an effort to counteract helplessness (e.g., Cook et al., 1986; Fridlund, Hatfield, Cottam, & Fowler, 1986). But it is possible that arousal is associated more narrowly at this point with Gray's behavioral inhibition system (see Chapter 2), because of the influence of a sense of uncontrollability and the matching or comparative function of self-focused attention. This state may be elicited by a broad range of stimulus and response propositions in the Langian sense. Alternatively, the cues may be very narrow, as is the case in sexual dysfunction or test anxiety, where implicit or explicit demands for performance and subsequent evaluation in the one situation serve to trigger the cycle of anxious apprehension. This affective core is cast in terms of propositions, since it is basically an affective or mood state. However, it is much more diffuse than clear-cut emotions such as fear or panic, and it is only a part of a structure that is greatly influenced by a number of cognitive processes.

At this point, a crucial shift from an external to a self-focused mode of attention occurs. Attention is directed specifically to the affective qualities of distress associated with the arousal and sense of uncontrollability characterizing the negative affective state. Self-preoccupation serves to increase further the intensity of negative affect and the arousal associated with it. In and of itself, this process forms a small negative feedback cycle, as represented in Figure 7.6. Of course, this self-focused attention more than likely becomes very much integrated with negative affect. That is, unexplained arousal and negative affect may initially trigger a shift to self-focused attention in vulnerable individuals, but eventually self-focused attention becomes an integral part of the core negative affect.

The arousal and activation associated with this process lead to a dramatic narrowing of attention to the content of the apprehension, as well as self-preoccupation with one's ability to obtain desired results in the upcoming situation(s). it is not arousal per se that is problematic in this process, since an external focus of attention and a sense of control combined with arousal may well produce effective performance. Rather, essential to this process are the arousal-driven apprehension and self-preoccupation. Extreme arousal, whatever the cause, will eventually result in deterioration of attention and performance (Korchin, 1964).

Hypervigilance, or the enhanced recognition of threat-related stimuli (MacLeod et al., 1986), is one consequence of attention narrowing. But hypervigilance will be directed differently, depending on the perceived source of threat. For example, in sexual dysfunction, any signs of demands for sexual performance will trigger anxious apprehension, leading to attention narrowing and hypervigilance to these cues. Similarly, simple phobics will be hypervigilant for environmental cues that provide a context for feared objects or situations. Sartory (1986) has confirmed the hypervigilance of simple phobics with fears of small animals to environmental stimuli. On the other hand, research from a variety of sources has highlighted the hypervigilance of patients with panic disorder to internal somatic cues that may signal the beginning of the next panic attack (see Chapter 6).

In its extreme state, narrowing of attention of apprehensive concerns leads to runaway, out-of-control, intense worry that individuals are unable to shut off or control in any effective way. Worry in turn leads to

259

disruptions in concentration, which constitute one of the hallmarks of clinical anxiety; these are accompanied by disruptions in performance, if performance is required. In sexual or test-taking contexts, disruptions in performance become the most salient part of the problem. When anxiety is generalized, difficulties in concentration may lead to inefficient performance at the job or at home, but patients place more emphasis on the unpleasantness associated with chronic unremitting states of anxious apprehension. Attempts to avoid a negative affective state are inevitable, but may not be successful. Avoidance may fail because of the diffuseness of the cues or because of the necessity of encountering the situation or context even if the cues are very restricted, as is the case with most individuals suffering from test anxiety.

Two issues remain. First, there is a complex but intriguing relationship among true alarms, false alarms, learned alarms, and anxious apprehension that comprises the essential feature of most anxiety disorders. I have suggested that alarms, in and of themselves, are not problematic unless they give rise to and combine with the process of anxious apprehension. It is this combination of learned alarms and anxious apprehension occurring in various contexts and situations that comprises the majority of the anxiety disorders.

Second, the process just described may represent the outline of an adequate model of the process of anxious apprehension, but does not really touch on how this process begins. Evidence is now accumulating on the variety of factors that may contribute to the etiology of anxious apprehension—a topic to which I now turn.

THE ETIOLOGY OF ANXIOUS APPREHENSION

ANXIETY IN ANIMALS

In the difficult area of etiology, the isolation of potentially important variables contributing to a disorder is often limited to a retrospective search of the patient's history. Short of longitudinal studies conducted over the course of decades to examine children at risk for the development of certain disorders, there are few methods available to help answer this most essential of all questions. For this reason, the ability to produce an emotional disorder in the laboratory is an enormously important step. Experimentally induced anxiety permits systematic exploration of the factors contributing to the disorder. Thus one chapter of this book (Chapter 4) has been devoted to the fledgling area of the laboratory provocation of panic, with all of its problems and promises.

While it would seem that there is no adequate laboratory analogue of the more diffuse phenomenon of anxious apprehension, the evidence actually suggests that we can produce severe anxious apprehension in the laboratory and that we have been doing so for over 50 years. In experiment after experiment, most of them now classic, investigators have produced behavior characterized by extreme agitation, restlessness, distractibility, hypersensitivity, increased autonomic responding, muscle tension, and interference with ongoing performance. The names of the investigators associated with these experiments occupy a prominent place in every textbook of introductory psychology: Pavlov, Masserman, Liddell, and Gantt. The phenomenon they produced was commonly termed "experimental neurosis."

Why has this work been largely ignored by clinical researchers? Probably because the subjects were animals rather than people, and these early investigators made few systematic attempts to match the phenomena they were producing in the laboratory with human clinical conditions. In addition, a wide variety of paradigms were used to produce what came to be called "experimental neurosis," and each was accompanied by sometimes radically different theoretical explanations, based on the biological, psychodynamic, or behavioral predilections of the investigator. For this reason, animal models of psychopathology in general were not popular for a number of years.

Now interest has been rekindled in possible animal models of anxious apprehension, because of the striking similarity of these emotional states produced in the laboratory to clinical anxious apprehension. Particularly notable is the persistence of these learned emotional states. Establishing a persistent, self-defeating emotional state begins to address the issue of Mowrer's "neurotic paradox" (see Chapter 1)

Anyone observing species closely related to humans, such as nonhuman primates, realized that in addition to displaying all of the behavioral and physiological signs of anxiety, these animals "look" extremely anxious in a number of more qualitative nonquantifiable ways (e.g., Suomi, Kraemer, Baysinger, & DeLizio, 1981). Of course, one must be cautious about generalizing too readily from animal models. Nevertheless, experimental neurosis would seem to be one of the best animal analogues of human psychopathology (Mineka, 1985a, 1985b). Therefore, it is important to determine possible causes of this laboratory phenomenon.

Experimental neuroses in animals are produced by a number of different procedures: the punishment of appetitive responses; the presentation of insoluble problems, accompanied by the punishment of mistakes; long periods of restraint and monotony; and the introduction of extremely difficult discriminations that are required to obtain food. Some of these models, such as the punishment of appetitive responses in the Geller–Seifter paradigm described in Chapter 5, are often used for testing the effects of anxiolytic drugs.

UNPREDICTABILITY AND UNCONTROLLABILITY

At first glance, it would seem very difficult to abstract common themes from the variety of paradigms used to produce experimental neurosis. Mineka and Kihlstrom (1978), in an important review, make a compelling case for the specification of one causal factor running through all paradigms. They suggest that the cause of anxiety in these animals is that "environmental events of vital importance to the organism become unpredictable, uncontrollable, or both" (p. 257).

A body of basic experimental work has demonstrated the markedly different consequence of exposing organisms to exactly the same stimuli in a predictable and controllable versus an unpredictable and uncontrollable way. For example, Weiss (1971a, 1971b) exposed rats to the same amount and intensity of electric shock and then examined their stomachs. He found greatly increased ulceration in rats whose shock was unpredictable, whether or not shock occurence or its absence was signaled. Similarly, providing rats with some control over the shocks (the capability of terminating the shock by pressing a bar) produced sigificantly less ulceration than in rats that received the same amount of shock without any control. Much of this early work was conducted by Seligman (1968) and his colleagues (see also Seligman, 1975).

The mention of Seligman's name will quickly recall to any student of psychopatholgy the concepts of learned helplessness and depression. but conceptions of helplessness and lack of control have long been thought to underlie anxiety. For example, Mandler (1966) suggested that perceptions of lack of control (caused by aversive interruptions) are central to all views of anxiety. Experiments with both animals and humans similar to those carried out by Weiss (1971a, 1971b) have repeatedly demonstrated the strong and crucial relationship between anxiety and perceptions of lack of control over events, particularly "stressful" events (Geer, Davison, & Gatchel, 1970, Haggard, 1943; Mowrer & Viek, 1948; Neale & Katahn, 1968; Pervin, 1963; Staub, Tursky, & Schwartz, 1971; see also Miller, 1979, for a review). In a particularly cogent experiment, Rodin and Langer (1977) informed one group of nursing home residents that they would exercise control and responsibility over the arrangement of items in their room and their time. After 18 months, residents receiving this message evidenced a significantly better mortality rate than did residents who did not have control and responsibiltiy. Miller (1979) suggests that it is not even control per se, but rather the "illusion" of control, that is important. Organisms may then "predict" that future danger will be held to a minimum. Seligman's important and influential observations on helplessness and depression have overshadowed the relationship of uncontrollability and anxiety.

In fact, experience with unpredictable and/or uncontrollable events consistently produces emotional disturbance in animals, but the form of the emotional disturbance varies considerably from animal to animal. In addition, the threshold for appearance of the emotional disturbance is different. In other words, some animals tolerate significantly more frequent or more intense unpredictable or uncontrollable events before showing signs of emotional disturbance. Many animals, under conditions of unpredictability–uncontrollability, first appear extremely anxious; this is followed by severe depression, as indicated by passive, retarded, apparently helpless behaviors. Some animals seem to develop depression as an initial response to stressful experiences. Reasons for these individual differences are not clear, but they have a marked parallel in human clinical psychopathology, as indicated below.

Seligman (1975) has suggested that there may be differences between unpredictability and uncontrollability. Specifically, unpredictability may lead to anxiety, whereas excessive amounts of uncontrollability may lead to depression. Mineka (1985a) suggests that these concepts necessarily overlap. Indeed, she has argued that many if all of the effects commonly attributed to the uncontrollability of the aversive event may be more appropriately attributed to the unpredictability of the event. This is true because animals who have control over shock termination are able to predict shock absence. This view is based on the observation that while controllable shock results in less fear conditioning than does equivalent exposure to uncontrollable shock, this difference can be removed by providing the animal with a "feedback" stimulus, which will predict shock absence, during the uncontrollable experience (Mineka, Cook, & Miller, 1984). This feedback stimulus is also called a "safety signal"—a term that appears subsequently in this book. Recently, however, Rosellini, Warren, and DeCola (1987) have demonstrated in animals that the effects of controllability and predictability are separable and do exert an independent influence. They have found that (1) the acquisition of fear follows a different pattern in animals having control than it follows in those having only prediction of shock absence; and (2) controllability of shock results in lower levels of fear conditioning under conditions where these effects cannot be mediated by predictability. Miller (1979) also concludes that the majority of human studies on this issue suggest that having control reduces emotional arousal after a stressful event, even when predictability is held constant. Investigators are continuing to untangle these effects and their relative importance in the generation of "anxiety."

Another interesting thread running through this research revolves around a comparison of losing control or predictability to never having had it in the first place. From their analysis of the early work on experimental neurosis, Mineka and Kihlstrom (1978) suggest that lack of experience with predictability in an organism may not result in the same dramatic effect as it does in animals accustomed to predictable, orderly lives.

In other words, if events never have been predictable, then subsequent unpredictable events have little impact.

In summary, it seems crucial that events important to the organism, such as the acquisition of food and escape from pain, occur in a predictable and/or controllable manner. Even aversive events of substantial intensity or duration will be better tolerated (with marked individual differences) if they occur predictably and if the organism at least perceives that some control over these events is possible. Lack of predictability or controllabiltiy of these "stressful" events seems to lead to chronic anxiety and/or depression. With this work from experimental laboratories in mind, it is possible to examine more closely factors in the etiology of anxious clinical apprehension.

STRESSFUL LIFE EVENTS

Although experiments on uncontrollability and unpredictability have been carried out with a variety of laboratory animals, some of the most compelling evidence comes from experiments with our close relatives, the primates, particularly rhesus monkeys. For example, Suomi and his colleagues have been studying "anxiety" in rhesus monkeys for years (e.g., Suomi, 1986). In particular, they have been interested in chronic displays of anxiety in the absence of any specific fear stimulus, and factors that increase or decrease the intensity of this anxiety. Monkeys display all of the signs and symptoms of anxiety: tension, agitation, vigilance, and autonomic hyperactivity. Additonal evidence that these behaviors and reactions represent anxiety comes from observations of similar or identical behavior on the part of the monkeys when faced with a feared stimulus. Of course, rhesus monkeys have species-specific expressions of anxiety, in addition to more general manifestations that seem to be shared by several species. Nevertheless, preliminary work by this group of investigators and others examining causes of chronic anxiety in monkeys provides useful, suggestive evidence to guide a search for causes of anxiety in humans.

What these investigators have found (e.g., Suomi et al., 1981) is that stressful negative life events during development produce long-term increases in anxiety levels. These events are characterized as potentially life-threatening, such as separation from a primary caregiver or introduction to a group of strangers. In each case a "panic-like" reaction in the young monkey occurs, followed by long-term chronic anxiety that may last several years. Anxious behavior over the long term is likely to occur in novel or stressful situations to which the monkey is subsequently exposed. Introduction to strangers is a particularly interesting event, in terms of the evidence reviewed in Chapter 2 on the seemingly innate (if short-lived) fear of strangers that develops in human infants at approximately 8 months of age. Fear of strangers in rhesus monkeys is an adaptive response, since young monkeys attempting to join a new group in the wild are often severely beaten or killed by these "strangers" if the newcomer does not display the appropriate submissive behaviors. In any case, this sequence seems to be an example of a stressful event leading to an alarm reaction (panic?), which is followed by chronic anxiety.

INTERACTION OF STRESS AND UNCONTROLLABILITY

There are marked individual differences in these responses, which can be traced to a combination of experiential and biological/genetic factors. For example, rhesus monkeys seem to inherit varying levels of autonomic hyperreactivity in response to stress (e.g., Suomi, 1986). High reactivity predisposes them to more severe anxiety. In addition, experiencing stress of various sorts prior to the experience of an unpredictable life-threatening experience also seems to produce more intense anxiety subsequently.

Recently, some fascinating research from Mineka, Insel, and their colleagues has begun to illustrate not only the seeming importance of negative life events in the production of anxiety in rhesus monkeys, but also their interaction with uncontrollability or unpredictability in what would seem to be a very unlikely context. For example, Insel, Champoux, Scanlan, and Suomi (1986) reared two groups of rhesus monkeys identically except for their control over nonaversive stimuli. One group (the control group) had free access to toys and food treats, but identical items were presented to a yoked group only when they were first selected by an animal in the control group. When these two groups were exposed to a traumatic social separation in their third year of life, the yoked group exhibited more anxiety.

In an interesting twist, these investigators then administered a benzodiazepine inverse agonist (see Chapter 5) in order to examine responses to this pharmacological anxiogenic substance in the two groups of monkeys. This drug seems to produce a severe burst of negative affect. Once again, the yoked group displayed significantly more anxiety, as indicated by social withdrawal and distress vocalizations. The monkeys that had control over their environment, on the other hand, made more aggressive threats under these conditions, rather than showing anxious behavior. The authors conclude that these anxiogenic compounds have differential behavioral effects depending on rearing history. Specifically, experiences of control and mastery early in life may have long-term consequences for the development of anxiety and coping behavior.

Mineka, Gunnar, and Champoux (1986) conducted a similar but even more sophisticated experiment, with similarly defined groups as well as a group receiving no reinforcers (toys or treats). Between 7 and 9 months of age, all groups were presented with a toy monster. The group with the experience of control and mastery evidenced far less fear and more exploratory behavior than the comparison groups.

Several features of these experiments are particularly interesting. First, exposure to traumatic negative experiences (social separation, threatening objects) resulted in the predictable alarm response followed by long-term anxious apprehension. This result seems to dramatically replicate previous animal work on exposure to uncontrollable aversive events. But prior experiences with *nonaversive* events, in which some of the animals learned to experience control over their environment, predicted response to subsequent aversive events. This differential response was even more clearly indicated with administration of a drug causing anxiety. In fact, the animals in the group that learned control over an aspect of their environment dealt with this anxiogenic compound by becoming more aggressive—certainly one way of coping with difficult situations or experiences.

A pause to speculate on possible connections with research reviewed earlier in humans is in order here. Scheier *et al.* (1983) observed that Type A personalities respond to stress by focusing totally on external circumstances, such as tasks at hand, in a seeming attempt to reassert control over their world. Type A personalities are also known for frequent angry outbursts. In fact, a consensus is developing that irritability and angry outbursts *are* the crucial components of so-called "Type A personality" (e.g., Chesney, 1986; MacDougell, Dembroski, Dimsdale, & Hackett, 1985). It has been noted in Chapter 2 that the affective components of anger and anxiety are more closely related in any dimensional analysis of emotion than even anxiety and depression, since both are negative affective states sharing similar action tendencies (fight or flight) and supportive physiology. Perhaps anger in stressed Type A individuals (and related stress disorders) and anxiety in our anxious patients have similar roots in aversive interruptions. One type of individual may become angry and the other anxious as a function of early experience with control and direction of self-focused attention.

On the basis of evidence presented in Chapter 6, it is likely that both types of individuals experience false alarms after stress. However, in anxious patients such a false alarm would result in a panic attack, while in Type A individuals it might result in an angry outburst or temper tantrum. An interesting clinical vignette illustrates the close relationship between anger and anxiety. Two individuals recently presented in our clinic with panic associated with attending and making presentations at committee meetings. Both men were successful but pressured professionals. In each case, the individual's difficulty started during a meeting where he was particularly angry with fellow committee members regarding an issue before the committee. During this period of extreme anger, it occurred to each individual that he might be unable to control his temper or speak coherently. Each was experiencing a false alarm, representing, most likely, an aggressive action tendency (fight). But in both cases, perceptions of possible lack of control quickly turned anger into anxiety. Subsequently, a full-blown social phobia developed.

The findings of Mineka *et al.* (1986) and others have important implications for the relationship of experiences with unpredictability and uncontrollability to fear. Mineka's monkeys evidenced more extreme fear (alarm, panic) when confronted with a potentially life-threatening situation if they had experienced unpredictability or uncontrollability over important life events. Presumably, they were already in a cycle of anxious apprehension. We also know from evidence reviewed in Chapters 4 and 5 that the best (and only) predictors of successful panic provocation in the laboratory are the high baseline anxiety and arousal characteristic of the "chronically" anxious. It is possible that the results described above comprise an animal analogue of the common clinical observation that panic attacks tend to "spike off" a platform of high baseline anxiety, leading to a classic vicious spiral of anxious apprehension and panic. More precisely, chronic anxious apprehension lowers the threshold for panic. It is also possible that panic attacks represent learned alarms to the arousal cues associated with the catecholamine surges and neurotransmitter activity of anxiety, as detailed in Chapter 6.

Taken together, this evidence indicates that, in animals at least, negative life events—particularly uncontrollable and/or unpredictable life events—can lead to stress and alarm reactions. Subsequently, chronic anxious apprehension may develop, including the perception that "This terrible event may happen again at any time, and I'm not sure I can deal with it." Animals seem to be biologically vulnerable to the experience of being stressed in some ways, but a sense of mastery or control during development seems to decrease the likelihood of an anxious response. Other evidence indicates that monkeys receiving social support from a monkey peer group will have fewer anxiety reactions than will monkeys reared in isolation (Mineka, 1985a, 1985b). The development of coping responses that imply a sense of control (whether real or apparent) also buffers anxiety (Suomi, 1986). With this suggestive evidence from our close primate relatives in mind, it becomes possible to examine evidence on the etiology of human anxious apprehension from the perspective of the model outlined above.

A MODEL OF THE DEVELOPMENT OF ANXIOUS APPREHENSION

As Mineka (1985a, 1985b) points out, this animal model of anxiety may be one of the best-fitting animal models of psychopathology currently available. Furthermore, among Martin Seligman's many contributions is his suggestion that unpredictability and uncontrollability are important for subsequent emotional reactions (Seligman, 1975). Nevertheless, the bulk of theorizing by Seligman and his students over the past decade has been limited to depression and the perception of helplessness that develops when negative uncontrollable events are perceived to be caused by internal, stable, and global factors. This is the reformulated learned helplessness model of depression (Abramson, Seligman, & Teasdale, 1978). But what has happened to anxiety?

In basic research, the first and primary reaction to negative life events seems to be anxiety, although retardation and helplessness may develop initially in some animals and subsequently in many animals who at first appear anxious. This once again brings up the intriguing and perplexing relationship between anxiety and depression, discussed in some detail in Chapter 2. While this issue is discussed fully below, it is important first to test the animal model of anxious apprehension for applicability to the development of human anxiety.

STRESSFUL LIFE EVENTS

Central to this model is the importance of traumatic or negative life events, and one's prior experience with these events. The remarkable association of negative or "stressful" life events with an alarm reaction in panic patients has been described in Chapter 6. This association is all the more notable, since individuals presenting with panic are seldom able to point to a temporal association between their alarm and a negative life event. Of course, I cannot proceed further without emphasizing once again that the data supporting this association are limited, in that they are confined to retrospective reports by patients presenting with panic.

In fact, as noted in Chapter 6, work on the relationship of stressful life events and clinical depression is more advanced in demonstrating the important etiological contribution of these events. For example, Lewinsohn and his colleagues conducted a prospective study of antecedents or risk factors for unipolar depression in over 400 subjects who were interviewed and diagnosed according to the Schedule for Affective Disorders and Schizophrenia and the Research Diagnostic Criteria, respectively. These subjects were closely followed for 1 year. Although some subjects were lost, 85 developed a depressive episode during the course of the study, and 269 remained nondepressed throughout.

A variety of interesting data are available from the preliminary report of this important comparison (Lewinsohn et al., in press). For example, frequency of pleasant life events did not predict the onset of depression, contrary to Lewinsohn's own earlier hypotheses (Lewinsohn, 1974). People with higher depression scores did engage in fewer pleasant activities;

however, reduction in pleasant activities may be a concomitant rather than a cause of depression. Although there was no evidence in this study that pre-existing cognitive sets predicted depression, a strong association emerged between the occurrence of stressful life events during the past year and the development of depression. People who became depressed reported a significantly greater amount of life change than did people who did not become depressed. This association was particularly strong for stressful events occurring in the month preceding the onset of their depression. The relationship became weaker with the passage of time. This finding on the temporal relationship replicated retrospective work reported by Paykel (1978, 1979), as well as a study by Hammen *et al.* (1986) with college students. Other controlled studies are also appearing confirming this finding (e.g., Monroe, Bromet, Connell, & Steiner, 1986).

Hammen *et al.* (1986), in another prospective study, also found a relationship between recent life events and depression in subjects who had either a history of depression or existing low-level intensities of depression. Hammen *et al.* suggest that prior experience, as represented in current "cognitive schemas," may mediate vulnerability to stress-related depression.

Prior episodes of depression or depressive symptoms did not seem to be responsible for an "overreporting" of life events in Lewinsohn *et al.*'s data, as some investigators have theorized (e. g., Depue & Monroe, 1986; Monroe, 1983). Stressful life events were not magnified by pre-existing depressive symptoms, resulting in a greater (retrospective) report of these events at the time of the depression. Rather, negative life events clearly preceded the occurrence of a depressive episode, rather than being consequences of that episode. It can be assumed for the moment, on the basis of retrospective reports of patients suffering from panic, that similar strong relationships will emerge in the anxiety disorders—an assumption that is beginning to receive confirmation (e.g., McKeon, Roa, & Mann, 1984; Roy-Byrne *et al.*, 1986).

PRELIMINARY DESCRIPTION OF THE MODEL

What, then, would be the process of the development of anxiety? Now that the crucial role of negative life events has been considered, the model can be summarized here briefly to provide a basis for elaboration below. In my view, a biological vulnerability to stress exists. This vulnerability is nonspecific, but may involve an overactive hypothalamic–pituitary–adrenocortical system and/or labile neurotransmitter systems. The occurrence of a negative life event produces marked disruptions in the individual's ongoing activity. These disruptions or interruptions are prominently highlighted in some theories of anxiety (e.g., Gray, 1982; Mandler, 1975).

The result is diffuse stress-related increases in arousal. In biologically vulnerable individuals arousal is particularly intense, involving, as it does, a number of neurobiological systems (see Chapter 5). The function of this neurobiological activity, which is not yet "anxiety," is to prepare the individual for action or coping. Up to this point, a similar process may be operative in individuals with certain stress disorders, in whom the same biological vulnerability may also exist, but they do not become apprehensively anxious. But neurobiological activation, particularly at intense levels, may trigger false alarms. What may happen is that the threshold for an alarm reaction (fear), which is fundamentally a set of action tendencies, is lowered as suggested in Chapter 5. This may occur because various response (and/or stimulus) propositions of a coherent emotion are tapped, particularly by biological aspects of the more diffuse stress response when experienced intensely. Alternatively, the two responses may share common neurotransmitter pathways. But this does not suggest that the alarm represents a random biological dysregulation. Rather, it is, at least initially, functionally related to stressful events and the ensuing stress response. As such, the alarm is simply another one of many examples of physiological and psychological (pathological) responses showing a stress diathesis.

These negative events and/or the alarms themselves may then produce a negative affective state characterized by a sense of unpredictability and uncontrollability in psychologically vulnerable individuals. This affective state may be associated with more specific monoaminergic activity, such as increased noradrenergic impulses to the septo-hippocampal system (e.g., Gray, 1985; see Chapter 5 and below). It is not yet clear whether this monoaminergic activity differs fundamentally in a neurobiological sense from the initial response to stress or whether it simply reflects a "chronic" expression of the stress response, based on the necessity to be continually prepared for upcoming events. In any case, the elicitation of negative affect is followed by a shift to self-focused attention and entry into the chronic cycle of anxious apprehension depicted in Figure 7.6.

UNEXPLAINED AROUSAL

Several aspects of this model need further reiteration and elaboration. There is strong evidence, reviewed above, that unexplained physiological arousal produces negative affect and subsequent self-focused attention. The experiments by Wegner and Giuliano (1980) form part of the data base for this conclusion. In addition, important reinterpretations of the Schachter and Singer (1962) hypothesis by Maslach (1979a, 1979b) and Marshall and Zimbardo (1979) indicated that unexplained or inadequately explained physiological arousal reliably produces negative affect. This induction of negative affect is true even if the context of the unexplained arousal consists of positive affective experience where others are happy. Other evidence supporting the importance of attributing the causes of unexplained arousal to an external versus an internal locus comes from well-known experiments in social psychology. For example, Storms and Nisbett (1970) administered placebo pills to insomniac subjects a few minutes before they went to bed. Some subjects were told that the pills would cause arousal; others were told that the pills would reduce arousal. Subjects told that the pills would cause arousal actually fell asleep more quickly than those who were told that the pills would be relaxing. Storms and Nisbett presume that subjects "attributed" their arousal to the pills in the aroused condition, and therefore became less "emotional" about it. Subjects who were expected to relax experienced more unexplained arousal, which (as the present model would have it) led to increased anxious apprehension and interference with sleep. Based on these conclusions, a unique aspect of the genesis of chronic anxiety is that the unpredictable and unexpected alarm reaction, with its accompanying massive arousal response, may be a major contributing factor to intense anxious apprehension. The intensity of this reaction (and one's attribution about it) may be a function of one's psychological vulnerability to unpredictable or uncontrollable events.

UNPREDICTABILITY–UNCONTROLLABILITY

A final link is required in this causal feedback cycle. The alarm (or other negative life event) must be sensed as unpredictable and/or uncontrollable, and therefore likely to happen again in an unpredictable fashion. If alarms are seen as predictable or are clearly connected with an antecedent that is no longer operable, the cycle of anxious apprehension will be unlikely to develop, even if this attribution is inaccurate. A sense of predictability–controllability may be one reason why the majority of individuals experiencing false alarms do not develop clinical anxiety disorders (Norton et al., 1986). These individuals may well attribute the intense, unexplained arousal characteristic of a false alarm to a fight with their boss, something they ate, or, perhaps more accurately, to a recent period of stress that is now behind them.

Perhaps it is here that a source of individual vulnerability can be identified. It is also possible that individuals experiencing events as unpredictable will feel less able to control or cope with unpredictable events. For example, a relatively common finding in the literature (e.g., Johnson & Sarason, 1978; Sarason, Johnson, & Seigel, 1978) is that individuals experiencing high levels of negative change become more anxious if they are externally oriented. That is, they perceive themselves as exerting less control over contingencies in their environment, as assessed by a locus of control measure. It is not clear from this work whether locus of control is a cause or an effect. But it is possible that the source of these attributions is historical and connected with prior experience of mastery or control over the environment, as demonstrated with Mineka's and Insel's monkeys (e.g., Insel et al., 1986; Mineka et al., 1986). In other words, early training of behaviors that are associated with mastery and control (coping behaviors) may result in a sense of control (cognitive schema) over unpredictable life events, including false alarms, even if this control is illusory. This hypothesis links up with some influential thinking on the etiology of phobia espoused by Andrews (1966). He has suggested that excessive dependency as a result of a markedly overprotected childhood may predispose one to phobic behavior. In the context of data from the developmental experiences of monkeys, being overprotected as a child may deprive one of the opportunity to develop a sense of mastery and control. Development of a specific focus of anxious apprehension may be a function of the negative event experienced and/or the subsequent alarm. For example, sexually dysfunctional males experience erectile failure; this is a common experience among males, but a minority who are vulnerable develop anxiety to sexual-performance-related cues. As noted in Chapter 6, many people experience false alarms, but only a few develop anxiety over the possibility of future panic attacks. In individuals vulnerable to anxiety, focusing anxious apprehension on the unexplained arousal of false alarms may be partly a function of the location of the first panic, as noted in Chapter 6. But individuals may also be predisposed to this focus through strong dispositions to self-focused attention, as reviewed above. In any case, the greater the vulnerability to anxious apprehension, the less severe the negative life event needs to be in order to initiate the cycle of anxiety.

Can "cognitive sets" of mastery and control versus helplessness or lack of control (and possibly cognitive sets reflecting more specific foci of anxious apprehension) be detected as pre-existing cognitive schemata (Beck & Emery, 1985)? Our theory predicts that Beck and Emery are correct. In fact, there may be a very good reason behind the widespread failure to identify cognitive schemata as pre-existing in either anxious or depressed persons (e.g., Lewinsohn et al., in press). On the basis of important personality research by Walter Mischel, it seems that human "traits" such as aggression are not consistently detectable through personality tests or other measures across situations. Rather, these traits are detectable only in certain situations—specifically, when these individuals are stressed (e.g., Mischel & Peake, 1982).

Interestingly, Suomi's biologically vulnerable, anxious monkeys only behaved "anxiously" while under stress. At other times they were indistinguishable from their "nonanxious" peers (Suomi et al., 1981). It may be that hypervalent cognitive schemata reflecting behavioral tendencies of vulnerability and helplessness will appear only during periods of stress. The fundamental importance of a sense of uncontrollability receives independent confirmation from a number of diverse sources. For example, Richard S. Lazarus (1966) has made perceived control of stress the cornerstone of his influential cognitive theory of stress and anxiety.

In summary, the disruption of negative events and the resulting diffuse stress response in biologically vulnerable individuals is often followed by intense unexplained arousal associated with false alarms. This process produces anxious apprehension if the individual is also psychologically vulnerable as the result of prior behavioral experiences with unpredictable and uncontrollable events, and of a learned inability to cope with these events. A disposition may also exist for a specific focus of anxious apprehension. This vulnerability is reflected in a variety of current attributions, but its source is past behavior. Other current factors, such as social support, may buffer this response by providing some sense of control in a difficult situation. This, then, becomes the negative affective core of the loose cognitive–affective structure of anxious apprehension.

ANXIETY WITHOUT ALARMS; ALARMS WITHOUT ANXIETY

But what of individuals with anxiety disorders that are not characterized by alarms? According to current knowledge, many individuals with generalized anxiety disorder may fall into this category. Here the disorder is characterized by intense chronic worry diffused across a number of life situations. Many individuals with generalized anxiety disorder report having experienced alarms (panic attacks) in the past, although panic is neither the focus of their problem nor the source of their concern. In any case, whether the experience of false alarms contributed to the process of anxious apprehension that in turn emerged in different life situations, or whether negative life events in the absence of false alarms began the negative feedback cycle of anxious apprehension, it seems clear that anxiety is in place and is chronic and intense. In the absence of false alarms, attributions of unpredictability and uncontrollability seem related to the negative life events alone. In this sense, generalized anxiety disorder is closer to models of depression, although important differences are described below.

Before presenting a diagram of this model, I must return to a consideration of the relationship between learned alarms and anxious apprehension, mentioned at the end of Chapter 6. That learned alarms are a common occurrence is apparent in any survey of fears and phobias. For example, up to 50% of the population reports common but irrational fears of insufficient severity to qualify as phobias, as defined in the ECA study (see Chapter 1). But alarms in themselves, whether true, false, or learned, are not problematic *unless* they become strongly associated with anxious apprehension. If alarms are seen as predictable and controllable, either because one can control access to the cues of alarm or because coping mechanisms are well in place (e.g., the nearly perfect avoidance present in the animal laboratory), then little subjective distress over the possibility of having an alarm will occur. In this way, learned alarms are similar to false alarms that are attributed to predictable–controllable or no-longer-operative events. As noted above, false alarms in this instance seem to cause minimal distress.

This fact accounts, most likely, for the marked differences observed between simple phobias and other anxiety or depressive disorders. For example, evidence has been presented in Chapter 5 that (many) simple phobics do not present with chronic hyperarousal, as seen in other anxiety disorders. Also unlike individuals with other anxiety disorders, simple phobics are seldom if ever depressed. For this reason, simple phobics seldom seek treatment, but when they do, they almost always present with additional emotional disorders that are causing clinical complications. Only when learned alarms become associated with a strong cycle of anxious apprehension is a clinical anxiety disorder manifested. Thus, the essence of clinical anxiety disorders consists not of alarms, but of severe and chronic anxious apprehension. For individuals in difficult and dangerous situations, the issue is not whether they experience fear or alarms, but whether it is acceptable and tolerable to experience an alarm.

With these distinctions in place, it is possible to return to definitional issues outlined in Chapter 1. "Fear," whether mild or in its severe alarm form ("panic"), is a transient, relatively automatic emotional reaction to a variety of perceived dangers and threats, either rational or irrational. "Anxious apprehension" is a diffuse cognitive–affective structure with characteristics that include chronic overarousal or activation, a sense of unpredictability and/or uncontrollability, and attentional shifts to self-evaluation modes that cycle toward chronicity. The difference between fear and anxiety is not to be found in the presence or absence of cues, although cues are always less obvious in anxiety. Rather, crucial differences can be found in the complex cognitive–affective relationships present in anxious apprehension, in its tendency toward chronicity due to a vicious-cycle effect, and in the all-important meaning propositions (in the Langian sense) found in the affective core of anxiety. Fear is a fundamental, survival-oriented, ethologically significant emotion with clear escapist action tendencies. But the essence of the affective component of anxiety is a personal loss of control over crucial events in one's internal or external environment. Among these events is the basic emotion of fear itself. That is, the experience of fear, if unexpected and unpredicted, can pro-

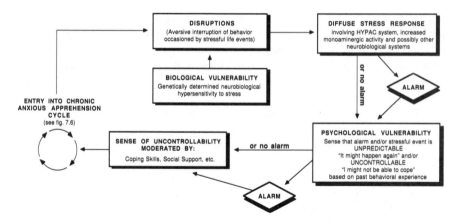

FIGURE 7.7. The origins of anxious apprehension.

duce anxious apprehension. This etiological model of anxious apprehension is represented schematically in Figure 7.7.

FULL DESCRIPTION OF THE MODEL

A full description of the model of the etiology of anxious apprehension, based on the evidence presented above and in preceding chapters, can now be presented. At the core of this model is a biological vulnerability to stress, most likely genetically transmitted, which may manifest itself across several neurobiological systems. This vulnerability is activated by disruptions—that is, aversive interruptions of behavior occasioned by negative stressful life events. These stress-produced reactions, at sufficient intensities, often result in false alarms. Whether an alarm is true or false depends on the nature of the negative event—specifically, the degree to which life-threatening danger is present in the situation. True alarms occur immediately; false alarms or other emotional responses are more probable immediately following the stressful incident, but it is not unusual for false alarms to be delayed by days, weeks, or even months. In some individuals, severe alarms do not occur.

In any case, the alarm and/or stressful event is experienced as unpredictable ("It may happen again") and possibly uncontrollable ("I may not be able to deal effectively with it"). The experience of uncontrollability and associated negative affect, in turn, may lower the threshold further for alarms, allowing for an initial occurence if an alarm has not yet been experienced. Attributions of predictability and controllability seem to be a function of early developmental experiences in one's environment. If one develops a sense of control or mastery, one may well be relatively im-

275

mune to the onset of the cycle of anxious apprehension. Other moderating variables may include the amount of social support available and the number and quality of coping skills at the disposal of the individual. A sense of "helplessness" may lead to chronic activation of the diffuse biological stress response, or, more likely, of Gray's behavioral inhibition system.

Thus, a complex interaction of biological, psychological, and environmental events is required for the genesis of anxious apprehension. Most important are the dual biological and psychological vulnerabilities, which must line up correctly. Once this cycle begins, it becomes self-perpetuating: A sense of unpredictability and uncontrollability increases emotionality, which in turn increases the probability of learned alarms in the negative feedback cycle outlined in Figure 7.6. The basic automatic quality of this cognitive–affective structure makes systematic intervention very difficult indeed (see Chapter 8). In any case, the best explanation of what happens next is that the affective core of this newly emerging cognitive–affective structure is stored deep in long-term memory as a series of propositions (Lang, 1984, 1985). These propositions become subject to further alterations as a function of the development of new associative networks. Thus, it is no longer a "rational" process dependent on fresh cognitive appraisals in each new context.

ANXIETY AND DEPRESSION

I begin to draw this chapter to a close by summarizing and elaborating on the relationship of anxious apprehension, depression, and stress. Delineating crucial differences among these three loosely defined constructs is essential if we are to develop precise and effective systems of classification and treatment. Some important differences are suggested by recent data collected in our clinic.

In one experiment (Heimberg, Vermilyea, Dodge, Becker, & Barlow, 1987), 33 patients received a DSM-III diagnosis of dysthymic disorder on the basis of a Schedule for Affective Disorders and Schizophrenia interview. These patients were compared to 75 anxious patients, whose diagnosis included agoraphobia with panic (n = 19), panic disorder (n = 8), generalized anxiety disorder (n = 17), social phobia (n = 24), and simple phobia (n = 7). What is important about this study is that the presence of depressive disorders was documented in the anxiety disorders group. All anxiety patients with an additional depressive disorder were eliminated from analyses, resulting in the above-described 75 patients. Furthermore, to control more precisely for the influence of depression among the anxiety patients, subjects were arrayed on the basis of their severity of depressive symptoms as measured by the Beck Depression Inventory. An additional control group of age-matched adults without any anxiety or depressive disorders was also tested.

The results indicated clear differences between anxious and depressed patients, *once the presence and severity of depressive symptoms were controlled for by covariation procedures.* That is, depressed patients displayed internal, global, and stable attributions for negative outcomes, based on scores on the well-known Attributional Style Questionnaire (Peterson *et al.*, 1982). Some anxiety patients also demonstrated this attributional style, *but only if they were also depressed.* Anxiety patients, despite the severity of their anxiety disorder, had scores almost identical to those of the normal group if they were not depressed. In fact, our anxious patients who were not depressed differed from normal subjects on only one measure involving negative outcomes: They attributed negative outcomes to significantly more global sources, believing that negative events were more likely to occur across multiple areas of concern. This global attribution for negative outcomes may well reflect their concern with the unpredictability of negative events. But the overall resullts with negative events suggest that they did not attribute them to internal or stable causes. Nor did they believe that negative events were necessarily their responsibility.

These attributional patterns became even clearer in an analysis of attributions for positive events on the Attributional Style Questionnaire. Nondepressed anxious subjects attributed positive outcomes to significantly more internal and stable causes and saw themselves as more responsible for obtaining positive outcomes. They also predicted greater success at controlling future positive outcomes than the depressed group.

This report is the first to demonstrate specific attributional styles for depressed and anxious groups. At least two methodological factors may account for this demonstration of specificity. First, the patients were clinical subjects who were carefully diagnosed on the basis of an up-to-date structured clinical interview. Second, accompanying diagnoses of depression in the anxious patients, as well as intensity of depressive symptoms, were carefully specified and controlled.

In Chapter 2, I have asserted that depression and anxiety are different cognitive–affective structures with essentially different underlying mood states. I have also suggested that the primary differences are emotional and reflected in different "action tendencies" or readiness to cope, as well as in underlying supportive physiology. The lack of action tendencies in depressed individuals is reflected in the terms "helpless" or "hopeless," which clearly discriminate between anxiety and depression. On the basis of this information and the data presented above, it is possible to "sketch out" the psychopathological processes leading to either depressed or anxious states.

Anxious patients deal with unpredictable negative life events by apprehensively anticipating the next occurrence of these (or similar) events and preparing for action. Evidence for these findings is found in data on hypervigilance for future threats (MacLeod *et al.*, 1986). Fridlund *et al.* (1986) and Fowles (1986), in an important line of research, also demonstrated on the basis of psychophysiological analysis that anxiety is best described as activation rather than as generalized arousal. Also, the concept of "worry" as elucidated by Borkovec and his colleagues may reflect anxious action tendencies, in which problem-solving activities regarding upcoming sources of concern are continually rehearsed, albeit imperfectly and incompletely. Anxious patients feel incapable of coping with unpredictable events, yet are driven to anticipate the next event and to prepare for some type of action. But because of the events' unpredictable nature, the patients do not feel any responsibility for them. Thus, an anxious response in an individual could be characterized as follows: "That terrible event [false alarm/life situation] is not my fault, but it may happen again. I may not be able to cope with it, but I've got to be ready and try."

Depression can be characterized in a similar manner, but depressed patients feel responsibility for negative events and have lost all hope of coping. In extreme depression, behavioral and cognitive retardation reflects the lack of action tendencies necessary to cope with the impact of negative life events. A depressed response would be as follows: "That terrible event may happen again, and I won't be able to cope with it, and the state of affairs is my fault, so there is really nothing I can do." Anxious patients trying to cope with aversive stimuli (especially unpredictable false alarms) fight the good fight; they are continually preparing to cope, however ineffectively, with the various noxious events in their lives. The depressed individual has given up.

I speculate with Weissman (1985) that the development of depression and the development of anxiety share a common diathesis. Specifically, the development of both disorders is largely a function of experience with perceived unpredictable or uncontrollable negative life events. Even the experience with false alarms is not really unique to anxiety, since 50% or more of individuals with major depression experience false alarms (Benshoof, 1987; Breier, Charney, & Heninger, 1986). The crucial difference seems to be in the action tendencies and supportive physiology continually marshaled to cope with and control aversive events. The assumption of responsibility and guilt for negative events implicit in the intense and stable attributions made by depressed individuals may be either a cause or an effect of their reduced action tendencies and accompanying sense of helplessness and loss.

This common diathesis is reflected in the close relationship among anxiety, depression, and panic that has been found in studies of familial aggregation of these disorders, using both adults and children as probands (Puig-Antich & Rabinovich, 1986; Weissman, 1985). The more signs and symptoms of anxiety and depression, the greater the rate of anxiety or depression or both in first-degree relatives and children (e.g., Leckman *et al.*, 1983). Future research efforts must determine whether these differential aggregations are a function of the severity of the underlying vulnerabilities, both biological and psychological, as seems likely. This research, in turn, will have to await clearer, more discriminating measures of anxiety and depressive disorders.

The relationship of these mood states to potential differences in monoaminergic activity (e.g., Gray, 1985) is also an important area for investigation, since differences may reflect fundamental aspects of an anxious or depressed response to identical events. Current evidence suggests that no differences exist; this would corroborate the views of a common diathesis. For example, evidence reviewed by Gray (1985) and discussed in Chapter 5 suggests that learned helplessness in laboratory experiments, construed as an animal model of depression, may be identical in its neurobiological underpinnings to models of anxiety. Specifically, enhanced hippocampal function as a result of increased noradrenergic input to this and other regions of the forebrain seems to underlie both anxiety and depression. As suggested in Figure 7.7, this activity may actually reflect the sense of uncontrollability or helplessness that is shared by both disorders. As Gray suggests, increased noradrenergic input may be due to reduced locus ceruleus autoreceptor-mediated inhibition or to reduced GABA-ergic presynaptic inhibition of noradrenaline release, or to both. In fact, our best direct evidence with clinical populations of panic disorder and major depression supports the notion of identical underlying noradrenergic activity (e.g., Breier, Charney, & Heninger, 1985). Moreover, tricyclic antidepressants reverse helplessness in both laboratory analogues of helplessness and clinical depression. These drugs also alleviate the anxious apprehension regarding false alarms in agoraphobia and panic, while not necessarily affecting the false alarms (panic) themselves (see Chapter 11). This finding likewise suggests a common neurobiological process. Finally, recent evidence suggests that patients with generalized anxiety and patients with major depression show similar rates of nonsuppression on dexamethasone suppression tests (Schweizer, Swenson, Winokur, Rickels, & Maislen, 1986). Confirmation of these findings will also have to await better and purer measures of anxiety and depression.

Future research efforts should not remain blind to the real world of the clinic, in which the loose cognitive–affective structures of anxiety and depression are seldom seen in isolation. While it seems possible to find anxious patients who are depressed, it is far more difficult (and perhaps impossible) to find depressed patients who are not anxious. This remarkable fact is also evident in children carefully diagnosed for major depression (e.g., Hershbert, Carlson, Cantwell, & Strober, 1982; Puig-Antich & Rabinovich, 1986). Depression may simply reflect an extreme psychological vulnerability to experiences of unpredictability and uncontrollability, based on early experience or a lack of experience with attempts to cope with uncontrollable events.

But another factor may be complicating the presentation of depression. If panic is the fundamental, evolutionary significant emotion of fear, and some individuals become anxious about this uncontrollable experience, perhaps a similar phenomenon is present in depressive disorders. A symmetrical proposition would be that some individuals experience a fundamental basic emotion of sadness in the same way they experience fear. Sadness may also be experienced as unpredictable or uncontrollable and thus may lead to anxiety or depression. Clinically, this seems to happen. It is not uncommon for patients to say something like "I just feel like there's a heavy weight on my shoulders that's keeping me from moving, and it's scaring the hell out of me."

The phenomenon of "double depression" may well describe the phenomenon of being depressed about being sad (Keller & Shapiro, 1982). Teasdale (1985) makes just such an observation, based on his clinical experience:

> It is not uncommon for depressed patients to misinterpret symptoms of depression as signs of irremediable personal inadequacy: for example, the lack of energy, irritability or loss of interest and affection that characterize depression are seen as signs of selfishness, weakness or as evidence that the person is a poor wife or mother. Such interpretations, as well as making the symptoms more aversive, imply that they are going to be very difficult to control. (p. 160)

Psychological treatment, then, according to Teasdale, should involve education about symptoms of depression and either a direct attack on the symptoms (through mood-elevating activities) or other procedures to instill a sense of "control" over depressive symptoms. These come close to the recommendations for treating panic within the anxiety disorders that are made in subsequent chapters of this book.

It is possible that what is commonly referred to as "psychotic depression," with delusions of guilt and motor retardation, reflects the basic emotion of depression. Furthermore, as originally postulated by Schildkraut (1965), the (lack of) action tendencies evident in the "retarded" aspect of severe depression may be associated with a functional exhaustion of central monoaminergic systems such as the noradrenergic system. This monoaminergic exhaustion, in turn, may differentiate the basic emotion from the loose cognitive–affective structure of depression, which I now refer to exclusively as "dysthymia." This monoaminergic activity may also account for the complete remission of severe depression, seldom seen with anxiety or dysthymic disorder, since increased synthesis of these neurotransmitters eventually occurs. Differential monoaminergic activity associated with depression, if someday discovered, may also be a consequence of the development of different action tendencies reflected in varying amounts of activation, rather than a cause of depression. Differential action tendencies may be based on individual differences in thresholds for expression of underlying basic emotions of sadness and fear, or, more likely, on differences in the environmental events triggering these emotions. If intense sadness (depression) is appropriate to the situation, as in a severe grief reaction after the death of a loved one, a proper attribution will be made, and a clinical disorder is not likely to develop. But if the emotion is sufficiently intense and is experienced as unpredictable or uncontrollable, a clinical disorder is much more likely to develop.

To complete the symmetry, one can also posit the presence of "false sadness" (endogenous depression) to parallel the phenomenon of false alarms. False sadness may be a stress-related reaction resulting in an intense but inappropriate (to the situation) emotion not directly related to personal loss. As we have seen, the basic emotions of fear (alarms) and depression can coexist. Furthermore, each can be learned or conditioned to a variety of internal and external events or stimuli. Some investigators have recently demonstrated this phenomenon in the context of manic–depressive disorder (e.g., Post, Rubinow, & Ballenger, 1986).

Thus, one can experience the basic emotions of fear or sadness (alarm or depression), but most clinical emotional disorders present with a complex picture of fear and/or sadness over which individuals have developed anxiety or dysthymia, in part because the action tendencies have been experienced as uncontrollable. Anxiety or dysthymia may exist long after the basic emotions of fear and sadness have run their course. This arrangement is depicted in Figure 7.8.

Clearly, the account above is speculative. For now, we need to sharpen our descriptions of dysthymia and anxiety and of the basic emotions of fear and depression. For example, when better instruments are developed, agitated depression with its clear behavioral and physiological signs may be better considered as severe generalized anxiety (J. P. Kahn, Stevenson, Topol, & Klein, 1986; Klerman, 1980) (see Chapter 9). We may draw similar conclusions about "neurotic" depression or dysthymia. Obviously, it will be essential to continue the exploration of crucial differences between clinically anxious and depressed individuals.

To take another example, investigators have long recognized that the primary content of anxious patients' cognitions concerns future threats (Beck, Laude, & Bohnert, 1974; Gentil & Lader, 1978; Sewitch & Kirsch, 1984). Unfortunately, no study has yet appeared contrasting the cognitive content in cases of dysthymia or pure depression with that in pure anxiety. Such a study is obviously an essential step. Butler and Mathews (1983) found no difference between anxious patients and those who were anxious but also depressed in terms of the frequency of their threat-related

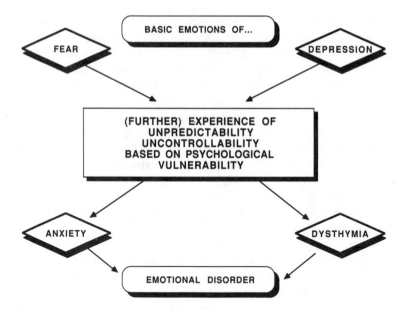

FIGURE 7.8. The relationship of fear (alarm), depression (sadness), anxiety, and dysthymia.

thoughts. When proper comparisons are made and the presence of panic or the basic emotion of depression is ascertained, one will find thoughts reflecting the different action tendencies, with hopelessness being the prime example. Nevertheless, comparisons of clearly defined samples must be made.

ANXIETY AND STRESS

To complete this speculative odyssey on etiology, consider the processes transpiring in severely stressed individuals, as suggested in the basic research reviewed in Chapter 2 and in comments by Scheier et al. (1983) and Chesney (Chesney, 1985, 1986; Chesney & Black, 1986). It is acknowledged that stress disorders are heterogeneous. (By "stress disorders," I am referring to the loosely defined "Type A syndrome" and presumably some other stress-related disorders presenting with moderate to severe physical disabilities, such as hypertension.) Individuals with these personality traits or disorders seem to display little or no anxiety or dysthymia over the stress they experience. Indeed, the process of anxious apprehension never seems to begin, since their focus of attention remains external and task-oriented. In fact, their method of coping with stress seems characterized by hard work, continual attention to achievement, and remarkable confidence in their abilities to deal with problems. Many individuals with stress disorders have an exaggerated sense of mastery and control, and deal with stressors by increasing their coping and problem-solving behavior at the expense of their physical well-being. Frequent bouts of irritability and anger in these individuals are reminiscent of the otherwise healthy rhesus monkeys who experienced mastery and control during their upbringing before displaying aggresive and angry outbursts when injected with a benzodiazepine inverse agonist. Anger seems to be the crucial defining characteristic of Type A individuals in terms of risk for physiological stress disorder, such as cardiovascular disease (Chesney, 1985, 1986). Thus, a more accurate and symmetrical name for this disorder might be "anger disorder." In this light, anger disorder would be analogous to anxiety and depressive disorders as another emotional disorder. Once again, this process would not characterize all stress disorders, as evidence developed in our clinic indicates. Disorders such as irritable bowel syndrome would be closer to anxiety disorders (Neff & Blanchard, 1987; see Chapter 9).

Since anger and fear (or anxiety) share more basic emotional dimensions than mood states of anxiety and depression, stress and anxiety patients may have more in common than depressed and anxious patients. But stress-disordered individuals, with their sense of mastery and control, do not seek treatment until evidence of clear physical deterioration is present. It is interesting that panic disorder patients are also at risk for cardiovascular disease (e.g., Coryell et al., 1986). This increased risk may likewise reflect a common diathesis, although stress patients may be at greater risk because of their tendency to ignore the symptoms.

Patients developing stress disorders may have some of the same experiences and vulnerabilities as anxious patients, and may share the same action tendencies, but stress patients never lose their illusion of control (Alloy, Abramson, & Viscusi, 1981). Dysthymic and depressed patients, on the other hand, share perceptions of unpredictability and uncontrollability with anxious patients, but evidence fundamentally different action tendencies. Hypothetical similarities and differences among anxious, depressive, and stress disorders are presented in Table 7.1. As with anxiety and depressive disorders, the close relationship between anxiety and stress disorders insures that individuals may present with considerable overlap between the two. Deffenbacher, Demm, and Brandon (1986) used regression analysis to demonstrate that general anxiety, coping through verbal antagonism, and daily anger levels accounted for 70% of the variance of general anger. Lee and Cameron (1986) reported that almost 75% of a group of anxiety disorder patients had Type A behavior (based on a questionnaire). Type A behavior was significantly more prevalent in male anx-

TABLE 7.1. Hypothetical Similarities and Differences among Anxiety, Depressive, and Stress Disorders

	Stress disorders	Anxiety disorders	Depressive disorders
Biological vulnerability	Yes	Yes	Yes
Stressful events	Yes	Yes	Yes
Stress-related neurobiological reactions	Yes	Yes	Yes
False alarms	Yes	Yes	Yes
Psychological vulnerability resulting in a sense of unpredictability–uncontrollability	No	Yes	Yes
"Coping" action tendencies and associated arousal	Yes	Yes	No

iety patients (92%) than in females (52%). Clinically, excessive anger is treated in a very similar fashion to anxiety (e.g., Novaco, 1975). This area needs considerably more investigation.

Finally, no account of the development of anxiety and anxiety disorders can fail to consider the marked sex differences evident in the epidemiological surveys reviewed in Chapter 1; these surveys found that most agoraphobics and a majority of individuals with other anxiety disorders are females. These differences stand out even more clearly in contrast to findings for hypothetical "anger disorder": The vast majority of individuals with Type A syndrome and other anger-linked stress disorders are male (Chesney & Rosenman, 1985). Reference to Table 7.1 suggests what may be the crucial etiological factor. Sex differences in anxiety (and depression) may not be due to any biological differences, but rather to psychological vulnerabilities associated with an acquired sense of uncontrollability and ineffective coping. Nolen-Hoeksema (1987) has come to a similar conclusion regarding unipolar depression.

With these theories of panic and anxiety in place, it is now possible to consider the validity of diverse explanations for successful reduction of panic and anxiety. It is to theories underlying the variety of treatments, both biological and psychological, that I now turn.

8

The Process of Fear and Anxiety Reduction: Affective Therapy

Now that models of the process and etiology of panic and anxiety have been set forth, it is possible to examine the implications of these models for treatment. The enormous strides made in recent years in developing psychological and pharmacological treatments for anxiety have not, for the most part, been guided by our knowledge of emotions. Rather, most treatments have been developed serendipitously. An example cited earlier was the discovery of drug treatments for panic. Other treatments developed as outgrowths of general schools of psychotherapy or behavior therapy; in these cases, more attention was often devoted to the therapeutic approach than to the disorder in question. Of course, influential theorists and therapists such as Wolpe and Beck have made important contributions to our knowledge of emotion therapy and theory, since their therapeutic approaches were developed in the context of emotional disorders. For this reason, the major psychotherapeutic approaches to emotional disorders that have received empirical support are outgrowths of procedures developed by pioneers such as Wolpe and Beck. Nevertheless, our knowledge of the mechanisms of action involved in the modification of intense maladaptive emotional responding is rudimentary at best. In fact, in the entire area of psychotherapy, much is made of the importance of emotional expression, whether the disorders are emotional disorders or not. And yet few approaches are guided by a knowledge of emotion theory and fact. Greenberg and Safran (1987) have begun to rectify this deficit with an important and scholarly book. But their emphasis is not on emotional disorders, or on the modification of maladaptive emotions.

The purpose of this chapter is to survey, briefly and critically, the strengths and weaknesses of current theories of fear or anxiety reduction.

285

The survey is limited to theoretical conceptions that have attempted to account for the process of fear or anxiety reduction in general as it occurs in a number of different therapeutic techniques. Implications for the modification of affect from emotion theory are suggested. The chapter concludes with a general therapeutic approach to fear and anxiety reduction, based on the models of panic and anxiety developed earlier. Since anxiety and fear have not been distinguished in most models of therapeutic change (see Chapter 1), I refer to the techniques surveyed in this chapter as "anxiety reduction procedures." Differential therapeutic targets within fear (panic) and anxious apprehension based on the models described earlier are specified below.

THEORIES OF FEAR AND ANXIETY REDUCTION

Most of the development and evaluation of treatments for anxiety have taken place in the context of phobic disorders. An integral part of anxiety reduction procedures when treating phobic disorders is the process of exposure to fearful or anxiety-producing situations. A major difference among psychosocial treatments is the manner in which exposure is arranged, and the additional procedures (strong suggestion, relaxation, the presence of a therapist, modeling, etc.) that are implemented to facilitate exposure. But exposure is not a theory of therapeutic action; it is simply an observation of a common procedure in many treatments. While some in the past have treated exposure as an explanatory concept for anxiety reduction, objections arose to this atheoretical stance very early. For example, Rosenthal and Bandura (1978) criticized this explanation as deficient on several accounts. They pointed out that patients with similar intensities of anxiety often respond very differently to identical amounts of exposure to their feared objects or situations. They suggested that exposure does not take into account the information-providing properties of the therapeutic situation, which may differ substantially from patient to patient. For example, watching an agoraphobic model enter a feared setting such as a department store and then faint may have an effect on the patient that is quite different from the effect of watching the same model enter the same department store and not faint. Nevertheless, the amount of actual exposure to the model in the department store is exactly equal.

Wolpe (1976) also pointed out that most exposure-based treatments contain elements that are likely to inhibit anxiety; examples include the presence of a therapist or some other significant person or instructions to relax. Such elements, he argued, are more critical than exposure per se. This notion is difficult to untangle from the alternative explanation that these elements (e.g., presence of a therapist) merely serve to increase the probability that exposure rather than escape or avoidance will occur, therefore facilitating anxiety reduction. Some have even suggested that exposure does not necessarily play a major role in the process of anxiety reduction, and have cited other procedures as more essential. For example, de Silva and Rachman (1981) have pointed out several instances in which exposure does not seem necessary to explain anxiety reduction.

At present, there is no clear answer to the question of why some people experience reductions in anxiety during therapy. At least five distinct theories have evolved to explain the general process of anxiety reduction. The theory of anxiety reduction underlying pure exposure is usually based on one of two closely related processes: habituation or extinction.

HABITUATION

As early as 1966, Lader and Wing first proposed that what was then the most popular anxiety reduction procedure, systematic desensitization, could be accounted for through the process of habituation. "Habituation" refers to a decline in fearful reactions, particularly psychophysiological aspects of fearful reactions, with repetitive exposure to fear-provoking stimulation. The literature on habituation, although it has developed independently, resembles the literature on systematic desensitization as originated by Wolpe (1958) in many ways. For example, habituation occurs more readily if the subject's baseline level of psychophysiological arousal is low. A corollary to this finding is that habituation will not occur if baseline arousal is too high. In this case, further increases in arousal, or "sensitization," will occur under some conditions.

Habituation, in its simplistic laboratory model, is also usually considered to be short-term, with physiological responses returning after a suitable rest period (Lader & Wing, 1966; Thompson & Spencer, 1966). This feature of habituation was overlooked by many early theorists, although it is also clear that habituation can occasionally be longer-lasting (Watts, 1979). The primary dependent variables in classical studies of habituation, as mentioned above, are psychophysiological measures such as GSR during orienting responses. In the context of anxiety reduction, attempts to correlate individual rates of habituation to experimental stimuli (such as auditory tones) with rate of anxiety reduction are often not successful (e.g., Gillian & Rachman, 1974; Klorman, 1974). In other words, physiological measures may decrease, but other indices of anxiety, including subjective reports, do not change.

There are several problems with habituation as a satisfactory theory of anxiety reduction. To take one example, most studies describing the treatment of agoraphobia have utilized prolonged direct *in vivo* exposure.

Among the consequences of prolonged exposure are maximum anxiety and arousal, as, for example, would occur during a panic attack. A strict adherence to habituation theory would predict that sensitization would occur under these conditions. And yet, according to all the evidence to date, this does not seem to happen. Recently, habituation theories have been extended in such a way that decrements in response as a function of massed, high-intensity, long-term exposure can be accommodated. These "dual-process" theories describe a complex interaction between habituation and sensitization, in which prolonged high-intensity arousal will eventually reduce sensitization, allowing habituation to occur (Groves & Thompson, 1970; Watts, 1979). There is some emerging evidence from the animal laboratories that different neural processes underlie these two phenomena (Davis, Parisi, Gendelman, Tischler, & Kekne, 1982).

Now, evidence emerging from studies examining an important new aspect of the anxiety reduction process also raises questions about habituation (as well as other theories) as a satisfactory explanation. After successful anxiety reduction, either in the laboratory or in the natural environment, a number of people—perhaps as many as 50%—demonstrate a return of anxiety as measured by self-report. Rachman and his colleagues have been studying this phenomenon for years and refer to it as "return of fear" (Craske & Rachman, 1987; Grey, Rachman, & Sartory, 1981). What they have found, in general, is that subjects who later evidenced a return of fear showed the same amount of fear reduction on all measures of anxiety after treatment as those subjects who did not evidence a return of fear. The one consistent predictor of return of reports of fear appeared to be elevated heart rate measured *before treatment*. It is important to note that heart rate in both experiments was not assessed during treatment itself or in a fearful situation. Thus, heart rate was probably reflecting "anticipatory" anxiety.

On the surface, it might seem that these data support habituation theory, which would predict that those subjects with higher physiological arousal to begin with might not "habituate" as quickly. However, the results differ on several counts from the pattern of results that would be predicted by habituation theory. First, habituation theory would predict that subjects with high heart rate would not show the same reduction in physiological measures of anxiety as those with low heart rate, and yet the results clearly indicate that they did show the same reductions in these measures during treatment. Second, when subjects have shown substantial anxiety reduction on both physiological and subjective measures, habituation theory would predict a return of fear on both measures after a suitable interval. But return-of-fear studies have found increases only in subjective measures. Craske and Rachman (1987) speculate that the explanation for the return-of-fear phenomenon may be found largely in the period after the fear has been reduced. They suggest, for example, that some form of disturbance of consolidation of information occurs at this time. Information-processing accounts of anxiety reduction are discussed further below.

EXTINCTION

A similar process often cited as underlying the effects of exposure is extinction. "Extinction" refers to decrements in the strength of learned responses through repetition of unreinforced responding. In the context of anxiety reduction, this rather technical explanation means that subjects repeatedly encounter feared situations without experiencing the fearful consequences, whatever they may be. This is derived directly from laboratory work on classical fear conditioning.

While the literature on extinction is broad and deep, most of the basic experimental work on extinction of fear has concerned itself with avoidance behavior as the primary dependent variable, as contrasted to the work on habituation, in which physiological indices of fear have been highlighted. But there are some subtle differences between habituation and extinction that may or may not be relevant to theories of anxiety reduction (Rachman, 1978). Basically, "habituation" refers to decrements in the strength of unlearned responses, probably controlled at a relatively low neurological level such as the brain stem (Davis *et al.*, 1982; Groves & Lynch, 1972). "Extinction" refers to decrements in the strength of learned responses. Also, habituation is often thought to be temporary, with the return of response (usually GSR in humans) occurring after the habituation process has been discontinued for a suitable time. In other words, nothing is really "learned." Extinction is considered more permanent. Procedurally, repetitive exposure to the feared situation is sufficient for habituation to occur, although other factors (such as initially low psychophysiological activity) are desirable. In the extinction process, exposure must occur in the absence of the aversive consequence. More recently, procedural differences between habituation and extinction have been questioned, because it seems that both may be permanent under certain conditions such as habituation to a novel stimulus, as in the orienting response (Watts, 1979). But the notion that something is learned during the process is clearly associated with extinction and not habituation.

Extinction has proved to be by far the most popular theory of anxiety reduction over the years, although, in fact, little work has appeared directly testing the adequacy of this theory in clinical populations. Nevertheless, an extinction-based model of anxiety reduction has several strengths. First, there is an extensive series of studies (reviewed in subsequent chapters) indicating that long-term intensive exposure, in which phobics are required to remain in the feared situation until anxiety decreases, is more effective than shorter or more widely spaced periods of exposure (e.g., Chaplin & Levine, 1981; Marshall, 1985; Stern & Marks, 1973). According to extinction theory, patients presumably learn, by staying in the situation until anxiety decreases substantially, that the feared consequences do not occur. Implicit in this explanation is the idea that new learning takes place—an idea that is also found in the extensive literature on extinction from the animal laboratories (e.g., Rescorla, 1979). The traditional account of precisely what is learned, stemming from Pavlov's (1927) original work, is that avoidance responding is associated with a process of inhibition after repeated unreinforced trials.

While there is some disagreement over exactly what is learned, there is agreement that extinction is not a passive process, and therefore that it has something in common with more cognitive models of anxiety reduction that stress information processing. In fact, some basic researchers are beginning to speculate about cognitive processes in animals to account more adequately for what is learned during extinction (Hulse, Fowler, & Honig, 1978), while other have speculated on similar cognitive processes in humans (Martin & Levey, 1985; Reiss, 1980).

In 1973, Seligman and Johnston suggested that what is learned during the extinction of avoidance behavior associated with anxiety is disconfirmation of outcome expectations. Outcome expectation is a cognitive construct that may be influenced by many factors in addition to length of exposure. In that sense, it is closely related to self-efficacy, another cognitive construct that is taken up below. In this regard, one could also postulate that what is learned during extinction in clinical populations is enhanced self-efficacy.

But there are also pieces of evidence that undermine extinction theory. Foremost among these is the conflicting series of studies (described more fully in Chapter 11) demonstrating that anxiety reduction can occur even though subjects are allowed to escape from the feared situation early in the "trial" before reaching maximum anxiety (e.g., Agras et al., 1968; Emmelkamp, 1982; Rachman, Craske, Tallman, & Solyom, 1986). If subjects do not have a chance to "learn" that there are no untoward or aversive *consequences* to remaining in the feared situation, then it is not clear how classical extinction can occur. Also problematic for extinction theory are some of the early studies utilizing implosion, in which the most terrible consequences of the feared situation were presented (at least symbolically), and yet anxiety decreased (Stampfl & Lewis, 1968). This outcome contradicts the basic premise of extinction, which is stimulus presentation without reinforcement (aversive consequences). Of course, it is possible that symbolic or imaginal consequences do not assume the same importance as real consequences. For example, imagining that one is fainting or losing control is obviously not the same as actually experiencing it. On the other hand, few if any agoraphobics ever really faint or lose control during their ventures out; most only imagine they are about to do so. Thus, the problems for extinction theory remain.

One possible path out of this morass of conflicting evidence is to conclude that the feared consequences have been improperly conceptualized to begin with. It is possible—and indeed likely, according to the models of panic and anxiety presented in Chapters 6 and 7—that the feared consequence in panic disorder and perhaps other phobic disorders as well is the perceived effect from somatic cues previously associated with alarms. An early study by Watson and Marks (1971) provided intriguing hints that this is the case. In this study, phobics showed equivalent anxiety reduction from relevant imagery specific to their phobic condition and from irrelevant imagery (being eaten by tigers). But the imagery in both cases resulted in equal exposure to cues associated with increased arousal. Therefore, it is possible that patients "learned" that there is little to fear from this increased arousal. Nevertheless, findings from the series of studies mentioned above, demonstrating that escape or the experience of less than maximum arousal is as effective as intense exposure with maximum arousal, are still problematic for a theory of extinction based on exposure to arousal cues. Presumably, one should confront maximal arousal cues to "learn" that the consequences of arousal (e.g., dying or losing control in the case of panic patients) are not there. The fact that subjects do not seem to have to experience maximal arousal, during which the feared consequences are most likely to occur, again brings into question the adequacy of extinction accounts of fear reduction.

TOUGHENING UP

A biological model of fear reduction exists that closely parallels habituation and extinction. In 1976, Weiss, Glazer, and Pohorecky suggested a biochemical explanation for the phenomenon of learned helplessness (referred to briefly in Chapter 7), based on changes in noradrenaline levels. In 1982, Weiss and colleagues elaborated on the specific biochemical mechanisms of action associated with these changes in noradrenaline levels. In this revised view, chronic stress, as simulated by exposure to repeated electric shocks in animals, results in a rise in tyrosine hydroxylase activity (an enzyme associated with noradrenaline synthesis). This, in turn, facilitates increased noradrenaline levels in the locus ceruleus. The important step in this process then follows: The increased noradrenaline causes a rise in autoreceptor-mediated inhibition in the locus ceruleus, and therefore a drop in noradrenergic transmission in the forebrain. To simplify this a bit, brief exposure to stressful or fearful stimuli will result in overall increases in noradrenaline, whereas more chronic exposure to the stimuli will eventually result in overall decreases in noradrenaline. These biochemical changes are associated with a variety of behavioral effects in animals (Gray, 1985). Generally, these effects can be described under the heading of "resistance" or "toughness." Specifically, animals will show greater tolerance for aversive stimuli; hence the name "toughening up."

In a fascinating preliminary experiment on the process of toughening up, Holt and Gray (1983) seemed to demonstrate that this result could be produced biologically as well as behaviorally. They electrically stimulated the septal area of the brain in rats. This process produced results that seemed to mimic the effects of toughening up. Specifically, animals with this stimulation also showed increased resistance to a variety of stimuli that would normally be considered anxiogenic.

The data on toughening up demonstrate once again the influence of learning and experience on neurobiology, and the inevitable interaction between these two systems (e.g., Bandura et al., 1985). That is, the behavioral process of repeated exposure is associated with biochemical changes, which in turn are associated with further behavioral changes. Of course, it seems to be necessary for some "learning" to occur at each stage. Specifying and isolating a specific biochemical mechanism underlying the effects of exposure also have the potential advantage of explaining differential results of exposure-based treatments among patients with seemingly similar levels of anxiety. It is possible that individual differences at a neurobiological level result in different rates of toughening up. For example, some individuals may be unable to reach the same levels of receptor desensitization that are quickly reached by others. While this result is certainly what would be expected, further evaluation would be required to see whether the individual differences are substantial enough to account at least partly for the wide intersubject variability in response to exposure.

It is also interesting, as noted in Chapters 5 and 11, that the mechanisms of action of some successful drug treatments for anxiety seem to involve roughly similar mechanisms of receptor desensitization and alteration of noradrenaline levels (e.g., Charney & Heninger, 1985). On the other hand, it would seem a bit naive to take the reductionistic view that all manifestations of anxiety—behavioral, physiological, and subjective—can be accounted for by alterations in levels of noradrenaline or related monoaminergic activity. In view of the enormous influences of learning and other environmental and cognitive events on anxiety, as reviewed in Chapter 5, the relative level of noradrenaline is most likely only one of many influences on the process of anxiety reduction. To take just one example, noradrenergic depletion has been cited as a possible neurobiological process associated with depression, as described in Chapter 7 (Gray, 1985; Schildkraut, 1965). Assuming that this is true, what accounts for positive outcomes associated with noradrenergic depletion in some patients, as seems to happen during exposure therapy, and negative outcomes (depression) in other contexts? In animal laboratories, the difference seems to be whether the encounter with the aversive stimulus is brief or prolonged. If it is brief, noradrenergic synthesis is increased in a seemingly compensatory fashion (Weiss *et al.*, 1982). One speculative possibility is that when toughening up occurs in therapy, the patient is in a context where behaviors associated with control and perception of control are systematically learned over a relatively prolonged period. When the individual is not in therapy, the same buffeting with aversive stimuli and the resulting noradrenergic depletion quickly result in depression. Of course, one still has to explain the initial development of depression versus anxiety in etiological accounts. That is, why do some individuals become depressed and others anxious as the result of seemingly identical stress-related experiences? As suggested in Chapter 7, both the emotional disorder and the associated action tendencies, as well as (possibly) differing monoaminergic activity, may be a function of differential developmental experiences with stress and perceptions of control.

In any case, the biological process of toughening up is closely related to habituation. Both "theories" have little theoretical "meat," and are just descriptions of processes. Both toughening up and habituation predict a return of fear if contact with the fearful object or situation ceases for a period of time. In other words, there is no specific provision for new learning or alteration of response patterns per se. Of course, it is an easy enough matter to consider that something is learned during these periods of low responding. What may be learned is a response that competes with anxiety. The addition of learning to toughening up and habituation would make habituation, extinction, and the underlying biological process of toughening up very similar in many ways, although one would expect some disagreement among various theorists over what specifically is learned.

Nevertheless, the biochemical data on toughening up, while seemingly compatible with extinction (if one is willing to consider that something may be learned during the process of toughening up), also cannot account for the series of studies mentioned above. These studies demonstrated that short-duration exposure with less than full evocation of arousal seems as effective as intense exposure. In order to accommodate these data, one must go beyond the usual types of simple learning associated with extinction and consider more complex explanations.

In reviewing some of the literature on toughening up and the various parameters that affect this phenomenon, Gray (1985) raises an important issue with clinical implications. Specifically, Gray describes a number of animal experiments indicating that the administration of drugs with arousal-reducing properties interferes with the process of toughening up. Essentially, animals are more sensitive to anxiety-producing situations after the removal of anxiolytic drugs than they would be if they had never received drugs at all, despite similar amounts of exposure to these situations. This evidence suggests that administration of drugs in the context of clinical exposure-based treatments may short-circuit the biological toughening-up process, and therefore may interfere with short-term anxiety reduction. This anticipates several clinical studies described in Chapter 11, in which the administration of drugs seemed to interfere with exposure-based treatments.

On the other hand, a number of additional studies reviewed in that chapter do not indicate that combined drug–exposure treatments produce weaker effects then exposure-based treatments administered without drugs. But clinical studies, of necessity, are rather broad-based in their strategies; this raises the possibility that some detrimental effects of combined treatment may exist in some individuals that are masked or lost in the overall variance. For example, few of these studies systematically evaluated patients after withdrawal of drugs. Cleaner experimental analyses of the interactions of exposure and drug treatments will be required to determine whether anxiolytic drugs interfere with the biological bases of long-term anxiety reduction in human clinical subjects.

EXTINCTION, HABITUATION,
AND TOUGHENING UP: SUMMARY

Neither extinction, habituation, nor the neurobiological process of toughening up seems fully satisfactory at this time as an explanation of fear or anxiety reduction. Most likely, clinical exposure-based treatment and its underlying theoretical rationales of habituation, extinction, or toughening up are oversimplified means of explaining the reduction of anxiety, although each may make some contribution. In addition to poor specification of what is "learned" during exposure, none of these theories easily accommodates the notion of anxiety as a construct of three relatively independent response systems. For example, for both agoraphobics and obsessive–compulsives, exposure and the prevention of avoidance or escape seem particularly effective in reducing avoidance behavior; however, the subjective experience of anxiety, and to some extent physiological indices, do not always respond as well (Mavissakalian & Barlow, 1981a; Rachman et al., 1979). Any comprehensive theory of anxiety reduction will require an explanation of the effects of successful clinical procedures on the integrated construct of anxiety. It is not clear that this is yet forthcoming. As noted above, it may be possible to "habituate" physiologically to a feared stimulus but still to report overwhelming fear. Another common observation is that someone will approach a feared situation despite physiological arousal and the subjective experience of fear; when this happens, it has been characterized as "bravery" or "courage" (Rachman, 1978). Similarly, it seems possible to eliminate avoidance behavior and even subjective reports of fear without resulting habituation of physiological responses. It is not clear that anxiety (in the sense that we understand it) is really occurring when physiological responses remain high, but when avoidance behavior and subjective experiences of anxiety are reduced or eliminated. In the model presented in Chapter 7, this may be a very normal and relatively unemotional response to an upcoming event reflecting a preparatory set.

Finally, any theory of anxiety reduction—particularly theories postulating gradual decrements in anxiety, such as habituation, extinction, or toughening up—must consider panic. The introduction of panic into a consideration of theories of anxiety reduction is akin to introducing the phenomenon of mass extinctions into the orderly theory of evolution. Until several years ago, natural selection occurring in a very gradual fashion seemed adequate to account for the current status of living organisms on earth. But evidence of mass extinctions produced by cataclysmic upheavals has altered and diminished our view of the importance of natural selection. Now Rachman and Levitt (1985), in a study described in Chapter 4, have pointed out how the occurrence of unexpected panic can disrupt the process of anxiety reduction in simple phobics. In their experiment, the occurrence of unexpected panic resulted in marked return of anxiety and greater escape from the feared situation subsequent to the panic than did the occurrence of expected panic.

It is difficult for extinction and related theories to deal with unexpected panics unless one considers that unexpected panics *are* in fact the feared consequences of exposure to certain objects or situations, as suggested above. For successful extinction to occur, then, patients should *repeatedly* confront feared situations without panicking. As Rachman and Levitt (1985) have demonstrated, this is hard to arrange. A related possibility mentioned above is that panic itself with its associated intense arousal is the feared "situation," and that the aversive "consequences" of panic are the experience of loss of control sensations. In this sense, extinction can only occur if an unexpected panic or its equivalent is presented repeatedly until one "toughens up" to it or perhaps learns that the expected but never-experienced consequences of losing control do not occur. However, the current weakness of this argument in regard to the effectiveness of exposure to less than full arousal has been reviewed above. Thus, one is left, once again, with the possibility that something more complex is learned during exposure than simply a disconfirmation of feared consequences while experiencing maximally fearful conditions.

SELF-EFFICACY

A theory of anxiety reduction that meets this requirement is receiving increased attention as well as some empirical verification. This theory is

Bandura's model of perceived self-efficacy as a determinent of fear and avoidance. Essentially, Bandura (1977a) theorized that increasing one's sense of self-efficacy or competence in mastering a feared situation is the single result of all successful anxiety reduction treatments. He observed that direct behavioral experience and accomplishment probably constitute the most powerful means of increasing one's sense of self-competence and efficacy, but that many other procedures may also contribute to this perception. These may include verbal instructions to the effect that one will be successful, as well as watching other people perform successfully. All of these various inputs then summate to produce self-efficacy. Early experiments with analogue subjects seemed to confirm the predictive power of self-efficacy (Bandura, 1977a). But it was not long before critics such as Borkovec (1978) observed that the theory is unparsimonious and circular. For example, Borkovec suggested that self-efficacy is more likely to be a reflection of behavioral change mechanisms than to be the mediator of such change. Teasdale (1978) also suggested that it may be impossible to separate self-efficacy from outcome expectations.

One sign of the health of a theory is the amount of attention and controversy it generates, and in this regard self-efficacy theory is doing very well indeed. Periodically, Bandura (1983, 1984) answers accumulated criticisms. In the meantime, evidence continues to accumulate on the usefulness of this construct. For example, Williams and colleagues (Williams, Dooseman, & Kleifield, 1984; Williams, Turner, & Peer, 1985) have provided some evidence with simple phobics that perceived self-efficacy predicts therapeutic outcome more accurately than does arousal during treatment, anticipated danger, or perceived danger. These clinical investigators suggest that constructing a treatment to target perceived self-efficacy by arranging conditions to instill a sense of mastery will be more effective than will simple exposure-based procedures without these conditions. They provide some evidence from work with their simple phobics that supports this notion. Lee (1984) also found that self-efficacy was a better predictor of outcome in an analogue experiment with snake phobics than were reports of outcome expectations. On the other hand, Biran and Wilson (1981) and others (e.g., Feltz, 1982; Kendrick, Craig, Lawson, & Davidson, 1982), working with simple phobias and performance anxiety, found much more modest correlations between self-efficacy and eventual outcome of treatment.

Early evidence contradicting the predictive power of self-efficacy was provided by Rachman (1978, 1983a). Rachman observed that while self-confidence predicted fearless performance in combat in a number of U.S. veterans in the Pacific theatre during World War II, approximately 17% of these soldiers continued to experience intense fear reactions during combat, despite a strong sense of self-competence or self-efficacy preceding combat. Like other studies cited earlier, this would seem to reflect discordance between the subjective experience of anxiety (or expectation of this experience) and responses in other systems during stressful events. Thus, desynchrony and discordance again pose some difficulties for any one postulated mechanism of action underlying current fear reduction procedures. It is also possible, of course, that the soliders were experiencing occasional panic attacks or true alarms during particularly difficult combat circumstances. These alarms might have been fully attributed by them to the circumstances in which they found themselves, such as a close brush with death. In this case, it is within the realm of possibility that these "expected" panics did not affect subsequent anticipatory anxiety or performance, much as in the Rachman and Levitt (1985) analogue study with claustrophobics. Of course, like other theories of anxiety reduction, self-efficacy theory has yet to attempt to accommodate the newly discovered functional relationship between panic and anxiety. Also, Craske and Rachman (1987), in a study cited above, noted that perceptions of self-efficacy bore little relationship to the *return* of subjective reports of performance fears in musicians. High heart rate prior to treatment was the only successful predictor of return of subjective fear.

Wilson (1984) observes that self-efficacy theory is undergoing occasional elaborations as new data appear. For example, he notes after reviewing some of Lee's work that accurate feedback during performance is critical to the formation of realistic and useful perceptions of self-efficacy. Furthermore, it is often overlooked that Bandura (1983, 1984) emphasizes that self-efficacy is predictive of *behavior* rather than intensity of anxiety or arousal:

> [P]erceived self-efficacy does not include anxiety in either the definition or the measuring devices. Self-efficacy scales ask people to judge their performance capabilities and not if they can perform nonanxiously. Indeed, considering the confused relationship that exists between anxiety arousal and behavior (Barlow, Leitenberg, Agras, & Wincze, 1969; Leitenberg, Agras, Butz, & Wincze, 1971; O'Brien & Borkovec, 1977; Orenstein & Carr, 1975; Schroeder & Rich, 1976), to include nonanxiety as a defining property of self-efficaciousness would diminish its predictive value. (Bandura, 1984, p. 238)

Thus, it is possible that studies reporting a low correlation between anxiety (or panic) and self-efficacy may not necessarily contradict other studies showing that self-efficacy can predict the accomplishment of certain tasks in a behavioral frame of reference. In fact, the data reviewed above generally indicate that the relationship between self-efficacy and performance is the strongest, while the relationship between self-efficacy and anxiety or arousal is the weakest. This supports Bandura's contention.

The difficulty with restricting self-efficacy theory to predicting performance capabilities is that these capabilities play little or no role in many of the major clinical anxiety disorders. By all estimates, the most common clinical anxiety disorders are the anxiety states—panic disorder and generalized anxiety disorder. Of course, panic disorder may be accompanied by the complication of varying amounts of avoidance behavior, but unless the avoidance behavior is extensive and accompanied by an elaborate network of safety signals, this is not the focus of concern. Rather, the focus, in terms of both complaints by the patient and the target of treatment, is the anxiety itself. Furthermore, evidence is reviewed in Chapter 11 that the most important predictor of outcome in clinical populations with panic disorder with or without avoidance behavior (agoraphobia) is a reduction in the intensity of anxiety occurring during treatment (e.g., Barlow, O'Brien, & Last, 1984; Michelson, Mavissakalian, Marchione, Dancu, & Greenwald, 1986).

It may be possible to extend self-efficacy theory to include performance capabilities in dealing with intense anxiety and panic. Although the definition of "performance" is not particularly clear in this context, since there are few behavioral referents, successful experiences of coping with the sudden increases in somatic sensations that form the beginning of the spiral into panic might somehow be formulated in self-efficacy terms.

More recently, Bandura (1986) seems to have made this extension by suggesting that "inefficacy sometimes involves perceived vulnerability to total loss of personal control" (p. 426). With this extension, constructs such as perception of self-efficacy and a sense of control may blend together, although each has a different emphasis.

A sense of predictability and controllability may be more useful in predicting fluctuations in intensity of anxiety, while self-efficacy relates more clearly to performance. To anticipate a later discussion a bit, a sense of control seems to play an important role in panic attacks (Rapee *et al.*, 1986), and it is possible that this cognitive construct may describe more accurately one's capacity to experience sensations of increased physiological arousal in a nonanxious manner.

But the tests have not been done, and with the clear emphasis of self-efficacy theory on performance capabilities, it has been misleading to assume that self-efficacy predicts intensity of emotions—something Bandura himself (1984, 1986) would not claim. This state of affairs seems to provide yet another example of the difficulties encountered in any theorizing about a construct such as anxiety, with multiple points of reference that necessarily differ in their expression from one clinical manifestation to another.

EMOTIONAL PROCESSING

One of the newest theories of fear and anxiety reduction is based on the bioinformational theory of affect proposed by Lang (1977a, 1977b, 1979,

1985) and reviewed in some detail in Chapter 2. This is a model that encompasses desynchrony to some extent and puts more emphasis on emotional aspects of anxiety than on behavioral aspects such as avoidance behavior. This model underscores the importance of exposure, but observes that what is important about exposure, whether *in vivo* or in imagination, is the information processing that occurs when all components or elements of the affective structure are present. Like bioinformational theory itself, this derivative emphasizes physiological indices of anxiety as the most direct measure of the cognitive activity underlying anxious responding and anxiety reduction. In this sense, it resembles habituation in that it requires the initial elicitation of, and gradual decrements in, physiological responding during exposure to a feared situation. What is different, however, is the suggestion that something is learned during this process. This model of anxiety reduction derived from Lang's theorizing is called "emotional processing," a term coined by Rachman (1980). Rachman (1980) and Foa and Kozak (1985, 1986) have elaborated on this model, providing greater specificity to the predictions.

Briefly reviewing the underlying bioinformational theory of affect, Lang rejects the long-held view that images are basically "pictures in the mind" or iconic representations in storage, and that imagining involves the inward perceiving of these images. Lang cites Pylyshyn (1973), who suggested that images in the brain are more like elaborated descriptions. In short, the image is a functionally organized, finite set of propositions. In the context of emotional, fearful images, it is hypothesized that these images contain at least three fundamental classes of statements: stimulus propositions, response propositions, and meaning propositions. "Stimulus propositions" include those sensory (auditory, visual, tactile, etc.) details of the feared object or situation. "Response propositions," on the other hand, are broken down into the specifics of the now familiar triple-sponses associated with the stimuli and responses. "Meaning propositions" are the interpretations associated with the stimuli and responses. Fear, then, is a program for fear behavior existing in memory (much like a computer program), comprising stimulus, response, and meaning structures. This fear program must be fully accessed if any important therapeutic change is to occur. In other words, to modify fear or anxiety, the individual must first become fearful or anxious.

Analyzing imagery-based anxiety reduction procedures in particular (but not limiting this model to those procedures), Lang proposes that different techniques, such as desensitization and imaginal flooding, may call forth different parts of these propositional statements. Thus, vividness of the image and intensity of the affect elicited are determined by the completeness of the propositional statement presented. For example, systematic desensitization, with its emphasis on imagining feared situations arranged in a hierarchy of intensity, concentrates on stimulus propositions. Flooding, on the other hand, concentrates on response propositions, since details of anxious responding ("Your heart is racing; you feel like running") are emphasized in imagination. The therapeutic effectiveness of an image, then, is determined in part by its propositional structure, the balance between stimulus and response elements, and the interrelated characteristics of vividness and affective intensity. Lang notes that the effectiveness of desensitization with specific fears, such as fear of small animals, may be due to the circumscribed nature of the stimulus propositions of these fears. The seemingly greater success of flooding with the more complex problems such as agoraphobia, in which anxiety associated with somatic responses is a major problem, may be due to the relative emphasis on response propositions (particularly visceral reactions) typically described in a flooding session. The greater success of *in vivo* exposure compared to imaginal exposure may be due to the more certain (although still not definite) elicitation of all stimulus, response, and meaning propositions comprising the phobia.

The fundamental strategy of treatment is to "process" information comprising the emotional image, and the emotional image is, for Lang, the prototype fear image stored in long-term memory. This "template" can be elicited for emotional processing in a variety of ways, either imaginal or *in vivo*, but all aspects of it should be processed for successful therapy. This processing may make possible the formation of a new response prototype preliminary to overt behavior change. This new prototype would contain a less anxious or nonanxious response to the stimulus propositions.

The Process of Anxiety Reduction during Emotional Processing

Lang does not actually suggest a specific process by which something new is learned, but Rachman (1980) and Foa and Kozak (1985, 1986) have begun to address this issue. In a stimulating heuristic, Rachman first suggested indices of unsatisfactory emotional processing that would be observable over time. These indices are listed in Table 8.1. The term "test probes" refers to the occasional presentation of aspects of the original emotional experience to determine whether unprocessed elements of the emotional template remain in memory. Rachman then suggested factors that may impede or promote the transformation or "neutralization" of emotion-provoking stimuli. These factors are presented in Table 8.2. Many of the listed factors that may promote processing are familiar ingredients of current therapies, particularly exposure-based therapy. But a crucial ingredient is autonomic reactivity. In other words, to modify an emotion one must elicit emotion, as indicated by autonomic indices in the emotional situation. This and other issues raised by Rachman are discussed

TABLE 8.1. Indices of Unsatisfactory Emotional
Processing Observable over Time

A. Direct signs
　　1. Test probes elicit disturbances
　　2. Obsessions
　　3. Disturbing dreams
　　4. Unpleasant intrusive thoughts
　　5. Inappropriate expressions of emotion (as to time/place)
　　6. Behavioral disruptions, distress (e.g., crying)
　　7. Pressure of talk
　　8. Hallucinations (e.g., after bereavement)
　　9. Return of fear

B. Indirect signs
　　10. Subjective distress
　　11. Fatigue
　　12. Insomnia
　　13. Anorexia
　　14. Inability to direct constructive thoughts
　　15. Preoccupations
　　16. Restlessness
　　17. Irritability
　　18. Resistance to distraction

Note. Adapted from Rachman, S. (1980). Emotional processing.
Behaviour Research and Therapy, 18, 51–60. Copyright 1980 by Pergamon Journals, Ltd. Adapted by permission.

further below. But Rachman provided only an outline of the therapeutic
process, and did not specify therapeutic targets in this early paper.

Foa and Kozak (1986) expand and extend some of these ideas, particularly in the context of exposure-based therapy. They suggest that the
process of fear or anxiety evocation that is part of any exposure-based
treatment must contain information that is incompatible with at least some
of the elements that exist in the patient's anxiety structure. These new
elements must then be perceived and integrated into the existing structure for an emotional change to occur. Specifically, during exposure-based
treatments, patients learn through short-term habituation of physiological
responding (usually during a single session) that anxiety will not last for-
ever. They learn through repeated exposure over several sessions that the
probability of harm or danger is low. This particular change in the anxiety
structure is reflected in between-session, long-term habituation. Negative
affect or the "aversiveness" associated with a situation also diminishes
with repeated exposure. In other words, they learn that the experience
itself is not so bad. These three pieces of corrective information constitute
what is "learned" during emotional processing, according to Foa and Kozak.

In vivo exposure is a particularly good way to access the anxiety and

TABLE 8.2. Factors That Promote or Impede Emotional Processing

Promote	Impede
Engaged exposures	Avoidance behavior
Calm rehearsals (especially of coping)	Agitated rehearsals (especially of not coping)
Talk	Silence
Habituation training	Distractions
Extinction	Poorly presented material
No distractions	Excessively brief presentations
Catharsis	Inadequate practice
Vivid presentations	Excessively large "chunks"
Long presentations	Immobility
Repeated practice	Fatigue
Relaxation	Irregularity of stimulation
Autonomic reactivity	Unresponsive autonomic reactions

Note. Adapted from Rachman, S. (1980). Emotional processing. *Behaviour Research and Therapy, 18*, 51–60. Copyright 1980 by Pergamon Journals, Ltd. Adapted by permission.

transmit new information or elements, but, for various reasons, it may not always be successful at either accessing the anxiety structure in memory or communicating new information. For example, simple distraction or misinformation during exposure procedures should interfere with anxiety reduction, as also suggested by Rachman (1980). There is some evidence that this happens (e.g., Grayson, Foa, & Steketee, 1982; Sartory, Rachman, & Grey, 1982). In addition, the feared situation may be better accessed by imaginal presentations for a variety of reasons, such as technical difficulties that arise in reproducing the actual situation. Other factors that Foa and Kozak (and Rachman) suggest may interfere with emotional processing include the duration of exposure. For example, longer exposure should produce more habituation, and consequent change in the fear structure should also facilitate change. Adequate matching of situations and information presented during exposure to the actual anxiety structure should also facilitate change. In addition, if the patient is depressed or is "cognitively avoiding" the feared stimulus during exposure by self-distraction, emotional processing will be incomplete. Finally, emotional processing will be hindered if initial arousal is so high that short-term habituation cannot occur, thus communicating to the patient that anxiety may continue indefinitely. Over the long term, high arousal is seen as reflecting continuing erroneous evaluation of the probability of danger or harm; this has been termed "overvalued ideation."

This model, as outlined by Rachman (1980) and Foa and Kozak (1986), has many implications for behavior change procedures. For example, it suggests that physiological responding must occur during therapy for the emotional image to be fully processed. Similarly, lack of autonomic reactivity, reflecting incomplete accessing of the anxiety structure among some patients, may explain the wide intersubject variability during otherwise similar exposure trials. While this model is certainly preliminary, it has the virtue of being testable.

Evidence Supporting Emotional Processing

Evidence is now beginning to appear supporting the theory of emotional processing, although the very nature of the theory, with its emphasis on deep cognitive structures and the relationship between these cognitive structures and psychophysiological responses, guarantees that the road to confirmation or disconfirmation will be long and hard.

Lang (1979, 1985) has demonstrated, mostly with analogue subjects, that training these subjects to process response information as well as stimulus information leads to increased physiological activity during imagery. According to the theory, this suggests successful processing of the emotional image, although this fact alone may simply reflect the results of training in imagining response information. Recently, Robinson and Reading (1985) demonstrated with simple phobics that imagery with response propositions produced stronger physiological responses and increased concordance with already declining subjective measures of these phobias than did imagining of stimulus propositions alone. Once again, this suggests successful processing.

Finally, this theory may accommodate the otherwise puzzling finding to be reviewed in Chapter 10 (J. A. Vermilyea, Boice, & Barlow, 1984)— namely, that initial high heart rate in feared situations predicted a positive outcome among a group of agoraphobics. This finding is reminiscent of analogue studies by Lang (1985) and others, in which higher physiological responding to feared images at pretreatment predicted better outcome from treatment. Presumably, what has been happening in these studies, according to emotional processing theory, is that subjects with higher physiological responses have been processing the anxiety cues more effectively and efficiently. This in turn has allowed for successful formation of new propositions (after the response has habituated) and the reduction of anxiety.

Foa and her colleagues have also found initial physiological responding predictive of positive outcome from therapy (Foa & Kozak, 1985, 1986). But Foa and Kozak (1985) cite evidence from both basic and applied studies that high arousal during the initial stages of treatment may interfere with outcome. They suggest that moderate arousal that is neither too high nor too low is required for successful processing. But it will be very difficult to decide in a given individual what is "moderate" and what is not, particularly with physiological measures.

Craske and Rachman (1987) also provide what may be contradictory evidence on the therapeutic predictive power of initial high arousal. They demonstrated that initial high heart rate was the one variable that predicted return of fear in a group of musicians suffering performance anxiety. In this study high heart rate did not predict response to treatment at posttest, but did predict the self-reported return of fear 3 months after treatment was completed. Of course, heart rate was not high in an absolute sense, as would be required to support the notion that moderate heart rate is optional for emotional processing. That is, heart rate in these individuals was not categorized as high, moderate, or low on the basis of predetermined criteria. Rather, individuals whose average heart rate was above the median evidenced return of fear. But this was also true in the J. A. Vermilyea et al. (1984) study, where high heart rate did predict successful outcome immediately after treatment (at posttest).

There are many barriers to a full understanding of these results at present. For example, relatively high heart rate seemed to predict successful outcome in the J. A. Vermilyea et al. (1984) study, but not the Craske and Rachman (1987) study. However, there *was* some evidence of return of fear in individuals in the former study at follow-up. Thus, initial high heart rate may predict both positive responding after treatment *and* return of fear at follow-up when these issues are fully explored. An additional difficulty with a clean interpretation of the Craske and Rachman study is that heart rate was not measured during the actual feared situation (in this case, during a musical performance); rather, heart rate was measured before the performance. Presumably, this reflected preparatory or anticipatory arousal. This arousal may have had little or no correlation with arousal during the feared situation itself, which might, in turn, have indicated more accurately whether the emotional structure was being processed. In the J. A. Vermilyea et al. (1984) study, on the other hand, initial heart rate *was* measured in the actual feared situation.

In several earlier experiments, where return of fear was also observed, emotional processing received stronger support. Both Grayson et al. (1982) and Sartory et al. (1982) demonstrated that subjects who were distracted in some way during the exposure process showed less between-session habituation and a return of fear several days after individual exposure sessions. While it is not entirely clear how return of fear within a day or two relates to return of fear months later, the data deserve further investigation. Craske and Rachman's (1987) observation that the process of consolidating new information after exposure seems to be disrupted in those whose anxiety later returns underlines the importance of these data. In other words, distraction somehow prevents full attention to and adequate processing of the fear structure. But there was no overt distraction in the Craske and Rachman experiment that could account for return of fear in some subjects and not in others. The theory would predict that some sort of covert distraction or some other factor inhibited effective processing in this instance. But both within-session and between-session habituation seemed to be going as well in those whose fear later returned as in those whose fear reduction was more permanent. The reasons for these discrepancies are not clear.

Difficulties with the Theory

Discordance

By now, the similarities that emotional processing shares with many elements of the habituation process are obvious: Each theory relies on a gradual decrement in physiological responding, both within and between sessions, for evidence of successful processing. Unfortunately, the theory also shares several weaknesses with habituation. Among these is one example of the phenomenon of courage, described above (Rachman, 1987). In this example, people are able to perform dangerous tasks very effectively and with little or no report of fear, despite the presence of marked physiological responding that would otherwise be indicative of fear, in a situation where fear is appropriate. This phenomenon is also apparent in patients, where it is the most common manifestation of posttreatment discordance among response systems (J. A. Vermilyea et al., 1984). Specifically, patients report substantial reductions in fear, but evidence no change whatsoever in physiological responding such as heart rate. For years, it was thought that these people were at risk for relapse. This would be consistent with emotional processing theory, since the assumption is made that the images have not been completely processed. However, there is little evidence as yet that this happens (Craske, Sanderson, & Barlow, 1987a; J. A. Vermilyea et al., 1984). Of course, studies required to document this fact are few and far between and very difficult to carry out. In any case, there are many clinical examples of patients who seem to do very well, despite the continuing presence of high physiological responding in feared situations. In an early example, Leitenberg et al. (1971) described a claustrophobic who demonstrated increasing heart rate during treatment, which remained very high at a 1-year follow-up. Nevertheless, she was able to enter small enclosed places quickly and with seeming ease, and reported little subjective disturbance. What she said was that she had learned to be "brave" and that carrying out her formerly feared behavior was no longer a problem, despite awareness that her heart was beating faster. What is difficult about this situation for emotional processing theory is not that the woman was performing well *in spite* of her fear (something that might have been predicted by self-efficacy theory). Rather, the problem is that the woman evidenced high physiological responding without any report of fear at a 1-year follow-up. It goes without saying that this is an isolated case; one can find an anecdotal report to support or undermine any theoretical position. The full implications of posttreat-

305

ment discordance for the theory of emotional processing will have to await new data.

Lang, of course, is fully aware of the poor correlation among the three major response systems comprising an emotion, since he was the first to propose this trichotomy among response systems (Lang, 1968). As noted above, he would presumably point out that these examples of long-term discordance, which are otherwise clinically satisfactory, represent cases in which the phobic emotional propositions stored in memory are incompletely processed or somewhat weaker but are still present. Another possibility (mentioned in Chapter 2) is that in some cases, the propositions are so diffuse that arousal may no longer be strongly connected to the phobic structure.

If future research determines that discordance after treatment predicts relapse, then these data not only will support the theory but will have substantial clinical implications. On the other hand, if it is enough to reduce subjective disturbance and behavioral manifestations of anxiety by, for example, instilling a sense of control despite the presence of physiological reactivity, then it is not clear that these ideas will be useful in the long run as a comprehensive theory of fear reduction in clinical situations. In other words, heightened physiological responding may not have any functional or clinical implications.

Gradual Decrements in Physiological Responding

The requirement of a gradual decrement in physiological responding as evidence of emotional processing is also inconsistent with other data. Evidence has been presented in Chapter 5 (see Figure 5.3) that changes in heart rate are not a valid indicator of anxiety reduction in the sense of discriminant validity. We (Holden & Barlow, 1986) found that gradual decrements in heart rate occurred over time in both a group of agoraphobics and a matched group of normal controls who were simply tested at identical intervals. No differences were evident in their rate of habituation. The only clear differences that emerged were that agoraphobics registered stronger physiological responding during resting baseline; thus, somewhat higher responding continued all the way through treatment. But normals reported no fear whatsoever, despite initial high heart rate and similar rates of habituation. If gradual decrements in physiological responding signify successful emotional processing and anxiety reduction, then what can be said about the group of normals showing a similar response? There are no easy explanations. The issue of response to "novelty," which is considered by some to be closely related to fear (at least physiologically), does not seem explanatory: Normals were very quickly bored by the standardized behavioral approach test designed for agoraphobics, which consisted of walking away from a safe place.

Identification of Fear Structures

Other issues arise at this early stage of analysis of emotional processing as a theory of anxiety reduction. In laboratory studies, Lang and his colleagues have been most successful at eliciting coherent and concordant responses, presumably reflecting feared prototypes, in simple phobics compared to social phobics or agoraphobics (Lang, 1985). Lang suggests that the emotional prototypes are generally less coherent or more diffuse for the latter groups. On the other hand, it is possible that Lang's experiments have not tapped the emotional prototypes in these groups in the most effective manner. For example, the variety of laboratory panicogenic procedures described in Chapter 4 would seem far more appropriate then simply imagining moving away from a feared situation, which was often the test in early experiments. Rather than the diffuse, fluid response structures proposed by Lang for the anxiety states, the context of fear for patients with panic disorder may have to be specified more carefully. Only in this way can emotional processing theory be fully tested with these disorders.

For a patient with generalized anxiety disorder, it is somewhat more difficult to envision emotional processing, since the response seems so diffuse that it is not clear what is being processed in terms of stimulus and response propositions. Here action tendencies and underlying arousal are associated, by current definition, with numerous situations and areas of functioning, making identification of stimulus propositions problematic.

Non-Exposure-Based Treatments

In addition, Rachman (1985) points out a number of factors, including the provision of new information, that seem to result in reductions in fear without any exposure taking place whatsoever. Certainly, this raises some difficulty for emotional processing—or, for that matter, for any of the theories mentioned above except perhaps self-efficacy theory. Rachman suggests, however, that emotional processing can easily incorporate this phenomenon. What is "processed" in this instance is new information. This new information contributes to the formation of a different propositional structure in relation to the object or situation that formerly evoked fear. If emotional processing means accessing the memory structure that contains the irrational fear and arranging for "reality testing" to occur, then it is entirely possible that simple provision of additional information will occasionally have some impact on that memory. This assumes that the memory is accessed to begin with. Of course, it seems that non-exposure-based methods of fear reduction, such as the provision of new information, seldom have more than moderate effects on severe irrational fears

(Barlow & Beck, 1984). But it is important to make this modification to emotional processing theory if it is to be comprehensive. This modification could be tested by observing rates of habituation and initial levels of arousal during these non-exposure-based methods.

Psychophysiological Methods

A final difficulty with emotional processing, as with the bioinformational theory of affect from which it derives, is its reliance on psychophysiological data collected under a variety of different conditions. Studies reporting unreliability of these data, even in the best of circumstances, are reported in subsequent chapters (see Chapter 10). A number of different factors influence states of arousal. Also, a number of different factors in addition to arousal account for psychophysiological responding. Unfortunately, we have known for years that psychophysiological responses are not well correlated even with each other, reflecting, as they do, different bodily functions. Building a precise theory of anxiety reduction based on psychophysiological responding, no matter how promising, will be time-consuming and difficult.

Summary of Emotional Processing

Despite the richness and comprehensiveness of Lang's theory of emotion, the evidence supporting the derivative of this theory, emotional processing, as an adequate explanation for anxiety reduction is very sparse at this time. As noted above, the requirement of decrements in physiological responding to formally feared situations does not necessarily occur, or if it does occur, it does not seem to be specific to the fear reduction process (e.g., Holden & Barlow, 1986). This leaves us with the findings on high physiological responsiveness before treatment predicting successful outcome. But once again, as reviewed above, the results are inconsistent. This has led Foa and Kozak (e.g., 1986) to propose that physiological responsiveness pretreatment can be neither too high nor too low, but must be somewhere in between. This may be either an elegant or a disingenuous solution, depending on future data, but it will be very difficult to disconfirm in view of the enormous variability and the individual nature of physiological responsiveness in terms of what is high, low, or moderate. Lang's theories will generate years of research, but the derivative process of anxiety reduction may need considerably more elaboration before it forms an adequate explanation of anxiety reduction. Nevertheless, it is clearly the most comprehensive theory yet to appear, and the only one to rest firmly on a foundation of emotion theory.

AFFECTIVE THERAPY

Peter Lang was not the first to call for a coherent and consistent therapeutic approach to emotional disorders based on emotion theory. Emotion theorists (including Darwin, James, and Cannon) have for years suggested therapeutic strategies for modifying maladaptive emotions, based on their theories (e.g., Izard, 1971). For a variety of historical reasons, these suggestions did not take root; thus, later elaborations into detailed coherent therapeutic approaches were not forthcoming. In 1981, Rachman, reacting to Zajonc's comments on the primacy of affect reviewed in Chapter 2, suggested that conceptual development in the area of affect modification would be a necessary task for any psychotherapy or behavior therapy in the 1980s. Wilson (1982) suggested that attention to cognitive aspects of psychopathology reflected in the development of cognitive therapy would have to be accompanied by similar developments in the modification of affect. It is clear that a comprehensive approach to therapeutic intervention must consider affect, particularly in the context of the emotional disorders, where problems with affect predominate. As noted above, Greenberg and Safran (1987), in an important book, have outlined a general approach to psychotherapy that is based on emotion theory. The construction of Lang's bioinformational theory of affect set the stage for the first theoretical statement on anxiety reduction to be based on a theory of emotion, as outlined above (Foa & Kozak, 1986; Rachman, 1980). Of course, creative and knowledgeable therapists approaching emotional disorders from a clinical perspective have attended to the implications of basic theories of emotion. In the best-known example, Aaron Beck based his theory of pathological anxiety as a function of distorted information processing on his clinical observations. With these exceptions, there have been few attempts to integrate emotion theory with therapy for emotional disorders.

In preceding chapters, the beginnings of models of panic and anxious apprehension, based on present knowledge of emotion theory and associated cognitive–affective processes, have been presented. I have suggested that the phenomenon of panic (emotional alarm) is not in and of itself pathological unless it becomes associated with the process of anxious apprehension. But once it becomes associated with anxiety, panic requires therapeutic intervention. The model of the process of anxious apprehension is presented in Figure 7.6. This model, in conjunction with a specification of factors implicated in the etiology of anxious apprehension (Figure 7.7), suggests the possibility of intervening at many different points in the cycle of anxious apprehension. In other words, therapeutic procedures directed at any one of the many components of the loose cognitive–affective structure of anxious apprehension have the potential for therapeutic benefit if the negative feedback cycle is disrupted. However, in my view, some components of the cycle make more crucial contributions to the ongoing spiral of anxiety than others. Therefore, these components comprise more essential targets for therapeutic action. Targeting other components, although helpful, should not prove to be as efficient therapeutically in decreasing the intensity of the cycle.

According to the reasoning developed in previous chapters, the core of anxiety disorders is negative affect—characterized in dimensional analyses of emotion as high arousal supporting a preparatory coping set, accompanied by a marked sense of uncontrollability and helplessness. This is experienced subjectively as unpleasant (i.e., it has a negative valence). The closely related cognitive process of attentional shifts to a self-evaluative focus is also part of the core of anxiety. The essential targets for therapeutic action are thus (1) efforts to cope, as well as the emergency action tendencies associated with alarms; (2) a sense of lack of control; and (3) attentional shifts to self-evaluative affective content.

Targeting a number of additional components of anxiety may be useful or helpful, but perhaps not as essential, according to both evidence and theory. Among these additional targets are (1) "hot" apprehensive cognitions; (2) hypervalent cognitive schemata and the associated cognitive–affective structure of attention narrowing; (3) associated coping skills, social support networks, or other factors capable of moderating the intensity of negative affect in response to personal stressors; and (4) physiological arousal and other somatic processes supporting the action tendencies.

A truly comprehensive therapy should target all components. But I suggest that without marked change in the essential components, affective modification will not be successful. The remainder of this chapter consists of evidence for these assertions. Specification of these therapeutic components forms the framework for a discussion of effective therapeutic interventions for each anxiety disorder in subsequent chapters. Finally, it is important to note that individual therapeutic procedures are not necessarily associated with one component of anxiety or another. For example, popular procedures such as relaxation or coping skills training may not have their primary effect through decreasing arousal or teaching specific new skills. Rather, both procedures may instill a sense of control or may change action tendencies or foci of attention.

ESSENTIAL TARGETS FOR CHANGE

Action Tendencies

Bandura, one of the foremost proponents of cognitive explanations of behavior change, stated as early as 1977 in reference to anxiety reduction:

On the one hand, explanations of change processes are becoming more cognitive. On the other hand, it is performance based treatments that are proving most powerful in effecting psychological changes. Regardless of the method involved, the treatments implemented through actual performance achieve results consistently superior to those in which fears are eliminated to cognitive representations of threat. (1977b, p. 78)

For years, therapists of all persuasions have agreed that a necessary step in the treatment of clinical phobia is to encourage contact with the feared object or situation. The well-known statement of Freud on the necessity of having phobic patients eventually face their fears has often been used to support exposure-based treatments: "One can hardly ever master a phobia if one waits till the patient lets the analysis influence him to give it up. . . . one succeeds only when one can induce them through the influence of the analysis . . . to go about alone and struggle with the anxiety while they make the attempt" (Freud, 1919/1959, pp. 165–166). In fact, exposure to feared situations has become the sine qua non of any therapeutic approach to phobia, as reviewed above.

Exposure has been viewed by many as simply a vehicle to reduce or eliminate "anxiety" connected with phobic situations. "Anxiety" usually refers to subjective or physiological aspects of the affect in this instance, and habituation or extinction processes are usually invoked as mechanisms of action. But emotion theorists such as Lang or Izard have long recognized that emotions are primarily action tendencies (Izard, 1977). To the extent that one can counteract these action tendencies, emotions will change. As Izard (1971) points out, theories and evidence from emotion theory indicate that "the most efficient and generalized principles and techniques for emotion control [are] focused on the neuromuscular component of emotion. . . . striate muscle action can initiate, amplify, attenuate, or inhibit an emotion" (p. 415). In other words, "the individual learns to act his way into a new way of feeling." (p. 410).

It is possible that the crucial function of exposure, instead of facilitating extinction, is to prevent the action tendencies associated with fear and anxiety. As our measurement procedures become more precise and sophisticated, investigations are beginning to pinpoint the action tendencies associated with emotion. For example, Fridlund et al. (1986), in a study referred to above, determined that physiological elevation during anxiety did not represent generalized arousal, but rather specific action tendencies associated with the effect. Further evidence reviewed above indicates that the expression of action tendencies intensifies the specific emotion with which they are associated. Thus, allowing action tendencies associated with fear and anxiety to occur is countertherapeutic. What are these action tendencies?

For the ancient, basic emotion of fear (panic), the behavior is clearly escape or flight. As noted in previous chapters, patients experiencing panic

311

are preoccupied with an overwhelming urge to escape, which is usually irrational and maladaptive. An example is the fictional character Mrs. Thayer's urge to rush headlong into the ocean during the winter blizzard, described in Chapter 1 (Fisher, 1978). There is nothing volitional about this action tendency. Preventing it may be the single most important therapeutic means of directly countering panic. It is here that patients may be able to act their way into a new way of feeling.

But I have noted above that anxious apprehension may be more central to anxiety disorders. What is the action tendency associated with the negative affective core of this cognitive–affective structure? In Chapter 7, this tendency is described as a preparatory coping set. This is the general "activation" observed by Fridlund et al. (1986) and Fowles (1986), which they have differentiated from generalized arousal. It is the chronic state of readiness that is referred to as "vigilance" in most accounts of anxiety. The purpose of chronic hyperarousal, mentioned so often in previous chapters, is to support this coping set. But it is not a specific behavior, such as escape; it is the readiness to behave. It is this activation that becomes an important target for change.

It is possible that attention to action tendencies forms an important part of the treatment of other emotional disorders. For example, Beck, Rush, Shaw, and Emery (1979) and others (e.g., Lewinsohn & Lee, 1981) spend a considerable amount of time countering the tendencies of their depressed patients to behave in a passive, retarded, and apathetic manner.

In any case, the majority of therapeutic approaches to anxiety disorders in general and phobia in particular have stumbled on the necessity of directly countering the action tendency of escape associated with panic. Escape behavior may be blatant, as is the case with phobic avoidance, or more subtle, as with the variety of cognitive avoidance strategies seen in panic disorder (see Chapter 11). One must prevent escape or other avoidance responses, both cognitive and behavioral, and must strongly encourage approach behavior. Overwhelming evidence supporting the usefulness of this approach is presented throughout this book.

Assuming that the prevention of chronic preparatory coping sets is also a primary goal in the modification of anxiety disorders, it is possible to interpret the role of other direct interventions a bit differently. For example, all emotion theorists believe that the physiological or neurobiological processes associated with varying emotions are there for a reason, which is to support behavior associated with the affect. If this is true, procedures directly targeting physiological or neurobiological aspects of anxiety may only be indirectly effective. That is, procedures such as relaxation, biofeedback, or anxiolytic medications may be effective only to the extent that they alter the action tendencies associated with chronic vigilance through undermining the supportive physiology. On the other hand, a procedure such as relaxation may be useful not because of any arousal-reducing properties, but because it directly substitutes a different action tendency for chronic vigilance.

In summary, the overwhelming evidence from emotion theory is that an essential step in the modification of emotional disorders is the direct alteration of associated action tendencies. Laughter, humor, and associated facial expressions induced during successful paradoxical intention (Frankl, 1960)—a technique successfully used to counteract fear and anxiety (e.g., Ascher, 1980)—may be effective not because of changes in self-statements, as is often assumed. Rather, prevention of behavioral responses (including facial expressions) associated with fear and anxiety, and the substitution of action tendencies associated with alternative emotions, may account for the effectiveness of this technique.

Control

I have suggested that at the core of the affective component of the complex cognitive–affective structure of anxiety is a sense of uncontrollability and unpredictability. As noted in Chapter 2, "control" is one of the three essential elements of emotion, according to dimensional analyses (e.g., Lang, 1985). A sense of lack of control may also be a "meaning proposition" in the Langian sense. Furthermore, a useful tradition of experimental analyses of the consequences of lack of control has been established within the context of another emotional disorder. This is the literature on learned helplessness associated with depression (Abramson et al., 1978). Helplessness or a sense of uncontrollability is common to anxiety and depression; these differ in other ways, such as in basic action tendencies, as outlined in Chapter 7. Preceding chapters have also described the close relationship between anxiety and anger in terms of their affective components. That is, anxiety and anger (and perhaps excitement) seem to share similar action tendencies, but differ in the all-important feature of perceptions of control. Angry and excited people are emotional but perceive that they are in control; anxious people perceive themselves as lacking control. For this reason, altering perceptions of control becomes an essential part of the therapeutic effort directed at anxious apprehension.

Altering perceptions of uncontrollability is also important from an etiological perspective, as outlined in Figure 7.7. These perceptions seem to comprise one of the major etiological contributions to the formation of the cognitive–affective structure of anxiety. That is, experiences of lack of control during development in biologically susceptible individuals may be a crucial etiological step in the origins of anxiety. For this reason, changing perceptions of helplessness is central to any therapeutic endeavor.

It should be clear from the preceding comments that altering action tendencies may be a good beginning to altering a sense of control. Modification of action tendencies should have an impact on the affective core of anxiety in general. Nevertheless, there are many instances where preventing phobic (or cognitive) avoidance with exposure-based procedures is only partially effective and sometimes totally ineffective. It is possible that some of these exposure-based treatments may have been ill-designed. For example, I have suggested in Chapter 6 that when learned alarms are involved in an anxiety disorder, it may be essential to prevent escape from somatic cues associated with panic, in addition to escape from any external situations associated with phobic behavior.

Nevertheless, these therapeutic attempts will not be completely successful unless the patient begins to feel in control of potential upcoming events, whether environmental or somatic. This may explain the puzzling series of studies with phobics described in Chapter 11 and alluded to above, demonstrating that anxiety reduction can occur even if subjects escape from the feared situation before reaching maximum anxiety. These studies are puzzling because one of the basic assumptions of extinction (or emotional processing) is that the patient must learn that there are no untoward or aversive consequences to remaining in the feared situation. But this would seem difficult if the patient does not stay in the situation long enough to learn this. It is possible that what is "learned" during these experiences is that events are not out of control. That is, whether aversive consequences occur or not, or whether unwanted physiological arousal occurs or not, the individual is in control of his or her world. This may be true even if the sense of control is illusory (Alloy et al., 1981). In this conceptualization, it is not important if high arousal supporting a coping set remains, as long as the action tendencies themselves are altered and a sense of control is instilled. Discordance, as indicated by the continuation of high physiological activation, is relatively unimportant. Of course, in the majority of cases, one would not expect the supportive physiology to continue on indefinitely in an autonomous manner if other, more essential aspects of the affect have been eliminated.

There is additional evidence that what may be learned during the variety of treatment procedures for anxiety disorders is a sense of control. The centrality of the issue of control is also evident in emerging data on the emotional effects of expected versus unexpected noxious events, particularly alarms (reviewed in Chapter 4). For example, Rachman and Levitt (1985) have indicated quite clearly that the occurrence of false or learned alarms does not necessarily increase anxiety subsequently. Only if the alarms are unexpected does anxiety subsequently increase. Similarly, Rapee et al. (1986) have demonstrated that provocation of panic in the laboratory through CO_2 procedures seem to be a function of whether one expects the various somatic sensations associated with CO_2 inhalation or not. If the effects are fully described in advance, reports of panic do not occur. In other words, if events are seen as predictable or controllable, there is little or no anxiety. Sanderson *et al.* (1987c) confirmed this finding by directly manipulating a sense of control, which affected reports of anxiety and panic.

Finally, what may be the strongest evidence for the importance of a sense of control comes not from the anxiety disorders, but from the stress disorders. Although a subset of patients with stress disorders seem to have a strong sense of mastery and control, as exemplified in Type A personalities, a large number of individuals within this heterogeneous group of disorders seem to resemble patients with anxiety disorders in many essential ways (see Chapter 9). For example, patients with chronic tension headache and irritable bowel syndrome, to take two common stress disorders, present with a great deal of emotionality. This emotionality can be characterized as anxiety surrounding their somatic symptoms. One of the most popular and effective treatments for these disorders is biofeedback targeted to the specific disturbances. But one of the most puzzling findings from biofeedback research is that the mechanism of action does *not* seem to be in the reduction of the physiological response presumably underlying the symptoms. For example, biofeedback of tension headaches has as its goal the reduction of muscle tension in crucial areas of the face and head. But recent investigations have shown that reductions in headache when they occur are not associated with specific reductions in muscle tension in these areas (Andrasik & Holroyd, 1980; Holroyd *et al.*, 1984). This raises a major paradox in the field of biofeedback today. What accounts for therapeutic success when it occurs? One possibility is that these patients undergoing the technically sophisticated treatment of biofeedback, with all of its electronic gadgetry, begin to develop the sense that their unpredictable and uncontrollable aversive somatic experiences are at last coming under some sort of control. As Blanchard points out in discussing his clinical success with irritable bowel syndrome (Neff & Blanchard, 1987), it seems that at last these patients begin to feel some control over an area of their functioning that has been unpredictable and uncontrollable for years. In view of the seeming similarity in the etiology of anxiety and stress disorders, it is possible that common mechanisms of action underlie the success of the variety of treatments used for both disorders.

Self-Focused Attention

The last aspect of treatment seen as essential in the modification of anxiety is the necessity of shifting attention away from an internal affective self-evaluative focus. In Chapter 7, I have observed that one of the major differences between "normal" and pathological anxiety involves the persistence of an internal self-evaluative focus of attention. In the model presented in Figure 7.6, this leads to further intensification of arousal, even-

315

tual disruptions in performance, and the creation of the vicious cycle of anxious apprehension. Furthermore, patients fail to habituate when in a self-evaluative attentional mode. Patients without pathological anxiety, on the other hand, may experience similar levels of arousal and even unpleasant affect, but their attention is easily shifted when necessary to the task at hand or to a more objective nonaffective focus, and "anxiety" disappears.

Evidence presented above indicates that distraction during exposure-based therapies may interfere with the process of anxiety reduction (e.g., Grayson et al., 1982; Sartory et al., 1982). This is also consistent with an emotional processing view of anxiety reduction (Foa & Kozak, 1986). But it is possible that one of the essential steps in successful anxiety reduction is the redirection of attention to more external or mechanical aspects of the anxious situation, perhaps because it contributes to the development of a sense of control. This does not involve diverting one's attention away from the situation or escaping it. Rather, the focus of one's attention is on other aspects of the situation or more mechanical stimulus aspects of one's responding. Once again, this process may have been implicated in Rapee et al.'s (1986) demonstration that providing full information on the sensory qualities of the somatic effect of CO_2-induced panic reduced reports of panic and anxiety. This different focus of attention may have contributed to a greater sense of control.

Suls and Fletcher (1985a) have reviewed studies on differential focus of attention in the context of health psychology. They also conclude that focusing on the sensory or mechanical aspects of the stressor and one's reaction to it ("nonavoidant strategy") will be more adaptive in the long run than distracting oneself from the situation ("avoidant strategy"). Certainly, the development of an external focus of attention is crucial to increasingly effective performance in the situation, which, of course, is another essential step in breaking the cycle of anxious apprehension.

I have hypothesized in Chapter 7 that shifts in attention to an internal self-evaluative affective focus, while originally a cognitive component of the complex cognitive–affective structure of anxiety, eventually becomes an integral part of the negative affective core of anxiety. In view of the enormously important role this component seems to play, according to hard evidence from my colleagues' and my sexually dysfunctional patients (see Chapter 7), it seems that targeting self-focused attention is essential during therapy.

HELPFUL TARGETS FOR CHANGE

Targeting a number of additional components of the cognitive–affective structure of anxiety may well be helpful or useful, but is probably not sufficient to effect major changes in anxiety, in the present view. Among these components are self-statements or the "hot" apprehensive cognitions associated with intense worry, and the process of attention narrowing that increases the salience and intensity of these "hot" cognitions. Evidence mentioned above and reviewed in some detail below indicates that altering anxious cognitions per se, either as an exclusive treatment or as an addition to more basic treatments, seems to have little effect on anxiety. As Bandura eloquently pointed out a decade ago, the process of emotional change does not seem to be accomplished through "cognitive interventions," by which he meant altering self-statements or the like. Simple persuasion is seldom effective. On the other hand, some evidence is beginning to appear that these cognitive components to treatment may serve something of a protective function in terms of preventing relapse (Marshall, 1985). The precise role of cognitive interventions in the anxiety disorders awaits future research, and it may well be that these procedures will prove to be helpful in some aspects of the therapeutic endeavor. It is unlikely, however, that they will be as essential as those described above.

Similarly, intervening in social support networks or teaching coping skills may well be useful, particularly in terms of preventing relapse. In some future community mental health endeavor, teaching effective coping skills may even prevent the development of severe anxiety. Nevertheless, it is unlikely that these efforts in themselves will strongly affect the structure of anxious apprehension unless they contribute in a major way to the modification of action tendencies, alterations of focus of attention, of the instilling of a sense of control. Of course, the development of strong and adequate coping procedures will probably have a major effect on a sense of control in the long run. In fact, teaching adequate coping strategies may be one of the most powerful therapeutic approaches available to us (e.g., Goldfried, 1986). But this strategy will probably be useful in the direct modification of anxiety only to the extent that a sense of control is instilled.

Finally, as mentioned above, altering physiological or neurobiological responding, which seems to play such an important role in supporting the action tendencies of various emotions, is more or less helpful in some disorders. But this strategy in isolation is not seen as essential. The example of prolonged heightened physiological responding, despite elimination of clinical "anxiety," has been mentioned above. Almost all individuals, including people without "anxiety," respond to challenges or stressors with arousal. This arousal serves a very functional purpose in terms of increasing the efficiency of performance, even at high levels, and is seldom accompanied by "anxiety." Therefore, this is not an essential target of therapeutic change in anxiety disorders. Rather, direct attacks on the action tendencies associated with this supportive physiology seem more crucial.

TABLE 8.3. Components of Any Affective Therapy

A. Essential targets for change
   1. Action tendencies
   2. A sense of uncontrollability–unpredictability
   3. Self-focused attention
B. Helpful but not essential targets for change
   1. "Hot" apprehensive cognitions
   2. Hypervalent cognitive schemata and attention narrowing
   3. Coping skills and social support
   4. Elevated physiological responding and altered neurobiological functions

---

There is one exception to this guideline, based on evidence developed in Chapters 4 and 5. Panic attacks seem to "spike off" a platform of high baseline anxiety and arousal. Therefore, reduction or elimination of somatic responding may reduce the cues that trigger the alarm. But whether this is done through medication or through psychological procedures such as relaxation, it is unlikely that any permanent effect will occur unless the patient also develops a sense of control concerning future false alarms, along with different action tendencies. Otherwise, anxiety and panic will recur as soon as the medication is stopped or during the next stressful event when relaxation or meditation procedures are not immediately available. This is not to say that pharmacological approaches to anxiety may not form a very important component of treatment. Succeeding chapters review the role that these agents can play in successful therapy. The point here is that the long-term beneficial effects of either pharmacological or psychological procedures aimed at reducing arousal, activation, or specific underlying monoaminergic processes associated with anxiety may be initially helpful, but are not necessarily essential.

Both essential and helpful components of any affective therapy are outlined in Table 8.3. With these principles in mind, it is now possible to apply these guidelines to individual anxiety disorders—a task that occupies the remainder of this book. First, however, Chapter 9 briefly discusses principles underlying the current nomenclature for specific anxiety disorders as represented in DSM-III-R. New definitions for the anxiety disorders found in this revision of DSM-III are placed in the context of the models of anxiety and panic presented above.

9

Classification

Classification is at the heart of any science. Without some objective ordering and labeling of objects or experiences, investigators would be unable to communicate with each other, and knowledge would not advance. Each individual would then have to develop his or her own personal science, which could not be applicable beyond his or her own subjective experience. In dealing with rocks or insects, these ideas are fundamental. But when the subject matter is human behavior, particularly emotional or behavioral disorders, controversy surrounds all aspects of the endeavor, including the basic issue of whether classification should even be attempted. For example, major controversies have arisen surrounding what is normal or abnormal in emotional expression; the boundaries among the various proposed categories; and/or which features of the anxiety disorders should be dimensionalized or scaled to provide a more complete picture. Since diverse phenomena such as the somatic manifestations of panic, the percept of derealization, intrusive thoughts, and massive agoraphobic avoidance behavior are all subsumed under the broad heading of "anxiety disorders," deciding on logical and useful groupings is difficult, to say the least. Problems are not limited to the practical issue of what features to be grouped together. The organization or classification of emotional disorders involves issues fundamental to the conceptualization of human behavior.

The classification of anxiety disorders, as the old adage goes, has a long past but a very recent history. While observations of phobic, obsessive–compulsive, and other anxiety-based phenomena stretch back to the earliest recorded observations of human behavior, only recently have these problems been defined and included in nosological systems. For example, as late as 1959, only three out of nine systems for classifying psychiatric disorders in various countries listed "phobic disorder" as an independent diagnosis (Marks, 1969). Even the term "anxiety" did not appear in the

International Classification of Diseases (ICD) until the seventh revision, published in 1955. At that time, the listing was "anxiety reaction without mention of somatic symptoms" under the general heading of "psychoneurotic disorders" (Jablensky, 1985).

Any reasonable system of classification, whether dimensional or categorical, should accomplish several important goals. First, it should describe specific subgroups of symptoms or dimensions of behavior that are readily identifiable by independent observers on the basis of operational definitions ("reliability"). Second, there should be some usefulness or value in identifying these subgroups or dimensions. Within the area of emotional and behavioral disorders, this usefulness ("validity") usually refers to predicting specific response to treatment, course of the disorder, and possibly etiology. That is, someone with social phobia, for example, not only should differ from someone with simple phobia by definition, but should also present with a different etiological picture, require somewhat different psychological or pharmacological treatment, and follow a somewhat different course over the years in regard to fluctuations and the possibility of spontaneous recovery. If the major features of all the anxiety disorders alluded to above are classified dimensionally, rather than categorically, then these distinctions should apply to individuals whose symptoms are more severe on some dimensions and less severe on others. In summary, diagnostic categories should include defining features that permit differentiation among the categories and preferably show some differences in etiology, course, prognosis, choice of treatment, or all of the above. Investigators working in the area refer to successful categorization of natural objects or events as "cutting nature at the joints" (e.g., Kendall, 1975).

As with everything else in the study of anxiety disorders, this is easier said than done. Currently, we are not at an advanced state in this area of investigation. One reason is the recency of this effort. Formal classification systems for most anxiety disorders did not begin to appear until close to 1950, as noted above; at that time, they were deeply influenced by prevailing theoretical conceptions of anxiety disorders. Therefore, full attention to the presenting descriptive characteristics of anxiety disorders, as well as empirical data on the validity of these disorders, received little attention.

This chapter reviews and integrates current knowledge on the organization and classification of anxiety disorders and associated phenomena. This knowledge is related to the models of panic and anxiety developed above. This information is a prelude to a detailed description of the nature, etiology, assessment, and treatment of each of the anxiety disorders, based on the theoretical conceptions developed in this book and on current evidence.

CURRENT NOSOLOGICAL SYSTEMS

This book is organized around the categories found in DSM-III-R (American Psychiatric Association, 1987), for convenience. But clinicians and investigators should not assume complacently that this system represents reality, or even the best thinking available in the world today on classification. In fact, as one travels from country to country, numerous differences emerge in categorizing the major features of anxiety disorders. As the cultural gaps become broader, these differences are accentuated to the point where the presenting disorder itself may seem to have little or no parallel in another culture. Essential questions regarding marked cross-cultural differences in presentation, as described in Chapter 1, go to the heart of basic controversies concerning the nature of anxiety.

Even in the West, substantial differences exist in the categorization of individuals presenting with (presumably) similar problems. The ICD is an attempt to compromise among various schools of thought regarding classification around the world, particularly in Europe. But the current (ninth) version of the ICD (ICD-9) groups most DSM-III anxiety disorders under the very general heading of "anxiety states." In the French system, these disorders are grouped under the term "anxiety neurosis" without further subcategorization. The unofficial diagnostic classification system of the Soviet Union regards these anxiety states as components of "psychasthenia" or "obsessional neurosis." Specific syndromes identified in one nosological system are not easily identifiable in others. What is specific in one system is general in another, and it is not obvious that disorders with roughly similar names across systems, such as "obsessional disorder," refer to quite the same thing.

For example, Table 9.1 presents the major ICD-9 categories in which anxiety plays a prominent role. The first five categories listed under I subsume current DSM-III-R descriptions of anxiety disorders, for the most part. The difference between this type of comparison and those made in the cross-cultural studies of anxiety described in Chapter 1 is that the presenting features of the individual with, for example, agoraphobia, are nearly identical in Europe and the United States by all accounts. But in DSM-III-R, the individual would be classified as having "panic disorder with agoraphobia"; in ICD-9, the category would be "phobic state."

Do such differences matter? Personal preferences aside, there are really only two ways to answer this question as suggested above: First, is the system reliable? Second, is the system useful? One would think that answers to these questions would have been established decades ago. In fact, investigators are only beginning to establish answers to these questions, and most of the data are in a very preliminary form indeed. In this regard, the DSM-III descriptions of anxiety disorders have provided a

TABLE 9.1. The Classification of Anxiety (Including States of Anxiety, Fear, Dread, Panic, Phobias, Apprehension, and Worry) in ICD-9

I. Categories for which anxiety is a major defining feature
    300.0 Anxiety states (include panic attacks, disorder, or state)
    300.2 Phobic state (includes agoraphobia, animal phobias, anxiety hysteria, claustrophobia, phobia NOS[a])
    308.0 Acute reaction to stress, with predominant disturbance of emotions
    309.2 Adjustment reaction, with predominant disturbance of other emotions (includes abnormal separation anxiety, culture shock)
    312.3 Mixed disturbance of conduct and emotions

II. Categories in which anxiety is a contributory defining feature
    291.1 Delirium tremens
    291.3 Other alcoholic hallucinosis
    292.0 Drug withdrawal syndrome
    296.1 Manic–depressive psychosis, depressed type
    300.3 Obsessive–compulsive disorders
    300.4 Neurotic depression
    300.6 Depersonalization syndrome
    300.7 Hypochondriasis
    301.1 Affective personality disorder
    302.7 Frigidity and impotence
    310.2 Postconcussional syndrome
    316.0 Psychic factors associated with diseases classified elsewhere

III. Categories in which anxiety is a defining feature by implication (though not specifically mentioned in glossary)
    306.0 Physiological malfunction arising from mental factors
    307.4 Specific disorders of sleep

Note. From Jablensky, A. (1985). Approaches to the definition and classification of anxiety and related disorders in European psychiatry. In A. H. Tuma & J. D. Maser (Eds.), *Anxiety and the anxiety disorders* (p. 754). Hillsdale, NJ: Erlbaum. Copyright 1985 by Lawrence Erlbaum Associates. Reprinted by permission.
[a]Not otherwise specified.

substantial advantage to those studying the classification of anxiety disorders.

THE REVISIONS OF DSM

The DSM of the American Pyschiatric Association has undergone three revisions over the decades, but the third edition (American Psychiatric Association, 1980) departed radically from its predecessors. While controversial, DSM-III has been widely used because of several advantages over alternative systems—notably, its relatively atheoretical approach and its specificity. Many clinicians have objected to the implementation of a nosological system that not only departed radically from accepted customs (including the custom of not diagnosing at all), but also introduced new categories without full empirical support. Their objections are understandable. Nevertheless, DSM-III has proven to have enormous heuristic value for clinical investigators. For the first time, diagnostic criteria within the anxiety disorders were specified in sufficient detail to allow studies of reliability and validity. In addition, investigators have been enabled to communicate with each other more accurately on the subject matter of their investigations, in areas of both psychopathology and treatment outcome. This should advance science.

DSM-III-R was published in 1987. While specific features of each DSM-III-R anxiety disorder category are reviewed in subsequent chapters, it is informative to have an overview of the development of these criteria from DSM-II to DSM-III-R. The major categories present of each of these three versions of DSM are presented in Table 9.2.

TABLE 9.2. The Classification of Anxiety Disorders in DSM-II, DSM-III, and DSM-III-R

DSM-II	DSM-III	DSM-III-R
Phobic neurosis	Phobic disorders (or phobic neuroses)	Phobic disorders
		Social phobia
	Agoraphobia with panic attacks	Simple phobia
		Agoraphobia without history of panic disorder
	Agoraphobia without panic attacks	
	Social phobia	
	Simple phobia	
Anxiety neurosis	Anxiety states (or anxiety neuroses)	Anxiety states
		Panic disorder with agoraphobia
	Panic disorder	Panic disorder without agoraphobia
	Generalized anxiety disorder	
Obsessive–compulsive neurosis	Obsessive–compulsive disorder (or obsessive–compulsive neurosis)	Generalized anxiety disorder
		Obsessive–compulsive disorder
	Posttraumatic stress disorder	Posttraumatic stress disorder
	Acute	
	Chronic or delayed	
	Atypical anxiety disorder	Anxiety disorder not otherwise specified
Neuroses not classified as anxiety disorders in DSM-III (or DSM-III-R)		
Hysterical neurosis	Somatoform disorders	
	Dissociative disorders	
Depressive neurosis	Affective disorders	
Neurasthenic neurosis	[Eliminated]	

The major shift in DSM-III, of course, was conceptual: The time-honored term "neurosis" was deleted. For most of the past 75 years or so, it was enough to say that anxiety was a major part of the neurotic condition. Automatically, this shifted the focus from the observable features of anxiety disorders to hypothetical, underlying, unconscious conflicts maintaining the anxiety. Several developments led to deletion of the term "neurosis." First, new theories regarding etiological and maintaining factors for anxiety disorders were suggested, as detailed in earlier chapters. Some of these were biological, while others were based on psychological and social learning concepts that departed from specific theoretical conceptions underlying the term "neurosis." Second, many pointed out that the term "neurosis" did not facilitate research in classification. "Neurosis" was too general a term and one that could not be defined reliably. This generality also made it difficult to answer questions concerning the usefulness or validity of the concept. DSM-III encouraged clinicians and investigators to look at anxiety more descriptively. This, in turn, highlighted a number of specific problems or major features de-emphasized within the neuroses. These features became the basis for DSM-III categories.

The neuroses were based on hypothetical etiological constructs. These constructs were associated not only with observable symptoms of anxiety, such as obsessions or phobic avoidance, but also with anxiety that was controlled unconsciously and automatically by conversion, displacement, and various other psychological mechanisms. Many disorders were subsumed under this broad heading, and therefore the listing of DSM-II "neurotic disorders" in DSM-III ranged far and wide. Only those neurotic disorders in which anxiety is experienced directly were grouped together in the new class of DSM-III anxiety disorders. Remaining DSM-II neurotic disorders were distributed among other classes, such as somatoform disorders, dissociative disorders, and affective disorders. Greater specificity has been achieved in DSM-III anxiety disorders through the provision of precise descriptions of narrower, more manageable categories. Panic disorder and post traumatic stress disorder were new to DSM-III.

The revisions in DSM-III-R have been limited to clarifications, with the exception of panic disorder, agoraphobia with panic attacks, and generalized anxiety disorder. In these categories, more substantial revisions have been introduced. Specifically, agoraphobia with panic attacks has been subsumed under panic disorder. Agoraphobic avoidance within the new category of panic disorder with agoraphobia is rated on the basis of severity, from mild to severe (see Chapter 10). The definition of generalized anxiety disorder is specified to a much greater extent. This allows the identification of generalized anxiety disorder in addition to other anxiety disorders; previously, it was a residual category diagnosed only when no other anxiety disorders were identifiable. These changes, as well as clarification in the definitions of other disorders, are discussed in some detail in subsequent chapters on these disorders.

In a final major revision, almost all hierarchical exclusionary rules have been eliminated. In DSM-III, hierarchical conventions dictated that a patient could not receive an anxiety disorder diagnosis if he or she was depressed. Similarly, a more pervasive anxiety disorder, such as obsessive–compulsive disorder, would automatically exclude a less pervasive anxiety disorder, such as simple phobia. These hierarchical exclusionary systems, which are characteristic of most classification systems, greatly distort the presenting clinical picture in a manner to be discussed below. DSM-III has prompted new research on the reliability and validity of this system, as well as other issues relevant to the classification of anxiety disorders.

RELIABILITY

With the increasing specificity and complexity of diagnostic criteria as evident in DSM-III, standardized interview protocols have become increasingly important. These protocols are necessary to test fairly the reliability of these categories, as well as to sample the broad range of phenomenology present even in the most discrete categories, such as simple phobia. The Schedule for Affective Disorders and Schizophrenia, which permits differential diagnosis within the schizophrenic and affective disorders, is probably the best example (Endicott & Spitzer, 1978, 1979). Unfortunately, neither this instrument nor other newly developed structured interviews, such as the Diagnostic Interview Schedule (Robins, Helzer, Croughan, & Ratcliff, 1981), cover sufficient information to permit differential diagnoses among all of the anxiety disorders. For example, the early version of the Diagnostic Interview Schedule, designed for quite a different purpose, did not cover generalized anxiety disorder, social phobia, or posttraumatic stress disorder; furthermore, it is designed for administration by a layperson. More recently, Spitzer, Williams, and Gibbon (1985) constructed the Structured Clinical Interview for DSM-III. Preliminary data indicate that this a very useful instrument for general screening purposes. However, to make it manageable, it is necessary to collect the minimum amount of information on each of the major DSM-III disorders. This makes it particularly valuable for screening in a general outpatient clinic, but less valuable for detailed inquiry into any one set of disorders, such as anxiety disorder.

THE ANXIETY DISORDERS INTERVIEW SCHEDULE

In order to proceed more effectively with our own research in 1981, my colleagues and I began developing a detailed structured interview specifically for the anxiety disorders, which we termed the ADIS (Di Nardo *et al.*, 1983). Since much of the new information on classification presented in this chapter involves data collected with the ADIS, I describe this instrument in some detail here and present guidelines governing its use. The ADIS was designed not only to permit differential diagnoses among the DSM-III anxiety disorder categories, but also to provide data beyond the basic information required for establishing the diagnostic criteria. To this end, information regarding history of the problem, situational and cognitive factors influencing anxiety, and detailed symptom ratings provide a data base for investigation of the clinical characteristics of the categories. Since depression is often associated with anxiety, a fairly detailed examination of depressive symptoms as well as their relationship to symptoms of anxiety disorders is included in the interview. Screening questions for addictive, psychotic, and relevant organic disorders are also included.

While many of the items have been developed by our own staff, some items have been adapted from the Schedule for Affective Disorders and Schizophrenia, as well as from the Present State Examination (Wing, Cooper, & Sartorius, 1974). Also embedded in the interview are the Hamilton Anxiety Rating Scale (Hamilton, 1959) and the Hamilton Rating Scale for Depression (Hamilton, 1960). To insure the continuity of the interview, the items of the Hamilton scales are grouped according to content so that similar items can be rated simultaneously. The ADIS has been revised several times in the intervening years, based on experience in our center and many other research clinics. The latest version (ADIS-R; Di Nardo *et al.*, 1985) makes it fully compatible with DSM-III-R. The ADIS-R has been translated into four languages and is in use in over 150 clinical and clinical research settings around the world.

There are several other features of the ADIS that are relevant to issues in classification. First, since one of our major goals was to gather as much detailed information as possible for purposes of later descriptive studies, there are very few cutoff questions that would enable one to skip sections of the interview. In this regard, we did not adhere to the hierarchical organization that was present in DSM-III, where, for example, any anxiety disorder such as panic disorder could be subsumed under an affective disorder if an affective disorder were also found. This turned out to be an important step in describing as fully as possible the complete phenomenology of those presenting with one or another of the anxiety disorders. On the basis of experience in our center and elsewhere, these hierarchical questions have been deleted, for the most part, in DSM-III-R, as noted above. For example, we now know that there are many instances where two anxiety disorders seem to exist independently, as in a patient who reports a long history of social fears and a recent history of panic in a wide variety of situations, many of which are not social situations. In these cases the clinician makes a distinction between a primary and a secondary disorder, based on severity and interference with functioning. The temporal relationship between or among the disorders is noted and often helps to establish their independence, but does not in and of itself determine the primary–secondary status of the disorders. We do not assume that the more long-standing disorder is necessarily the primary problem, unless the information indicates that the more recent problem can be subsumed under the long-standing one (see below). Furthermore, as many secondary diagnoses as can be ascertained by the clinician after administration of the ADIS are given. This allows an analysis of patterns of comorbidity, which describes more fully the true presenting characteristics of each patient.

Occasionally a patient presents with two distinct anxiety disorders, both of which are severe and interfere with functioning. In these cases, two primary diagnoses are given, although secondary diagnoses are still assigned if present. On the other hand, if symptoms that would meet the criteria for one anxiety disorder are clearly part of another anxiety disorder, no separate diagnosis is given. For example, many agoraphobics report fears of heights or enclosed places, because such situations represent the unavailability of an escape route in case of panic. A diagnosis of simple phobia is not assigned in this case. In another example, simple phobics or obsessive–compulsives may "panic" when confronted with a specific phobic object or an intrusive thought, respectively; however, panic attacks are not diagnosed as panic disorder even if the criteria are otherwise met. Thus, the ADIS is not designed for administration by a layperson, but requires clinical judgments and some experience with the anxiety disorders.

To summarize, if one disorder can be clearly subsumed under another, the subsumed disorder is neither diagnosed nor given a secondary status. But if two anxiety disorders are judged to be independent, primary status is determined on the basis of relative severity and interference with functioning, rather than on the basis of temporal relationships or other hierarchical assumptions.

RELIABILITY STUDIES

With these guidelines in mind, an extremely stringent test of the reliability of DSM-III anxiety disorders was conducted. In a preliminary study, each of 60 consecutive admissions was administered the ADIS at different times by two different and independent interviewers. The second interviewer was blind to the results of the first interview. Furthermore, diagnostic agreement was defined as an exact match of the two clinicians' primary diagnosis. For example, in our sample there were several cases

TABLE 9.3. Kappa Coefficients for Specific Diagnostic
Categories after 125 Consecutive Admissions

Diagnosis	n	Kappa
Agoraphobia with panic	41	.854
Social phobia	19	.905
Simple phobia	7	.558
Panic disorder	17	.651
Generalized anxiety disorder	12	.571
Obsessive–compulsive disorder	6	.825

Note. Adapted from Barlow, D. H. (1987). The classification of
anxiety disorders. In G. L. Tischler (Ed.), Diagnosis and classification in psychiatry: A critical appraisal of DSM-III (p. 226).
Cambridge, England: Cambridge University Press. Copyright
1987 by Cambridge University Press. Adapted by permission.

in which the interviewers arrived at the same two anxiety disorders, but
did not agree on which of the two was the primary diagnosis. In the
calculation of kappa coefficients (a conservative statistic for determining
extent of agreement over and above chance), these cases were scored as
disagreements. When disagreements occurred, a consensus diagnosis was
arrived at after a detailed discussion of the case at a staff meeting; at this
meeting, the apparent reasons for the disagreement were also identified.
Preliminary reliability data on 60 patients can be found in Di Nardo et al.
(1983). Table 9.3 presents kappas calculated on the first 125 consecutive
admissions (Barlow, 1987). The sample size enabled the calculation of the
kappa on a reasonable number of cases in each of the DSM-III anxiety
disorders, with the exception of posttraumatic stress disorder.[1]

Ignoring simple phobia for a moment, one can see that the lowest
kappas were in the categories of panic disorder and generalized anxiety
disorder. There are few behavioral referents in these two disorders, and
the clinician must rely on evidence, mostly self-reports, of somatic or cognitive phenomena. On the other hand, the kappa for agoraphobia was
quite high and represents about as good an agreement as one could expect in a study of diagnostic reliability. Similarly, the kappa for obsessive–compulsive disorder was high, despite the fact that we had fewer
cases in this category than any other. The low number of cases reflects
the relative rarity of this disorder in anxiety clinics, despite seemingly
high prevalence in the general population (see Chapter 16). But the high
kappa highlights the fact that, at least in its severe form, it presents as a
distinctive, recognizable disorder.

1. More recently, a study examining reliability of posttraumatic stress disorder has been
completed using the ADIS (Blanchard, Gerardi, Kolb, & Barlow, 1986). With a somewhat
different procedure, in which diagnoses ascertained by an ADIS interview were matched
against a criterion diagnosis, a very satisfactory kappa of .857 was obtained.

With this in mind, the rather low kappa for simple phobia would seem somewhat surprising. In fact, difficulties and disagreements were not due to inability to recognize a simple phobia, but rather to the fact that almost all of our simple phobics also presented with other anxiety disorders, making the clinical weighting of the primary and secondary disorder somewhat difficult. In other words, if a patient presented with both a simple phobia and panic disorder, both interviewers might have recognized the simple phobia, but one might have rated it as primary and the other as secondary, resulting in a disagreement.

Clinicians disagreed on the primary diagnosis for 29 out of 125 patients. Six different reasons or categories of disagreement were identified, and the frequency of disagreements for each of these categories is presented in Table 9.4. "Subject variance" in the table refers to an actual change in the patient's condition or status between the two interviews (which occurred a median of 2 weeks apart, and 4–5 weeks apart or more in a few cases). For example, a patient might have been severely depressed during the first interview, but less depressed during the second interview several weeks later. One of the most common sources of disagreement was "information variance," where patients provided different, or at least considerably more detailed, information to one clinician than to the other. The other common source of disagreement, termed "differential weighting of aspects of clinical picture," refers to the fact

TABLE 9.4. Frequency of Sources of Diagnosis Disagreement

Source	n
1. Subject variance	6
2. Information variance	13
3. Insufficient information provided by ADIS	1
4. Insufficient specification of criteria in DSM-III	1
5. Differential weighting of aspects of clinical picture	11
6. Clinician's error	1
Total	33[a]

Note. Adapted from Barlow, D. H. (1987). The classification of anxiety disorders. In G. L. Tischler (Ed.), Diagnosis and classification in psychiatry: A critical appraisal of DSM-III (p. 227). Cambridge, England: Cambridge University Press. Copyright 1987 by Cambridge University Press. Adapted by permission.

[a]Clinicians disagreed on primary diagnosis in 29 of 125 cases. Total number of sources of disagreement is more than this, because in some cases more than one source of disagreement was identified.

that both clinicians might have identified the same two disorders in a patient but might have assigned them in different orders of severity. This, or course, was scored as a disagreement.

In summary, this study showed that the DSM-III categories of anxiety disorders were good to excellent descriptions of the phenomenology presenting to clinicians. This was particularly true if the hierarchical decision rules within the anxiety disorders were deleted (as is the case in DSM-III-R). The only exceptions were generalized anxiety disorder and, somewhat surprisingly, simple phobia. It is also worth noting that the first wave of 60 patients yielded no cases of agoraphobia without panic, and that out of a total of 41 patients in the initial sample of 125 with agoraphobia, only one met the definition of agoraphobia without panic. The relationship of panic to agoraphobic avoidance, and the data relevant to the new DSM-III-R category of panic disorder with agoraphobia, are discussed in some detail in Chapter 10.

In the case of simple phobia, the problem may not lie with the definition, but rather with complex patterns of comorbidity present in any individual with a simple phobia who is distressed enough to seek out help. This issue is examined in some detail below.

For generalized anxiety disorder, on the other hand, the source of the low kappa did seem to be the definition. Treating generalized anxiety disorder as a residual diagnosis, to be specified only if other anxiety disorders were judged not to be present but the patient was still severely anxious, created problems. Definitions since developed in our center and adopted in DSM-III-R (Barlow, Blanchard, et al., 1986) eliminate the residual status of generalized anxiety disorder and permit its diagnosis as an additional anxiety disorder independent of other disorders. The essentials of this new definition have been presented above. Preliminary estimates of the reliability of certain aspects of the new definition are promising, but more formal estimates must be ascertained. A full discussion of these preliminary data and other aspects of generalized anxiety disorder can be found in Chapter 15.

VALIDITY

Studies of the validity of anxiety disorders have been greatly hindered by the lack of reliable definitions. With more precise definitions now in place for the majority of anxiety disorders, these studies may proceed. Questions bearing on the validity of diagnostic categories can be addressed in many different ways. Some, but not all, of those questions have been mentioned above. For instance, current definitions of anxiety disorders revolve around specific presenting problems; to take one example, fear of social evaluation characterizes social phobia. On the face of it, fear of social evaluation seems different from alternative presenting problems, such as severe intrusive thoughts and accompanying rituals. But direct comparisons have not always been carried out. Many questions regarding validity in this context involve direct comparisons among different groups to ascertain whether important differences exist. Areas where important differences should exist involve etiology, course, prognosis, and choice of treatment, as well as descriptive differences (distinctiveness).

But before one examines for important distinguishing features, a more basic question concerns the definition of the disorder itself. In other words, do the various features describing a disorder form a coherent whole? This is one form of construct validity. For example, social phobics could be defined as individuals sensitive to evaluation, with accompanying delusions of grandeur and motor retardation. But it is unlikely that factor-analytic solutions to the variety of anxiety symptomatology would confirm that these features are grouped together in a meaningful way. Evidence relevant to this type of validity is presented in subsequent chapters dealing with each disorder (see Chapters 10–16). Suffice it to say that what little work has been done in this area generally supports the construct validity of the categories. For example, studies of the agoraphobic syndrome described in Chapter 10 suggests that fears that have come to be called "agoraphobic," such as avoiding crowded places or places far from home, tend to occur together and are associated with a factor of panic–anxiety (Arrindell, 1980; Hallam, 1985). Naturally, studies such as this are most useful if they concentrate on features that, by definition, are different from category to category. Since all categories share the experience of anxiety, it is not usually informative to determine whether these categories differ in manifestations of basic features of anxiety.

DISTINCTIVENESS

Examining for differences among disorders has produced data that, in general, support the distinctiveness of anxiety disorders. But very few of these investigations have targeted DSM-III (or DSM-III-R) categories, and most comparisons among disorders have been limited. For example, a variety of data suggest that these categories have a different course. The strongest data indicate a different age of onset among several disorders. For example, many simple phobias arise in childhood; intense social anxiety first appears in adolescence; and anxiety states, specifically panic disorder and generalized anxiety disorder, have a modal age of onset in the 20s. This evidence is reviewed in more detail in subsequent chapters.

There is less evidence on the long-term course of these disorders, but what evidence exists suggests a somewhat different fate for simple phobia than for agoraphobia (e.g., Agras et al., 1969). While all phobias run a prolonged course, panic disorder with agoraphobia seems subject to marked fluctuations characterized by nearly full remissions, only to be followed by severe exacerbations. Sex differences also emerge among some categories. For example, panic disorder with agoraphobia is an overwhelmingly female disorder, accounting for 75% or more of patients presenting with this problem. Social phobia, on the other hand, presents with a more nearly equal distribution between the sexes.

Differential age of onset or sex differences may reflect something important about etiology. On the other hand, these differences may be due to rather trivial differences in the context of biological and psychological vulnerabilities contributing to the risk of developing an anxiety disorder. Discussions of etiology of each anxiety disorder are developed in subsequent chapters.

Choice of treatment and responsiveness to treatment have probably had undue influence on the formation of diagnostic categories. The logical fallacy of inferring a cause from an effect has been discussed in Chapter 3. In that context, the inference referred to is assuming a certain etiology as a function of response to treatment. In the area of validation of diagnostic categories, this issue is not as serious. If two categories respond differentially to treatment, regardless of their etiology, this is an important fact distinguishing them. Nevertheless, efforts at discriminating categories based on response to treatments are preliminary, because of the recent development of the categories themselves. While there is some evidence for differential response to both drug and psychological treatments among the categories (also reviewed in subsequent chapters), there is not yet enough evidence from treatment studies to contribute strongly to the validation of the categories themselves.

More recently, data have begun to appear demonstrating differentiation among DSM-III and DSM-III-R categories on a large array of demographic and psychometric variables (Sanderson, Rapee, & Barlow, 1987a). In Table 9.5 are descriptive data from 131 consecutive patients seen in our clinic and diagnosed according to DSM-III-R definitions. As one can see, the sex differences mentioned above are apparent in these data. Among patients with panic disorder with agoraphobia, there was an increasing proportion of females as agoraphobic avoidance behavior became more severe. Other anxiety disorders showed the characteristic female-to-male ratio, with social phobics showing the greatest proportion of males in this sample.

Data across the categories are also arrayed for the Hamilton scales and for ratings on Axes IV and V of DSM-III. Axis IV refers to ratings of the severity of psychosocial stressors. A rating of 1 indicates "none" and a rating of 7 indicates "catastrophic." Axis 5 refers to highest level of adaptive functioning in the past year (1 = "superior," 5 = "poor"). As might be expected, simple phobics evidenced the best functioning, and

TABLE 9.5. Descriptive Data on 131 Patients Given DSM-III-R Anxiety Disorder Diagnoses

	Diagnosis (n)							
Variable	PDA:MILD (25)	PDA:MOD (21)	PDA:SEV (9)	PD (1)	SOCIAL (24)	SIMPLE (17)	O-C (12)	GAD (22)
Sex (% female)	72	81	89	0	58	76	67	64
Mean age	34	37	32	28	33	38	34	43
Current medication use								
Anxiolytics (%)	52	58	22	0	17	24	25	55
Antidepressants (%)	14	14	11	0	17	0	17	9
Beta-blockers (%)	12	5	11	0	17	0	17	9
Hamilton Anxiety Rating Scale	16	20	21	21	16	16	17	21
Hamilton Rating Scale for Depression*	12_{ab}	15_{ab}	17_{ab}	10_{ab}	10_a	8_a	18_b	16_{ab}
Axis IV	2.9	3.4	2.3	4.0	2.9	1.9	3.4	3.6
Axis V*	3.3_{ab}	4.0_{ab}	4.6_a	2.0_{ab}	3.7_{ab}	2.9_b	3.9_{ab}	3.6_{ab}

Note. Key to abbreviations in table heads: PDA:MILD, panic disorder with agoraphobia, mild avoidance; PDA:MOD, panic disorder with agoraphobia, moderate avoidance; PDA:SEV, panic disorder with agoraphobia, severe avoidance; PD, panic disorder; SOCIAL, social phobia; SIMPLE, simple phobia; O-C, obsessive–compulsive disorder; GAD, generalized anxiety disorder. Means sharing subscripts are not significantly different by Scheffe test. From Sanderson, W. C., Rapee, R. M., & Barlow, D. H. (1987, November). *The DSM-III—Revised anxiety disorder categories: Description and patterns of co-morbidity.* Paper presented at the annual meeting of the Association for Advancement of Behavior Therapy, Boston.

*$p < .05$.

patients with panic disorder with severe agoraphobic avoidance showed the worst. Cameron, Thyer, Nesse, and Curtis (1986) also examined ratings on Axes IV and V across DSM-III groups. On both axes, agoraphobics were most severely impaired and simple phobics least impaired, replicating our findings. To return to Table 9.5, differences also emerge on severity of depression among groups, but not severity of anxiety on the Hamilton scales—an issue to be taken up below.

A rather interesting descriptive analysis of patterns of current medication use is presented in Table 9.5. Medication usage reflected, for the most part, drugs prescribed by primary care physicians for the various disorders. The majority of patients with panic disorder or generalized anxiety disorder were on benzodiazepines. Only a small percentage in any category were on antidepressants or beta-blockers.

Descriptive studies also present a variety of evidence demonstrating a lack of discriminability between the DSM-III categories of panic disorder and agoraphobia with panic. This finding supports the revision in DSM-III-R of subsuming agoraphobia with panic under panic disorder (Barlow, 1986d). For example, Turner, McCann, Beidel, and Mezzich (1986) administered a number of questionnaires (listed in Table 9.6) to patients meeting criteria for DSM-III anxiety disorder categories. DSM-III agoraphobics were more "anxious," according to these inventories, than were patients with other phobic disorders (simple and social phobia). Levels of anxiety in agoraphobia were similar to those in the anxiety states (generalized anxiety disorder, panic disorder, obsessive–compulsive disorder). The similarities of agoraphobia to panic disorder (and the anxiety states) are evident in Table 9.6. Other evidence supporting the DSM-III-R panic disorder with agoraphobia revision is reviewed in detail in Chapter 10. Generally, the patients with anxiety states were more severely anxious on these self-report inventories in the Turner, McCann, et al. (1986) study; the authors suggest that this validates the differentiation of anxiety states from phobic disorders.

This type of comparison was also reported by Cameron et al. (1986) on 316 patients representing all specific DSM-III anxiety disorders except posttraumatic stress disorder. Data from this study indicate the ubiquity of anxiety symptoms across the categories, but also support the finding by Turner, McCann, et al. (1986) of more severe anxiety symptoms in the anxiety states than in the phobic disorders. Cameron et al. (1986) conclude that all of the disorders share the descriptive features of anxiety, and that few differences exist among the categories on anxiety symptomatology. A difficulty here is that major features tending to define the disorders, such as social phobic features or intrusive thoughts, were generally not included in this analysis. On the other hand, Turner, McCann, et al. (1986) did assess some of these major features by administering the Maudsley Obsessional–Compulsive Inventory and various social phobia

TABLE 9.6. One-Way Analysis of Variance on Groups with Agoraphobia, Simple and Social Phobias, and Anxiety States

Measure	Simple and social phobias (n = 44)		Agoraphobia (n = 18)		Generalized anxiety disorder; panic disorder; obsessive–compulsive disorder (n = 27)		F
	M	SD	M	SD	M	SD	
State–Trait Anxiety Inventory							
A-State	37.46	11.49	51.06	12.34	55.93	10.56	24.39***
A-Trait	37.68	11.07	51.83	15.38	55.93	14.42	22.61***
Beck Depression Inventory	7.50	7.73	16.94	9.78	21.78	9.53	23.88***
Cornell Medical Index	24.00	14.06	39.89	23.17	52.22	22.90	18.86***
Maudsley Obsessional–Compulsive Inventory	4.80	3.83	8.22	7.06	10.85	6.71	10.27**
Fear Survey Schedule	66.84	44.42	145.83	77.00	140.93	48.77	22.40***
Social Avoidance and Distress Scale	7.73	7.61	17.94	8.67	17.48	7.69	17.83***
Fear of Negative Evaluation Scale	12.52	9.38	19.33	9.79	18.41	8.29	5.26*

Note. From Turner, S. M., McCann, B. S., Beidel, D. C., & Mezzich, J. E. (1986). DSM-III classification of the anxiety disorders: A psychometric study. Journal of Abnormal Psychology, 95, 168–172. Copyright 1986 by the American Psychological Association. Reprinted by permission.

* p < .01.
** p < .001.
*** p < .0001.

335

scales. Marked differences appeared among anxiety disorder groups on these measures. For example, obsessive–compulsive patients reported the highest scores on the Maudsley Obsessional–Compulsive Inventory, as might be expected. But scales measuring social phobic features (e.g., the Social Avoidance and Distress Scale) were paradoxically lower for patients with social (and simple) phobias. Issues involved in the distribution of major features of each anxiety disorder across all anxiety disorders and the general population are discussed in more detail below.

In summary, studies examining for descriptive differences among the various anxiety disorder categories have begun to produce some evidence supporting the distinctiveness of the categories. The evidence is strongest (although very limited) at the level of descriptions of presenting problems, such as social phobic features. Demographic information, such as sex distribution and age of onset, also differentiate among some disorders. Discriminations are less clear when one compares more basic anxiety symptomatology among groups, which is not surprising, since all categories are classified under the broad heading of anxiety disorders. Nevertheless, patients with anxiety states (including obsessive–compulsive disorder) are generally more severely anxious than simple and social phobics, particularly simple phobics (see also Solyom, Ledwidge, & Solyom, 1986). More severe anxiety in the anxiety states may be directly related to the greater pervasiveness of cues associated with anxiety in these disorders than in phobic disorders.

Some efforts have been made to dimensionalize basic anxiety symptoms. For example, investigators have dichotomized cognitive and somatic anxiety symptoms (e.g., Schwartz, Davidson, & Goleman, 1978). Tyrer (1976) has proposed that a preponderance of cognitive or somatic anxiety may have pharmacological treatment implications. Other studies have suggested that the heavy somatic component of panic disorder may have implications for the nature of this problem (see Chapter 10). Nevertheless, identification of a preponderance of cognitive versus somatic anxiety symptoms has not proved to be a useful distinction as yet. It seems that one must go a step further and establish functional relationships among a cognitive or somatic focus of anxious apprehension and other aspects of a specific anxiety disorder. Therefore, endorsement of cognitive versus somatic symptoms on questionnaires may be epiphenomenal and associated with the focus of anxious apprehension, rather than an inherent dimension of anxiety itself (see Chapter 7). For example, patients with panic disorder focus on somatic events; patients with obsessive–compulsive disorder, on the other hand, focus on intrusive cognitions. These patients may report predominantly somatic or cognitive symptoms, respectively, on questionnaires designed to dimensionalize these components. But on objective examination, both groups may present with similar cognitive and somatic features of anxiety.

DISTINGUISHING ANXIETY AND DEPRESSION

In Chapters 2 and 7, I have speculated on the nature of anxiety and depression, and have suggested a distinction between the loose cognitive–affective structure of anxiety and the more fundamental emotion of panic. Similarly, the cognitive–affective structure of depression, termed "dysthymia," may be distinct from the more fundamental emotion of sadness or depression present in a major depressive episode. But current rating scales or self-report instruments designed to measure anxiety or depression overlap considerably. As noted in Chapter 2 specific questions in current versions of the widely used Hamilton scales overlap by approximately 70%. An essential step in elucidating the nature of anxiety and depression, either as loose cognitive–affective structures (anxiety and dysthymia) or as more basic emotions (panic and depression), will be the development of measures that assess what is unique in these mood states or emotions, rather than what is overlapping.

A few years ago, I reported on the existence of several items from the Hamilton scales that discriminated anxiety patients from depressed patients (Barlow, 1983). Among these items, in addition to suicidal thoughts, were feelings of hopelessness and motor retardation. Recently, Riskind *et al.* (1987) revised the two Hamilton scales to discriminate more clearly between major depressive disorder and generalized anxiety disorder, as noted in Chapter 2. Patients in this study were also characterized as being relatively "pure"; that is, patients with generalized anxiety disorder were not depressed.

Items were reassigned after factor analysis and point–biserial correlational analyses. Items were assigned to the new anxiety or depression scales if their highest salient loading was on either "anxiety" or "depression," as long as this did not conflict with the results of the point–biserial analysis. This allowed for the assignment of 82% of the items. The remaining decisions were made on a case-by-case basis with redundant items deleted. As in our clinic, items most closely associated with depression included suicidal thoughts, feelings of hopelessness and helplessness, and motor retardation. On the other hand, apprehension and worry were more strongly associated with anxiety, along with agitation during the interview and various somatic symptoms associated with arousal and tension.

Many of the changes in the scales have immediate face validity, while others may be more puzzling. For example, reassigning agitation from the Hamilton Rating Scale for Depression to the Hamilton Anxiety Rating Scale eliminates the phenomenon of agitated depression. In view of the conception of depression outlined in Chapters 2 and 7, the change is probably long overdue; this item accounted for considerable conceptual confusion. Obviously, the Hamilton scales continue to be incapable of diagnosing anxiety or depression. However, to the extent that there is something pure about the constructs of anxiety and depression, these scales will be better able to assess the presence, as well as the severity and intensity, of these constructs.

Recently, we examined the utility of these revised scales with a wide variety of DSM-III anxiety and affective disorder diagnoses (McCauley, Di Nardo, & Barlow, 1987). Between 15 and 20 patients in each of the following categories were studied; panic disorder, agoraphobia with panic, social phobia, simple phobia, generalized anxiety disorder, obsessive–compulsive disorder, dysthymic disorder, and major depressive disorder. Anxiety patients were excluded from the sample if they received an additional diagnosis of either dysthymia or major depression. Similarly, depressed patients were excluded if they received an additional anxiety disorder diagnosis. For purposes of comparison, a mixed group of patients, with a primary diagnosis of panic disorder as well as an additional diagnosis of either dysthymia or major depression, was included.

Table 9.7 presents mean scores (and standard deviations), as well as the pattern of statistically significant differences among groups, on the revised Hamilton scales. One-way analyses of variance were calculated for the scores on the revised scales by diagnostic group. The group with DSM-III agoraphobia with panic demonstrated significantly higher Hamilton Anxiety Rating Scale scores than any other diagnostic group. Those with simple phobia, social phobia, and major depression showed the lowest scores on this scale (patients with major depression were selected on the basis of no additional anxiety disorder diagnoses). These scores were significantly different from those for the mixed and panic disorder groups. Hamilton Rating Scale for Depression scores for major depression and dysthymia were significantly higher than for all other groups. Scores on this scale for the agoraphobia, mixed, and obsessive–compulsive groups were intermediate and significantly higher than those for patients with simple phobia, social phobia, panic disorder, and generalized anxiety disorder.

Findings from our center (Barlow, Di Nardo, et al., 1986; Benshoof, 1987) as well as other centers (Riskind et al., 1987; Roth & Mountjoy, 1982) consistently specify individual items that differentiate anxiety from depression. These items are psychomotor retardation; feelings of helplessness, hopelessness, and worthlessness; and depressed mood. Depressed patients are significantly more impaired on each of these variables. Patients with major depression manifesting the basic emotion of sadness most likely account for most of these differences, particularly retarded action tendencies.

Anxiety, on the other hand, is characterized by arousal and behavioral agitation. This is consistent with views reviewed in Chapter 2 from the emotion theorists that depression, in its pure form, is characterized by withdrawal and diminished activity or disengagement. Anxiety, on the

TABLE 9.7. Comparison of Anxiety Disorder and Depressed Groups on Revised Hamilton Scales

n	Score M	Score SD	Group	Simple phobia	Social phobia	Major depressive disorder	Dysthymic disorder	Generalized anxiety disorder	Obsessive–compulsive disorder	Panic disorder	Mixed	Agoraphobia with panic
			Hamilton Anxiety Rating Scale (revised)									
20	17.3	3.8	Simple phobia									
19	19.3	4.5	Social phobia									
15	20.3	6.5	Major depressive disorder									
15	21.0	6.0	Dysthymic disorder	*								
20	21.2	3.3	Generalized anxiety disorder	*								
17	23.4	5.8	Obsessive–compulsive disorder	*	*							
19	23.7	4.5	Panic disorder	*	*	*						
19	25.3	3.8	Mixed	*	*	*	*	*	*			
18	27.1	4.7	Agoraphobia with panic	*	*	*	*	*	*	*		
			Hamilton Rating Scale for Depression (revised)									
20	16.3	2.2	Simple phobia									
19	19.9	4.4	Social phobia	*								
19	20.2	2.3	Panic disorder	*								
20	20.3	3.5	Generalized anxiety disorder	*								
18	22.6	3.4	Agoraphobia with panic	*	*							
19	23.9	3.3	Mixed	*	*							
17	24.4	4.4	Obsessive–compulsive disorder	*	*							
15	28.9	6.1	Dysthymic disorder	*	*			*	*	*		
15	29.9	3.8	Major depressive disorder	*	*			*	*	*	*	*

Note. Asterisks denote pairs of groups significantly different at the .05 level. From McCauley, P. A., Di Nardo, P. A., & Barlow, D. H. (1987, November). *Differentiating anxiety and depression using a modified scoring system for the Hamilton scales.* Poster presented at the annual meeting of the Association for Advancement of Behavior Therapy, Boston.

other hand, is characterized as active, if unpleasurable, engagement, implying an effort to cope with difficult situations (Tellegen, 1985). Once again, it is at the level of action tendencies that primary distinctions are found. Of course, identification of rating scale items more clearly measuring anxiety and depression is only a beginning; additional independent replications in other centers are needed. Furthermore, these systematic rating scales are only one component along which these two constructs or emotions may be distinguished. Preliminary data describing differential attributions for negative events (Heimberg, Vermilyea, et al., 1987), presented in Chapter 7, suggest another method of discriminating anxiety and depression. I have also hypothesized that developmental histories may provide the context for the evolution of psychological vulnerabilities unique to either anxiety or depression. Others have hypothesized that patients who become anxious or depressed may be vulnerable to different types of negative life events reflecting either loss or threat (e.g., Beck & Emery, 1985). A fuller exploration of all aspects of affect and cognition associated with depression and anxiety in their pathological expression is needed.

COMORBIDITY: THE DISTRIBUTION OF ADDITIONAL DIAGNOSES

Now that systems of nomenclature such as DSM-III are relying increasingly on presenting or descriptive features rather than theories of etiology for classification, several additional consequences emerge. In order to achieve the levels of reliability now possible for at least some disorders, as described above, disorders are defined in a specific and rather narrow fashion. While the old category of "neurosis" was so heterogeneous that the label communicated very little, the new categories within the anxiety disorders describe the nature of a presenting problem precisely. However, clinicians have known for years that patients seldom present with just one problem, and trying to "force" patients into one and only one category is not a good way to represent the reality of clinical presentation. Nonetheless, the hierarchical exclusionary systems present in most systems of classification often require one and only one diagnosis.

HIERARCHICAL EXCLUSIONARY SYSTEMS

Explicit or implicit hierarchies of disorders are introduced into classification systems to assist in choosing among related diagnoses when decisions are difficult. Associated with these hierarchies are often complex exclusionary rules reflecting the assumptions of the hierarchies. For some DSM-III disorders, a diagnosis is excluded if, in the clinician's judgment, its symptoms are "due to" a coexisting disorder that occupies a higher position in the hierarchy. Thus, a diagnosis of simple phobia may be excluded by a number of disorders, including major depression and obsessive–compulsive disorder. As noted above, generalized anxiety disorder may be excluded by any other anxiety disorder as well as by major depression. More generally, any of the anxiety disorders may be excluded by major depression. The primary difficulty in establishing these hierarchical relationships among various disorders for any given patient is that DSM-III provided no guidelines for determining when a particular disorder is "due to" another. Excellent discussions of the origin and nature of hierarchical exclusionary systems within diagnostic categories are provided by Kendall (1975), Surtees and Kendall (1979), Sturt (1981), and Boyd et al. (1984).

Below the level of organic disorders, few of these exclusionary systems in their totality have any empirical support (Surtees & Kendall, 1979). Their most important function is to allow clinicians to assign only one diagnosis. However, Sturt (1981) makes a convincing argument, based on an analysis of data from the Present State Examination, that even exclusionary systems with some face validity may simply reflect the tendency of every symptom to show a highly significant association with the total symptom score. A recent study by Boyd et al. (1984) indicates that when diagnoses are applied without exclusionary restrictions, individuals who meet the basic criteria for any one DSM-III disorder are likely to meet the criteria for one or more additional diagnoses. Such findings suggest that arbitrary exclusionary systems may obscure true relationships among disorders or syndromes.

On the other hand, the results of the Boyd et al. study also indicate that the practice of simply listing all of the diagnoses for which a patient meets the basic criteria also obscures existing relationships among syndromes, since such a procedure makes no provision for recording these relationships. That is, in some cases, symptoms fitting the criteria for two different diagnoses either may be part of the same problem or may not be. For example, in a severe obsessive–compulsive with washing rituals, fear of dirt is not a separate simple phobia. But a fear of heights may be, particularly if it had a different time of onset or otherwise has nothing to do with feelings of contamination, which are an integral part of many obsessive–compulsive syndromes. Automatically including every "simple phobia" that happens to be present in an obsessive–compulsive would be as misleading as automatically excluding every simple phobia. Thus, the issue becomes one of carefully delineating the exclusionary guidelines used in a diagnostic system, rather than eliminating hierarchical or exclusionary assumptions altogether.

Recognizing these difficulties, Spitzer and Williams (1985) have critically evaluated some of the assumptions underlying the hierarchical organization of DSM-III anxiety disorders. For example, they note that DSM-III excluded a diagnosis of agoraphobia in the presence of obsessive–compulsive disorder, because individuals with the latter disorder are often fearful of going out of the house alone. This exclusionary rule fails to recognize that the agoraphobic and the obsessive–compulsive may be housebound for different reasons. In agoraphobia, fear of leaving the house is mediated by anticipation of panic attack or sudden incapacitation; such fears are not a part of the obsessive–compulsive picture.

THE FUNCTIONAL RELATIONSHIP AMONG DISORDERS

These issues, as well as new data presented below, have resulted in the deletion of the hierarchical exclusionary system in DSM-III-R. But it has not been replaced with the practice of simply listing all diagnoses, for reasons mentioned above. Rather, clinicians must examine the functional relationship of problems or disorders. A central element in this version is the distinction between "associated features" of a disorder and "coexisting complications" of a disorder. An "associated feature" refers to a symptom that is a typical aspect of the clinical picture of a more pervasive disorder. In the presence of the more pervasive disorder, the associated symptomatology does not warrant a separate diagnosis. For example, as noted above, phobic avoidance of dirt is a typical feature in patients with obsessive thoughts about contamination, so a separate diagnosis of simple phobia is not warranted. Similarly, in our work, my colleagues and I have found that fear and avoidance of heights or enclosed places, sufficient to meet the criteria for simple phobia, are often reported by agoraphobics. These symptoms usually prove to be an associated part of the agoraphobic symptomatology, because the feared situations represent the unavailability of an escape route in the case of panic. That is, a fear of heights is "functionally related" to the agoraphobic syndrome.

"Coexisting complications," on the other hand, are additional disorders that are also present but cannot be subsumed under the primary disorder. These additional diagnostic entities may have implications for etiology, treatment, or prognosis. For example, Leckman, Merikangas, Pauls, Prusoff, and Weissman (1983) demonstrated that a history of panic attacks in patients with depression was associated with a greater family prevalence of depression, anxiety disorders, and alcoholism than in depressed patients who were not panicking. That is, panic is not an integral part of depression, but if it is present it seems to represent a coexisting complication, with different implications for familial aggregation (and, perhaps, etiology and treatment). In fact, any time two or more distinct diagnoses are present, treatment approaches may be different than they would be for one disorder. In such cases, it is important to be able to assign joint diagnoses. Various specific examples in which assigning multiple diagnoses have proven important in choice of treatment are described below and in subsequent chapters. Since fixed hierarchies and automatic exclusionary rules cannot reflect the full presenting picture, decisions about the assignment of diagnoses must be made on a case-by-case basis, through considering the functional relationships among various symptom clusters in a given patient.

PATTERNS OF ADDITIONAL DIAGNOSES

In a preliminary study, we examined the distribution of additional diagnoses or patterns of comorbidity in 108 consecutive patients presenting at our clinic (Barlow, Di Nardo, et al., 1986). The number of patients in this study and their primary DSM-III diagnoses are presented in Table 9.8. These diagnoses were arrived at in the manner described above for the reliability studies. Table 9.9 presents the number and percentage of anxiety disorder cases in which additional but secondary anxiety diagnoses were assigned in a substantial number of cases, and the number of additional diagnoses appears related to the primary diagnosis. In approximately half of the cases of social phobia and agoraphobia, no additional diagnoses were assigned. However, there were relatively few cases of panic disorder, generalized anxiety disorder, and obsessive–compulsive disorder in which no additional diagnoses were assigned. For example, only 12% of the panic disorder cases and 17% of the cases of generalized

TABLE 9.8. Number of Patients in Each Diagnostic Category

Diagnosis	n
Agoraphobia with panic	41
Social phobia	19
Simple phobia	7
Panic disorder	17
Generalized anxiety disorder	12
Obsessive–compulsive disorder	6
Major depressive disorder	6
Total	108

Note. From Barlow, D. H., Di Nardo, P. A., Vermilyea, B. B., Vermilyea, J. A., & Blanchard, E. B. (1986). Co-morbidity and depression among the anxiety disorders: Issues in diagnosis and classification. Journal of Nervous and Mental Disease, 174, 63–72. Copyright 1986 by Williams & Wilkins. Reprinted by permission.

TABLE 9.9. Number of Anxiety Disorder Cases in Which Additional Diagnoses Were Assigned

Number of additional diagnoses	Primary diagnosis (n)						
	Agoraphobia with panic (41)	Social phobia (19)	Simple phobia (7)	Panic disorder (17)	Generalized anxiety disorder (12)	Obsessive–compulsive disorder (6)	Major depressive disorder (6)
None	20 (49%)	10 (53%)	3 (43%)	2 (12%)	2 (17%)	0	0
One	8 (20%)	7 (37%)	2 (29%)	11 (65%)	5 (42%)	3 (50%)	3 (50%)
Two	9 (22%)	2 (11%)	2 (29%)	3 (18%)	3 (25%)	3 (50%)	2 (33%)
Three or more	4 (1%)	0	0	1 (6%)	2 (16%)	0	1 (17%)

Note. From Barlow, D. H., Di Nardo, P. A., Vermilyea, B. B., Vermilyea, J. A., & Blanchard, E. B. (1986). Co-morbidity and depression among the anxiety disorders: Issues in diagnosis and classification. *Journal of Nervous and Mental Disease, 174,* 63–72. Copyright 1986 by Williams & Wilkins. Reprinted by permission.

anxiety disorder did not receive an additional diagnosis. None of the cases of obsessive–compulsive disorder went without an additional diagnosis, although only six cases were in this category.

Table 9.10 shows the distribution of specific additional diagnoses among the anxiety disorder cases. The first number of each entry indicates the total number of cases in which the particular additional diagnosis was assigned by either or both raters. The parenthetical figure indicates the number of those cases in which the diagnosis was independently assigned by both raters or by consensus of the staff. Of particular interest in this table is the frequency with which a depressive diagnosis (either major depressive disorder or dysthymic disorder) appeared as an additional diagnosis among the anxiety disorders. If one counts a diagnosis by either clinician of these two affective disorders, then this diagnosis occurred in 16, or 39%, of the 41 cases of agoraphobia; 6, or 35%, of the 17 cases of panic disorder; 4, or 21%, of the 19 cases of social phobia; and 2, or 17%, of the 12 cases of generalized anxiety disorder. Finally, 4 out of 6 cases of obsessive–compulsive disorder received a diagnosis of depression, and in all 4 cases each interviewer agreed that this was a major depressive disorder. On the other hand, none of the simple phobics was depressed.

Now we have similar data from a later series of 132 patients receiving DSM-III-R diagnoses (Sanderson, Rapee, & Barlow, 1987a). The numbers and percentages of anxiety disorder cases in which additional diagnoses were assigned are presented in Table 9.11. The number and percentage of patients in each DSM-III-R category receiving each additional diagnosis are presented in Table 9.12. The fact that only one patient received a diagnosis of panic disorder without agoraphobia demonstrates how rare it is for an individual to present with no avoidance whatsoever. The diagnosis of panic disorder with agoraphobia with mild avoidance better describes those patients who would be diagnosed with panic disorder according to DSM-III.

While some differences were apparent, the overall patterning was roughly similar. For example, a depressive diagnosis was most likely to be associated with obsessive–compulsive disorder and least likely to be associated with simple phobia. Social phobia and simple phobia were the most common additional diagnoses for all disorders except obsessive–compulsive disorder, where a depressive disorder was likely. Panic disorder with agoraphobia was an additional diagnosis for 17% of social phobics but none of the simple phobics. Interestingly, 27% of patients with generalized anxiety disorder received an additional diagnosis of panic disorder with agoraphobia. The implications of this association are discussed more fully in Chapter 15.

It seems clear from these data that a number of distinct anxiety disorders varying in severity may occur at the same time in any one individ-

TABLE 9.10. Additional Diagnoses among Anxiety Disorder Cases

Additional diagnoses	Primary diagnosis (n)						
	Agoraphobia with panic (41)	Social phobia (19)	Simple phobia (7)	Panic disorder (17)	Generalized anxiety disorder (12)	Obsessive–compulsive disorder (6)	Major depressive disorder (6)
Agoraphobia	—	0	1 (1)	0	2 (2)	1 (1)	2 (0)
Social phobia	7 (5)	—	2 (2)	6 (4)	4 (2)	0	0
Simple phobia	7 (4)	1 (1)	—	5 (4)	5 (3)	1 (1)	3 (3)
Panic disorder	0	0	1 (1)	—	0	1 (0)	1 (0)
Generalized anxiety disorder	1 (0)	1 (1)	0	0	—	1 (1)	1 (0)
Obsessive–compulsive disorder	3 (1)	2 (2)	0	1 (1)	0	—	1 (1)
Major depressive disorder	6 (4)	1 (1)	0	2 (2)	0	4 (4)	—
Dysthymic disorder	10 (3)	3 (2)	0	4 (1)	2 (0)	0	0
Somatization disorder	0	0	0	1 (1)	0	0	0
Axis III	2 (2)	1 (1)	1 (1)	0	4 (1)	0	1 (1)
Alcohol abuse	0	1 (1)	0	0	0	0	1 (1)
Conversion	0	0	0	0	0	1 (1)	0
Cyclothymic disorder	0	1 (1)	0	0	0	0	0
Axis II	2 (1)	0	1 (1)	0	0	0	0

Note. Additional diagnoses assigned independently by both raters before consensus was determined at a staff meeting appear in parentheses. From Barlow, D. H., Di Nardo, P. A., Vermilyea, B. B., Vermilyea, J. A., & Blanchard, E. B. (1986). Co-morbidity and depression among the anxiety disorders: Issues in diagnosis and classification. Journal of Nervous and Mental Disease, 174, 63–72. Copyright 1986 by Williams & Wilkins. Reprinted by permission.

TABLE 9.11. Comorbidity within the DSM-III-R Anxiety Disorder Categories: Number of Additional Diagnoses Received by Each Category

Number of additional diagnoses	Primary diagnosis (n)							
	PDA:MILD (25)	PDA:MOD (21)	PDA:SEV (9)	PD (1)	SOCIAL (24)	SIMPLE (17)	O-C (12)	GAD (22)
None	9 (36%)	5 (24%)	3 (33%)	1 (100%)	10 (42%)	8 (47%)	2 (17%)	2 (9%)
One	12 (48%)	7 (33%)	5 (56%)	—	9 (38%)	9 (53%)	7 (58%)	8 (36%)
Two	2 (8%)	6 (29%)	1 (11%)	—	4 (16%)	—	3 (25%)	9 (41%)
Three	2 (8%)	2 (9%)	—	—	1 (4%)	—	—	3 (14%)
Four	—	1 (5%)	—	—	—	—	—	—

Note. For key to abbreviations, see Table 9.5. From Sanderson, W. C., Rapee, R. M., & Barlow, D. H. (1987, November). *The DSM-III—Revised anxiety disorder categories: Description and patterns of co-morbidity.* Paper presented at the annual meeting of the Association for Advancement of Behavior Therapy, Boston.

TABLE 9.12. Comorbidity within the DSM-III-R Anxiety Disorder Categories: Percentage Receiving Each Additional Diagnosis

Additional diagnoses	Primary diagnosis (n)							
	PDA:MILD (25)	PDA:MOD (21)	PDA:SEV (9)	PD (1)	SOCIAL (24)	SIMPLE (17)	O-C (12)	GAD (22)
PD	0	0	0	0	0	0	0	0
PDA	—	—	—	—	17	0	8	27
SOCIAL	24	33	0	—	—	29	8	59
SIMPLE	36	52	44	0	25	—	33	23
O-C	4	0	0	0	4	6	0	9
GAD	16	14	0	0	8	24	0	—
Major depressive disorder	8	19	0	0	8	6	33	0
Dysthymic disorder	12	23	22	0	21	12	33	27

Note. For key to abbreviations, see Table 9.5. From Sanderson, W. C., Rapee, R. M., & Barlow, D. H. (1987, November). *The DSM-III—Revised anxiety disorder categories: Description and patterns of co-morbidity.* Paper presented at the annual meeting of the Association for Advancement of Behavior Therapy, Boston.

347

ual. These additional diagnoses also seem to have important treatment implications in many cases. For example, an agoraphobic in one of our groups also presented with a distinct blood and injury phobia, which would be categorized as a simple phobia. This complicated treatment by graduated exposure. When confronted with a phobic object, such as a dead squirrel in the road during her practice sessions, she experienced the bradycardia and hypotension that are paradoxically characteristic of this particular simple phobia (Connolly, Hallam, & Marks, 1976; Yule & Fernando, 1980); she also occasionally would faint, something agoraphobics almost never do (see Chapter 12). In this case, the specific phobia had to be treated before substantial progress could be made with the agoraphobia.

This method of examining comorbidity requires that all DSM-III criteria for a secondary diagnosis be present before that diagnosis is added to the patient's list of problems. When the clinician is through, a fuller picture of the patient's presenting clinical condition is obtained; this picture may well have implications for choice of treatment as well as prognosis, as suggested above. We are only just beginning to uncover the implications of many of these relationships, since establishing the full range of diagnoses for which any one patient may qualify is a very recent development. Specific implications for treatment of comorbidity are discussed within the context of each disorder in subsequent chapters.

COMORBIDITY WITH SOMATOFORM
AND PERSONALITY DISORDERS

Of course, analyses of comorbidity are not restricted to other emotional disorders. Recently, investigators have begun to examine patterns of comorbidity with other Axis I disorders, as well as personality disorders. The somatoform disorders are among the most interesting, since they have always been thought to be closely related to anxiety disorders. In Table 9.2, it can be seen that several disorders classified under the general heading of neuroses became somatoform disorders in DSM-III. Marks (1970) refers to some somatoform disorders, particularly hypochondriasis, as "illness phobia."

Somataform disorders are understudied. Thus the degree to which major features are shared among somataform and anxiety disorders is not clear at this time. King *et al.* (1986) have begun to examine this issue. These investigators constructed a questionnaire, the Self-Report Inventory for Somatic Symptoms, to ascertain somatization, and visceral sensitivity. This scale also contains a symptom checklist of 37 physical symptoms that make up the DSM-III diagnosis of somatization disorder. This scale was administered to 44 females with the DSM-III diagnosis of agoraphobia with panic attacks. Fully 12 of the 44 agoraphobic patients reported 14 or more symptoms, thereby meeting the cutoff for somatization disorder. This was in contrast to the results for a control group, where none met the criteria.

Descriptively, patients with panic disorder are defined in DSM-III-R as those with an extreme sensitivity to and fear of somatic symptoms that may signal the next panic attack. Since somatization disorder also features visceral sensitivity as one of its defining features, it is not surprising that some overlap occurs. But somatization disorder is thought to represent a more broad-based sensitivity to illness-related phenomena, while panic disorder is very specific. Only future research will clarify these distinctions. Another interesting somataform disorder is called dysmorphic somatoform disorder in DSM-III-R, but has been referred to more commonly as "dysmorphophobia" (Marks, 1981a). Generally, these individuals are particularly horrified or repulsed by an aspect of their physical presentation, such as a facial feature or body odor. These negative qualities are not apparent to others, or, if noticeable, are very insignificant. Information disputing their beliefs has little effect. Often they seek out plastic surgeons. The reaction of these individuals to their "repulsive" physical attribute seems characterized by distress and anxiety in the same way that an intrusive thought concerning contamination or illness evokes distress and anxiety in obsessive–compulsive disorder. But their thoughts are not resisted or seen as unrealistic. Once again, precise similarities and differences between dysmorphophobia and other anxiety disorders requires closer scrutiny.

Determining the association of personality disorders with the anxiety disorders may have substantial treatment implications. Nevertheless, investigation in this area suffers from difficulties in diagnosing personality disorders in a reliable fashion. The development of structured interviews and other methods of diagnosing broad clusters of personality disorders may soon correct this deficiency. In the meantime, what data we have on the association of anxiety disorders and personality disorders are preliminary and uncertain.

Tyrer, Casey, and Gall (1983) administered an interview schedule for assessing personality disorders to a vaguely defined group of 316 outpatients. They discovered that "anxiety neurosis" was strongly related to passive, dependent personalities, and that the presence of a personality disorder significantly impaired clinical outcome in a drug treatment trial. Koenigsberg, Kaplan, Gilmore, and Cooper (1985) found that anxiety and somatoform disorders, along with substance abuse disorders, were most commonly associated with personality disorders. For example, approximately 50% of phobic and panic disorder groups received additional personality disorder diagnoses, as did 36% of the obsessive–compulsive group. Although thousands of subjects were included, this study was based on chart reviews and is therefore likely to be particularly unreliable. Nevertheless, establishing the presence of certain personality disorders may have substantial implications for treatment outcome research and is a task that lies ahead of us.

THE ASSOCIATION OF DIMENSIONS OF ANXIETY

Studies of "comorbidity," or the association of certain problems with other problems, need not be limited to diagnostic categories. The association of various prominent features of anxiety and anxiety disorders can also be examined within a more dimensional framework. We have even less evidence from this particular approach then we do for comorbidity. But some of the evidence we do have is particularly interesting. For example, in Chapter 3 the incidence of panic across the anxiety disorder categories, as well as in major depressive disorder, has been presented (see Table 3.5). The table shows that panic is a ubiquitous phenomenon, differing only in reported frequency across the disorders. As noted below, panic is also very frequent in patients with affective disorders who do not necessarily present at an anxiety disorders clinic. One recent study designed to answer this question found that 50% of patients with primary diagnoses of affective disorders also reported panic attacks (Benshoof, 1987). Thus, reports of panic attacks are not in themselves sufficient to earn a diagnosis of panic disorder (see Chapter 10). However, the point here is that panic seems to be an important feature that can be dimensionalized across the anxiety disorders according to ratings of intensity and frequency. In Chapter 15, data are presented demonstrating that generalized anxiety is also a feature present in most anxiety (and depressive) disorders to varying degrees. Once again, it can be dimensionalized on the basis of frequency and/or intensity of its components.

We are only beginning to explore the distribution of other salient anxiety-related features across patients with various primary anxiety disorders. For example, data recently collected in our clinic (Rapee, Sanderson, & Barlow, 1987) indicate that features of social phobia are also present in other anxiety disorders, although they are far more frequent and intense if the primary diagnosis is social phobia. These data are presented in Table 9.13. For each anxiety disorder, the percentage of patients who presented with social phobic features (according to questions in the ADIS-R) and the percentage of patients who met DSM-III-R criteria for social phobia are given. Scores on the Social Phobia subscale of the Fear Questionnaire (Marks & Mathews, 1979) and mean impairment ratings are also presented.

Other data presented in subsequent chapters indicate quite clearly that many features of anxiety disorders are present in normal popula-

TABLE 9.13. Subject Characteristics and General Social Phobia Descriptors across Diagnostic Categories

Variable	Social phobia ($n = 35$)	Agoraphobia ($n = 35$)	Panic disorder ($n = 35$)	Generalized anxiety disorder ($n = 35$)	Simple phobia ($n = 19$)	df	Statistics
Percentage of females	37	74	80	67	84	χ^2 (4)	20.1**
Mean age (years)	33.5	37.8	34.1	40.3	34.2	F (4, 153)	2.42
Fear of observation (%)	94.3	48.6	48.6	75.0	36.8	χ^2 (4)	28.8**
Concern re: humiliation (%)	91.4	31.4	31.4	75.0	21.1	χ^2 (4)	48.6**
Avoidance of social situations (%)	62.9	25.7	29.4	30.6	15.8	χ^2 (4)	17.2*
DSM-III-R social phobia (%)	100.0	31.4	22.9	41.7	21.1	—	—
Fear Questionnaire (Social Phobia subscale)	17.1_a	16.1_a	11.0_{ab}	12.3_{ab}	5.4_b	F (4, 80)	6.28**
Mean impairment (0–4)	2.6_a	1.6_{ab}	1.3_b	1.3_b	1.0_b	F (4, 66)	7.58**

Note. Means sharing subscripts are not significantly different at the .05 level using a Scheffe procedure. From Rapee, R. M., Sanderson, W. C., & Barlow, D. H. (1987, November). *Social phobia symptoms across the DSM-III anxiety disorders categories.* Paper presented at the annual meeting of the Association for Advancement of Behavior Therapy, Boston.

*$p < .01$.
**$p < .001$.

tions, most often less intensely or severely. Examples are intrusive thoughts, ritualistic checking (see Chapter 16), panic attacks (see Chapters 3 and 10), and social anxiety (see Chapter 14). It is also well known that many individuals have simple phobias with associated avoidance, which nevertheless does not interfere sufficiently with functioning to earn the status of a "disorder" (see Chapters 1 and 12).

While we are just beginning to develop this type of data, it seems likely that the major features defining most DSM-III-R anxiety disorders, such as social phobic features or intrusive thoughts, may be identified in patients presenting with any one of the anxiety or affective disorders. In addition, these major features may exist in the normal population at lower intensity or frequency. Theoretical conceptions developed earlier emphasize the focus of anxious apprehension as a determining factor of the type of emotional or stress disorder with which a given patient may present. In any case, it may be useful in the future to develop a type of dimensional comorbidity, in which primary presenting problems are clearly identified for each individual but additional salient features of anxiety, depression, or stress are arrayed or dimensionalized. Examining this dimensional array may have more treatment implications for a clinician than simply listing comorbidity of DSM-III-R categories.

CONCLUSIONS ON COMORBIDITY

Whether we arrive eventually at a categorical or a dimensional method of ascertaining comorbidity, or both, it seems clear that this task will be very important if we are to reflect clinical reality and increase the precision and validity of our treatment outcome research. Of course, it is not surprising that patients present with multiple disorders or features of a variety of disorders. Indeed, almost every study examining this phenomenon has observed marked overlap among clinical features in various mental disorders (P. C. Kendall & Butcher, 1982; R. E. Kendall, 1975; Masserman & Carmichael, 1938; Nathan, 1967; Sheehan & Sheehan, 1982). Since all nonorganic categories are now classified by presenting clinical features rather than by etiology, substantial overlap should be expected. The question remains, however: Should researchers and clinicians continue to act as if diagnostic categories are actual "entities" by choosing one category and excluding others, or should they attend more closely to presenting coexisting problems and the overall pattern of psychopathology?

On a more basic level, there remains the issue of whether classification should be categorical or dimensional. With the marked overlap in symptomatology, it is tempting to turn to more dimensional analyses for anxiety disorders, as described above. On the other hand, there seems to be increasing evidence, in my opinion, of the importance of identifying at least some of the clusters of symptoms specified in DSM-III anxiety disorder categories. If one can forego the notion that these are distinct entities with single causes and no particular relation to other descriptive psychopathology, then identifying certain disorders seems more useful than does a strictly dimensional analysis. For example, there is growing evidence for the importance of identifying fear of panic in panic disorder (see Chapter 10). The performance anxieties currently grouped under the category of social phobia seem to have a particularly strong cognitive mediating process that may distinguish them from other phobias (Beck & Barlow, 1984; Sarason, 1982) (see Chapter 14). Additional discontinuities between social phobia and agoraphobia have recently been reported (Amies, Gelder, & Shaw, 1983). Blood and injury phobia is characterized by a physiological response different from that of other simple phobias (Öst, Sterner, & Lindahl, 1984), and perhaps deserves its own category for this reason (see Chapter 12). The relationship of blood and injury fears to somatization disorder has yet to be explored. Finally, it is useful to know whether someone with obsessive–compulsive disorder is depressed, and to know the functional relationship between the obsessive–compulsive features and the depression (see Chapter 16).

Gross quantifiable rating scales, such as the Hamilton Anxiety Rating Scale (Hamilton, 1959), do not seem very useful in this regard, since the items within such scales simply sample the broad range of features currently thought to be associated with anxiety in general (or depression in general). With the growing specificity of treatments, both psychological and pharmacological, few implications can be gleaned from simply observing higher Hamilton scores. Questionnaires that examine for the specific categories more systematically, such as the Fear Questionnaire, seem to provide more information.

Thus, diagnostic categories such as those specified in DSM-III-R, while not qualifying in any sense as real entities (P. C. Kendall & Butcher, 1982; R. E. Kendall, 1975), seem to be useful concepts or constructs that emerge as "blips" on a general background of a varying mixture of anxious and depressed symptomatology. Tyrer (1984) has adequately described the somewhat confused state of the classification of anxiety disorders and has called for longitudinal studies to determine the patterns and relationships of these symptoms over time. This will be an important step. In the meantime, in view of the relatively good reliability of DSM-III (and, most likely, DSM-III-R) anxiety disorder categories, a full description of these problems as they exist in each individual—a description based on functional relationships, but without regard to arbitrary hierarchical exclusionary systems—seems an important step in both clinical and research settings.

FUTURE CLASSIFICATION SYSTEMS

One issue in the area of classification on which everyone can agree is that DSM-III-R will not represent the last word on classifying anxiety disorders. We have concluded that, at present, a combination of categorical and dimensional classification best represents reality and should be most helpful in clinical planning. But the defining features of the categories, as well as the choice of which aspects of anxiety are dimensionalized, are likely to change as new data appear. It is likely that the improved reliability of the DSM-III-R system will facilitate research in this area. In addition, the emergence of new and important features within the anxiety disorder categories may force a different perspective, much as the new emphasis on panic has reorganized our thinking in the decade of the 1980s. By the early to middle 1990s, DSM-IV and ICD-10 are due for an appearance. According to current planning, these two systems should be more closely coordinated than were DSM-III and ICD-9. Thus, we are likely to see an increasing flurry of activity surrounding issues of classification for the next decade. It is possible that the next set of revisions will accord panic an even more important role, based on theorizing set forth in preceding chapters and our emerging knowledge of the nature of panic.

Data have been presented in Chapter 3 on the ubiquity of panic in all anxiety disorders as well as in the general population. The results of future research may indicate that most currently identified anxiety disorders, as well as some DSM-III-R disorders not characterized as anxiety disorders, are basically panic disorders that differ only in terms of the pervasiveness of the antecedents, the perception of cues, and whether the panic is expected or not. Posttraumatic stress disorder and some simple phobias with traumatic etiologies may represent true alarms transformed into learned (conditioned) alarms. That is, an identifiable traumatic event associated with a true alarm reaction may develop into simple phobia or posttraumatic stress disorder on the basis of specific biological and psychological vulnerabilities. Current antecedents in these conditions may be quite pervasive and include thoughts or dreams of the natural disaster, war, or traumatic encounter with an animal. But the major difficulty may be anxious apprehension over the prospect of another alarm (panic) occurring when one is confronted with the antecedents.

Panic disorder with and without agoraphobia, as well as other phobias without a traumatic etiology (such as most social and some simple phobias), may follow a different etiological path, as suggested in Chapter 6. These disorders may begin in a biologically vulnerable individual with stress-related false alarms that are transformed into learned alarms. These alarms may become more or less highly discriminated (cued). But the focus of anxiety is also on the next alarm. An individual experiencing a false alarm while flying on a plane after years of successful and enjoyable flying may be said to have a phobia of flying, when in fact it is a highly discriminated panic disorder emerging out of an experience with a false alarm. Similar analyses may apply to certain social phobics. While the learned alarm may be more or less discriminated (depending on a variety of circumstances surrounding the initial event, as well as specific psychological vulnerabilities), what is actually feared is the unexpected alarm itself, representing as it does a breakdown of control over future events. All that differ are the cues. Similarly, in obsessive–compulsive disorder, alarms become learned to and associated with certain patterns of thoughts (Barlow et al., 1985; see Chapter 3), making the antecedents in this disorder the most pervasive and unavoidable of any of the anxiety disorders. The pervasiveness of the antecedents here may insure heroic attempts at magical avoidance in the form of rituals, as well as the demoralization, dysphoria, and depression that often accompany this severe anxiety disorder. In this sense, all anxiety disorders described above are panic disorders, because learned alarms (panic) play a central role in each disorder.

The one anxiety disorder that cannot be characterized by inappropriate learned alarms is generalized anxiety disorder. Generalized anxiety disorder is characterized by pervasive anxious apprehension concerning multiple life events, or chronic worry. Anxious apprehension is, of necessity, a part of the panic disorders in the form of anticipatory anxiety (with the exception of some highly discriminated simple phobias, where complete avoidance is possible). But when anxious apprehension becomes the primary focus, it is, in many ways the most difficult of all anxiety disorders to treat. Of course, patients with generalized anxiety disorder also panic, as described in Chapter 15, but panic is not the focus of their anxious apprehension as it is in other disorders. A full elaboration of the etiology of each anxiety disorder, based on the conceptions of anxiety and panic developed in earlier chapters, comprises the remainder of this book.

10

Diagnosis and Assessment of Panic Disorder and Agoraphobia

After years of relative obscurity, agoraphobia has become perhaps the most widely recognized anxiety disorder in the eyes of the public, second only to simple phobia. As late as the early 1970s, this was not the case. People who suffered from anxiety attacks resulting in immobilization to the point of being housebound were most often considered to be extremely nervous or perhaps odd. As the condition of agoraphobia became widely publicized during the late 1970s and the 1980s, many people remembered an "eccentric" aunt who seldom if ever left home. Family reunions would be difficult for this aunt, as well as visits to church, trips downtown to the shopping center, or long rides away from home in a car. It is now widely known that agoraphobia is a fear of leaving a safe place or venturing into crowded areas and that the multitude of "eccentric" aunts suffered from this condition. This is consistent with the original suggestion of Westphal (1871), who coined the term "agoraphobia" or "fear of the marketplace." The aptness of this term, bringing to mind as it does the *agora* or Greek marketplace, is never more apparent than when current agoraphobics consistently describe the modern-day *agora*, the shopping mall, as one of their most frightening situations.

THE RELATIONSHIP OF PANIC AND AVOIDANCE

The view of agoraphobia as a fear of venturing into crowded areas does not fit neatly with the model alluded to in previous chapters, which highlights the centrality of panic in agoraphobia. In fact, on the basis of our emerging model and evidence available at this time, it would seem that

356

the term "agoraphobia" is misleading to some extent. Were it not for an accident of history, this seeming misdirection might not have occurred. In 1870, a year before Westphal, Benedikt suggested another name for what was certainly the same condition. The German term *Platzschwindel*, referring to the sensation of dizziness in public places, conveys what now seems to be a more accurate conception of the disorder: We now know that these individuals focus on and attempt to avoid internal physical sensations associated with panic, and that dizziness is one of the primary symptoms of panic (see Chapter 3).

Over the years, other clinicians have suggested alternative labels to capture this essential fact of panic disorder and agoraphobia, as did Roth (1959) when he referred to agoraphobia as the "phobic anxiety–deperson-alization syndrome." In any case, what these clinicians were communi-cating was that the central problem in agoraphobia with panic is fear of the symptoms of panic; hence the well-known and accepted characteri-zation of agoraphobia as fear of fear. In keeping with Greek traditions, another name might be "panphobia" (Ley, 1985a). As described in Chap-ter 3, the Greek god Pan, with his habit of suddenly jumping out of the bushes and scaring people to death, was the origin of the term "panic."

The growing realization that agoraphobic avoidance is basically a complication of anxiety about a fear of panic is supported by reasonably strong evidence, some of it reviewed in previous chapters (Barlow, 1986d). To summarize, there is both physiological and phenomenological evi-dence that panic attacks are descriptively and functionally unique events. First, panic attacks present differently than does generalized or anticipa-tory anxiety and are experienced differently by patients (Barlow *et al.*, 1985; Cohen *et al.*, 1985; Rapee, 1985b; Taylor *et al.*, 1986). Second, re-search suggesting how unexpected panic attacks are functionally related to subsequent anticipatory anxiety and avoidance (e.g., Rachman & Lev-itt, 1985) is beginning to appear (see Chapter 4). Third, detailed timelines constructed by both behavioral and pharmacological researchers point to a developmental course that is identical from study to study. Specifically, an individual will experience one or more unexpected panic attacks, which are followed some time later by the development of varying degrees of avoidance (Thyer & Himle, 1985; Uhde, Roy-Byrne, *et al.*, 1985). Fourth, patients presenting with either panic disorder or agoraphobia with panic (DSM-III) seem identical in terms of descriptive characteristics (e.g., Hal-lam, 1978; Thyer, Himle, Curtis, Cameron, & Nesse, 1985; Turner, Mc-Cann, *et al.*, 1986; Turner, Williams, Beidel, & Mezzich, 1986). For exam-ple, the age of onset of panic disorder, with or without extensive avoidance behavior, seems to be identical (Thorpe & Burns, 1983; Thyer, Parrish, Curtis, Nesse, & Cameron, 1985) (see below). Fifth, evidence reviewed below suggests that the main determinant of whether avoidance behavior will accompany panic attacks or not may be cultural. Typically, over three-quarters of panic-disordered patients manifesting extensive avoidance are women, but the sex ratio is closer to 1:1 in panic-disordered patients without avoidance behavior (Myers *et al.*, 1984; Thyer, Parrish, *et al.*, 1985). New data (presented in Table 9.5) also demonstrate the correlation of agoraphobic avoidance with gender.

It is my basic assumption—based on this evidence, as well as other evidence reviewed below and clinical experience—that agoraphobic avoidance behavior is simply one associated feature of severe unexpected panic. This avoidance behavior is multiply determined and maintained, but is closely associated at least initially with the escapist action tendencies of the basic emotion of fear (panic). Eventually, agoraphobic avoidance, if it is feasible, becomes one way of coping with anxiety over the possibility of additional unexpected panics. Other methods of coping with panic include resorting to the use (and eventually the abuse) of drugs and/or alcohol, as described in Chapter 1; employing a number of cognitive rituals to avoid or dissociate from the panic; or simply enduring the panic in whatever situation occurs as best one can. But we have seen in Table 9.5 that few, if any, patients with panic disorder display no avoidance or escape. Rather, avoidance behavior associated with panic is more accurately depicted as being on a continuum from mild to severe.

Costello (1982), in a community survey of fears, also found evidence for the relative independence of avoidance behavior and the occurrence of panic in his subjects. In those subjects who reported marked fears of public places in the manner of agoraphobia, avoidance was uncorrelated with the severity of reports of anxiety. It would seem, once again, that other factors are responsible for the extent and type of avoidance within agoraphobia.

My colleagues and I (Craske, Sanderson, & Barlow, 1987b) have illustrated that neither the greatest frequency of panic during the course of the disorder nor the amount of time since the first unexpected panic is necessarily related to current avoidance behavior. Specifically, a series of 57 patients, categorized by amount of avoidance (mild to severe), did not differ in the amount of time that had elapsed since their first panic. Nor did fear of having another attack or history of the severity of panic discriminate degree of current avoidance in patients. In fact, all patients feared having another attack, whether they avoided or not. Only current panic frequency seemed related to degree of avoidance. But even this relationship was not statistically significant, because of large intersubject variability. The relationship between greatest panic frequency and avoidance in these patients is presented in Figure 10.1.

Avoidance is always idiosyncratic to the individual, in terms of patterns as well as amount (ranging from slight to very extensive). But most patients fall somewhere in between, as noted above: They avoid some situations and not others, depending on the particular circumstances of

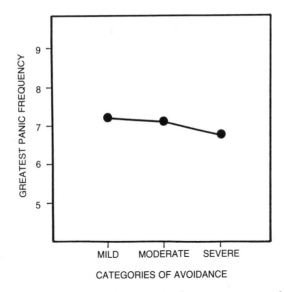

FIGURE 10.1. Panic frequency at the greatest frequency per week for each level of avoidance ($n = 57$). Adapted from Craske, M. G., Sanderson, W. C., & Barlow, D. H. (1987). The relationships among panic, fear, and avoidance. *Journal of Anxiety Disorders, 1,* 153–160. Copyright 1987 by Pergamon Journals, Ltd. Adapted by permission.

their lives, such as job requirements, the tolerance of social support systems (including families), and the development of individual safety signals permitting greater mobility (Rachman, 1984). Specific patterns of coping with panic would also be a function of methods that have been learned in the past for coping with stress and anxiety. As highlighted in Chapter 1 and mentioned above, one of the major determinants of which coping methods are utilized seems to be some factor connected with sex roles—an issue to be discussed more fully later.

For all of these reasons, agoraphobia with panic is now subsumed under panic disorder in DSM-III-R, as described in Chapter 9. For these reasons, also, the assessment and treatment of panic disorder and agoraphobia are integrated in this book.

PREVALENCE

The mystery of agoraphobia and the tendency for other problems to mask panic and agoraphobia are never more evident than in the vastly different estimates of the prevalence of these problems. As observed in Chapter 1, the prevalence of agoraphobia was formerly estimated at approximately 0.5% on the basis of probability samples of the population as late as the

1960s (e.g., Agras *et al.*, 1969). More recent estimates, based on the extensive ECA study carried out under the sponsorship of NIMH, found that between 2.8% and 5.7% of a random sample of the population met the criterion for agoraphobia, with another 1% on the average presenting with panic disorder (Myers *et al.*, 1984) (see Table 1.2).

It is not entirely clear what accounts for this 10-fold discrepancy in population prevalence. Presumably, this does not reflect an actual increase in prevalence in the space of 10 years. More likely, it is due to differing definitions of agoraphobia; to the use of somewhat different criteria to arrive at these definitions; and perhaps to a greater awareness in the population at large of the symptoms that comprise agoraphobia. Of course, even within the ECA survey, there are wide discrepancies from catchment area to catchment area; these most likely reflect somewhat different populations, differences in interviewer techniques, or possibly a combination of the two. These issues require clarification from epidemiologists.

Finally, both DSM-III and its recent revision reserve a category for agoraphobia without panic attacks. This is a controversial category about which we know very little. During the committee discussions on which DSM-III-R was based, a difference of opinion arose between the clinicians on the one hand and the epidemiologists on the other. Clinicians reported almost never seeing a case of agoraphobia without panic. For example, over a 1-year period of time in our clinic, we saw 41 patients who received a diagnosis of agoraphobia with panic, but only 1 patient with agoraphobia without panic. Even this one case clearly presented with the limited symptom attacks (fewer than three symptoms) described in Chapter 3, and reported that her major fear concerned having one of these limited symptom attacks while away from home. Therefore, she was not diagnosed as having agoraphobia with panic only because of a nosological technicality. Swinson (1986) saw 300 consecutive agoraphobics without encountering one who did not report an initial panic attack. Thyer, Himle, *et al.* (1985) reported 95 out of 115 agoraphobics meeting the criteria for agoraphobia with panic attack. This left 20 agoraphobics who technically met the criteria for agoraphobia without panic. But these investigators also found that all 20 of these patients suffered from some somatic ailment of an unpredictable or sporadic nature, such as epilepsy or colitis. It is very possible that those with colitis and related symptoms also met the criteria for limited symptom attacks. In any case, an unpredictable somatic event (whether functional or organic) seems to serve as a functional equivalent to panic attacks, in that patients learn to fear the somatic event and avoid situations where it may occur. Since the event is unpredictable, the avoidance can become extensive.

Despite these observations from clinics, epidemiologists report a substantial percentage of people with extensive avoidance who do not present with panic attacks (Weissman, 1985). For example, in the ECA survey, from 25% to 50% of agoraphobics did not report panic attacks (Weissman, Leaf, Blazer, Boyd, & Florio, 1986). The reasons for this discrepancy between epidemiological and clinical experience are not clear, but at the very least it seems that these people do not come in for treatment.

PRESENTING CHARACTERISTICS

SEX RATIOS AND AGE OF ONSET

One of the most fascinating mysteries about agoraphobia, as illustrated in Chapter 1 and mentioned above, is that 75% or more are women. This finding is reported consistently in studies of agoraphobics from around the world, and seems to hold up whether these studies are based on patients coming for treatment (Mathews et al., 1981) or agoraphobics found in random samples of the population (Myers et al., 1984; Thorpe & Burns, 1983). A variety of reasons have been offered to explain this discrepancy. The most common explanation involves cultural factors. Based on this hypothesis, it is more culturally acceptable for women to report fear and to act on this report by avoiding a large number of situations. Men, on the other hand, are expected to be stronger and braver and to "tough it out" by neither reporting fear nor demonstrating avoidance.

Some support for this cultural hypothesis can be found in comparisons of panic disorder patients with different amounts of agoraphobic avoidance. In one of our recent matched samples of DSM-III-diagnosed agoraphobics with panic compared to panic disorder patients, 13 out of 15 agoraphobics were women, compared to 8 women out of 15 with panic disorder. Thyer, Himle, et al. (1985) observed that 76 out of 95 agoraphobics with panic attacks, or 80%, were women. On the other hand, the percentage of patients with panic disorder who were women was 35 out of 52, or 57%. Finally, sex differences within DSM-III panic disorder were much smaller than those found in agoraphobia and were usually not statistically significant in the large ECA survey (Myers et al., 1984).

Now two studies using DSM-III-R criteria have arrayed panic disorder patients on extent of avoidance and examined sex ratios. In data reported earlier (see Table 9.5), extent of avoidance was correlated with gender. Reich, Noyes, and Troughton (1987) have also reported an increasingly greater percentage of females in categories with more extensive agoraphobic avoidance.

The tendency for panic disorder with only mild agoraphobic avoidance to be distributed somewhat more equally among men compared to women suggests that men may be finding ways other than extensive avoidance to cope with panic, such as alcohol use/abuse. In this respect, the few studies that have directly compared men and women with agoraphobia with panic are also interesting. In the largest and most comprehensive study of this type, Chambless and Mason (1986) reported data from 334 female and 68 male clients treated in the Temple University Agoraphobia Program. The authors found few, if any, differences on a wide range of measures of psychopathology and personality—a finding replicated on a smaller scale in other centers (Mavissakalian, 1985). Nevertheless, one fascinating finding mentioned above appears in Chambless and Mason's data. The tendency to avoid situations while alone for agoraphobics, whether male or female, was significantly correlated with masculinity scores on a sex-role scale. That is, the less "masculine" one's scores on a sex-role scale, the more agoraphobic avoidance, regardless of gender. This supports further the notion that avoidance behavior within agoraphobia is in large part culturally determined, and it highlights the potential importance of associated personality characteristics described below.

A related observation is the high proportion of individuals with anxiety and panic who resort to self-medication by means of alcohol, as described in Chapter 1. The majority of these individuals are male. This suggests that males turn to alcohol to help them through situations in which they are likely to panic. There is little support for the hypothesis that biological differences between men and women—specifically, greater hormonal fluctuations surrounding menstrual periods and births—may predispose women to panic attacks and resulting agoraphobia, thus accounting for sex differences.

There is also wide agreement across studies examining the historical development of panic and agoraphobia that the origins are most often found early in adult life. This is in contrast to other phobic disorders, such as simple phobia and social phobia. For example, Marks and Gelder (1966) found two periods of time during which the greatest number of patients reported their first panic attack: (1) in late adolescence, and (2) at about age 30. However, Thorpe and Burns (1983), in their large survey of over 900 agoraphobics, reported a mean age of onset of 29 years, without the bimodal distribution noted by Marks and Gelder. Almost all surveys report a mean age of onset in the 20s for panic disorder and agoraphobia (e.g., Thyer, Parrish, *et al.*, 1985). The comparative ages of onset for different phobias, from a study by Öst (1987), are presented in Chapter 12 (Figure 12.1).

DEPENDENCY AND OTHER PERSONALITY CHARACTERISTICS

Aside from age of onset and the remarkable sex ratio, there is little evidence that patients with panic disorder and agoraphobia differ in any systematic way from other anxiety-disordered patients with respect to presenting characteristics. Some studies have indicated increased difficulties with sexual functioning in agoraphobics (Marks & Gelder, 1965). Systematic comparisons with other anxiety disorders have not been made. But panic disorder patients present with greatly increased sensitivity to and fear of somatic events compared to patients with other anxiety disorders, as discussed in Chapter 6 and below. Not all panic disorder patients are afraid of sexual arousal, but it is common clinically for these patients to begin avoiding sexual activity after the onset of their panic. Many report feeling as if they are going to panic during sexual relations. It is possible that the somatic signs of sexual arousal resemble panic for some of these patients.

A common and more important clinical observation is that phobics in general and agoraphobics in particular present with overly dependent personalities. It is also widely assumed that agoraphobics were overprotected as children (Andrews, 1966). These clinical reports form part of the basis for the interest in separation anxiety in children as a precursor to the development of panic and agoraphobia, since separation anxiety may occur in the content of an overdependent relationship. As noted in Chapter 6, the separation anxiety hypothesis is ripe with implications for the etiology of panic, although the evidence is weak at this time.

Much of the impetus for assumptions regarding phobic dependency has come from a well-done early study by Webster (1953), who judged that agoraphobics were more overprotected during childhood than a comparison group of anxiety neurotics. Mathews et al. (1981) have summarized the evidence from seven studies, all of which examine the issue of overprotection as well as stability of family background in agoraphobics and some comparison group (see Table 10.1). Several other studies also bear on this finding: For example, the Raskin et al. (1982) study reviewed in Chapter 5 found panic patients to have more "unstable" family backgrounds than patients with generalized anxiety disorder.

As Table 10.1 indicates, the studies listed have produced relatively contradictory results, with no firm conclusions possible. Mathews et al. (1981) point out that much of this contradiction is due to the fuzziness of the concepts of dependency and overprotection, and to the difficulty of retrospectively nailing down "instability" in family background. This difficulty was also evident in the Raskin et al. (1982) study, where raters had to rate retrospectively whether the subject reported a home environment that was "grossly deviant from one in which support for the child was consistent and appropriate" (p. 688). These ratings were based on records of previous interviews. No attempt was made to determine the reliability of these judgments, and, on the face of it, obtaining adequate reliability would be a difficult task indeed. Thorpe and Burns (1983) have also reported a seemingly high incidence of shyness and lack of family stability;

TABLE 10.1. Overprotection, Dependency, and Stability of Family Background: Summary of Seven Studies

Study	Subject groups	Measures	Results
Webster (1953)	Agoraphobics, anxiety neurotics; conversion hysterics	Ratings taken from therapy case notes	Higher proportion of agoraphobics judged as over-protected and as having unstable fathers.
Snaith (1968)	Agoraphobics; other phobics	Standard ratings by interview	Higher proportion of agoraphobics with unstable families; no difference in overprotection.
Shafar (1976)	Agoraphobics; other phobics	Subjective ratings (unspecified)	No difference in frequency of unhappy, disrupted childhood; more dependency in general.
Solyom, Beck, Solyom, & Hugel (1974)	Mixed phobics; volunteer subjects	Ratings and questionnaires	Tendency for agoraphobics to report greater maternal overprotection.
Solyom, Silberfeld, & Solyom (1976)	Mothers of agoraphobics; overprotective mothers	Standardized self-report questionnaires	Mothers of agoraphobics more overprotective than validation group.
Buglass, Clarke, Henderson, Kreit-man, & Presley (1977)	Agoraphobics; matched controls	Structured interview	Agoraphobics come from more "anomalous home situations"; no objective evidence of dependency; but agoraphobics feel more dependent and ambivalent.
Parker (1979)	Agoraphobics; social phobics; matched controls	Standardized questionnaire by mail	Agoraphobics report less maternal care; no differ-ence from controls in overprotection.

Note. From Mathews, A. M., Gelder, M. G., & Johnston, D. W. (1981). *Agoraphobia: Nature and treatment.* New York: Guilford Press. Copyright 1981 by The Guilford Press. Reprinted by permission.

upon reflection, however, they conclude that the frequency of those events seems no greater than that occurring in samples of normal children.

More recent studies are beginning to correct the definitional vagueness and methodological problems of earlier studies, at least in terms of presenting characteristics associated with dependency, if not developmental history. Reich, Noyes, and Troughton (1987) administered structured and well-validated questionnaires to ascertain personality disorders in 88 DSM-III-R panic disorder patients with varying amounts of agoraphobic avoidance. Patients with more extensive avoidance presented with more dependent personality disorder specifically and a greater number of third-cluster personality disorders (dependent, avoidant, compulsive, passive, aggressive) than did panic patients with less agoraphobic avoidance. In another study, Reich, Noyes, Hirschfeld, Coryell, and O'Gorman (1987) demonstrated that even recovered panic disorder patients (with or without agoraphobia) were more dependent and had less "emotional strength" than control subjects. Interestingly, panic disorder patients and depressed patients did not differ from each other on these characteristics, either before or after recovery. On the other hand, Mavissakalian and Hamann (1986b) noted improvement in personality disorder characteristics, particularly dependent personality disorder traits, after successful treatment.

Generally, the prevalence of diagnosed personality disorders in panic patients ranges from 25% to 50% in recent studies using up-to-date methods. Most of these personality disorders are the "anxious" third-cluster type, including dependent personality disorder (e.g., Koenigsberg et al., 1985; Mavissakalian & Hamann, 1986b; Reich, Noyes, & Troughton, 1987).

Of course, many of the features comprising these personality disorders are common to the "neurotic" personality, described in some detail in Chapter 2 (Eysenck, 1981; Gray, 1982). We know that these anxious traits are familial and almost certainly inherited. Thus, to the extent that trait anxiety and third-cluster personality disorders overlap, the frequency of personality disorders may seem low. Furthermore, studies comparing the prevalence of personality disorders across the anxiety disorders (reviewed in Chapter 9), although preliminary and suffering from methodological problems, suggest that an elevated prevalence of third-cluster personality disorders is common across all anxiety disorders (with the possible exception of simple phobia). There is no reason to assume, at this time, that panic disorder is unique in this regard.

This leaves us with the interesting, if preliminary, finding that panic disorder patients with extensive avoidance are more dependent, at least at time of presentation, than panic patients without avoidance. This may relate to the correlation of agoraphobic avoidance with "feminine" sex-role scores, noted above. If so, it may reflect once again a learned style of coping with aversive events such as panic. Alternatively, both dependency and extensive avoidance may be consequences of some other factor. It is also possible, although unlikely, that memories of dependence in childhood follow the development of panic rather than precede it. The possibilities for distortion in the collection of retrospective accounts of events occurring years ago in a group of emotionally disturbed patients are always large. In any event, prospective studies in children at risk for the development of anxiety disorders are necessary.

But dependency and overprotection during childhood may play a more basic role in the etiology of anxiety than the tentative connection with phobic behavior. As noted in Chapter 7, extreme overprotectiveness during childhood may deprive children of the opportunity to develop a sense of mastery and control (Andrews, 1966). This may create a psychological vulnerability to experience subsequent negative life events in an anxious manner.

A MODEL OF PANIC DISORDER

In Chapters 6 and 7, models for the development of panic and anxiety have been presented. The role of false alarms and the subsequent development of anxious apprehension concerning false alarms have been highlighted as important in the development of most anxiety disorders. While alarms, either true or false, seem to play a major role in the development of most anxiety disorders, the association of false alarms with interoceptive or somatic cues is particularly crucial in the development of panic disorder. Subsequently, the degree and extent of avoidance behavior, as described above, are functions of particular coping skills employed by the individual to cope with unexpected panic. The development of avoidance behavior to deal with panic is determined at least partly by experiential and cultural factors. Fluctuations in avoidance behavior subsumed under the label "agoraphobia" are largely functions of perceptions of safety on the part of the individual: That is, does a place exist where it is relatively safe to have a panic attack, or does an individual exist with whom it is relatively safe to have a panic attack (Rachman, 1984)?

Before specific assessment and treatment procedures for panic disorder and agoraphobia are discussed in detail, it is useful to refer to the etiological model presented in Figure 10.2. The first vulnerability is a tendency to be neurobiologically overreactive to the stress of negative life events. This biological response forms a platform for an initial hard-wired alarm reaction, for reasons detailed in Chapter 5. This hairtrigger alarm response to stress is false, since the "fight or flight" action tendencies associated with the alarm are not functional. That is, there is no real danger, as there would be in the case of a true alarm. The tendency for individuals to react to negative life events with exaggerated neurobiological

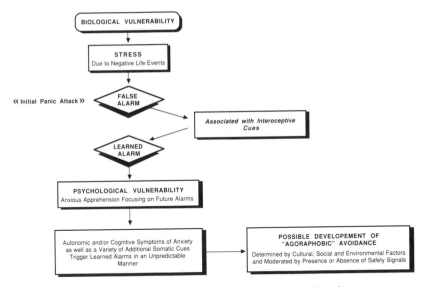

FIGURE 10.2. A model of the etiology of panic disorder.

activity and inappropriate false alarms seems to be genetically based. But this reaction would quickly diminish without the subsequent association of false alarms with interoceptive cues, resulting in learned alarms to interoceptive cues. This association, in turn, must be followed by the all-important development of anxious apprehension over having additional alarms. The propensity to develop anxiety over negative events or subsequent alarms is a crucial psychological vulnerability. This vulnerability arises out of developmental experiences with predictability and controlability. The focus of anxious apprehension is determined by the negative event experienced, including the subsequent alarm. For example, potentially sexually dysfunctional males react to the all-too-common experience of an initial erectile failure with anxiety; most men do not. That the focus in panic disorder is on potential upcoming false alarms may be due partly to the location of the first false alarm, as described in Chapter 6. But a more substantial determinant may be a pre-existing disposition to focus anxiety specifically on somatic events. This disposition to increased self-awareness or somatic sensitivity may interact with the shift to self-focused attention inherent in anxious apprehension to produce a particularly vicious cycle, and may make these individuals exquisitely sensitive to false alarms. This disposition to increased self-awareness boosted by emotional learning may be the reason why so many patients with panic disorder end up in the offices of cardiologists or other nonpsychiatric physicians, as reviewed in Chapter 1, while patients with other anxiety disorders, (often with equal frequencies of panic) do not. It is for this reason also that a large overlap exists between panic disorder and somatization disorders, as detailed in Chapter 9 (King *et al.*, 1986).

Thus, panic disorder patients are biologically predisposed to react to negative life events with neurobiological lability. They are psychologically predisposed to develop anxiety with a sense that events are proceeding out of control. And many are predisposed specifically to focusing anxiety on internal somatic events. With this model in place, the specific reasons and strategies for assessment described below should be clear.

ASSESSMENT

ORGANIC CONDITIONS ASSOCIATED WITH PANIC AND ANXIETY SYMPTOMS

Any time someone walks into the office of a mental health professional with panic attacks or severe anxiety, there is a chance that many of the symptoms may be due to one of several physical disorders (Hall, 1980; Mackenzie & Popkin, 1983; McCue & McCue, 1984; Taylor, 1987). Usually this is not an issue, since patients most often bring their first panic attack to emergency rooms or the offices of their primary care physicians where they are screened for these disorders. Only then are they referred to mental health professionals, very often to the surprise of the patients, who have assumed that the causes are organic. Nevertheless, every clinician should be aware of the major physical disorders responsible for anxiety-like symptoms. For that reason, brief descriptions of some of the primary disorders that mimic panic are presented here. It should also be noted at the outset that any one of the following conditions may coexist with panic disorder and interact with panic in a way that exacerbates its effect. Therefore, the diagnosis of one of these physical disorders should not rule out the coexistence of panic disorder and the necessity of treating panic attacks directly.

Hypoglycemia

Hypoglycemia, which refers to low blood sugar levels, is one of the more common disorders associated with panic. The symptoms of hypoglycemia include sweating, palpitations, weakness, dizziness, faintness, and tremor. Hypoglycemia has various causes, some acute, others more chronic; however, patients ordinarily very quickly come to recognize hypoglycemic symptoms and take corrective action to alter blood sugar levels, usually though more frequent intake of foods. One of our recent patients reported that she had numerous panics, but that one would occur quite predictably at 4:00 P.M. every day. In fact, it seemed that the symptoms of hypoglycemia were triggering this particular attack and that a small snack prevented it. However, the panic disorder remained and required treatment. That hypoglycemia plays a relatively small role in panic disorders was illustrated in two recent studies where panic disorder patients were made hypoglycemic in the laboratory (Schweizer, Winokur, & Rickels, 1986; Uhde, Vittone, & Post, 1984). In both studies, patients reported "nervousness" along with somatic symptoms of panic, but no panic.

Hyperthyroidism

Hyperthyroidism is a common endocrine disorder that causes restlessness, shortness of breath, palpitations, and tachycardia, as well as tremor and sweating. These symptoms can be very similar to panic. It is also noteworthy that this disorder occurs eight times more frequently in women than in men, with an age of onset similar to that of panic disorder.

Hypoparathyroidism

Hypoparathyroidism is characterized by deficiencies in secretions of the parathyroid hormone. The biological results are a depressed concentration of calcium and elevations of phosphate in blood plasma. In extreme cases, "panic attacks" may occur.

Cushing Syndrome

Cushing syndrome, which results from increased circulating levels of cortisol, can sometimes develop during a prolonged period of psychological stress. While acute anxiety and panic are sometimes observed during this disorder, depression is a more common reaction.

Pheochromocytoma

Pheochromocytoma refers to a tumor, generally found in the adrenal glands, that causes excessive secretion of the catecholamines noradrenaline and adrenaline. This disorder very closely mimics panic disorder, since the effects of the disorder are to exaggerate the normal secretion of catecholamines that would occur during stressful periods or preparation for purposeful activity. The symptoms, of course, are identical to those that would occur with any sudden increase in catecholamines as a result of stress or anxiety.

Temporal Lobe Epilepsy

Temporal lobe epilepsy has been associated with a wide range of emotional and sexual disorders, including anxiety. Once again, many of the symptoms of panic—sweating, palpitations, and also derealization—can result from temporal lobe epilepsy, which requires EEG recordings for proper diagnosis.

Caffeine Intoxication

In addition to the disorders described above, other conditions that have been used to provoke panic in the laboratory may be consistently associated with panic attacks and should be ruled out at initial interview. Prominent among these is an excessive intake of caffeine.

The effects of caffeine in provoking panic have been reviewed in Chapter 4. As Boulenger *et al.* (1984) point out, most people with panic avoid sources of caffeine, since they have learned that it exacerbates their panic symptoms. But some have not made the connection. Recently, we administered the ADIS to a woman who presented with panic attacks after referral from her primary care physician. When asked about coffee-drinking habits or other sources of caffeine intake, she replied that she liked coffee but did not drink to excess. Specification of intake, as required on the ADIS, revealed that she prepared and consumed three 10-cup vats of coffee per day! She was referred back to her physician for supervised withdrawal before her panic symptomatology was reassessed. Detailed questions regarding caffeine consumption are included in the ADIS and should be a routine part of any examination of anxiety disorders.

Audiovestibular System Disturbance

In a very interesting pilot study with potentially important implications, Jacob, Moller, Turner, and Wall (1985) administered an otoneurological examination to 21 patients with either DSM-III panic disorder or agoraphobia with panic attacks who also reported dizziness, fear of falling, or unsteadiness during their panic attacks. The results indicate that up to two-thirds of the patients had abnormal findings on two or more vestibular tests, while almost half were found to have a positive audiological test. The authors point out that it is not yet clear whether these findings are specific to patients with panic disorder, compared to those with other psychiatric diagnoses. In addition, even if the findings do turn out to be specific for panic patients, the implications are not yet clear. The authors note that it is very possible that anxiety influences the parameters of vestibular tests rather than the reverse (i.e., frightening endogenous sensations of disturbed audiovestibular functioning cause panic attacks).

Mitral Valve Prolapse

The condition that has unquestionably received the greatest attention in relation to possible organic etiologies of panic is MVP, and not just because it is also called Barlow syndrome (no relation)! MVP is characterized in its extreme form by chest pain, palpitations, headaches, and "giddiness," accompanied by an unusual and difficult-to-characterize systolic murmur.

The early excitement concerning the relation of panic disorder to MVP was caused by the fact that a series of early studies reported a high percentage of patients with recurrent panic attacks who also presented with MVP (Crowe et al., 1980; Gorman, Fyer, Gliklich, King, & Klein, 1981; Grunhaus, Gloger, Rein, & Lewis, 1982; Kantor, Zitrin, & Zeldis, 1980; Pariser et al., 1979). These early data excited a flurry of speculation that MVP might be a biological marker for panic in a substantial number of patients. However, more recent and more sophisticated examinations using echocardiogram procedures have failed to confirm the earlier reported high prevalence of MVP. Studies from around the country—notably by Shear, Devereux, Kramer-Fox, Mann, and Frances (1984), as well as Mavissakalian, Salerni, Thompson, and Michelson (1983)—found the prevalence of MVP in panic disorder patients to be no greater than that found in the normal population.

From a different perspective, Mazza, Martin, Spacavento, Jacobsen, and Gibbs (1986) surveyed the incidence of panic or other anxiety disorders in MVP patients. They found no difference in prevalence of anxiety disorder in MVP patients versus controls without MVP. Hartmann, Kramer, Brown, and Devereux (1982), who found similar results, suggest that the high prevalence of MVP in anxiety disorders found in earlier studies was due to biased screening.

Sophisticated studies also point to ascertainment bias and erroneous classification of differences as reasons for early positive findings (e.g., Devereux, Kramer-Fox, Brown, et al., 1986). On close examination, Devereux, Kramer-Fox, Shear, et al. (1988) found that overdiagnosis of MVP in panic patients was often due to misidentification of inconsequential midsystolic murmurs. Another major difficulty pointed out by Dager, Comess, Saal, and Dunner (1986) is that expert cardiologists cannot agree on the presence or absence of MVP, as reflected in kappa coefficients below .20. Also, Gorman et al. (1981) reported that panic patients with and without MVP responded equally well to imipramine. Finally, Crowe et al. (1980) found a similar pattern of inheritance for panic disorder whether MVP was present in the index case or not, suggesting that MVP is not related in any important way to panic. As cardiological diagnostic techniques improve, research in this area will continue, but Dager et al. (1986) reasonably conclude that at present there is no reason to attempt to diagnose MVP in panic patients.

Summary of Organic Conditions

There is little question that the various physical disorders described above can produce symptoms that mimic panic. For this reason, it is under-

371

standable that various clinicians suggest from time to time that a substantial proportion of panic disorders may be caused by one or another of these physical problems. What is overlooked is that a physical condition may well coexist with panic disorder, as more recent evidence has suggested is the case with MVP. What is also often overlooked, even in the case of MVP, is that the presence of a physical disorder producing several anxiety-like symptoms may exacerbate an existing panic disorder by contributing to the maintenance of panic disorder in a manner outlined in Figure 10.3. Whether the organically caused symptoms are endocrinological (as in hyperthyroidism), vestibular, or cardiovascular (as in MVP), a panic disorder patient is overly sensitive to and vigilant of certain patterns of internal physical changes. Patients who develop learned alarms to one or more of these patterns through the process of interoceptive conditioning are more likely to experience the spiral into a full-blown panic attack than if the sensations produced by the physical disorder are not present. Similarly, those patients without panic disorder presenting with one or more of these physical problems do not experience the subjective sensations of anxiety or panic once the underlying reasons for the physiological sensations have been thoroughly explained by a health professional—something that is not true for panic disorder patients. The ultimate test is whether the patient with a physical disorder stops panicking once the disorder is properly diagnosed and treated. If not, then it is probably time to deal with the panic disorder in its own right.

ASSESSING PANIC DISORDER AND AGORAPHOBIC AVOIDANCE

Preliminary Considerations

Recognizing panic disorder with agoraphobia does not seem to be particularly difficult, although panic disorder in the absence of agoraphobic avoidance presents somewhat more of a problem. I have described in Chapter 9 a structured interview, the ADIS (Di Nardo et al., 1983), for diagnosing the major anxiety disorders as outlined in DSM-III; a revised version, the ADIS-R (Di Nardo et al., 1985), is compatible with DSM-III-R. Of all of the major anxiety disorders in DSM-III, a classification of agoraphobia with panic attacks was agreed upon as the *primary* diagnosis most often by two clinicians in our clinic interviewing a patient independently on two different occasions. As noted in Table 9.3, the kappa was .854, which is very high indeed. The kappa for DSM-III panic disorder was also reasonably good at .651. The lack of clear behavioral referents (avoidance behavior) probably accounted for the somewhat lower rate of agreement for panic disorder, as did the issue present in DSM-III concerning how much avoidance behavior is required to discriminate between panic disorder and agoraphobia with panic. this issue is no longer present in DSM-III-R.

Clinicians in practice may not wish to administer the entire structured interview on a routine basis, since it was designed primarily to enable investigators to differentially diagnose subcategories of anxiety disorders, as well as to rule out affective disorders and other major problems. But clinicians may wish to adopt some of the carefully worded questioning developed in this interview over a period of several years when dealing with anxiety-related problems.

Although recognizing agoraphobia as defined in DSM-III seemed straightforward, problems with assessment became apparent. Many people we saw in our clinic had the features of agoraphobia with panic, but reported only limited avoidance behavior. For example, one patient in our clinic reported that she was able to get around quite well, particularly if a friend accompanied her, but she was unable to drive outside of an approximate 5-mile radius surrounding her home. In this case avoidance was not widespread nor were most normal activities constricted, but there was a very specific pattern of avoidance. This case would now fall into the category of panic disorder with agoraphobia with mild avoidance in DSM-III-R, as outlined in Chapter 9.

The more usual case is that patients will present with extremely variable patterns of avoidance and anxiety. That is, several months ago they were doing well, whereas at present they have an increasing pattern of avoidance that is making it difficult for them to function. Often this variable pattern of avoidance occurs against a background of chronic anxiety with occasional panics. For this reason, a detailed description of the course of the disorder is important, since examination focusing on only one particular point in time may be misleading.

Another problem often coexisting with panic is depression, as noted in previous chapters. Nevertheless, my colleagues and I have not found depression, even in fairly severe form, to interfere with response to the treatment described in the next chapter. But others have found that depression interferes with treatment (e.g., Zitrin et al., 1980), and clinicians may want to make a judgment on whether a major affective disorder should be treated before tackling the panic disorder or vice versa. One issue that we consider in making this decision is the chronology as well as the severity of the two disorders. If a major depressive disorder has its onset well before the onset of the panic with or without avoidance, then one might consider dealing with the depression first to see whether the panic disorder lifts on its own. Sometimes this happens clinically, although there are few data to predict when it may happen or when it may not. On the other hand, if the panic disorder preceded the depression or if the depression is not particularly severe, then it would seem clinically logical to attend to the panic or agoraphobia first.

Classification and Behavioral Assessment

With these considerations in mind, it is possible to begin the process of assessing panic disorder. Initial classification, as determined during the interview, should always be followed by an elaboration of the character-istic and idiosyncratic responses with which the patient presents. This process is often called "behavioral analysis" or "behavioral assessment," although it is routine in most clinical situations. While classification will give the clinician some very good clues as to which problematic behaviors to assess, the behavioral analysis is the actual process of assessing each patient individually to determine the manner in which the disorder pre-sents itself. For example, two people who are panicking may present with very different pictures, depending on their age, social support system, sex, and socioeconomic status, as well as on the presence or absence of other associated problems. Number and types of panic attacks and their antecedents, as well as particular patterns of avoidance behavior or other coping responses, also require additional individual assessment. To as-sume that every patient stereotypically fits the criteria as described in the broad and general classification scheme, and that no further information is necessary before beginning treatment, would be naive. Detailed steps involved in this process are outlined elsewhere (Barlow, 1981; Nelson & Barlow, 1981). Thus, an initial classification of panic disorder will point the clinician in the proper directions for additional assessment.

For present purposes, "behavioral assessment" simply means that each patient's behavior is carefully observed, measured, and analyzed. More importantly, relationships between these problematic behaviors and environmental or organismic variables that may be maintaining them are continually sought. This is really something that most clinicians do rou-tinely; it is just that behavioral assessment formalizes the activity and in-sures a continuing close interaction between the processes of assessment and treatment until the case is terminated.

Another crucial step in assessment is a comprehensive approach to measuring all presenting problems in what have been termed the three major response systems: behavioral or motoric; cognitive or subjective; and physiological or somatic (Barlow, 1981; Lang, 1968, 1977b). In panic disorder, the application is particularly clear. Within the behavioral re-sponse system, one must carefully assess avoidance or other behavioral attempts at coping with panic. Subjective or cognitive aspects requiring assessment include reports of subjective disturbance or intensity of the various symptoms and feared consequences of panic. Physiological or so-matic assessment most often involves monitoring autonomic nervous sys-tem reactivity accompanying anxiety and panic, such as increased heart rate, respiration, and other physiological signs of arousal that most likely underlie action tendencies associated with these emotions or affective states.

A goal of assessment, then, is to examine all three of these components of panic disorder as they relate to one another and as they relate to particular features of each individual's environment, resulting in an individualized idiosyncratic pattern for each patient. For example, an elderly woman living in a third-floor walk-up in an urban area will obviously have different problems with different goals for treatment than will a male with a large family living in a rural area who must drive 30 miles round-trip to work each day. With these considerations in mind, it is possible to outline the actual steps of assessment, beginning with the specifics of the clinical interview.

The Clinical Interview

I have already mentioned the existence of the ADIS. Once again, administration of this full schedule is not called for in every clinical setting, particularly in those settings where clinicians are seeing patients with a variety of disorders. Nevertheless, some of the specific questions from this structured interview that pertain to panic disorder are recommended. Naturally, some special considerations apply when interviewing clients with potential panic disorder with or without agoraphobia, as opposed to other disorders. Panic disorder patients are often terrified of the first interview. Patients who have difficulty leaving their houses in order to come to a clinic or office setting will anticipate this visit for hours, days, or even weeks in advance. We have had patients turn around and return home after coming within sight of the clinic door. Most often these people are accompanied by a spouse or friend, and this alone will require some special logistical considerations. Occasionally we make a home visit for the first interview, but we avoid this if at all possible, since we are already at a considerable advantage if a patient learns that he or she can make it to the clinic.

Therapy often begins during the first 10 minutes of this initial interview, when some patients will report experiencing a "full-blown" panic. Naturally, the experienced clinician will interrupt the proceedings only to say that he or she is well aware of how the patient is feeling before continuing with specific questions, and will make every attempt to get the client to focus on the material at hand. While it may appear that the clinician is simply proceeding with the interview, the secondary purpose of diverting the patient's attention from symptoms of panic to questions of the moment will have its therapeutic effect.

In terms of the structure of the initial interview, we recommend the "graduated-funnel" approach (Nelson & Barlow, 1981) for obtaining information. This approach initially involves asking relatively global questions about many areas of the individual's life, including such topics as presenting complaints, existence of other problems, history and functioning in major areas such as family and marital relationships, and so on. Following the initial board inquiry, the interviewer gradually focuses on and asks more detailed questions about issues and problems that have been identified as requiring further information. As any clinician knows, it is not at all uncommon to discover that the client's initial complaints are not his or her primary concerns, but that more serious problems exist in other areas of functioning. In the special case of panic disorder, clients will occasionally present with extensive avoidance when, in fact, a severe obsessional process, a psychotic process, or perhaps even unrelated substance abuse is more prominent.

To assess for panic disorder, we use the sequence of questions from the June 1987 version of the ADIS-R (Di Nardo *et al.*, 1985) shown in Figure 10.3. The first series of questions assesses for the existence of panic, with the aim of establishing or disconfirming a diagnosis of panic disorder; these are followed by questions on the degree and extent of avoidance behavior or other coping responses.

Variability across time in the pattern of panic and avoidance behavior is also examined directly in the interview. Almost all panic patients report that they experience both good days, on which they are more active with less avoidance, and bad days, when they may end up totally housebound. Similarly, patients may report panicking more frequently on certain days. Many female patients report that they are at their worst im-

FIGURE 10.3. ADIS-R questions for DSM-III-R panic disorder. From Di Nardo, P. A., Barlow, D. H., Cerny, J. A., Vermilyea, B. B., Vermilyea, J. A., Himadi, H. G., & Waddell, M. T. (1985). *Anxiety Disorders Interview Schedule—Revised (ADIS-R)*. Albany: Phobia and Anxiety Disorders Clinic, State University of New York at Albany. Copyright 1985 by the State University of New York at Albany. Reprinted by permission.

PANIC DISORDER

Establishing Diagnosis

1. a. (Have you had times when you have felt a sudden rush of intense fear or anxiety or feeling of impending doom?)

                                                          YES ___   NO ___

****

   If YES, or uncertain, continue inquiry. Otherwise, skip to generalized anxiety disorder [see Figure 15.4].

****

2. a. (In what situation(s) have you had these feelings?)

---

   b. (Have you had these feelings come "from out of the blue," or while you are at home alone, or in situations where you did not expect them to occur?)

                                                          YES ___   NO ___

   If patient indicates that panic symptoms occur only in a specific situation (public speaking, heights, driving, etc.), further inquiry is necessary to determine if symptoms occur immediately upon exposure to the situation.

c. (When you are faced with [phobic situation], does the anxiety come on as soon as you enter it, or is it sometimes delayed, or unexpected?)

Delayed: YES ___   NO ___

****

If YES to 2b or 2c, or if there is any uncertainty about the existence of panic symptoms, continue inquiry. Otherwise, skip to generalized anxiety disorder [see Figure 15.4].

****

3. (How long does it usually take for the rush of anxiety to peak?)

___ minutes

4. (How long does the anxiety usually last at its peak level?)

___ minutes

Symptom Ratings

In this section rate symptoms *only* for anxiety attacks that occur *unpredictably,* in a variety of situations. Anxiety symptoms that are limited to a single stimulus (enclosed places or heights, social situations, obsessional content, etc.) should be rated in the appropriate section.

In some mixed cases, ratings might be completed in both this section and a later section.

A. Rate the severity of each symptom which is *typical* of the most recent attacks, and during the period of most severe attacks. If a symptom is experienced during only some attacks (i.e., it does *not* typically occur during an attack), enclose the rating in parentheses.

DSM-III-R requires at least one attack in which four symptoms were present. If typical attacks do not include four symptoms, determine if *any* attack has included four symptoms.

B. If the most recent attacks are also the worst attacks, indicate this and enter severity ratings under the "most recent" column only.

C. Use the following inquiry when rating symptoms:

1. (During the most recent period of attacks, did you experience _____? How severe was it?) If there is any doubt about whether the symptom is typical, ask: (Do you experience this nearly every time you have an attack?)
2. (When the attacks were the most severe, did you experience _____?)
3. (When were the attacks the most severe?) From _____ to _____
   a. (How frequent were the attacks during this period?) _____
   b. (What made the attacks the most severe you have had?)

4. (When was your most recent attack?) _____
5. Rate the severity of typical symptoms for each period on the following scale:
Note: Symptoms which are occasionally experienced, but are not typical, should be rated parenthetically.

```
0 - - - - - 1 - - - - - 2 - - - - - 3 - - - - - 4
None         Mild       Moderate    Severe      Very Severe
```

(Did/do you *usually* experience _____ during the attacks?)

	Most recent	Most severe	Limited symptom attack
1. Shortness of breath (dyspnea) or smothering sensations	___	___	___
2. Choking	___	___	___
3. Palpitations or accelerated heart rate (tachycardia)	___	___	___
4. Chest pain or discomfort	___	___	___

(*continued*)

377

FIGURE 10.3. (*Continued*)

5. Sweating	—	—	—
6. Dizziness, unsteady feelings, or faintness	—	—	—
7. Nausea or abdominal distress	—	—	—
8. Depersonalization or derealization	—	—	—
9. Numbness or tingling sensations, paresthesias	—	—	—
10. Flushes (hot flashes) or chills	—	—	—
11. Trembling or shaking	—	—	—
12. Fear of dying	—	—	—
13. Fear of going crazy or doing something uncontrolled	—	—	—

6. If patient reports four or more symptoms per *typical* attack, ask:

(Do you have periods [attacks, spells] when you have only one or two of these symptoms?)

If YES, go back and rate severity of symptoms under "Limited Symptom Attack" column.

Note: Diagnosis of panic disorder requires presence of four symptoms during at least one attack. If typical attacks do not include four symptoms, determine if *any* attack has included four symptoms.

7. a. (During the time that the attacks were most frequent, how often did they occur?)

           ___ per week for ___ weeks

   b. (When was this period?)

           From _____ to _____

If patient reports full panic attacks (four or more symptoms) and limited attacks, obtain frequencies for both types in c and d below.

   c. (During the past month, how many panics have you had?)

           ___ per week for ___ weeks

   d. (How many attacks have you had in the last 6 months?)

           ___ per month for ___ months

   e. (Since your first attack, has there been a period of time when you were afraid that you might have more attacks?)

           YES ___ NO ___

   (When was this?)   From _____ to _____

   f. (In the last month, how much have you been worrying, or how fearful have you been about having another attack?)

0 -- 1 -- 2 -- 3 -- 4 -- 5 -- 6 -- 7 -- 8				
No	Rarely	Occasionally	Frequently	Constantly
worry/	worried/	worried/	worried/	worried/
no fear	mild fear	moderate fear	severe fear	extreme fear

8. (Have there been times when you awoke from sleep in a panic?)

           YES ___ NO ___

If YES, (When did this occur?)

           From _____ to _____

(How often?)

           ___ per night

           ___ nights per week

9. a. (Do you have any specific thoughts before an attack?)

   b. (Do you have any specific thoughts during an attack?)

10. History:
    (Tell me about your first panic):
    a. (When did it happen?)   Month _____ Year _____
    b. (Where were you?) _____
    c. (Whom were you with?) _____
    d. (How did it start?) _____
    e. (What did you do?) _____
    f. (Were you under any type of stress?)   YES ___ NO ___
       (What was happening in your life at the time?)
       Specify _____
       _____
       (Were you taking any type of drug?) Include alcohol, caffeine.
                                              YES ___ NO ___
       Type _____ dose/amount _____
       (Did you have any physical condition such as inner ear problems, hyperthyroidism,
       mitral valve prolapse, pregnancy, hypoglycemia, or temporomandibular joint dysfunc-
       tion?)
                                              YES ___ NO ___
       Specify _____
    g. (Do you remember having similar feelings [maybe milder] any time before this?)
                                              YES ___ NO ___
       If YES, (When?)   Month ___ Year ___
       (What was the feeling?) _____

11. (Have you had periods when the panics became less intense or less frequent?)
    If YES, continue. If NO, go to Question 12.

(When): From–to month and year	(What was going on in your life? How did you get over it?) That is, did stressor let up or did person develop coping strategy?	(How did they come back?) Changes in life circumstances? Stressor-related?

12. (How do you handle the panics now?)
    _____
    _____
    _____
    _____
    _____

13. Distress/interference:
    (How much have the panics interfered with your life, job, traveling, activities, etc.?)
    _____
    _____
    _____

    Rate interference on 0–4 scale ___
    0 – – – – – – 1 – – – – – – 2 – – – – – – 3 – – – – – – 4
    None   Mild   Moderate   Severe   Very severe/
                                                            grossly disabling

mediately before or during menstruation, which seems to provide yet another pattern of heightened physiological sensations capable of spiraling into panic.

One problem that is quite variable across panic disorder is depersonalization or derealization. In our experience, only a minority of panickers report this problem (see Table 3.2), but when they do, it is usually reported as the prominent feature of panic and often requires some special therapeutic attention.

Finally, every clinician will want to examine patterns of cognitions associated with panic and avoidance behavior. Initial questions on this topic are specified on the ADIS-R. Several issues frequently arise in this context. Despite the increasing publicity given to panic and agoraphobia in popular magazines and newspapers, many patients have avoided seeking out health professionals because they believe that they are the only persons in the world with such symptoms and that diagnosis will mean quick institutionalization in the nearest state hospital! Once patients are relieved of this concern, thoughts of impending catastrophic consequences associated with anxiety and panic most often fall into one or two categories. First, some agoraphobics will report that if they fall prey to their panic while away from their safe place or person, they will eventually lose control and "go crazy" or "go insane." Second, others report that the ultimate catastrophic consequence is a severe physical problem, usually a "heart attack" followed by death. As noted in Chapter 3, these catastrophic consequences have been separated for more accurate specification on the DSM-III-R symptoms list.

The most important part of the assessment, as mentioned above, is a determination of the functional relationship between avoidance behavior, cognitive patterns, and panic on the one hand and associated internal or external cues on the other hand. This is the well-known "functional analysis," in which maladaptive behaviors and feelings are related to specific events, resulting in an individual and idiosyncratic pattern of responses. For example, in one patient, health concerns such as apprehension over heart attacks and increases in avoidance behavior may be tightly tied to unexpected panic attacks. In another patient, health concerns and avoidance behavior may be more independent of unexpected panic, resulting in a more functionally autonomous pattern of responses. It is this determination, over and above the initial classification, that is necessary if the clinician is to tailor a standardized set of therapy principles to the individual patient.

The Assessment of Safety Signals

Once the interviewer establishes the strong possibility of panic disorder and agoraphobia, several other areas should be covered during the initial interview. While exploring specific patterns and severity of avoidance be-havior, the clinician should be particularly concerned about the degree of reliance on safety signals, such as a safe place, person, or thing (Rach-man, 1984). The interviewer should be sure to clarify the identity of the person(s), place(s), or object(s) the patient considers safe. Most often a safe person is a spouse, but occasionally it is another family member or a friend. A "safe" person, of course, is one in whose company the agora-phobic feels comfortable in going places, to a degree not achievable either alone or with other people. Usually, a person is considered "safe" be-cause he or she knows about the panics. Even if the safe person does not approve of the panics (as is the case with some spouses), the patient feels that this person would take him or her to the hospital or be able to help in some way if the patient were incapacitated by panic. Often animals or inanimate objects also serve as safety signals. The most common talisman by far is the unused or even empty bottle of pills. A summary of safety signals (excluding safe people) from 125 consecutive patients with panic disorder with agoraphobia seen in our clinic is presented in Table 10.2. One can see that seldom used or even empty pill bottles were the most widely used items, but that a variety of other items had substantial safety value.

Once the range of safety signals is determined by interview, it is as-

TABLE 10.2. Safety Cues (Excluding Safe People) of 125 Consecutive Patients with Panic Disorder with Agoraphobia

Cue	Frequency
Anxiety medication	60
Food/drink	17
Bags, bracelets, objects	8
Smelling salts/antacid	5
Paper bag	5
Religious symbols	5
Flashlight/money/CB radio	4
Reading material	3
Cigarettes	3
Alcohol	3
Relaxation tapes/coping statements/ therapist's phone number	2
Pets	0
No safety cues (excluding a safe person)	32
1 safety cue	58
2 safety cues	29
3 safety cues	6

sumed that these will remain relatively constant, since they often represent habits of long standing. Therefore, they are not assessed on a repeated basis, although attention to safety signals becomes an integral part of the treatment program as patients are gradually weaned from these ritualistic props. Naturally, particular attention is paid to a safe person, such as a spouse, another family member, or a close friend. But one must also be careful to continue to monitor the use of inanimate objects, such as empty bottles of pills, to determine that no new safety signals are picked up along the way. One relatively common problem, as described below, is that sheets of paper containing coping statements or other new cognitive strategies become substitutes for empty bottles of pills and pick up ritualistic overtones in their own right. By the end of treatment, clinicians must insure that these have become fully incorporated into the patients' day-to-day functioning, so that forgetting a sheet of paper with cognitive strategies written on it not in and of itself provoke a panic attack.

Unfortunately, assessing panic, as well as the complications of avoidance behavior and the idiosyncratic safety signals that a patient may employ, is not a straightforward task. From the point of view of convenience, the ideal procedure would involve asking patients periodically how much they are panicking and how much they are avoiding. A more structured way of accomplishing this is to administer psychometrically sound questionnaires periodically that do the asking, but in a manner that is consistent from time to time and asks the questions in just the right way. Structured questionnaires also have the advantage of allowing the clinician to compare a patient's response to some well-established norm for patients with similar problems.

Unfortunately, both periodic informal questions and structured questionnaires require that the desired information be filtered through the patient's view of how things seem to be going in that moment of time. For example, asking a patient how many times he or she has panicked in the past week requires, first, that the patient remember each and every panic. This is a task that research on assessment has demonstrated time and again to be very, very difficult, even for the best-intentioned patient (Barlow, Hayes, & Nelson, 1984). In addition, the patient must remain immune to the ever-present demands inherent in this type of situation, the most common of which is a desire to please the therapist by reporting things as somewhat better than they actually are.

This situation is illustrated by the case of an agoraphobic treated several years ago in our clinic (Last, Barlow, & O'Brien, 1984a). This patient was a male in his 40s who presented with a particularly severe case of agoraphobia associated with panic disorder. He was panicking at a high frequency, and the avoidance behavior was beginning to keep him from his job in a local factory. Progress during treatment was assessed, as always, by self-report measures, as well as by a behavioral measure of time spent away from home alone (which was confirmed by the patient's wife). The results of this assessment are presented in Figure 10.4. Data from Figure 10.4 show substantial improvement on self-report measures during treatment; this progress was maintained during a 1-year follow-up. However, data from Figure 10.5, presenting the results of direct behavioral observations, indicate that most of the initial gains during treatment were largely lost at follow-up.

Despite these caveats, a number of questionnaires now exist with demonstrated reliability and validity that can be very useful for assessing panic and agoraphobia.

Questionnaires

Fear Questionnaire

The Fear Questionnaire (Marks & Mathews, 1979) appears to possess adequate psychometric properties and yields four main scores: Main Pho-

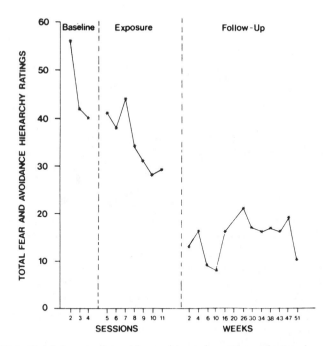

FIGURE 10.4. Total fear and avoidance hierarchy ratings during baseline, treatment, and follow-up phases. From Last, C. G., Barlow, D. H., & O'Brien, G. T. (1984). Cognitive changes during in vivo exposure in an agoraphobic. *Behavior Modification, 8,* 93–113. Copyright 1984 by Sage Publications, Inc. Reprinted by permission.

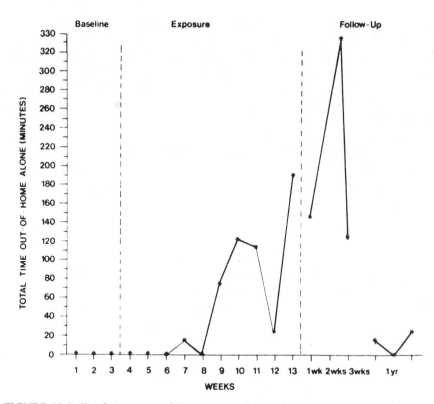

FIGURE 10.5. Total time out of home alone during baseline, treatment, and follow-up phases. From Last, C. G., Barlow, D. H., & O'Brien G. T. (1984). Cognitive changes during in vivo exposure in an agoraphobic. *Behavior Modification, 8,* 93–113. Copyright 1984 by Sage Publications, Inc. Reprinted by permission.

bia rating, Total Phobia rating, Anxiety–Depression rating, and a global measure of phobic symptoms. In addition, three particularly useful subscores (Agoraphobia, Blood–Injury Phobia, and Social Phobia) are derived (Marks, 1981a). This measure requires only a brief administration time, and the Agoraphobia subscale, because of its wide acceptance, allows comparison of the severity of agoraphobia to published standards. For example, Mavissakalian (1986a) provided data on the validity of the scale and suggested that a cutoff point of 30 on the Agoraphobia subscale would identify a severe agoraphobic. Additional investigation (Mavissakalian, 1986b) suggests that a posttreatment score below 10 identifies an excellent clinical response to therapy, achieved by those patients also classified as "high end-state functioners" (see below). Mizes and Crawford (1986) have provided normative information from the general population on this questionnaire.

Mobility Inventory for Agoraphobia

The Mobility Inventory for Agoraphobia (Chambless, Caputo, Jasin, Gracely, & Williams, 1985) is a 27-item questionnaire designed primarily to assess agoraphobic avoidance behavior. Instructions require ratings of the severity of avoidance both when alone and when accompanied, which is a particularly useful feature, since these ratings are often very different. In addition, ratings of panic frequency during the last week are obtained. Adequate reliability and validity data are reported for this inventory, which also discriminates agoraphobics from patients with other anxiety disorders (Craske et al., 1986).

Agoraphobia Cognitions Questionnaire; Body Sensations Questionnaire

The Agoraphobia Cognitions Questionnaire and the Body Sensations Questionnaire (Chambless, Caputo, Bright, & Gallagher, 1984) are two companion questionnaires designed to assess the cognitive and physiological aspects of anxiety concerning panic; this makes them unique and particularly useful for assessing progress during the treatment of panic disorder with either limited or extensive avoidance. Both questionnaires possess sound psychometric properties, although Craske et al. (1986) report an inability of the Agoraphobia Cognitions Questionnaire to discriminate panic disorder from other anxiety disorders.

Despite the utility of these two and other questionnaires, a word of caution must be offered regarding the assessment of cognitions associated with panic or anxiety. A number of reports have implicated catastrophic or negative thoughts in the maintenance of pathological anxiety (Beck et al., 1974; Last & Blanchard, 1982; May, 1977a, 1977b; Wade, Malloy, & Proctor, 1977). Furthermore, when these negative or catastrophic cognitions are assessed on a pre–post basis, it seems that a number of treatments for panic disorder and agoraphobia result in the amelioration of these thoughts. Of course, as alluded to earlier, cognitive procedures in and of themselves do not seem particularly successful in the treatment of clinical phobias (Biran, Augusto, & Wilson, 1981; Biran & Wilson, 1981; Emmelkamp, 1982; Emmelkamp, Brilman, Kuiper, & Mersch, 1986; Williams & Rappoport, 1983). But the modification of panic-related cognitions may yet prove to be an important index of progress, whatever the treatment.

In any case, the assessment of catastrophic thoughts proves to be a very slippery task, since these cognitions are extremely variable from time to time and do not seem to covary reliably with treatment effectiveness. In an attempt to look very closely at the pattern of phobic cognitions across time, we (Last, Barlow, & O'Brien, 1984b) repeatedly assessed cognitions in agoraphobics under two conditions. During an *in vivo* cognitive assessment, cognitions were directly recorded on a microcassette recorder as subjects freely verbalized any thoughts during exposure sessions at a local shopping mall. In addition, immediately following each *in vivo* assessment occasion throughout treatment, subjects recorded thoughts they recalled having during the exposure period in written form, using a thought-listing procedure (Cacioppo & Petty, 1981). All cognitions were classified by several raters, using a previously developed and reliable categorization system, into negative, positive, and neutral thoughts.

The results of this investigation revealed decreases in negative and catastrophic thoughts from the beginning to the end of therapy, whether cognitive therapeutic procedures were included with the exposure-based treatment or not. However, the changes in catastrophic thinking were not directly related to therapeutic success. Many of the changes occurred during baseline, when no treatment was in effect. At other times during treatment, cognitions would show marked fluctuations that seemed to bear no relation to progress. It is entirely possible that any changes occurring when these thoughts are sampled infrequently, such as before and after treatment, may simply be artifacts of the timing of the assessment. For this reason, it seems that the major emphasis of assessment is best placed on panic and avoidance behavior, rather than on cognitions per se.

Anxiety Sensitivity Index

The Anxiety Sensitivity Index, developed by Reiss *et al.* (1986), measures sensitivity to and discomfort with a number of physical sensations commonly associated with anxiety. It appears to have good reliability and validity (Maller & Reiss, 1987). For example, patients with panic disorder with agoraphobia have been found to score high on the scale and to decrease their scores significantly following successful treatment. This questionnaire has an emphasis slightly different from that of the Body Sensations Questionnaire, since it specifically targets discomfort with bodily sensations associated with anxiety, as well as closely related feelings (e.g., distress over being nervous).

Patient and Therapist Ratings

In addition to formal, psychometrically sound questionnaires, a number of strategies have emerged for ongoing patient and therapist ratings of varied aspects of panic disorder.

Fear and Avoidance Hierarchy

Following directly from the clinical interview, an idiosyncratic fear and avoidance hierarchy of 10 situations is developed in our clinic with each patient. My colleagues and I strongly recommend this procedure, since it forms one of the most convenient ways of assessing progress from the point of view of the patient. This hierarchy is usually constructed at the second session after the initial interview in our clinic. This hierarchy, in fact, also plays a prominent role in treatment, since items from it will be assigned for "homework" during treatment. The patient is not specifically informed of this beforehand, however, since the explanation will be accompanied by a complete rationale for treatment. Also, this information without the treatment rationale may cause the patient to withhold reporting difficult items in his or her environment, for fear of being "forced" to deal with the items before he or she is ready.

In developing the hierarchy, the clinician should utilize information from the structured interview as well as from the patient's report during the initial appointment. The clinician may begin by saying, "I know from your last interview that you're having difficulty getting to a number of places [or that you're frequently panicking in certain situations]. Could you tell me some of the things that you would like to do that are currently difficult or impossible for you [or situations that seem to frequently evoke panic]?" Generally, the patient will then list places or tasks that he or she is unable to go to or complete but that the patient feels should be part of his or her daily life, if avoidance behavior is present; or the patient will list situations that provoke panic, if avoidance behavior is not present.

The clinician then uses these reports, as well as items noted during the interview, to develop 10 items or situations that have particular relevance for the patient. For example, if a patient with avoidance wants to be able to go to the local mall, and also feels that he or she should be able to do the grocery shopping or go to a small store a few blocks from home, all of these items are included. Ultimately all of these items are rated on a scale of 0–8, where 0 represents no anxiety, panic, or avoidance and 8 represents the probability of extreme anxiety and panic and/or avoidance. For some patients, one of the items lower on the hierarchy may be driving to a small store only two blocks from home and then back again. For others, in order to derive items that will be rated a 2 or 3 on the hierarchy, simply walking outside the door and down to the end of the front walk may be sufficient. Items higher in the hierarchy may include traveling longer distances and/or visiting places that are typically crowded, such as malls or restaurants during the lunch hour. Other typically difficult items are waiting in lines at banks or at checkout counters in grocery stores.

It is very important to have a wide variety of items, in terms of avoidance and/or anxiety ratings, on the hierarchy. For patients with very severe avoidance, it may be necessary to break down individual trips in order to obtain a variety of anxiety ratings. For example, if simply walking down the front walk would be rated a 3, then walking or driving halfway to a nearby small store may be a 5, going into the store may be a 6 or a 7, and so on. Thus, each step involved in "getting there" must be included. When the items are broken down more thoroughly, patients will not have a sense of failure from attempting items that are too difficult for them too early in treatment. On the other hand, it is also important to include the most difficult items on the severe end of the hierarchy which often comprise some of the most important goals for the patient. If avoidance is not present, situations involving some tension or stress are often panicogenic. All hierarchies also include liberal reference to interceptive cues, such as dyspnea and palpitations.

If one is planning on assessing avoidance behavior directly using items on this hierarchy, one must be careful to include only items that can, in fact, be accomplished during routine practice sessions. Therefore, one should try not to include items such as shopping during the Christmas rush, going on vacation, or going to the movies, which depend on time of year or the schedule of the movie theater. Other items that are dependent on external circumstances may include attending a neighbor's party or going to dinner at a friend's house. Naturally, these items will be addressed during treatment as they arise, but should not be part of this initial hierarchy.

Patients often have difficulty compiling this hierarchy for a number of reasons, and therefore it must be constructed with the help of the therapist. However, after a bit of initial practice, most therapists are able to accomplish this goal in as little as 20 minutes. It is quite useful to provide patients with a copy of this hierarchy approximately weekly, so that they can rate each item for avoidance and/or anxiety, thereby providing a repeated measure of progress.

Therapist Ratings

When a therapist resorts to "asking" a patient how he or she is doing, a well-known and often used method of quantifying the patient's answers consists of the 9-point rating scales devised by Watson and Marks (1971) for assessing the severity of avoidance behavior and the severity of anxiety. These ratings can also be made by the patient. While these ratings are reliable among raters, particularly in a phobia clinic where therapists have extensive experience in doing this sort of thing, the information is ultimately subject to the type of distortions mentioned above.

Self-Monitoring Measures

Years of research in behavioral assessment (e.g., Barlow, 1981) have demonstrated that continuous monitoring of behavioral and emotional events is far preferable in terms of accuracy and reliability to periodic recall of these events. These procedures have now been fully incorporated into the assessment and treatment of panic and agoraphobia. Before typical self-monitoring procedures for panic and avoidance behavior are described, it is only fair to warn the clinician that there are a number of drawbacks to self-monitoring. Particularly problematic is the issue of compliance with recording, since this activity does require a certain amount of effort on the part of the patient. Procedures have been developed to enhance recording compliance in order to increase the reliability of the obtained data (cf. Barlow, Hayes, & Nelson, 1984).

There are several ways in which we deal with problems of compliance at our clinic. First, we emphasize the importance of the daily record when we first start seeing a patient. Second, we have at least 1 and sometimes 2 weeks of training and practice with the form during assessment before treatment begins. Third, we examine systematically the records as they are handed in, particularly in the first few weeks, and provide detailed corrective feedback on the accuracy and completeness of each record at the time of the session, thus highlighting in a very positive way compliance with the record-keeping activity.

Despite the effort involved in self-monitoring, on the part of both the patient and the therapist, the importance of this type of monitoring has emerged clinically time and time again. Accurate record keeping by the patient at or near the time of the event often provides important information that may seem routine to the patient and/or the spouse or other family member, and therefore is not reported at weekly sessions. Particular strategies and emphases within therapy will often turn on this information.

In treating panic disorder, we employ two self-monitoring forms for assessing panic (see Figure 10.6) and generalized anxiety and depression

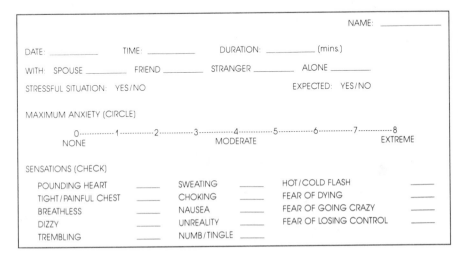

FIGURE 10.6. Panic Attack Record. From the Phobia and Anxiety Disorders Clinic, State University of New York at Albany.

(see Figure 10.7) on a day-to-day basis. If the complication of avoidance behavior with accompanying safety signals is present, we also employ a Daily Activity Form (see Figure 10.8). These forms have been developed after years of trial and error in our clinic to provide us with the type of information that we find most useful, as well as to make it as easy and

FIGURE 10.7. Weekly Record of Anxiety and Depression. From the Phobia and Anxiety Disorders Clinic, State University of New York at Albany.

Name: _____   Week ending: _____

Each evening before you go to bed please rate your *average* level of anxiety (taking all things into consideration) throughout the day, the *maximum* level of anxiety that you experienced that day, your *average* level of depression throughout the day, and your average feeling of pleasantness throughout the day. Use the scale below. Next, please list the dosages and amounts of any medication you took. Finally, please rate, using the scale below, how worried or frightened you were, on average, about the possibility of having a panic attack throughout the day.

Level of Anxiety/Depression/Pleasant Feeling

| 0 | – – | 1 | – – | 2 | – – | 3 | – – | 4 | – – | 5 | – – | 6 | – – | 7 | – – | 8 |
| None | | | | Slight | | | | Moderate | | | | | A lot | | | As much as you can imagine |

Date	Average anxiety	Maximum anxiety	Average depression	Average pleasantness	Medication type, dose, number (mg)	Fear of panic attack

FIGURE 10.8. Daily Activity Form. From the Phobia and Anxiety Disorders Clinic, State University of New York at Albany.

Name: _____   Weekly Record: (_____ to _____)

Date	Time left home	Time returned home	List each activity (including transportation) and place traveled to while away from home*	Total time spent	Time alone	Anxiety rating (0–8) Average ¦ Maximum

*Please put a check mark by any activity that was an assigned practice for this week.

convenient for the patient as possible. All of the information has proved useful at one time or another.

The Weekly Record of Anxiety and Depression (see Figure 10.7) allows one to assess daily background or generalized anxiety and depression. To obtain a general index of positive affect, the patient also records pleasant feelings. A very important piece of data also recorded on this form is the "fear" of having a panic attack that day. Finally, medication use is recorded. On the accompanying Panic Attack Record (see Figure 10.6), patients record information each time they have an attack. Specifically, they record the time of onset, duration and intensity, of each attack and the number of symptoms comprising it. Perceived antecedents or cues (termed "stressful situations") associated with these panic attacks are also recorded, as well as whether the attack was stressful or not.

Prior to the initiation of self-monitoring, illustrations that assist patients in remembering the distinction between panic and heightened generalized anxiety are provided. These illustrations, which were devised for the Upjohn Cross-National Collaborative Panic Study, have proven very useful in helping patients make this distinction if it is not already clear to them.

The Daily Activity Form (see Figure 10.8) allows recording of behavior relevant to agoraphobic avoidance. The most important data from this daily measure include total time away from home, total time away from home alone, total time spent practicing, and the number of practice sessions conducted alone and whether they were successfully completed. Anxiety ratings during these sessions are also recorded. Recent data (Michelson et al., 1986), described more fully in Chapter 11, confirm that amount of self-initiated exposure is an important predictor of successful treatment.

Since the self-monitoring of panic is so critical to clinical and research strategies, several issues reflecting recent developments in research clinics around the world are worth noting. First, as mentioned above, it is clear that it is unsatisfactory to ask for reports of panic retrospectively—that is, "How many panic attacks have you had for the last 3 days [or the last week, or the last month]?" This results in marked distortion and exaggeration (Turner et al., 1988). A clinician must use prospective self-monitoring of some type.

Second, it has become apparent that simple recording of frequency of panic results in an extremely variable record that is often inadequate for data analysis and probably misleading clinically (e.g., Chambless et al., 1986). What happens, for example, is that after becoming sensitive to what is a panic and what is not, patients often correctly record less intensive "bursts" of anxiety as panic attacks. This results in little or no change in frequency over time. Panic attacks may also decrease considerably in duration. These less intense, shorter "panics" comprise the "rumblings" that usually remain to some extent in patients even after successful drug or behavioral treatment. At this point patients have difficulty deciding whether this is a true "panic" or not, resulting in wide variability from day to day in the same patient or between patients in frequency of panic. Alternatively, a patient might decide that only the most severe burst (8 on a scale of 0–8) qualifies as panic, and may not record somewhat less intense instances of panic, thereby providing a misleading picture. Occasionally, these definitions may change from week to week in the mind of the same patient. Therefore, several centers, including ours, record self-monitored panic as the product of frequency × intensity × duration. This results in what seems to be a more valid and satisfactory measure that eliminates the extreme variability and reflects clinical reality.

Third, as noted in Chapter 3, some confusion has developed among the terms "spontaneous," "unpredictable," "unexpected," and "situational" as modifiers of panic. "Spontaneous," of course, is not a scientifically accurate description, since nothing is truly "spontaneous." Also, panics may be "predicted" on the basis of either situational or cognitive factors. "Unpredictable," therefore, lacks precision. As illustrated in Chapter 3 (see Table 3.9), we believe the terms "expected" and "cued" and their antonyms are more descriptive. A panic attack, whether it occurs within the context of panic disorder or a simple phobia, may be expected or unexpected (Rachman & Levitt, 1985). In addition, a panic may tend to occur after the same cue or not. In simple phobia, all panics are cued by definition. In panic disorder, multiple cues can be identified, including interoceptive cues as well as situational cues (e.g., crowds, shopping malls); the latter may be more properly considered as discriminative stimuli or "learned settings" where safety signals are not present (Rachman, 1984). In the early stages, panic may not be associated with obvious cues (which is the origin of the term "spontaneous"). Thus, the "expected–unexpected" and "cued–uncued" nature of panic attacks may vary independently, and both factors should be noted and recorded.

Behavioral Measures

For the reasons discussed above,, it is preferable to assess the avoidance behavior component of agoraphobia directly—that is, by observing this behavior where it makes a difference, in the local environment of the patient. Figure 10.5 above highlights the importance of behavioral measures, since avoidance behavior had deteriorated despite reports by the patient to the contrary. On the other hand, direct behavioral assessment can be expensive and time-consuming, and can be subject to strong demand characteristics (Mavissakalian & Hamann, 1986a). Certain strategies discussed below can yield the information that the therapist needs without direct involvement by the therapist. The two major types of behavioral tests used are standardized behavioral avoidance tests (SBATs) and individual behavioral avoidance tests (IBATs).

Prior to a discussion of the specifics of these behavioral tests, some general issues deserve attention. Williams (1985) has pointed out that the behavioral tests must incorporate a wide range of differentially difficult items if they are to handle demand effects adequately and to be sensitive to treatment-produced change. Another critical issue involves the imposition of an anxiety-based criterion for the termination of the behavioral test. Some investigators include instructions to patients to conclude their performance upon experiencing excessive anxiety. These instructions, unfortunately, introduce a confound between the behavioral and subjective components of anxiety: That is, the patients are subjectively judging what is "excessive." Rather, patients should be instructed to do as much as they can. Williams (1985) also notes the importance of minimizing active treatment elements from the behavioral test procedure; these include modeling, distraction, and protracted exposure to the feared situation.

Another important consideration involves the assessor's function as a safety signal for the patient. As noted above, agoraphobics are able to perform certain behaviors when accompanied by someone whom they perceive as "safe" (cf. Barlow & Waddell, 1985; Gray, 1971; Rachman, 1984). Thus, if at all possible, the assessor should not accompany the patient on the test itself. The patient's behavior may be unobtrusively observed by clinic personnel or verified through some other means. For example, odometer readings have been obtained for driving items (Williams & Rappoport, 1983). An additional possibility would require the patient to note certain landmarks on a portable tape recorder during trips away from a safe place (J. A. Vermilyea et al., 1984). These strategies also allow the therapist to assess behavior relatively inexpensively.

Finally, it has often been observed that patients will "push" themselves under the implicit demands of an in vivo behavioral test to accomplish goals they would not even attempt ordinarily. While this is true, it may not be a disadvantage. Under these conditions, the assessor can be confident that the true behavioral capacity of the patient is being assessed. In addition, SUDs scores should reflect how hard the patient is pushing himself or herself. Finally, a measure of ongoing day-to-day behavior is available in the self-monitoring measure as well as in patient (and perhaps spouse) ratings of avoidance. Thus, the assessor should insure that the behavioral test samples the maximally difficult items for a given patient in order to provide a true indication of the patient's behavioral capacity. If a patient completes all items before treatment (a very unusual occurrence in our experience), but still meets the criteria for panic with severe agoraphobia on the basis of interviews, then the assessor has learned something useful about the behavioral capacity of this (presumably) somewhat less severely disordered patient.

Standardized Behavioral Avoidance Tests

SBATs have been been used in agoraphobia research for years (Agras *et al.*, 1968; Bandura, Adams, Hardy, & Howells, 1980; Barlow, O'Brien, & Last, 1984; Emmelkamp & Wessels, 1975; J. A. Vermilyea *et al.*, 1984; Williams & Rappoport, 1983). One useful standardized test for agoraphobics involves the "behavioral walk." The administration of this procedure is relatively straightforward and can readily be incorporated into clinical practice. This test involves a walking course divided into approximately equidistant units. For instance, the course described in the J. A. Vermilyea *et al.* (1984) report was 1.2 km in length and divided into 20 stations. Patients are instructed to walk along the course and return when they either complete the course or are unable to proceed further. The actual measure from this test is the number of stations completed. In addition, subjective anxiety ratings and heart rate can also be monitored. While this test allows for a standardized measurement situation, it involves only one behavior that may not be problematic for some agoraphobics. It is important, therefore, that this walking course incorporate a range of increasingly difficult contexts.

Investigators have used different SBATs in assessing the behavioral component of agoraphobia. Examples include driving a car along a progressively more difficult route (Williams & Rappoport, 1983) and behavioral assessment across multiple areas of functioning (Bandura *et al.*, 1980). An advantage of the behavioral walk over other types of standardized tests is its relative ease of administration.

Individualized Behavioral Avoidance Tests

The oft-noted heterogeneity of phobic difficulties for agoraphobics renders the SBATs somewhat artificial and limited in scope. The IBAT remedies this difficulty through assessment of personally relevant behaviors in naturalistic situations. The individualized assessments can be conducted from the patient's home (Barlow, O'Brien, & Last, 1984; Mathews *et al.*, 1981; Mathews, Teasdale, Munby, Johnston, & Shaw, 1977), or the clinician can arrange for assessment to occur in a number of situations close to the clinic (Mavissakalian & Michelson, 1983). Obviously, the home environment is more relevant, since that is where the problems exist; however, arranging a number of behavioral tasks around the clinic that are relevant to the individual patient is a good substitute.

At our clinic, we often visit the home. While there, we choose items for assessment from the 10-item hierarchy of phobic situations discussed above. Five items are selected from this hierarchy, representing a range of severity. The five items chosen are those that are feasible to carry out in a 1- to 2-hour session, which may be administered by the therapist or by an assistant trained to carry out this task. For example, walking or driving to a local store is feasible, but attending a weekly meeting at a local school is not.

The patient is instructed to attempt all five items in the order of their difficulty for him or her. Each item is scored on a 3-point scale with the interpretation of each score as follows: 0, patient refused the item (avoidance); 1, partial completion of the item (escape); and 2, successful completion of the item. The total score, therefore, has a range from 0 to 10 if five items are chosen. In addition, SUDs ratings on a scale of 0–8 may be obtained for each item. An example of how we recorded data from one IBAT is presented in Figure 10.9.

IBATs have a number of positive features. An IBAT allows assessment in a variety of personally relevant situations and should, if the pho-

FIGURE 10.9. IBAT home visit form for one patient. From the Phobia and Anxiety Disorders Clinic, State University of New York at Albany.

Individualized BAT—Home Visit

Name: _____   Date: _____

Address: _____   Administered by: _____

_____   Circle one: Pretest

Group: _____   Posttest

Follow-up ____ months

0	-- 1	-- 2	-- 3	-- 4	-- 5	-- 6	-- 7	-- 8
No anxiety	Slightly/ somewhat anxious		Definitely anxious			Markedly or very anxious		Severe anxiety— never panic

	Item completed				Rating
Item	Yes	No; avoided	No; escaped		Rating
1. Drive alone to Stuyvesant Plaza	×				5
2. Drive alone to Mohawk Mall	×				4
3. Drive alone to Clifton Country Mall	×				4
4. Drive to Clifton Park with a friend		×			
5. Take a bus to downtown Albany alone			×		

bia hierarchy is properly constructed, possess a high enough ceiling to deal with demand characteristics present in such tests (i.e., the tendency of patients to "push" themselves). Naturally, this makes the assessment a conservative measure. Other advantages of IBATs include their sensitivity to treatment changes and their generalizability to other situations.

Physiological Assessment

The assessment of physiological responding is of theoretical as well as practical interest, and until recently many have considered it an essential component in the assessment of clinical anxiety. Recent data collected in our clinic, however, have changed our thinking somewhat on the usefulness of physiological assessment as a measure of clinical change. Physiological assessment may have other equally important uses that are not necessarily connected with clinical change. Since this is an important area in which views are rapidly changing, I spend some time here describing the state of the art of physiological assessment of panic and anxiety.

There are obvious reasons why most anxiety researchers suggest assessing physiological responding (Agras & Jacob, 1981; Barlow & Wolfe, 1981; Jansson & Öst, 1982). The panic attack, with its surge of physiological activity, is the defining characteristic of panic disorder. Physiological, behavioral, and subjective responding in a fearful situation comprise the well-known three response systems of anxiety, which are correlated only loosely (Lang, 1968). In our view, as outlined in previous chapters, physiological responding may well represent the all-important action tendencies associated with any emotion or affective state. Therefore, all three should be assessed to obtain a complete picture of the anxiety.

The call for routine physiological recording has not been without its critics. A minority of those attending an NIMH-sponsored conference on anxiety disorders questioned the usefulness of physiological data and suggested that "the collection of such data should reflect the precise aspects of behavior that are expected to change or should be tied to an important theoretical question" (Barlow & Wolfe, 1981, p. 454). A related point was offered by Schwartz (1978), who noted that physiological measures obtained in complex (i.e., minimally controlled) clinical situations may produce only complexity and confusion.

Now there is evidence that these measures are not reliable when taken repeatedly as measures of change (Arena et al., 1983; Holden & Barlow, 1986; Sturgis, 1980; Sturgis & Arena, 1984). Thus, for example, Arena et al., (1983) found poor reliability estimates for the majority of their laboratory-based measures. Also, in a study described in detail in Chapter 5 and having more direct relevance for the treatment of panic with agoraphobia, we (Holden & Barlow, 1986) found low reliability estimates and, more importantly, a lack of discriminant validity for heart rate measured *in vivo* as a measure of treatment outcome. That is, heart rate declined over the course of repeated assessments as much for normals as for agoraphobics, for whom this measure is supposed to reflect decreases in anxiety.

Michelson and Mavissakalian (1985) reported some locally interesting effects but found few physiological changes over time in agoraphobics who otherwise improved. Although decreases in some measures of heart rate were found for some groups during treatment, particularly those who received flooding *in vivo* or instructions to practice systematically between sessions, baseline measures of heart rate also decreased at these points. This resulted in little or no change in the difference score between resting heart rate and heart rate in a feared situation as a result of treatment. This seems to replicate our results (Holden & Barlow, 1986) and to strengthen the conclusion that heart rate may not change systematically in agoraphobics during treatment. Rather, baseline or resting heart rate may decrease during treatment, possibly reflecting either generalized habituation to the testing situation or decreases in the preparatory action set associated with anxiety. However, normals, who presumably are not generally anxious, showed similar decreases in the Holden and Barlow experiment. This lends support to the hypothesis of nonspecific habituation.

This idea is buttressed further by the findings of Woods *et al.* (1987), who reported no physiological or endocrinological differences on a wide range of measures at any point in time between normals and agoraphobics, both of whom were confronting situations *in vivo* that were very frightening for the agoraphobics. That is, both groups evidenced similar increases in these measures. Naturally, these studies require replication prior to reaching any firm conclusions regarding the adequacy of these measures for clinical research.

At this point we cannot readily recommend the use of any particular physiological measure *as an index of treatment outcome,* although heart rate would still appear to be a readily obtainable measure, given the availability of inexpensive and portable heart rate monitors (Leelarthaepin *et al.,* 1980). Arena *et al.* (1983) suggest that researchers determine the reliability estimates of physiological measures for each subject population of interest and select only the most reliable for research purposes. Sturgis and Arena (1984) also stress the importance of experimental control and recommend against the exclusive use of psychophysiological measures as dependent variables in treatment outcome research.

Nevertheless, there seem to be other, equally important uses of physiological assessment, over and above the basic theoretical research on emotion described in preceding chapters. Two issues in particular arise in this context. One is the assessment of synchrony–desynchrony (or concordance–discordance), and the other involves utilizing pretreatment physiological measures to predict outcome.

As noted in Chapter 2, the relationship among various aspects of anxiety has aroused deep theoretical interest in regard to the basic nature of anxiety and emotion. It has also been suggested that the occurrence of desynchrony or discordance may be practically relevant in predicting outcome. Basically, Rachman and Hodgson (1974) and others (Barlow & Mavissakalian, 1981; Barlow, Mavissakalian, & Schofield, 1980) have suggested that a finding of desynchrony may predict relapse. In an extensive investigation of desynchrony in agoraphobics described briefly in Chapter 8, we (J. A. Vermilyea *et al.*, 1984) found that when desynchrony occurred, the most typical pattern involved improvement on subjective measures, but lack of improvement on physiological measures such as heart rate. These responses were assessed during an SBAT. If a panic patient reports that he or she is improved, as the thinking goes, but continues to demonstrate very high physiological responding during stressful situations, then he or she may be at greater risk for relapse.

There is certainly some common sense to this notion. If a panic patient enters a formally difficult situation and perceives marked changes in physiological responding, it would seem that this might reactivate the feedback cycle, which would spiral into a panic attack. Unfortunately for the theory, there is no firm evidence that this happens. According to our data (J. A. Vermilyea *et al.*, 1984), desynchronous subjects seemed to do as well as synchronous subjects by the end of treatment on the whole. Extended follow-up assessment of these subjects has not yet revealed any differential pattern of outcome. That is, even at follow-ups of a year or more, desynchronous subjects seem to be doing as well as synchronous subjects (Craske, Sanderson, & Barlow, 1987a). Follow-up is continuing.

Michelson and Mavissakalian (1985) examined the relationship of discordance rather than desynchrony to treatment outcome. That is, rather than assessing the relative change in heart rate and SUDs as treatment progressed, they examined the relationship of heart rate, SUDs, and behavioral avoidance *at one time only:* the 1-month follow-up. Subjects who were much improved on all three measures were termed "synchronous" (a term the authors have now changed, more accurately, to "concordant"; L. Michelson, personal communication, 1986), while subjects who were relatively unimproved on at least one measure were classified as "desynchronous" ("discordant"). Some subjects were eliminated from the analyses—for example, those who were unimproved on all three measures. The results indicated that subjects who improved on all three measures were also significantly more improved on a variety of unrelated measures than were discordant subjects. Therefore, this study really does not address the issue of predicting outcomes based on desynchrony, but rather speaks more to the correlations among various measures of agoraphobia.

There are many problems with research on desynchrony, including a very basic one—the definition of desynchrony itself. In fact, the criteria for defining desynchrony seem to differ considerably from one research center to another. It is possible that continued research in this area may clarify this issue, but at the present time there is no firm evidence that the existence of desynchrony has any practical implications.

Physiological measures assessed in a different way do seem related to outcome, and these data would seem to have both practical and theoretical import. Specifically, we (J. A. Vermilyea et al., 1984) found that absolute levels of responding recorded in a phobic situation before treatment began did predict outcome, but not in the way one might expect. Specifically, those patients who responded with the highest heart rates while walking away from a safe place were significantly more likely to respond to treatment than those with lower heart rate. This finding has been discussed in some detail in Chapter 8 in relation to theories of anxiety reduction. This, of course, is a very different way of using physiological measures than as indices of clinical change.

One other use for physiological assessment that has proved important has recently emerged. As described above and in Chapter 3, Taylor et al. (1983, 1986) have begun assessing panic attacks using a 24-hour ambulatory physiological monitoring device. This seems to be a valuable addition to the monitoring of panic attacks by means of a diary, although there are many puzzling findings. For example, the lack of relationship of panic attacks as measured by heart rate changes to reports of panic by the patient raises issues concerning the definition of panic, discussed in Chapter 4. One possibility mentioned in Chapter 6 is that this discordance is present only in learned alarms, where reports of panic become associated with a wider range of physiological referents. The details and parameters of these measures still need to be worked out before optimal methods for monitoring panic become clear. But ambulatory physiological monitoring looks very promising.

Composite Measures of Change

We are always left with the question of how best to represent change in panic disorder with or without agoraphobia. Usually the therapist simply estimates the overall amount of change on the basis of his or her perception of progress. These perceptions are based on reports from the patient and/or significant other concerning degree of anxiety and panic, and the amount of remaining avoidance behavior. As noted above, these observations can be formalized in terms of a 9-point rating scale, where 0 represents normal functioning (Watson & Marks, 1971). Some clinicians and investigators think that even 9 points are too many, since any one point may not convey adequate information on the status of the patient. These clinicians would suggest that clinical change be divided into three major categories: "unchanged," "improved," and "cured" or "normal functioning."

There is little question that this type of rating is more clinically useful than what we so often see in research studies—that is, tests of statistical significance. Knowing that a group of patients with panic disorder changed to a statistically significant degree more than a comparable control group did communicates little to clinicians. Clinicians are more concerned with how well the clinical group responded, or, more importantly, with what percentage of patients in the clinical group reached an adequate level of functioning after treatment. This issue of clinical versus statistical significance has been elaborated in great detail elsewhere (e.g., Barlow, Hayes, & Nelson, 1984), and I do not belabor it here.

In regard to panic disorder, as well as other disorders, there is no question that what we want to demonstrate through our assessment procedures is clinically significant improvement, as well as overall level of functioning at the end of treatment and at follow-up. The difficulties with simply estimating this information on a global basis, relying on reports from patients, have been discussed above. A patient may well be influenced by demands of the situation or may be misperceiving progress, as seems to have been the case with our patient in Figure 10.6. Overall clinical ratings undoubtedly will continue to be made and will be of some use. In addition, for determining changes in panic disorder, it would seem that careful monitoring of the frequency, intensity, and duration of panic attacks, as recorded in panic diaries, would be essential. The questionnaires described above should also be useful, particularly the Body Sensations Questionnaire (Chambless *et al.*, 1984) or the Anxiety Sensitivity Index (Reiss *et al.*, 1986). Pre- and posttreatment physiological measures such as heart rate and EMG have also been demonstrated to be responsive in successfully treated panic patients (Barlow, Cohen, *et al.*, 1984); however, in view of the cautions reviewed above concerning reliability and validity of physiological recording, it seems that these indices should not be relied on as the major measures of change. When avoidance behavior is a complication, one needs to monitor a much large number of clinically relevant issues simultaneously.

To determine clinically significant change after treatment in panic disorder with moderate to extensive avoidance, several clinical research groups, including ours, have established composite indices of change. These composite indices possess the potential for an overall measure that incorporates the multidimensional nature of clinical change. Since these change indices have only recently emerged in the literature, no established guidelines exist as to which measures to include. For instance, Hafner and Ross (1983) used a combination of the patient's and an independent assessor's ratings of the patient's two main phobias. We (Barlow, O'Brien, & Last,

1984) used a composite measure to assess the degree of agoraphobics' improvement during treatment. Patients were considered to be "treatment responders" if they attained 20% improvement from pre- to posttreatment on at least three of five outcome measures from both the behavioral and self-report domains. Mavissakalian and Michelson (1983) also devised a composite criterion that included behavioral, self-report, and clinician ratings to provide a composite of clinical change, as well as to identify agoraphobics with high and low levels of "end-state functioning."

Currently, we use two composite change measures in calculating clinical change in panic disorder with moderate to extensive agoraphobic avoidance. One is concerned with the degree of change during treatment, the other with the patient's end-state functioning. The measures used to define these composites have been selected to reflect the following major phenomenological components of panic disorder: avoidance behavior, subjective anxiety, and panic. We have also included therapist's and significant others' ratings of a client's phobic severity as additional measures of clinical significance. Another reason for the selection of these measures is that they are either currently in use or can be readily incorporated by anxiety researchers and clinicians throughout the world. And, as is consistent with an idiographic assessment strategy, these measures emphasize individual change.

Treatment Responder Status

To assess whether a patient may be considered a treatment responder, we use a composite criterion composed of five individual measures; these measures comprise behavioral, subjective, and therapist ratings of severity. Treatment responder status is attained if a patient demonstrates 20% improvement from pre- to posttreatment on at least three of the following five outcome measures:

1. Total score from the 10-item fear and avoidance hierarchy, rated by patients on a scale of 0–8.
2. Behavioral avoidance on the five-item IBAT.
3. Total SUDs ratings on a scale of 0–8 for the IBAT items.
4. Frequency, duration, and intensity of panic attacks from the Panic Attack Record (see Figure 10.6)—2 weeks of recording per assessment period.
5. Therapist ratings on the Watson and Marks (1971) 9-point scale of agoraphobic severity.

In addition to the 20% improvement criterion, a decrement criterion is also required for treatment responder status. That is, a patient is considered a *non*responder if there is deterioration of 20% or greater on any

one of the five measures from pre- to posttreatment. This is a fairly conservative criterion for treatment response. For example, using a similar
composite, we (Himadi, Cerny, Barlow, Cohen, & O'Brien, 1986) found
that out of a total sample of 42 agoraphobic women who had received
treatment, 64% were considered treatment responders.

End-State Functioning

Any evaluation of clinically significant change must also consider the absolute level of functioning following a treatment intervention (Mavissakalian & Michelson, 1983). We use a five-measure composite to determine
end-state functioning. A patient must meet at least three of the following
five criteria to be considered a high end-state functioner:

1. Total score of 20 or less on the 10-item fear and avoidance
   hierarchy, with a score of no greater than 3 for the top 5 items—
   rating by patient.
2. Total score of 20 or less on the 10-item fear and avoidance
   hierarchy, with a score of no greater than 3 for the top 5 items—
   rating by designated significant other (usually the spouse).
3. Completion of all five items from the IBAT, plus a total IBAT
   SUDs score of 10 or less, with a SUDs score of no greater than
   3 for any one item.
4. A zero frequency of panic attacks with intensity over 4 on the
   0–8 rating scale from the Panic Attack Record (see Figure 10.6)—
   2 weeks of posttreatment recording.
5. A score of 2 or less on therapist ratings using the Watson and
   Marks (1971) scale of agoraphobic severity.

My colleagues and I believe that end-state functioning status is meaningful only for those patients who are treatment responders. It is possible, because of poorly defined inclusion criteria, that a patient may have
a high pretreatment level of functioning and not improve during treatment. In this case, the patient would not be a treatment responder at
posttreatment, but would have achieved high end-state functioning status. Thus, limiting the analysis of end-state functioning to treatment responders anchors this classification to change during treatment. Application of similar end-state criteria to our agoraphobic sample (Himadi, Boice,
& Barlow, 1986) revealed that 19% were considered high end-state performers at posttreatment; this figure seems to represent the customary
results in terms of "cure" from phobia clinics around the world as of 1985
(Barlow & Waddell, 1985; see below). Although we have not yet devised
a similar composite for panic disorder with limited avoidance behavior,
the task should be relatively straightforward.

Predicting Outcome of Therapy

As noted above, there is some promise that physiological measures recorded during pretreatment experience with anxiety-provoking situations may predict overall outcome from psychosocial treatments (e.g., Jansson, Öst, & Jerremalm, 1987; J. A. Vermilyea *et al.*, 1984). In addition, there is evidence that specifying response profiles at pretreatment in terms of severity of behavioral versus physiological versus subjective aspects of panic and agoraphobia may be useful in choosing the most efffective treatment (e.g., Michelson, 1986; Öst, Jerremalm, & Johansson, 1981). That is, if individuals are reacting more strongly in somatic as compared to behavioral response systems of panic disorder and agoraphobia, treatments targeting somatic responding may be indicated (see Chapter 11). Surprisingly, there are few additional variables that seem to predict outcome at this point in time. For example, Stern and Marks (1973) noted no consistent pattern of predictors emerging from their agoraphobia assessments. Jansson and Öst (1982) examined the agoraphobia literature for prognostic variables and found no consistent findings for the areas of marital functioning, depression, assertiveness, and initial response to treatment. The only variable with any prognostic significance was patient expectancies, and even these results were mixed. In a later study, Jansson *et al.* (1987) also discovered few positive prognostic factors, with the exception of high heart rate during a pretreatment behavioral test (as mentioned above), as well as self-rated anxiety during the same test. Like heart rate, higher reports of anxiety at pretreatment correlated with better outcome. Presumably, further experience with the multimethod assessment strategies that are increasingly used in clinics and research centers will provide us with more information on the accurate prediction of outcome in various patients, as well as the tailoring of individual treatments to individual variations of panic disorder.

11

Treatment of Panic and Agoraphobia

TREATING AVOIDANCE BEHAVIOR

THE DISCOVERY OF EXPOSURE

As late as the 1960s, there were no proven effective treatments for agoraphobia or panic. Donald Klein had begun his work with imipramine, with only preliminary results available. At about the same time, pioneering behavioral investigators were experimenting with possible behavior therapy approaches to agoraphobia. For example, Meyer and Gelder (1963) began encouraging agoraphobics to venture away from their homes or the clinic along routes that were very difficult for them. However, they cautioned their patients to avoid experiencing any anxiety and to turn back if this occurred. This resulted in very limited improvement in a few patients at an excruciatingly slow rate of progress (Mathews *et al.*, 1981).

This procedure was soon given up in favor of the predominant behavioral treatment for phobia in those days, systematic desensitization in imagination. Evidence began to accumulate at that time that systematic desensitization was effective with simple and mixed phobics, at least some of whom were agoraphobics, when compared to psychotherapy (Gelder & Marks, 1968; Gelder, Marks, & Wolff, 1967). Nevertheless, in studies confined to severe agoraphobics, systematic desensitization did not provide a significant advantage over psychotherapy, and overall improvements were small with both treatments (Emmelkamp, 1982; Gelder & Marks, 1966; Marks 1971). Although an occasional study appeared suggesting some advantage for systematic desensitization in imagination over no treatment under certain circumstances, particularly at follow-ups of 6 months or more (Mathews *et al.*, 1976), it was generally assumed at this time that systematic desensitization was not particularly effective with agoraphobia.

In the late 1960s, we experimented with the possibility of strongly encouraging agoraphobics to expose themselves to real-life frightening situations (e.g., Agras, *et al.*, 1968). A course was set up, as described in Chapter 10, which led from the clinic to an increasingly busy downtown area about 1 mile away. As agoraphobics walked further along this course, and therefore began to experience and tolerate greater anticipatory anxiety and panic, the value of this exercise was discussed with them and they were effusively praised. If they were unable to make progress on a given trial, very little was said, although they were encouraged to try harder next time. While these patients were told to return if they experienced what was vaguely defined as "undue anxiety," in fact the demands of the situation produced Herculean efforts on the part of many of these patients.

According to behavioral observations of distance walked along this course, the initial three patients in this series did extremely well in a rel-

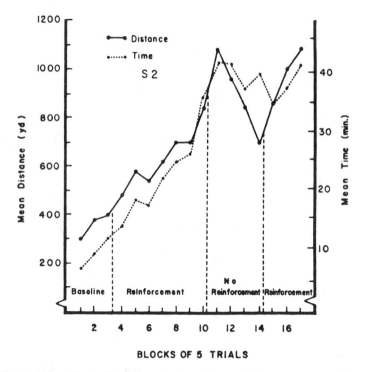

BLOCKS OF 5 TRIALS

FIGURE 11.1. The effect of reinforcement and nonreinforcement upon the performance of an agoraphobic patient (Subject 2). From Agras, W. S., Leitenberg, H., & Barlow, D. H. (1968). Social reinforcement in the modification of agoraphobia. *Archives of General Psychiatry, 19,* 423–427. Copyright 1968 by the American Medical Association. Reprinted by permission.

atively short period of time (Agras *et al.*, 1968). But a surprising finding began to emerge, which we were to isolate experimentally only in later years. Although we were betting on the therapeutic value of praise and encouragement from a therapist with whom a patient had a good relationship, many of these patients began improving in a "baseline" phase before this encouragement was even introduced. That is, the opportunity to practice by walking further along this difficult course seemed therapeutic in and of itself. These results are graphically demonstrated in Figure 11.1 for one of the patients in this early series. As one can see, this patient was already improving in terms of distance walked and time away from a safe place in baseline. The slope of this improvement was not substantially affected by the introduction of social reinforcement, although removal of this reinforcement in a systematic way at a later date did exert some control over agoraphobic behavior. In fact, later studies in this series indicated quite clearly that the opportunity to practice in a systematic way by exposing oneself to feared situations accounted for the largest part of therapeutic benefit (e.g., Leitenberg, Agras, Edwards, Thompson, & Wincze, 1970; Mavissakalian & Barlow, 1981b).

THE EFFECTIVENESS OF EXPOSURE

Since that time, investigators around the world have demonstrated very clearly that exposure *in vivo* is the central ingredient in the behavioral treatment of agoraphobia and that this process is substantially more effective than any number of credible alternative psychotherapeutic procedures (Emmelkamp, 1982; Mathews *et al.*, 1981; Mavissakalian & Barlow, 1981b). In the few studies where this has not proved to be the case, either exposure *in vivo* was not the prime therapeutic modality (Klein, Zitrin, Woerner, & Ross, 1983), or treatment comparisons were confounded because patients were systematically encouraged to practice exposing themselves *in vivo* in their home environment between sessions in all comparison groups (Mathews *et al.*, 1976). Of course, in any controlled trial of differing therapeutic procedures, we now know that there is a possibility (indeed, a strong probability) that agoraphobic patients are being systematically encouraged to gradually confront their feared situations between sessions. Once again, Klein *et al.* (1983) observed this phenomenon while delivering supportive therapy in a phobia clinic. They concluded that almost any treatment delivered within the context of a phobia clinic is likely to instigate graduated self-paced exposure *in vivo*, and therefore to lead to improvement. This is due in part to the wide publicity exposure-based treatments have received of late. This publicity results in a general expectancy or demand for agoraphobic patients to engage in these types of exercises when they arrive at a phobia clinic. For this reason, the only theoretically sound manner in which to evaluate the effects of exposure, either direct or indirect, is to arrange for exposure not to occur. This can be accomplished through therapeutic instructions or other therapeutic procedures.

When this is accomplished, the results of exposure are even more dramatic. As early as 1971, Leitenberg et al. alternated periods of exposure with periods of "psychotherapeutic activity" where exposure was actively prevented. They found no further improvement whatsoever in phobic behavior in a series of severe simple and social phobias during "psychotherapeutic activity." Greist, Marks, Berlin, Gourney, and Noshirvani (1980) also instructed their 13 phobic patients, 5 of whom were agoraphobics, to avoid phobic situations rather than to confront them. They likewise found that exposure resulted in substantially more benefit than antiexposure instructions, which seemed to cause a slight deterioration. Since patients thought both treatments were credible, the results could not be attributed to expectancies.

More recently, in a well-designed experiment, Telch, Agras, Taylor, Roth, and Gallen (1985) administered imipramine to a group of agoraphobics who were also given antiexposure instructions. In this study, which is reviewed more fully below, the group in the exposure-based condition achieved the usual level of benefit. But the group receiving antiexposure instructions showed no improvement whatsoever, despite the presence of imipramine. The theoretical implications of this study, in terms of drug–behavior interactions, are taken up below. It is sufficient to point out now that the importance of exposure as a basic therapeutic ingredient in the treatment of agoraphobia seems well established.

This is further supported in an indirect way by the well-documented observation that agoraphobics do not improve over time without treatment. This was demonstrated first by Agras et al. (1972), who followed a group of agoraphobics for 5 years before widespread publicity on exposure-based treatment was available. They found no improvement whatsoever in the absence of treatment.

In fact, the outcome of exposure-based treatments has been fairly consistent over a number of different studies conducted by clinicians in various parts of the world. If dropouts are excluded, the best estimates of outcome indicate that from 60% to 70% of those agoraphobics completing treatment have shown some clinical benefit. Follow-up studies reveal that these effects have been maintained, on the average, for periods of 4 years or more (Emmelkamp & Kuipers, 1979; Jansson & Öst, 1982; McPherson, Brougham, & McLaren, 1980; Munby & Johnston, 1980). More recent follow-up studies confirm this result (Burns, Thorpe, & Cavallaro, 1986; Cohen, Monteiro, & Marks, 1984; Jansson, Jerremalm, & Öst, 1986). In view of the consistency of this outcome, and the fact that the effectiveness of this approach has been demonstrated repeatedly in controlled experimentation when compared to no treatment or some good placebo (e.g., Mathews, 1978; Mavissakalian & Barlow, 1981b; O'Brien & Barlow, 1984), this development represents one of the success stories of behavior therapy or psychotherapy.

THE LIMITATIONS OF EXPOSURE

Nevertheless, having demonstrated that this approach is successful, investigators are beginning to examine its limitations. It is now becoming increasingly apparent that the outcome of these treatments is characterized by many examples of failure, relapse, and limited clinical improvement. For example, one major problem most often overlooked in the treatment of agoraphobia is the dropout rate. A review of a large number of studies indicates that the median dropout rate from exposure-based treatments is 12% (Jansson & Öst, 1982). Furthermore, data reporting success rates of 60–70% are also reflecting the fact that 30–40% of all agoraphobics who complete treatment fail to benefit. Of the remaining 60–70%, a substantial percentage may not reach clinically meaningful levels of functioning. For example, Marks (1971) reported that only 3 of 65 clients (4.6%) were completely symptom-free at follow-up, as determined by assessors' clinical ratings. McPherson et al. (1980) reported that among clients who showed some improvement following behavioral treatment, only 18% who were reached at follow-up rated themselves as being completely free of symptoms. Finally, Munby and Johnston (1980) observed relapses occurring in as many as 50% of clients who had benefited clinically, although in most cases these clients were evidently able to return to a level of clinical improvement previously reached in treatment.

TYPES OF EXPOSURE TREATMENT

As noted above, it has also become increasingly clear that literally scores of therapeutic procedures for agoraphobia are *not* described as exposure-based. Rather, these alternative approaches to agoraphobia, whether pharmacological or psychotherapeutic, are delivered in such a way that exposure is encouraged. For this reason, it seems useful for descriptive purposes to divide exposure-based treatments into two categories: direct and indirect. "Direct exposure" involves arranging for the patient to be exposed to feared situations, such as walking or driving away from a safe place or safe person or entering a crowded shopping center. In the most usual form, this procedure is termed "prolonged *in vivo* exposure." A therapist often accompanies the patient. The patient is expected to remain in a difficult situation until anxiety diminishes; one example would be remaining in a shopping mall for as long as 4 hours or more. The primary therapist can accompany the patient, but often the therapist is an assistant or an ex-phobic who is trained in facilitating this type of activity (Marks, 1981a).

Direct exposure, however, can also occur on a graduated basis. In its "mildest" form, direct exposure need not require the presence of a therapist or a therapy aide. For example, the patient can be requested to move up a hierarchy of fear-producing situations very gradually, in a self-paced manner. This can be done on the instructions of the therapist, usually between sessions, with the patient reporting back to the therapist each week to discuss progress (e.g., Mathews et al., 1976).

A second type of exposure can be labeled "indirect exposure." In this procedure the patient is not directly exposed to the phobic situation, but rather is presented with fear-arousing cues in imagination or symbolically. Systematic desensitization is included in this category, since this procedure is characterized by the gradual, imaginal presentation of a hierarchy of feared situations paired with relaxation. Other imaginal procedures, such as imaginal flooding, can be included here (Mavissakalian & Barlow, 1981b).

WHAT MAKES EXPOSURE WORK?

The Role of Practice

Several studies, in addition to those mentioned above, seem to demonstrate the superiority of direct exposure to indirect exposure just after treatment (Barlow et al., 1969). However, the picture changes considerably if one looks at the outcome of treatment at a follow-up point of 3–6 months. At this point any differences disappear, since either more graduated, self-paced direct exposure or even indirect exposure techniques produce therapeutic gains that "catch up" to those obtained with prolonged in vivo exposure (Mathews et al., 1976, 1977; Munby & Johnston, 1980). Klein et al. (1983) found that self-paced exposure taking place in the context of supportive therapy delivered within a phobia clinic was as effective as imaginal exposure (systematic desensitization) at follow-up. These authors point out (correctly, I think) that almost any treatment delivered within the context of a phobia clinic will "instigate" graduated self-paced direct exposure in vivo, and therefore will lead to improvement.

Occasionally, a study appears that shows no differences between direct and indirect exposure even at posttest, contrary to the majority of studies, which clearly demonstrate the superiority of direct exposure at posttest. Mathews et al. (1981) offers a very plausible analysis of why one of their major studies (Mathews *et al.*, 1976) did *not* reveal any differences between direct and indirect exposure at posttest (as opposed to at a follow-up). They observe, cogently, that their direct exposure was carried out around the clinic, rather than in the home environment. Thus, the location of practice would seem to be important. During indirect exposure (in this case, systematic desensitization in imagination), patients were practicing in their home environment between sessions. But since direct exposure was implemented in a novel situation proximal to the clinic, no *additional* practice occurred in the home environment, where the problem was located. Thus, practice in the home environment was most likely equal in both conditions. In contrast Emmelkamp and Wessels (1975), who *did* find an advantage for direct exposure at posttest, carried out their treatment in the home environment.

To extend this analysis, these observations may well contribute in large part to the lack of differences between direct and indirect exposure at follow-up. That is, after treatment of whatever modality, patients continue practicing in their home environment in the very situations that are most difficult for them. Any differences that exist at posttest between direct and indirect exposure, therefore, disappear in the face of continued practice or direct exposure in the home environment after treatment. Once again, then, the combination of practice with the appropriate location of practice seems to be the core of successful exposure-based procedures.

More recently, larger and particularly well-done studies have demonstrated quite clearly that the amount and quality of "practice" engaged in between contacts with the therapist is extremely important. This finding has been made possible by the detailed collection of diary data between sessions at various anxiety research clinics. For example, we (Barlow, O'Brien, & Last, 1984) noticed a trend suggesting that a greater amount and duration of between-session practice correlated with overall improvement. We also (B. B. Vermilyea, Barlow, & O'Brien, 1984) observed, in a process analysis, that improvement in phobic behavior was strongly correlated with practice, regardless of the type of treatment. More recently, Michelson *et al.* (1986) demonstrated that patients falling into the category of high end-state functioning at posttest practiced substantially more and substantially longer than did those patients who also improved, but were categorized as low end-state functioners.

Two major issues emerge from this analysis. First, exposure, particularly direct exposure, is clearly an effective treatment for agoraphobia. Direct exposure seems to owe much of its effectiveness to practice between sessions. But this approach leaves much to be desired in terms of the extent of change. A substantial proportion of people do not improve, and those who do improve very seldom reach optimal levels of functioning. Second, the widely varying methods in which exposure-based procedures have been delivered, both direct and indirect, raise a major question concerning the optimal manner of administering exposure-based treatments.

The Intensity of Exposure

One major issue is the optimal speed or "intensity" of exposure. Unfortunately, while it seems clear that exposure must occur, it is not yet clear how long the patient must stay in the feared situation or how frequently the trials should be scheduled. For years, studies suggested that exposure delivered in an intense or massed way was more effective than gradual shorter periods of exposure (e.g., Chaplin & Levine, 1981; Marshall, 1985; Mathews et al., 1981; Stern & Marks, 1973). If massed exposure was not more effective than exposure delivered more gradually, then it was at least as effective; the argument was thus made, "Why not get it over as quickly as possible?" (Foa, Jameson, Turner, & Payne, 1980; Yuksel, Marks, Ramm, & Ghosh, 1984).

The idea that exposure should be administered long enough for anxiety to diminish substantially, no matter how long it takes, fit well with the then-prevailing principles of learning theory discussed in Chapter 8. Specifically, long periods of exposure were thought to result in greater habituation or extinction of anxiety, both within and between sessions. Short periods of exposure, on the other hand, were seen as running the risk of sensitization if the patient were to leave a phobic situation while still anxious (Eysenck, 1976, 1982). Data supporting this notion came from the laboratories of experimental psychology, as well as Mowrer's (1939) two-factor theory of learning, and have been reviewed thoroughly in Chapter 8. In this view, escape from the phobic situation while the patient is still anxious must be prevented at all costs to insure elimination of avoidance behavior and fear.

In the clinical area, Stern and Marks (1973) and Marshall (1985) provided some support for these assumptions. For example, Stern and Marks (1973) found a continuous 2-hour session better than four 30-minute sessions within the same day in the treatment of agoraphobics. Marshall (1985), treating a group of simple phobics with fear of heights, found little benefit from brief periods of exposure, but substantial benefit from longer periods of exposure in which there was time enough for the patients' anxiety to drop to nearly zero. This study is described in more detail below. Yet work by Agras et al. (1968) reviewed above, and a long series of studies by Emmelkamp and his colleagues (see Emmelkamp, 1982), indicate that treatment is also successful if patients are encouraged to expose themselves to feared situations only until "undue anxiety appears," at which time they may remove themselves from the feared situation. On the face of it, this approach would seem to "reinforce" the fear, since there is no opportunity for habituation to occur. Escaping the situation while one is still anxious would seem to reinforce escape and avoidance. Nevertheless, Emmelkamp (1974) found this approach—which is essentially the reinforced practice procedure originated by Agras et al. (1968)—at least as effective as, if not more effective than, prolonged flooding in vivo when the results were assessed at a 3-month follow-up.

Now some recent evidence suggests why intensive exposure might not be as effective in the long run as more gradual spaced exposure. Both de Silva and Rachman (1984) and Rachman et al. (1986) demonstrated that exposure was equally effective with agoraphobics whether they were allowed to escape from the feared situation during exposure or not. Essentially, the patients in the escape group were instructed to leave their feared situation if their anxiety reached 70 on a self-estimated fear scale of 0–100. This was very similar to the "undue anxiety" instructions given by Agras et al. (1968). Subjects in the no-escape group, however, were instructed to experience peak anxiety and not to leave the situation (e.g., supermarket, etc.) until their anxiety had dropped by at least half from its peak. Both groups of patients showed significant and equivalent improvement on all measures of agoraphobia, which were maintained at a 3-month follow-up. The authors analyzed both fear and feelings of control very carefully during the sessions and found that patients in the escape condition reported greater control and less fear than those in the no-escape condition. Furthermore, escapes were not followed by increases in fear or increases in estimates of danger. What is particularly noteworthy is that patients in the escape group showed a significant increase in their presession estimates of control. Therefore, knowing that they could escape if they chose seemed to increase their sense of control and reduce their fear at subsequent trials. In fact, they chose to escape very seldom.

The reasons for the discrepancies among these studies are not clear, but several possibilities exist. For example, Marshall's (1985) experiment was carried out with simple phobics rather than agoraphobics. While it is clear that differential intensities of exposure produced differential outcome at a 1-month follow-up, it is possible that these simple phobics had fewer opportunities to practice between sessions than agoraphobics, who, after all, would have been exposed to the somatic fear cues associated with panic every time they got anxious. Nevertheless, Foa et al. (1980) and Stern and Marks (1973) tested groups of subjects who were exclusively or mostly agoraphobics, and yet found an advantage for more intense exposure.

Until these discrepancies are resolved by further experimentation, it seems important to insure that sufficient exposure to difficult situations occurs. But there seems no reason to take control away from the patient as long as he or she is willing to endure some anxiety—for example, 70 or more on a SUDs scale as tested by Rachman et al. (1986). With these

413

requirements in mind, a more gradual, self-paced, self-initiated series of exposure sessions carried out by the patient between meetings with the therapist would seem to have the most likelihood of producing long-term benefit. This approach is consistent with the views presented in Chapter 8. Specifically, two of the primary goals of affective therapy are preventing escapist action tendencies and instilling a sense of control.

In fact, it now seems possible that prolonged *in vivo* exposure, carried out in an intensive fashion may be less effective than previously assumed and may even be detrimental if viewed in a broader context. For example, intensive *in vivo* exposure administered over a short period of time seems to produce a dropout rate considerably higher than the median 12% (e.g., Emmelkamp & Ultee, 1974; Emmelkamp & Wessels, 1975). On the other hand, a more gradual, self-initiated exposure program carried out over a longer period of time produces a very low dropout rate (Jannoun, Munby, Catalan, & Gelder, 1980; Mathews *et al.*, 1977). Another possible disadvantage to intensive exposure is the fact that dramatic behavioral changes sometimes have deleterious effects on the interpersonal system of the client (e.g., Hafner, 1977; O'Brien, Barlow, & Last, 1982). Since at least 75% of agoraphobics are women, the majority of whom are married, these effects most often show up in husbands (Himadi, Cerny, *et al.*, 1986; Mavissakalian & Barlow, 1981b). The issue here is that any dramatic change in the social system is going to have an impact on that system. In this case, family and close friends will be most affected if they are not prepared for the change. Fuller consideration of this issue is provided below.

In addition, it has been consistently observed that continued progress after treatment is terminated does not occur with intensive, therapist-assisted, *in vivo* exposure. This is a serious problem, since it has already been noted that improvement is often far less than desired. Other investigators suggest that therapist-assisted, *in vivo* exposure may produce a dependence on the therapist, which in and of itself precludes further improvement once the therapist is absent (e.g., Mathews *et al.*, 1977). The specific effect of this dependence may be a tendency to practice less in the home environment or to refrain from initiating any positive changes. Instead, the patient waits in vain for continued guidance from the therapist. Finally, and perhaps most importantly, intensive, massed *in vivo* exposure is associated with a higher relapse rate than are less intensive treatments (Hafner, 1976; Jansson & Öst, 1982).

One implication of these findings is that the most common and popular method for administering exposure in phobia clinics around the country is probably not the most effective. Typically, agoraphobic patients will gather together in a phobia clinic and then travel to a nearby shopping mall or some other equally frightening place in a group led by a therapist or therapeutic aide. They will remain in this setting for as long as 4 hours or more. Most often the therapist remains with the group, coaching first

414

one and then another of the agoraphobics as they experience intense anticipatory anxiety and panic. Many of these programs are completed in 2 weeks. It seems clear that the weight of the evidence is now against this intensive approach to exposure and in favor of a more gradual self-initiated program of exposure based practices.

The Role of the Therapist

A variety of additional procedures have been tested for their ability to enhance the effects of systematic direct exposure programs. One of the more frequently tested additions to exposure-based programs is the involvement of a therapist or a therapeutic aide who may accompany the agoraphobic to the feared situation. At the very least, the therapist will meet frequently (e.g., on a weekly basis) with the agoraphobic to review progress, provide guidance, and so on. Recently, a number of studies have examined the importance of the role of the therapist in these programs.

At one extreme lie the self-help manuals now widely available around the world. With these manuals, agoraphobics can construct their own direct exposure program without therapeutic assistance (Weekes, 1968, 1972, 1973, 1976). Usually these programs involve arranging a hierarchy of difficult situations where panic is likely to occur, ranging from least difficult (involving the least anticipatory anxiety and avoidance) to most difficult. Patients then gradually work their way through these procedures until they can accomplish the most difficult items on a consistent basis with reduced anxiety. Weekes (1968) sampled over 500 agoraphobic patients who had simply read her book without any further contact by mail. Results from the mail questionnaire indicated that between 49% and 73% of the patients reported satisfactory results, although the criteria for improvement were not clearly specified. Results also depended on tallying responses from those agoraphobics who bothered to return the questionnaire. Weekes classified phobics as showing good results if they indicated that they "were able to move much more freely and if they panicked they could cope with the panic and were not especially deterred by it" (Weekes, 1968, p. 9). Mathews et al. (1981) also reported in a pilot study that a self-help manual without any therapeutic contact could provide therapeutic benefit.

This type of program can also be supplemented by varying degrees of therapist contact (as well as by other therapeutic ingredients to be discussed below). This contact can range from a few hours (Ghosh, Marks, & Carr, 1984; Mathews et al., 1977, 1981) up through almost continual contact with the therapist during a process of prolonged in vivo exposure. After a decade of research, it now seems clear that very little therapist time is required to provide patients with the same amount of benefit as more intensive therapeutic contact if these patients are provided with a structured program of direct exposure in the form of a manual or some other suitable medium (Ghosh & Marks, 1987; Jannoun et al., 1980; Mathews et al., 1981). However, it is not entirely clear at this point that no therapeutic contact is required. For example, we (Holden, O'Brien, Barlow, Stetson, & Infantino, 1983) provided six severely avoidant female agoraphobics with a self-help manual containing instructions for arranging a direct exposure program, as well as suggestions for cognitive restructuring. The results indicated that the self-help manual was not effective.

What we found to be the major difficulty with the manual was that subjects did not perform the direct exposure practices required by the manual after the first week or so. The same treatment then conducted by the therapist did produce moderate improvement in the majority of the patients. Graphic illustration of this is provided in Figure 11.2 for one of the patients. Measures of phobias, fear, and avoidance, represented in the left-hand side of the figure, showed no change during the manual-only phase. Improvement began when the therapist started conducting the treatment program outlined in the manual. Practice sessions, represented in the right-hand side of the figure, showed a decline to near zero after an initial burst of activity, but then rose substantially under the direction of the therapist. It does seem that some people improve with self-help books alone, but these may be less severely affected patients than the ones in this experiment.

This suggestion seems to be confirmed in a new study by Ghosh and Marks (1987), who treated three groups of agoraphobics. One group received a well-worked-out self-help program, preceded by 1.5 hours of therapist time during which the program was explained. The same program delivered by the therapist was accomplished with 4.6 hours of the therapist's time. The same program adapted for computer interaction also took 4.7 hours of therapeutic time (some of it, presumably, to explain the operation of the computer). The heart of the program was self-paced exposure practice, the occurrence of which was documented in diaries. All groups improved equally. The amount of improvement was similar to that reported in other studies using drugs or exposure-based programs with prolonged therapist contact. The patients were, however, less severely affected than those we studied (Holden et al., 1983).

In summary, it seems that minimal therapeutic time is necessary unless patients are severely impaired, in which case more intensive therapeutic assistance may be necessary. When therapists do assist with exposure, it would seem important to withdraw the therapist gradually from exposure sessions, in order to enable the patients to make attempts on their own and develop a sense of control and independence. In fact, Williams et al. (1984) did just that in a well-done experiment with simple

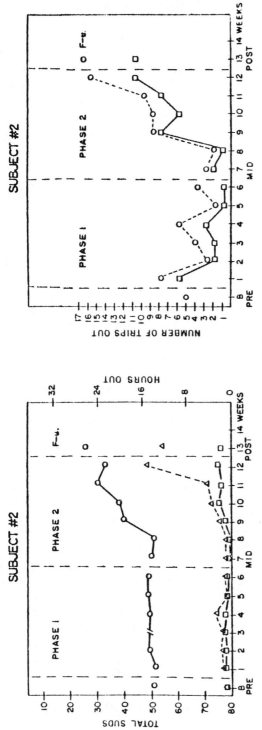

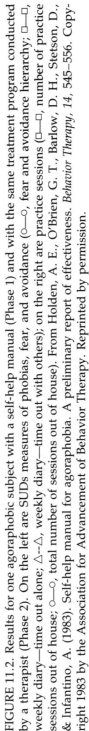

FIGURE 11.2. Results for one agoraphobic subject with a self-help manual (Phase 1) and with the same treatment program conducted by a therapist (Phase 2). On the left are SUDs measures of phobias, fear, and avoidance (○—○, fear and avoidance hierarchy; □—□, weekly diary—time out alone; △--△, weekly diary—time out with others); on the right are practice sessions (□--□, number of practice sessions out of house; ○—○, total number of sessions out of house). From Holden, A. E., O'Brien, G. T., Barlow, D. H., Stetson, D., & Infantino, A. (1983). Self-help manual for agoraphobia. A preliminary report of effectiveness. *Behavior Therapy, 14,* 545–556. Copyright 1983 by the Association for Advancement of Behavior Therapy. Reprinted by permission.

417

phobics afraid of heights or driving. Therapists accompanied patients on their exposure sessions, giving detailed advice and helping them over rough spots. Eventually the therapists withdrew, allowing the patients to do it on their own. The groups with therapist assistance had improved more at posttest, although no follow-up was provided. Thus, a conservative strategy would dictate the inclusion of a therapist to structure the session and provide feedback on progress, but to participate directly only if progress is not satisfactory.

PARTNER- AND SPOUSE-ASSISTED EXPOSURE

A related strategy tested in various ways over the years involves the inclusion of a partner in an exposure-based program. The notion here, of course, is that a motivated partner, usually a relative or friend of the patient, will help the patient over the "rough spots" and insure that practice in the home environment is accomplished.

Before conclusions we can draw from studies completed are summarized, it is important to note that this strategy has not received a great deal of attention. For example, in many exposure-based programs it is our experience that patients often involve a spouse, family member, or friend in an informal manner as they go about facing their feared situations. This would be understandable, since direct exposure in the home environment takes place in the social system in which a patient exists on a day-to-day basis. Thus, some degree of involvement with family or friends is likely. It also seems clear that this can be a very uneven experience when left to the devices of the patient. Most of the experiments that have looked at the role of partners in a systematic way have attempted to structure the partners' participation in order to examine the effects more clearly. However, even these studies have not precluded in any way the informal participation of additional partners.

The first investigators to examine this issue were Hand, Lamontagne, and Marks (1974). They noted that agoraphobics treated in what became a cohesive group stayed in touch with one another and supported each other after treatment; this evidently resulted in further improvement after completion of treatment. Mathews *et al.* (1977), in an uncontrolled clinical trial, included spouses of agoraphobics as cotherapists and noted that over 90% were much improved at the end of treatment, with improvement continuing at follow-up. Munby and Johnston (1980) followed up a series of studies carried out by the same group of investigators. They concluded that the treatment in which spouses were directly included produced continuing improvement. The results were superior at a 4- to 9-year follow-up to the results of treatments where agoraphobics were treated in separate clinical trials, but more intensively and without spouses. Sinnott, Jones,

Scott-Fordham, and Woodward (1981) also noted that agoraphobics selected from the same neighborhood and treated as a group were superior on many outcome measures to a group composed of agoraphobics from diverse geographical regions who presumably did not meet, socialize, or generally support each other during or after therapy. It seems likely that the reason for greater improvement in these experiments lies in support and motivation for continued "practice" in facing feared situations between sessions and after treatment is over.

Recently we tested the feasibility and benefit of including the spouse directly in treatment (Barlow, O'Brien, & Last, 1984; Barlow, O'Brien, Last, & Holden, 1983). In this program, 28 agoraphobic women received the core self-paced exposure-based treatment, which encouraged them to practice exposing themselves to feared situations around their homes in a systematic way. At 12 weekly treatment sessions they received a variety of suggestions for accomplishing these practice sessions in a systematic manner. In addition, they initially received basic education on the nature of agoraphobia, as well as cognitive restructuring procedures for altering negative attitudes and thought processes occurring during both anticipatory anxiety and panic.

The husbands of all 28 women agreed to accompany their wives to the 12 weekly treatment sessions if necessary, but only 14 were invited to do so; the others were told that in their particular cases it would not be necessary. All of these women were then treated in small groups of three to six, either with or without their spouses. A typical spouse group consisted of four agoraphobic women and their husbands for a total of eight, as well as one to two therapists.

As one might expect, all subjects improved after receiving direct exposure consisting of practice in the home environment. Overall, the improvement rate was in line with typical improvement rates from around the world (Jansson & Öst, 1982). However, there was a significantly greater number of treatment responders, according to the criteria discussed in Chapter 10, in the spouse group than in the nonspouse group. These results are presented in Table 11.1. A variety of additional methods for

TABLE 11.1. Treatment Responders and
Nonresponders in Spouse and Nonspouse Groups

	Responders	Nonresponders
Spouse	12	2
Nonspouse	6	8

Note. From Barlow, D. H., O'Brien, G. T., & Last, C. G.
(1984). Couples treatment of agoraphobia. *Behavior Therapy*,
15, 41–58. Copyright 1984 by the Association for Advancement of Behavior Therapy. Reprinted by permission.

computing therapeutic outcome also showed either a statistically significant advantage for the spouse group or a trend in that direction. The fact that 12 out of 14, or 86%, of the patients in the spouse group "responded" to treatment replicated the high percentage of success reported by Mathews et al. (1977).

It is also important to reiterate that the rate of attrition in studies employing a graduated self-paced direct exposure program seems to be extremely low, remaining under 5% for studies of this type (Arnow, Taylor, Agras, & Telch, 1985; Jannoun et al., 1980; Mathews et al., 1977). Once again, this is in contrast to the more intensive therapist-directed massed exposure treatments, where considerably higher attrition is evident (Jansson & Öst, 1982).

There was a statistically nonsignificant trend for the group of responders to engage in a greater number of practice sessions than those who were classified as nonresponders. The lack of clear differences in this measure—a finding also reported by others (Jansson et al., 1980; Mavissakalian & Michelson, 1983; Solyom, Solyom, LaPierre, Pecknold, & Morton, 1981)—may well be due to the relative crudeness of these diary measures in the early 1980s. As noted above, Michelson et al. (1986), analyzing these measures in a more sophisticated manner than in their 1983 study (Mavissakalian & Michelson, 1983), did find that amount of practice between sessions predicted positive outcome.

Patients from our study have now been followed for 2 years (Cerny, Barlow, Craske, & Himadi, 1987). Consistent with our hypothesis, the data indicate that the spouse group demonstrated an increasingly more positive response than the nonspouse group at the 1- and 2-year follow-ups, confirming and extending the differences found at posttest. That is, they continued to improve, and the gap between them and the nonspouse group became wider than it was at posttest. Some of the results are presented in Table 11.2.

Spouse group members were significantly less phobic on a number of measures. They also completed a greater number of items in the behavioral test at the 1-year follow-up. At 2 years, the low number of patients in the nonspouse group on some measures limited the analyses somewhat. But on clinical ratings and the IBAT, where numbers were more satisfactory, the spouse group remained superior. Presumably, the support and knowledge of the spouses helped these patients deal successfully with phobic and panic situations that arose over the years.

Despite the potential promise of these findings, replication is necessary in other clinics. Now two studies have appeared addressing the same topic. One study by a highly competent group of investigators evaluated the effect of including the spouse in a very similar manner to the Barlow, O'Brien, and Last (1984) experiment (Cobb, Mathews, Childs-Clarke, & Blowers, 1984). This experiment failed to reveal any positive effect of in-

TABLE 11.2. Average Client Scores at 1- and 2-Year Follow-Ups for Spouse and Nonspouse Treatment Formats: Phobia Measures

| | Spouse group | | | | Nonspouse group | | | | t | |
| | 1 year | | 2 years | | 1 year | | 2 years | | | |
Variable name	$\bar{x}$	n	$\bar{x}$	n	$\bar{x}$	n	$\bar{x}$	n	1 year	2 years
Clinical rating	3.30 (1.35)	23	2.85 (1.56)	17	4.81 (1.86)	14	4.37 (1.56)	14	−2.87**	−2.70*
Fear Questionnaire	36.90 (17.33)	19	31.47 (16.27)	17	51.96 (27.24)	12	39.60 (18.00)	5	−1.89	−0.96
Phobia self-rating	2.81 (1.51)	18	2.53 (1.63)	17	4.04 (2.55)	12	2.80 (1.10)	5	−1.67	−0.35
Fear and avoidance hierarchy	18.71 (12.57)	17	16.79 (12.96)	14	35.55 (21.34)	10	24.40 (19.24)	5	−2.60*	−1.00
Percent of IBAT items completed	100.00 (0.00)	14	89.50 (14.62)	10	85.00 (19.31)	12	67.00 (32.16)	13	2.69*	2.06**

Note. Standard deviations appear in parentheses. From Cerny, J. A., Barlow, D. H., Craske, M. G., & Himadi, W. G. (1987). Couples treatment of agoraphobia: A two year follow-up. *Behavior Therapy, 18,* 401–415. Copyright 1987 by the Association for Advancement of Behavior Therapy. Reprinted by permission.
*$p < .05$.
**$p < .01$.

cluding the spouse at posttest or a 6-month follow-up. One procedural difference stands out that might account for this discrepancy. In this study all treatment took place in the patients' homes, with the therapist spending approximately 5 hours in each home. During the first visit, as well as all measurement sessions, spouses in both groups were included interacting with both patients and therapists. Therapists reported that spouses in the nonspouse group "showed an interest" in therapy during this initial session. Possibly they were more active during therapy in view of their attendance at the first treatment session and measurement sessions. In our study (Barlow, O'Brien, & Last, 1984), all groups met at the clinic and therapists never met the spouses, although questionnaires were sent home for them to return by mail. Thus, they may not have become as "interested" or active as in the Cobb *et al.* (1984) study.

A second study approached the question in a somewhat different way. Arnow *et al.* (1985) exposed agoraphobics and their spouses to phobic situations in a standard manner for 4 weeks. Patients were then divided into two matched groups according to their change scores on behavioral measures of agoraphobia. These groups were determined by random assignment. One group then received a communication training package, which focused on dealing with agoraphobic situations. The other group received relaxation training in a couples format. At both posttest and an 8-month follow-up, a significant advantage existed for the communication group over the relaxation group on measures of agoraphobia. Figure 11.3 graphically illustrates these important differences for several standard measures.

This study would seem to confirm the hypothesis that intervening in the social system of the agoraphobic exerts a positive influence on out-

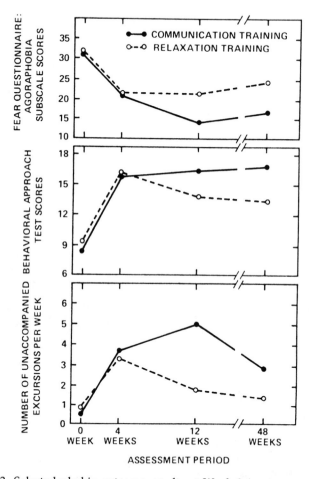

FIGURE 11.3. Selected phobia outcome results at Week 0 (pretreatment), Week 4 (postexposure), Week 12 (postcommunication/relaxation), and Week 48 (8-month follow-up). From Arnow, B. A., Taylor, C. B., Agras, W. S., & Telch, M. J. (1985). Enhancing agoraphobia treatment outcome by changing couple communication patterns. *Behavior Therapy, 16*, 452–467. Copyright 1985 by the Association for Advancement of Behavior Therapy. Reprinted by permission.

come. Spouse groups in both the Barlow, O'Brien, and Last (1984) and the Arnow *et al.* (1985) experiments were trained to practice self-initiated exposure between sessions and to improve communications and problem-solving skills regarding agoraphobic situations. But the Arnow *et al.* experiment isolated communication training as an important therapeutic ingredient in a particularly elegant way. In their experiment, both groups were trained to work on between-session practice as a couple, but only one group was specifically trained to improve communication and problem-solving skills. The fact that an advantage on measures of agoraphobia was evident for this group attests to the seeming power of this intervention.

The experimental strategy of matching subjects on progress after initial exposure sessions and before administering communication training and its control treatment was clever. But it would seem to make more sense clinically to train couples in communication and problem solving before they begin exposure sessions. In this way, they might take advantage of their newly developed skills during treatment. This remains to be evaluated experimentally.

There is no question that agoraphobia is a problem that impinges on the social system of the patient. For this reason, the family of the agoraphobic almost always has to become involved in some way or another in the problem. As noted above, it is possible that the type of support and encouragement present from the family exerts differential effects in all treatment studies, whether these interactions are formally monitored or not. Evidence from our study (Barlow, O'Brien, & Last, 1984) indicates that in a well-adjusted marriage, the formal inclusion of the spouse in the treatment process makes little difference. However, in a more poorly adjusted marriage, inclusion of the spouse seems to override the influence of a poor relationship. In the Arnow *et al.* (1985) experiment, however, most of the marriages were well adjusted to begin with, and yet communication training improved the effectiveness of treatment. These experiments underline the importance of considering the social system that provides the context for the treatment of agoraphobia—a topic to be discussed further below.

ALTERING DEPENDENCY

For decades, clinicians have observed that neurotic patients by and large are unassertive and overly dependent. As a result, much of the emphasis in traditional psychotherapy is placed on searching for the cause of and modifying overly dependent interpersonal relationships, particularly among family members (Andrews, 1966). Unfortunately, there has been very little systematic testing of this hypothesis. For example, evidence presented in Chapter 10 makes it unclear whether agoraphobics are overly dependent or not (see Table 10.1), although more recent evidence suggests that agoraphobics (as well as individuals with other anxiety disorders) are dependent to some extent. Nevertheless, one can surmise that altering this seemingly prominent interpersonal feature in the personalities of agoraphobics may reduce phobia, perhaps through encouraging more independence. This, in turn, may result in more self-initiated exposure and the inclination to venture away more readily from a safe person. Only Paul Emmelkamp has tested this in a systematic way. In one experiment (Emmelkamp, van der Hout, & de Vries, 1983), three small groups of agoraphobics were treated with either assertive training, prolonged exposure *in vivo*, or a combination of the two. The investigators observed that assertive training did indeed increase assertiveness, but no differential effects were evident on phobic behavior. Nor did increased assertiveness contribute anything to direct exposure over and above exposure alone. In a related experiment, Emmelkamp (1980) found that assertive and unassertive agoraphobics benefited equally from exposure *in vivo*.

Despite the lack of any meaningful findings from these two experiments, it is certainly possible that attention to interpersonal factors in general and to dependency or unassertiveness in particular may still play a role in the treatment of panic disorder and agoraphobia. Evidence reviewed above underlines the role of stress, interpersonal and otherwise, in potentiating panic. Interpersonal problems, particularly marital difficulties, are a common source of stress. It is possible that therapeutic attention to assertiveness and dependency may well buffer the occurrence of stress and resulting panic after treatment, thereby reducing the possibility of relapse.

ELIMINATING SAFETY SIGNALS

An overlooked treatment target is the elimination of safety signals—the "talismans" that are so prominent a feature in the lives of agoraphobics (Rachman, 1983b, 1984). While few therapists would ignore the necessity of attending to the functional impairment that results from requiring the presence of a "safe person" such as a spouse on ventures out, other safety signals receive less attention. As described in Chapter 10, empty pill bottles, sheets of paper containing coping self-statements, or even pets may be unobtrusive companions most of the time. Therefore, an agoraphobic may be considered "recovered" despite continuing dependence on these items—a dependence that is readily acknowledged to be irrational.

The difficulty with ignoring this residue of extensive avoidance lies in the danger of the former agoraphobic's misplacing or otherwise forgetting the item after treatment is over. This, of course, may result in anxiety, a return of some avoidance, or even a complete relapse if circumstances line up correctly. At the very least, it will bring the agoraphobic to a realization that he or she has not recovered and that loss of control and panic may be just around the corner, depending on the presence or absence of a small piece of paper or an empty pill bottle.

Since it is a rather small matter, in our experience, to wean patients from the variety of safety signals as part of their structured, self-paced exposure exercises, there seems little reason not to do it. The discovery of the optimal methods for eliminating safety signals and the best way to integrate these methods with standard exposure exercises awaits further research.

THE CONTRIBUTION OF COGNITIVE THERAPY

In Chapters 2 and 7, I have reviewed evidence characterizing cognitive processes and content in anxious apprehension. Cognitive features of anxiety disorders are conspicuous in clinical presentation and quite naturally emerge as a prime target for treatment. This is particularly true with panic disorder and agoraphobia, where reports of exaggerated fears of losing control or dying are prominent defining characteristics of the disorders. For that reason, there have already been a number of studies testing the utility of cognitive therapy or cognitive restructuring in combination with exposure for agoraphobia. Since none of these studies used antiexposure instructions, all studies are more properly construed as testing the addition of cognitive procedures to self-directed *in vivo* exposure. The cognitive procedures most often studied are paradoxical intention and coping self-statement training.

In paradoxical intention, patients are instructed to exaggerate the most feared consequences of panic attacks. For example, a patient who is afraid of fainting in a public place is told to make every possible effort to faint; to imagine himself or herself fainting; and to attempt to faint in a way so dramatic that it will draw everyone's attention. As originally envisioned, this is meant to be conveyed in a manner so exaggerated as to bring some humor to the situation (Frankl, 1960). The function of paradoxical intention within exposure therapy seems to be to keep people in their feared situation, thereby prolonging exposure not only to the feared situation itself, but also to the catastrophic consequences anticipated by these patients—a form of cognitive exposure. Coping self-statement training, of course, attempts to substitute more positive thoughts for the negative and/ or catastrophic thoughts that occur during anxiety and panic.

Several investigators have examined the clinical utility of these procedures with agoraphobics and found them to be effective in uncontrolled clinical replication series (e.g., Ascher, 1981); others have compared cognitive procedures directly. For example, Mavissakalian, Michelson,

Greenwald, Kornblith, and Greenwald (1983) compared paradoxical intention to self-statement training and found the former slightly better at posttest. But differences disappeared at a 6-month follow-up, presumably due to the overriding effects of subsequent exposure practice.

When more direct comparisons are undertaken, cognitive therapy does not fare as well. For example, when cognitive therapy of whatever form is compared with structured direct exposure, exposure treatments are consistently more effective (Biran & Wilson, 1981; Emmelkamp, Kuipers, & Eggeraat, 1978). Of course, even the most ardent cognitive therapist would not suppose that cognitive therapy alone would outshine exposure-based treatment in a direct comparison (Ellis, 1979). But cognitive therapists do believe that cognitive therapy should make exposure-based exercises more effective and efficient. Therefore, a more interesting question concerns the potential benefit of adding cognitive procedures to exposure therapy.

The best evidence we have to date indicates that cognitive therapy does not seem to add anything to a structured exposure-based program in the treatment of agoraphobia (e.g., Emmelkamp & Mersch, 1982; Williams & Rappoport, 1983). In fact, Michelson, Mavissakalian, and Marchione (1985) reported that adding a cognitive procedure, paradoxical intention, to exposure-based treatment was detrimental compared to other variants of exposure. In this study, Michelson et al. (1985), using instructed self-initiated exposure as the basic treatment component, added either (1) relaxation training, (2) a therapist to guide in vivo exposure or (3) paradoxical intention. All groups improved, but paradoxical intention was significantly less effective on a number of measures at posttest. Particularly interesting is the analysis of patients who could be categorized as high end-state functioners at a 3-month follow-up: 73% of the guided exposure group and 70% of the relaxation group, but only 40% of the paradoxical intention group, were high end-state functioners.

Ladouceur (1983) also found that cognitive restructuring did not contribute to an exposure-based treatment for phobia. In fact, it actually seemed to interfere with progress during direct exposure. He has hypothesized that attempting to alter self-statements during exposure may distract one from the beneficial effects of exposure.

The fact that cognitive procedures do not seem to contribute anything to exposure is a bit of a puzzle. Of course, this is not to say that threat-related cognitions associated with anxiety do not change during exposure; in fact, when monitored, they do seem to decrease substantially after successful therapy. But this decrease seems to occur without the addition of cognitive procedures per se to the program (Williams & Rappoport, 1983). The apparent lack of a contribution from cognitive procedures is all the more interesting, because clinically these procedures seem very useful to both therapists and patients. For example, patients often attribute their therapeutic gains to the use of cognitive coping procedures (O'Brien & Barlow, 1984). Furthermore, there do seem to be individual cases where no change is apparent in catastrophic cognitions, even after successful exposure therapy (Last *et al.*, 1984a). These patients would seem to be prime candidates for relapse. For this reason, it is possible that cognitive therapy may be useful primarily in preventing relapse or prolonging therapeutic gains after treatment is over, rather than in providing immediate benefit.

Now one study seems to support this hypothesis for cognitive therapy, although the subjects in this study were not agoraphobics. Marshall (1985) held total exposure constant while treating height phobics. In one group the exposure sessions, which were conducted on top of a tall building, varied in duration. Longer-duration exposures produced more benefit than exposures of shorter duration. For present purposes, however, the most interesting finding is that when cognitive coping procedures were added in a well-controlled fashion to long-duration exposure, no differences appeared at posttest. But the group with cognitive coping procedures continued to improve during a follow-up period and were superior to those receiving long-duration exposure alone at the follow-up test. If this finding is replicated with agoraphobics, the importance of cognitive procedures will be demonstrated.

Marshall (1985) makes an interesting suggestion, albeit one without experimental support at this time. He notes that his cognitive restructuring took place in the feared situation (on top of the building) *after* a relatively low state of anxiety and arousal had been reached. As he notes, this is consistent with basic research on cognitive processes in anxiety (Spielberger & Sarason, 1978) demonstrating that optimal learning occurs during low arousal states. Pending future experimentation, particularly with agoraphobics, Marshall's strategy on the timing of cognitive intervention may prove useful in maximizing the effects of exposure-based treatments.

In any case, based on the essentials of therapy outlined in Chapter 8, directly attacking threat-related cognitions is not essential unless it brings about substantial changes in the affective core of anxiety—specifically, the action tendencies or sense of loss of control. Although cognitive intervention may be helpful in this regard, as suggested by Marshall (1985), the evidence would suggest that it is not a primary ingredient of treatment.

TREATING PANIC

Despite the realization that direct exposure seems to be the core of any treatment program for agoraphobia, and despite the ingenuity of clinical investigators in devising therapeutically helpful additions to this core program, the results remain less than satisfactory. The improvement rates from exposure-based programs have been reviewed in some detail above. Briefly, the majority of clients (approximately 90%) are not "cured," and a substantial minority (approximately 35%) fail to receive any benefit whatsoever. When a spouse is systematically included, the rates of clinical improvement seem to increase from approximately 65% to 90% (Arnow et al., 1985; Barlow, O'Brien, & Last, 1984; Mathews et al., 1977), but the cure rate is still low. Although preliminary evidence in the context of simple phobia suggests that cognitive procedures may facilitate continued improvement after treatment is over and possibly prevent relapse, this remains to be confirmed with agoraphobics.

If the models of panic and agoraphobia presented in earlier chapters are even close to accurate, the reason for these results should be obvious: Exposure-based programs concentrate on avoidance behavior, but ignore or at least downplay panic. My colleagues and I now believe that panic is the central feature of agoraphobia (and panic disorder), and good evidence exists that avoidance behavior is a subsequent complication of initial panic. Of course, avoidance behavior may well become functionally autonomous after a period of time. In addition, the development of strong safety signals or rituals seem to strengthen avoidance behavior even if panic attacks have long since disappeared. Therefore, treating avoidance behavior will always be necessary. Nevertheless, the primary goal should be the treatment of panic.

PANIC REDUCTION DURING EXPOSURE TREATMENTS

One obvious question is this: Why are exposure-based treatments as successful as they are? What happens to panic during exposure treatments? The answer is that direct exposure does seem effective in reducing panic, although we are not sure why. Evidence for this is relatively sparse, since very few of the scores of studies examining the effects of exposure in the treatment of agoraphobia have even measured panic. For those studies reporting these data, clear reductions in panic are evident.

For example, Chambless, Goldstein, Gallagher, and Bright (1986) chose 35 agoraphobic patients from a larger series for whom they had suitable measures of both avoidance behavior and panic frequency. These 35 patients were chosen from the larger series because they were entirely drug-free at all times during the treatment program. These patients were assessed during intake and then again just before treatment began approximately 1 month later. Little change in avoidance or panic was evident during this month. Data were collected on panic frequency and avoidance during a 1-week period 6 months after treatment. "Panic frequency" refers to the number of panics during the 1-week period as reported by the patient. Avoidance was measured by the Mobility Inventory for Agoraphobia (Chambless et al., 1985), which samples a large number of situations and is therefore a very conservative measure. Frequency of panic was substantially reduced, with 64% reporting no panic during the 1-week period. Avoidance was also reduced.

Similarly, in the Barlow, O'Brien, and Last (1984) study, ratings of overall frequency, duration, and intensity of spontaneous panic for the preceeding 3-day period were collected both at pretest and posttest. In those patients who responded to treatment (the majority), significant reductions in panic occurred. In one-third or 6 out of 18 of these patients, panic was essentially eliminated. By contrast, 10 patients who did not respond to this treatment deteriorated on these ratings. Of these 10 patients, 6 actually reported increases on ratings of panic.

Reductions in panic after exposure-based treatments comparable to those produced by imipramine or relaxation treatment, as determined by direct comparisons of the treatments, have also been reported by Marks and his colleagues (e.g., Cohen et al., 1984; Marks et al., 1983) and by Michelson and his colleagues (e.g., Michelson, 1988). Ghosh and Marks (1987) noted marked reductions in ratings of panic after exposure treatments in their large series of 40 agoraphobics. Michelson et al. (1985) also reported that approximately 50% of 39 agoraphobics reported no spontaneous panics while alone at home for a 1-week period preceding a 3-month follow-up; substantial reduction was still evident at a 2-year follow-up (Michelson, 1988).

Reductions in panic are also evident in studies examining in more detail the effects of exposure in the context of pharmacological studies (e.g., Mavissakalian & Michelson, 1983; Zitrin et al., 1980, 1983). In the Zitrin et al. (1983) study, behavior therapy, which in this case consisted of indirect imaginal exposure, was administered with either imipramine or placebo. Imipramine and behavior therapy produced a slightly greater effect on patient and therapist ratings of spontaneous panic than did behavior therapy with placebo; however, this differential effect was not evident on ratings by a blind independent assessor, according to which spontaneous panic improved in both conditions. This implies a clear antipanic effect of behavior therapy. Mavissakalian (1983) also found equal reductions in panic when comparing direct exposure and imipramine. In a subsequent study comparing imipramine with and without intensive exposure (Mavissakalian, Michelson, & Dealy, 1983), greater reductions in panic were noted when exposure was added to imipramine than when imipramine alone was given.

It seems clear that exposure reduces panic. Why should exposure treatments reduce panic? This is a fascinating question from both a theoretical and a practical point of view, and one for which there are no satisfactory answers. It is true that some exposure-based programs include panic management procedures such as distraction, breathing retraining, and relaxation procedures to be used either while panic is occurring or if it is imminent (e.g., Chambless et al., 1986). But most studies also reporting marked reductions in panic have not routinely employed these procedures, or even construed them as treatment as opposed to temporary management (Barlow, O'Brien, & Last, 1984; Mavissakalian & Michelson, 1983). This issue is discussed further below in connection with psychological treatment of panic.

Now evidence has appeared indicating that reductions in panic and anxiety during exposure-based treatments may be the single most important predictor of successful outcome, outranking even amount of practice between sessions. Specifically, Michelson et al. (1985), in the study reviewed above, reported that reductions in anxiety during self-directed practice were strongly related to the success of all three psychologically based treatments. In fact, reductions in anxiety accounted for more of the variance within regression analyses than did amount of practice. This also seems to have been the case in the Barlow, O'Brien, and Last (1984) study, as mentioned above.

If treating panic is as important as it would seem from our model, as Klein suggested many years ago (Klein, 1967; Mendel & Klein, 1969), and if the success of exposure-based treatment is due in large part to reductions in anxiety and panic that may occur almost as an afterthought in the context of these programs, then it makes sense to take a closer look at treatments that target panic directly. This targeting should occur not only in the treatment of panic disorder without agoraphobia or avoidance behavior, but also in the treatment of panic with agoraphobia, where (at least in the context of exposure-based programs) these treatments have not been emphasized. In fact, a number of approaches target panic directly. Among these are pharmacological treatments and newly developing psychologically based treatments designed to reduce the phobic value of interoceptive cues, in line with the model elaborated on in Chapter 6. The approach that has been investigated more thoroughly is the use of drugs.

DRUG TREATMENTS

One of the true revolutions in the treatment of anxiety disorders over the past decade has been the dramatic increase in the use of drugs. This development has been accompanied by an equally dramatic increase in controlled research evaluating the effects of drugs on anxiety and panic. These developments have been accompanied by the conveyence of large amounts of information through the media on the potential effectiveness of drugs for emotional disorders.

If drugs are effective, this public relations campaign is very important, because the public in general does not believe that drugs are useful or desirable in dealing with emotional disorders. Well-done surveys (e.g., Norton, Allen, & Hilton, 1983; Norton, Allen, & Walker, 1985) indicate that both the general public and agoraphobic patients rate pharmacological treatments as generally less acceptable and (potentially) less effective than alternative treatments.

Despite the explosion of research on drug treatments, results from clinical trials have only begun to appear during the past several years. Several early studies of imipramine, initiated in the mid-1970s, were rather methodologically primitive by current-day standards. However, these studies served an important purpose by stimulating the field; for this reason, some of these early studies are reviewed briefly. After more recent imipramine studies with methodological improvements are summarized, investigations of other drugs (particularly a very large and well-done study examining the effects of alprazolam on panic) are reviewed.

Imipramine

Early Studies

In 1972 Charlotte Zitrin, Donald Klein, and their colleagues began a major controlled outcome study comparing the effects of imipramine and behavior therapy with phobic patients. Eventually, 218 adult phobic patients completed treatment in one of three treatment conditions: behavior therapy plus imipramine, behavior therapy plus placebo, or supportive therapy and imipramine. As noted above, behavior therapy consisted largely of imaginal systematic desensitization. Patients were classified as either agoraphobics, simple phobics, or a category termed "mixed phobics." In the "mixed" category, patients reported experiencing at least "one spontaneous panic" during the course of their disorder, although they did not otherwise meet the DSM-III criteria for panic disorder or agoraphobia with panic. This distinction was important to the investigators, in view of their hypothesis regarding the effects of imipramine on "spontaneous" panic.

The final report on this project did not appear until 1983, attesting to the enormous scope and complexity of this study (Zitrin *et al.*, 1983), although an interim report had appeared in 1978 (Zitrin, Klein, & Woerner, 1978). The appearance of the interim article, as well as developments in the field during the late 1970s, sensitized these investigators to the belief prevalent at the time that imaginal desensitization was considerably less effective for agoraphobia than direct *in vivo* exposure. For this reason, they conducted a similar yet smaller study directly comparing *in vivo* exposure with or without imipramine to appropriate placebo control conditions (Zitrin *et al.*, 1980).

The results were essentially the same in both studies. Using therapists' ratings of overall clinical improvement as a representative measure, the addition of imipramine to exposure-based treatments, whether imaginal or *in vivo*, resulted in a somewhat higher percentage of patients improving to a "marked or moderate" degree in these ratings. In the Zitrin *et al.* (1983) study, 84% of those who completed treatment improved to a marked or moderate degree with imipramine plus imaginal exposure, compared to 70% with imaginal exposure plus placebo. Similarly, in the Zitrin *et al.* (1980) study, 93% of those completing treatment receiving exposure *in vivo* plus imipramine improved to a marked or moderate extent, compared to 72% of those receiving *in vivo* exposure alone.

These results are important for several reasons. First, the 70% improvement rate from exposure-based treatments essentially replicates the improvement rates from numerous applications of this treatment reviewed above. Second, adding imipramine to exposure seemed to confer an additional benefit by increasing the percentage of success somewhat. These studies are discussed in more detail below.

Since Zitrin and colleagues failed to find any additive benefit of imipramine in simple phobics, they concluded that the drug effects (compared to the effects of exposure alone) were specific to those patients experiencing "spontaneous" panic, and hypothesized that the drugs acted directly on the panic attacks. In fact, as reviewed in Chapter 3, the evidence for this is very weak. These effects were apparent only for some ratings of panic and not others. In addition, levels of statistical significance were set unconventionally low ($p < .10$). If these had been set at the more conventional .05 level, it is possible that even for those measures of panic where results seemed apparent, statistical significance would have disappeared. Furthermore, overall statistical analysis revealed no differential effect *on panic attacks* between patients with spontaneous panic (agoraphobics and mixed phobics) and simple phobics. Thus, we have the first hint that the beneficial effects of adding imipramine to exposure may *not* be due to a direct blockade of panic over and above that achieved by exposure.

Despite the marked lack of clarity concerning the direct effects of drugs on panic in this study, the major impact clearly concerns the benefit of adding imipramine to exposure treatments. These studies have been roundly and soundly criticized many times (e.g., Emmelkamp, 1982; Telch, Tearnan, & Taylor, 1983) on methodological grounds, and rightly so. The primary reason is that these studies share the problems of pioneering studies in any field. With the hindsight of a decade of experience, the measures and methodologies chosen left much to be desired. Thus, there is little question that these studies are more interesting for their historical contribution rather than for substantive value at this point in time. Among the understandable methodological weaknesses is what the authors themselves would now consider to be an unacceptable measure of panic. For example, patients were simply asked to give an estimate of frequency and severity of panic attacks during the last month, they were also asked to compare these estimates with experiences of the previous month. In view of the distortion inherent in recall even during the past week, as discussed in Chapter 10, the validity of these data is very questionable. Nevertheless, the number of subjects treated, the wealth of data collected, and the hard-nosed empirical approach to a problem that had not enjoyed this attention before all contributed to the enormous impact of this study in promoting a new generation of research on the effects of drugs and drug–behavioral interactions in the treatment of panic and anxiety.

In the context of research on drug treatments, several questions have been pursued since the Zitrin et al. studies. First, can their results be replicated? Second, if imipramine is effective, particularly in contributing to the effects of exposure-based treatments, why is it effective? That is, what is its mechanism of action? Third, may other drugs also be effective, and if so, why? Finally, are there any specific problems associated with the use of drugs in the treatment of anxiety disorders? I address each of these questions in turn.

Recent Studies

Several well-done studies have essentially replicated the aims of the Zitrin et al. studies, with mixed results. In one well-controlled study by Issac Marks and his colleagues (Marks et al., 1983), agoraphobics were treated in a 2 × 2 factorial design in which imipramine and therapist-assisted exposure were analyzed singly and in combination. All four groups also had the advantage of receiving a manual with structured self-exposure homework assignments. Generally, the results immediately after treatment, as well as at 1- and 2-year follow-ups (Cohen et al., 1984), revealed no differences whatsoever among the four treatments. Thus, there was no advantage in this initial analysis for adding imipramine to exposure as compared to placebo, even immediately after treatment. Since these results were so strikingly different from those reported in the Zitrin et al. studies, they attracted a great deal of attention. In fact, Raskin, Marks, and Sheehan (1983) carefully analyzed the data and did find that imipramine contributed to the effects of exposure over and above placebo on a number of outcome measures. But, again, these differences had disappeared by follow-up.

The other well-done study examining the effects of adding imipramine to exposure was also carried out in a 2 × 2 factorial design by Mavissakalian and Michelson (1986a, 1986b). This study was very similar to that of Marks et al. (1983), in that all four groups also received systematic instructions on self-directed exposure between sessions. As in the Marks *et al.* study, all four groups demonstrated substantial improvement; however, in this study an imipramine effect was evident on several outcome measures immediately after treatment. Patients in this study were also followed for 2 years. Once again, any pretreatment advantage to adding imipramine to exposure-based treatments at posttreatment disappeared within 1 month of treatment termination.

Several additional issues concerning these studies are worth noting at this time. In both the Marks *et al.* (1983) and the Mavissakalian and Michelson (1986b) studies, therapist-assisted exposure provided little if any advantage at follow-up over self-paced graduated exposure guided by detailed instructions. This finding replicates, in the context of drug interaction studies, the conclusion reached above regarding the optimal means of delivering exposure-based treatments. That is, less intense, self-paced exposure is at least as effective as exposure delivered more intensively. Second, the Marks *et al.* (1983) study, which attracted so much attention, was criticized for administering relatively low doses of imipramine. Indeed, Mavissakalian and Perel (1985) did find a relationship between dose of imipramine and the effects of treatment, suggesting that optimal responses may require doses of 150 mg per day or more. Furthermore, the relationship of drug to treatment response was not limited to total dosage, but was also correlated with plasma tricyclic concentrations, as ascertained in a small group of patients (Mavissakalian *et al.*, 1984).

But one fascinating finding from this series of analyses stands out. There was no relationship whatsoever between drug dosage or plasma concentrations of drug and panic! That is, panic responded equally well to all treatments in both the Marks *et al.* study and the Mavissakalian and Michelson study. Drug relationships were found only for global response to treatment, and then only at posttreatment.

Since the failure to find differential reductions in panic as a function of a treatment designed to reduce panic is an interesting and potentially important issue from a theoretical point of view, most investigators have agreed that it deserves further investigation. The studies mentioned above have all confounded the administration of imipramine with exposure-based treatments, which might somehow mask the antipanic effects of the drug. One reason for this, as mentioned above, is that exposure-based treatments alone seem to have antipanic effects. Therefore, several studies have begun to examine the effectiveness of imipramine without exposure. The difficulty here is that there are many ways of arranging for exposure not to occur. One way is simply to administer the drug without any formal instructions to enter feared situations systematically (e.g., Garakani, Zitrin, & Klein, 1984). This would be the most clinically realistic way of exploring the effects of a drug, since drugs are often administered this way in clinical settings. But a common clinical observation is that patients will begin entering feared situations on their own to "test" themselves, either because the drug is working or because the demands implicit in a phobia clinic require this type of activity (Klein *et al.*, 1983). Thus, to examine more clearly the mechanisms of action of imipramine, it is necessary to prevent self-initiated exposure temporarily.

Studies along both of these lines have now appeared. For example, Mavissakalian, Michelson, and Dealy (1983) compared imipramine plus self-directed exposure homework to imipramine alone in a small group of agoraphobics. Imipramine plus exposure was clearly superior in terms of both overall global response and reductions of panic. Some reductions in panic with imipramine alone were observed; even these subjects probably engaged in some self-initiated exposure. Also, there was no placebo group to ascertain the source of the reductions in panic.

One study has examined the theoretically interesting question of temporarily preventing exposure during the administration of imipramine. Telch *et al.* (1985), in a study mentioned briefly earlier, administered imipramine alone with antiexposure instructions for the first 8 weeks of treatment. That is, subjects were simply administered the drug but told not to confront feared situations until blood levels of the drug were sufficient to exert a therapeutic effect. The other two groups both received intensive *in vivo* exposure with imipramine or with placebo. The results indicated that after 8 weeks patients receiving imipramine with antiexposure instructions showed little or no improvement on panic attacks, phobic avoidance, or anxiety, although they did show a reduction in depressed mood. Patients in exposure conditions with or without imipramine displayed marked improvements on these measures. But in a finding reminiscent of the Zitrin *et al.* studies, as well as the Mavissakalian studies, imipramine did seem to potentiate *in vivo* exposure by the time treatment was over, compared to the effects of exposure alone.

The methodological difficulties inherent in these complex studies will probably insure inconsistency for the short term. However, it seems doubtful at this point that imipramine is effective for the reasons most clinicians would assume. That is, there is little or no evidence from these studies that imipramine directly and differentially reduces panic, followed by a reduction in avoidance behavior.

Mechanisms of Action

If imipramine does potentiate exposure-based treatment but does not directly affect panic, then how does it achieve its effects? In 1983, Marks formally suggested an idea that many had suspected all along. He surmised that when tricyclics or other antidepressants were effective with agoraphobics, it was only with agoraphobics who were depressed. In other words, the drugs did not affect anxiety or panic per se; rather, the effects were indirect results of the alleviation of depression.

Marks's retrospective survey of past studies provided some support for the contention that agoraphobics with higher levels of depression responded more favorably to drugs. However, more direct examination of evidence from more recent studies does not fully support this interpretation. For example, Mavissakalian and Michelson (1986a) excluded patients with major depression and did not find higher initial depression levels predictive of outcome in their remaining patients. In a subsequent study, Mavissakalian (1987) demonstrated no effect of depression on response to imipramine in a group of 37 agoraphobics. Telch *et al.* (1985) found that patients receiving imipramine with antiexposure instructions improved significantly on measures of depressed mood, without any concomitant changes in central measures of agoraphobia.

If there is no direct relationship between changes in depression and phobic behavior, perhaps there is an indirect relationship between the effects of imipramine and improvement. Telch and his colleagues (Telch, 1988; Telch *et al.*, 1983, 1985) have proposed what they call the "dysphoria–efficacy hypothesis," which is really an extension of self-efficacy theory (referred to in Chapter 8). The first possibility is straightforward: Elevations of mood caused by imipramine (and other antidepressants) may increase the likelihood that agoraphobics will engage in self-directed exposure, either between sessions or after termination of therapy. The increasing evidence that self-initiated exposure between sessions is an important component of treatment (Michelson *et al.*, 1986) has been reviewed above. Anything that facilitates this type of practice is probably useful. Clinicians have long observed that patients will attribute lack of motivation to practice to mild bouts of depression or dysphoria occurring during exposure-based treatments.

But Telch and colleagues propose a second, potentially more interesting, effect that relates to the theory of anxiety reduction outlined in Chapter 8. Relying on self-efficacy theory, they suggest that performance accomplishments during actual practice sessions may not be judged as positively if a patient is mildly depressed or dysphoric than if a patient's mood is normal. Citing evidence that elevating mood raises perceived self-efficacy, Telch *et al.* suggest that patients may judge themselves as more efficacious after successful exposure-based practice sessions if they are not dysphoric or depressed. In other words, the dysphoria–efficacy hypothesis suggests that even mildly depressed mood prevents optimal increases in self-efficacy during treatment, either by reducing the number of self-initiated exposure practice sessions or by altering self-evaluative judgments of one's success (efficacy) during the practice sessions. This would be quite different from ascertaining clinical levels of depression as predictors of outcome. Almost all agoraphobics are somewhat demoralized by their condition, but only (approximately) 40% are clinically depressed (Barlow, Di Nardo, *et al.*, 1986).

In support of his position, Telch *et al.* (1985) reported that estimates of self-efficacy correlated very well with therapeutic changes. That is, exposure plus imipramine produced greater changes in self-efficacy than did exposure plus placebo. Little or no change in judgments of self-efficacy was noted in the imipramine-only condition. This is reminiscent of the Williams *et al.* (1984) study reviewed in Chapter 8, where similar correlations were found with variations of exposure treatments.

The thrust of this argument is that the effects of imipramine are restricted to potentiating the effects of exposure, and the evidence thus far would seem to support this interpretation. Both treatment components in turn are effective inasmuch as they increase judgments of perceived self-efficacy. Some of the difficulties with self-efficacy theory have been outlined in Chapter 8, including its restriction to actual judgments of anticipated performance capabilities. To test the dysphoria–efficacy hypothesis, one must examine the mediating effect of changes in dysphoria on central measures of panic, anxiety, and avoidance. Since alleviation of clinical levels of depression does not seem responsible for treatment effects, it may be difficult to tease out the more subtle and vague concept of dysphoric mood. One must also insure that changes in dysphoria do not just constitute another correlate of changes in self-efficacy (as well as overall improvement in phobic behavior), but are causally related to self-efficacy in some way.

Yet another possibility seems more likely, in my view. Imipramine may contribute to exposure-based procedures by directly reducing anxious apprehension (rather than panic). Thus, the somatic sensations associated with anxiety that seem to serve as cues for panic would decrease, as well as levels of anxious self-preoccupation (self-focused attention). A sense of control would increase. Panic attacks would then decrease because the platform of anxious apprehension from which panic attacks emerge would be removed (see Chapter 5).

Solid evidence for the anxiolytic effects of imipramine are now beginning to appear (R. J. Kahn *et al.*, 1986). In this study, imipramine produced substantial anxiolytic effects that were superior to those of a standard benzodiazepine on most measures. Furthermore, this effect was observed despite the exclusion of patients with clear panic and phobic components to their anxiety. Although the self-report measures utilized are subject to confounds involving overlap with measures of depression (as mentioned in Chapter 2), clinicians' and patients' ratings would seem to confirm the anxiolytic effect of imipramine pending further replication.

In addition, some evidence now exists that drugs for panic disorder do not block naturally occurring alarms or fear. In one study, patients reported that "alarming" events such as near-accidents in automobiles provoked the same response as they did when the patients were not on drugs (Nesse, Cameron, Curtis, & Lee, 1986). To return to self-efficacy for a moment, if the concept of self-efficacy is altered to include perceptions of abilities to control future unpredictable negative events of any kind, it comes extremely close to what I have proposed as one of the three essential components of affective therapy. It may be that correlated changes in self-efficacy are simply reflecting the anxiolytic effects of imipramine. It is the development of this sense of control, along with changes in action tendencies and alterations in focus of attention, that may ultimately be the target of all drug and behavioral treatments. All drug and behavioral treatments may be effective only to the extent that they reduce anxiety or anxious apprehension.

Alternative Drug Treatments

Additional Antidepressants

While imipramine has received the most attention from a scientific point of view, a number of other drugs have been tested in clinical trials with panic disorder and agoraphobia. Primary among these are other antidepressants, beta-blockers such as propranolol, and various benzodiazepines. The drug receiving the most attention has been the monoamine oxidase (MAO) inhibitor phenelzine (Buigues & Vallejo, 1987; Lipsedge et al., 1973; Mountjoy, Roth, Garside, & Leitch, 1977; Sheehan et al., 1980; Solyom et al., 1973; Tyrer, Candy, & Kelley, 1973). Results from studies with this drug look very much like the results with imipramine, although there are fewer and less sophisticated experiments available. Essentially, although some studies have found no contribution of phenelzine to exposure-based treatments (Solyom et al., 1981), others have found that phenelzine seems to potentiate self-initiated exposure (e.g., Sheehan et al., 1980). Clomipramine, a close relative of imipramine, has also been used on occasion for agoraphobics (Beaumont, 1977), but firm experimental tests have been undertaken only with obsessive–compulsives. Therefore, examination of the effectiveness of this drug is taken up in Chapter 16. Recent evidence also suggests that trazodane, with a primarily serotonergic mechanism of action, may be effective in panic disorder (Mavissakalian, Perel, Bowler, & Dealy, 1987).

One of the more surprising turns of events in clinical psychopharmacology has been the lack of experimental attention accorded to two classes of drugs that, on the face of it, would seem particularly well suited for anxiety and panic attacks: the beta-blockers and the benzodiazepines. Beta-blockers such as propranolol act by blocking peripheral manifestations of cardiovascular activation, as described in Chapter 4. Benzodiazepines such as diazepam, on the other hand, are marketed as antianxiety drugs. In the case of benzodiazepines, shared clinical experience convinced many experts that these agents were ineffective for panic attacks, despite the extremely widespread patterns of use of this drug for panic and anxiety, as described in Chapter 1.

Benzodiazepines

On the basis of clinical experience, Klein, Zitrin, and their colleagues concluded that benzodiazepines were ineffective for panic. They suggested, however, that benzodiazepines might be effective for generalized or anticipatory anxiety. In Chapters 3 and 4, the flaws in this "pharmacological dissection" analysis have been highlighted. It now seems, according to the analyses presented above, that tricyclics may not exert their effects by blocking panics. It has even been suggested that tricyclics may be potent anxiolytics. But then why wouldn't benzodiazepines also be effective? Until recently, very little research has appeared on the potential usefulness of benzodiazepines with panic and agoraphobia (Marks, 1983). For example, three early studies combined benzodiazepines with exposure-based therapies (Hafner & Marks, 1976; Johnston & Gath, 1973; Marks, Viswanthan, & Lipsedge, 1972). In two studies slight temporary gains were observed, but in the only study to follow up these patients for a month, the gains dissipated. Similar results were reported by Chouinard, Annable, Fontaine, and Solyom (1982) with alprazolam.

In an important but widely overlooked study, Noyes *et al.* (1984) examined the effects of high doses of a benzodiazepine (diazepam) on patients meeting the DSM-III criteria for panic disorder and agoraphobia. Clinical ratings indicated that 18 out of 21 patients showed at least moderate improvement after 2 weeks of administration, at which time patients were crossed over into another experimental condition and began receiving propranolol (see below). What was remarkable about this study was that patients received a median daily dose of 30 mg of diazepam, far above what is normally prescribed. Ratings of moderate improvement were based on overall performance, including retrospective ratings by patients of frequency and severity of panic attacks during the past week. These retrospective ratings are, of course, far less desirable than diary measures described above. Nevertheless, 18 out of 21 patients were rated as at least moderately improved, and these ratings included what seemed to be substantial reductions in panic attacks. These results were far superior to those in the comparison condition, propranolol. This study provided the first indication that benzodiazepines might be effective for severe anxiety and panic, at least in the short term. Obviously, there were no follow-ups in this crossover design.

The major result of this study was the realization that benzodiazepines in high enough dosages might be effective in panic disorder. Concurrently, a new generation of high-potency benzodiazepines was developed and tested in open (uncontrolled) clinical trials with panic disorder—for example, clonazepam (e.g., Fontaine Chouinard, & Annable, 1984; Spier, Tesar, Rosenbaum, & Woods, 1986) and alprazolam. All reports suggest substantial benefit from these drugs for panic disorder. But the drug receiving by far the most attention is alprazolam.

Alprazolam (Xanax)

A number of studies have reported success with alprazolam in uncontrolled trials (e.g., Alexander & Alexander, 1986; Liebowitz, Fyer, et al., 1986). But this drug has received very wide publicity, making it one of the most frequently prescribed medications for panic. Much of this publicity is due to a comprehensive and interesting study coordinated by the Upjohn pharmaceutical company, called the Upjohn Cross-National Collaborative Panic Study (Ballenger et al., in press). In the first phase of the study, 500 carefully diagnosed patients with panic disorder were randomly assigned in a double-blind fashion to either alprazolam or placebo. Diagnoses were based on structured interviews and stringent exclusion criteria. This study, coordinated by a central committee, was administered at multiple sites around the world. In the second phase of the study, now under way, the alprazolam and placebo conditions are being repeated and a third condition, imipramine, has been added. The results of the first phase of the study have been presented widely and are now available (Ballenger et al., in press). Of the patients on alprazolam, 60% were panic-free after 8 weeks of treatment at levels up to 10 mg per day. This compares to 30% of the placebo group who were panic-free. Furthermore, this drug acts very quickly, often in a matter of days, and this provides enormous relief to patients. Dropout rates due to side effects also appeared manageable at approximately 12%.

Problems with high-potency benzodiazepines have become apparent in this and related studies, however. First, it is very difficult to remove patients from this drug because of strong withdrawal reactions. For example, Sheki and Patterson (1984) reported that only 2 out of 16 patients were able to discontinue alprazolam when asked. When patients are withdrawn more forcefully, they experience a recurrence of panic, including some attacks more intense than they had ever experienced previously. These are termed "rebound panics." Fyer et al. (1987) observed a return of panic (relapse) in 15 out of 17 patients who were withdrawn. Of these, 4 experienced rebound panics. Similar data have been reported from the Upjohn study, with close to 90% experiencing relapse after withdrawal and 30% suffering rebound panic. These percentages are nearly identical to those reported by Fyer et al. (1987). Fontaine et al. (1984) report that rebound panic (but not relapse) can be avoided by very slow withdrawal. Results from the first study comparing alprazolam with the new generation of psychological treatments targeting panic directly are presented below.

The primary indication for the benzodiazepines has been generalized anxiety rather than panic and agoraphobia. For that reason, far more evidence is available on the pattern of effects of these drugs with generalized anxiety disorder than with panic disorder. Numerous studies evaluating benzodiazepines for generalized anxiety disorder are summarized in Chapter 15.

Propranolol

On the basis of models of panic describing enhanced sensitivity to interoceptive or somatic cues, one would think that a beta-blocker such as propranolol might be useful. Some enthusiasm for beta-blockers was generated in a study by Tyrer (Tyrer, 1976; Tyrer & Lader, 1974), where it was suggested that propranolol might be effective for somatic aspects of anxiety, while benzodiazepines might be more effective for cognitive aspects. Nevertheless, the results have been extremely disappointing. For example, Hafner and Milton (1977) reported that adding propranolol to an *in vivo* exposure treatment produced significantly worse results than exposure with placebo. Similarly, Noyes *et al.* (1984) reported that only 7 out of 21 panic or agoraphobic patients receiving propranolol evidenced even moderate improvement, according to overall clinical ratings. In addition, propranolol appeared to have no influence on the retrospectively reported number and severity of panic attacks. On the other hand, the use of beta-blockers is receiving increased attention in the treatment of social phobia, where intense cardiovascular symptoms during performances of various sorts seem very disruptive to the patient. Thus, the use of these drugs is taken up again in Chapter 14.

If panic patients have developed an extreme sensitivity to various somatic symptoms, why wouldn't a beta-blocker be useful, at least in the short run? Several answers are possible. First, as Tyrer (1976) points out, beta-blockers selectively block only certain peripheral indices of arousal (mostly cardiovascular). Respiratory, muscular, or audiovestibular signs are relatively unaffected. In view of the prominence of respiratory cues, particularly in unexpected panics (see Chapter 3), these peripheral blocking actions may be incomplete. This information is fully consistent with the panic provocation studies reviewed in Chapter 4, where acute administration of beta-blocking agents had little or no effect on laboratory-provoked panic. Second, since beta-blockers do not seem to cross the blood–brain barrier, there is little chance for them to affect the hypothetical neurobiological basis of anxiety, which seems to play such an important role in panic disorder. Thus, by any estimation, the outlook for the use of beta-blockers in the treatment of panic is bleak.

Limitations of Drug Treatment

With the exception of the beta-blockers, the emerging question in the drug treatment of panic disorder and agoraphobia is this: Which drugs are *not* effective? Any number of antidepressant and anxiolytic drugs at appropriate dosages seem effective initially. There is no reason to believe at this time that any of these drugs will be differentially effective on the whole when proper comparisons are made, although an individual patient may always respond differently to one or another drug. The major difference is that high-potency benzodiazepines will act very quickly, often in several days, while antidepressants may take several weeks. But it is important to review some difficulties that have emerged from these studies in regard to the treatment of panic disorder. Generally, five different problems can arise in the course of pharmacological treatment: side effects, dropouts, relapse, long-term dependence, and potential interference with the effects of nondrug treatments. Some of these issues are more important than others and certainly must be considered if we are to devise truly comprehensive treatments in the future.

Side Effects, Dropouts, and Relapse

Some data are now available on the issue of dropouts and relapse with antidepressants, particularly tricyclics, and benzodiazepines. The group of drugs with by far the fewest problems in this area are the tricyclics, although difficulties have also been encountered with these drugs (Marks et al., 1983; Telch et al., 1983). For example, Tables 11.3 and 11.4 present

TABLE 11.3. Therapist Ratings of Improvement after *In Vivo* Exposure plus Placebo or Imipramine

	In vivo exposure + placebo	*In vivo* exposure + imipramine
n	35	41
Improved: Marked or moderate	18/25 = 72%	27/29 = 93%
Dropouts	10 = 29%	12 = 29%
Relapses	1 = 6%	7 = 29%
Total improved	17/35 = 49%	20/41 = 49%

Note. From Zitrin, C. M., Klein, D. F., & Woerner, M. G. (1980). Treatment of agoraphobia with group exposure in vivo and imipramine. *Archives of General Psychiatry, 37*, 63–72. Copyright 1980 by the American Medical Association. Reprinted by permission.

TABLE 11.4. Therapist Ratings of Improvement after Imaginal
Exposure plus Placebo or Imipramine

	Imaginal exposure + placebo	Imaginal exposure + imipramine
n	24	23
Improved: Marked or moderate	15/21 = 70%	15/18 = 84%
Dropouts	3 = 12.5%	5 = 22%
Relapses	2 = 14%	3 = 19%
Total improved	13/24 = 54%	12/23 = 52%

Note. From Zitrin, C. M., Klein, D. F., Woerner, M. G., & Ross, D. C. (1983). Treatment of phobias: I. Comparison of imipramine hydrochloride and placebo. Archives of General Psychiatry, 40, 125–138. Copyright 1983 by the American Medical Association. Reprinted by permission.

data derived from the two major studies by Zitrin and Klein and their colleagues (Zitrin et al., 1980, 1983). The data in each table are abstracted from just two groups, exposure plus placebo and exposure plus imipramine. Here one can see, once again, the differences in the percentage of patients who were marked or moderately improved at posttest. For example, in the Zitrin et al. (1980) study 35 patients began the exposure plus placebo treatment, while 41 began the exposure plus imipramine. Of 25 who finished treatment, 18, or 72%, demonstrated marked or moderate improvement on therapists' ratings in the exposure group, while fully 27 out of 29 who finished treatment, or 93%, demonstrated a similar rate of improvement in the exposure plus imipramine group.

When one considers dropouts and relapses in terms of percentage improved, the picture changes considerably. Fully 29% dropped out of both groups in the Zitrin et al. (1980) study. One must remember that the in vivo exposure treatment here was the intense group exposure variety lasting several hours a day, which consistently produces high dropout rates (see above). But at a follow-up period, 29% of those taking imipramine had relapsed versus only 6% (1 patient) in the exposure group. While Zitrin et al. (1980) note that the difference between relapses is not statistically significant, the more proper comparison is to examine the percentage of improvement of those who started treatment at the follow-up point. When this is done, the percentages of success in both groups in the Zitrin et al. (1980) study are almost identical.

In contrast to the high dropout rates in the exposure plus placebo condition of the Zitrin et al. (1980) study, results from numerous exposure-based studies reviewed above suggest that very few patients drop out (fewer than 10% if the treatment is self-initiated and self-paced), and that improvement on the whole remains stable or continues at various follow-up periods ranging from 4 to 10 years.

Thus, the dropout rate with antidepressant medications in panic disorders is a concern. In the Marks *et al.* (1983) study, fully 38% of the patients on imipramine dropped out; dropout rates in the Sheehan *et al.* (1980) study of MAO inhibitors were even higher. Most of these dropouts are due to side effects of the medications. In the case of imipramine, these include anticholinergic side effects (such as dry mouth, agitation, and constipation), as well as amphetamine-like effects (such as irritability, insomnia, and jitteriness). In the case of MAO inhibitors, not only are the side effects more severe, but the patient must adhere to strict dietary prescriptions involving a wide range of foods. The major difficulty here, of course, is that many of these symptoms mimic anxiety symptoms, which are so disconcerting to the patient to begin with.

It seems possible that with very careful management and close clinical attention, the problem with dropouts might be minimized. For example, Mavissakalian and his colleagues are one of the few groups to report manageable dropout rates from imipramine of approximately 25% (Mavissakalian & Michelson, 1986a). But they put considerable effort into keeping people in treatment. For example, they take frequent calls to the clinic during the first week and go to some length to persuade the patients to stay on "at least one pill until the next session." They note that for a subset of patients it takes a great deal of negotiation, sometimes to no avail, to increase the dose by even one tablet (Mavissakalian & Perel, 1985). Mavissakalian and Perel raise another important issue, which arises even if patients are effectively managed and kept in treatment. They report that in their study the side effects of imipramine prevented optimal dose administration in 13 (43%) of 30 motivated and compliant patients.

These findings raise an interesting issue in regard to those patients who survive the anxiety-mimicking side effects of imipramine in order to reach a therapeutic dose. Neurobiological hypotheses regarding the anxiety-reducing properties of imipramine have been mentioned in Chapter 5. Another possibility is that the side effects of imipramine provide a convenient and continuous period of anxiety to the very somatic symptoms to which these patients are so sensitive. For those who endure the side effects and learn to manage them effectively, any naturally occurring anxiety is by contrast less severe, since some desensitization to the somatic symptoms has occurred. But this interpretation is weakened by the high relapse rate after withdrawal from imipramine. If subjects learn to manage and be less afraid of somatic symptoms associated with both anxiety and imipramine, this learning should continue past the point of removal of medications. In fact, the relapse rate in studies of antidepressants for panic ranges from 27% to 50% (Telch *et al.*, 1983). This issue is discussed again below.

A final concern revolves around the actual process of withdrawal from drugs. This issues has arisen primarily in the context of benzodiazepine treatment rather than treatment with antidepressant drugs, as noted above. Well-known consequences of chronic benzodiazepine use are decreasing effectiveness, increasing tolerance, and ultimately psychological and physical dependence. These issues have raised serious questions in the minds of many physicians concerning the long-term efficacy and safety of these drugs (Lader, 1985; Laughren, Battey, & Greenblatt, 1982; Noyes *et al.*, 1984; Petursson & Lader, 1981; Tyrer, Rutherford, & Huggett, 1981). For this reason, the long-term administration of benzodiazepines in anxiety disorders, which are known for their chronicity, is often discouraged. Basically, symptoms of withdrawal from benzodiazepines mimic anxiety (and may well be anxiety neurobiologically), much as side effects of antidepressants mimic anxiety upon initial administration. This issue becomes more salient with extremely high doses of diazepam, such as those prescribed in the Noyes *et al.* (1984) study. It also seems to be an issue at relatively low dosages (Mellman & Uhde, 1986). Data from attempts to withdraw patients from the high-potency benzodiazepines, reviewed above, seem to illustrate the problem at its worst. The development of a new nonbenzodiazepine anxiolytic, buspirone, may address some of these problems (Eison & Temple, 1986). This drug is associated with fewer side effects and does not seem to be addicting. But it may not be powerful enough to alleviate panic.

Interference with Nondrug Treatments

One concern raised periodically in the literature is that drugs and psychosocial treatments may interact adversely to produce either less responding than would occur from exposure-based treatments alone, or higher rates of relapse. The arguments are most often based on theories of state-dependent learning or attributions. The concept of "state-dependent learning" is the notion that anything learned while on a drug will not transfer to a nondrug state. Therefore, any anxiety reduction based on learning while on a drug may disappear when the drug is withdrawn, causing relapse (e.g., Overton, 1977). This is a complex and sophisticated question that is difficult to address in the clinical area. Nevertheless, there is increasing evidence (as reviewed in Chapters 2 and 7) that learning and memory may be mood-dependent, and these concepts may have increasing relevance to clinical work in years to come.

The more common objection is that patients may attribute any therapeutic gains to medications rather than to their own personal efforts. Thus, when drugs are withdrawn the patient may expect therapeutic gains to disappear also, as suggested by Zitrin (1981). This certainly seems to happen clinically, although no firm data support this phenomenon in studies of panic and agoraphobia. Furthermore, this attributional problem, if it exists, may not be limited to drugs. As we have seen above, similar attributions may be made concerning the presence of a therapist or phobia aide; these attributions may limit further improvement, at least after the end of therapy. In view of the seeming potentiating effect of imipramine and perhaps other antidepressants to exposure in the short term, there is little evidence that these drugs interfere with the actual process of treatment. However, either one or both explanations, in addition to any biochemical explanations, may account for the high rates of relapse.

Finally, evidence reviewed in Chapter 8 raises potentially more important questions about the compatibility of psychological and pharmacological treatments, specifically in regard to the use of benzodiazepines. In animal laboratories, the process of exposure to feared situations results in the biological process of "toughening up," which basically seems to involve a desensitization of the noradrenergic neurotransmitter system. Benzodiazepines interfere with this process. This may account for the extraordinary high relapse rate and the phenomenon of rebound panics after withdrawal of benzodiazepines. Tricyclic antidepressants, on the other hand, may work more synergistically with exposure therapies, at least in the short term. Specifically, tricyclics may facilitate the same desensitization of monoaminergic systems as happens during the "toughening-up" process.

For this reason, the treatment recommendations for panic and agoraphobia at our clinic *do not* include a recommendation for benzodiazepines unless withdrawal is carefully planned and occurs early in the treatment program. If drug treatment regimens are chosen, tricyclics seem preferable at this point in time.

Summary of Drug Treatments

In summary, the best evidence indicates that antidepressants, particularly tricyclics such as imipramine, confer an advantage on exposure-based treatments for panic disorder and agoraphobia. The effects are generally anxiolytic rather than specifically panicogenic. Dropout rates are high because of anticholinergic side effects during the first few weeks of treatment. Relapse rates after withdrawal are problematic but far better than for high-potency benzodiazepines.

High-potency benzodiazepines reduce anxiety and panic quickly in many patients, usually within the first week. It is not clear whether these drugs affect panic directly or only indirectly through generally anxiolytic action. On the basis of neurobiological evidence reviewed in Chapter 5, a generally anxiolytic effect is the best bet. Dropout rates due to side effects are manageable, but these drugs are strongly addictive; therefore, it is very difficult to remove patients from them. In those patients who are withdrawn, relapse approaches 100%. Cognitive and motor impairment while on these drugs, affecting routine behavior such as driving, is also becoming a concern (see Chapter 15).

Nevertheless, we are still in the early stages of evaluating the effectiveness of these potentially valuable therapeutic agents, particularly in combination with new nondrug treatments for panic disorder.

PSYCHOLOGICAL TREATMENT

During the past several years, we may have discovered something unprecedented in the annals of psychotherapy research. Preliminary evidence from a number of centers around the world suggests that we can eliminate panic. Of course, the exposure-based treatments for agoraphobia mentioned above eliminate panic in some cases. Drugs also seem to eliminate panic as long as the patients remain on the drug in the majority of cases; for example, 60% of patients receiving alprazolam in the Upjohn study were panic-free just after treatment. But with specifically targeted psychological treatments, panic is eliminated in close to 100% of all cases, and these results are maintained at follow-ups of over 1 year. If these results are confirmed by additional research and replication, it will be one of the most important and exciting developments in the history of psychotherapy.

Unfortunately, we cannot yet conclude that these results have been confirmed; the data are still very preliminary, consisting mostly of clinical series of patients treated with appropriate controls or comparisons. Early uncontrolled clinical series evaluating any new treatment often yield similar results. All too frequently, the optimism engendered by these early findings turns to disappointment when proper controlled comparisons are carried out. For we have learned one important lesson in the development of successful treatments for the variety of human afflictions: Nothing can substitute for the slow, inexorable process of science.

Background

At the heart of the psychological treatment of panic are reproduction of and exposure to the somatic symptoms of panic. The reproduction–exposure process has been accomplished in a variety of different ways, accompanied by different explanations for its effectiveness. Nevertheless, all psychological treatments for panic with any demonstratable success have this process as a core ingredient.

As with all new discoveries, some interesting early examples of this approach were either misinterpreted or ignored. In Wolpe's classic early work, CO_2 inhalations were a common but largely overlooked component of his anxiety reduction procedures. Generally, inhaling CO_2 was conceptualized as facilitating relaxation, and therefore promoting the reciprocal inhibition of anxiety. In fact, this may have been a very effective procedure for systematically exposing panic-ridden patients to their feared cues in the benign setting of the therapist's office (Wolpe, 1958). Other early reports can also be interpreted in this sense. Orwin (1973) treated eight agoraphobics with "the running treatment." In his procedure, patients were instructed to sprint until breathless and then to approach or enter a feared situation. Running, of course, produced many of the somatic signs of panic, resulting in systematic exposure to these cues. This recalls some of the early panic provocation work using exercise (e.g., Cohen & White, 1950; see Chapter 4). Watson and Marks (1971), in a study with agoraphobics cited earlier, reported the then-puzzling finding that imaginal flooding to relevant phobic cues (imagining an intensely vivid scene depicting phobic cues) was no more effective than irrelevant flooding (visualizing being eaten by tigers). In fact, irrelevant flooding produced significantly greater therapeutic effects on patients' subjective anxiety while imagining a phobic scene! This is understandable if one considers that arousal cues produced by irrelevant flooding *are* the primary phobic cues.

One of the most interesting early reports along these lines was that of Bonn *et al.* (1971). Following up on the origins of provoking panic in the laboratory using lactate (see Chapter 4), Bonn *et al.* carried this procedure to its logical conclusion from the point of view of treatment by administering it repeatedly to 33 patients. While panic was not directly measured, this procedure seemed quite successful. Interestingly, this result was totally ignored. In another early series, Haslam (1974) treated 16 subjects, 10 of whom panicked following a sodium lactate challenge with repeated CO_2 inhalation. Of the 10 patients who panicked with lactate, 9 demonstrated marked improvement after 6 weeks of CO_2 inhalation treatment. Other early case reports or clinical series by Latimer (1977) and Lum (1976) reported on diverse procedures such as CO_2 inhalation or voluntary hyperventilation, which seemed to result in substantial improvement in cases of what we would now call panic disorder.

Theories of Treatment

Generally, three explanations are offered for the success of these clinical trials (e.g., Rapee, 1987). One tradition, espoused by Lum (1976) and Ley (1985), attributes panic to the effects of chronic hyperventilation. The biological basis of this hypothesis has been discussed in Chapters 4 and 5. Treatment then involves breathing retraining, such that hyperventilatory episodes are precluded (e.g., Kraft & Hooguin, 1984).

A second school of thought focuses on the catastrophic misinterpretations of otherwise normal somatic events as the cause of panic. Treatment then involves the correction of these cognitive distortions (e.g., Beck & Emery, 1985). Several investigations have combined these rationales. For example, Clark *et al.* (1985), Salkovskis, Jones, and Clark (1986), and

Rapee (1985a) used voluntary room-air hyperventilation and subsequent breathing retraining to educate their patients on more proper attributions for their somatic symptoms. These investigators all emphasize cognitive reattribution, but also suspect, much as do Lum (1976) and Ley (1985), that a vulnerability to hyperventilation exists in these patients. This vulnerability would be reflected in low resting pCO_2 measures.

In a preliminary report recalling the early work of Mendel Cohen (e.g., Cohen & White, 1950), Salkovskis and his colleagues (Salkovskis, Jones, & Clark, 1984; Salkovskis et al., 1986) replicated the finding that panic patients presented with low resting pCO_2. In an interesting twist, they observed that pCO_2 levels rose to within the normal range after successful treatment. Future efforts must be directed at determining whether changes in pCO_2 levels are specifically due to changes in breathing retraining or are simply a consequence of any successful panic reduction procedure. Similarly, it will be important to determine, as noted in Chapter 5, whether the often-observed low pCO_2 levels imply something specific about the nature of panic or comprise just another one of many biological markers of chronic overarousal associated with anxiety.

Finally, pure exposure to somatic cues, occasioned by any number of provocation procedures (hyperventilation, CO_2 inhalation, lactate infusion, etc.), has been advocated as the important component for treatment for all of the reasons discussed in Chapter 8.

At the present time it is difficult to untangle different explanations for the success of treatment, since all case studies and clinical replication series advocating one or the other of these approaches have typically included all three components. For example, clinicians emphasizing exposure to either CO_2 inhalation sensations or room-air hyperventilation also employ cognitive procedures in which patients are educated about the source of their somatic symptoms (Clark et al., 1985; Griez & van den Hout, 1983, 1986). Typically, current treatment protocols quite purposely include a combination of breathing retraining, cognitive therapy, and interoceptive exposure (e.g., Barlow, Cohen, et al., 1984). At this early state in the development of psychological treatments for panic, investigators have not yet begun to dismantle the treatment package in an attempt to identify the essential components. Therefore, I assume for the moment that various treatment approaches mentioned below are very similar in their operations.

Controlled Studies

Because of the recovery of this emerging conceptualization of the psychological treatment of panic, controlled studies are only beginning to appear. In an early study at our center, we treated patients with panic disorder, as well as patients with generalized anxiety disorder, with a broad-based treatment approach including all of the components listed above.

When compared to a waiting-list control group, treated patients demonstrated significant improvement on all measures (Barlow, Cohen, et al., 1984). More importantly, these treatment gains were maintained and even strengthened during a follow-up period averaging a year. Several other early studies also suggest an advantage for this approach. For example, Bonn, Readhead, and Timmons (1984) added a respiratory control training procedure to a standard in vivo exposure treatment for a group of agoraphobics. This approach was compared to the standard in vivo exposure treatment alone. While few differences emerged at posttest, the small group of individuals receiving respiratory control training were significantly better at a 6-month follow-up.

In a clinical replication series with a similar goal, we treated 32 patients with panic disorder either with ($n = 16$) or without ($n = 16$) agoraphobia (Klosko & Barlow, 1987). While this was not a controlled study, both groups of patients received nearly identical treatments, with the following exception: The patients with panic disorder without agoraphobia received systematic exposure to interoceptive cues. The patients with agoraphobia, on the other hand, received more standard exposure-based treatments to external situations. Up-to-date diary measures of panic episodes revealed some interesting differences between the two groups in terms of reductions in panic. Of the agoraphobics, 40% were panic-free after treatment, which is consistent with results on the elimination of panic from other studies of exposure-based treatments for agoraphobia. But fully 80% of the patients with panic disorder were free of panic after treatment. These data suggest that directly attacking panic by exposure to and reinterpretation of internal somatic cues may be a crucial factor in treatment.

Finally, Griez and van den Hout (1986), following up their earlier work, carried out a crossover comparison in 14 patients where CO_2 inhalation was compared with a beta-blocker, propranolol. Both treatments were administered for the very brief period of 2 weeks, and were separated by a 2-week intermission. Perhaps because of this brevity, no significant differences in reduction of panic attacks were apparent. CO_2 inhalations reduced panic by approximately 50%, while propranolol produced a 38% reduction. However, even in this brief 2-week period, systematic CO_2 inhalations almost eliminated the fear of having another panic attack. Reductions in this measure were significant when compared to reductions on propranolol. Therefore, it is possible that panic attacks themselves would have been eliminated if treatments were extended, in view of the elimination of anxiety about panic.

The Albany Study

Now we have preliminary results from one large controlled trial on the psychological treatment of panic that has been ongoing in our center since

1983. This study has been restricted to patients suffering from panic disorder without the complication of substantial avoidance behavior. In other words, individuals with agoraphobia have been excluded. Thus, the focus is very clearly on assessing and treating panic.

At the heart of our treatment program is systematic structured exposure to feared internal sensations. At the outset, patterns of fear are assessed by having patients engage in a variety of exercises designed to produce different physiological symptoms. To activate cardiovascular symptoms, we use exercise. For respiratory symptoms, we induce voluntary hyperventilation. For audiovestibular symptoms, we induce dizziness. Tension in the chest, which so often signifies an impending heart attack for a panic patient, is produced by tightening of the intercostal muscles. When feared patterns or combinations of patterns are identified, these become targets for treatment. Exposure to these cues occurs via visualization as well as symptom induction within the clinic, and subsequently during assigned exposure tasks (e.g., running up a flight of stairs, engaging in vigorous exercise, entering a sauna, etc.). We place strong emphasis upon between-session practice in order to have patients consolidate and generalize what is learned in the sessions themselves.

After careful screening via the ADIS, patients are assigned to one of four groups consisting of at least 15 patients each. One group is comprised of patients assigned to a waiting-list condition to provide appropriate comparisons at posttreatment. Thus, these patients undergo all assessments but receive no treatment during a 15-week period. To the basic interoceptive exposure strategy, cognitive procedures based largely on the work of Beck and Emery (1985), are added, and one group receives this protocol; another group receives extensive training in relaxation. A third group receives a combination of the two treatment protocols.

Cognitive procedures involve identifying automatic catastrophic thoughts concerning physical sensations and attributing them to normal bodily processes. More basic cognitive errors are also addressed. Relaxation procedures involve extensive training in individual muscle relaxation and control, and generally follow the outline provided by Bernstein and Borkovec (1973). A detailed session-by-session description of our combined treatment program can be found elsewhere (Barlow & Cerny, 1988).

The number of patients who have completed the study to date is too small to permit us to analyze the separate effects of the cognitive protocol, the relaxation protocol, and the combined protocol compared to the waiting-list condition. Therefore, the combined results for 32 patients in the three treatment protocols, compared to 18 waiting-list patients, are presented at this time. Follow-ups of from 3 to 6 months are also available for a few patients.

The results indicate that clinicians' severity ratings dropped from 5.3 to 2.9 in the treatment group, reflecting a significant change. While some patients in the waiting-list group also demonstrated some improvement, others deteriorated a bit. In contrast, over 90% of the treatment group improved and none deteriorated. These results are presented in Figure 11.4. One of the most dramatic effects, however, is the almost total elimination of panic that seems to have occurred in the treatment group by posttest. These results, presented as percentage of group reporting no panic, are shown in Figure 11.5. A related measure, average intensity of panic attacks, dropped to zero at posttest in the treatment group, as represented in Figure 11.6. But potentially the most exciting findings are the data on follow-up, which, of course, are extremely preliminary at this time. Follow-up of 9 patients from 3 to 6 months after treatment suggests that they may have learned something. This is reflected in continuing improvement on clinicians' rating of severity (presented in Figure 11.7); as well as relative stabilization in the percentage of group reporting no panic (presented in Figure 11.8).

It is also interesting to note, on the basis of our preliminary data, that our combined treatment seems to be producing therapeutic effects that are superior on a number of measures to either the somatic or cognitive treatment components alone. This trend will be followed closely as we

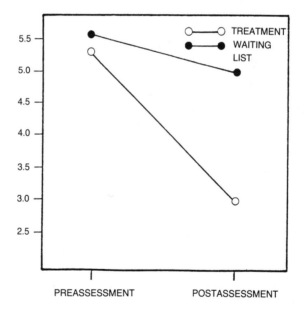

FIGURE 11.4. Clinicians' ratings of severity (on a scale of 0–8) at pretreatment and posttreatment for 32 patients receiving treatment and 18 waiting-list patients. From Craske, M. G., & Barlow, D. H. (1986, August). *Psychological treatments of panic disorder*. Paper presented at the annual meeting of the American Psychological Association, Washington, DC.

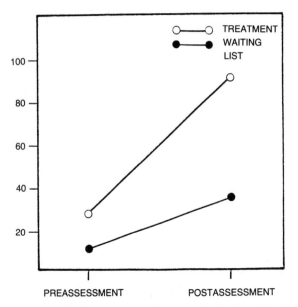

FIGURE 11.5. Percentage of group reporting no panic at pretreatment and post-treatment for 32 patients receiving treatment and 18 waiting-list patients. From Craske, M. G., & Barlow, D. H. (1986, August). *Psychological treatments of panic disorder*. Paper presented at the annual meeting of the American Psychological Association, Washington, DC.

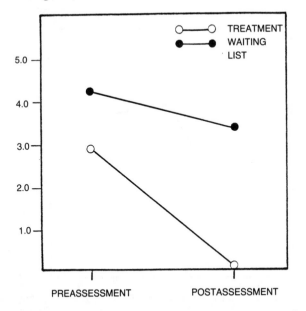

FIGURE 11.6. Average intensity (on a scale of 0–8) of panic attacks at pretreatment and posttreatment for 32 patients receiving treatment and 18 waiting-list patients. From Craske, M. G., & Barlow, D. H. (1986, August). *Psychological treatments of panic disorder*. Paper presented at the annual meeting of the American Psychological Association, Washington, DC.

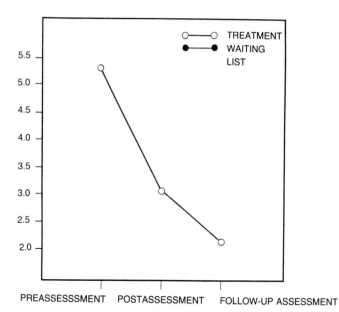

FIGURE 11.7. Clinicians' rating of severity (on a scale of 0–8) at pretreatment, posttreatment, and follow-up for 9 patients receiving treatment. From Craske, M. G., & Barlow, D. H. (1986, August). *Psychological treatments of panic disorder.* Paper presented at the annual meeting of the American Psychological Association, Washington, DC.

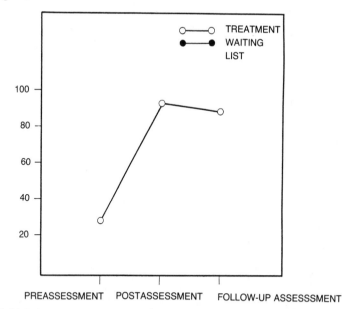

FIGURE 11.8. Percentage of group reporting no panic at pretreatment, posttreatment, and follow-up for 9 patients receiving treatment. From Craske, M. G., & Barlow, D. H. (1986, August). *Psychological treatments of panic disorder.* Paper presented at the annual meeting of the American Psychological Association, Washington, DC.

continue to accumulate cases. Full analysis, of course, will await completion of the study. Extended follow-up, where potentially the most important findings from this study will emerge, will continue to occur over the next several years of this project.

Percentage of Success in Other Centers

These are dramatic results. But despite a careful experimental analysis and the resulting confidence with which we can attribute the results to treatment, the information would be of little value if the evidence for treatment effectiveness came only from our center alone. Now there are series of cases treated with this general approach in other centers around the world; these series, while largely uncontrolled, provide equally dramatic evidence on the reduction or elimination of panic.

For example, Gitlan *et al.* (1985) treated 11 patients with panic disorder and reported complete elimination of panic in 10 of these patients at posttreatment. These results are displayed in Figure 11.9. Clark *et al.* (1985), as well as Salkovskis *et al.* (1986), treated panic directly in a number of patients suffering from panic either with or without agoraphobia. These patients were termed "situational" if their panics occurred in primarily agoraphobic situations that they tended to avoid, or "nonsituational" if no avoidance was present. Their results, presented in Figure 11.10, also indicate nearly total elimination of panic continuing through a follow-up

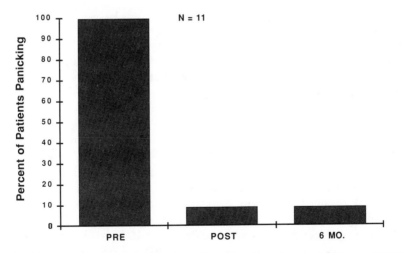

FIGURE 11.9. Percentage of patients with panic disorder panicking at pretreatment, posttreatment, and a 6-month follow-up. From Gitlan, B., Martin, M., Shear, K., Frances, A., Ball, G., & Josephson, S. (1985). Behavior therapy for panic disorder. *Journal of Nervous and Mental Disease, 173,* 742–743. Copyright 1985 by Williams & Wilkins. Reprinted by permission.

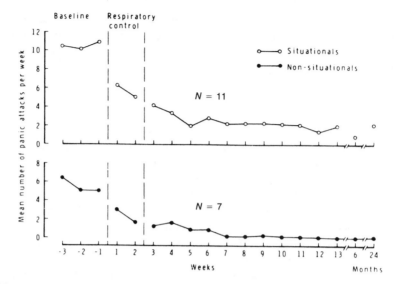

FIGURE 11.10. Effect of respiratory control on panic attacks. From Clark, D. M., Salkovskis, P. M., & Chalkley, A. J. (1985). Respiratory control as a treatment for panic attacks. *Journal of Behavior Therapy and Experimental Psychiatry, 16,* 23–30. Copyright 1985 by Pergamon Journals, Ltd. Reprinted by permission.

of 2 years. A recent series reported by Beck also demonstrates elimination of panic; these results with 16 patients are presented in Figure 11.11 (Beck, 1988). A follow-up of 1 year indicated no return of panic. In a preliminary controlled study, 13 patients were treated in a similar fashion and compared to 16 patients who received brief supportive therapy lasting 8 weeks. The results, presented in Figure 11.12, also reflect elimination of panic with cognitive therapy but little change with supportive therapy. Öst (1987) eliminated panic in 8 patients, using a somewhat similar treatment termed "applied relaxation." The gains were maintained at an average follow-up of 19 months. Although largely uncontrolled, these outcome statistics from different centers around the world seem to demonstrate the generality of the findings observed under controlled conditions in our center.

One obvious question concerns the efficacy of these new treatments compared to better-established drug treatments. The first study comparing these treatments has now appeared (Klosko, 1987; Klosko, Barlow, Tassinari, & Cerny, 1988). A combined treatment group, where the identical treatments described above were administered to mostly different patients, was also contrasted to a waiting-list control group. These two groups were compared to groups receiving alprazolam (Xanax) or placebo administered in a double-blind fashion. There were 15 or more patients in each group. Of 18 patients beginning the placebo condition, 7 dropped out, leaving 11 patients whose data could be analyzed at the end of treat-

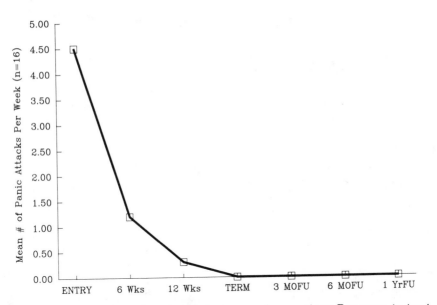

FIGURE 11.11. Number of panic attacks per week over time: Response to treatment. From Beck, A. T. (1988). Cognitive approaches to panic disorder: Theory and therapy. In S. Rachman & J. D. Maser (Eds.), *Panic: Psychological perspectives* (p. 107). Hillsdale, NJ: Erlbaum. Copyright 1988 by Lawrence Erlbaum Associates. Reprinted by permission.

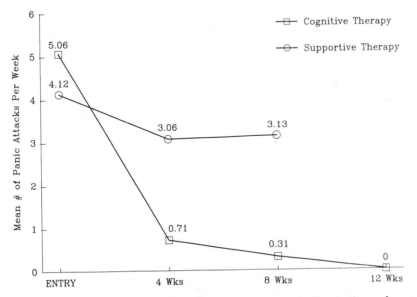

FIGURE 11.12. Number of panic attacks per week over time: Comparison of groups receiving cognitive therapy or brief supportive therapy. From Beck, A. T. (1988). Cognitive approaches to panic disorder: Theory and therapy. In S. Rachman & J. D. Maser (Eds.), *Panic: Psychological perspectives* (p. 108). Hillsdale, NJ: Erlbaum. Copyright 1988 by Lawrence Erlbaum Associates. Reprinted by permission.

ment. This most likely biased the results in a favorable direction for this group. Dropouts from other conditions were minimal.

No differences emerged on pretest measures. Each treatment condition lasted 15 weeks, at which time all patients, including those in the waiting-list group, were reassessed. Table 11.5 presents global clinical ratings of outcome on the scale of 0–8. Patients in the alprazolam and combined therapy groups were significantly better than the waiting-list group on this measure (they did not differ significantly from each other or the placebo group). We determined the percentage of patients in each group who were functioning well (a score of 3 or less on the global rating scale). Therapy patients (those who completed treatment, as well as the total sample) were significantly more likely to obtain high end-state functioning than waiting-list patients, whether or not dropouts were included in the analysis.

Percentages of patients with and without panic attacks at posttreatment are presented in Table 11.6. The combined therapy group did significantly better than the placebo or the waiting-list group. On intensity of panic symptoms, as well as the important symptom of dyspnea, the therapy patients did significantly better than the alprazolam group. Generally, the therapy group demonstrated a much broader pattern of positive therapeutic change than the alprazolam group.

TABLE 11.5. Posttreatment Clinical Assessment Measures of Treatment Groups: Global Clinical Ratings and End-State Functioning

	Group			
Measure	1 Alprazolam	2 Placebo	3 Therapy	4 Waiting list
Study completers	$n=16$	$n=11$	$n=15$	$n=15$
Global clinical rating				
M*	3.56_a	3.55_{ab}	2.73_a	4.80_b
SD	1.90	1.51	1.53	1.47
End-state functioning				
n (%) nonclinical severity*	$8(50.0)_{ab}$	$5(45.5)_{ab}$	$11(73.3)_a$	$3(20.0)_b$
n (%) clinical severity	8(50.0)	6(54.5)	4(26.7)	12(80.0)
Total sample	$n=17$	$n=18$	$n=18$	$n=16$
End-state functioning				
n (%) nonclinical severity	$8(47.1)_{ab}$	$5(27.8)_{ab}$	$11(61.1)_a$	$3(18.8)_b$
n (%) clinical severity	9(52.9)	13(72.2)	7(38.9)	13(81.3)

Note. Groups sharing subscripts are not significantly different. From Klosko, J. S., Barlow, D. H., Tassinari, R. B., & Cerny, J. A. (1988). Comparison of alprazolam and cognitive behavior therapy in the treatment of panic disorder: A preliminary report. In I. Hand & H. U. Wittchen (Eds.), *Treatments of panic and phobias: Modes of application and variables affecting outcome.* Berlin: Springer-Verlag. Copyright 1988 by Springer-Verlag. Reprinted by permission.

*$p<.05$.

TABLE 11.6. Posttreatment Panic Attack Measures of Treatment Groups

	Group			
	1	2	3	4
	Alprazolam	Placebo	Therapy	Waiting list
Measure	($n=16$)	($n=11$)	($n=15$)	($n=15$)
Frequency of panic attacks				
n (%) with zero panic				
attacks	$8(50.0)_{ab}$	$4(36.4)_b$	$13(86.7)_a$	$5(33.3)_b$
n (%) with panic attacks	$8(50.0)$	$7(63.6)$	$2(13.3)$	$10(66.7)$

Note. Groups sharing subscripts are not significantly different. Therapy versus placebo: $\chi^2=5.05$, $p<.05$; therapy versus waiting list: $\chi^2=6.80$, $p<.01$. From Klosko, J. S., Barlow, D. H., Tassinari, R. B., & Cerny, J. A. (1988). Comparison of alprazolam and cognitive behavior therapy in the treatment of panic disorder: A preliminary report. In I. Hand & H. U. Wittchen (Eds.), *Treatments of panic and phobias: Modes of application and variables affecting outcome.* Berlin: Springer-Verlag. Copyright 1988 by Springer-Verlag. Reprinted by permission.

A long road lies ahead of us if we are to confirm and extend these preliminary findings. Procedural questions revolve around the relative contribution of various components of these sometimes diverse psychological procedures. While all psychological techniques seem to have exposure to interoceptive sensations at their core, different emphases are placed on cognitive components, respiratory control components, and basic education on the origins of somatic symptoms associated with the nature of panic. In addition, the contribution of pure exposure is not clear at this time. To echo themes developed in Chapter 8, answers to these procedural questions may move us further along in our quest to understand the nature of anxiety reduction.

For example, it is possible that prevention of escapist action tendencies, whether cognitive or behavioral, is a crucial mechanism of action of treatment, along with developing perceptions of control. In this regard, evidence cited in Chapter 4 (Rapee *et al.*, 1986; Sanderson *et al.*, 1987b) is relevant. In the Rapee *et al.* (1986) study, patients inhaling CO_2 panicked at a high frequency under usual and customary conditions of administration. However, if they were told in some detail exactly what symptoms to expect, panic did not occur. It is possible that a full description of what to expect imparted a perception of control (and safety) that would not otherwise have been present. This manipulation may have brought about shifts in self-focused attention sufficient to attenuate intense affective experiences, as outlined in Chapter 8. In a more direct test (Sanderson *et al.*, 1987b), it was demonstrated that instilling a sense of control all but eliminated panic during CO_2 provocation.

Panic Reduction during Exposure Treatments Revisited

One remaining question raised above can now be considered: Why does *in vivo* exposure to external situations have a moderate panic reduction effect in agoraphobics? One possibility is that for those patients with "situational" panics, exposing them to these feared settings has the same effect as inhaling CO_2 or experiencing the effects of sodium lactate infusions. That is, panic attacks are repeatedly provoked under rather benign therapeutic conditions. To the extent that panics or periods of intense anxiety occur, this may be one of the major indicators for successful outcome. As noted above, Michelson et al. (1985), and to a lesser extent my colleagues and I (Barlow, O'Brien, & Last, 1984), demonstrated that reductions in anxiety and panic during in vivo exposure were the best predictors of outcome. Furthermore, high autonomic responding, which may reflect an increased tendency to experience anxiety and panic, has been a significant predictor of outcome in many studies (e.g., Jansson et al., 1987; J. A. Vermilyea et al., 1984), as described in Chapter 10. It is possible, then, that one important procedural contribution of in vivo exposure is the ability of this technique to provoke panic repeatedly.

Finally, this line of thinking may account for one other puzzling finding noticed in both the animal and the human literature and mentioned above. That is, anxiolytic pharmacological agents under certain conditions (specifically, benzodiazepines) seem to impede rather than facilitate exposure-based anxiety reduction procedures in both animals and humans. Once again, it is possible that exposure to the interoceptive symptoms characteristic of anxiety is a necessary condition for the process of long-term anxiety reduction.

We have made great strides in treating both avoidance behavior and panic in recent years, although much remains to be done. Nevertheless, what may ultimately turn out to be an equally important advance is a more detailed consideration of the interpersonal system in which these phenomena occur. In view of recent developments, no treatment would be complete without a full consideration of this issue.

THE CONTEXT OF THE SOCIAL SYSTEM

BACKGROUND

While the primary focus of treatment for panic disorder with or without agoraphobia has been on the symptoms themselves, clinicians and clinical investigators have recognized that the interpersonal system of the patient cannot be ignored during treatment. For these reasons, both clinicians and researchers have begun to observe carefully the interaction of interpersonal issues with treatment. In fact, we have more evidence on issues involving the interpersonal context of treatment for this disorder than for any other disorder, including depression. The improved outcomes as a result of including spouses in treatment have been reviewed above. This section ventures beyond the issue of immediate reduction in symptoms and discusses additional reasons why it is important to consider the patient's social system during treatment. Of course, the primary social context of treatment is the marital relationship, if one is present. For this reason, most of the evidence reviewed below centers on marital issues.

Interest in the interpersonal system of the agoraphobic has at least three different origins. First, clinicians faced with the problem of agoraphobia have long noted that agoraphobics seem to be relatively dependent, with low self-sufficiency, and to have a marked lack of assertiveness (e.g., Webster, 1953). Often, these interpersonal qualities have manifested themselves in the context of an unsatisfactory marriage. Thus, clinicians for years hypothesized that important etiological information is contained in this interpersonal picture. They assumed that agoraphobia is basically an exaggerated form of dependency in which patients rely excessively on those around them. In fact, as noted in Chapter 10, most reports pointing to excessive dependency on the part of agoraphobics are uncontrolled clinical reports. Studies employing well-constructed comparison groups have generally failed to find greater dependency or increased marital problems (Kleiner & Marshall, 1985; Thorpe & Burns, 1983), although there seems to be a somewhat higher frequency of dependent personality disorders than in the general population. Nevertheless, there are many treatment approaches to agoraphobia that maintain a primary focus on these issues.

Second, the analysis of successful treatments for agoraphobia presented above strongly suggests that practice between sessions, of sufficient amount and duration, is one of the central components of any effective treatment. These findings indicate that all treatments should have a goal of motivating and facilitating this activity. But this activity takes place in the patient's home environment and inevitably has an impact on the interpersonal system. Obviously, if family and/or friends show little interest—or, worse, actively discourage this type of activity—then progress may be impeded. On the other hand, a supportive social system encouraging and facilitating this activity should result in greater improvement during treatment, and, more importantly, in continuing improvement once contact with the therapist has terminated.

Third, evidence regarding the relationship of stressful life events to false alarms or panic attacks has been reviewed in Chapter 6. While we need much more information on this, a very consistent observation is that a substantial number of stressful life events can be found in the marital situation. For example, Thorpe and Burns (1983), in surveying types of stresses related to panic attacks, found marital and family difficulties to be high on the list. In view of the relationship of stress to panic, relatively greater amounts of stress in the social system may lead to greater instances of panic and therefore to more difficulty in overcoming the problem initially, as well as in maintaining gains after treatment terminates.

461

Several studies examining the effects of activating the social system in a positive way to facilitate exposure-based treatments have been reviewed above. The rather consistent finding is that such activation is useful, since therapeutic gains are greater in groups with this assistance, both at posttest and at follow-up. Improvement also continues past the point of posttest. Now, the study reported by Arnow et al. (1985) suggests the mechanism that may account for this advantage. Improvement in communication and problem-solving skills within the marriage seems responsible for the superior outcome. For these reasons, we need to attend more closely to the social context of treatment.

This is a trend that is not limited to the phobic disorders. Investigators in the areas of schizophrenia, alcoholism, obesity, and depression, to name only a few disorders, are recognizing that maximum benefit from treatment and long-term therapeutic gains may well depend on the active cooperation and participation of the interpersonal system of the patient in the treatment process (e.g., Paolino & McCrady, 1977). For example, Brownell, Heckerman, Westlake, Hayes, and Monti (1978) found that direct training of the spouse and inclusion of the spouse in the treatment program produced more weight loss both at posttreatment and at follow-up in a group of obese patients. Several studies have replicated this finding (e.g., Pearce, LeBow, & Orchard, 1981). In the area of depression, many clinicians are putting equal emphasis on dealing with the interpersonal context of the disorder. For example, Rounsaville, Weissman, Prusoff, and Herceg-Baron (1979) observed that marital distress seemed to prevent any useful progress in depressed patients being treated with psychotherapy. They suggest that progress in these patients may not be possible unless the distressed interpersonal system is attended to and perhaps altered. Klerman and Weissman (1982) suggest that renegotiating the interpersonal context associated with the onset of symptoms is important not only for the depressed patient's initial recovery, but also for the prevention of further episodes. Clinical investigators are also finding it very useful to include the spouse in the treatment of problem drinking (McCrady, 1985). Finally, in the area of schizophrenia, investigators have discovered that families who engage in continual conflict and other behaviors associated with high "expressed emotion" will put a schizophrenic member of that family at greater risk for relapse. To counter this detrimental interpersonal effect, Falloon et al. (1985) devised a family therapy program that successfully prevented subsequent psychotic episodes.

THE RELATIONSHIP OF MARITAL STATUS TO TREATMENT

With agoraphobia, the marital system is the most frequent and salient interpersonal context. Much of the evidence that we have on this issue has come from examining marriages of agoraphobics. As already noted, many clinicians feel that marital relationships play a role in the development and maintenance of agoraphobia (Agulnik, 1970; Andrews, 1966; Fry, 1962; Goldstein, 1970; Goldstein & Chambless, 1978; Lazarus, 1966; Webster, 1953; Wolpe, 1970). From a more behavioral point of view, Goldstein and Chambless (1978) formulated a well-known conceptualization that "complex" agoraphobia (i.e., agoraphobia that is not secondary to a drug experience or physical disorder) virtually always develops in a climate of marked interpersonal conflict. This idea has received wide attention. According to Goldstein and Chambless, individuals with low levels of self-sufficiency experience conflict concerning a desire to escape from an unsatisfactory marriage on the one hand and fears of independence on the other. This conflict produces anxiety and panic, which is solved by withdrawing into the home. As noted above, this conception has not yet been empirically validated. That is, there is no evidence that agoraphobics are less self-sufficient, are less assertive, or have a greater number of marital problems than other comparable groups with different emotional or behavioral disorders (Thorpe & Burns, 1983). On the other hand, it is entirely possible that these individuals are more susceptible to the stress of a difficult marriage, which may increase the likelihood of panic.

In addition to possible contributions to etiology, two other issues concerning the marriages of agoraphobics deserve comment. The first issue concerns the effects, if any, that successful treatment has on the marital relationship. The second issue is the possibility of predicting outcome of treatment as a function of a relatively satisfied or dissatisfied marriage.

Effects of Treatment on the Marital Relationship

In a series of early papers, clinicians reported several instances where husbands and/or marriages deteriorated as agoraphobic wives achieved increasing independence. Some of these reports were very dramatic. For example, there were observations of suicide attempts by husbands and extreme pressure on recovered agoraphobic wives to return to their dependent role after successful treatment (Hafner, 1977; Hudson, 1974). Hand and Lamontagne (1976) also observed acute marital crises in seven couples after the removal of the clients' phobic symptoms. In an interesting paper along these lines, Hafner (1979) describes seven cases of agoraphobic women married to abnormally jealous men. These men seemed to equate improving behavior in their wives with sexual infidelity. They reasoned that since their wives were now going out alone, they must be having affairs with other men.

Of course, the deeper implication in these clinical reports is that something in these marriages may have been responsible for the onset of the agoraphobia in the first place. But these early reports were really just clinical anecdotes. Now we have relatively strong evidence, from numerous studies involving hundreds of agoraphobic couples, that successful treatment has little or no effect on spouses. Furthermore, the most consistently observed reaction to successful treatment within the interpersonal system is a marked increase in marital satisfaction (e.g., Himadi, Cerny, *et al.*, 1986).

The Influence of Marital Satisfaction on Outcome of Treatment

Before possible reasons for this discrepancy are discussed, it is informative to examine the other side of the coin—the influence of the quality of the marriage on subsequent treatment outcome. Early studies looking at this issue also found that outcome was influenced by pre-existing marital satisfaction or lack of it. In this case, however, the pattern of results was stronger and deeper. For example, early studies (e.g., Hudson, 1974; Hafner, 1976, 1977, 1979; Milton & Hafner 1979) provided suggestive evidence that improvement in agoraphobic symptoms was less if a marriage was poor to begin with. Bland and Hallam (1981) make the very reasonable suggestion that improvement is less likely in a poor marriage because the spouse cannot or will not provide the necessary support and encouragement during and after treatment. Of course, it is also possible that patients may be less likely to accept such support even if it is offered in poor marriages.

Even recent studies have observed this phenomenon on occasion. For example, Monteiro, Marks, and Ramm (1985) found the greatest improvement and the most positive results at follow-up in patients who had the best initial marital and sexual adjustment. These investigators concluded that the ability of couples to solve problems probably had a great deal to do with their eventual success.

The consistent findings from this series of studies conducted by different investigators around the world is striking. Nevertheless, there is an equally impressive series of studies in which this finding is not apparent (Barlow, Mavissakalian, & Hay, 1981; Barlow, O'Brien, & Last, 1984; Cobb, McDonald, Marks, & Stern, 1980; Cobb *et al.*, 1984; Mathews *et al.*, 1976, 1977). In none of these studies did level of marital satisfaction predict outcome. In fact, marital satisfaction increased markedly during treatment in most of these studies. Thus, in this series of studies, marital satisfaction prior to treatment did not predict outcome, and the effects of treatment on the marriage itself seemed to be quite positive.

The Importance of Spouse Participation

How can we account for the marked discrepancy between these two long series of studies, as well as for the discrepancy concerning the effects of treatment on the marriage? One overriding procedural difference becomes apparent. In the studies that found no adverse effects of treatment on marriages, spouses were actively involved in treatment. While the participation of the spouses differed somewhat from study to study, all spouses were informed of the nature of treatment and participated to some extent. It is possible that including the spouses in these studies precluded any disruption to the marital system, which had been noticed anecdotally from time to time previously. Indeed, it would seem to make sense that including the spouses in the treatment process would prevent any adverse effects on the spouses or the marriages.

However, results from the other side of the coin are even more interesting: It seems that the deleterious effects of pre-existing marital dissatisfaction on treatment outcome disappear when spouses are included in treatment. That is, no studies where spouses were included in at least the planning of treatment reported this effect. The best evidence for this is found in the Barlow, O'Brien, and Last (1984) study, where the agoraphobic wives in pre-existing satisfactory marriages did equally well whether their husbands participated in treatment or not. On the other hand, agoraphobics from dissatisfied marriages did significantly better at posttest if their husbands were included in treatment. Presumably, therapists were able to counteract and correct, to some extent, the potential negative effects of these dissatisfied marriages during treatment.

Yet another factor might be implicated in the discrepancy between these series of studies. Clinical reports of occasional negative effects on the patients' marriages were almost always associated with exposure-based treatments administered in an intensive manner. As noted earlier, many of these treatments were carried out in as little as 2 weeks, with 4 or more hours per day of intensive intervention. We have speculated previously (Barlow, O'Brien, et al., 1983) that the rapid and dramatic changes that can occur in this brief period of time, at least some of which are beyond the control of the spouse, may produce some negative effects. Even in our own groups, which are carried on in a rather gradual manner, we have observed occasional negative comments from husbands of patients who improve in a particularly rapid fashion. For example, as patients in this category begin to take their children to activities, make necessary purchases for the home, and so on, husbands have made comments such as "That used to be my job." While such concerns can be easily handled in a group format, it would not be surprising if occasional dramatic changes occurring in the space of 2-week periods without the participation of the spouses might have some untoward effect. In fact, Hafner (1983), treating patients in this intensive way without their spouses, also noted that "relatively large improvements in patients' phobias and general symptoms were negatively associated with husbands' subsequent well-being (p. 224). Hafner also reports some evidence that "confusion" on the part of husbands with regard to their wives' behavior changes predicted poorer results at follow-up. This undesirable effect, while admittedly occurring in only a few patients, is one of the several reasons why my colleagues and I recommend gradual rather than intensive exposure.

Recently, we (Himadi, Cerny, et al., 1986) looked carefully not only at the relationship of marital adjustment to treatment outcome, but also at the effect on spouses. A rather large series of 42 patients was included in this series, 28 of whom were treated with their spouses. The results reported above for studies utilizing gradual exposure and the inclusion of the spouses were strongly supported in this study. Specifically, overall marital adjustment improved, and pretreatment marital satisfaction (or dissatisfaction) did not predict outcome.

A close look at the effects of treatment on spouses reveals some interesting patterns. To enable us to assess these effects, spouses of agoraphobics filled out fear and avoidance hierarchies as described in Chapter 10, reflecting their perception of the amount of fear and avoidance present in the patients. They also filled out the Beck Depression Inventory and the Middlesex Hospital Questionnaire as measures of their own rather than their spouses' psychopathology. The results are presented in Table 11.7. These data are broken down according to whether spouses were in satisfied or dissatisfied marriages at pretreatment. At pretreatment, spouses who were in satisfactory marriages scored significantly higher on both the Beck Depression Inventory and the Depression subscale of the Middlesex Hospital Questionnaire than did spouses in dissatisfied marriages. They

TABLE 11.7. Mean Pre- and Posttreatment Scores of Spouses in Satisfied and Dissatisfied Marriages

Measure	Satisfied[a]		Dissatisfied[b]		df	Univariate F
	Pre	Post	Pre	Post		
FAH	51.93	27.27	38.79	30.29	1, 25	12.84**
	(7.93)	(16.01)	(14.49)	(14.14)		
BDI	6.40	3.60	3.14	3.21	1, 25	4.90*
	(6.77)	(4.93)	(2.41)	(4.10)		
MHQ	4.13	2.87	2.29	2.64	1, 25	7.43*
	(2.26)	(1.85)	(2.16)	(2.34)		

Note. Measures are the fear and avoidance hierarchy (FAH) completed by the spouses; the Beck Depression Inventory (BDI); and the Depression subscale of the Middlesex Hospital Questionnaire (MHQ). Standard deviations appear in parentheses. From Himadi, W. G., Cerny, J. A., Barlow, D. H., Cohen, S., & O'Brien, G. T. (1986). The relationship of marital adjustment to agoraphobia treatment outcome. Behaviour Research and Therapy, 24, 107–115. Copyright 1986 by Pergamon Journals, Ltd. Reprinted by permission.
[a]$n = 15.$
[b]$n = 14.$
*$p < .05.$
**$p < .002.$

also perceived their agoraphobic partners as significantly more avoidant and anxious on the fear and avoidance hierarchy than did spouses in dissatisfied marriages. At posttreatment, there were no significant differences between the groups. Of course, the depression scores of the husbands in satisfied marriages were subclinical and not indicative in any way of major psychopathology. One explanation might be that spouses in good marriages communicated well with their agoraphobic partners, and thus were more sensitive to their problems. This could, in turn, have produced slightly elevated measures of dysphoria in these husbands. With the amelioration of patients' phobic difficulties, the level of dysphoria in their spouses may have improved. Spouses in unsatisfactory marriages, on the other hand, seem not to have been as sensitive to difficulties experienced by their partners.

In regard to improvements in marital satisfaction, a trend in this study suggests that the couples group treatment format led to more positive changes in marital adjustment at follow-up than did the condition in which spouses were not involved. This was also evident in a marked shift from marital dissatisfaction to marital satisfaction for seven clients in the couples group; only one couple shifted in the reverse direction. Among those clients in the nonspouse treatment, on the other hand, one client shifted from a dissatisfied to a satisfied marriage and one shifted in the opposite direction. While these numbers are too small to achieve significance, they do support findings from the Arnow et al. (1985) study. Arnow et al. demonstrated that specific training in communication skills decreased negative behavior and increased positive behavior on the Marital Interaction Coding System (a behavioral measure of communication) during a contrived role-play situation. This finding indicates that couples develop an enhanced ability to discuss sensitive issues in ways less likely to lead to defensiveness or increased marital tension. More importantly, this may facilitate negotiating more successful task-oriented behavior connected with the ongoing treatment program.

Another critical issue raised in this study is the degree of independence achieved by agoraphobics after successful treatment that includes their spouses. Emmelkamp (1982) suggested that inclusion of the spouses may be counterproductive in the long run, since the agoraphobics, usually women, may never develop the requisite independence. Arnow et al. (1985) measured this directly through a structured interview and found that partner encouragement of independence and autonomy increased substantially in their study. The increase was significantly greater in those couples who experienced communication training. For those who did not receive such training, partner encouragement of independence declined slightly following treatment. Thus, one of the positive benefits of including the spouse in treatment may be, paradoxically, a greater increase in independence and autonomy.

TREATMENT OF ADOLESCENT AGORAPHOBICS

One study that has examined an interpersonal system other than the marriage was conducted in our setting (Barlow & Seidner, 1983). We treated three adolescent agoraphobics who were accompanied by their mothers. The treatment protocol was conducted along the line of the couples treatment protocol, wherein gradual self-paced exposure-based exercises were facilitated by the partners (in this case, the mothers). Two of the three adolescents showed substantial improvement, while the third showed no improvement whatsoever. This replicates the percentage of "success" reported above with adults. Ratings of phobic severity on the fear and avoidance hierarchies by both the adolescents and their mothers for the two subjects who improved are presented in Figures 11.13 and 11.14. The

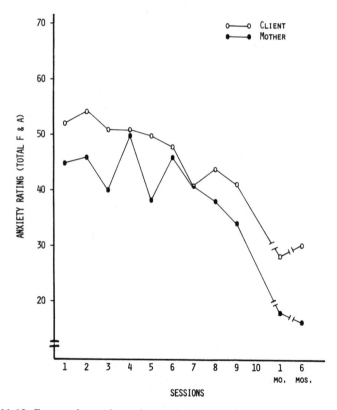

FIGURE 11.13. Fear and avoidance hierarchy ratings for one adolescent agoraphobic by the patient and her mother. From Barlow, D. H., & Siedner, A. L. (1983). Treatment of adolescent agoraphobics: Effects on parent–adolescent relations. *Behaviour Research and Therapy, 21,* 519–527. Copyright 1983 by Pergamon Journals, Ltd. Reprinted by permission.

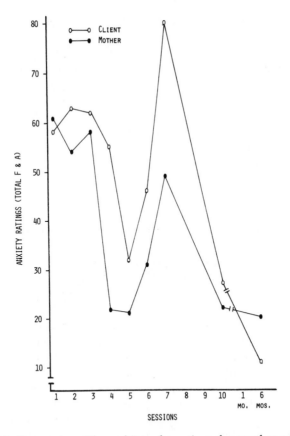

FIGURE 11.14. Fear and avoidance hierarchy ratings for another adolescent ago-raphobic by the patient and her mother. From Barlow, D. H., & Seidner, A. L. (1983). Treatment of adolescent agoraphobia: Effects on parent–adolescent rela-tions. *Behaviour Research and Therapy, 21,* 519–527. Copyright 1983 by Pergamon Journals, Ltd. Reprinted by permission.

girl in Figure 11.14 deteriorated in the middle of treatment as a result of overwhelming stress at school—a deterioration also noticed by her mother.

More interesting for our purposes here was the outcome on measures specific to parent–adolescent communication and conflict (Prinz, Foster, Kent, & O'Leary, 1979). The results indicated that improvements in the adolescents' phobic behavior were associated with reduced conflict and substantial improvement in relationships with their parents. Unfortu-nately, the third child came from a family beset by chronic and continuing conflict. This forced the mother to conclude that she simply could not deal with her daughter's treatment while at the same time trying to hold the rest of the family together.

What was unique about these adolescent agoraphobics is that, unlike our adults, they seemed unable to comprehend that their fear of panic attacks and associated thoughts that they were dying were unrealistic. Each time a new panic occurred, they would run to their parents exclaiming that they were dying and needed immediate assistance. However, with training, the parents were able to handle these concerns. This seems to underscore the necessity of including parents in this treatment program, although confirmation of this finding will have to await accumulation of a larger number of subjects.

CONCLUSIONS ON THE INTERPERSONAL SYSTEM

Evidence is building to support the common-sense notion that to maximize treatment benefit, clinicians must consider the interpersonal system in which behavior change takes place. Of course, prior to the development of powerful and effective behavior change technologies, this was not an issue (Barlow, Hayes, & Nelson, 1984). For the next several years, the effect of treatment on interpersonal systems will be a major focus of study across many different behavioral and emotional disorders. In the area of panic disorder, almost all studies concern panic disorder with severe agoraphobia rather than other forms of panic disorder. It seems that extensive avoidance has more of an impact on the patient's interpersonal system than panic disorder without avoidance. Nevertheless, debilitating panic and the variety of coping procedures other than extensive avoidance that are utilized by these patients suggest that consideration of the interpersonal system will also be beneficial in panic disorders without agoraphobia.

We are at a very preliminary stage in our knowledge of how best to integrate this issue into treatment programs. It is not yet clear exactly what aspects of the interpersonal system may be responsible for contributing to the success or failure of treatment. Preliminary results from our study as well as the Arnow et al. study (1985) indicate that improving communication skills may be very useful. Common sense also supports this notion. However, it is not always clear where improvements in communication will lead or whether participation by the spouse is always in the best interest of a patient's treatment program. Several of our agoraphobic women over the years have pulled us aside and said they would really prefer that their husbands not participate in the program, since they considered them more of a hindrance than a help. Cobb et al. (1984) noted that several patients from the poorest marriages in what was generally a group of well-adjusted marriages seemed to do somewhat better without their husbands, although this was little more than an anecdotal report. Arnow et al. (1985) also noted that training couples in communication skills produced vastly different results from couple to couple. In some couples, wives requested that their husbands encourage them and support them during practice. In other couples, wives specifically requested that their husbands not encourage them or even mention anything regarding their fears, since they interpreted this as being "pushy." One of our own patients negotiated with her husband early in treatment that he never ask her how she was feeling. She pointed out that this drew her attention to whatever bodily sensations she might be experiencing at the time, which increased her likelihood of panic. However, it was satisfactory to her if he asked her "where she was" on her 0–8 scale of anxiety.

It seems possible from these observations that communications training, such as that carried out in our study (Barlow, O'Brien, & Last, 1984) and more formally in the Arnow et al. (1985) study, may help patients to negotiate methods of dealing with treatment that work best for them. On occasion, this negotiation may lead to relatively little participation on the part of the spouse. If this is the case, then increased positive communication and support may not always be the most desirable goals in terms of eventual outcome. Cobb et al. (1984) cited one couple who increased their communication during treatment but then divorced approximately 3 months after treatment. The wife reported that as they began to talk, they realized they really didn't like each other and had very little in common. Thus, they were both happy with the divorce. Future studies should pinpoint how a spouse can best facilitate treatment as a function of initial marital satisfaction and personal style.

Finally, the interpersonal system certainly goes beyond the spouse, as evidenced in our study of adolescent agoraphobics. Nevertheless, few studies have considered other members of the system. Approximately 65% of our agoraphobics are married, which is roughly equivalent to statistics generated in other phobia clinics. For those who are not married, we often try to include another family member. On occasion, a very good friend is suggested as a confederate by some of our patients. Oatley and Hodgson (1987) found that a group of agoraphobics with good friends as cotherapists did as well as a group with husbands as cotherapists at a 12-month follow-up. In our clinical experience, daughters seem to work well with mothers, and good friends brought in by patients also seem to work quite well. In many cases, these partners seem to be more effective in helping the patients deal with problems during treatment than spouses, in that they can be more understanding and less judgmental. On rare occasions, we have had patients report that spouses are available but absolutely refuse to come in. In our experience, these are extremely poor marriages in older couples who have resigned themselves to coexisting for the rest of their days. In these situations, it seems important to have a friend or daughter come in to assist the agoraphobic. Clinical observations of these patients indicate that sustained progress in an interpersonal system characterized by extreme and continual conflict and stress is unlikely. Fortunately, out of the hundreds of patients who have come through our program, perhaps only four of five have fallen into this category. This is consistent with recent evidence that marriages of agoraphobics may even be slightly better adjusted, on the whole, than the average marriage (Arrindell & Emmelkamp, 1986).

One of the most useful and interesting areas of research, not only in the anxiety disorders but in all behavioral and emotional disorders, will concern the successful integration of our developing treatment technology into the interpersonal system of the patient. Only in this manner will our treatments be truly effective, not only in the office but in the actual world of the patient.

A TREATMENT OUTLINE FOR PANIC DISORDER
AND AGORAPHOBIA

During the 1970s, the Royal Australian and New Zealand College of Psychiatrists initiated a project to develop treatment outlines for various psychiatric disorders. In 1982, a treatment outline for agoraphobia was published. This treatment outline was developed by a project team headed by Dr. Gavin Andrews (Andrews, 1982). Specifically, the outline recommends treating both panic and agoraphobic avoidance if both are present. The treatment outline specifies occasional short-acting benzodiazepines for panic, but acknowledges in the body of the report the usefulness of other medications as determined on an individual basis. Long-term consistent use of benzodiazepines is discouraged. Involvement of the interpersonal system of the patient is clearly emphasized. In view of the continuing appropriateness of this general treatment outline, I adapt its structure here in presenting my colleagues' and my treatment recommendations.

Treatment must focus on the two major features of the disorder: panic attacks and avoidance behavior. Relative attention to these components must be individually determined. We recommend an approach that differs from the most popular treatment for avoidance behavior. Specifically, therapist-aided, intense *in vivo* exposure is de-emphasized in favor of self-paced exposure integrated into the interpersonal system of the patient. To treat panic, the psychological approach of exposure to interoceptive cues, accompanied by cognitive therapy and breathing retraining, is recommended. Evidence also indicates that relaxation procedures, particularly when these are taught as a coping skill (applied relaxation; Öst, 1987), are helpful. We recommend psychological approaches to panic as the first step before considering drugs, because of the greater rates of dropout and relapse associated with drugs and the possible demoralizing effect relapse might have on subsequent treatment.

The overall objectives of these approaches are in line with recommendations made in Chapter 8. Specifically, escapist action tendencies must be prevented at all costs. Exposure accomplishes this goal. Cognitive and breathing control procedures, and perhaps relaxation procedures as well, instill a sense of control over negative events that are otherwise perceived as uncontrollable. These techniques also redirect attention away from the negative affective core of anxiety. It remains for future research to determine which of these procedures in what combination will best achieve these goals. For the time being, we continue to recommend the comprehensive package (Barlow & Cerny, 1988).

On the basis of the cumulative evidence reviewed above, particularly the evidence on withdrawal and relapse, we do not recommend administration of benzodiazepines at any time, unless an overwhelming need for immediate relief is apparent and the therapist can contract with the patient for quick withdrawal. Rather, the selective use of tricyclic antidepressants remains the best choice. This recommendation is based on two pieces of evidence reviewed above. First, withdrawal from tricyclics is more easily managed. Second, initial evidence reviewed in Chapter 5 also suggests that the pharmacological action of tricyclics may be synergistic with the "toughening-up" process, which seems to be a neurobiological process associated with exposure therapy. Withdrawal from benzodiazepines, on the other hand, is extremely difficult because of the pharmacologically based rebound effect of the drugs, associated with addiction. Evidence also exists that these drugs interfere with the "toughening-up" process, thereby (possibly) working against the effects of psychological therapies.

If progress is less than optimal, we suggest assessing whether the individual is undergoing severe acute stress with all of its psychological and biological consequences. It is difficult to make this determination *a priori*. But if substantial progress is not forthcoming with the procedures outlined above, it is possible that the effects of stress are preventing full realization of the benefits of treatment.

Finally, one has to consider the possible influence of coexisting Axis I or Axis II disorders. As outlined in Chapter 9, it seems clear that several disorders may exist independently. While little evidence has yet been developed on the nature of the interaction of various disorders or the influence of multiple disorders on prognosis, it seems clear that treatment is complicated when additional disorders are present. For the time being, every clinician will have to judge how best to proceed under these circumstances.

The complete outline of treatment recommendations is presented in Figure 11.15.

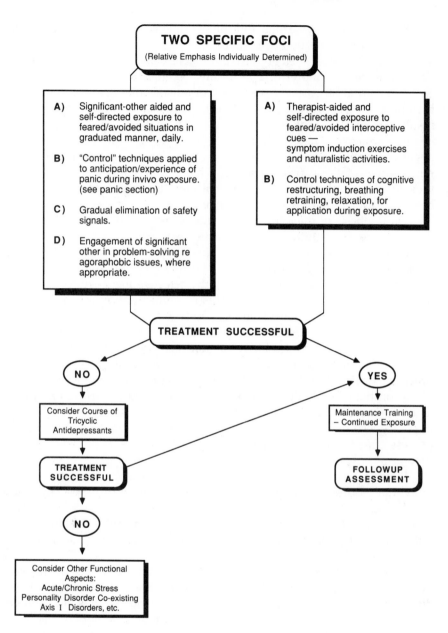

FIGURE 11.15. Outline of treatment recommendations for panic and agoraphobia.

12

Simple Phobia

Simple phobia is at once the most familiar and the most enigmatic of the anxiety disorders. Specific fears of a variety of objects or situations occur in a majority of the population, according to up-to-date epidemiological surveys. For somewhere between 5% and 10% of the population, these fears are severe enough to be classified as "disorders" and earn the label "phobias" (Myers *et al.*, 1984). The variety of Greek and Latin names contrived to describe these fears or phobias stuns the imagination. Table 12.1 gives phobias beginning with the letter "A" from a long list compiled by Jack D. Maser from three medical dictionaries and other diverse sources (Maser, 1985). The fact that so many phobias have been identified and named has been a source of inspiration to creative writers; an object of curiosity; and the cause of considerable consternation to behavioral scientists. Obviously, no meaningful classification system could incorporate this many terms, which are limited only by the number of Greek and Latin prefixes describing modern-day objects or situations. For that reason, as noted by Maser, this list is of more historical than practical interest. In fact, the number of different types of simple phobics appearing at phobia clinics is actually rather small, consisting primarily of claustrophobics; blood, injury, or injection phobics; dental phobics; and small-animal phobics.

Another anomaly drastically limits the clinical and research interest in simple phobia. Despite the overwhelming variety of phobias suggested by Table 12.1, and despite the large number of people reporting phobias in epidemiological studies, very few individuals with simple phobia come for treatment. When they do come for treatment, it is very seldom indeed that they complain only of an isolated simple phobia. As described in some detail in Chapter 9, individuals with simple phobia usually present with a variety of additional anxiety or affective disorders, making it diffi-

TABLE 12.1. Phobias Beginning with "A"

Term	Fear of:
Acarophobia	Insects, mites
Achluophobia	Darkness, night
Acousticophobia	Sounds
Acrophobia	Heights
Aerophobia	Air currents, drafts, wind
Agoraphobia	Open spaces
Agyiophobia	Crossing the street
Aichmophobia	Sharp, pointed objects; knives; being touched by a finger
Ailurophobia	Cats
Algophobia	Pain
Amathophobia	Dust
Amychophobia	Laceration; being clawed, scratched
Androphobia	Men (and sex with men)
Anemophobia	Air currents, wind, drafts
Anginophobia	Angina pectoris
Anthropophobia	Human society
Antlophobia	Floods
Apeirophobia	Infinity
Aphenphobia	Physical contact, being touched
Apiphobia	Bees, bee stings
Astraphobia	Thunderstorms, lightning
Ataxiophobia	Disorder
Atephobia	Ruin
Auroraphobia	Northern lights
Autophobia	Being alone; solitude; oneself; being egotistical

From Maser, J. D. (1985). List of phobias. In A. H. Tuma & J. D. Maser (Eds.), *Anxiety and the anxiety disorders* (p. 805). Hillsdale, NJ: Erlbaum. Copyright 1985 by Lawerence Erlbaum Associates. Reprinted by permission.

cult to decide whether the simple phobia is the primary problem or not, even if it is relatively severe.

PREVALENCE AND AGE OF ONSET

An earlier well-done epidemiological study mentioned in Chapter 1 categorized the most common fears and phobias found in the population at large, as well as those phobias severe enough to warrant a visit to a health care professional (Agras *et al.*, 1969). Using conservative criteria (including periods of marked disability), the investigators ascertained the prevalence of common fears, intense fears, and phobias in the general population. Only intense fears and phobias are presented in Table 12.2. The figures represent numbers per 1,000 of the population and the standard errors, as well as a breakdown by sex. Notice how the relative ranking of types of fear changes as one moves from intense fears to phobias. For example, one might have a consistent alarm reaction when confronted

TABLE 12.2. Prevalence and Standard Errors of Prevalence of Intense Fears and Phobia

Intense fear	Prevalence per 1,000 population	Sex distribution	SE by sex	Phobia	Prevalence per 1,000 population[a]	Sex distribution	SE by sex
Snakes	253	M: 118 F: 376	M: 34 F: 48	Illness/injury	31 (42%)	M: 22 F: 39	M: 15 F: 20
Heights	120	M: 109 F: 128	M: 33 F: 36	Storms	13 (18%)	M: 0 F: 24	M: 0 F: 15
Flying	109	M: 70 F: 144	M: 26 F: 38	Animals	11 (14%)	M: 6 F: 18	M: 8 F: 13
Enclosures	50	M: 32 F: 63	M: 18 F: 25	Agoraphobia	6 (8%)	M: 7 F: 6	M: 8 F: 8
Illness	33	M: 31 F: 35	M: 18 F: 19	Death	5 (7%)	M: 4 F: 6	M: 6 F: 8
Death	33	M: 46 F: 21	M: 21 F: 15	Crowds	4 (5%)	M: 2 F: 6	M: 5 F: 7
Injury	23	M: 24 F: 22	M: 15 F: 15	Heights	4 (5%)	M: 7 F: 0	M: 9 F: 0
Storms	31	M: 9 F: 48	M: 9 F: 22				
Dentists	24	M: 22 F: 26	M: 15 F: 16				
Journeys alone	16	M: 0 F: 31	M: 0 F: 18				
Being alone	10	M: 5 F: 13	M: 7 F: 11				

Note. Adapted from Agras, S., Sylvester, D., & Oliveau, D. (1969). The epidemiology of common fears and phobia. *Comprehensive Psychiatry, 10,* 151–156. Copyright 1969 by Grune & Stratton. Adapted by permission.

[a]Percentage of the total of those with phobias are in parentheses.

with a snake, but successful avoidance of snakes would result in no extended period of disability, and therefore no phobia according to the conservative definitions used by the authors. At the top of the phobia list is illness/injury phobia, including blood phobia.

Extending the Agras *et al.* (1969) findings, Öst (1987) has examined the age of onset in a number of different types of specific phobias as compared to agoraphobia or social phobia. Öst's sample is interesting, since it was comprised of a large number of individuals whose simple phobias were severe enough to compel them to seek treatment in Sweden over an 8-year period. The types of specific phobias represented were animal phobia, blood phobia, dental phobia, and claustrophobia. Ages of onset for the four groups of simple phobics, compared to those for social phobics and agoraphobics, are presented in Figure 12.1.

Simple phobics were clearly differentiated from social phobics and agoraphobics, with a much earlier mean age of onset. The age of onset was the earliest in animal phobics (mean = 7 years of age), followed by blood phobics (mean = 9 years of age) and dental phobics (mean = 12 years of age). Interestingly, the mean age of onset in claustrophobia (20 years of age) was much closer to that in agoraphobia, where the age of onset also peaked in the 20s (see also Chapter 10). Öst echoes Klein (1981) in suggesting that claustrophobia may well be descriptively and functionally the equivalent of agoraphobia, with a slightly more constricted range of avoidance. In other words, at least some cases of claustrophobia may best be considered panic disorder with moderate avoidance. This issue is discussed further below. It is also important to note for the moment that there are differences in age of onset among subgroups of simple phobics. For example, dental phobics have a significantly later age of onset than animal phobics.

The number of subjects in Öst's study makes it one of the most informative illustrations of the presenting characteristics of simple phobics yet published. The findings complement and extend the results of prior surveys of age of onset in simple phobics seeking treatment (Marks & Gelder, 1966; Sheehan *et al.*, 1981). It is also interesting to compare this large sample with that in the Agras *et al.* (1969) study, described in Chapter 1 (see Figure 1.1). In this study, rates of incidence (the beginning of the phobia) were very similar for injury/illness or blood phobia. But for fear of crowds, the pattern of incidence was different and resembled that for claustrophobia and agoraphobia.

MODES OF ACQUISITION AND A MODEL OF THE ETIOLOGY OF SIMPLE PHOBIA

In Chapter 6 I have observed that the etiology of most phobic disorders, according to descriptive evidence, seems to involve the association of either

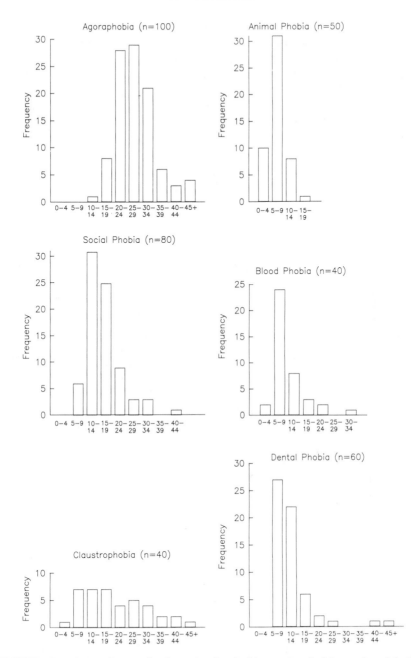

FIGURE 12.1. Ages of onset for four simple phobias, agoraphobia, and social phobia. Adapted from Öst, L. G. (1987). Age at onset in different phobias. *Journal of Abnormal Psychology, 96,* 223–229. Copyright 1987 by the American Psychological Association. Adapted by permission.

a true or a false alarm with an object or situation that has a high probability of acquiring phobic properties. Some of these objects or situations may have real danger or pain associated with them, or otherwise are "prepared" in some way for this type of association or learning (Seligman, 1971). Other objects or situations may have been the focus of mild anxious apprehension because of vicarious experiences or informational transmission prior to the association. For example, a child may have been warned repeatedly of the dangers of dogs. More frequently, objects or situations that hinder or prevent the powerful action tendency of escape during an alarm have a high probability of becoming phobic situations. In the case of panic disorder with or without agoraphobia, the overwhelming evidence from current descriptive studies as well as from retrospective reports suggests that an initial false alarm occurs, which then becomes associated primarily with interoceptive cues. Subsequent avoidance behavior, if it develops, involves situations from which escape to a safe place (or person) is difficult. Specific patterns of avoidance seem to depend on cultural and social factors, as well as the development of idiosyncratic safety signals.

For simple phobics, however, modes of acquisition seem somewhat more heterogeneous. For example, evidence reviewed in Chapter 6 indicates that both false and true alarms, as well as vicarious or instructional factors, are reported to be of etiological significance by simple phobics. Öst (1985) ascertained various modes of acquisition by means of a structured questionnaire across six groups of phobics. The results are presented in Table 12.3. The large number of subjects questioned and the structured nature of the questionnaire make this the best evidence we have to date on various modes of acquisition. Nevertheless, asking patients to attempt to recall something that occurred years ago is fraught with problems, and the results must be considered in that light.

TABLE 12.3. Ways of Acquisition for the Different Groups of Phobias

Way of acquisition	Type of phobia													
	Animal		Social		Claustro		Agora		Blood		Dental		Total	
	n	$\%$	n	$\%$	n	$\%$	n	$\%$	n	$\%$	n	$\%$	n	$\%$
Conditioning	19	48	18	58	24	69	65	81	10	45	35	68	171	66
Modeling	11	27	4	13	3	9	7	9	7	32	6	12	38	15
Instruction/ information	6	15	1	3	4	11	0	0	2	9	3	6	16	6
No recall	4	10	8	26	4	11	8	10	3	14	7	14	34	13

Note. From Öst, L. G. (1985). Mode of acquisition of phobias. *Acta Universitatis Uppsaliensis (Abstracts of Uppsala Dissertations from the Faculty of Medicine), 529*, 1–45. Copyright 1985 by the Faculty of Medicine, University of Uppsala, Sweden. Reprinted by permission.

DIRECT EXPERIENCE

Öst (1985) includes what we would now call both true and false alarms as examples of conditioning experiences. One can see in Table 12.3 that the largest percentage of conditioning experiences among Öst's subjects occurred within agoraphobia. Presumably these were all false alarms, as noted in Chapter 6. Claustrophobics also had a high percentage of conditioning experiences. Other simple phobias had a somewhat lower percentage. Although a high proportion of dental phobics reported conditioning experiences, fewer than 50% of animal and blood/injury phobics recalled such experiences. There is undoubtedly a mixture of true and false alarms in simple phobics. For example, the report from Munjack (1984) mentioned in Chapter 6 specifies the experiences of his series of driving phobics in such a way that they can be categorized into true or false alarms. Of his driving phobics, 40% reported an initial false alarm (unexpected panic) while driving; an additional 30% reported traumatic experiences that presumably resulted in a true alarm, such as collisions. In another case of a true alarm, a woman's headlights went out while she was driving at night on a winding mountain road with no guard rail! In any case, on the basis of the model presented in Chapter 6, both true and false alarms may lead to learned alarms that, in the case of simple phobics, become narrowly associated with the object or situation that comes to define the simple phobia.

The case of claustrophobia is particularly interesting, in view of the data on age of onset presented above. As noted, this particular disorder may be closer to agoraphobia in terms of the percentage of cases experiencing an initial false alarm in a situation from which escape is difficult. However, there are clearly exceptions. For example, Öst (1985) reports the case of a woman trapped in a small, hot closet in the midst of an air raid during World War II. One of our own claustrophobics was trapped in an elevator for an extraordinarily long period of time. In both situations, the danger seems to have been real enough to provoke a true alarm.

As also suggested in Chapter 6, the development of a learned alarm is not in and of itself sufficient to result in an emotional disorder. For this to happen, one must also be vulnerable to the development of anxious apprehension over the possibility of another alarm (or another extremely traumatic event). It is this anxious apprehension that occasions widespread and intense vigilance or attention narrowing in regard to upcoming potential encounters with phobic objects or situations. This, in turn, guarantees relatively widespread avoidance. Without anxious apprehension, the fear reaction would presumably fall into the category of normal fears experienced by over half of the population, which cause some mild distress during direct confrontation but are otherwise ignored and forgotten. In the present model, it is also anxious apprehension that sets the occasion for the other major modes of acquiring intense phobias: vicarious or instructional experiences.

VICARIOUS EXPERIENCE
AND INFORMATIONAL TRANSMISSION

There is little question that intense phobias can be learned vicariously. Based on the data presented above from Öst (1985), as well as years of experimentation by Bandura and his colleagues with nonclinical subjects (e.g., Bandura, 1969, 1986) and recent evidence from the primate laboratories (Cook et al., 1985; Mineka, Davidson, et al., 1984), it seems that vicarious learning may operate in at least two different ways. In the first mode, which is really modeling, a subject observes another individual experiencing intense emotion in a certain situation. Clinically, Öst (1985) gives a nice example of the acquisition of dental fear. An adolescent boy was sitting in the waiting room at the school dentist's office partially observing, but fully hearing, his friend, who was undergoing severe discomfort at the hands of the school dentist. Evidently, this discomfort resulted in sudden movement on the part of the dental patient; as a consequence, the drill partially punctured his cheek. The boy in the waiting room, upon overhearing this accident, bolted from the room and developed a severe and long-lasting fear of dental situations. Mineka, Davidson, et al.'s (1984) experience with primates seems similar. In that context, naive monkeys observed models becoming intensely fearful in the presence of a real or toy snake. Subsequently, they developed similar levels of fear themselves.

Why does this happen? It seems there are at least two possibilities. First, according to the well-known and long-established principles of emotion contagion established by the emotion theorists (e.g., Izard, 1977; see Chapter 2), it is possible that the observational situation alone is enough to trigger an alarm in the observer. The average person would probably find the experience of the boy in the dentist's chair sufficiently intense to trigger an alarm reaction, particularly if he or she were the next patient. This mode of acquisition, then, would not be essentially different from experiencing a true alarm directly. In support of this interpretation, Mineka, Davidson, et al. (1984) note that the primary determinant of individual differences in their modeling experiments with monkeys was the amount of fear shown by the model. In other words, the more fear shown by the model, the more "conditioning" demonstrated by the observer: If not enough fear was shown, the acquisition of fear by the observers did not occur in some cases. This seems to support an interpretation based on emotion contagion.

But a second possibility also seems likely. Evidence with both humans (Bandura & Rosenthal, 1966) and primates (Cook *et al.*, 1985) indicates that level of pre-existing disturbance or arousal (or perhaps anxiety) predicts the intensity of the acquired phobia. It is possible that pre-existing levels of anxious apprehension in those individuals biologically and psychologically vulnerable to this trait set the occasion for an intense alarm response during a vicariously frightening experience. In other words, consistent with the model presented in Chapter 7 (see Figure 7.7), the stress of the vicariously frightening experience, along with the opportunity for emotion contagion, may set the occasion for an initial alarm. It is also possible that the boy described by Öst was mildly anxious about dentists to begin with because of prior experience or information from others. This differs little from the process described above, except for the mediating role of pre-existing anxious apprehension. But this mediation may play an even more important role in what is probably the least common mode of the acquisition of intense phobias—the simple transmission of information.

As an example of the etiological role of informational transmission, Öst (1985) describes the case of a woman with extremely severe snake phobia who had never encountered a snake in her life. Rather, she had been told repeatedly while growing up of the dangers of snakes in the high grass. She was encouraged to wear high rubber boots to guard against this imminent threat. Wolpe (1981) also describes a number of cases from his files of patients whose phobias had evidently arisen as a result of misinformation. Many "normal" fears probably originate in this way. In the case of more severe phobias, however, it would seem that the intense anxiety and vigilance in someone repeatedly warned of the dangers of an object or situation may well lead to a full-blown alarm or panic when and if the person finally confronts the object or situation. Of course, the individual would have to be vulnerable to perceptions of unpredictability and uncontrollability, and to the development of anxiety in general, to begin with. In these cases, the anxiety precedes the alarm.

But the more interesting theoretical possibility is that an alarm need never occur. If the anxiety engendered by misinformation is intense enough to cause continual vigilance and avoidance of potential phobic situations, a phobia may develop without the occurrence of an alarm. Interestingly, this latter mode of acquisition, although seemingly infrequent, may have different treatment implications; this possibility is discussed more fully below (Öst, 1985; Wolpe, 1981).

As this discussion has made clear, the etiology of simple phobia is seemingly more varied and more complex than the origins of panic disorder. The various hypothetical modes of acquisition are outlined in Figure 12.2. The hypothetical pre-existing focus of mild nonclinical anxious apprehension on the (eventual) phobic object or situation in the alarm

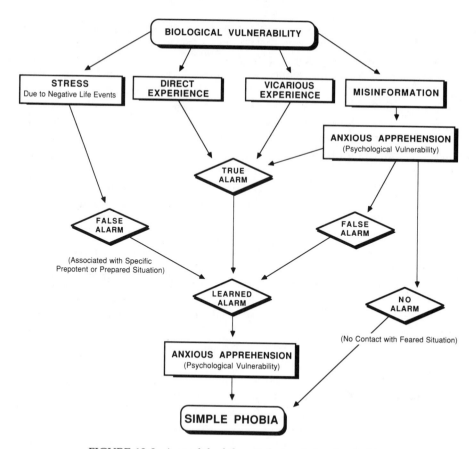

FIGURE 12.2. A model of the etiology of simple phobia.

etiology pathways is not represented. But it is assumed to exist in many cases, and may be an additional way in which phobic objects or situations become prepotent or prepared if events line up correctly.

ASSESSMENT AND TREATMENT

In contrast to the relative complexity involved in the acquisition of simple phobias as compared to panic disorder and agoraphobia, current recommendations regarding treatment are very straightforward. Both biological and psychological investigators and clinicians, as well as adherents of psychotherapy from all orientations and schools of thought, evidence remarkable agreement. The treatment of simple phobia requires structured, consistent, exposure-based exercises. Perhaps because of this unanimity of opinion, the treatment of simple phobia has been remarkably understudied. Therefore, despite the overwhelming agreement on treatment approaches, we are probably less sure about specific strategies for approaching the variety of simple phobias than we are about strategies for more complex or severe disorders. Some general assessment and treatment considerations are reviewed briefly here; attention is then focused in the remainder of the chapter on several specific phobias that either are commonly encountered clinically, or present unique examples of assessment or treatment issues.

DIAGNOSIS AND ASSESSMENT

As indicated in Chapter 9, the initial determination of the presence of a simple phobia may not be as straightforward as it would seem. This is due to the fact that very few individuals present for treatment with just a simple phobia. Most individuals seeking treatment for an anxiety disorder have multiple problems. These problems summate to produce the marked interference with functioning that causes them to seek treatment in the first place. Therefore, one of the first decisions required by a clinician is an assessment of whether the simple phobia is an independent problem or whether it is an associated feature of another disorder.

Early in my experience with anxiety disorders, I interviewed a woman who presented with a fear of sharp pointed objects, particularly kitchen knives. A routine interview revealed no particular complications. We proceeded to treat her for her fear of knives, using structured exposure-based exercises in the usual manner. After several sessions it became apparent that we were making no progress whatsoever. At that point, a reinterview revealed a severe obsessional process that was very difficult for the woman to admit. The patient's daughter, who had recently moved back to town, had begun to take advantage of her in regard to requests for babysitting services; the children (the patient's grandchildren) were rather loud and disruptive. One day, while in the kitchen preparing dinner, the thought flashed through her mind of running a knife through one of the children, who was being particularly disruptive. This thought then developed into a full-blown obsessive process. Thus, her fear of knives was an associated feature of an obsessive–compulsive disorder. The sight of knives, in this case, only set the occasion for the true source of her concern—her obsessional thoughts of killing her grandchildren.

A variety of other problems may also present as simple phobia. In one rather unusual case, a woman presented to our anxiety disorders clinic with a fear of shopping for various items of food and clothing. Further assessment rather quickly revealed that her fears involved difficulty in making decisions regarding various items. This feature clearly seemed to be an integral part of a major depressive episode. For this reason, the ADIS covers the most common simple phobias and examines them in the context of other anxiety and affective disorders.

In view of the diversity of simple phobias, assessment of progress is necessarily tailored to the individual. For this reason, there are no SBATs, as there are for agoraphobia (see Chapter 10). Rather, all direct behavioral assessments of simple phobias are idiosyncratic, or IBATs. Most usually, these involve arranging for the individual to proceed up a hierarchy of distance or intensity in the context of the feared object or situation. For example, fears of small animals or insects are easily tested by arranging for the patient to approach increasingly closer to the animal or insect. Final steps involve actual contact with the animal or insect (in the case of insects, allowing an insect to crawl unimpeded on one's skin). For height phobics, working one's way increasingly higher inside of a building, outside of a building on a fire escape, or on a ladder are most commonly used. For the dental phobics treated by Jerremalm, Jansson, and Öst (1986), an ordinary dental examination was divided into 15 steps, culminating in allowing the dentist to inject an analgesic and do a small restoration. Naturally, the dental phobic could stop at any point during this 15 step sequence.

Most simple phobias lend themselves to hierarchical arrangements based on intensity. For example, fear of draft or wind lends itself to confronting a fan with adjustable speeds; fear of noise or sounds of any kind can be easily assessed by gradually increasing the intensity of the sound on a tape recorder; and so on. Fears of thunderstorms are often treated in this way with lightning produced by flashing strobe lights or some less sophisticated arrangement.

Assessment of physiological responding can most conveniently be carried out in an ambulatory fashion in the context of the IBAT, as described above. However, in view of the uncertainties regarding the usefulness of this type of assessment as a measure of treatment outcome (see Chapter 10), the issue is not pursued here.

Finally, in view of the diversity of simple phobias that clinicians may encounter, questionnaires, of necessity, consist mostly of surveys of the most common fears. The best known is the Fear Survey Schedule (Wolpe & Lang, 1969), which samples a large number of fears and requires ratings of intensity. This is useful on occasion to determine the patterning of additional specific fears in individuals presenting with a clinical phobia.

TREATMENT

The few studies in the literature reveal no particular advantage for one type of exposure over another in the treatment of simple phobia (Linden,

1981). This is consistent with the information reviewed in Chapter 11 on exposure-based treatments for panic disorder and agoraphobia. For example, Bourque and Ladouceur (1981) compared five different exposure-based treatments for height phobics: participant modeling, in which the therapist first modeled climbing a fire escape and then actually physically assisted the phobic individual with the task; participant modeling without actual physical assistance from the therapist; and three other conditions requiring increasingly less participation by the therapist. The final condition was actually the self-initiated, self-paced exposure discussed at some length in Chapter 11. No differences were observed among these five conditions. Similarly, Öst and his colleagues demonstrated essentially similar benefits from several exposure-based treatments for thunder and lightning phobics (Öst, 1978) as well as blood phobics (Öst, Lindahl, *et al.*, 1984).

Tailoring Treatment to the Individual

Öst and his colleagues have investigated whether variations in individual response patterns predict differential success with treatment tailored to those response patterns. For example, Jerremalm *et al.* (1986) assessed 37 dental phobics who displayed more intense responding in either physiological systems (heart rates) or cognitive systems (catastrophic cognitions) during a behavioral test in the form of a dental examination. It was determined that 20 of the patients were primarily cognitive reactors and 17 were primarily physiological reactors. These patients were then assigned to exposure-based treatments that concentrated primarily on either physiological reactivity (applied relaxation) or cognitive reactivity (self-instructional training). In other words, half of the cognitive reactors and half of the physiological reactors received self-instructional training, while the other half of each group received applied relaxation. In applied relaxation, patients learned to relax deeply while exposing themselves to an increasingly greater number of steps in a dental examination procedure. During self-instructional training a similar procedure was in effect, but patients worked on altering self-statements rather than relaxing. The results indicated no beneficial effect of matching the treatment to the most reactive response modality. All groups improved equally.

On the other hand, Öst, Johansson, and Jerremalm (1982) found some support for tailoring exposure-based treatments for claustrophobia to particular features of the claustrophobics' response profiles. Using a design similar to that used with the dental phobics, Öst *et al.* treated primarily physiological reactors (high heart rate but not as much avoidance) or primarily behavioral reactors (considerable avoidance, but less physiological responsivity). These two groups of patients received either applied relaxation similar to that used with the dental phobics as described above, or direct behavioral training on entering a small room. The results were compared to waiting-list control groups. Both treatments produced significant benefit when compared to the waiting-list control groups. In addition, there were some hints that tailoring the treatment provided additional benefit. For example, applied relaxation was slightly better than exposure for physiological reactors; similarly, intensive practice upon entering a small room was somewhat more effective for behavioral reactors than for physiological reactors.

If replicated and extended, this finding would have important treatment implications. But this overall conclusion is weakened somewhat by the fact that "effectiveness" of treatment was determined by changes in the particular response system that defined the groups. For example, it is probably not too surprising that individuals with substantial avoidance who were assigned to the behaviorally reactive group did better on the behavioral tests after being trained to enter a small room than they did after applied relaxation. In the latter treatment, less training in entering a small room was provided. No differences on this particular measure were apparent for physiological reactors because of a ceiling effect (they all completed all of the behavioral items to begin with); this is understandable, since this group by definition did not demonstrate substantial avoidance. Similarly, physiological reactors evidenced lower posttreatment heart rate responding after relaxation training than after behavioral training. Nevertheless, there is clinical wisdom in tailoring treatment to problems that are more severe in individual patients.

Similar considerations apply to another often-cited response dichotomy within the anxiety disorders: cognitive versus somatic anxiety (e.g., Davidson & Schwartz, 1976; Schwartz et al., 1978). For example, Norton and Johnson (1983) demonstrated a small advantage for tailoring the treatment of analogue snake-phobic subjects according to their scores on the Cognitive and Somatic Anxiety Questionnaire (Schwartz et al., 1978).

Despite the misgivings expressed here, the work of Öst and his colleagues represents the most sophisticated therapeutic outcome research with simple phobics yet to appear. For the time being, it makes eminently good clinical sense to assess and tailor exposure-based treatments individually, based on particular patterns of responding that are notably problematic for the individual patient. Nevertheless, at a more basic level, the underlying principles of fear and anxiety reduction outlined in Chapter 8—that is, preventing escapist action tendencies and instilling a sense of control through exposure-based therapies—would seem primary.

In addition to suggestions on the usefulness of tailoring treatments to individual patterns of responding, there are some very intriguing hints on specifying different treatments for different modes of acquisition. For example, Wolpe (1981) first suggested that anxiety-disordered individuals with a traumatic conditioning etiology may require traditional behavioral exposure-based strategies. Those individuals who report acquiring their problems through misinformation, on the other hand, may benefit from cognitive correction, particularly in less severe cases. A retrospective analysis of a clinical series of cases provides some initial support for this recommendation. In Öst's (1985) large series of 370 phobics described above, he reported no difference in outcome among patients with different modes of acquisition. However, he did notice that among patients with a cognitive mode of acquisition (misinformation), significantly more patients reached a response status of clinical improvement with cognitively focused methods than with physiologically focused methods (applied relaxation) or more behaviorally focused methods. These effects are apparent in Table 12.4.

Using an arbitrary definition of clinical improvement on each measure as well as an overall treatment response composite, Öst calculated the percentage receiving each type of treatment as a function of their mode of acquisition. While it must be remembered that all treatments involved systematic *in vivo* exposure, the physiological treatment added relaxation training, whereas the cognitive treatment added self-instructional training concentrating on catastrophic misattributions. One can see a slight advantage for the behavioral and physiological treatments when conditioning was the mode of onset, but a significant advantage for cognitive treatments when the mode of onset was indirect (misinformation). Of course, these results are nothing more than suggestive, since they are based on retrospective post hoc groupings across different studies. In addition, the subjects themselves represented very different simple phobias, and the treatments varied somewhat from study to study. Nevertheless, these results suggest that it would be worthwhile to explore this issue more thoroughly and systematically.

TABLE 12.4. Proportion of Patients within Each Acquisition–Treatment Combination That Had Reached the Criterion for Clinical Improvement on the Different Measures

Acquisition–treatment combination	Measure			
	Behavior score	Self-rating of anxiety	Δ Heart rate	Overall
Conditioning–behavioral	63.2%	42.1%	47.7%	47.4%
Conditioning–physiological	68.0%	38.0%	34.0%	46.0%
Conditioning–cognitive	53.3%	36.7%	33.3%	40.0%
Indirect–behavioral	78.6%	42.9%	35.7%	50.0%
Indirect–physiological	56.3%	25.0%	25.0%	37.5%
Indirect–cognitive	88.9%	22.2%	66.7%	66.7%

Note. From Öst, L. G. (1985). Mode of acquisition of phobias. *Acta Universitatis Uppsaliensis (Abstracts of Uppsala Dissertations from the Faculty of Medicine)*, 529, 1–45. Copyright 1985 by the Faculty of Medicine, University of Uppsala, Sweden. Reprinted by permission.

Preliminary data from our clinic relate to another etiological issue that may have implications for treatment. We examined outcome in a small group of simple phobics according to whether they acquired their phobia by means of a false alarm or a true alarm (Rygh & Barlow, 1986). Specifically, three simple phobics were treated with interoceptive exposure, during which they were exposed to various somatic cues associated with panic (see Chapter 11), or more traditional exposure, during which they were confronted with their feared object or situation (exteroceptive exposure). The results are depicted in Figure 12.3. The first patient, whose phobia seemed to arise after an unexpected panic, responded to interoceptive exposure without any imaginal or *in vivo* exposure to her feared object. Unfortunately, the other two patients, with nonpanic etiologies, failed to respond to either treatment. If they had responded to exteroceptive exposure, as we had hypothesized, we would have had some hints on the usefulness of prescribing differential treatments based on etiology. The fact that the first patient responded to a panic treatment still suggests that this may be useful in some cases. Of course, we need to explore this issue more thoroughly to specify the relationship.

Drug Treatment

Just as there is near-unanimity of opinion among biological and psychological clinicians and investigators on the appropriateness of exposure-based procedures for simple phobia, near-unanimity of opinion also exists on the seeming lack of benefit of adding drugs to these procedures. For this reason, very little serious investigation on possible benefits of drugs in the treatment of simple phobia exists. The Zitrin *et al.* (1983) study mentioned in Chapter 11 reported no particular contribution of imipramine to the treatment of simple phobia by systematic desensitization in imagination.

A scattering of studies have examined possible contributions of benzodiazepines or beta-blockers (e.g., Bernadt, Silverstone, & Singleton, 1980; Campos, Solyom, & Koelink, 1984; Sartory, 1983; Whitehead, Robinson, Blackwell, & Stutz, 1978). While occasionally a transitory beneficial drug effect on one measure or another has been noticed and reported, the firm and consistent conclusion is that drugs do not contribute to therapy and may even hinder the effects of exposure-based therapy because of state-dependent learning (e.g., Sartory, 1983). These unpromising results can also be found in animal studies, where typically higher doses of drugs have been explored as a possible "treatment" for induced phobic avoidance behavior.

This state of affairs is somewhat curious, in view of emerging evidence reviewed in Chapter 11 on the beneficial effects of drugs on panic disorder, at least in the short term. Assuming that the conclusion on the lack of contribution of drugs to exposure-based treatments for simple phobia

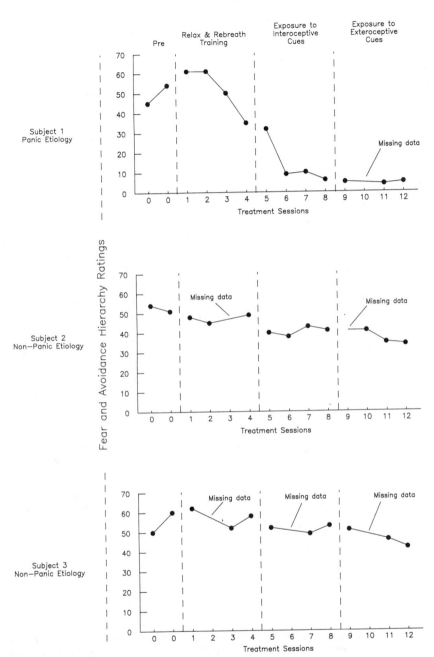

FIGURE 12.3. Fear and avoidance hierarchy ratings during various phases of treatment for three patients with simple phobias differing in etiology. From Rygh, J. L., & Barlow, D. H. (1986, November). *Treatment of simple phobias with panic management techniques.* Paper presented at the annual meeting of the Association for Advancement of Behavior Therapy, Chicago.

is correct, what could account for this marked difference? In the models of the development of panic and phobic disorders presented in this book, the occurrence of an alarm, either true or false, is an event common to all of these disorders. Furthermore, the subsequent development of anxiety over the possible occurrence of another alarm is also a shared feature of these disorders, although it seems that some simple phobias may have a slightly different mode of acquisition. Why, then, should drugs be effective for one condition and not the other?

One obvious difference lies in the nature of the hypothetical learned alarm in panic disorder. The interoceptive cues for learned alarms are not clearly discriminated, although a marked sensitivity to these interoceptive cues is apparent. As a result, anxiety seems to be more intense and more generalized, since the individual must be on guard for an uncontrollable and unpredictable event that may occur at any time. Simple phobics, on the other hand, also may develop severe anxiety concerning their phobic objects, but anxiety is limited to situations where the possibility of confronting the phobic objects or situations exists. Thus, the learned alarms themselves may be basically the same, but marked differences exist in the intensity and generality of anxiety over alarms. Since drugs with some evidence for effectiveness in panic disorder may act through their anxiolytic properties, this may well account for the differences observed. That is, the highly discriminated nature of simple phobia, with the resulting marked restriction of (anticipatory) anxious apprehension, renders drugs that are anxiolytic ineffective. In addition, the fact that anxiety hypothetically provides many of the cues for learned alarms within panic disorder would also lead to differential predictions on the effectiveness of these drugs, since somatic responses associated with anxiety may be phobic cues in panic disorder. Possible reasons why beta-blockers are not effective have been discussed in Chapter 11. This analysis also raises some interesting issues in regard to preliminary evidence on the effectiveness of beta-blockers for social phobia, to be discussed in more detail in Chapter 14.

BLOOD PHOBIA

ORIGINS OF BLOOD PHOBIA

While the potential varieties of phobias are limited only by the imagination, the most intriguing from a scientific and ethological point of view is blood phobia. In Chapter 1, I have described the vasovagal reaction that occasionally results in fainting at the sight of blood as one of several ethologically significant defensive reactions (Marks, 1969). What makes blood phobia so interesting is the markedly different physiology associated with this response compared to the common "flight" action tendency associated with fear (see Chapter 1).

Systematic observation and description of individuals who tend to faint at the sight of blood, some of whom become blood phobics, is a recent phenomenon (Connolly *et al.*, 1976; Curtis & Thyer, 1983; Yule & Fernando, 1980). One interesting feature of these reports is the observation that this reaction seems to have a strong familial tendency. For example, in a series of 18 patients treated by Öst, Lindahl, *et al.* (1984), fully 14, or 67%, also had close relatives with blood phobia, as noted in Chapter 5.

The physiological response associated with blood phobia has now been examined in some detail by Öst and his colleagues (Öst, Sterner, & Lindahl, 1984), who have studied the largest number of these patients. To examine this response closely, Öst and colleagues arranged for blood phobics to watch a film on surgical procedures (patients could turn off the film at any time by pressing a button). What the investigators confirmed in this study was the presence of a diphasic physiological response. Initial marked increases in heart rate and blood pressure were followed by dramatic bradycardia, hypotension, and occasionally fainting. Mean heart rate and systolic blood pressure for 18 of these patients are presented in Figures 12.4 and 12.5, respectively. Since an increasing number of patients found it necessary to turn off the film, numbers of

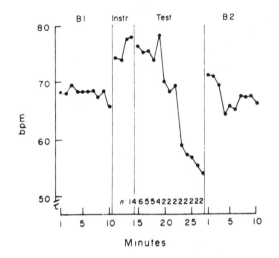

FIGURE 12.4. Mean heart rate during the different periods of the test. From Öst, L. G., Sterner, U., & Lindahl, I. L. (1984). Physiological responses in blood phobics. *Behaviour Research and Therapy, 22,* 109–117. Copyright 1984 by Pergamon Journals, Ltd. Reprinted by permission.

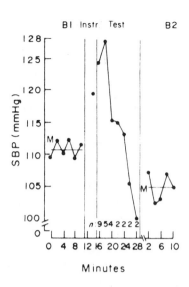

FIGURE 12.5. Mean systolic blood pressure during the different periods of the test. From Öst, L. G., Sterner, U., & Lindahl, I. L. (1984). Physiological responses in blood phobics. *Behaviour Research and Therapy*, 22, 109–117. Copyright 1984 by Pergamon Journals, Ltd. Reprinted by permission.

subjects contributing to the mean responses decreased over the course of the test. Nevertheless, the responses were quite consistent from subject to subject. Following a baseline, both heart rate and blood pressure rose sharply during the brief instruction period preceding the film and for the first few minutes of the film itself, followed by marked drops and a subsequent recovery after cessation of the film.

A number of theoretical explanations have been proposed for this unusual response. Some authors (e.g., Engel, 1962; Graham, Kabler, & Lunsford, 1961) think that the initial physiological increase represents the usual response to threat. However, because of surges in parasympathetic activity or a physiologically mediated generalized inhibition of sympathetic tone (to which some individuals are biologically vulnerable), marked physiological decreases occur. There are two difficulties with this type of theorizing. First, it does not take into account the stimulus specificity of this response in blood phobics. That is, blood phobics do not faint at other phobic or frightening situations, nor do other types of phobics faint under any circumstances. For example, Öst (1985) has now demonstrated that blood phobics show this characteristic response only in relation to blood stimuli. When studied in ordinary stress situations, they react with the more usual physiological increases. If this response really represented an idiosyncratic biological vulnerability during periods of stress, the response of fainting would be randomly distributed among the variety of phobic situations.

While these issues await further direct systematic investigation, it would seem that the vasovagal response represents a special defensive reaction. A tendency to respond in this manner should be distributed normally in the population; the extreme reactors at the end of the distribution would be vulnerable to fainting when confronted with minimal blood stimuli. The vasovagal response has a strong familial component, most likely as a result of underlying genetic contributions. As in other phobias, an individual must sense that this reaction is out of control and become anxious about it for a severe phobic reaction to occur. Sudden and unexpected fainting, of course, is likely to provoke this response in vulnerable individuals, but a large number of individuals undoubtedly exist who have learned to cope with (control) this response, perhaps through one of the methods described below. For these individuals, the response is just a nuisance rather than a disorder, as seems to be the case with nonclinical panickers.

One can see from Table 12.3 that blood phobias do not differ from other simple phobias, such as small-animal phobias, in regard to mode of acquisition. Slightly less than half of 22 blood phobics reported conditioning experiences, while almost an equal number reported modeling or misinformation modes of acquisition. It is interesting, however, that conditioning seems to play less of a role in the acquisition of blood phobia than in some other phobias, such as dental phobia, social phobia, or claustrophobia. On the other hand, a modeling mode of acquisition is more frequent. In view of the strong familial nature of this specific phobia, and the fact that almost everyone confronts blood at some time or another, opportunities for modeling are probably common.

TREATMENT OF BLOOD PHOBIA

For all of the intrigue and mystery of such a strange phobic reaction, the few reports in the literature on treatment of blood phobia have been rather routine until recently. That is, systematic structured exposure to hierarchies of blood and injury scenes or situations proved reasonably effective. The only clear procedural difference involved the desirability of having the patient lie down during the early stages of treatment, to prevent any untoward consequences of possible faints.

Now an exciting and theoretically interesting treatment has been devised specifically for blood phobia, with preliminary estimates of considerable success. On the basis of an early case report by Kozak and Montgomery (1981), Öst, Lindahl, et al. (1984) treated a group of blood phobics with what they have come to call "applied tension." Applied tension is theoretically interesting from the point of view of the principles of affective therapy described in Chapter 8. The major purpose is to counter directly the behavior of fainting. Specifically, blood phobics are taught to tense gross body muscles at the first signs of hypotension.

The therapeutic program, as devised by Öst and Sterner (1987), takes five sessions. In the first session, the patients are taught to tense their muscles systematically and hold the tension for 10–15 seconds. During the second and third sessions, patients practice applied tension while shown a series of slides depicting wounds and mutilated people. In the fourth session the patients are accompanied to the blood donor center, where they observe blood donors; subsequently, they give blood themselves. In the final session, they observe thoracic surgery. After completing this treatment, all of a group of 10 patients watched an entire 30-minute surgical film without any difficulty (Öst & Sterner, 1987). A 6-month follow-up revealed a maintenance of benefits.

Of course, an important step at this point is to determine the active ingredient of this treatment. Substantial amounts of systematic exposure *in vivo* are involved. Since exposure is also effective for blood phobia (Connolly *et al.*, 1976; Öst, Lindahl, *et al.*, 1984), it is possible that applied tension makes no further contribution. On the other hand, Öst and Sterner's 10 patients reported a greatly increased sense of control because of their newly developed capacity to counter directly the tendency to faint. In any case, pending further replication and extension, it seems that this treatment is very promising.

The applied tension method as elaborated by Öst and Sterner (1987) may have implications for improved treatment of phobia. What is common to all treatments of phobia is passive exposure to feared objects or situations. But we are only just beginning to attend to the inappropriate alarm or defensive response itself. Attending directly to the alarm response in a therapeutic way (as outlined in Chapter 11 in the case of panic) and to associated flight tendencies may be a crucial step in the successful treatment of phobia. In fact, it is possible that the success of more passive exposure-based therapies is dependent on the extent to which action tendencies associated with emotions or other defensive reactions are incidentally prevented, resulting in an increased sense of control in the face of runaway alarms of whatever type. For the essence of phobia, as concluded in Chapter 6, is anxiety over reactions or events that seem uncontrollable, particularly reactions within one's own body.

SPACE PHOBIA

Blood phobia is interesting because of the unique physiological reaction. Another simple phobia, seemingly more rare, is also interesting on theoretical grounds. Panic disorder has been conceptualized here as primarily a fear of unpredictable, uncontrollable alarm reactions involving flight. The evidence indicates that what a person with panic disorder comes to fear are patterns of physiological responses associated with the alarm reaction. To the extent that this is true, one might then expect theoretically that other phobic reactions to more specific or circumscribed interoceptive stimuli exist. Now it seems that such a phobia has been isolated, thanks to some clever clinical detective work by Isaac Marks (Marks, 1981b; Marks & Bebbington, 1976).

Marks's initial observation concerned a patient who presented with what appeared to be an agoraphobic pattern. However, on closer analysis, the pattern differed somewhat in that it was much more specific. Marks discovered that in this patient and others, the fear revolved around falling when no support was nearby, as would happen when the patients were in the middle of a room or corridor. Occasionally these individuals resorted to crawling on hands and knees across an open space. Physical support such as a cane was not necessarily helpful. This phobia was found most often in older people who had experienced a bad fall.

Recently we administered neuropsychological evaluations to two patients presenting with space phobia (McCaffrey, Rapee, Gansler, & Barlow, 1987). Although both of these patients had been referred by neurologists after a series of negative neurological workups, testing revealed mild right-hemisphere dysfunction in both cases. The results support a disturbance in visual–perceptual spatial functioning that may underlie this disorder; these symptoms are what patients come to fear. While exposure in open space is not helpful, it is possible, on the basis of our conceptualization, that systematic exposure to audiovestibular cues or other sensations of dizziness may be useful, along with neuropsychological rehabilitation procedures.

SIMPLE PHOBIA AND POSTTRAUMATIC STRESS DISORDER

Occasionally, very specific phobias can present with severe incapacitating symptoms, even though the phobic object is seldom encountered and easily avoidable. A fascinating case recently reported by Thyer and Curtis (1983) concerned a 26-year-old woman who developed a severe fear of frogs. Eighteen months earlier, she had been mowing thick grass in her yard, which was located on a riverbank. She was suddenly surrounded by a large group of jumping frogs. Several were chopped up in her lawn mower, and bloody pieces of frog were flung in all directions. She ran from the scene and was unable to mow the lawn henceforth. At night, the sounds of frogs croaking filled the air, and she suffered many nightmares and much insomnia. Occasionally a frog would work its way into her home, forcing her to leave and seek help from a neighbor.

The severity of the symptomatology, including nightmares and marked affective changes in the absence of the phobic object, is something all clinicians have encountered occasionally. Quite properly, this patient was classified using DSM-III criteria as having simple phobia and was treated as such. According to the conceptualization presented in this chapter, she experienced a true alarm during an initial traumatic conditioning experience, which then generalized widely along various stimulus dimensions associated with the experience.

But what if this patient's experience had not concerned running over a group of frogs, but rather witnessing a severe car accident where people were killed, or barely escaping from a tragic fire, or watching her friends maimed and killed by incoming rockets during an air attack? It would be unlikely in these cases that the woman would be classified so readily as having simple phobia. Rather, with exactly the same symptomatology, there would by quick agreement on the labeling of her psychopathology as posttraumatic stress disorder—a topic to which I now turn.

13

Posttraumatic Stress Disorder

One of the great questions in all of psychopathology concerns etiology. It is widely agreed that determining what causes emotional and behavioral disorders will be far more beneficial to society than devising new treatments. Discovering the cause of a problem may ultimately lead to preventing the problem from ever occurring. For this reason, the study of posttraumatic stress disorder (abbreviated hereafter as PTSD) becomes extremely important: This is the only disorder where we can clearly identify the onset. Despite this knowledge, one of the more fascinating aspects of PTSD is that few people appear to develop the disorder among the large number of individuals who experience traumatic stress. This belies the notion that we really know the "cause" of this disorder. To state it more accurately, we know the proximal event that activates the disorder in vulnerable individuals.

Individuals suffering from this disorder have experienced a traumatic event that is usually outside the range of normal human experience. Following the event, victims experience anxiety characterized by elevated autonomic activity and such cognitive symptoms as difficulty concentrating and memory impairment. This is accompanied by classic PTSD symptoms of re-experiencing the traumatic event and a suppression or numbing of emotional responsiveness.

Combat experiences during the war, as well as experiences in prisoner of war or death camps, were noted early on as situations provoking PTSD in some individuals. For this reason, early names such as "shell shock," "combat fatigue," or "war neurosis" identified what seems to be the same condition (Grinker & Spiegel, 1945). Even before the great wars of this century, anxiety as a response to severe stress was observed and labeled "traumatic neurosis" by Oppenheim (1892; cited in Kraepelin, 1896) or *Schreckneurose* ("fright neurosis") by Kraepelin (1896). Kraepelin considered this condition a separate clinical entity "composed of multiple nervous and psychic phenomena arising as a result of severe emotional upheaval or sudden fright which build up great anxiety; it can therefore be observed after serious accidents and injuries, particularly fires, railway derailments or collisions, etc." (Kraepelin, 1896; translation by Jablensky, 1985, p. 737). In view of the early and clear recognition of this emotional disorder, it is somewhat surprising that controversy over the existence of this diagnostic category emerged during the 1970s, when it was first proposed following the Vietnam war (Figley, 1978). Although this controversy has abated somewhat with the recognition of PTSD in DSM-III, it continues to be debated, particularly in the context of civilian disasters from a policy point of view (e.g., Quarantelli, 1985).

While war and its aftermath continue to provide a large group of individuals suffering from PTSD, we have learned to expect this response in some individuals after a wide variety of traumatic situations. For example, auto accidents, industrial accidents, natural catastrophes (e.g., earthquakes), physical assault (particularly rape), or death of a loved one (even a pet) are all capable of producing PTSD. Many early examples of these reactions have been recorded over the centuries by those inclined to write them down. One of the better-known descriptions is the reaction of the famous 17th-century diarist, Samuel Pepys, after the Great Fire of London in 1666. This catastrophe resulted in substantial loss of life and property and in marked disorganization in the city, all of which was very well described by Pepys. Fully 6 months after the fire, he recorded: "[I]t is strange to think how to this very day I cannot sleep a night without great terrors of fire; and this very night could not sleep to almost 2 in the morning through thoughts of fire" (quoted in Daly, 1983, p. 66). Insomnia, as well as recurring dreams of the event, of course, are prominent features of PTSD, but Pepys also demonstrated mild depersonalization, as well as some characteristic guilt concerning saving himself and his property while others died.

In addition to recurrent and intrusive recollection and dreams concerning the event, the individual may also experience "flashback" episodes, in which he or she seems to experience a recurrence of at least a portion of the traumatic event. Extreme distress and/or avoidance of events that resemble aspects of the traumatic event is also common. This avoidance may involve inability to remember certain aspects of the event. Interestingly, a part of this avoidance seems to include restriction or "numbing" of emotional experiences. This numbing may be disruptive to interpersonal relationships. According to the theories elaborated in Chapters 6 and 7, avoidance of intense emotional experience would seem to be similar to the avoidance of interoceptive cues in panic disorder (see below).

PTSD is not uncommon even in very young children undergoing an extremely traumatic event. Senior, Gladstone, and Nurcombe (1982) describe the unfortunate case of a 2-year-old boy who was "snatched" from his natural father and stepmother by his natural mother. The child subsequently developed a rather severe emotional reaction, with several posttraumatic emotional consequences that caused the natural mother to return the child after 5 weeks. Symptoms included difficulty sleeping; nightmares and frequent awakenings accompanied by terror and screaming; anorexia; and regression in toileting habits. These reactions persisted for over a year and even worsened in some ways as the boy began to confuse his natural mother and his stepmother. The situation was resolved with successful therapy. Newman (1976) also observed intense and long-lasting posttraumatic reactions in children after the disastrous Buffalo Creek flood.

While the emotional aspects of PTSD provide its defining features, the interpersonal consequences are also substantial. PTSD victims, particularly war veterans, evidence problems with intimacy and sociality and are often paranoid and hostile in their relationships. Substance abuse is common (Roberts *et al.*, 1982).

INCIDENCE, PREVALENCE, AND COURSE

At first blush one would think that ascertaining prevalence rates for PTSD would be a straightforward task. After all, victims of a trauma, whether war-related or civilian, can be counted and the percentage of those suffering from PTSD can be determined. Unfortunately, this problem has not yielded so simply to this type of calculation. Numerous articles have appeared attesting to the remarkably low prevalence of PTSD in populations of trauma victims. Unfortunately, an almost equal number of articles attest to the remarkably high prevalence. For example, analyzing the British psychiatric literature published during World War II, Rachman (1978) concluded:

> [T]he great majority of people endured the air raids extraordinarily well contrary to the universal expectation of mass panic. Exposure to repeated bombings did not produce a significant increase in psychiatric disorders. Although shortlived fear reactions were common, surprisingly few persistent phobic reactions emerged. (p. 182)

Even among combat soldiers, estimates of PTSD are often low. For example, Kettner (1972) retrospectively examined the records of 1,086 Swedish United Nations troops who saw action in the Congo (now Zaire) during the early 1960s and found only 35 soldiers who had apparently suffered from PTSD. Studying a similar number of Swedes who had been stationed in the Congo and had not experienced combat, Kettner (1972) found no differences in incidence of PTSD (or any psychiatric morbidity, for that matter) between combat and noncombat soldiers.

Findings from civilian disasters echo the surprisingly low rates of emotional casualities. For example, Green, Grace, Lindy, Titchener, and Lindy (1983) examined 147 survivors of the Beverly Hills Supper Club fire. Psychological and emotional symptoms ascertained by clinical interview, as well as questionnaire results, were within normal limits at the times they were assessed. Similarly, a group of 38 people living within 5 miles of the Three Mile Island nuclear power plant were compared to several well-constructed control groups either living near nuclear power plants where no accidents had occurred, or not living near any power plants (Baum, Gatchel, & Schaeffer, 1983). A year after the accident, the Three Mile Island residents did exhibit some symptoms of stress, but these were clearly subclinical.

In perhaps the most elegant series of studies on this topic, Philip Saigh, until recently a professor at the American University in Beirut, studied Lebanese students and civilians throughout various phases of the tragic civil war in Lebanon. What makes Saigh's work particularly important is that he was able to collect prospective data. In the best tradition of a scientist operating under adverse circumstances, Saigh took advantage of the Israeli siege of West Beirut to examine its effect on a selected group of students who had remained in West Beirut. This group was subject to continual bombings, rocket fire, and the usual consequences of being present in an active war zone. Another comparable group of students, however, had managed to evacuate West Beirut and was not subject to the same level of stress. Fortuitously, Saigh had administered a number of questionnaires assessing anxiety and fear to both groups prior to the invasion as part of another study. The surprising conclusion was that the postinvasion scores of the two groups were not significantly different. Thus, prolonged exposure to life-threatening events was not necessarily associated with higher levels of anxiety (Saigh, 1984a, 1984b).

An equally impressive group of studies has reported extraordinarily high rates of PTSD. For example, in their recent epidemiological study of prevalence of DSM-III disorders, Helzer, Robins, and McEvoy (1987) found that fully 60% of Vietnam veterans reported one or more combat-related PTSD symptoms, and that 20% of this sample met the full DSM-III criteria for a PTSD diagnosis. In clinical samples from Veterans Administration hospitals in Southern California, Foy, Resnick, Sipprelle, and Carroll (1987) observed the high rate of 70% meeting full DSM-III criteria for PTSD.

Similar findings are also evident after civilian traumas. In a very important study, Kilpatrick, Best, et al. (1985) sampled over 2,000 adult women about victimization experiences and mental health problems. Traumatic experiences included rape, sexual molestation, robbery, and aggravated assault. The investigators also determined whether the crime was completed, as opposed to attempted but not completed. Subjects were asked about suicidal ideation, suicide attempts, and "nervous breakdowns."

Almost 500 of these 2,000 women had been the victims of a serious crime; 100 had been raped. The results are presented in Table 13.1. Crime victims had a significantly higher frequency of nervous breakdowns, suicidal ideations, and suicide attempts than nonvictims. The crime with the most significant emotional impact was rape. Compared to 2.2% of nonvictims, 19.2% of rape victims had attempted suicide, and 44% reported suicidal ideation at some time following the rape. Suicide attempts by those experiencing attempted rape totaled 8.9%; almost 30% of this group reported suicidal ideation. Severe emotional reactions were generally somewhat less for other crimes, but still significantly higher than for nonvictims. The authors conclude that crime victims are at serious risk for severe emotional symptoms. The response they experience can probably be characterized as PTSD.

The large discrepancies in these surveys become understandable when one looks closely at the experiences of victims of war-related or civilian traumas, as the investigators finding high rates of PTSD have done. For example, the high rate of positive PTSD cases (70%) reported in the Foy, Resnick, et al. (1987) sample was for veterans with "high combat exposure," which was defined as having participated in combat and been wounded. The rate of positive PTSD diagnosis for clinical samples with low combat exposure was approximately 25%. Helzer et al. (1987) reported similar results. Thus, in the studies where low rates of emotional

TABLE 13.1. Proportion of Victimization Groups Experiencing Major Mental Health Problems

	Problem					
	Nervous breakdown		Suicidal ideation		Suicide attempt	
Group	n	%	n	%	n	%
Attempted rape	7	9.0	23	29.5	7	8.9
Completed rape	16	16.3	44	44.0	19	19.2
Attempted molestation	2	5.4	12	32.4	3	8.1
Completed molestation	1	1.9	12	21.8	2	3.6
Attempted robbery	0	0.0	3	9.1	4	12.1
Completed robbery	5	7.8	7	10.8	2	3.1
Aggravated assault	1	2.1	7	14.9	2	4.3
Nonvictims	51	3.3	106	6.8	34	2.2

Note. From Kilpatrick, D. G., Best, C. L., Veronen, L. J., Amick, A. E., Villeponteaux, L. A., & Ruff, G. A. (1985). Mental health correlates of criminal victimization: A random community survey. *Journal of Consulting and Clinical Psychology, 53,* 866–873. Copyright 1985 by the American Psychological Association. Reprinted by permission.

distress were reported, civilians and soldiers may have been present during war or during civilian catastrophes, but may not have directly experienced the horrors of death, dying, and direct attack.

This observation receives further confirmation in Saigh's Beirut studies (Saigh, in press-a). For example, on February 6, 1984, West Beirut experienced a particularly intense bombardment by various factions of Lebanese militias. Several days later, Saigh interviewed a number of undergraduates on whom he had previously collected questionnaire data on emotional functioning. Twelve of these students reported that they were forced to take shelter and were deprived of sleep for 36–48 hours. They had never experienced a more threatening situation. On February 14, 1984, and again on March 14, 1984, they filled out the various anxiety and depression questionnaires. The students were interviewed and questionnaires completed on a final occasion in December 1984.

The results from these timely assessments indicate that 9 of the 11 students experienced symptoms that probably would have warranted a diagnosis of acute PTSD immediately after the attack. For 8 of these students, the symptoms remitted spontaneously within 1 month of the bombardment (by March 14). One student, however, presented symptoms sufficient to earn a PTSD classification (nightmares, flashbacks, elevated anxiety, etc.) fully 9 months after the attack. This student had experienced continual stress for about 1 month after the February 6 bombardment, since her home was located near an area of continued fighting. Scores for this student on the State–Trait Anxiety Inventory, the Beck Depression Inventory, and the Rathus Assertiveness Scale are presented in Figure 13.1. One can see increasing emotionality from prebombardment to December 1984.

Other investigators have also noted a chronic course for PTSD. For example, Kluznick, Speed, VanValkenburg, and Magraw (1986) interviewed 188 men who had been prisoners of war during World War II. Of these men, 67% had experienced PTSD. According to a careful structured interview, 29% of these had fully recovered; 39% still reported mild symptoms; another 24% had improved somewhat but clearly evidenced moderate residual symptoms; and the condition of 8% either remained unchanged or had deteriorated. Of course, these interviews were conducted nearly 40 years after the trauma.

What all of these results suggest is that being present during a catastrophe or trauma is not sufficient by itself to produce PTSD. In fact, the overall incidence of PTSD in populations witnessing or experiencing a trauma seems little or no higher than in those not experiencing the trauma. Rather the disorder appears to be directly related to the intensity and severity of one's personal experience with the catastrophe or trauma.

But even knowledge of this information is not sufficient to predict the onset of PTSD fully. Many individuals experience traumatic events

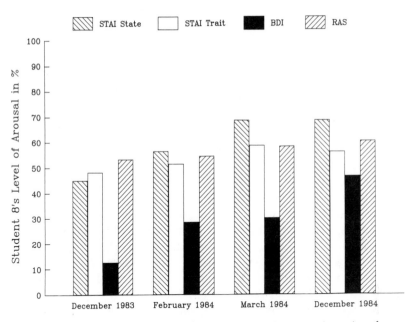

FIGURE 13.1. Results on several anxiety and depression questionnaires for a university student at points before and after a heavy bombardment of West Beirut. Adapted from Saigh, P. (in press). Anxiety, depression, and assertion across alternating intervals of stress. *Journal of Abnormal Psychology.* Copyright by the American Psychological Association. Adapted by permission.

beyond the realm of human imagination, with few if any emotional consequences. Others experience relatively mild traumatic events and yet develop full-blown PTSD. These observations lead directly into a discussion of the etiology of PTSD.

A MODEL OF THE ETIOLOGY OF PTSD

As noted above, we do not know the "cause" of PTSD, but identification of the precipitating event or proximal cause is simple. In this sense, the etiology of PTSD seems much more straightforward, based on the theoretical descriptions of anxiety and fear described in Chapters 6 and 7. Unlike simple phobia, where true alarms, false alarms, or (less often) simple transmission of information may develop into a simple phobic reaction, PTSD seems to emerge from one special chain of events. Intense basic emotions, such as true alarms (but also including rage or distress, resulting from the overwhelming effects of traumatic life events), lead to learned alarms. Learned alarms occur during exposure to situations that symbolize or resemble an aspect of the traumatic event. This is one of the defining features of PTSD in DSM-III-R.

Among occasions that symbolize aspects of the traumatic event are anniversaries of the trauma. As in any phobic reaction, the development of learned alarms results in persistent avoidance of stimuli associated with the trauma, which is another defining feature of PTSD in DSM-III-R. Other stimuli associated with the trauma include thoughts or feelings, as well as memories of the event.

Wirtz and Harrell (1987) provide support for the process of classical conditioning (learned alarms) within PTSD. They observed that victims of physical assault were *less distressed* 6 months after the assault if they had experienced exposure to situations or stimuli that were part of (or resembled) the context of the original assault without experiencing another assault. Victims who had not had the advantage of this exposure, on the other hand, maintained a high level of distress in the 6-month interim. This is what one would expect in classical conditioning. Others have noted the seeming importance of conditioning in the development of PTSD (Keane, Fairbank, Caddell, Zimering, & Bender, 1985), whether the trauma is combat-related or involves physical assault such as rape (e.g., Holmes & St. Lawrence, 1983; Kilpatrick, Veronen, & Best, 1985).

This suggests an important similarity to panic disorder that has been alluded to above. In PTSD, the experience of affect itself is avoided to some extent; this is characterized clinically as a numbing of general responsiveness. This seems to be similar to the tendency of patients with panic disorder to avoid feelings such as those occasioned by movies, whether they be frightening, sad, or exciting. According to the conceptualizations presented above, fear is associated with interoceptive cues signaling the possible occurrence of another false alarm (learned alarm). The numbing of general responsiveness in PTSD would seem to represent a similar avoidance of affect associated with the possibility of another aversive emotional reaction or alarm. Whether the sensitivity to or avoidance of interoceptive cues in panic and the numbing of general responsiveness in PTSD are identical psychopathological responses remains to be demonstrated.

In any case, the experience of alarm or other intense emotions in and of itself is not sufficient for the development of PTSD. Much as in other disorders, one must develop anxiety or the sense that these events, including one's own emotional reactions to them, are proceeding in an unpredictable, uncontrollable manner. When negative affect, including a sense of uncontrollability, develops, one enters the vicious cycle of anxious apprehension described in Chapter 7, and PTSD emerges.

This implies that a psychological and biological vulnerability to develop the disorder exists, as outlined in Chapter 7. There it is also noted that anxiety is always moderated to some extent by variables such as the presence of adequate coping skills and social support. In PTSD, as indicated below, evidence already exists that these moderating variables play a role in determining whether the disorder develops or not. Therefore, these factors are represented explicitly in the model presented in this chapter, although it is assumed that these factors moderate the occurrence of other anxiety disorders to an equal extent. A model of the etiology of PTSD is presented in Figure 13.2. An elaboration of evidence supporting various aspects of the model is presented below.

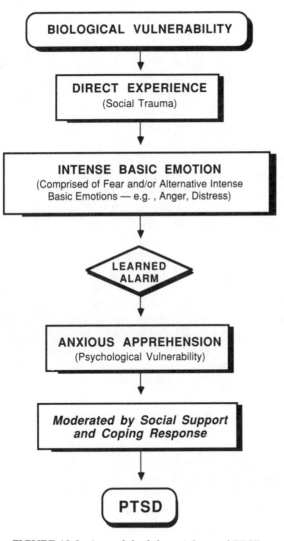

FIGURE 13.2. A model of the etiology of PTSD.

INTENSITY OF ONE'S EXPERIENCE OF THE TRAUMA

That intense emotional reactions to trauma are usually short-lived has been often observed and is illustrated above in the data from Saigh's (in press-a) Lebanese students. All of the students experienced marked emotional reactivity immediately after the shelling of their neighborhoods. For all but one, however, these emotions quickly subsided in a day or two. For the one student who experienced more intense emotion over a longer period of time (about a month), a full-blown disorder developed and was more severe when assessed 9 months later. Foy and his colleagues (Foy, Sipprelle, Rueger, & Carroll, 1984) have estimated that approximately 40% of the variance in PTSD scores in combat veterans is predicted by degree of combat exposure. Thus, the nature of the traumatic event—or, more accurately, the duration and intensity of the emotional reaction or alarm to the traumatic event—plays the major role in predicting the existence of PTSD at a later date. Once again, 70% of a clinical sample of combat veterans surveyed by Foy, Resnick, et al. (1987) who had experienced intense combat and had been wounded met full DSM-III criteria. Among prisoners of war, 67% developed PTSD, but less combat exposure resulted in fewer PTSD cases or symptoms. Thus, it seems clear that a major etiological factor is the severity of the trauma itself. This is clearly illustrated in Table 13.2, put together by Foy, Carroll, and Donahoe (1987), which summarizes studies examining etiological factors in combat-related PTSD; it was reported again in a study by Breslau and Davis (1987).

FAMILY STUDIES

In Chapter 5, evidence is reviewed that strongly suggests a biological predisposition to develop anxiety disorders. Although the current evidence suggests that this biological disposition may be relatively nonspecific, it is suggested in Chapter 7 that the disposition is activated by negative life events and plays a role in the development of anxious apprehension and, possibly, alarms. If the model of PTSD depicted in Figure 13.2 is correct, one would also expect anxiety disorders to aggregate in the families of PTSD victims. Now some evidence is beginning to appear suggesting that this is the case.

Davidson, Swartz, Storck, Krishnan, and Hammett (1985) conducted an important, although preliminary, family study on PTSD. These investigators compared the rates of familial psychopathology in the relatives of 36 veterans with PTSD to the rates in relatives of two other groups, using the family history method. Appropriately, the two other groups consisted of matched samples of nonveteran males with either generalized anxiety disorder or major depression. The rates of depression and anxiety in the

TABLE 13.2. Studies Examining Etiological Factors in Vietnam Combat-Related PTSD

Study	Variables	Findings	Population	Combat exposure measured	Comments
		Premilitary variables			
Egendorf, Kadushin, Laufer, Rothbart, & Sloan (1981)	Family stability[a] Minority status[a]	Although combat exposure was found to be the primary etiological variable, family stability and minority status were also significant factors. Black combat veterans and veterans with poorer family stability were more vulnerable to postwar stress problems.	A nonclinical sample ($n = 733$) was divided into Vietnam-era vets. Vietnam vets, and nonvets.	Yes	Although the study evidences considerable postwar adjustment difficulties among Vietnam combat vets, it may underestimate problem severity due to not sampling institutionalized vets (e.g., those who were hospitalized or in prison or jail) or those who lived in isolation. PTSD symptomatology as defined in DSM-III (1980) was not measured as a postwar variable.
Foy, Sipprelle, Rueger, & Carroll (1984) Carroll, Rueger, Foy, & Donahoe (1985)	Preliminary psychosocial adjustment	Combat exposure accounted for significantly more variance in postwar PTSD severity than premilitary adjustment variables.	Clinical samples (Foy: $n = 43$; Carroll: $n = 65$). Multiple regressions on PTSD severity utilized continuous variables rather than sample groupings.	Yes	Preliminary adjustment index included items assessing family stability, legal-authority problems, substance abuse, and social functioning. Subject response was cross-validated with relative report in the Carroll et al. (1985) study. Limitations include small sample sizes drawn from one geographic location and PTSD symptomatology assessed only by a symptom checklist method.

(Continued)

509

TABLE 13.2. (*Continued*)

Study	Variables	Findings	Population	Combat exposure measured	Comments
		Premilitary variables			
Worthington (1977)	Age of entry[a] Education[a] Authority problems[a]	Postwar adjustment problems were more strongly related to premilitary adjustment variables than military service in Vietnam. Earlier age of entry, lower education, and authority problems were most predictive.	A nonclinical sample of veterans who were recently released from service were divided into Vietnam service and nonservice groups ($n = 147$).	No	PTSD symptoms were not assessed; dependent variables were anomie, self-concept, and socialization. Combat exposure was not assessed and compared to other predictor variables.
Nace, O'Brien, Mintz, Ream, & Meyers (1978)	Premilitary psychosocial adjustment	Postmilitary social adjustment and depression were accounted for primarily by preservice adjustment variables.	A sample ($n = 202$) of Vietnam vets who sought medical help for drug abuse while in Vietnam were divided into heavy users, experimental users, and nonusers.	No	Premilitary adjustment index included items assessing criminal behavior, work history, education, family stability, SES, and substance abuse. Limitations include the absence of PTSD as an outcome variable, and combat exposure was not used as a control or predictor variable.
Penk *et al.* (1981)	Family Environment Scales (Moos, 1979)	Current PTSD symptomatology was more strongly related to combat exposure than demographic or premilitary variables.	A clinical sample ($n = 207$) of veterans seeking treatment for substance abuse was divided into heavy-combat, light-combat, and noncombat groups.	Yes	The Family Environment Scales were completed retrospectively for the premilitary time period. The measure includes a number of subscales such as Cohesiveness, Expressiveness, Conflict, Organization, Independence, etc. Findings may be limited to primary substance abusers.

510

Study	Variables	Findings		Description
Frye & Stockton (1982)	Education War attitudes Emotional stability Age of entry into service	Current PTSD symptomatology was more strongly related to military and post-military variables than premilitary variables.	A nonclinical sample ($n = 88$) of Vietnam-era officer candidate school graduates was divided into PTSD-positive and PTSD-negative groups.	Yes	Although findings were limited to Vietnam-era officers of one graduating class, it replicates the findings of other studies indicating the importance of combat exposure to subsequent development of PTSD symptoms, rather than premilitary adjustment variables. A considerable number of predictor variables were used ($n = 19$), given sample size; replication of findings is needed.

Military variables

| Worthington (1978) | "Enlisted" service[a]
Lack of promotion[a]
Disciplinary actions[a] | Poor postservice adjustment was related to the listed in-service variables. | Same as Worthington (1977). | No | Same as above. |
| Foy et al. (1984) | Military adjustment[a] | Military adjustment was significantly related to postmilitary adjustment and, to a lesser degree, PTSD symptomatology, whereas premilitary adjustment was not. | Same as above. | Yes | Military adjustment index included items assessing disciplinary actions, drug and alcohol use, awards, and psychiatric contacts.

Postmilitary adjustment examined postwar work history, social functioning, legal problems, and psychiatric help seeking.

(Continued) |

TABLE 13.2. (*Continued*)

Study	Variables	Findings	Population	Combat exposure measured	Comments
		Military variables			
Frye & Stockton (1982)	Combat wounds Marital status Age in service Duration of assignment Perceived stress	None of these variables was found to differentiate PTSD-positive and PTSD-negative vets or to predict PTSD severity.	Same as above.	Yes	Same as above.
Gallers, Foy, Donohoe, & Goldfarb (in press)	Traumatic violence[a] Drug use[a] Military adjustment Premilitary adjustment	PTSD-positive veterans reported significantly more exposure to traumatic violence and a greater evidence of drug use during combat duty than PTSD-negative veterans. Groups did not differ on premilitary or military adjustment.	60 high-combat vets were divided into PTSD-positive and PTSD-negative groups.	Yes	The exposure to traumatic violence index assessed exposure to atrocity and abusive violence to civilians and enemy soldiers (e.g., torture, physical abuse, rape, mutilation, etc.) Premilitary and military adjustment index same as Foy *et al.* (1984).
Laufer & Gallops (1982)	Participation in abusive violence[a] Exposure to abusive violence	Participation in abusive violence was found to result in a greater incidence of postwar stress. Results were negative for the exposure variable.	Same as Egendorf *et al.* (1981).	Yes	"Stress" variable was roughly analogous to DSM-III "PTSD." Abusive violence was measured on basis of open-ended questions about the "dirty side" of war.

512

		Homecoming variables		
Frye & Stockton (1982)	Family helpfulness on return[a] Immediacy of discharge after combat duty[a] Talking about Vietnam SES Education Locus of control[a]	Veterans with PTSD symptoms reported a significantly more negative view of their family's helpfulness, an external locus of control, and a more immediate discharge after the war. The other variables were not significantly related to PTSD.	Same as above.	Yes	Same as above.

Note. From Foy, D. W., Carroll, E. M., & Donahoe, C. P., Jr. (1987). Etiological factors in the development of PTSD in clinical samples of Vietnam combat veterans. *Journal of Clinical Psychology, 43,* 17–27. Copyright 1987 by Clinical Psychology Publishing Company. Reprinted by permission.

[a]Variable significantly related to postwar PTSD or postmilitary adjustment.

families of the PTSD group were similar to the rates observed in the families of the generalized anxiety disorder group; the rate of anxiety disorders was higher in the families of both of these groups than in the families of the depressed group.

Now even more interesting data on familial aggregation provide broad hints on the interaction of the negative life event that triggers PTSD with familial aggregation of psychopathology and perhaps biological predispositions. Foy, Resnick, *et al.* (1987) looked at the family history of veterans with either high or low combat exposure, as well as the presence of a PTSD-positive or PTSD-negative diagnosis. In two separate samples, rates of familial psychopathology were higher in the PTSD-positive patients than in the PTSD-negative patients. But the more interesting result became apparent when the groups were broken down by amount of combat exposure. In the face of high combat exposure (which, according to Foy, Resnick, *et al.*'s definition, included being wounded), rates of familial psychopathology made little difference. That is, a very high percentage of high-exposure veterans developed PTSD whether anxiety ran in their families or not. However, across two separate samples, the probability of a PTSD-positive diagnosis in the low-exposure group was considerably higher when family psychopathology was present. In one sample, 48% of a group with a family history of psychopathology were PTSD-positive, compared to 27% of a group without such a family history. In the other sample, the figures were 30% and 11%, respectively. These data support the interaction between a biological vulnerability and the experience of a traumatic event in the development of PTSD. As such, data supporting this interactional model may have important implications for the etiology of other anxiety disorders, where a false alarm rather than a true alarm plays a crucial role. Most recently, biological investigators are beginning to consider the specific relationship of PTSD and the neurobiological systems implicated in anxiety (e.g., Kolb, 1987; Van der Kolk, Greenberg, Boyd, & Krystal, 1985).

SOCIAL SUPPORT

Finally, the role of social support in buffering PTSD is worth mentioning, since there is more evidence on this topic within this specific disorder than exists for other anxiety disorders (e.g., Carroll, Rueger, Foy, & Donahoe, 1985). The results are quite consistent in supporting the buffering role of social support in the development of PTSD. The broader and deeper the network of social support, the less chance of developing PTSD. Once again, based on our theoretical models, this would be true of all anxiety disorders.

PTSD AND SIMPLE PHOBIA

Now that the literature on the development of PTSD has been briefly reviewed, it is interesting to reflect on the relationship of PTSD to simple phobia, as alluded to at the end of Chapter 12. According to the developing models of anxiety disorders presented in this book, it is no accident that the chapters on simple phobia and PTSD are paired. PTSD, by definition, describes an emotional disorder developing after an intense emotional experience in the context of a trauma outside the realm of typical human experience. But some phobic reactions characterized as simple phobia develop under similar conditions. For example, some people develop dog phobias after having been bitten by a dog; the resulting true alarm generalizes in the form of learned alarms to all dogs, even those known to be harmless, as well as real and symbolic representations of dogs. The case of the woman who developed a phobia of frogs, described at the end of Chapter 12, is another example. On the face of it, there seems little if any difference in terms of psychopathology between PTSD and simple phobias developing after true alarms, at least in extreme forms. This would exclude the multitude of phobic reactions that do not reach the status of clinical disorders. In support of the role of learned alarms in PTSD, Mellman and Davis (1985) reported that the most common symptoms accompanying a "flashback" were perspiration, tremulousness, palpitations, and dyspnea. They noted that the similarities to a panic attack were striking. Phobias developing after false alarms (e.g., phobias of flying in planes after an unexpected panic), as well as those few phobias that seem to develop after simple information transmission, may proceed a bit differently (more is said about modes of information transmission in the discussion of obsessive–compulsive disorder in Chapter 16). In any case, future classification systems may be realigned on the basis of whether the initial alarm is true or false.

COURAGE UNDER STRESS

Finally, some additional intriguing hints regarding a biological contribution to anxiety in general and to the development of PTSD in particular can be found in the creative and important series of studies on courage carried out by Rachman and his colleagues (e.g., Rachman, 1978). For example, Cox, Hallam, O'Connor, and Rachman (1983) studied a small group of individuals who had volunteered to be bomb disposal operators in Northern Ireland and who were decorated for their gallantry. By any criteria, these individuals were highly courageous. They were compared to a group composed of other members of bomb disposal units who were also experienced and highly competent operators and had achieved the same training standards as the decorated operators. Both groups were asked to make difficult discriminations under threat of shock. There were no differences between the groups on subjective reports of reactivity (or anxiety) or on their performance during the stressful situation. Both groups reported few, if any, fearful reactions in contrast to a small number of normal comparison subjects. However, the subjects decorated for gallantry maintained a lower cardiac rate when making difficult discriminations than did their confederates.

The results from this preliminary study suggest that the only difference between these two small groups of otherwise very closely matched subjects was physiological reactivity under stress. Of course, it is very possible that this finding was a consequence of the development of a sense of control and perceptions of self-efficacy learned in a variety of conditions far more stressful then the test in this experiment. But the other possibility is that they brought this lowered physiological activity with them to the test and that it reflected consitutional differences in reactivity to stress. These findings may lend some support to the contribution of a biological tendency to be reactive to stress. Of course, this vulnerability would have to line up with a variety of environmental and psychological factors to produce PTSD or any anxiety disorder.

DIAGNOSIS AND ASSESSMENT

DIAGNOSIS

In view of the controversy over the very existence of PTSD as a diagnostic category prior to 1980 (Figley, 1978), we have made remarkable progress in the area of diagnosis and classification. One reason, of course, is the relatively clear precipitant. Any time a trauma occurs, the potential for studying the development of PTSD exists. If a prospective patient has just witnessed a brutal murder, been raped, or been intensely exposed to the horrors of a natural catastrophe, initial complaints of anxiety and depression accompanied by deterioration in performance may well be associated with PTSD. Of course, it is never that simple. According to the model of the development of anxiety presented in Chapter 7, negative life events of some sort are often present in anxiety disorders. To consider PTSD, one must decide whether the negative life event is outside the usual range of human experience, as specified in DSM-III-R. The presence of other criteria suggesting a conditioned emotional response to this traumatic experience makes differential diagnosis a bit easier. The only conceptually inconsistent issue arises when one attempts to differentiate simple phobia with a traumatic conditioning etiology from PTSD. Most likely, this is not possible.

As reviewed in Chapter 9, comorbidity is often present in clinical samples. Comorbidity often has substantial treatment implications. A variety of additional emotional and behavioral disorders may accompany PTSD. Thus, we need to examine presenting patterns of comorbidity closely when PTSD is the primary diagnosis. This is true for any primary diagnosis.

Refinements to the category of PTSD in DSM-III-R are relatively minor, with one exception. The subtyping of acute versus chronic or delayed has been dropped; in its place, one simply notes whether the onset was delayed 6 months or more after the trauma. DSM-III and DSM-III-R criteria are counterposed in Table 13.3.

With more precise specification of PTSD, it seems that we can now diagnose the condition with some reliability. In a preliminary study we (Blanchard, Gerardi, et al., 1986) established a kappa coefficient of .857 for PTSD. In this procedure the (novice) interviewer utilized the ADIS (see Chapter 9), and diagnostic information was compared to a criterion diagnosis ascertained by an experienced clinician. The results support the reliability of PTSD as a diagnostic category and the utility of the ADIS in generating the necessary information.

A variety of studies from different points of view are also contributing to the validity of the category. Difficulties with the category as specified in DSM-III have revolved largely around issues of lack of specificity or comorbidity. For example, addictive behaviors and depression are common accompaniments of PTSD in clinical samples, as they are with all anxiety disorders. Of course, addictive behaviors are found more often in male patients, which might account for their prevalence in male combat veterans with PTSD. Nevertheless, this raises some difficulties when one is trying to determine the primary disorder, as noted by Green, Lindy, and Grace (1985).

The ADIS is providing useful information on the incidence of PTSD symptoms in other anxiety disorders, as well as the prevalence of other anxiety disorders in patients with a primary diagnosis of PTSD. Data from these studies will be forthcoming from our clinic. Suffice it to say for now that the overlap is not restricted to simple phobia. To take just one recent example, we assessed a severe social phobic who also met the Axis II criteria for avoidant personality disorder. This individual, who suffered as a child from poor social skills and a very awkward physical style, reported a very difficult adolescence. He had been brutalized both physically and psychologically by his peers during his difficult early adolescent years. At the time of examination in his mid-30s, flashbacks, nightmares, and the full range of emotional responding connected with rejection and

TABLE 13.3. DSM-III and DSM-III-R Diagnostic Criteria for PTSD

DSM-III[a]	DSM-III-R[b]
A. Existence of a recognizable stressor that would evoke significant symptoms of distress in almost everyone.	A. The person has experienced an event that is outside the range of usual human experience and that would be markedly distressing to almost anyone, e.g., serious threat or harm to one's life or physical integrity; serious threat or harm to one's children, spouse, or other close relatives and friends; sudden destruction of another person who has recently been, or is being, seriously injured or killed as the result of an accident or physical violence.
B. Reexperiencing of the trauma as evidenced by at least one of the following: (1) recurrent and intrusive recollections of the event. (2) recurrent dreams of the event (3) sudden acting or feeling as if the traumatic event were reoccurring, because of an association with an environmental or ideational stimulus	B. The traumatic event is persistently reexperienced in at least one of the following ways: (1) recurrent and intrusive distressing recollections of the event (in young children, repetitive play in which themes or aspects of the trauma are expressed) (2) recurrent distressing dreams of event (3) sudden acting or feeling as if the traumatic event were reoccurring (includes a sense of reliving the experience, illusions, hallucinations, and dissociative [flashback] episodes, even those that occur upon awakening or when intoxicated) (4) intense psychological distress at exposure to events that symbolize or resemble an aspect of the traumatic event, including anniversaries of the trauma
C. Numbing of responsiveness to or reduced involvement with the external world, beginning some time after the trauma, as shown by at least one of the following: (1) markedly diminished interest in one or more significant activities (2) feeling of detachment or estrangement from others (3) constricted affect	C. Persistent avoidance of stimuli associated with the trauma or numbing of general responsiveness (not present before the trauma), as indicated by at least three of the following: (1) efforts to avoid thoughts or feelings associated with the trauma (2) efforts to avoid activities or situations that arouse recollections of the trauma (3) inability to recall an important aspect of the trauma (psychogenic amnesia) (4) markedly diminished interest in significant activities (in young children, loss of recently acquired de-

velopmental skills such as toilet training or language skills)

(5) feeling of detachment or estrangement from others

(6) restricted range of affect, e.g., unable to have loving feelings

(7) sense of foreshortened future, e.g., child does not expect to have a career, marriage, or children, or a long life

D. At least two of the following symptoms that were not present before the trauma:

(1) hyperalertness or exaggerated startle response

(2) sleep disturbance

(3) guilt about surviving when others have not, or about behavior required for survival

(4) memory impairment or trouble concentrating

(5) avoidance of activities that arouse recollection of the traumatic event

(6) intensification of symptoms by exposure to events that symbolize or resemble the traumatic event

D. Persistent symptoms of increased arousal (not present before the trauma), as indicated by at least two of the following:

(1) difficulty falling or staying asleep

(2) irritability or outbursts of anger

(3) difficulty concentrating

(4) hypervigilance

(5) exaggerated startle response

(6) physiologic reactivity upon exposure to events that symbolize or resemble an aspect of the traumatic event (e.g., a woman who was raped in an elevator breaks out in a sweat when entering any elevator)

E. Duration of the disturbance (symptoms in B, C, and D) of at least one month.

Specify Delayed Onset if the onset of symptoms was at least six months after the trauma.

---

[a] Criteria from American Psychiatric Association. (1980). *Diagnostic and statistical manual of mental disorders* (3rd ed., pp. 137–138). Washington, DC: Author. Copyright 1980 by the American Psychiatric Association. Reprinted by permission.

[b] Criteria from American Psychiatric Association. (1987). *Diagnostic and statistical manual of mental disorders* (3rd ed., rev., pp. 250–251). Washington, DC: Author. Copyright 1987 by the American Psychiatric Association. Reprinted by permission.

"taunting" cues remained. Technically, these symptoms qualified him for the diagnosis of PTSD. While this individual clearly met the diagnosis for social phobia and avoidant personality disorder, his presentation was qualitatively different from that of a socially skilled individual presenting with fear of public speaking, or even a socially unskilled individual who avoids social situations. DSM-III-R, in which hierarchical considerations are eliminated, will help in addressing this issue.

The majority of studies approaching the problem from different points of view have found that PTSD has both construct and discriminant validity. For example, Laufer, Brett, and Gallops (1985) found that exposure to combat stress affected differentially the four major dimensions of posttraumatic stress comprising the diagnostic criteria. That is, the more exposure to stress, the more evident specific PTSD symptoms become. Pearce, Schauer, Garfield, Ohlde, and Patterson (1985) found similar results when comparing two groups that had undergone trauma with a group that had not. Analogously, Saigh (in press-b) found that children with a PTSD diagnosis had more symptoms of PTSD than comparable control groups of children with test anxiety or nonclinical controls. Also, Malloy, Fairbank, and Keane (1983) clearly distinguished PTSD patients from several well-constructed comparison groups on a variety of anxiety-related measures after presentation of mild combat stimuli. Other studies of this type are reviewed below. Of course, demonstrating that PTSD symptoms vary in intensity as a function of the initial trauma and that the symptoms discriminate patients from normals is only the beginning of a thorough assessment of the validity of the category. Fine-grained analyses of the importance of each of the defining criteria, as well as careful assessment of discriminant validity compared to other clinical groups, is required.

Preliminary estimates on the reliability and validity of PTSD insure that additional study of this disorder will be worthwhile. But as knowledge evolves and additional data on classification and comorbidity are forthcoming, nosological systems will undoubtedly undergo further change.

ASSESSMENT

In addition to assessment by structured interview, more specialized assessment procedures for the variety of PTSD symptoms have been investigated. These can be classified in the usual three categories of self-report instruments, measures of behavior, and physiological assessment procedures. In the case of PTSD, as in the special case of blood phobia described in the last chapter, physiological assessment has proved particularly promising. This brief survey begins with an examination of the most commonly used self-report instruments and questionnaires.

Questionnaire Measures

Many investigators have examined the utility of standard questionnaire measures in classifying and assessing PTSD patients. The most heavily used seems to be the MMPI (e.g., Foy et al., 1984; Penk et al., 1981). But using the MMPI or other similar questionnaires to "diagnose" known groups of subjects has proven difficult in the past with other disorders. This is because sometimes one group of subscales will significantly discriminate groups, while in a replication a second, entirely different group of subscales will be discriminating.

Keane and his colleagues (e.g., Keane, Malloy, & Fairbank, 1984) have made the most sophisticated analysis of the utility of the MMPI. In one study from this group (Fairbank, McCaffrey, & Keane, 1985), the MMPI successfully discriminated PTSD patients from those "feigning" PTSD symptomatology. Thus, it appears, pending replication, that it is possible to use existing psychometric questionnaires to identify PTSD patients. But the MMPI is a relatively lengthy instrument to employ, particularly if other structured interviews and assessment procedures are part of the battery.

A variety of structured questionnaires have been developed to assess specific situations often associated with PTSD, such as combat or rape. For example, Keane, Caddell, and Taylor (1986) developed a 35-item scale based on the DSM-III criteria for PTSD to assess combat-related PTSD. This scale has very adequate psychometric properties. Friedman, Schneiderman, West, and Corson (1986) also developed two questionnaires to assess combat-related PTSD. These questionnaires were labeled the Combat Exposure Scale and the Post Traumatic Stress Disorder Scale. Adequate psychometric properties were established for these scales. Resick, Veronen, Kilpatrick, Calhoun, and Atkinson (1986) developed a modified fear survey to assess the level and content of fear reactions in sexual assault victims. They also established the reliability and utility of this survey for these populations. In addition to structured questionnaires, simple quantitative ratings of emotional reactivity to various PTSD stimuli (e.g., war scenes, images of attack or assault) are often utilized as repeated measures of subjective responding during treatment.

Physiological Responding

An exciting development—from the point of view of establishing the validity of the category of PTSD, as well as that of providing a useful assessment procedure—involves newly devised physiological measures for PTSD. Typically, patients are exposed to a variety of PTSD-related stimuli (movies, audiotapes, etc.) as well as to non-PTSD-related stimuli in a psychophysiological laboratory while relevant physiological measures are administered. In an early example of this type of investigation, Dobbs and Wilson (1960) used this procedure to discriminate veterans who probably had PTSD from veterans who did not. Other preliminary studies testing these methods were carried out by Fairbank and Keane (1982), Blanchard, Kolb, Pallmeyer, and Gerardi (1982), and Malloy et al. (1983).

More sophisticated studies appearing recently seems to confirm the utility of psychophysiological assessment. For example, Pallmeyer, Blanchard, and Kolb (1986) recorded heart rate, blood pressure, skin conductance level, and forehead EMG during a series of conditions including combat sounds of gradually increasing intensity. Five groups were assessed in this manner: Vietnam veterans with PTSD; Vietnam veterans without PTSD but with comparable levels of combat experience; Vietnam veterans with other psychiatric disorders; Vietnam-era veterans who were not stationed in Vietnam at any time during their service experience; and nonveteran phobics. The authors found that heart rate response to low-intensity combat sounds discriminated very clearly between veterans with PTSD and other groups. Specifically, veterans with PTSD showed significant changes in heart rate to combat stimuli when compared to other groups, as indicated in Figure 13.3. Although group averages clearly revealed increased heart rate responsivity to all levels of intensity of combat sound, a discriminant-function analysis suggested that response to low levels of combat sound best predicted individual differences between veterans with PTSD and other groups.

This type of analysis was tested more systematically by Blanchard, Kolb, Gerardi, Ryan, and Pallmeyer (1986). The responses of 57 veterans with PTSD were compared to 34 without PTSD in a similar physiological test. Once again, veterans with PTSD demonstrated higher average heart rate across all conditions, as well as higher resting heart rate, which is so

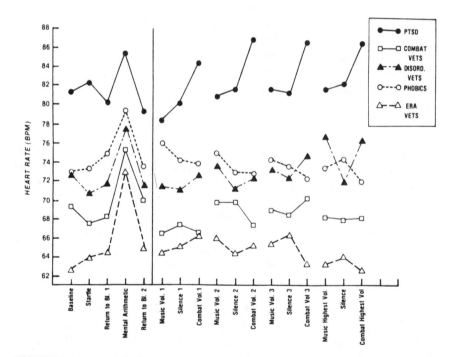

FIGURE 13.3. Average heart rate values of each group for each experimental condition. From Pallmeyer, T. P., Blanchard, E. B., & Kolb, L. C. (1986). The psychophysiology of combat-induced post-traumatic stress disorder in Vietnam veterans. *Behaviour Research and Therapy, 24,* 645–652. Copyright 1986 by Pergamon Journals, Ltd. Reprinted by permission.

characteristic of the anxiety disorders (see Chapter 5). Using a single cut-off score on the highest heart rate response to combat sounds, the investigators accurately identified 70% of the PTSD veterans, with only 9.7% false positives. They suggest that this assessment procedure may be useful in diagnosis, but should not be a single diagnostic index. The procedure may also be useful for determining improvement after treatment, although data demonstrating the validity of physiological indices as measures of change in PTSD are not available. Data presented in Chapter 5 (Holden & Barlow, 1986) found that a similar pattern of responses from agoraphobics was not particularly useful as a means of assessing therapeutic change.

Behavioral Measures

Simple phobics characteristically avoid representations of their phobic object or situation. Sometimes these representations may range far and wide across a number of generalization gradients, including images, thoughts, and objects that seem only remotely related to the original phobic object. By all reports summarized above, the same can be said for PTSD. Thus, one would expect substantial avoidance of trauma-related stimuli; this certainly seems to be the case. From this point of view, it is somewhat surprising that behavioral measures of avoidance have not been more widely utilized. When these assessment procedures have been employed, they are often part of another type of assessment procedure. For example, Blanchard et al. (1982) noted that the PTSD group tolerated less intense levels of combat sounds and turned off audiotapes of combat sounds more quickly than controls. In view of all the creative methods of establishing IBATs that have been devised for the various simple phobias, it would seem a small matter to extend this work to the area of PTSD.

TREATMENT

EXPOSURE

Chapter 12 has noted near-unanimity of agreement on the utility of exposure-based procedures in treating simple phobia. For that reason, treatment issues have not received the experimental attention they deserve. Much the same can be said for PTSD (Fairbank & Brown, 1987; Keane et al., 1985). Although most clinicians would agree on the advantages of re-exposing the victim to the trauma (exposure to trauma cues), our knowledge of the effectiveness of treatment has not advanced much beyond anecdotal case studies. Thus, imaginal exposure, in which the contextual and emotional experiences of the trauma are worked through systematically, has been used for decades with trauma victims under a variety of names. Perhaps the best-known example, described extensively by Grinker and Spiegel (1943), was the treatment of war neuroses by "abreaction."

With avoidance of situational and emotional cues of the trauma as complete as it often is, exposure-based treatments designed to facilitate re-experience of the trauma can have very dramatic results. For example, repeated systematic imagination of events associated with the trauma may elicit little or no affect for a number of sessions. But it is not unusual at some point for the full emotional experience to burst forth as if a dam had collapsed, resulting in a dramatic and sometimes frightening display of intense emotion. Since the object of therapy is to work through or "process" this emotion and prevent further avoidance of emotion-related (or situation-related) cues, it seems important to encourage this emotional "abreaction" rather than to attempt to dampen the emotion and comfort the patient. This can make for dramatic therapeutic sessions and often requires considerable therapeutic skill.

Many case studies have been reported along these lines (e.g., Fairbank, Gross, & Keane, 1983; Keane & Kaloupek, 1982; Schinder, 1980). Rychtarik, Silverman, Van Landingham, and Prue (1984) reported an interesting case of an incest victim treated with intensive imaginal exposure. Larger series of cases have also been reported, although specific interventions are often vaguely described. For example, Kuch, Swinson, and Kirby (1984) treated a series of 30 patients evidently suffering from PTSD after traumatic car crashes. Most patients responded positively to exposure-based treatments. Interestingly, the authors noted that initial anxiety in regard to the imagery was one of the best predictors of outcome. This clinical observation is consistent with experimental observations in other anxiety disorders as reviewed in Chapter 8.

Solomon and Benbenishty (1986), working with Israeli soldiers in the Lebanon war, have extolled the benefits of treating potential trauma victims as soon as possible. Relying on the principles of proximity, immediacy, and expectancy, these clinicians set up a treatment center near the front and allowed potential PTSD victims to rest and "ventilate" their experiences regarding the trauma for a few days. A strong expectation that they would return to the front was maintained. This treatment resembles the old adage of jumping back on the horse after a painful fall to prevent subsequent fear of riding. This adage has some truth to it.

THE TREATMENT APPROACH OF MARDI HOROWITZ

The clinical investigator with perhaps the most extensive experience in treating traumatic states is Mardi Horowitz (1986). Approaching the problem from a psychodynamic point of view, Horowitz has made some important contributions to our understanding of PTSD. The priorities of treatment, according to Horowitz. are listed in Table 13.4. As one can see, the emphasis is on systemic exposure to or reexperience of the traumatic event. If the patient is "frozen in [an] overcontrol state of denial and numbness," then Horowitz recommends "dosing" the re-experience or arranging the exposure along a hierarchy of intensity. This contrasts with the abreaction response sought after by those employing more intensive imaginal exposure procedures. Of course, there is as yet no evidence on which approach is better. However, consistent with our therapeutic recommendations for other anxiety disorders, my colleagues and I agree with Horowitz and see no reason to put the patient through an intensively

TABLE 13.4. Priorities of Treatment

Patient's current state	Treatment goal
Under continuing impact of external stress event.	Terminate external event or remove patient from contiguity with it. Provide temporary relationship. Help with decisions, plans, or working through.

Swings to intolerable levels:
  Ideational–emotional attacks.
  Paralyzing denial and numbness.
	Reduce amplitude of oscillations to swings of tolerable intensity of ideation and emotion.
	Continue emotional and ideational support.

Frozen in overcontrol state of denial and numbness with or without intrusive repetitions.	Help patient "dose" re-experience of event and implications that help remember for a time, put out of mind for a time, remember for a time, and so on. During periods of recollection, help patient organize and express experience. Increase sense of safety in therapeutic relationship so patient can resume processing the event.
Able to experience and tolerate episodes of ideation and waves of emotion.	Help patient work through associations: the conceptual, emotional, object relations, and self-image implications of the stress event. Help patient relate this stress event to earlier threats, relationship models, self-concepts, and future plans.
Able to work through ideas and emotions on one's own.	Work through loss of therapeutic relationship. Terminate treatment.

Note. From Horowitz, M. (1986). *Stress response syndromes* (2nd ed.). New York: Jason Aronson. Copyright 1986 by Jason Aronson. Reprinted by permission.

aversive emotional experience when more gradual exposure-based procedures seem to be just as effective in the long run.

What is particularly important about Horowitz's contributions is his emphasis on providing substantial (social) support during therapy and making every attempt to insure that adequate social support is arranged in the patient's environment following the trauma. In view of the established importance of social support networks in the etiology of traumatic reactions, this is an obvious area for intervention.

TREATMENT RESEARCH

Perhaps the closest approximation to an experimental analysis of the effects of treatment has recently been reported by Saigh (1987). Once again, working against the background of the crises in Beirut, Saigh assessed and treated three Lebanese children with PTSD. For example, one young girl, Layla, was referred for problems associated with PTSD that developed shortly after she witnessed the death of a man who was shot by a sniper. The other two children had had similar experiences. A variety of questionnaires were utilized, but this report is distinguished as one of the few to arrange for direct behavioral measures of trauma-related problems. IBATs (10 items each) were developed describing the approach to the situation where the trauma had occurred (which was now judged to be safe). In addition, self-monitoring of traumatic thoughts was initiated 1 week prior to the initial baseline probes and continued on a daily basis throughout baseline and treatment. Self-monitoring was maintained for 7 days after treatment and resumed once again for 7 days at a 6-month follow-up. In addition, for each child, a series of at least four traumatic scenes was constructed for later use in imaginal flooding; these scenes depicted a chronological sequence of trauma-related events. Layla's scenes were (1) walking to a neighborhood market, (2) hearing shouts and seeing people flee, (3) seeing a man's prostrate body in the street, and (4) running away.

Treatment involved presenting the scenes in imagination for 60 minutes. While this may seem lengthy to some clinicians accustomed to utilizing the briefer imaginal procedures of systematic desensitization, most clinicians report that a presentation of 30 or more minutes in length is very important to the success of imaginal flooding with PTSD. After the session, probes of all four scenes were taken, during which each child reported his or her levels of anxiety (SUDs). Data for Layla are presented in Figure 13.4; in addition, self-monitored frequencies of traumatic and intrusive thoughts for all three children are presented in Figure 13.5. On behavioral measures Layla accomplished 35% of her steps prior to treat-

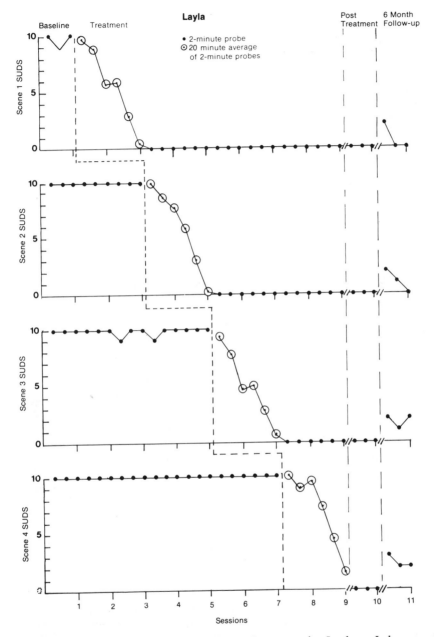

FIGURE 13.4. SUDs data on four traumatic scenes for Layla, a Lebanese child being treated for PTSD. From Saigh, P. (1987). In vitro flooding of childhood post-traumatic stress disorders: A systematic replication. *Professional School Psychology*, 2, 133–144. Copyright 1987 by Jason Aronson. Reprinted by permission.

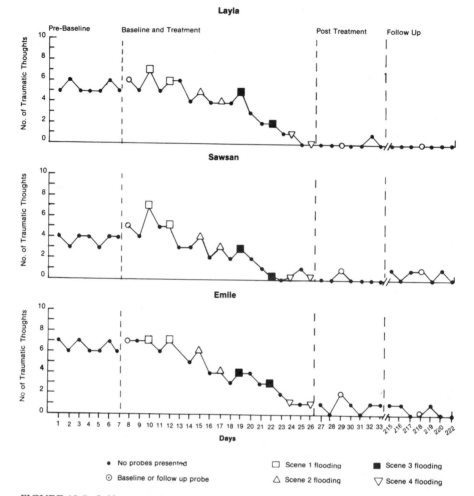

FIGURE 13.5. Self-reported number of traumatic thoughts for three Lebanese children being treated for PTSD. From Saigh, P. (1987). In vitro flooding of childhood post-traumatic stress disorders: A systematic replication. *Professional School Psychology, 2,* 133–144. Copyright 1987 by Jason Aronson. Reprinted by permission.

ment, 95% percent at the midpoint, and 100% by the end of treatment. The other children showed similar improvement. Intrusive thoughts were virtually eliminated for all three children; other measures, including performance in school, showed comparable improvement.

Saigh has constructed a sophisticated set of procedures to assess the effectiveness of his treatment for PTSD. From the multiple-baseline-across-scenes design, it also seems clear that his treatment has some specific effects on the trauma-related scenes. It is not clear in these case studies why the effects were quite so specific, since all scenes were components of the same traumatic experience. On the other hand, these kinds of very specific effects are not unusual with these types of treatments in the context of other disorders. There is certainly a need for a more systematic investigation of psychological treatments for PTSD.

DRUG TREATMENTS

Exploration of the potential effectiveness of various pharmacological agents for PTSD has been limited to the occasional case report or (more rarely) uncontrolled series of cases. The mix of drugs utilized has a familiar ring. Antidepressants, benzodiazepines, and occasionally beta-blockers have all been tried. For example, in a series of 25 retrospectively studied patients, Bleich, Siegel, Garb, and Lerer (1986) found that antidepressants had good or moderate results in 67% of the cases treated, but that major tranquilizers were much less effective. These investigators conclude that specific drug effects were not mediated by changes in panic attacks or depression. Similarly, Hogben and Cornfield (1981) observed some success in five patients treated with phenelzine. They speculate that this drug may have enhanced abreaction. Other series of cases reporting similar results with antidepressants include those of Burstein (1984) and Falcon, Ryan, Chamberlain, and Curtis (1985).

Finally, several reports have appeared on the potential usefulness of beta-blockers. In an interesting clinical series, Kolb, Burris, and Griffiths (1984) observed self-reports of improvement from 11 out of 12 veterans with combat-related PTSD after a trial of propranolol. Clonidine was equally effective in 9 additional patients, with 8 reporting some improvement. Interestingly, the authors report that trials of tricyclic antidepressants have been not nearly as effective in their experience. Of course, it is difficult to make much of these reports at this time, since none represents even a modicum of controlled investigation, and it is not entirely clear what other treatments may have been concurrently operative.

CONCLUSIONS ON TREATMENT

The treatment of PTSD has a long history. Nevertheless, from a scientific point of view, we have less evidence for the effectiveness of either psychological or pharmacological approaches than for any of the other anxiety disorders (or any other emotional disorder, for that matter). Clearly, the case studies reported above provide only suggestive evidence for the effectiveness of one treatment or another, and controlled investigation is urgently needed. On the basis of the model developed in Chapter 8 and clinical wisdom accumulated over the years, some form of re-experiencing the traumatic event seems necessary. Usually imaginal exposure of some type, combined with the provision of adequate social support, is administered. But regaining a sense of control over one's emotions, as well as preventing action tendencies and redirecting attention away from negative affect, will be the result of any successful treatment. The importance of these steps is suggested once again in what may be the most common and yet the most theoretically interesting example of PTSD.

GRIEF REACTIONS

Grief reactions are something everyone experiences sooner or later. It has long been recognized that grief reactions may become pathological and interfere with functioning over a long period of time. Among the names associated with this reaction are "pathological grief," "impacted grief," and "delayed grief reaction." Although the term "delayed grief reaction" implies that an individual did not grieve at the time of the death of a loved one, most clinicians would agree that there is probably a quantitative rather than a qualitative difference between normal and pathological expressions of grief. As early as 1944, Lindemann observed that grief could have either an immediate or a delayed onset and was composed of a number of psychological and somatic symptoms. He also noted characteristic denial and avoidance. Parkes (1970) observed denial of affect, reality, and some "numbing" in 22 widows showing typical grief reactions. Intrusive thoughts were a common accompaniment of this syndrome.

It will already have occurred to the reader that these symptoms are similar to, if not a part of, the usual human response to trauma or stress. In their exaggerated form, there is every reason to believe that severe grief reactions comprise a special instance of PTSD. There are several implications to this assumption. Since PTSD is categorized as an anxiety disorder, extremely pathological, long-lasting grief responses should also constitute an anxiety disorder. And yet we do not typically think of "grieving" as associated with anxiety.

One of the most interesting studies of the grief process was reported by Horowitz et al. (1981). They compared a group of patients seeking help at a clinic after the death of a parent with a similar group of individuals who had sustained the same loss but did not seek treatment. Distress associated with symptoms of PTSD was compared in both groups. Results demonstrated that the grief response in the patient group was more intense and prolonged and had a more substantial effect on functioning. The patient group also became alarmed (apprehensively anxious) at their seemingly uncontrollable and interminable emotional reaction. They were not sure that they were capable of enduring the intensity of their emotions.

This interesting study brings to mind the model of panic disorder described in Chapter 10 (as well as the models of other anxiety disorders described in other chapters). Specifically, both groups of bereaved individuals seemed to experience an intense basic emotion, although the emotions in the clinical group were probably more intense. However, only the clinical group seemed to develop anxious apprehension or perhaps dysthymia over the possibility that their emotional responding was out of control. Those in the clinical group would certainly seem a minority of all individuals experiencing grief. Among individuals who panic, only a minority develop anxiety over the possibility of having another panic attack, resulting in panic disorder. The concept of "double depression," referred to in Chapter 7, highlights a similar process. Patients with double depression seem to experience a basic intense emotion of sadness–distress that is perceived as uncontrollable. Subsequently, they develop chronic depression over the possibility of the recurrence of this basic emotion and their inability to control it. More frequently, it would seem that these depressed patients become anxious about the possibility of experiencing basic sadness once again.

In pathological grief reactions, a similar process may be taking place, and the Horowitz *et al.* (1981) data seem to support this fact. That is, individuals experiencing a death of a loved one in a very intense way, because of the circumstances surrounding the death and/or their own vulnerability to this loss, have an intense emotional reaction that may consist of sadness, distress, rage, fear, or some alternating combination of these emotions. This is not yet pathological. Only when these emotions are unacceptable and sensed as out of control, with associated features of anxiety and/or depression (dysthymia), does pathology develop. The anxiety and depression as specified above, in combination with the basic emotion, are what define the disorder of PTSD. Social support moderates the experience of these basic emotions, as it does after other trauma. It is interesting that our culture provides adequate rituals to insure that social support is available at the time of death. Nevertheless, for various reasons, these rituals are not always sufficient to prevent a pathological stress reaction.

Thus, we have the interesting possibility that pathological grief is an anxiety disorder. This is true not because one necessarily experiences fear or even anxiety during the trauma. Rather, as in other anxiety disorders and perhaps other emotional disorders as well, one experiences an emotion so intensely that with the proper lineup of biological and psychological vulnerabilities, an emotional (anxiety) disorder develops. The more intense the initial experience and the resulting emotion, the less contribution is required from either biological or psychological vulnerabilities. Future family studies may well establish the existence of emotionally based psychopathology in the families of those who develop pathological grief responses, much as seems to be true for other PTSD responses. This remains to be demonstrated.

Finally, some interesting but overlooked observations on the treatment of delayed grief reactions further strengthen a possible association with PTSD. Ramsay (1979) reports treating a number of pathological grief reactions with the type of intensive imaginal exposure described above for use with combat-related PTSD. Imaginal flooding with images of a loved one recently lost may seem counterintuitive to some. But, much as with combat veterans, it has proved very effective clinically. More gradual, "dosed" exposure as recommended by Horowitz (1986) may be just as effective.

14

Social Phobia

The neurotic paradox of self-defeating behavior has been described and illustrated in Chapter 1. Nowhere is this paradox more evident than in the case of famous and well-paid performers, including professional athletes whose very careers depend on repeatedly displaying their skill in front of admiring audiences. Consider the following report, which is representative of many appearing from time to time in the press:

In the second inning of this season's All-Star game, Los Angeles Dodger Second Baseman Steve Sax fielded an easy grounder, straightened up for the lob to first, and bounced the ball past First Baseman Al Oliver, who was less than 40 ft. away. It was a startling error even for an All-Star game studded with bush-league mishaps. But hard-core baseball fans knew it was one more manifestation of a leading mystery of the 1983 season: Sax, 23, last year's National League Rookie of the Year, cannot seem to make routine throws to first base. (Of his first 27 errors this season, 22 stem from bad throws.)

Sax is not alone. Over the years, a number of major league baseball players have developed odd mental blocks and sent psychologists scurrying for explanations. Among the most dramatic examples:

Mike Ivie, an outstanding catching prospect, was signed as a teenager by the San Diego Padres in 1970. In his first workout with the Padres, Ivie threw the ball too low to the pitcher and hit the screen used to protect pitchers during batting practice. A fellow catcher, Chris Cannizzaro, joked about it, and Ivie developed a block about throwing the ball back to the pitcher. Ivie switched to first base and, after a mediocre career with two other teams, is now a journeyman player for the Detroit Tigers.

Steve Blass, a World Series hero for the Pittsburgh Pirates in 1971 and an All-Star pitcher in 1972, mysteriously could not get the ball over the plate in 1973. As a result, he was out of baseball in 1974, at 32. Blass could throw with near-perfect control in practice, but apparently developed a phobia about facing hitters in a game. (Leo, 1983, p. 72)

Performers whose substantial incomes depend upon displaying their skills consistently will go to great lengths to overcome these anxieties. A variety of professionals promise quick cures. From nutritionists to hypnotists, all can claim at least one success, which reinforces further efforts. The desperation of the performers insures a ready queue of consumers for each new promise. One of the more recent promises receiving wide coverage involves drugs, specifically beta-blockers. The evidence on pharmacological approaches to social phobia is reviewed in some detail below. But the use of beta-blockers has not escaped the popular press. Consider the following tongue-in-cheek comments from the *New Republic:*

> Mrs. Reagan, where are you when we really need you? Use of a drug called propranolol is on the rise, according to a recent article in *The Wall Street Journal.* Last year Inderal (propranolol's brand name) was prescribed more often than any other drug in the country. Mostly it's used to treat migraine headaches, high blood pressure, and other related problems. But increasingly it's catching on as the cure for stage fright. Actors, musicians, and other performers are swallowing five or ten milligrams to steel themselves for the stage. Nervous public speakers have discovered the drug, too, and the popularity of propranolol is sure to rise. It's the chic cure for shyness. But apparently nobody has considered the social side effects of the drug, which seem to me quite serious. One thing the world does not suffer from is an excess of shyness. There is, in fact, a glut of false shyness—which makes propranolol all the more dangerous. Just about everybody thinks he or she is shy. Ask even the boldest, most sociable people you know. They'll confess with a becoming blush (though their hearts won't be pounding at all) that, yes, they have a bashful streak. Think what will happen when they, never mind the truly shy, find out about a drug that will make then poised to perform before thousands. It's painful to contemplate the ensuing roar and press of confidence. If Mrs. Reagan can intercede and at least warn America's youth about this drug, she will bequeath an important legacy. (Washington Diarist, 1985, p. 59)

The vignettes provided above may not always evoke the most common conception of social phobia. A skilled athlete's or a seasoned lecturer's difficulties with throwing a baseball to first base or appearing in front of a TV camera, respectively, certainly do not correlate with the concept of "shyness" with which we are all familiar. For, contrary to the report of the Washington diarist, the performers taking propranolol are not typically shy. In fact, many of them may well be among our more gregarious citizens. This underscores a distinction that is only recently emerging clearly: General interpersonal shyness, perhaps combined with social skill deficits, may not equate with social phobia. This issue is discussed further below.

ORIGINS AND PREVALENCE

Fears and anxieties in social situations are ancient history, but the definition of social phobia as we know it today dates back only to 1966. At that time, Marks and Gelder (1966) described a condition in which the individual becomes very "anxious" in situations where he or she may be subject to scrutiny by others while performing a specific task. The most common situation of this type to which most people can relate is public speaking. But other types of situations also meet the definitional criteria, such as eating at a lunch counter or in any public restaurant; writing one's signature in front of a bank clerk; or, for males, urinating in a crowded men's room. What is common about each of these examples is that the individual is required to *do* something while knowing that others will be watching and, to some extent, evaluating the behavior. That it is truly a "social phobia" is clear, because these patients report no difficulty whatsoever eating, writing, or urinating in private. Only when others are watching does the behavior deteriorate.

This concept was elaborated over the years by Isaac Marks (e.g., Marks, 1969) and proved useful enough to be adopted in a full-scale fashion within the definitions of anxiety disorders in DSM-III. As noted in Chapter 9, the definition remains essentially unchanged in DSM-III-R, except for the notation that individuals may well have more than one of these performance-related phobias at the same time. And, as with all phobic disorders, avoidance is not required. Enduring the situation with intense anxiety is sufficient.

With this definition, difficulties with throwing the ball to first base or other seemingly mysterious "mental blocks" among professional performers seem a bit more understandable. As was the case with Steve Blass, the pitcher, these individuals can perform flawlessly in practice, but their behavior deteriorates in the presence of other people. This also highlights once again the intriguing issue first raised in Chapter 7 regarding another very common difficulty encountered during a specific and frequent social behavior. On the basis of evidence developed there, I have suggested that sexual dysfunction, particularly erectile dysfunction in males, is simply another focal social phobia. As with urinating in public or throwing a baseball to first base, sexually dysfunctional individuals perform flawlessly in private (solitary masturbation), but their performance deteriorates rapidly in the presence of a sexual partner. The information developed in Chapter 7 specifying the pathological process involved in sexual

535

dysfunction bears on the conceptualization of social phobia presented below.

Data on the prevalence of social phobia are only beginning to appear and are complicated by some remaining confusion over what constitutes social phobia. Nevertheless, according to DSM-III criteria, epidemiological data presented in Table 1.2 suggest that social phobia occurs in from approximately 1.2% to 2.2% of the population, with a slightly (but not greatly) higher prevalence in females. On the other hand, Marks (1985) found the sex distribution of social phobics in clinical populations to be nearly equal when social phobics were separated out from individuals with social skills deficits or general patterns of social avoidance. In our own clinic, the sex distribution of all individuals receiving a diagnosis of social phobia is also nearly equal.

In a series of 125 patients seeking treatment at our center several years ago, 19, or 15%, were diagnosed as social phobics. During a recent 18-month period, 43, or 12%, of a series of 351 patients admitted to our Phobia and Anxiety Disorders Clinic were diagnosed as social phobics. Thus, individuals with social phobia present frequently for treatment, although not as frequently as those with panic disorder. In Marks's (1985) clinical sample, the mean age of onset of social phobia was about 20 years, which is about 5 years younger than the age for a comparable group of patients having panic disorder with agoraphobia.

SOCIAL PHOBIA AND AVOIDANT PERSONALITY DISORDER

I have noted above that deterioration of performance while under scrutiny may have nothing to do with "shyness" or difficulty in socializing generally. Marks points out that clinical populations of social phobics are composed of individuals whose symptoms are relatively "pure," as well as individuals who have varying amounts of difficulty socializing and mixing in groups of people. Implicit in Marks's and the DSM-III's conceptualizations is the notion that these problems are independent even if they overlap. Social phobias are discrete and typically limited to one or more specific situations where performance in front of one or more people deteriorates. On the other hand, shyness in its extreme form may have more trait- or character-like features that are more pervasive and long-lasting. In this sense, the Axis II classification of avoidant personality disorder may best capture this problem in its extreme form. The essential feature of avoidant personality disorder, according to DSM-III, is an exquisite sensitivity to rejection or humiliation. These individuals typically are devastated by the slightest hint of disapproval and cannot tolerate relationships that are anything but uncritically accepting. This results in few if any friendships despite a desire for acceptance and affection.

536

Marks conceptualizes the differences between these two hypothetically dissimilar types of social anxiety in a manner outlined in Table 14.1. Although he labels the latter problem as "social skill deficit," he may also be referring more specifically to the generalized trait of shyness. The role of social skill deficit in avoidant personality has not been made clear, although it would seem a common feature.

Heimberg, Dodge, and Becker (1987) suggest a potentially useful distinction between avoidant personality disorder and social phobia. Specifically, the distinction between the two groups may be found in whether the person has little desire to confront the phobic event and has adopted avoidance as a comfortable if unfulfilling lifestyle. This would be contrasted to a patient who frequently desires to confront avoided situations or does so at great sacrifice. Those who have adopted avoidance as a lifestyle would more nearly meet the criteria of avoidant personality disorder and would seem more difficult to treat. Of course, this distinction is only speculative at present and requires confirmation.

No one believes that the types of behavior subsumed in the categories of avoidant personality disorder or social phobia represent a unique psychopathological entity not found in the population at large. While additional careful investigation is necessary, it would certainly seem that the trait of shyness is on a continuum. Avoidant personality would represent one extreme of that continuum. For example, in a careful examination of shyness across cultures, Pilkonis and Zimbardo (1979) surveyed 1,000 individuals and found that 40% labeled themselves as shy, with 80% reporting that they had been shy at some point in their lives.

To return to more discrete social phobias, a fear of public speaking is often the most common type of fear among normal adults. For example, there are few of us who do not quiver a bit before a speech (Heimberg, Dodge, & Becker, 1987). Further evidence for the continuity of social anxiety was obtained in a study by Nyman and Heimberg (1985), who found that clinical social phobics differed very little in their responses to social

TABLE 14.1. Two Types of Social Anxiety: Social Phobia and Social Skills Deficit

	Social phobia	Social skills deficit
Sex incidence	M = F	M > F
Onset	Sudden from teens on	Gradual since childhood
Type of phobia	Focal	Diffuse
Associated problems	Occasional	Usually marked
Treatment needed	Exposure and anxiety management	Social skills training

Note. From Marks, I. (1985). Behavioral treatment of social phobia. *Psychopharmacology Bulletin, 21,* 615–618.

fear stimuli from nonclinical socially anxious volunteers. Data presented in Chapter 9 (Table 9.13) demonstrate that features of social phobia are often found in other anxiety disorders. While we may yet discover something unique and qualitatively different about individuals with severe cases of social phobia or avoidant personality disorder, the best bet for the time being is that these problems are at one end of a continuum of performance anxiety or shyness.

Furthermore, as noted above, it is sometimes difficult to untangle these problems, since they do overlap in individuals. For example, in a sample of 80 social phobics (60% males) studied by Amies *et al.* (1983), the situation feared most was being introduced to others. This was followed by meeting people in authority. Since these situations seemingly would require minimal behavior on the part of the individuals (other than saying hello or shaking hands), it is not clear whether these difficulties are part of a specific social phobia or a more generalized social deficit.

Despite this overlap, evidence is emerging supporting Marks's contention that these two types of social anxiety are different in some important ways. For example, in a preliminary study, Turner, Beidel, Dancu, and Keys (1986) compared 21 social phobics (15 women and 6 men) with 8 patients with avoidant personality disorder (7 men and 1 woman). According to the now-discarded DSM-III hierarchical decision rules, avoidant personality disorder superseded social phobia. Thus, patients with avoidant personality disorder might have presented with specific social phobias, which would have increased the likelihood of some overlap among the groups. Nevertheless, significant differences on a number of measures were found. For example, patients with avoidant personality disorder had significantly higher social avoidance and distress scores on questionnaire measures of social anxiety such as the Social Avoidance and Distress Scale (Watson & Friend, 1969). This group also scored significantly higher on a number of Hopkins Symptom Checklist 90—Revised scales reflecting general psychopathology. Thus, the avoidant personality disorder group had generally more severe symptoms, reported a greater number of somatic anxiety symptoms, and were more socially sensitive and distressed in a greater range of social situations.

Similarly, in a series of carefully constructed role-play situations, the avoidant personality disorder group displayed significantly less overall social skill than did the social phobic group. More specifically, the social phobic group was rated as having significantly more appropriate gaze in social interactions, as well as higher ratings for voice tone. Ratings on overall anxiety did not differ significantly but were somewhat higher for the avoidant personality disorder group. What is particularly interesting about this behavioral assessment is that the avoidant personality disorder group did very poorly on tasks requring simple social interactions with either the same sex or the opposite sex. Their performance in these situations was significantly less skilled than when they were asked to give an impromptu speech. These data are presented in Table 14.2.

Evidence from our own clinic also supports this distinction (Heimberg, Hope, Dodge, & Becker, 1987). Specifically, 22 patients with a circumscribed public speaking phobia were compared to 35 patients with "generalized" social phobia, who feared and avoided most if not all social situations. This generalized social phobia overlapped considerably with avoidant personality disorder, although no patients with a pretreatment diagnosis of avoidant personality disorder were included in this group. The generalized social phobics were significantly younger, less educated, and more likely to be unemployed. Their phobia was rated as more severe, and their behavior during a simulation was rated as more anxious and less socially skillful; these results resemble those for the avoidant personalities in the Turner, Beidel, et al. (1986) study. The generalized phobics also showed more negative internal dialogue on two cognitive

TABLE 14.2. Comparison of Patients with Social Phobia and Avoidant Personality Disorder on Behavioral Ratings of Skill and Anxiety

	Social phobia	Avoidant personality	F
Gaze			
Opposite sex	4.5	2.8	10.27**
Same sex	4.5	2.9	
Speech	4.2	3.1	
Volume			
Opposite sex	4.5	4.0	1.83
Same sex	4.6	4.0	
Speech	4.6	4.3	
Tone			
Opposite sex	4.2	2.7	9.38*
Same sex	4.2	2.9	
Speech	4.1	3.3	
Overall skill			
Opposite sex	4.1	2.1	5.59*
Same sex	4.2	2.1	
Speech	4.0	3.1	
Anxiety			
Opposite sex	4.1	5.0	3.88
Same sex	3.6	5.0	
Speech	4.3	4.7	

Note. From Turner, S. M., Beidel, D. C., Dancu, C. V., & Keys, D. J. (1986). Psychopathology of social phobia and comparison to avoidant personality disorder. Journal of Abnormal Psychology, 95, 389–394. Copyright 1986 by the American Psychological Association. Reprinted by permission.
$*p < .01.$
$**p < .005.$

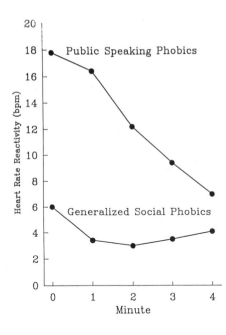

FIGURE 14.1. Heart rate response by two groups of phobics to idiosyncratically constructed behavioral simulation. From Heimberg, R. G., Hope, D. A., Dodge, C. S., & Becker, R. E. (1987). *DSM-III-R subtypes of social phobia: Comparison of generalized social phobics and public speaking phobics.* Unpublished manuscript. Reprinted by permission of the authors.

assessment measures. Finally, the public speaking phobics evidenced significantly higher heart rate response to an idiosyncratically constructed behavioral simulation than did the generalized social phobics. Heart rate data are presented in Figure 14.1.

A MODEL OF THE ETIOLOGY OF SOCIAL PHOBIA

No analysis of social phobia would be complete without acknowledgment of one very special consideration for which there is increasing evidence. Much as we seem to be "prepared" in an evolutionary sense to fear certain wild animals, we are also prepared to fear angry, critical, or rejecting faces (Öhman, 1986). Evidence is mentioned in Chapter 6 on the increased facility with which individuals are conditioned to fear angry faces. According to years of evidence developed by Öhman (1986) and others, there seems nothing particularly volitional about this. That is, responses to what Öhman suggests are evolutionary fear-relevant stimuli—in this case, angry faces—can be elicited after only a very quick "unconscious" or preattentive stimulus analysis. Similarly, fear conditioning to angry faces shows much more resistance to extinction than do responses to happy or neutral expressions (Öhman & Dimberg, 1978). As Öhman points out, this conditioning effect is amazingly specific. It is obtained only when the stimulus person directs his or her anger towards the subject; angry faces looking away are as ineffective as happy faces (Dimberg & Öhman, 1983).

What seems crucial in all of the analyses is eye contact. In species such as our close relatives, the primates, direct eye contact seems to be very frightening. Among humans this response is obviously greatly altered by contextual and learning factors, but it seems to be there nevertheless.

On the basis of these observations, it is not surprising that social fears and sensitivities are common in the population at large. What is surprising is that severe social phobias are not more common in comparison to other disorders, such as panic disorder. There are several possible explanations for this. One is that many social phobics do not come to treatment, since they conceptualize themselves as being "shy" in a characterological kind of way that is not subject to modification (Heimberg, Becker, & Dodge, 1987). But a more likely possibility, according to the conceptualization of the anxiety disorders presented in this book, is that a majority of individuals to not develop intense anxiety over their occasional social fears even if a learned alarm is involved, much as a majority of those with occasional simple fears and panics do not develop other phobic disorders and panic disorder. But here the phobic disorders begin to differ among themselves.

I have postulated that simple phobics and individuals with PTSD experience true or false alarms and develop anxiety over possible loss of control of their emotions on the basis of psychological and biological vulnerabilities. This anxiety is limited to anticipating the possibility of experiencing the fear or intense emotion once again in the form of flashbacks, panic attacks, and so on. Within the category of social phobia, an additional complication develops. Because of arousal-driven negative cognitive activity (or worry), the individual actually becomes distracted from the task at hand if some performance is necessary. It is this process that causes the deterioration in performance present in focal social phobics.

This process has been schematically depicted in Figure 7.5 in the case of individuals with erectile dysfunction. Evidence supporting the fact that social phobics essentially distract themselves is also present in that context. Within other phobic disorders, this phenomenon is seen less often. This is because performance is not usually required or a part of the disorder. For example, claustrophobics do not really have to *do* anything in a small enclosed space except follow their action tendencies and try to escape. But in social phobia, the individual experiences a dread of being unable to perform a specific behavior, based on past experience. All too often this develops into a self-fulfilling prophecy.

Thus the present model of the etiology of social phobia follows very closely the models presented for other anxiety disorders in prior chapters. Specifically, for reasons of evolutionary significance, we seem sensitive to anger, criticism, or other means of social disapproval. Therefore, most of us are socially fearful at one time or another, particularly in adolescence, but few develop social phobia. To develop social phobia, one must be biologically and psychologically vulnerable to anxious apprehension. If so, relatively minor negative life events involving performance or social interactions can lead to anxiety, particularly if an alarm is associated with these social events. Furthermore, there is evidence that at least some social phobics are predisposed to focus anxious apprehension on events involving social evaluation, when and if they occur. For example, Bruch, Heimberg, Berger, and Collins (1987) have recently produced some preliminary data from our center suggesting that the parents of social phobics are significantly more socially fearful and concerned with evaluative opinions of others than the parents of agoraphobics. I have suggested in Chapter 10 that patients with panic disorder, on the other hand, have a disposition to self-awareness, and therefore focus anxiety (when it develops) on the somatic sensations of alarms themselves.

In any case, social anxiety or stress from negative life events involving performance forms the platform from which a false alarm develops in specific social situations. Alternatively, but probably rarely, a true alarm may be experienced if one is subjected to a particularly virulent form of social rejection or humiliation. Occasionally this happens in adolescence, but it can also happen in adulthood. A patient in our clinic once reported "panicking" while making a presentation to a very critical group of supervisors who he believed were about to fire him (in fact, this was what happened). A fear of panicking once again, as well as of performing poorly during presentations, remained with this individual but was limited to these types of situations. As Öhman (1986) points out, it is unusual for social fears to be acquired vicariously. This is in contrast to other fears such as specific animal phobias, which also seem to have an evolutionary prepared component.

Another pathway to the acquisition of social phobia is probably based on the specific and unique feature of performance deficits. Individuals experiencing social anxiety may occasionally experience some deficits in performance during a task without an encounter with an alarm, true or false. Performance deficits may then be apprehensively expected in future circumstances. This may set off the vicious cycle of anxious apprehension outlined in Chapter 7; performance deficits may then continue to occur.

The process of anxiety without alarms seems to be more likely to occur among social phobics than among those with other phobic disorders. Once again, erectile dysfunction appears to be a particularly good example of this. On the other hand, most social phobics presenting at our clinic report panic attacks, either cued (social situations) or uncued. Much as with simple phobia instigated by the transmission of misinformation, the very process of anxious apprehension may be sufficient to trigger a false alarm in susceptible individuals, leading to learned alarms and so forth. But this may not be necessary for the development of social phobia, since the presence of intense anxiety itself may be sufficient to disrupt performance.

Further support for the importance of this mode of acquisition is provided in the descriptive data of Amies *et al.* (1983). As noted above, they replicated the findings of Isaac Marks concerning the relatively early onset of social phobia (middle to late adolescence). They point out that the second half of the teenage years is the period when social embarrassment and lack of social confidence are most common and experienced most intensely. They also observe that social phobias seem to have a more gradual onset than other problems such as panic disorder. They conclude that social phobia evolves from normal social anxiety, exacerbated by the need to face new social expectations. As I have suggested may be the case with simple phobia, it is possible that these hypothetically different modes of acquisition have different treatment implications.

While the data are only suggestive at this time, it seems that the experience of social anxiety without alarms may play a far greater role in the etiology of social phobia than does the transmission of misinformation in simple phobia. Nevertheless, once established, severe social anxiety may trigger alarms accounting for the high proportion of existing social phobics who report (cued) panic attacks, as noted above. This model of the etiology of social phobia is presented in Figure 14.2.

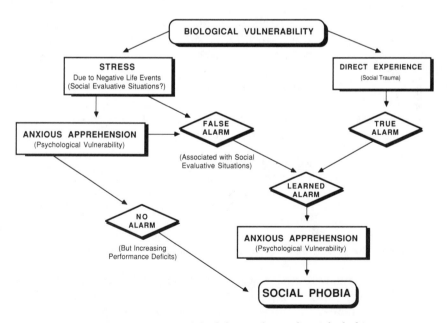

FIGURE 14.2. A model of the etiology of social phobia.

DIAGNOSIS AND ASSESSMENT

DIAGNOSIS

In a clinical setting, it is often difficult to discriminate social phobics from patients with panic disorder. This difficulty occurs despite the clear divergence in DSM-III-R definitions, because social phobics panic. Of course, panic is a common phenomenon in a wide number of anxiety and affective disorders, as noted in some detail in Chapters 3 and 9. Thus, it is not the occurrence of panic itself that is confusing; rather, it is the situation in which panic occurs. The types of social evaluative situations that define social phobia often occur away from a safe place or a safe person (i.e., restaurants, banks, public halls, public restrooms, etc.). But these are situations often associated with panic in patients who have panic disorder with agoraphobia. Amies *et al.* (1983) looked very closely at types of situations provoking panic and phobic symptoms in the two groups, in an attempt to provide a clearer discrimination. While finding considerable overlap, the investigators were able to specify several situations that were rated as consistently more severe by one group or the other. For example, social phobics had little difficulty being alone, crossing streets, riding public transport, or the like, but consistently rated situations such as being introduced, using the telephone, and being teased as more "phobic" than did patients with panic disorder with agoraphobia. Nevertheless, the agoraphobics had often experienced difficulties in situations associated with social phobia, and even rated those situations the same as did social phobics in terms of degree of difficulty. A similar overlap in phobic symptoms between social phobics and agoraphobics was reported by Solyom *et al.* (1986).

That social phobics panic in social situations has long been acknowledged. For example, Nichols (1974), in an early descriptive study of social phobics that is widely cited, observed that the detection of somatic sensations of anxiety by a social phobic provokes greater anxiety and panic:

> A person troubled by anxiety in social situations almost inevitably acquires a preoccupying fear of the response itself. To him it is an ever present threat that carries the alarming possibility of attracting attention and causing others to think him odd. In the feared situations he closely monitors his body state watching for "another attack." Detections of the sensations of anxiety may than provoke alarm and buildup of that response. The person thus becomes anxious about being anxious. (p. 304)

This sounds suspiciously like panic disorder and is in line with assertions in Chapter 9 that all phobic disorders have strong associations with alarms. In this sense, all phobic disorders can be considered panic disorders.

The distinction most often used by investigators working in this area (e.g., Liebowitz, Gorman, Fyer, & Klein, 1985) to discriminate social phobia from panic disorder with agoraphobia is to determine whether uncued panics occur outside troublesome situations involving social evaluation. Panics occurring across a broad range of situations, many of which may be unexpected and without cues (Amies *et al.*, 1983) may then differentiate panic disorder with agoraphobia from social phobia, particularly if an agoraphobic pattern of avoidance is present. Amies *et al.* (1983) note that social phobics report concern with a somewhat different pattern of somatic symptoms (such as blushing or twitching) than their agoraphobic sample, which tended to report the more standard pattern of panic symptoms. This may be a specific marker for social phobia, but not because such symptoms actually occur. For example, McEwan and Devins (1983) observed that socially anxious subjects reported significantly more visual signs of anxiety than were actually noticed by their peers. Therefore, what Amies *et al.* have noted may simply be another reflection of a phobic response to being observed by others.

Despite the confusion that can and does occur in individual cases, the distinction is apparently not as difficult as it may seem when aggregated across groups. For example, the kappa coefficients reported in Chapter 9 for social phobia and panic disorder with agoraphobia, describing the reliability with which each disorder can be identified, are consistently above .850. Specific questions from the June 1987 version of the ADIS-R regarding social phobia are present in Figure 14.3. Note particularly the questions regarding the origins of the phobia, which become important during assessment and treatment.

FIGURE 14.3. ADIS-R questions for DSM-III-R social phobia. From Di Nardo, P. A., Barlow, D. H., Cerny, J., Vermilyea, B. B., Vermilyea, J. A., Himadi, W., & Waddell, M. (1985). *Anxiety Disorders Interview Schedule—Revised (ADIS-R).* Albany: Phobia and Anxiety Disorders Clinic, State University of New York at Albany. Copyright 1985 by State University of New York at Albany. Reprinted by permission.

SOCIAL PHOBIA
Establishing Diagnosis
1. a. (In social situations where you might be observed or evaluated by others, do you feel fearful/anxious/nervous?)
   YES ___ NO ___
   b. (Are you overly concerned that you may do and/or say something that might embarrass or humiliate yourself in front of others, or that others may think badly of you?)
   YES ___ NO ___
   c. (Do you try to avoid these situations?)
   YES ___ NO ___
2. (I'm going to describe some situations of this type and ask you how you feel in each situation.)

(continued)

545

FIGURE 14.3. (*Continued*)

Find out how much fear, discomfort, and avoidance exists for each situation and rate on the 0–4 scale for fear and avoidance.

0	1	2	3	4
No fear/ never avoids	Mild fear/ rarely avoids	Moderate fear/ sometimes avoids	Severe fear/often avoids	Very severe/ always avoids

	Fear	Avoid	Comments
a. Parties	___	___	_____
b. Meetings	___	___	_____
c. Eating in public	___	___	_____
d. Using public restrooms	___	___	_____
e. Talking in front of a group/formal speaking	___	___	_____
f. Writing in public (signing checks, filling out forms)	___	___	_____
g. Dating situations	___	___	_____
h. Talking to persons in authority	___	___	_____
i. Being assertive, e.g.:			
1. Refusing unreasonable requests	___	___	_____
2. Asking others to change their behavior	___	___	_____
j. Initiating a conversation	___	___	_____
k. Maintaining a conversation	___	___	_____
l. Other situations	___	___	_____
1. _____	___	___	_____
2. _____	___	___	_____

3. (What do you anticipate before going into _____? What do you think will happen before/during?)

_____

4. (Do you experience the fear nearly every time you encounter _____?)

YES ___ NO ___

5. (Does the fear come on as soon as you encounter _____?)

YES ___ NO ___

****

If no evidence is found for fear/avoidance, or if fear/avoidance is clearly related to fear of panic, skip to obsessive–compulsive disorder.

****

6. (In these situations, does it make a difference if the people are:) Note which is easier:

Male ___	Female ___	No difference ___
Older ___	Younger ___	No difference ___
Attractive ___	Less attractive ___	No difference ___
Married ___	Unmarried ___	No difference ___
Friends ___	Strangers ___	No difference ___
Large group ___	Small group ___	No difference ___
Informal (i.e., parties) ___	Formal (e.g., meetings) ___	No difference ___

7. a. (When did you first experience this fear?)

_____ Month _____ Year

  b. (What was the situation?) _____

  c. (Has there been a time since then when you were not bothered by these fears?)

YES ___ NO ___

    If YES, (When?) From _____ to _____

8. (Has the fear interfered with your life, work, social activities, family, etc.? Has your current job or educational attainment been influenced by the fears?)

YES ___ NO ___

If YES, (How?) _____

Rate impairment on 0–4 scale. ___

Etiology

1. (Do you think that your fear was caused by:)

   a. (Observing or imagining someone else experience fear or trauma in this situation?)

   YES ___ NO ___

   If YES, (Where did you observe this [i.e., on TV, in a movie, in real life, in imagination, etc.] and what did you observe?)

   _____

   b. (Being warned or told unpleasant things about this situation?)

   YES ___ NO ___

   If YES, (Where/what was the information you received?)

   _____

   c. (Being frightened by something in the situation or being embarrassed or humiliated in this situation?)

   YES ___ NO ___

   If YES, specify:

   _____

   d. (Suddenly experiencing a rush of intense fear, anxiety, and/or a feeling of impending doom for no apparent reason in this situation?)

   YES ___ NO ___

   If YES, (Rate [0–4] the intensity of the following sensations for the very first time this occurred:)

   1. Shortness of breath (dyspnea) or smothering sensations ___
   2. Choking ___
   3. Palpitations or accelerated heart rate (tachycardia) ___
   4. Chest pain or discomfort ___
   5. Sweating ___
   6. Dizziness, unsteady feeling, or faintness ___
   7. Nausea or abdominal distress ___
   8. Depersonalization or derealization ___
   9. Numbness or tingling sensations (paresthesias) ___
   10. Flushes (hot flashes) or chills ___
   11. Trembling or shaking ___
   12. Fear of dying ___
   13. Fear of going crazy or doing something uncontrolled ___

   (Were you able to enter this situation, without fear, before this particular experience?)

   YES ___ NO ___

   e. (Unknown cause?)

   YES ___ NO ___

   f. (Other cause?)

   YES ___ NO ___

2. (What distresses you most about this phobia?) Check one:

   ___ The sensations of fear

   ___ Aspects of the object or situation

ASSESSMENT

Simulation of Performance Situations

The performance hall quiets. The curtain opens to reveal a concert pianist ready to play. Video cameras start whirring. But this is no usual performance: The pianist has electrodes attached from head to foot to measure heart rate, respiration, and skin conductance. Furthermore, the person is told, "Accomplished pianists and experts in behavioral assessment who have copies of your music will be evaluating your performance. At the sound of the buzzer, begin playing."

While this scenario might be daunting even to Vladimir Horowitz, it is, in fact, a standard assessment procedure for a specific social phobia—in this case, music performance anxiety (Craske & Craig, 1984). Unlike PTSD, where traumas are essentially recreated in imagination with the occasional use of simulated audio–visual aides, most socially phobic situations can be closely approximated in the clinic or laboratory. This provides a considerable advantage to the therapist and the patient in terms of observing crucial features of the problem. For example, the scenario described above was actually arranged by Craske and Craig (1984), who assessed musical performance anxiety among a group of accomplished pianists.

Telemetry procedures and ambulatory monitoring equipment are increasingly available for the measurement of physiological responding in contrived or real-life situations. In the experiment reported above, Craske and Craig used telemetric procedures with electrode placement arranged so as not to interfere with the behavior necessary for performance. For example, skin conductance electrodes were placed on the foot. Other social phobias, such as those centering on public speaking, eating, urinating in public lavatories, or introducing oneself to a group of strangers require only the collection of a few people to role-play the audience and the appropriate placement of electrodes. When first presented with this task, many patients will suggest that it will not be very useful. They note that since it is occurring in the clinic and is not "the situation where it really happens," they doubt whether they will become anxious. After experiencing the assessment procedure, however, many patients change their minds very quickly. It is not unusual for patients to report emotional intensity at or near levels they are accustomed to experiencing in socially phobic situations in their day-to-day lives. Recruitment of a suitable audience is made all the easier if social phobics are to be treated in groups, as is the case in our center (see below). The fact that the audience in front of whom the phobic must perform is known to be composed of other social phobics does little to reduce the effectiveness of the situation. When difficulties arise, they may as often as not reflect the fact that the contrived socially phobic situation is too intense. For example, in our center one woman preparing to perform her socially phobic behavior excused herself to visit the ladies' room. After some time had passed, it seemed clear that she was not coming back. The therapist then had to spend a considerable amount of time persuading her to unlock the door to the ladies' room, to return to the situation, and to attempt a less intense situation. Of course, some individuals will initially report the situation as too unreal to be useful. In such a case, it is often a matter of working with the individual to construct the situation in such a way as to make it as real as possible.

In the case of the Craske and Craig (1984) assessment procedure, no such concerns were voiced by the 20 overly anxious concert pianists. The very real situation contrived by these investigators allowed comparison of the responses of 20 overly anxious performers with those of 20 counterparts who were relatively nonanxious. In addition to physiological measures, the assessment procedure lends itself to the administration of a variety of self-report and behavioral measures. SUDs can be collected continually within the constraints inherent in the task, and are very useful in gauging the subjective experience of anxiety. In the Craske and Craig experience, this was obviously not possible during the performance itself, but SUDs were collected immediately prior to the performance. After the performance was completed, the pianists retrospectively estimated their SUDs during the performance itself.

Questionnaires

Specific questionnaires have also been devised to assess social phobia in a standardized way. For example, the Performance Anxiety Self-Statement Scale (Kendrick, 1979) was developed to assess pianists' positive and negative thoughts before, during, and after a performance. Another popular questionnaire devised to assess both positive and negative self-statements that may occur during social interactions is the Social Interaction Self-Statement Test (Glass, Merluzzi, Biever, & Larsen, 1982). Other popular questionnares for assessing aspects of social phobia include the Social Phobia subscale of the widely used Fear Questionnaire, described in Chapter 10 (Marks & Mathews, 1979). For specific aspects of social anxiety and phobia, the Social Avoidance and Distress Scale and the Fear of Negative Evaluation Scale (Watson & Friend, 1969), both of which are true–false inventories, are useful. These questionnaires are typically administered periodically during assessment and treatment.

Behavioral Measures

As noted above, the contrived role-play situation lends itself to direct behavioral observations. Typically, these observations will be individually structured for the specific type of performance under scrutiny. For example, in the Craske and Craig (1984) study, experienced musicians rated the performance of the pianist under different conditions, much in the way they would during any competition. A more standardized behavioral measure of performance anxiety, based on Paul's (1966) timed behavioral checklist, was also used. Items in this widely used checklist include ratings of trembling, posture, facial expressions, and movements. The checklist is not a direct measure of the quality of performance, but may be useful nonetheless. A number of studies exist demonstrating that social skills of highly anxious individuals are typically poorer during contrived social interactions (e.g., Arkowitz, Lichtenstein, McGovern, & Hines, 1975; Beidel, Turner, & Dancu, 1985; Twentyman & McFall, 1975).

Direct behavioral measures need not be limited to observations of the quality of performance or observable indices of "anxiety." In a clever observational procedure, Oei (1986) serendipitously observed positive and negative self-statements in a group of socially anxious females just prior to a performance. Using audio–visual monitoring equipment, Oei recorded the preperformance conversations of females both high and low in social anxiety. Conversations were prompted by a confederate in the room. High-anxiety females made significantly more negative self-statements, conversed less, and made fewer initiations of conversations, than low-anxiety females. This direct observation of high-frequency negative self-statements replicates findings using questionnaires (Heimberg, Dodge, & Becker, 1987). The psychometric properties of contrived behavioral assessments for social phobia and social anxiety have been examined and are satisfactory (Farrell, Curran, Zwick, & Monti, 1983).

In the few experiments conducted to validate these measures of social phobia, social phobics have been compared with relatively nonanxious counterparts in a variety of contrived situations such as those mentioned above. For example, in the Craske and Craig (1984) experiment, not only were anxious pianists compared with relatively nonanxious counterparts, but both groups were observed either playing in front of an audience or playing alone. The audience condition elicited more intense emotional responses in the anxious group than in the relatively nonanxious group of pianists. In fact, almost all behavioral and self-report measures reflected increased anxiety and decreased performance in the anxious group when playing in front of an audience. Interestingly, the only measures that did not display consistent differences either between the groups or in reaction to the audience condition were physiological measures. This finding is consistent with the large body of data reviewed in Chapter 5, demonstrating that both anxious and nonanxious individuals show increased and equivalent physiological responding when presented with a task. For example, a well-known experiment by Dimsdale and Moss

(1980) demonstrated the extent to which normals evidence a surge in physiological responding before a task such as public speaking. Once again, the only consistent between-group physiological finding in these studies is a relatively higher resting baseline of physiological arousal in anxious groups. But the Craske and Craig (1984) experiment is only one study.

Beidel et al. (1985) did find somewhat greater physiological reactivity in a socially anxious analogue group than in a similar but less anxious group. Whether this will hold true for more severe social phobics in their setting remains to be seen. In any case, the physiological response system requires careful interpretation. Much as with agoraphobics, it seems that both normals and social phobics demonstrate elevated physiological responding prior to performing a task. Thus, decrements in this responding may not be differentially indicative of therapeutic success, at least on the basis of comparison across groups. However, individual differences in physiological responding to specific tasks assessed before treatment may well have predictive implications. It is observed in Chapter 10 that relatively high physiological responding during an assessment task seems to predict successful outcome. To the best of my knowledge, no such data yet exist in the context of social phobia, but it would not be surprising if some turned up.

TREATMENT

As with all phobic disorders and PTSD, some variant of exposure forms the heart of any psychosocial treatment for social phobia. The relative ease with which most socially phobic situations can be approximated in the clinic makes *in vitro* behavioral rehearsal the treatment of choice at this point in time. But this may change as we begin to accumulate more facts on treatment outcome. All clinical investigators would agree that evidence on the effectiveness of treatment is scanty.

Alternative treatment approaches are beginning to appear. Some of these may be important, according to the model presented in Figure 14.2. For example, in those social phobics who present with panic, directly treating the panic with either drugs or psychosocial treatments has yet to be tested systematically (see Salkovskis, Jones, & Clark, 1986, described below, for some preliminary data). As with simple phobia, this treatment target may be particularly important for some people (see Chapter 12). The model also highlights the importance of cognitive and performance decrements caused by cognitive interference during periods of high anxiety. According to this conception, forms of cognitive therapy directed at the distracting effects of cognitive interference may well be useful with this disorder. Evidence is beginning to accumulate along these lines. After describing briefly the standard treatment protocol for social phobia employed in our center, I review the potential importance of some of these emerging ideas.

A SOCIAL PHOBIA TREATMENT PROGRAM

The Social Phobia Treatment Program in the Center for Stress and Anxiety Disorders, under the direction of Richard G. Heimberg, emphasizes exposure and cognitive restructuring. Homework assignments are an important part of treatment, as they are in many exposure-based therapies (Heimberg, Dodge, & Becker, 1987). In this approach, social phobics are treated in small groups, typically composed of from five to seven patients. Weekly sessions are 2 hours long and continue for 12 weeks. If possible, two therapists, one male and one female, lead the group therapy sessions. Having a therapist of each sex available provides the opportunity for role-playing heterosocial interactions, which are so often a component of social phobics' problems.

Exposure

Exposure exercises begin by constructing a realistic simulation of the socially phobic situation. If the situation involves making a presentation at a business meeting, other group members are arranged around a conference table or in a circle. Members are coached on relevant behaviors that may prove particularly difficult for the patient. For example, negative comments, looks of boredom or disapproval, and other relevant gestures should be incorporated into the simulation. Participation in these simulations serves several purposes. In addition to exposing the patient to relevant phobic cues, the simulation provides the opportunity to prevent escape and encourage continued performance while the patient is experiencing the distracting cognitive effects of anxiety. Relevant cognitions that occur while the patient is anxious are also listed for use during cognitive restructuring, as detailed below.

During rehearsal, patients are repeatedly requested to provide SUDs ratings on a scale of 0–100. They are encouraged to continue in the situation until SUDs ratings drop to an acceptable level, usually at or below initial levels of anxiety. When repetitions of the simulation result in virtual elimination of anxiety, variations in the simulation are attempted or new simulations based on other socially phobic concerns are constructed.

Cognitive Restructuring

The first two group sessions concentrate on identifying negative or catastrophic cognitions that typically occur in socially phobic situations. At the conclusion of each simulation, the patient is asked to provide a complete account of negative or catastrophic cognitions experienced during rehearsal. Reports of core negative cognitions are then discussed in terms of the logic of the cognitions. Rational alternative responses or thoughts more appropriate to the situation are considered.

A second goal involves examining the patient's perception of standards of performance implicit in the situation. Typically, these are unrealistically high. The group assists in setting more realistic standards of performance. For example, rather than making a flawless, spellbinding, and dramatic presentation during a staff conference that results in quick adoption of the recommendations, the phobic is taught that simply providing the information clearly is sufficient, whether the conferees are listening or not. Behavioral experiments much like those outlined by Beck and Emery (1985) can be conducted during therapy sessions. For example, if a phobic feels that everyone can detect extreme anxiety as soon as he or she begins to speak, this can be tested in the group by having each member record signs of anxiety after the phobic initiates conversation. Typically, the worst fears of the phobic are discounted by the evidence.

While it has not been systematically tested, the importance of treating social phobics in a group seems apparent. Not only do group members provide the necessary audience for simulations, but each group member should learn from other simulations principles that should apply to his or her own situation.

Homework assignments are considered an important part of this program. Typically, these take the form of patient-initiated exposure sessions similar to those proven effective with other disorders, such as panic disorder with agoraphobia (see Chapter 11). These exercises are planned during group sessions and reported on at the next session. All skills acquired during sessions are applied and practiced during the self-paced exposure exercises so that difficulties can be ascertained and corrected.

Clinical reports have suggested the effectiveness of this treatment (Heimberg, Becker, Goldfinger, & Vermilyea, 1985). A preliminary report on a long-term controlled investigation of this approach is presented below.

Problems Arising during Treatment

While the approach to treating social phobia described above is unique in some ways, it also bear similarities to other exposure-based programs for social phobia that are employed in several centers around the world. Butler (1985) has described typical problems that arise in the conduct of this therapeutic effort. For example, Butler notes that it is more difficult to arrange situations along a hierarchy of difficulty or intensity for social phobia than it is for simple phobia or agoraphobia. This may not be a crucial issue, as long as social phobics engage in the requisite amount of practice between sessions. For example, they can attempt exposing themselves to several entirely different situations, or to different aspects of the same situation. These practical or strategical considerations are probably more important than any strict hierarchical approach in arranging which specific situations to employ for exposure exercises on a given day. Similarly, many social situations are too brief to allow prolonged exposure; examples include shaking hands with a new acquaintance or signing checks. Nevertheless, it is useful to practice these brief situations repeatedly, perhaps combining them with other situations as noted above to insure adequate practice.

A more interesting difficulty encountered by Butler (1985), from both a conceptual and a practical point of view, is the tendency of patients who must engage repeatedly in their socially phobic behavior (e.g., salespersons who must make repeated approaches to new clients despite the dread this engenders) to distract themselves in some way. When presented with a rationale for treatment emphasizing exposure, these patients protest that they are continually exposing themselves with no benefit. What many clinicians, including Butler, have discovered is that these individuals are using what Butler refers to as a kind of "internal avoidance." For example, some pretend that they are someplace else; others attend strictly to internal cues; still others may not participate in the situation (i.e., they may avoid talking during a group social interaction). Thus, anxiety persists despite the fact that the patients are physically present in their phobic situation repeatedly. The solution is to take any and all steps to engage such individuals more fully in difficult situations.

Finally, fear of negative evaluation, or the perception by social phobics that others are thinking negative things about them, may be resistant to change by simple exposure. Cognitive procedures such as those used in the program described above seem particularly important from a clinical point of view in overcoming this difficult aspect of social phobia.

TREATMENT RESEARCH

Psychosocial Studies

As noted above, experiments evaluating the effectiveness of treatment are only beginning to appear. Early studies had the difficulty of including a very heterogeneous mix of patients. Many presented primarily with social skill deficits rather than a primary phobic reaction. For example, Falloon, Lindley, McDonald, and Marks (1977) treated 30 patients with either social phobia and/or social skills deficits. Patients received either social skills training plus homework assignments emphasizing exposure or social skills training without specific homework assignments. Yet another group was administered a control procedure. Patients receiving social skills training alone, as well as those receiving social skills training and exposure homework, did better than patients in the control condition. No differences were apparent between treatment groups. Of course, social skills training alone contains exposure elements, since it resembles the types of simulations described above. But for those social phobics without social skills deficits, explicit skills training seems superfluous.

In a similar vein, Stravynski, Marks, and Yule (1982) examined the effects of treatment in the context of a heterogeneous group of anxious and socially unskilled patients. Adding cognitive therapy to social skills training resulted in no additional benefit to the group receiving both treatment components. Each group improved significantly and reported increased social interaction with less anxiety.

Most studies until recently have included this diffuse mix of patients with social inadequacy, social skills deficits, social anxiety, and/or phobic reactions in social situations (Brady, 1984a, 1984b; Emmelkamp, 1982). But some investigators have separated out these groups in order to try to enhance differential treatment effectiveness. In a preliminary study addressing this question, Trower, Yardley, Bryant, and Shaw (1978) classified patients as either predominantly socially phobic or predominantly deficit in social skills. Patients received either social skills training or systematic desensitization. As might be predicted, those patients with social skills deficits benefited substantially from social skills training and also evidenced some reduction in social anxiety. Their gains were greater with social skills training than with desensitization. Phobic patients, on the other hand, reported substantial reduction in anxiety with either treatment. Shaw (1979) extended this experiment by adding another phobic group that received imaginal flooding. Results were very similar to those for the group receiving systematic desensitization in the Trower et al. (1978) study. The amount of therapeutic change in all groups, however, was relatively small.

Öst et al. (1981) addressed this issue more systematically but arrived at similar conclusions. As in similar studies with simple phobia, Öst et al. divided social phobics into those with or without social skills deficits, based on a social interaction test that was videotaped. Half of the patients in each category received social skills training and the other half received relaxation training. As might be expected, social skills training was significantly better on most measures for those patients with social skills deficits. On the other hand, relaxation training (the alternative treatment) was somewhat better for those without social skills deficits.

In view of the effectiveness of exposure-based treatments with other anxiety disorders, most clinicians have recognized that the exposure elements of social skills training may be the important ingredient for those patients suffering primarily from social phobia. Recently, several studies have evaluated this issue with more homogeneous groups of social phobics. For example, we (B. B. Vermilyea *et al.*, 1984) reaffirmed the importance of exposure while treating two social phobics in a series of single-case experimental designs. These patients received a variety of cognitive and exposure-based treatments during the course of the experiment. Repeated measures of progress indicated that improvement took place at different times for different patients. A careful examination of measures of practice outside the sessions indicated that treatment was not always received as intended. That is, the application of exposure-based treatments, including instructions to practice outside sessions, did not necessarily result in adherence to the instructions. A careful analysis of records of practice suggested quite clearly that improvement was correlated with the amount of practice that did occur outside the sessions.

Biran *et al.* (1981) treated three patients with the classic social phobia concerning writing in public. Exposure-based treatments along the lines described above, in which patients practiced writing in front of small groups, proved substantially effective in three cases. For two subjects who initially received five sessions of cognitive restructuring without rehearsal (exposure), no immediate effects were observed, although it is possible that cognitive restructuring enhanced the value of exposure-based exercises when they began.

Two major outcome studies have now been completed, using up-to-date diagnostic procedures and appropriate control groups. Butler, Cullington, Munby, Amies, and Gelder (1984) treated 45 socially phobic outpatients who were divided into three groups of 15 each. Patients with avoidant personality disorder were specifically excluded. One group received exposure-based exercises. A second group received "enriched" exposure-based exercises. "Enrichment" consisted of cognitive and distraction strategies, as well as some relaxation training; these techniques were taught in an anxiety management format, in which patients practiced managing and coping with anxiety. These two conditions were compared to a waiting-list control group. Both groups were superior to the waiting-list control at posttreatment. But at a 6-month follow-up, the group receiving "enriched" exposure proved superior to the group receiving exposure alone. These results are graphically illustrated in Figure 14.4; they are extremely important, since this is one of the few treatment studies with any of the phobic disorders where basic exposure treatments have been significantly enhanced by the addition of other techniques. These findings are discussed below in connection with the unique aspects of social phobia that may make cognitive techniques useful.

In a second study conducted at our center (Heimberg, Dodge, Hope, Kennedy, Zollo, & Becker, 1988), 39 social phobics were carefully diagnosed with the ADIS. Of this group, 20 completed the cognitive–behav-

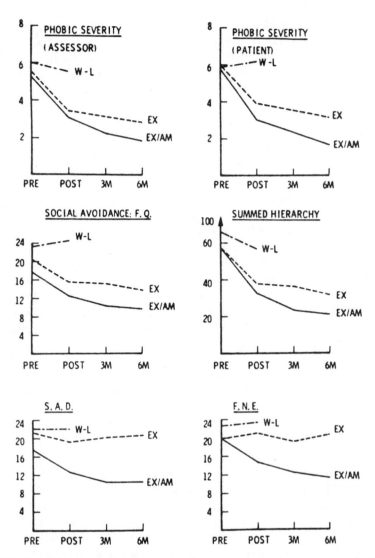

FIGURE 14.4. Measures of social anxiety before and after treatment, and at 3- and 6-month (3M and 6M) follow-ups. EX/AM, exposure and anxiety management; EX, exposure; WL, waiting list; FQ, Fear Questionnaire; SAD, Social Avoidance and Distress; FNE, Fear of Negative Evaluation. From Butler, G., Cullington, A., Munby, M., Amies, P., & Gelder, M. (1984). Exposure and anxiety management in the treatment of social phobia. *Journal of Consulting and Clinical Psychology, 52,* 642–650. Copyright 1984 by the American Psychological Association. Reprinted by permission.

ioral treatment outlined above. The other 19 completed an educational/ supportive group therapy program that took the same amount of time. This treatment package was designed to deliver all of the therapeutic ingredients in the cognitive behavioral treatment except the enactive behavioral and cognitive components; it consisted of the presentation of didactic material pertinent to social phobia, group discussion, and therapeutic group support. The didactic presentations covered such topics as fear of negative evaluation, anticipatory anxiety, and assertive behavior.

Not surprisingly, both groups improved and maintained their improvement at a 6-month follow up. But patients in the cognitive–behavioral group improved significantly more on many of the measures. On ratings of overall improvement, 75% of the cognitive behavioral group had improved by posttest. At a 6-month follow-up, 80% were rated as improved. The comparable figures for the educational/supportive group were 42% improved at posttest and 50% at 6 months.

In summary, the evidence is extremely preliminary at this time regarding the effectiveness of psychosocial treatments for social phobia. Some of this has been due to the confusion and lack of clarity regarding the nature of social phobia. For that reason, individuals with social skills deficits and/or what is now referred to as avoidant personality disorder were routinely included in most early studies. Although some overlap is inevitable, social skills deficits seem relatively independent of socially phobic responses. Thus, these early treatments have been confounded. Only a few studies have examined pure social phobia, and only the Butler *et al.* (1984) and Heimberg, Dodge, Hope, *et al.* (1988) studies provide clear evidence for substantial treatment effectiveness.

Drug Studies

Studies examining the effects of various pharmacological agents on social phobia are no further along than are studies of nondrug treatments. To date, only one clinical trial seems to exist examining drug effects in a homogeneous group of clinical social phobics. Falloon, Lloyd, and Harpin (1981) completed treatment with 12 social phobics all of whom were administered exposure-based treatment. In addition, half received the beta-blocker propranolol while the other half received a placebo. All patients showed benefits at posttest and at follow-up, with no differences between drug and placebo.

Nevertheless, enthusiasm is high for the potential of beta-blockers in the treatment of social phobia. This enthusiasm is reflected at the beginning of this chapter in the quotation from the *New Republic*. Where does this enthusiasm come from? Almost all of it comes from the experimental use of beta-blockers applied acutely to otherwise normal or nonclinical individuals with mild performance anxiety. After reviewing the literature, Liebowitz, Gorman, Fyer, and Klein (1985) found 11 controlled studies, 8 of which reported a beta-blocker to be superior to placebo in reducing some aspect of performance anxiety. The other 3 studies found no differences. The types of problems most frequently encountered in these 11 studies are those with which many of us may be personally familiar. Among subjects included were professional and amateur bowlers, students with test anxiety, public speakers, and professional and amateur musicians (musicians were the subjects of 5 of the 11 studies). In all cases, the drug was administered just before the performance. None of these individuals had recurring, chronic social phobia.

Typical of these studies is one reported by Brantigan, Brantigan, and Joseph (1982). The subjects were primarily music performance students from local colleges and universities who underwent a simulation remarkably similar to that described at the beginning of the chapter. Two groups of subjects were evaluated at two different sites. The audience consisted of fellow study participants and interested faculty members. Some of the trials were videotaped.

The results indicated that subjects generally rated themselves as less anxious while on propranolol, although reductions on the State–Trait Anxiety Inventory were not significant. More interesting were the blind evaluations of the performances by three judges during either propranolol or placebo (see Table 14.3). For 16 subjects, who comprised the group

TABLE 14.3. Performance Preferences (New York Study)

Subject no. and self-evaluation	Evaluators		
	Thomas Brantigan	Carlos Moseley	Bertha Melnik
1,B	—	B	B
2,B	B	B	B
3,—	B	—	—
4,—	B	—	—
5,B	B	—	—
6,A	B	B	B
7,A	—	—	—
8,B	—	B	B
9,A	B	—	B
10,B	B	A	B
11,A	A	B	—
12			
13,B	—	—	—
14,B	B	B	—
15,B	B	B	B
16,B	B	B	B

Note. B = preference for performance with beta-blocker; A = preference for performance with placebo. Subject 12 had adverse reaction to placebo. From Brantigan, C. O., Brantigan, T. A., & Joseph, N. (1982). Effect of beta blockade and beta stimulation on stage fright. American Journal of Medicine, 72, 88–94. Copyright 1982 by the American Journal of Medicine. Reprinted by permission.

at one site, the judges found propranolol to produce better musical performance than placebo. If one ignores "no-preference" decisions (indicated by dashes in Table 14.3), the judges favored the propranolol performance significantly over the placebo performance (25 out of a possible 28 decisions). While it is statistically inappropriate to ignore the no-preference decisions, the trend did favor propranolol. Evaluations of performances by the remaining subjects at the other site were not significantly different under propranolol or placebo conditions.

While this is a very preliminary study, it is an intriguing finding that has been replicated with other beta-blockers (e.g., James, Griffith, Pearson, & Newby, 1977; Liden & Gottfries, 1974). Not all of these studies measured performance, but some that did reflected better performance on beta-blockers. On the other hand, some studies reporting subjective decreases in anxiety observed no differences in performance (e.g., James, Burgoyne, & Savage, 1983). Nevertheless, it is interesting to note that all five studies reviewed by Liebowitz, Gorman, Fyer, and Klein (1985) that targeted musical performance anxiety specifically reported some benefit from beta-blockers—either performance-related, subjective, or both.

Studies of other drugs in the treatment of social phobia are very limited. Several studies have been reported on the use of MAO inhibitors (e.g., Mountjoy et al., 1977; Solyom et al., 1981). Unfortunately, agoraphobics were also included in all studies of MAO inhibitors, making it impossible to determine the effects on social phobia alone. No studies involving tricylics or benzodiazepines have been reported with social phobia, although it is interesting to note that those favoring beta-blockers express concern that benzodiazepines might lower overall quality of performance. Of course, this has not been tested.

The possible effectiveness of beta-blockers is intriguing, although the results are only suggestive at best. Many factors limit the generalizability of the findings. Among these are the analogue nature of the studies. Subjects in almost all studies were not particularly anxious to begin with; rather, they were simply those musicians from a large group who happened to volunteer for the study. For this reason, any changes in self-reported anxiety are very hard to interpret. The only study involving volunteer musicians who were somewhat anxious to begin with did not examine for differences in performance (Liden & Gottfries, 1974). In addition, the simulation was relatively nonstressful in some studies. For example, Brantigan et al. (1982) were concerned that their simulation was not stressful enough to performers who were accustomed to playing in front of much larger audiences. Furthermore, as Liebowitz, Gorman, Fyer, and Klein (1985) point out, treatment with beta-blockers has not been tried with clinical social phobics who frequently encounter their socially phobic situation (e.g., salespersons making repeated calls), and therefore must be medicated on a more chronic basis. Preliminary data from a large trial comparing beta-blockers with MAO inhibitors in populations of clinical social phobics suggest that beta-blockers are not necessarily effective under these conditions (Liebowitz, 1986).

Nevertheless, the results from analogue studies with musicians are interesting and intriguing, and warrant investigation with more severe populations under better-controlled conditions. If these results hold up, several fascinating questions arise about possible differences between social phobia and other phobias. Evidence reviewed in Chapter 11 suggests that beta-blockers such as propranolol have no appreciable effect on panic disorder and agoraphobia. In addition, results reviewed in Chapter 4 on the provocation of panic point to propranolol's lack of effectiveness in blocking laboratory-provoked panic. Why, then, should beta-blockers be effective with performance anxiety (if they are effective)? What can account for improvements in performance when it does occur?

In the model of anxious apprehension presented in Figure 7.6, arousal-driven off-task cognitive activity may interfere with performance through disrupting concentration. On the other hand, at least moderate levels of arousal are necessary for peak performance in almost any task one may undertake. The musicians in the studies mentioned above had not sought out treatment and were not particularly anxious even when compared to other musicians, according to the selection criteria. It is possible, then, that peripheral manifestations of arousal including slight tremors may interfere with performance for physical rather than psychological reasons. As Brantigan et al. (1982) point out, it is difficult to play Bach with a tremor, however slight. To this may be added that it is difficult to play Bach while relaxed or unaroused. Thus, it is interesting to note that of the three studies reporting negative results with beta-blockers, none involved musicians. Rather, the subjects were bowlers, public speakers, or test-anxious students.

It is within the realm of possibility that the effects of beta-blockers on performance anxiety have nothing to do with the severe clinical anxious apprehension that one may find in social phobics. Rather, if beta-blockers are effective, the positive results may be limited to those types of performance requiring fine motor coordination of a type that may be somewhat disrupted even by moderate levels of peripheral arousal. In other words, beta-blockers may act on peripheral tremors. For anxious apprehension of clinical proportions (presumably a more central function), other, more traditional anxiolytic drugs such as tricylics, MAO inhibitors, or even benzodiazepines may be needed.

COGNITIVE THERAPY AND COPING SKILLS FOR ANXIETY REDUCTION IN SOCIAL PHOBIA

An interesting phenomenon is emerging in the context of social phobia: Cognitive therapy in the absence of exposure may be useful, as it does not appear to be for other phobic reactions, including panic disorder and PTSD. As with all evidence regarding the treatment of social phobia, the results are only suggestive at this time, but enough data have been collected to warrant further investigation.

The first line of evidence comes from replications with social phobia of methodologies used with other phobic reactions where cognitive therapy has been found wanting. For example, Emmelkamp, Mersch, Vissia, and van der Helm (1985) compared rational–emotive therapy and self-instructional training to exposure *in vivo* in the treatment of 34 DSM-III social phobics. Treatments were relatively brief, consisting of six sessions of $2\frac{1}{2}$ hours each. Exposure was conducted through simulated situations, much as described above, and was accompanied by instructions to practice between sessions. Self-instructional training involved helping patients change what they said to themselves. In rational–emotive therapy, the major emphasis was on disputing irrational beliefs common among social phobics. All three treatments produced similar therapeutic benefits. What is interesting about this finding is that it does not replicate very similar studies by Emmelkamp and his colleagues with agoraphobics (e.g., Emmelkamp & Mersch, 1982), where exposure *in vivo* was clearly superior to cognitive intervention.

Similarly, Jerremalm et al. (1986) replicated some of their earlier procedures, attempting to tailor treatments to the individual characteristics of patients. Thirty-nine social phobics were divided into either physiological reactors or cognitive reactors on the basis of a pretreatment assessment. Half of each group then received self-instructional training and the other half received applied relaxation. Unlike previous studies with claustrophobics or with socially anxious individuals with social skills deficits, no significant trends emerged. That is, cognitive therapy was as good with the physiological reactors as with the cognitive reactors.

While these results provide only suggestive evidence, data from the Butler et al. (1984) study presented in Figure 14.4 provide stronger evidence for the utility of adding cognitive procedures to exposure-based strategies. As in the pioneering work of Richard Suinn (Suinn & Richardson, 1971), all patients in the group receiving exposure plus anxiety management were trained to identify negative or self-defeating thoughts and to substitute more constructive thoughts (self-instructional training). But other coping techniques were also taught, such as cue-controlled relaxation and (perhaps more important) distraction techniques in which subjects were taught to shift their focus away from anxiety symptoms to the task at hand.

It is not yet clear why additional procedures such as these seem to enhance the effects of exposure procedures with social phobia and not with agoraphobia (see Chapter 11). One reason may be that not enough emphasis has been placed on utilizing additional procedures as coping skills in the context of agoraphobia as a recent study seems to suggest (Kleiner, Marshall, & Spevack, 1987). In this study, the addition of "problem-solving" techniques did seem to enhance exposure. It is possible that the coping procedures of distraction and relaxation directly attack the distracting effects of anxious apprehension on performance, resulting in performance enhancement.

As outlined above and in Chapter 7, the usefulness of these additive procedures, particularly cognitive coping procedures, suggests that anxious apprehension plays a more central role in social phobia than in other phobias (or that these techniques have not been adequately tested in other phobias). Specifically, it is suggested in Chapter 7 that arousal-driven off-task cognitive activity, often reflecting the sense that events are proceeding in an unpredictable and uncontrollable manner, may become intense enough to interfere with ongoing performance. This may not be a major issue in other phobic disorders, where requirements for performance are minimal. But in social phobia, which by definition involves difficulty in performing some behavior in front of an audience, any procedures that diminish distracting negative and catastrophic cognitions and that redirect attention to the task at hand may be particularly important. Some interesting supportive evidence for this idea is presented in an important but often overlooked study that brings us back to a repeated focus in this chapter—the performance anxiety of experienced musicians (Kendrick *et al.*, 1982).

A total of 53 pianists were selected from a large group on the basis of extreme musical performance anxiety that was judged to be "debilitating." In other words, anxiety clearly disrupted performance among these musicians. Of these pianists, 18 were assigned to a waiting-list control group. The remaining musicians were randomly assigned to an attentional training treatment or a behavioral rehearsal treatment. Both treatments were relatively brief in duration; subjects met in small groups once weekly for 3 weeks. Attentional training consisted, for the most part, of subjects' viewing videotapes of their performance while anxious. This was followed by a discussion of the need to substitute task-oriented positive thoughts for negative and task-irrelevant thoughts. In subsequent sessions and between sessions, this attentional refocusing was rehearsed. At first, subjects verbalized thoughts out loud; this was followed by "internalizing" the task-relevant attentional process. The subjects in the behavioral rehearsal group did not receive specific attention-refocusing techniques, but engaged in repeated rehearsals in front of live audiences who were instructed to be friendly, supportive, and encouraging.

Both treatment groups were superior to the waiting-list control group after 3 weeks on a variety of measures, including judged quality of playing. No differences were apparent at that time between the treatment groups. However, an important follow-up evaluation took place some time after treatment: Performance was evaluated at either a music festival, a concert, or a music examination that was perceived as particularly demanding by the musician. At this evaluation, the attentional training procedure produced significantly greater decreases in visual signs of anxiety and greater increases in expectations of personal efficacy than did behavioral rehearsal. A trend in favor of the attentional training group was also evident for overall quality of performance.

These results, like those of studies with beta-blockers, are only suggestive at this time. Although the Kendrick *et al.* (1982) study was particularly well done, it is only a single study and requires replication. One strength of the Kendrick *et al.* study is that the subjects were musicians who presented with debilitating performance anxiety. Thus, these effects can be generalized to other social phobics with more confidence. But again, replication is required both within the specific problem of musical performance anxiety and with other socially phobic conditions.

This study provides some evidence for the potential importance of targeting the disruptive and distracting cognitive activity that forms a part of anxious apprehension. According to the models presented in this book, procedures that redirect the focus of attention and instill a sense of control (coping) should be important in treating any anxiety disorder. But social phobia may be the one phobic condition in which directly targeting cognitive components of anxious apprehension that interfere with performance produces the most obvious benefit. In this manner, behavioral and other psychosocial approaches to social phobia may share important components with successful treatments for generalized anxiety disorder, to be taken up in the next chapter.

THE TREATMENT OF PANIC

We know from evidence presented in Chapter 3 and elsewhere in this chapter that many social phobics panic. Of course, these attacks are restricted to their socially phobic situations. But any time panic occurs, it can disrupt and complicate psychosocial treatments (see Chapter 11). For example, experiencing panic will quickly shift the focus of anxious apprehension from the task itself to the possibility of experiencing another panic attack.

In Chapter 11, emerging evidence on the effectiveness of treating panic attacks directly is discussed. In Chapter 12, preliminary evidence is presented on the benefits of directly treating cued panic in simple phobia. Now some anecdotal evidence exists on the potential usefulness of treating panic directly within the context of social phobia (Salkovskis, Jones, & Clark, 1986). Specifically, measures of pCO_2 were taken during a variety of behavioral and imaginal challenges in two social phobics and two controls with other types of phobia. The social phobics complained of frequent panic attacks in their phobic situation. When assessed, these patients evidenced significant reductions in pCO_2 just prior to or during both imaginal and *in vivo* exercises involving the socially phobic situation. The control phobic patients undergoing similar assessment revealed no changes in pCO_2 levels. Both socially phobic patients were treated with exposure to the physical symptoms associated with hyperventilation, and were also taught rebreathing. Both recovered.

As noted in previous chapters, hyperventilation does not seem a sufficient condition for the occurrence of panic, but it does seem to be one physical manifestation of the basic emotion of fear and its associated action tendencies. In these cases, the direct treatment of panic and the associated anxious apprehension over panic attacks was successful. This suggests (but certainly does not prove) that these patients might have had a panic etiology to their social phobia, wherein panic attacks or false alarms became associated with social situations, as depicted in Figure 14.2. In any case, it seems that clinicians must pay careful attention to the role of panic in all phobic conditions.

15

Generalized Anxiety Disorder

Chapter 1 has described the overwhelming number of patients descending on the offices of primary care health professionals with complaints of "anxiety." Statistics presented there suggest that 30–40% of the population may experience anxiety to a sufficient degree of severity that clinical intervention would be useful (Shepherd *et al.*, 1966). In the past, these practitioners cried out for some assistance in managing these complaints. When the benzodiazepines became available, they were seized upon as a relatively quick solution for a problem that primary care practitioners had neither the time nor the training to deal with in depth. By the mid-1970s, benzodiazepines were the most widely prescribed drugs in the United States (Solomon & Hart, 1978). In 1978, Greenblatt and Shader estimated that between 10% and 20% of adults in the Western world used prescription drugs on a regular basis for anxiety and tension.

Chapter 1 raises the question of who all of these people could be; it is concluded there that they must be a loose collection of patients experiencing a variety of emotional and stress-related symptoms. But when these individuals have been described more fully, a substantial proportion have seemed to fall within the definition of the DSM-II category of anxiety neurosis (see Chapter 9). This was a rather vague category that referred to patients who were experiencing excessive anxiety over a prolonged period of time without marked phobic avoidance—in other words, people who were generally anxious, as well as those who would meet current definitions of panic disorder without severe agoraphobic avoidance.

With the advent of DSM-III, panic disorder was designated as separate from anxiety neurosis. As detailed in previous chapters, this has proved a useful distinction. One would suppose that the remaining anxiety neurotics would fall into the category of generalized anxiety disorder (abbreviated hereafter as GAD). It would also seem that these individuals would be numerous and frequently encountered clinically. After all, DSM-III required only that individuals be excessively nervous for a 1-month period to meet criteria for GAD. But this has not proved to be the case. In fact, the category of GAD in DSM-III produced so much confusion that few clinicians or investigators could agree on individuals who would meet this definition. For that reason, among others, this category has been subjected to substantial changes in DSM-III-R. Whether it will now prove more descriptive and useful remains to be seen.

This dilemma is merely a by-product of our efforts to classify pathological anxiety-related phenomena discretely. By definition, anxiety is at the heart of all anxiety disorders. Therefore, it would seem that adequately defining and assessing anxiety, whether generalized or specific, should not be difficult. In fact, a number of valid rating scales and questionnaires—some described in previous chapters, and some described below—have existed for years. These instruments measure anxiety as a continuous function. Thus, it seems all the more surprising that attempts to categorize people with severe, chronic anxiety have proved so difficult and elusive.

PREVALENCE

Because of this confusion, attempts to profile the DSM-III GAD patient are sparse. Even estimates of prevalence are few, and those that do exist are conflicting. For example, in contrast to estimates of anxiety neurosis totaling 40–50% in general medical practice (e.g., Dunn, 1983), the figures seem to be considerably smaller when DSM-III criteria are used. Prevalence of GAD was not ascertained in the first wave of the NIMH ECA study. However, preliminary data from the second wave in St. Louis are now available. Estimates from these data place the prevalence of DSM-III GAD at approximately 4% (L. N. Robins, personal communication, May 29, 1986). Other studies estimate prevalence at approximately 2.5% (Anderson et al., 1984).

The ECA data are particularly interesting, since this effort represents the most sophisticated epidemiological study yet to appear. The figure of 4% in the St. Louis catchment area suggests that GAD is approximately four times as prevalent as panic disorder. Other studies also suggest that GAD is three to five times more frequent than panic disorder in people reporting some emotional symptoms in the general population, as well as among those seeking help from primary care physicians (Barrett, 1981; Uhlenhuth, Baltzer, Mellinger, Cisin, & Clinthorne, 1983).

What makes these figures interesting is that they are the reverse of the experience of anxiety disorder clinics. For example, in our own Center for Stress and Anxiety Disorders, 11% of 125 consecutive referrals were diagnosed as having GAD (Barlow, 1985). Even with the revisions to DSM-III GAD discussed below, the number diagnosed as having GAD out of 351 patients receiving an anxiety disorder diagnosis was 36, or 10%. Similarly, the members of the University of Iowa group report that approximately 10% of patients in their anxiety clinic are diagnosed as having GAD. This contrasts to panic disorder (with or without agoraphobia), where over 50% received this diagnosis in the most recent series of patients in our clinic.

The reasons for the discrepancy between population surveys and the experiences of clinics are not yet clear. The most obvious explanation is that more severe cases with the more distressing and disabling symptoms of panic find their way to specialty clinics. Individuals with GAD, on the other hand, may construe themselves as "chronic worriers," only seeking out treatment when somatic symptoms become severe enough to interfere with functioning. Most of these individuals may not get beyond their primary care physicians.

Among the few remaining findings characterizing GAD patients is one from our clinic regarding the duration of generalized anxiety in GAD compared to panic disorder (Barlow, Blanchard, et al., 1986). Comparisons of a small number of patients revealed that individuals with GAD reported generalized anxiety for a significantly longer period of time than did patients with panic disorder. To express the data as percentages of patients' lives, patients with GAD reported severe generalized anxiety for 56% of their lives, whereas patients with panic disorder reported severe generalized anxiety for 16% of their lives. This difference in duration was also reported by Anderson et al. (1984). As we have noted (Barlow, Blanchard, et al., 1986), reports of generalized anxiety in panic patients may be confounded with reports of panic and therefore artifactual.

CLASSIFICATION

In retrospect, the enormous confusion generated by the DSM-III category of GAD seems to have been due to its status as a residual category (See Chapter 9). That is, patients could not be diagnosed as having GAD unless they did not meet the criteria for any other anxiety or affective disorder. Diagnosis by exclusion, of course, is certain to produce fuzzy discriminations and difficult decisions. Such was the case with GAD. Estimates of reliability for DSM-III categories using the original version of the ADIS (Di Nardo et al., 1983) revealed that two independent interviewers could not agree on the presence or absence of GAD to a satisfactory degree. The kappa coefficient for 6 patients receiving a consensus diagnosis of GAD out of 60 consecutive patients was .470. In a larger sample of 125 consecutive patients (Barlow, 1987), 12 patients received a consensus diagnosis of GAD, but the kappa coefficient remained low at .571. As noted in Chapter 9, the methods used in this study were very rigorous and conservative, but the low kappa coefficients are striking, particularly in view of the satisfactory kappas for most other anxiety disorders.

Reasons for disagreement between the two independent interviewers were examined. A number of reasons were pinpointed, but one cause for disagreement unique to GAD was an inability to determine whether GAD was severe enough to be classified as a disorder. In other words, a number of people would present with sufficient symptoms of anxiety lasting 1 month or more, but the interviewers would disagree as to whether the anxiety was severe enough to warrant labeling it a disorder.

Clinicians working with DSM-III definitions of GAD also reported difficulty in setting the duration criterion at 1 month. Many pointed out correctly that experience with any number of negative life events may produce temporary adjustment reactions lasting a month or more. While these reactions result in only temporary emotional distress, they technically qualify as DSM-III GAD if the duration is 1 month or more. Breslau and Davis (1985) examined the utility of extending the duration criterion to 6 months. Using both 1-month and 6-month duration criteria, they found that the latter cut prevalence rates dramatically in 357 women surveyed from the general population. Specifically, prevalence rates were reduced from a (very high) estimate of 11.5% to 2.4%. Extending the duration to 6 months also yielded a group that reported a greater number of symptoms, as well as more severe symptoms. Thus, extending the duration to 6 months seemed to approximate more closely the popular clinical conception of GAD as *excess* anxiety experienced *chronically*. This is consistent with data on duration of GAD in patients who seek help at specialty clinics, where chronicity of several years or more is the rule.

WHAT IS GAD?

Conceptualizing GAD as a residual disorder implies that the symptoms of generalized anxiety are, in fact, present in the remaining anxiety disorders. To test this, we examined for DSM-III GAD symptoms across the variety of anxiety disorders as well as major depression (Barlow, Blanchard, et al., 1986).

The results are presented in Table 15.1, which contains the mean severity ratings for the four GAD symptom clusters rated within each anxiety disorder category (see Table 15.2, below, for the DSM-III definition of GAD). Although patients with GAD had arithmetically higher severity ratings for two of the four symptom clusters (muscle tension and autonomic hyperactivity), in no instance did the difference between ratings across groups reach statistical significance.

TABLE 15.1. Severity of Generalized Anxiety Disorder Symptoms for Each Primary Diagnosis of 99 Anxious Patients

| | Severity of generalized anxiety disorder symptom clusters[a] | | | | | | |
| | Muscle tension[b] | | Autonomic hyperactivity[c] | | Vigilance and scanning[d] | | Apprehension expectation[e] | |
Primary diagnosis	Mean	SD	Mean	SD	Mean	SD	Mean	SD
Agoraphobia with panic (n=39)[f]	1.46	0.908	1.95	0.804	1.81	0.775	2.22	0.785
Social phobia (n=17)	1.53	1.138	1.62	0.993	1.85	0.897	2.12	0.839
Simple phobia (n=6)	1.08	1.357	1.00	0.949	1.25	1.084	1.58	1.357
Panic disorder (n=17)	1.56	0.796	2.04	0.705	1.78	0.825	2.25	0.925
Generalized anxiety disorder (n=11)	2.18	0.902	2.18	0.513	1.81	0.751	1.77	0.876
Obsessive–compulsive disorder (n=4)	1.38	0.479	2.13	0.629	2.50	0.577	2.63	0.479
Major depressive episode (n=5)	2.10	1.245	1.70	1.204	2.40	0.894	2.40	0.822

Note. From Barlow, D. H., Blanchard, E. B., Vermilyea, J. A., Vermilyea, B. B., & Di Nardo, P. A. (1986). Generalized anxiety and generalized anxiety disorder: Description and reconceptualization. *American Journal of Psychiatry, 143,* 40–44. Copyright 1986 by the American Psychiatric Association. Reprinted by permission.

[a] 0 = none, 1 = mild, 2 = moderate, 3 = severe, 4 = very severe.

[b] $F = 1.34$, $df = 6, 90$, n.s.

[c] $F = 1.92$, $df = 6, 91$, n.s.

[d] $F = 1.36$, $df = 6, 92$, n.s.

[e] $F = 1.13$, $df = 6, 92$, n.s.

[f] For muscle tension, $n = 37$; for autonomic hyperactivity, $n = 38$.

Thus, it seems clear that almost all of these patients with anxiety disorders presented with the four basic features that define GAD in DSM-III. The one exception was the category of simple phobia, where only 40% met criteria for GAD. Even this proportion may be artifactually high, since very few patients come to our Phobia and Anxiety Disorders Clinic with simple phobia as their only problem. Most often, additional anxiety disorder or affective disorder diagnoses are assigned, even though simple phobia is the primary diagnosis. It may be that in the case of simple phobia without additional problems, an even lower percentage of patients would meet the criteria for GAD. But very few of these people come in for treatment, as discussed in Chapter 12.

Not only did a relatively high proportion of each diagnostic category meet the criteria for GAD, but we were not able to discriminate reliably among the various anxiety disorders on the basis of severity ratings for GAD symptom clusters. Thus, GAD meets the requirement of a "residual" category, in that symptoms of GAD are found in all of the remaining anxiety disorder categories. On the basis of these data, it seemed clear that there was little reason to note the existance of GAD symptoms, with the possible exception of cases where simple phobia was the primary diagnosis.

DEVELOPING A NEW DEFINITION OF GAD

Nevertheless, our own experience suggested that a number of patients successfully treated at our clinic for one or another of the anxiety disorders (e.g., agoraphobia) continued to experience severe discomfort due to more generalized anxiety after treatment had concluded. Others did not. It seemed that the former individuals were suffering from generalized anxiety that was independent of their presenting disorder. On the basis of these observations, GAD could be conceptualized as a separate anxiety disorder category diagnosable in addition to other anxiety disorders. We accomplished this by differentiating between the anticipatory anxiety that is almost always part of a panic or phobic disorder, and generalized anxiety.

Part of the evidence supporting this strategy came from a study in which patients were assigned all of the DSM-III anxiety and affective disorder diagnoses for which they qualified. In other words, the diagnostic exclusionary rules that were part of DSM-III procedures were dropped. This practice allows the establishment of patterns of comorbidity. A description of comorbidity, along with the data from the study where patterns of comorbidity among the anxiety disorders were detailed (Barlow, Di Nardo, et al., 1986), can be found in Chapter 9. What was surprising to us in that study, in light of the prevalence of GAD symptom clusters noted above, was how few additional diagnoses of GAD were assigned when the primary diagnosis was another anxiety disorder, such as social phobia or panic disorder.

From the data presented in Table 15.1, one would assume that GAD would be a very common additional diagnosis. The reason it was not had to do with the way diagnoses were made in that study. In making a decision as to whether an additional diagnosis of GAD was warranted, clinicians determined whether symptoms of GAD were an associated feature or an integral part of the primary diagnosis, or whether they represented a coexisting independent problem. In order to make this determination with GAD symptoms, clinicians had to determine the focus of apprehensive expectation—one of the four symptom clusters of GAD. In other words, what were the patients worrying about? If they were worrying about the next panic attack, or perhaps their next encounter with a socially phobic situation (depending on their primary diagnosis), this would be anticipatory anxiety and was judged as such by our clinicians. Anticipatory anxiety is, of course, an integral part or associated feature of a primary diagnosis of phobia or panic disorder. However, if the focus of apprehensive expectation was on multiple life circumstances, many of which were unrelated to the primary diagnosis, and the patients also presented with the other three symptom clusters (muscle tension, autonomic hyperactivity, and vigilance or scanning), an additional diagnosis of GAD was assigned. In this case, GAD would be a coexisting independent problem. This required a determination of the functional relationship among anxiety features, as described in some detail in Chapter 9. As also noted in Chapter 9, this practice, along with fully establishing patterns of comorbidity, has been incorporated into the revisions of DSM-III.

In devising a new definition of GAD based on the considerations described above, we thought it best to work with a conservative definition at first. For that reason, we required identification of two general areas or life situations that were serving as the focus of chronic apprehensive expectation. Future research may demonstrate that only one "sphere of worry" is necessary and sufficient to discriminate the syndrome of GAD. But requiring identification of two spheres of worry should separate out the problem more clearly from other anxiety disorders and insure that this anxiety is truly "generalized."

Thus, we came to the conclusion that the cardinal feature of GAD is apprehensive expectation. Distinguishing a syndrome of GAD from the anticipatory anxiety often found in other anxiety disorder categories depends on determining the focus of apprehensive expectation or worry. When this is done, a group of patients emerge who can be characterized as "chronic worriers" with sufficient severity ratings and accompanying autonomic symptoms to meet criteria for GAD.

Conceptualizing GAD in this way removes it as a residual category and bases classification on a cardinal symptom not necessarily present in other anxiety disorders. This strategy is consistent with our experience / (and that of other clinicians) that chronic pathological "worrying" does not necessarily covary with symptoms of other anxiety disorder during treatment, such as panic or intrusive thoughts. These conceptualizations form the basis for the DSM-III-R category of GAD. DSM-III and DSM-III-R criteria for GAD are presented in Table 15.2.

TABLE 15.2. DSM-III and DSM-III-R Diagnostic Criteria for GAD

DSM-III[a]	DSM-III-R[b]

300.02 Generalized Anxiety Disorder
A. Generalized, persistent anxiety is manifested by symptoms from three of the following four categories:
  (1) *motor tension:* shakiness, jitteriness, jumpiness, trembling, tension, muscle aches, fatigability, inability to relax, eyelid twitch, furrowed brow, strained face, fidgeting, restlessness, easy startle
  (2) *autonomic hyperactivity:* sweating, heart pounding or racing, cold clammy hands, dry mouth, dizziness, lightheadedness, paresthesias (tingling in hands or feet), upset stomach, hot or cold spells, frequent urination, diarrhea, discomfort in the pit of the stomach, lump in the throat, flushing, pallor, high resting pulse and respiration rate
  (3) *apprehensive expectation:* anxiety, worry, fear, rumination, and anticipation of misfortune to self or others
  (4) *vigilance and scanning:* hyperattentiveness resulting in distractibility, difficulty in concentrating, insomnia, feeling "on edge," irritability, impatience
B. The anxious mood has been continuous for at least one month.
	300.02 Generalized Anxiety Disorder
	A. Unrealistic or excessive anxiety and worry (apprehensive expectation) about two or more life circumstances, e.g., worry about possible misfortune to one's child (who is in no danger) and worry about finances (for no good reason), for a period of six months or longer, during which the person has been bothered more days than not by these concerns. In children and adolescents, this may take the form of anxiety and worry about academic, athletic, and social performance.
	
	B. If another Axis I disorder is present, the focus of the anxiety and worry in A is unrelated to it, e.g., the anxiety or worry is not about having a panic attack (as in Panic Disorder), being embarrassed in public (as in Social Phobia), being contaminated (as in Obsessive Compulsive Disorder), or gaining weight (as in Anorexia Nervosa).

C. Not due to another mental disorder, such as a Depressive Disorder or Schizophrenia.	C. The disturbance does not occur only during the course of a Mood Disorder or a psychotic disorder.
	(Continued)

TABLE 15.2. (*Continued*)

DSM-III[a]	DSM-III-R[b]
D. At least 18 years of age.	D. At least 6 of the following 18 symptoms are often present when anxious (do not include symptoms present only during panic attacks):
	Motor tension
	(1) trembling, twitching, or feeling shaky
	(2) muscle tension, aches, or soreness
	(3) restlessness
	(4) easy fatigability
	Autonomic hyperactivity
	(5) shortness of breath or smothering sensations
	(6) palpitations or accelerated heart rate (tachycardia)
	(7) sweating, or cold clammy hands
	(8) dry mouth
	(9) dizziness or lightheadedness
	(10) nausea, diarrhea, or other abdominal distress
	(11) flushes (hot flashes) or chills
	(12) frequent urination
	(13) trouble swallowing or "lump in throat"
	Vigilance and scanning
	(14) feeling keyed up or on edge
	(15) exaggerated startle response
	(16) difficulty concentrating or "mind going blank" because of anxiety
	(17) trouble falling or staying asleep
	(18) irritability
	E. It cannot be established that an organic factor initiated and maintained the disturbance, e.g., hyperthyroidism, Caffeine Intoxication.

[a]Criteria from American Psychiatric Association. (1980). *Diagnostic and statistical manual of mental disorders* (3rd ed.). Washington, DC: Author. Copyright 1980 by the American Psychiatric Association. Reprinted by permission.

[b]Criteria from American Psychiatric Association. (1987). *Diagnostic and statistical manual of mental disorders* (3rd ed., rev.). Washington, DC: Author. Copyright 1987 by the American Psychiatric Association. Reprinted by permission.

RELIABILITY, VALIDITY, AND PRESENTING CHARACTERISTICS OF DSM-III-R GAD

We have now had an opportunity to collect descriptive information from the last 22 patients meeting the DSM-III-R criteria for GAD. Of these patients, 14, or 64%, were female and 8, or 36%, were male. The mean age was 43 years, with a range of 31–63 years. Marital status was as follows: 64% were married, 9% were divorced, 9% were separated, and 18% were single. The mean Hamilton Anxiety Rating Scale score for these patients was 21.1, with a range of 14–26, the mean Hamilton Rating Scale for Depression score was 16.3, with a range of 7–26.

Central to the definition of GAD is the identification of specific spheres of worry that are judged excessive. The most common spheres of worry are presented in Figure 15.1 (Sanderson & Barlow, 1986). As one can see, family, money, and work were the most common life circumstances eliciting chronic and excessive worry from these GAD patients. We determine whether these particular spheres of worry could be reliably identified by interviewers. Interviewers agreed exactly on each of the two spheres of worry for 9 out of 11 patients for whom data were available, producing an agreement rate of 82%. In the remaining 2 patients, the interviewers disagreed on at least one of the particular spheres of worry.

The other crucial defining feature of GAD is whether these concerns are excessive and/or unrealistic. Independent ratings of these dimensions produced agreement 80% of the time. While these data are preliminary, it seems that it is possible to obtain satisfactory agreement among raters

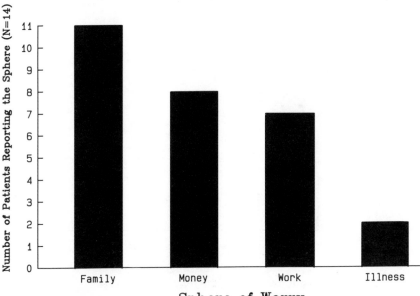

FIGURE 15.1. Content of worries reported by GAD patients that were judged to be excessive and/or unrealistic by the interviewer. From Sanderson, W. C., & Barlow, D. H. (1986, November). *Domains of worry within the DSM-III-R generalized anxiety disorder category: Reliability and description.* Paper presented at the annual meeting of the Association for Advancement of Behavior Therapy, Chicago.

on specific areas of worry, as well as whether the worry or concern is of clinical proportion (i.e., excessive or unrealistic).

Other findings from this preliminary series also look promising for the reliability, validity, and usefulness of the new definition of GAD. For example, we examined the frequencies with which 10 consecutive patients from each anxiety disorder category answered "yes" to the question "Do you worry excessively about minor things?" (This is a standard question on the ADIS.) The results are presented in Figure 15.2. One can see that the answer to this question significantly differentiated GAD patients from other anxiety disorder patients, about half of whom tended to respond affirmatively to this question. The severity and chronicity of this disorder are also clear when one examines the average amount of time during the day that patients reported feeling tense, anxious, or worried. These data are presented in Figure 15.3 and reflect the fact that 19 out of 22 GAD patients reported spending more than half of an average day anxious and worried.

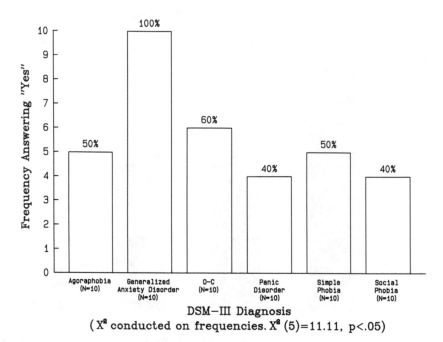

FIGURE 15.2. Clients' answers to interviewer's question "Do you worry excessively about minor things?" From Sanderson, W. C., & Barlow, D. H. (1986, November). *Domains of worry within the DSM-III-R generalized anxiety disorder category: Reliability and description.* Paper presented at the annual meeting of the Association for Advancement of Behavior Therapy, Chicago.

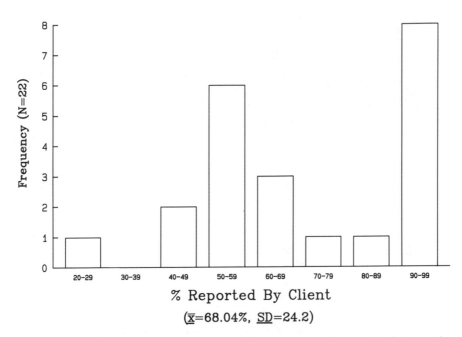

% Reported By Client

($\bar{x}$=68.04%, $\underline{SD}$=24.2)

FIGURE 15.3. Clients' answers to question "On an average day over the last month, what percent of the day do you feel tense, anxious, worried?" From Sanderson, W. C., & Barlow, D. H. (1986, November). *Domains of worry within the DSM-III-R generalized anxiety disorder category: Reliability and description.* Paper presented at the annual meeting of the Association for Advancement of Behavior Therapy, Chicago.

THE RELATIONSHIP OF PANIC AND GAD

One of the most interesting findings of our early look at DSM-III-R GAD concerns the relationship of panic to GAD. In DSM-III, panic disorder superseded GAD under the hierarchical conventions present in that system. But some patients with a diagnosis of GAD were panicking, albeit at frequencies or intensities insufficient to earn a diagnosis of panic disorder Careful questioning of the 22 patients described above, in the context of administration of the ADIS, revealed specific information on the incidence of panic among these patients. Surprisingly, fully 16 out of 22, or 73%, reported experiencing at least one panic attack in their lifetime. Furthermore, as noted in Chapter 9, 27% actually earned a secondary diagnosis of panic disorder with agoraphobia (Sanderson *et al.*, 1987a). According to the hierarchy-free conventions of DSM-III-R, these patients received a primary diagnosis of GAD because this was judged to be the more severe clinical disorder at the time of presentation.

Patterns of comorbidity have been fully discussed in Chapter 9. In this particular instance, the comorbidity data raise some fascinating questions about the relationship of panic and generalized anxiety. The issue is particularly salient in regard to GAD patients, because, by definition, their "anxiety" is focused primarily on areas other than their next panic attack. In other words, they are presenting with chronic, excessive, unrealistic anxious apprehension focusing on work, school, money, and so forth. But many also report a history of panic and a few report current panic attacks, although this is not now their major concern. In fact, many of these GAD patients with current panic attacks exclaim that these attacks are of little concern to them at the present time. In this respect, they seem to resemble many nonclinical panickers described in Chapter 3. These nonclinical panickers notice the attacks but attribute them for the most part to contemporary events. They are not particularly worried about them. GAD patients, on the other hand, seem to be so totally preoccupied with their current problems that panic attacks, when they occur, are only a passing nuisance. Their overriding concerns remain the current focus of worry (e.g., "Will I pass this exam?" "Can I pay this bill?" "Will my children turn out all right?").

Timelines for patients (e.g., Cloninger *et al.*, 1981; Uhde, Boulenger, Roy-Byrne, *et al.*, 1985) suggest that panic attacks follow a prolonged period of chronic generalized anxiety. Panic attacks then become the major clinical syndrome that comes to the attention of mental health professionals. Indeed, it is observed in Chapter 4 that the best predictor of laboratory-provoked panic attacks is high baseline anxiety preceding the laboratory provocation. Thus, there is a considerable amount of evidence that panic attacks are associated with high generalized anxiety, at least initially. But our experiences with the patients described above suggests that panic disorder does not necessarily develop. That is, one can have a panic attack in the context of GAD without necessarily going on to develop panic disorder or some other phobic disorder. This is reminiscent of the clinical picture of panic attacks associated with depressive disorders. In major depression, panic attacks also seem to occur in approximately 50% of patients, but they do not dominate the clinical picture (although they may reflect greater overall severity). Clinicians are able to designate the major depressive episode as the primary clinical problem. Similarly, from our small number of patients, it seems that panic attacks can occur in patients with GAD without dominating the clinical picture. That is, GAD is clearly the primary problem.

Chapter 7 has suggested that initial panic attacks or false alarms may spike off a platform of elevated anxiety and/or stress precipitated by negative life events. The degree of anxiety and stress experienced may, in turn, be related to both biological and psychological vulnerabilities. The initial panic attack may then occur because of shared neurotransmitter pathways, shared response propositions or memory traces in a Langian sense, or some combination of these. Some sort of further psychological elaboration or learning is necessary for panic to become the central feature of an anxiety or phobic disorder. In the absence of that learning, and given the right combination of circumstances, severe generalized anxiety or depression may just as easily dominate the clinical picture. These speculations tie in directly with the model of the development of GAD presented below. Of course, as noted in Chapter 9, the "cutting points" between diagnoses such as GAD and panic disorder with agoraphobia are never as clear as suggested by categorical classification. In addition to the approximately 25% who are "comorbid" for these disorders, many more have features of one or the other. As long as one keeps this in mind, my colleagues and I continue to believe that it is useful to consider these disorders as separate problems for treatment purposes.

A MODEL OF THE ETIOLOGY OF GAD

The new emphasis on apprehensive expectation in the DSM-III-R definition of GAD emphasizes what appears to be the central feature of GAD—arousal-driven worry. In GAD, where the cognitive–affective structure of anxiety reaches its full clinical manifestation, combining therapeutic processes that target cognitive and affective aspects of the problem seems essential. In this sense, GAD may be very similar to those forms of social phobia in which panic does not play an etiological role. Rather, as seems to be the case with erectile dysfunction, the primary problem is intense, excessive, chronic anxiety, with its strong sense of loss of control and inappropriate attentional focus. In the case of erectile dysfunction, the focus of anxious apprehension is solely on sexual performance. This process and the evidence supporting it have been described fully in Chapter 7. In GAD the focus is more diffuse, since, by definition, at least two different spheres of excessive and unrealistic worry must be present. Furthermore, specific foci may change from time to time as a function of changing life events, this is not the case in social phobia. Increasing vulnerabilities to anxiety insure that relatively small disruptions in one's life (hassles) become the focus of anxious apprehension, resulting in a number of shifting, excessive, and unreasonable worries.

In depicting this etiological process, one cannot improve on Figure 7.7. Based on what is by now a familiar pattern of biological and psychological vulnerabilities, stress-related neurobiological reactions are triggered by negative life events. Within GAD, the focus remains on various life events, and an exquisite sensitivity to otherwise relatively minor events is manifested. Reactions to these events are accompanied by negative affect, which is comprised of physiological arousal associated with stress-related neurobiological reactions and a sense that events are proceeding in an unpredictable, uncontrollable fashion. This, in turn, is associated with a maladaptive shift in focus of attention from the task at hand to self-evaluative modes, resulting in further increases in arousal. Increased vigilance results, along with narrowing of attention to the focus of worry or concern, including one's inability to cope with the source of concern. This arousal-driven cognitive process continues to spiral in a negative feedback loop until one is worrying intensely and excessively about the focus of concern as well as one's inability to cope with it (control it). At extreme levels, attention narrowing is such that concentrating on alternative tasks is difficult or impossible. Performance is then disrupted.

The clinician can intervene at many points in this cycle. Pharmacological approaches and relaxation procedures target the somatic components of anxiety associated with activation. Psychosocial approaches other than relaxation (or biofeedback) may target cognitive processes associated with the hypervalent cognitive schema reflecting a sense of loss of control. Both of these general approaches also provide the patient with new methods of coping with or controlling events that are seen as proceeding out of control, as well as anxious reactions to them. This may be the important mechanism of action in all successful treatments, for reasons described in Chapter 8.

DIAGNOSIS AND ASSESSMENT

DIAGNOSIS

Diagnostic issues have been convered in the beginning of this chapter, in explicating the revised definition of GAD. There I have speculated on the similarities of GAD to some forms of social phobia. Below, I draw stronger parallels between GAD and obsessive–compulsive disorder. This distinction, in fact, becomes the most difficult differential diagnosis in severe cases of GAD.

Several other issues relevant to initial diagnosis remain. One issue requiring further elaboration and research concerns the number of spheres of worry required to qualify for a GAD diagnosis. Some individuals come to our clinic for evaluation meeting the criteria for GAD in all respects but one: The focus of their worry is centered on one and only one life event, such as finances or a child's welfare. As noted above, the requirement for two spheres of worry was an attempt to be conservative by insuring that anxiety is truly "generalized" across at least two areas of concern. Through careful questioning devised over the years and included in the ADIS-R (see below), it is usually not difficult to ascertain two or more spheres of worry. But many of those individuals with only one focus of concern almost certainly qualify for GAD on the basis of a functional or more qualitative analysis. Future research may determine that requiring one sphere of worry still allows sufficient specificity in diagnostic practice to be useful.

Occasionally, individuals present at our clinic reporting that they do not worry about anything. Rather, they report being "a bundle of nerves." Upon closer examination, they seem to be presenting with a variety of somatic complaints without any specific apprehension, except over the somatic events themselves. This, of course, reflects that fact that they are apprehensive over their somatic condition, which qualifies as one sphere of concern. These individuals are diagnosed as having "anxiety disorder, not otherwise specified." Out of the past 30 patients otherwise meeting the DSM-III-R diagnostic criteria for GAD, 2 have presented with either one sphere of worry or no specific worries other than somatic complaints. While this is a small number, other clinics report seeing larger numbers, particularly of the type presenting with only somatic complaints. It remains to be seen whether this is due to differences in interviewing strategies or to other, as yet unspecified factors. In any case, we should know much more about these people in years to come. Listed in Figure 15.4 are the questions from the June 1987 version of the ADIS-R designed specifically to ascertain DSM-III-R GAD.

FIGURE 15.4. ADIS-R questions for DSM-III-R generalized anxiety disorder. From Di Nardo, P. A., Barlow, D. H., Cerny, J., Vermilyea, B. B., Vermilyea, J. A., Himadi, W., & Waddell, M. (1985). *Anxiety Disorders Interview Schedule—Revised (ADIS-R)*. Albany: Phobia and Anxiety Disorders Clinic, State University of New York at Albany. Copyright 1985 by State University of New York at Albany. Reprinted by permission.

Questions in this section should be used to establish the presence of tension or anxiety with no apparent cause, or anxiety which is related to excessive worrying about family, job performance, finances, etc., and minor matters. This tension or anxiety is not part of, or anticipatory to, panics or phobic anxiety.

1. a. (What kinds of things do you worry about?)

_____

If patient identifies anxiety or tension which is *anticipatory* to panics or exposures to phobic situations—e.g., "I worry about having an attack; I worry whenever I know I will have to cross a bridge"—as a major source of anxiety:
1. (Are there things other than _____ which make you feel tense, anxious, or worried?)

                              YES ___ NO ___

If YES, (What are they?)

_____

b. (During the last 6 months, have you been bothered by these worries more days than not?)

                              YES ___ NO ___

2. (Are you a worrier? Do you worry excessively about small things such as being late for an appointment, repairs to the house or car, etc.?)

                              YES ___ NO ___

3. (Do you feel tense or nervous or jittery for no apparent reason?)

                              YES ___ NO ___

(continued)

FIGURE 15.4. (*Continued*)

---

4. (On an average day over the last month, what percent or how much of the day do you feel tense, anxious, worried?)

_____ %

5. (Last time you experienced an increase in tension, anxiety, or worry, aside from panics or phobic exposures, what was happening/what were you thinking?)
   When _____
   Situation _____
   Thoughts _____

6. *Generalized Anxiety Disorder Symptom Rating*
   Persistent symptoms (continuous for at least 6 months). Do *not* include symptoms present *only* during panic.

   Inquire about each symptom listed in each category:

   (During the past 6 months, have you often been bothered by _____ when you are anxious?)

   (How severe is it?)

   ```
   0 - - - - - - 1 - - - - - - 2 - - - - - - 3 - - - - - - 4
   None          Mild          Moderate      Severe        Very severe/
                                                            grossly disabling
   ```

   a. *Motor Tension*
      Trembling, twitching or feeling shaky ___   Restlessness   ___
      Muscle tension, aches, or   Easy fatigability   ___
      soreness   ___

   b. *Autonomic Hyperactivity*
      Shortness or breath or smothering   Nausea, diarrhea, or other abdominal
      sensations   ___   distress   ___
      Palpitations or accelerated heart rate ___   Flushes (hot flashes) or chills   ___
      Sweating, or cold clammy hands   ___   Frequent urination   ___
      Dry mouth   ___   Trouble swallowing or lump in throat ___
      Dizziness or light-headedness   ___

   c. *Vigilance, Scanning*
      Feeling keyed up or on edge   ___   Difficulty concentrating or mind
      Exaggerated startle response   ___   going blank because of anxiety   ___
      Trouble falling or staying asleep ___   Irritability   ___

7. How long has the tension, anxiety, worry been a problem?

   From _____ to _____
   Duration in months _____

   Note: If patient responds "all my life," inquire further, e.g.: (Can you remember feeling this way in school? What grade?)

---

8. (How much does this interfere with your life, work, social activities, family, etc.?)
   Rate interference:

   ```
   0 - - - - - - 1 - - - - - - 2 - - - - - - 3 - - - - - - 4
   None          Mild          Moderate      Severe        Very severe/
                                                            grossly disabling
   ```
   ****

   If Hamilton scales are to be administered, go to next page. If Hamilton scales are not to be administered, skip to PTSD.
   ****

ASSESSMENT

Questionnaires and Rating Scales

There are as yet no questionnaire measures designed specifically for DSM-III-R GAD, as there are for panic disorder with agoraphobia and some other anxiety disorders. On the other hand, some of the most widely used and best-known rating scales and questionnarires for assessing "generalized" anxiety are often utilized to assess progress in GAD patients. For example, the Hamilton Anxiety Rating Scale is frequently used as will be evident from many treatment studies reviewed below. The Hamilton Anxiety Rating Scale is a clinician's rating scale that is integrated into the ADIS. This scale has been described more fully in Chapter 9. Other questionnaires based on self-report are also widely used.

The State–Trait Anxiety Inventory, an inventory originally developed by Spielberger et al. (1970), was recently revised (Spielberger, 1983). This is a self-report measure of both state and trait anxiety in normal adults as well as individuals with anxiety disorders. The State–Trait Anxiety Inventory is one of the most frequently used self-report measures in the assessment of subjective anxiety. The revised version also provides subscores for both cognitive and somatic anxiety.

The Cognitive and Somatic Anxiety Questionnaire, devised by Schwartz et al. (1978), permits derivation of separate scores for cognitive anxiety and somatic anxiety. In our center we use it chiefly as a treatment outcome measure. While a variety of other self-report questionnaires exist, many of them are redundant to some extent with the two described above. In fact, using just one of these questionnaires, such as the revision of the State–Trait Anxiety Inventory, would also be sufficient to assess cognitive and somatic aspects of anxiety. On occasion we also employ the Beck Depression Inventory (Beck, Ward, Mendelson, Mock, & Erbaugh, 1961), as we do with many anxiety disorders. However, as noted in Chapter 9 and elsewhere, the Beck Depression Inventory and the State–Trait Anxiety Inventory also correlate highly with each other and are redundant to a large extent.

Self-Monitoring Measures

For ongoing self-monitoring of generalized anxiety, we use our Weekly Record of Anxiety and Depression, described in some detail in Chapter 10 and illustrated in Figure 10.7. This form also allows recording of fear of any panic attacks that might occur. Obviously, this is less of a concern for patients with GAD. Nevertheless, panic occurs frequently enough to make this information useful.

Behavioral Measures

By definition, patients with GAD do not manifest extensive avoidance. But GAD patients do evidence subtle avoidance in a variety of idiosyncratic situations. Some of the avoidance is situational; other avoidance is similar to the avoidance of somatic cues in panic disorder. During treatment of GAD, we take any avoidance behavior into consideration during construction of a hierarchy of situations associated with anxiety. This hierarchy forms an integral part of treatment, and is very similar to the one utilized in the assessment and treatment of panic disorder (see Chapter 10). This process is illsutrated in the presentation below of preliminary data on the treatment of GAD in our center.

Physiological Measures

Monitoring changes in physiological aspects of anxiety during treatment would seem an important topic for assessment, particularly within GAD, where, by definition, excessive and sometimes severe physiological over-reactivity is a major component of the disorder. The notion of GAD as excessive and unrealistic worry driven by arousal also seems to underline the importance of directly assessing arousal. Furthermore, in one of our early treatment studies described below (Barlow, Cohen, et al., 1984) physiological responding decreased significantly from pre- to posttreatment. Thus, it would seem to be another useful index of change.

However, Chapter 10 has discussed in some detail the current status of physiological assessment of anxiety *as a measure of treatment outcome.* It is observed there that the precise utility of physiological measures of change is not clear, for a variety of practical and conceptual reasons. The chapter thus concludes that *routine* assessment of physiological responding in clinical situations cannot be recommended until some of these issues are clarified. Nevertheless, for those clinicians with the requisite technology, there is no reason not to administer these measures—particularly with GAD patients, since reductions in overall arousal *seem* important within GAD. As a result of positive changes in physiological measures, patients may also acquire a greater sense of control over somatic responses that are often perceived as out of control. Further research should be directed at answering some of these important questions concerning the assessment of GAD.

TREATMENT

DRUG TREATMENT

Pharmacological approaches to GAD or its predecessor, anxiety neurosis, have consisted almost entirely of the use of benzodiazepines. There is no anxiety disorder for which drug treatments have been as extensively and competently tested. Since the 1970s, leading investigators have conducted well-designed, double-blind, placebo-controlled studies of the effects of benzodiazepines on generalized anxiety. The results have been reported clearly and accurately in most instances. Therefore, it is all the more surprising that the general impression among the lay community, as well as some professionals, is that benzodiazepines are a "cure" for GAD. In fact, what clinical investigators have reported all along is that the benzodiazepines have, at best, a limited therapeutic effect lasting no more than several weeks. Furthermore, benzodiazepines have a number of problematic effects, including psychological dependence, physical addiction, sedation and impairment of cognition and performance.

As early as 1978, Solomon and Hart reviewed 78 double-blind studies, including 29 testing the effects of diazepam alone. They concluded that although some rather small effects were present in some studies, the benzodiazepines had not been demonstrated to be clinically more effective than placebo for the treatment of neurotic anxiety. That same year, Greenblatt and Shader (1978) concluded that "the spread of anti-anxiety drug use appears to be attributable to neither changes in the environment (e.g., increase in stress) nor to advances in pharmacology, but rather to skillful and timely promotion of pharmaceutical products" (p. 1381).

Since that time, additional well-controlled studies have been conducted. Pharmacological advances have also resulted in the introduction of new anxiolytic drugs. Furthermore, a number of nonbenzodiazepine agents have been tested for their anxiolytic effects, with promising results. A few of these studies are reviewed selectively here. In the process, the promise of some of the newer nonbenzodiazepine drug treatment approaches to GAD is assessed.

Recent Studies

Table 15.3 summarizes a number of well-controlled studies evaluating the effects of benzodiazepines on anxiety since 1978. Most of these large studies were begun before the introduction of DSM-III. Therefore, "anxiety neurosis" was the most common categorization of the patients involved. However, these studies were very careful for the most part in specifying the patients so as to exclude marked depression, panic attacks, and so on. For example, Feighner, Meredith, and Hendrickson (1982), Rickels *et al.* (1983), and Shapiro, Streuning, Shapiro, and Milearek (1983) examined their patients retrospectively and concluded that all or almost all would meet the DSM-III criteria for GAD. Additional studies, many with only minimal controls, are reviewed by Klein, Rabkin, and Gorman (1985).

The studies shown in Table 15.3 were included because all investigators utilized one common and widely used measure of effectiveness, the Hamilton Anxiety Rating Scale. Of course, this is not a diagnostic

TABLE 15.3. A Number of Studies since 1978 Using the Hamilton Anxiety Rating Scale to Evaluate the Effects of Benzodiazepines on Anxiety

Study	Comparison	% reduction on HARS	% dropout	Daily dosage	Length of treatment	Total n
Doongaji et al. (1978)	Diazepam	62	43	17.5	4 weeks	60
	Clobozapam	62	23	35		
Rickels et al. (1980)	Diazepam	55	21	25	6 weeks	222
	Ketazolam	57	29	35		
	Placebo	41	44	—		
Aden & Thein (1980)	Alprazolam	41	9	1.5		162
	Diazepam	41	12	18.6	4 weeks	
	Placebo	21	35	—		
Hallstrom, Treasaden, Edwards, & Lader (1980)	Diazepam	27	0	22.5		24
	Propranolol[a]	18	0	180	2 weeks	
	Placebo	18	0	—		
	Combination[a]	36	0			
Bjertnaes et al. (1982)	Placebo	48	31	—		96
	Chlordiazepoxide	58	19	45	6 weeks	
Feighner, Meredith, & Hendrickson (1982)	Diazepam	33	NR[b]	15	4 weeks	100
	Buspirone[a]	35	NR	16.5		
Rickels et al. (1982)	Diazepam	58	NR	16		240
	Buspirone[a]	50	NR	16	4 weeks	
	Placebo	21	NR			
Rickels et al. (1983)	Alprazolam	52	4	2.1		151
	Diazepam	50	18	27	4 weeks	
	Placebo	31	31	—		
Shapiro, Streuning, Shapiro, & Milearek (1983)	Diazepam	22	40	21.4	6 weeks	224
	Placebo	32	35	—		

Note. My appreciation to William C. Sanderson for compiling this table.
[a]Not a benzodiazepine.
[b]NR = not reported.

instrument, but it is useful for comparative purposes in measuring changes in severity of clinical anxiety. Table 15.3 presents the specific drugs used in the studies and the average percentage of reduction by the end of treatment on the Hamilton scale for each drug. Most reductions for patients on benzodiazepines were statistically significant, compared to those for patients on placebo. Also presented are the percentage of patients dropping out, the daily dosage of the drug, the length of treatment, and the total number of patients (*n*) in each study.

Few studies on any topic have accumulated as many patients per condition or group as these studies have. There are two implications of very large *n*'s such as these. First, adequate statistical power was available for these studies. That is, any reliable effect of the drugs worth noting was statistically significant. But statistical power is a two-edged sword. That is, the larger the *n*, the smaller the absolute size of the effect required for statistical significance. Unlike some other areas of science, this is a serious consideration for therapy outcome studies, since results can be statistically significant but fall far short of clinical significance. In other words, one may witness a small effect averaged over a very large group of subjects, the size of which will provide little or no clinical benefit to the patient.

The size of the treatment effect from these drugs compared to placebo is plotted in Figure 15.5. Specifically, the figure plots the percentage of reduction of the Hamilton Anxiety Rating Scale for each group in all nine studies. There were a total of 7 placebo groups and 13 benzodiazepine groups (excluding nonbenzodiazepine drug conditions; see footnote *a* to Table 15.3). The marked overlap between the benzodiazepine and placebo groups is obvious in this figure. The range of reduction on the Hamilton scale fell between 18% and 48% for the placebo group, compared to between 22% and 62% for the benzodiazepine groups. The mean reduction on the Hamilton scale for patients in the benzodiazepine treatment groups was 47.5%, compared to 30.3% for placebo groups. To put it another way, for patients with a pretreatment score of 20 on the Hamilton scale, the predicted decrease for those on the active drug treatment would be 3.4 points greater than the decrease for those on placebo. This could be accounted for by a change in one symptom.

Conclusions on the marginal effects of benzodiazepines (compared to placebo) are underlined by noting that scores on the clinician-rated Hamilton scale seemed to produce the strongest pattern of differences. Self-report data from patients revealed a weaker and often nonsignificant pattern of differences between drug and placebo in many studies. For example, 50% of the studies reviewed above did not find a significant difference between drug and placebo on self-report measures from patients.

One other noteworthy finding communicated earlier and often by leading investigators concerns the relatively short-lived nature of any therapeutic effects. Of the studies in Table 15.3, for example, the longest

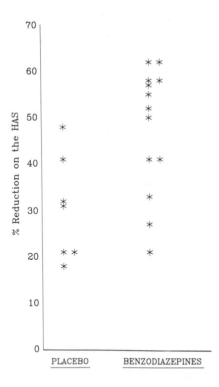

FIGURE 15.5. Each asterisk represents the percentage of reduction on the Hamilton Anxiety Rating Scale in either a placebo or a benzodiazepine group of the studies reviewed in Table 15.3. My appreciation to William C. Sanderson for organizing the data.

follow-up was 6 weeks. In the Shapiro *et al.* (1983) study, which was particularly well done with a large number of subjects, statistically signif- icant drug effects were present 1 week after the beginning of treatment but not thereafter. This reflects the well-known tendency of benzodiaze- pines to produce rapid tolerance requiring increased dosages.

On the basis of these studies, most investigators conclude that these drugs may have some temporary palliative value in reducing anxiety over the short term, but not over the long term. Conventional clinical wisdom suggests prescribing these drugs for a short time during a particularly difficult or stressful situation and then removing the drug very quickly. In these circumstances, benzodiazepines can be a useful tool.

The Risks of Benzodiazepines

The use of benzodiazepines involves two major risks: impairment of cog- nitive abilities and performance, and problematic withdrawal reactions. Some of these issues have been covered in Chapter 11 in the context of studies utilizing benzodiazepines for panic disorder. For example, many investigators have noted "rebound anxiety" after abrupt withdrawal of benzodiazepine treatment (e.g., Fontaine *et al.*, 1984); this refers to more severe manifestations of anxiety after drug withdrawal than observed before treatment began. Studies documenting this phenomenon with alprazolam, a triazolobenzodiazepine often used to treat panic, have been mentioned in Chapter 11.

This effect is most obvious in benzodiazepines with a short half-life. Therefore, most clinicians are advised to withdraw benzodiazepines extremely slowly. Petursson and Lader (1981) present data suggesting that the return of anxiety after withdrawal, whether gradual or abrupt, represents a true withdrawal syndrome and not just a return of the original anxiety symptoms. In all likelihood, it is this effect that makes it so difficult for patients to discontinue the use of benzodiazepines. The neurobiological basis for this physical dependence has been explored by Lukas and Griffiths (1982), who conclude that benzodiazepines may produce clinically relevant functional changes in the central nervous system more rapidly than heretofore expected.

Specific cognitive impairments have been documented by Lader and others. For example, Petursson and Lader (1981) noticed gradual improvement on subscales of the Wechsler Adult Intelligence Scale during withdrawal from chronic benzodiazepine usage. They interpret these data as implying psychological impairment during chronic benzodiazepine ingestion. More problematic are impairments in performance while driving, which have been interpreted as potentially dangerous (e.g., O'Hanlon, Haak, Blaauw, & Riemersma, 1982). These risks are additional reasons for the strong recommendations that benzodiazepines be administered for only a short time (Tyrer, 1980; Tyrer & Owen, 1984).

New advances in anxiolytic drugs may begin to address some of these concerns. For example, buspirone is a nonbenzodiazepine that appears to have anxiolytic properties. In Table 15.3, data from Rickels et al. (1982) suggest that busiprone's anxiolytic properties are approximately equivalent to those of benzodiazepines. Goldberg and Finnerty (1982) report similar results. Significantly, buspirone does not appear to be sedating, nor does it interact with central nervous system depressants such as alcohol. Additional research will determine whether it has other advantages over benzodiazepines in terms of risk factors. It will also be important to determine whether the effects last longer than several weeks as with the benzodiazepines.

In view of the prevalent misconceptions concerning benzodiazepines, I have highlighted research findings implying a more cautious interpretation of the effects of this class of pharmacological agents. However, the benzodiazepines are certainly not without their advantages. If used appropriately, they can provide very fast relief from overwhelming anxiety associated with a difficult or stressful situation. As noted above, in the ideal case, they would then be withdrawn very quickly. Finally, among various drugs widely used in our society, benzodiazepines seem to have a very low potential for involvement in suicide. Thus, like any other tool, benzodiazepines when used appropriately may be of some assistance in the symptomatic treatment of anxiety. But there is general agreement that there are many risks and few benefits from long-term usage. Therefore, this class of drugs is not a comprehensive treatment for GAD.

Additional Drugs

As with other anxiety disorders, a few scattered studies have evaluated the effects of the beta-blockers as well as clonidine on GAD (e.g., Hallstrom, Treasaden, Edwards, & Lader, 1981; Hoehn-Saric et al., 1981). Although occasional hints of positive reactions are found in some patients (e.g., Hoehn-Saric et al., 1981), the more usual finding is that propranolol is little or no better than placebo (e.g., Hallstrom et al., 1981). Thus, beta-blockers are not highly regarded as a potential treatment for GAD.

Results are just beginning to appear on what may be the most powerful anxiolytic drug available. Chapter 11 has mentioned a study by R. J. Kahn et al. (1986), who reported a significant anxiolytic effect from imipramine. Imipramine, of course, has been thought to be a specific treatment for panic. However, the possibility is raised in Chapter 11 that the effects of imipramine may well be generally anxiolytic rather than specifically panicolytic. Klein et al. (1985) review a number of minimally controlled trials for vaguely defined "anxious" patients suggesting the efficacy of antidepresants. On the basis of these preliminary findings, this class of drugs deserves vigorous investigation in regard to their potential effectiveness for GAD.

Finally, there have been surprisingly few investigations of the interactions of drug and nondrug treatments for GAD. In an early study, Lavallée, Lamontagne, Pinard, Annable, and Tétreault (1977) reported results indicating that EMG biofeedback and diazepam had additive effects on outpatients suffering from chronic anxiety, but that the effects of biofeedback were stronger and more prolonged than the effects of diazepam. To date, a greater number of studies have examined the interaction of benzodiazepines with exposure-based treatments for phobia, as noted in Chapter 11. While it is possible that benzodiazepines and psychosocial treatments may have an overall additive effect if used properly, the somewhat more pessimistic conclusion in Chapter 11 is that benzodiazepines seem to interfere with the effects of exposure-based treatments for phobic reactions. Whether this is true for GAD remains to be seen. A fuller investigation of the interactive effects of drugs and psychosocial treatments for GAD would be desirable.

PSYCHOSOCIAL TREATMENT

Compared to investigations of the pharmacological treatment of GAD, studies on the efficacy of psychosocial treatments are just beginning. Relatively few reports have appeared. The overwhelming majority of those treated have been analogue volunteer subjects rather than clinically anxious patients.

Early Studies

Early studies can be divided into two types: those treating somatic aspects of generalized anxiety and those targeting cognitive aspects. Techniques targeting somatic manifestations of anxiety have included biofeedback and general relaxation procedures. The literature on biofeedback approaches to GAD has been thoroughly reviewed previously (Rice & Blanchard, 1982) and includes several studies with clinical populations (e.g., Canter, Kondo, & Knott, 1975; LeBoeuf & Lodge, 1980; Mathew, Ho, Kralik, Weinman, & Claghorn, 1981; Raskin, Bali, & Peeke, 1980; Rupert, Dobbins, & Mathew, 1981). Most biofeedback studies have also included some form of relaxation training, either in combination with biofeedback or as a comparison group. Generally, Rice and Blanchard (1982) conclude that consistent evidence exists for the effectiveness of only frontal EMG feedback. However, while an occasional study suggests superiority of EMG feedback training over relaxation (e.g., Canter et al., 1975), other forms of relaxation training have most often yielded comparable clinical effects in controlled studies.

Relaxation training in its many forms, including meditation, is probably the most popular and oldest treatment for anxiety and tension. As noted above, relaxation procedures also reduce anxiety (as measured by rating scales or questionnaires) as effectively as EMG biofeedback. Occasionally the results for relaxation are superior to those for biofeedback (e.g., Beiman, Israel, & Johnson, 1978). Additional research indicates that relaxation is more effective than no treatment or a placebo control group in reducing tension (Borkovec, Grayson, & Cooper, 1978; Borkovec & Hennings, 1978; Hutchings, Denney, Basgall, & Houston, 1980; Jannoun, Oppenheimer, & Gelder, 1982; Lewis, Beglan, & Steinblock, 1978; Sherman & Plummer, 1973). But with a few exceptions (e.g., Jannoun et al., 1982), most studies treated only mildly anxious college students.

Three issues derived from these studies deserve comment. First, at least two studies mention specifically the inclusion of patients reporting acute panic attacks in groups experiencing more chronic anxiety (Canter et al., 1975; Jannoun et al., 1982). While it is not clear whether any of these patients would have met DSM-III criteria for panic, and panic attacks were not specifically measured, this is a common occurrence, as noted above. No differential response to treatment was observed in these two groups as a function of the occurrence of panic. Second, many studies were unable to document a relationship between increased muscle relaxation and

591

clinical improvement (e.g., Raskin *et al.*, 1980; Rice & Blanchard, 1982; Rupert *et al.*, 1981), suggesting that other factors may have accounted for any anxiety reduction that did occur. I have speculated on the nature of these other factors in Chapter 8. Finally, in the few studies where detailed clinical ratings of improvement were collected in addition to questionnaire measures, results were very weak. For example, LeBoeuf and Lodge (1980) reported only 4 out of 26 patients showing more than marginal improvement; Raskin *et al.* (1980), in a thorough and comprehensive study, suggest that an improvement rate of 40% on a composite measure of change is probably overgenerous. As Raskin *et al.* (1980) have observed, relaxation-based treatments appear to be insufficient by themselves in treating chronic anxiety; one must also incorporate other interventions, such as cognitive approaches.

Beck *et al.* (1974) pointed out specific sets of cognitions associated with free-floating anxiety states. Those observations coincided with the advent of behaviorally oriented treatments that included explicit attempts to alter clients' cognitions (e.g., Goldfried, Decenteceo, & Weinberg, 1974; Mahoney, 1974; Meichenbaum, 1974).

Two early studies evaluated cognitive–behavioral approaches with clinically anxious patients. Woodward and Jones (1980) found the combination of cognitive restructuring and modified applied relaxation treatment superior to either treatment alone on one measure (out of eight)—intensity of fear on the Fear Survey Schedule. It is not clear why this measure, designed primarily to assess phobias, would reflect changes in nonphobic anxiety states. On another measure, daily self-monitoring of anxiety levels, both applied relaxation and this combined treatment were superior to cognitive restructuring alone. However, the *n* in each group was small, and the extent of clinical change is not clear. Ramm, Marks, Yuksel, and Stern (1981), in a pilot study, found positive self-statement training somewhat more effective than negative self-statement training when comparing two groups of six anxiety state patients each. These differences emerged only on some measures at some points in time, but, notably, included patient ratings of panic at posttest. The authors note that the gains were not impressive compared to results with analogue subjects.

Recent Studies

Recent studies evaluating cognitive–behavioral treatments show considerably more promise in their application to GAD. One study comes from Oxford University; a second is currently in progress at our center; and a third is in progress at Penn State University.

Based on an earlier successful pilot study (Jannoun *et al.*, 1982), Butler, Cullington, Hibbert, Klimes, and Gelder (1987) evaluated an anxiety management package for GAD. This package was very similar to their treatment for social phobia, described in Chapter 14. Specifically, patients were taught to cope with various aspects of their anxiety in a number of ways. Tape-recorded instructions for relaxation were provided during the first session so that patients could practice both during sessions and at home throughout treatment. Patients were also given a booklet describing the major procedures at the first session. To deal with cognitive aspects of anxiety, patients were taught distracting techniques and the control of upsetting thoughts. The latter technique is similar to self-instructional training. Butler *et al.* (1987) also observed that avoidance, while not the major problem in GAD, does exist to some degree and can be problematic; therefore, graded exposure practice sessions were incorporated into treatment. Patients were encouraged to take control of their lives by scheduling more pleasurable activities and noting areas in their life in which they were functioning well.

This rather heterogeneous package was administered in a very clinical manner, such that patients could stop treatment after the minimum of 4 sessions provided they were no longer distressed by symptoms of anxiety. In fact, the average length of treatment was 8.7 sessions.

Although the Research Diagnostic Criteria definition was used to classify patients as having GAD, this definition, as modified by the investigators, comes extremely close to the DSM-III-R definition. Specifically, patients were included not only if they had occasional panic attacks, but also if they met the criteria for panic disorder, provided that GAD was the primary disorder in terms of severity.

A total of 45 consecutive patients meeting these criteria were randomly allocated to the anxiety management condition or a waiting-list group. Of these patients, 22 were initially assigned to the anxiety management group and 23 to the waiting-list group. After 12 weeks, waiting-list subjects began treatment. Due to attrition at various points, results are available at the 6-month assessment point for 20 subjects in the anxiety management group and 18 in the waiting-list group. The results are presented in Table 15.4. Data from the Leeds Anxiety Scale, the State and Trait Anxiety subscales of the State–Trait Anxiety Inventory, the Hamilton Anxiety Rating Scale, and the standard 9-point clinical rating scale developed by Watson and Marks (1971) are illustrated. Groups differed significantly at the 3-month assessment on every measure. At this time, the waiting-list group began receiving treatment. Changes in the waiting-list group after treatment then approximated those of the anxiety management group. At a 6-month follow-up, improvement on all measures was either maintained or increased further.

A more informal follow-up at 1 year was collected from the records of the patients' primary care physicians. Just under two-thirds of the patients had had no further contact with their general practitioners. Nine

TABLE 15.4. Means of the Main Outcome Measures

	Assessment 1		After wait	After treatment		6-month follow-up	
	Anxiety management	Waiting list	Waiting list	Anxiety management	Waiting list	Anxiety management	Waiting list
n	22	23	23	22	19	20	18
Age	36.5	38.3					
Anxiety ratings							
0–8 (assessor)	5.5	5.6	5.2	2.6	2.7	1.9	2.4
0–8 (patient)	4.9	5.0	4.5	2.0	2.3	1.6	1.7
Leeds Anxiety Scale	11.5	12.7	12.4	6.7	6.8	5.0	6.4
Hamilton Anxiety Rating Scale	16.0	17.4	15.4	6.6	7.6	5.0	8.0
State Anxiety[a]	58.0	54.6	57.1	43.9	41.8	38.9	41.5
Trait Anxiety[a]	55.8	54.8	—	—	—	43.7	38.9

Note. Adapted from Butler, G., Cullington, A., Hibbert, G., Klimes, I., & Gelder, M. (1987). Anxiety management for persistent generalized anxiety. British Journal of Psychiatry, 151, 535–542. Copyright 1987 by the Royal College of Psychiatrists. Adapted by permission.
[a]Subscales of the State–Trait Anxiety Inventory.

patients, on the other hand, had received more extensive treatment for anxiety in the interim, including medication. Overall, 46% of the patients were taking regular medication at the beginning of treatment; 6 months after treatment, this figure had dropped to 13%. Panic attacks also improved. Before treatment, 20 of the 41 patients who received treatment had recurrent attacks; the mean attack frequency was 1.76 per week. After treatment, the mean attack frequency per week was 0.23, and it was 0.10 at the 6-month follow-up. Fourteen of the 20 patients reported that they had had no attacks for a period of at least 3 months.

Currently, this package is a very complex combination of a number of procedures. As the investigators point out, it is not at all clear why this treatment works, or what procedure or combination of procedures contributes most to its effectiveness. Furthermore, it will be difficult to replicate until procedures are specified more clearly. In any case, pending replication and the inclusion of appropriate control conditions, the results are very promising.

One further result is particularly interesting in the context of data reported above for the benzopdiazepines. The widely used Hamilton Anxiety Rating Scale was a dependent measure in this study. This is the standard measure in benzodiazepine studies reported in Table 15.3. In the anxiety management treatment group, Hamilton scores showed an average 59% reduction immediately following treatment, and a 69% reduction by the 6-month follow-up. The latter figure exceeds the greatest benefit reported in any drug study reviewed in Table 15.3. Of course, this difference may not reflect differential treatment effectiveness, but rather methodological differences in rating. Direct comparisons within the same study are essential. In addition, an average of 30.3% reduction in all placebo groups, with some reductions up to 50%, should give appropriate caution to those who may be overconfident about the specific effects of psychosocial treatment. It is very possible that any number of psychosocial treatments may be effective for GAD as a result of positive expectancies, renewed hope, and increased sense of control, or other psychological or cognitive efffects occasionally engendered by placebo treatment. Appropriate comparison treatments are required.

In 1984, my colleagues and I published a pilot study demonstrating the effectiveness of a package combining cognitive and relaxation procedures for a group of patients with GAD or panic disorder (Barlow, Cohen, et al., 1984). Compared to controls, treated patients improved—not only on clinical ratings, but also on psychophysiological measures, daily self-monitoring measures of background anxiety and panic, and questionnaire measures of anxiety. The waiting-listed group did not improve. At follow-ups averaging 6 months, the treated group showed additional improvement. This latter result was particularly encouraging, since it suggested that these patients had learned something during treatment.

Now we have preliminary results from a large study in progress comparing three different treatment procedures for GAD to a waiting-list control group. Specifically, cognitive and relaxation procedures are administered separately to each of two groups of patients. A third group receives a combination of both treatments. These three groups are contrasted to a waiting-list control group. Treatment procedures in our combined group include relaxation and cognitive strategies, both used as coping procedures. Thus patients are specifically taught to cope with anxiety and anxiety-related situations. This approach has some similarities to that of Butler *et al.* (1987), described above. Any avoidance behavior that may be present, as well as sensitivity to or avoidance of somatic cues associated with anxiety (which are also considered to be anxiety-related situations), are routinely assessed and treated. After construction of a hierarchy of anxiety-related situations in a manner similar to that described in Chapter 10, relaxation and cognitive strategies are taught systematically to these patients, who then practice these procedures in the context of situations found on their hierarchies. Examples of two hierarchies for GAD patients who received treatment in our setting are presented in Table 15.5. The

TABLE 15.5. Hierarchies of Anxiety-Related Situations for Two GAD Patients

Anxiety rating	Situation
	K. M.—33-year-old white male
1	Getting up in the morning and getting ready for work
2	Driving to work
3	Going to a physician for a checkup
5	Talking to a stranger about yourself
5	Going in to talk to your boss during the afternoon
5	Going to dinner with people you do not know very well
5	Your wife just spent a large amount of money
5	You must give a customer negative news (e.g., no loan)
6	Interviewing for a job
7	You are having a physical pain and are contemplating death
	G. W.—38-year-old white female
2	Getting dinner together, general household responsibilities
2	Teaching at school
5	Waiting for phone calls (e.g., from a doctor, husband is late)
5	Visit your mother
6	Your husband is traveling on a plane
6	You and your family are taking a vacation
7	You need to go to the doctor for a checkup
7	Driving in areas with which you are not familiar
8	You must take your children to the doctor
8	Your husband is ill

patients' anxiety ratings for the situation prior to treatment are on the left (based on a 0–8 scale). As one can see, some of these situations imply mild or even moderate avoidance, while others imply a sensitivity to or fear of somatic cues. But these patients clearly meet DSM-III-R criteria for GAD, which was their primary diagnosis.

While the full data set is not yet available, some interesting preliminary results are in. All treatments appear to be beneficial, but cognitive coping procedures seem particularly powerful with this group of patients, producing the greatest percentage of change on major measures of outcome. Preliminary results from Borkovec and his colleagues also suggest a strong effect of cognitive components of therapy, and an overall sizeable clinical benefit from these treatments with GAD patients. Confirmation of these findings will await full analysis of the data.

In Chapter 14, I have noted the potential importance of instilling a sense of control and redirecting the focus of attention away from negative affect in social phobia. This should be important in all anxiety disorders. But in certain cases of social phobia and all cases of GAD, where interference with performance and concentration is the major clinical problem, treatments involving cognitive coping components may assume central importance.

16

Obsessive–Compulsive Disorder

If a patient with an anxiety disorder needs hospitalization, chances are that the patient has obsessive–compulsive disorder (abbreviated hereafter as OCD). If a patient is referred for psychosurgery because every psychological and pharmacological treatment has failed and the suffering is unbearable, chances are that the patient has OCD. If one evaluates a patient with unbearably severe generalized anxiety, recurrent panic attacks, debilitating avoidance, and major depression all occurring simultaneously, the diagnosis is probably OCD. For OCD is the devastating culmination of the most intense manifestations of emotional disorders. It is the disorder in which establishing even a foothold of control and predictability over the dangerous events in one's life seems so utterly hopeless that one resorts to magic and rituals in a vain attempt to re-establish a small haven of safety. In OCD the dangerous event is a thought, image, or impulse. But this thought or image must be avoided as assiduously as a snake phobic avoids snakes. If it occurs even once, it can have the same impact as re-experiencing a trauma. Usually, it occurs many times a day. In more severe cases, this process goes on continuously. The chapter on OCD is the last chapter in this book because readers can more fully grasp the dimensions of this disorder if they are familiar with the other anxiety disorders discussed earlier.

The intensity, severity, and occasional bizarre quality of OCD are hard to appreciate without case illustrations. Some time ago, a 32-year-old married woman from a middle-class family was referred to our clinic. Accompanied by her husband and her 6-year-old child, she reported a 5-year history of severe compulsive behavior, consisting primarily of washing rituals. The woman was attractive and well dressed, and seemed reasonably calm if slightly worried during the initial interview. She and her husband were very affectionate during the interview, touching and smiling at each other frequently. They mentioned that their life centered around their church and their fundamental Protestant religion. Shortly thereafter, her husband told us privately that he was absolutely at his wits' end. As much as he loved his wife, he was ready to consider a divorce. He mentioned that he had communicated this to his wife, which was the primary motivation for her seeking treatment again at this time.

In fact, the wife's reluctance to seek further treatment, although a relatively common state of affairs in OCD, was understandable in this case. On several prior occasions, at her husband's urging, she had entered treatment. Twice she was hospitalized, each time receiving a series of electroconvulsive treatments with only a temporary positive effect. Thus, she had lost some confidence in the promise of treatment.

Her difficulties had begun 5 years prior to her visit, when she first suspected she was pregnant with a second child. She remembered being distressed by this, feeling she was not ready for the rigors of childbirth and another young infant. One day, while standing by the picture window in her living room, she had the thought that she really did not want another baby and pressed her abdomen against the window. Several weeks later she experienced some bleeding and discomfort and eventually lost the baby. In the context of her fundamental religious beliefs, she felt sinful and guilty over ever having the thought that she did not want the child. She associated this thought and her behavior at the window with the miscarriage.

Her fears and doubts centered on two areas: cleanliness of her environment, and excessive concern with "salvation." She was continually calling her minister to check on the moral appropriateness of every thought and action. Her minister, who ultimately arranged for the referral to our clinic, attempted to be understanding and reassuring. More significantly, she was washing her hands and arms up to the elbow from 30 to 60 times a day. Her hands and arms were raw and scabbed in places from excessive scrubbing with strong disinfectants. Her contamination fears, which led to the washing, centered on cleanliness in general, but also included fear of x-rays from television, fears associated with a variety of food preservatives, and many others. As with many severe washers, her concern did not center on the danger of contaminating herself, but rather on the possibility of spreading contamination and/or poison to her family, causing their illness or death.

The second case to be described here was more complex and more severe, and illustrates the wide range of behavior encountered in OCD. The patient was a 19-year-old single white male, a college freshman majoring in philosophy, who had withdrawn from school because of incapacitating ritualistic behaviors. The patient had an 8-year history of severe compulsive rituals. These included excessive hand washing and showering; ceremonial rituals for dressing and studying; compulsive placement of any objects handled; grotesque hissing, coughing, and head tossing while eating; and shuffling and wiping his feet while walking. These rituals interfered with every aspect of his daily functioning. The patient had steadily deteriorated within the past 2 years, isolating himself from family and friends, refusing meals, and neglecting his personal appearance. His hair was very long, as he had not allowed it to be cut in 5 years. He had never shaved or trimmed his beard. When he walked, he shuffled, taking small steps on his toes while continually looking back, checking and re-checking. On occasion he would run quickly in place. He had withdrawn his left arm completely from his shirt sleeve, as if he were crippled and his shirt was a sling.

Seven weeks prior to admission, his rituals had become so time-consuming and debilitating that he refused to engage in any personal hygiene for fear that the associated rituals would interfere with the time needed to study. Almost continual showering became no showering. He stopped washing his hair, brushing his teeth, or changing his clothes. He left his room infrequently and, to avoid rituals associated with the toilet, had begun defecating on paper towels, urinating in paper cups, and storing the waste in a corner of the closet in his room. His eating habits had degenerated from eating with the family, to eating in an adjoining room, to eating in his own room. In the 2 months prior to admission, he had lost 20 pounds and would only eat late at night when others were asleep. He felt that eating was "barbaric"; this well described his grotesque eating rituals, consisting of hissing noises, coughs and hacks, and severe head tossing. His food intake had been narrowed to ice cream or a mixture of peanut butter, sugar, cocoa, milk, and mayonnaise. He considered several foods (e.g., cola, beef, and butter) contaminating, and would not eat these foods. He also had a long list of checking rituals associated with the placement of objects. Excessive time was spent checking and rechecking to see that wastebaskets and curtains were in place. These rituals had progressed to tilting of wastebaskets and twisting of curtains, which were checked periodically throughout the day.

These two cases are discussed further below in connection with treatment. Both of them fit very clearly within the definition of OCD in DSM-III-R, where the disorder is characterized as "recurrent obsessions or compulsions sufficiently severe to cause marked distress, be time consuming, or significantly interfere with the person's normal routine, occupational functioning, or with usual social activities or relationships with others" (American Psychiatric Association, 1987, p. 245). Obsessions are defined as "persistent ideas, thoughts, impulses, or images that are experienced, at least initially, as intrusive and senseless (for example, a parent having repeated impulses to kill a loved child, or a religious person having recurrent blasphemous thoughts)" (American Psychiatric Association, 1987, p. 245). The definition specifies that attempts must be made to ignore or suppress such thoughts or to neutralize them, and that the individual must recognize that the obsessions are the product of his or her own mind and not imposed from without. This last point is a small but important clarification not present in DSM-III.

Compulsions are defined as "repetitive, purposeful, and intentional behaviors that are performed in response to an obsession, according to certain rules or in a stereotyped fashion" (American Psychiatric Association, 1987, p. 245). It is also noted that the behavior is designed to neutralize or to prevent discomfort or some dreaded event or situation, and that the individual recognizes that his or her behavior is obsessive or unreasonable (unless it has become overvalued ideation; see below). This definition also is a simple clarification of the DSM-III definition. In fact, the definition of OCD in DSM-III-R is essentially unchanged from definitions in DSM-II, DSM-I, and even earlier descriptions, going back to Westphal in 1878 (Insel, 1984).

PHENOMENOLOGY

OBSESSIONS

A number of investigators have attempted to delineate different types of obsessions and compulsions. Typically, these investigators have accumulated a large number of cases and examined types of obsessions and compulsions according to form and content. For example, Akhtar, Wig, Verma, Pershad, and Verma (1975) categorized the symptoms of 75 patients with OCD. The obsessional symptoms most frequently revolved around the subject of dirt and contamination. This topic was followed by aggression and violence, religion, and sex. In fact, studies examining obsessional content consistently verify that these themes are the most common. For example, Jenike, Baer, and Minichiello (1986) also observed in a sample of 100 patients that the most frequent themes of obsessions were contamination (55%) aggressive impulses (50%), sexual content (32%), somatic concerns (35%), and the need for symmetry (37%). Sixty percent of their sample displayed multiple obsessions.

Most studies attempting to categorize obsessions by form rather than content refer to a number of related phenomena. For example, as noted above, DSM-III-R defines obsessions as (recurrent, persistent) ideas, thoughts, images, or impulses. Akhtar et al. (1975) divided obsessions into doubts, obsessive thinking, obsessive fears, obsessive impulses, and obsessive images. For example, "a woman who worries about her child's safety might have an obsessive doubt (has something happened to him), or an obsessive fear (something might happen to him because of my negligence), or an obsessive image (over and over I see him drowning!), or obsessional thinking (if he plays outside he might catch cold that might turn into pneumonia, and if that goes undiagnosed, then . . .)" (p. 345). As they point out, the content of the obsession is the same in each case, but the form is different.

Attempts to determine the relative frequency of these different forms of obsessions have resulted in a great deal of inconsistency. This is probably due to difficulties in differentiating among the forms. For example, Reed (1985) reported that 65% of 48 patients presented with obsessional fears, 40% with ruminations, 38% with doubts, 35% with impulses, and only 2% with images. Akhtar et al. (1975) however, found that 75% of the obsessions were in the form of doubts in their sample. In order of decreasing frequency, 34% were thoughts, 25% fears, 15% impulses, and 7% images. de Silva (1986), on the other hand, thinks that images are far more common relative to other types of obsessions. He suggests that if investigators were to examine more carefully for these phenomena, as did Parkinson and Rachman (1981b), then images would rank second only to thoughts among forms of obsession.

de Silva points out properly that images (and other obsessions) can be both obsessions and compulsions. For example, images of blasphemous acts, mutilated bodies, and the like can serve as obsessions. Images can also serve as compulsions designed to somehow relieve the distress of the obsessive image. For example, Rachman (1976) describes a young woman with the recurrent image of four people lying dead in an open grave. The compulsive or neutralizing image involved imagining the same four people standing or walking, quite healthy. The importance of a functional classification of obsessive or compulsive images is discussed further below.

It is not clear at this time that differentiating the forms of obsessions has any value. In our clinic, we have little difficulty separating images from impulses. Patients often report an "impulse" to shout something blasphemous in church or touch a stranger sexually; this impulse is strongly resisted and often subject to neutralizing rituals. Similarly, many patients report horrific images of sexual or aggressive content. We have more difficulty distinguishing thoughts, fears, and doubts. For example, the woman who hears a sound or feels a slight vibration while driving her car develops the obsession that she has run over somebody. This, in turn, leads to elaborate checking rituals. It is not clear whether this is a thought, doubt, or fear.

In the extreme, these thoughts, doubts, or fears may evolve into a seemingly endless pattern of rumination characterized by preoccupation, anxiety, and guilt. For example, the woman who reads a story in the newspaper about the death of a young family in a fire may ruminate over being responsible for this in some way and dwell on ways she could have prevented it. A student we saw recently ruminated continually on whether his studying and concentration were adequate. This rumination extended to the appropriateness of his behavior in social situations. Interspersed with these ruminations were innumerable corrective thoughts. At one time, the obsessions concerning studying and adequate social behavior may have produced the type of horrific emotional reaction that we see in many patients with obsessive images or impulses. But in this case, where the problem had been going on for many years, intense anxiety was not associated specifically with a particular part of the process. Rather, the whole process itself was continually distressing. As noted above, determining differential treatment implications for the various forms of obsessions is an area yet to be studied. At the present time, both pharmacological and psychological interventions would be similar, whatever the form.

COMPULSIONS

Investigators have classified ritualistic behavior in a variety of ways. But it is possible that the various categories can be subsumed under the larger headings of cleaning and checking, as well as the less frequent category of primary obsessional slowness. Several studies report somewhat different percentages of these types of rituals, although many patients present with both types. For example, Hodgson and Rachman (1977), using a factor-analytic technique, found that 52% of their patients displayed what could be called checking rituals, while 48% evidenced cleaning rituals. These were clearly the major forms of ritualistic activity, although 52% also demonstrated some obsessional slowing of activity. Stern and Cobb (1978) examined 45 patients and found that 51% had cleaning rituals, whereas another 51% had "avoiding" rituals that were similar to the avoidance behavior manifested in phobic disorders. The majority of these patients may have been avoiding contaminating substances. If so, this behavior would be in the same functional category as cleaning or washing rituals. Stern and Cobb also found that 38% of the patients presented with checking rituals and 40% demonstrated rituals characterized as repeating (doing things by numbers, regardless of the type of activity being carried out).

Jenike et al. (1986) found that 79% of their 100 patients had checking rituals, while 58% presented with cleaning rituals and 21% with counting rituals. (Functionally, checking and counting rituals can probably be categorized together.) In contrast to the preponderance of checkers in Jenike et al.'s (1986) sample, Rachman and Hodgson (1980) and Foa et al. (1983) found that 86% and 66% of their patients, respectively, presented with washing rituals.

There is an obvious difference between washers and checkers (Rachman, 1976). The fears of washers are centered on contact with objects or situations that may be contaminating; washing restores a sense of safety and control. Checking rituals, on the other hand, serve to prevent some future imagined disaster or catastrophe. Nevertheless, systematic examination has not revealed any additional substantive differences between patients with these two types of rituals (Steketee, Grayson, & Foa, 1985). Therefore, much as with obsessions, it is not clear that these demonstrably different types of rituals have any implications for treatment or course of the disorder.

A far less frequent but seemingly distinct form of ritualistic behavior referred to as "primary obsessional slowness" was first identified and labeled by Rachman (1974). Essentially, this refers to a condition in which the individual behaves in slow motion. For example, Bilsbury and Morley (1979) described a patient who took 4 hours to get up in the morning. This patient did not repeat activities, but subdivided each activity involved in getting ready in the morning into a number of stages. He then narrated his progress through these stages. In this way, it took him 1 hours to get out of bed, 35 minutes to wash his face, and so on. What is unique about this behavioral pattern is that the excessive mental rehearsal involved in meticulously carrying out each small portion of behavior is not intrusive, unpleasant, or resisted. The patient was simply making sure that he did everything properly by paying excessive attention to detail. For reasons discussed below, it is not clear that this problem should be considered a variant of OCD.

Finally, 25% of all patients presenting with OCD seem to have no motoric compulsions. But these patients almost always present with neutralizing thoughts, which serve as compulsions in a manner described below (Mavissakalian, Turner, & Michelson, 1985).

Before continuing, it is interesting to note that clinicians, greatly puzzled by the bizarre content of many of these rituals, have often attributed them to excessive concern with cultural preoccupations. For example, it has been noted that the high percentage of cleaning rituals in Egypt or India may be due to the dictates of the Moslem religion in Egypt or the emphasis on cleanliness in India. In fact, patients from a variety of different cultures display remarkably similar forms of the disorder (e.g., washing, checking). Even the frequencies of specific forms of the disorder are similar across cultures. For example, Insel (1984) reviews studies from England, Hong Kong, India, Egypt, Japan, and Norway showing the characteristic cluster of OCD phenomena, such as fears of contamination accompanied by cleaning rituals; pathological doubt accompanied by checking; obsessional thoughts accompanied by neutralizing thoughts but no behavioral rituals; and, more rarely, primary obsessional slowness.

FUNCTIONAL CLASSIFICATION OF OBSESSIONS
AND COMPULSIONS

I have noted above that thoughts or images can be both obsessions and compulsions, according to the usual definition of these terms. These definitions, in turn, are based in large part on the supposed functions that they serve. That is, obsessions are typically considered to be internal, intrusive, noxious stimuli that are anxiety-provoking or distressing. Compulsions, on the other hand, may be cognitions, behaviors, or combinations of the two that are designed to neutralize the obsessions and reduce the subjective distress. Washing and checking rituals certainly serve a "neutralizing" function most of the time (Rachman & Hodgson, 1980). But other cognitive neutralizing thoughts or images, such as saying a prayer or magical word or imagining people alive (as described above), may also reduce anxiety or distress. Most of the time this relationship holds, making this a useful way of conceptualizing obsessions and compulsions. But there are exceptions. For example, Rachman and Hodgson (1980) note that compulsions may on occasion increase distress or anxiety, or they may have no relationship whatsoever to affect. Mavissakalian (1979) refers to compulsions that serve to increase distress or anxiety as "obsessionalized compulsions"; that is, they can functionally be considered obsessions. In fact, they are unsuccessful compulsions or failed compulsions. Compulsions that have become functionally autonomous from affect are referred to by Mavissakalian as "rituals." As early as 1949, Maier demonstrated that animals could develop functionally autonomous rituals that had originally served to reduce anxiety or distress.

In any case, establishing the functional relationship of obsessive and compulsive behaviors has useful treatment implications, at least for behavioral treatments. This makes it a more valuable determination than establishing forms or types of obsessive or compulsive complaints, at least for the time being. For example, the exposure procedures described below are usually applied to anxiety-provoking phenomena. Response prevention procedures, on the other hand, are systematically applied to anxiety-reducing phenomena. For functionally autonomous rituals, procedures involving shaping, pacing, and prompting have proven useful (Mavissakalian & Barlow, 1981a).

PREVALENCE AND CONTINUITY WITH NORMAL BEHAVIOR

> Whenever I walk in a London street,
> I'm ever so careful to watch my feet;
>   And I keep in the squares,
>   And the masses of bears,

Who wait at the corners all ready to eat
The sillies who tread on the lines of the street,
  Go back to their lairs,
  And I say to them, "Bears,
  Just look how I'm walking in all of the squares!"
And the little bears growl to each other, "He's
  mine,
As soon as he's silly and steps on a line."
And some of the bigger bears try to pretend
That they came round the corner to look for a
  friend;
And they try to pretend that nobody cares
Whether you walk on the lines or squares.
But only the sillies believe their talk;
It's ever so portant how you walk.
And it's ever so jolly to call out, "Bears,
Just watch me walking in all the squares!"
               —A. A. Milne[1]

Do the fanciful games of children so eloquently depicted by A. A. Milne have anything to do with the grotesque and debilitating life lived by the 19-year-old boy described earlier? Are the clinical manifestations of obsessive–compulsive behavior common or rare?

Prior to the major NIMH ECA study described in Chapter 1, OCD was thought to be a very rare condition indeed, with prevalence estimated at only a small fraction of a percent (American Psychiatric Association, 1980). One of several startling findings from the NIMH ECA study is that the 6-month prevalence of OCD in the general population is greater by a factor of 10 or 20 then was previously assumed. In fact, 6-month prevalence rates of 1.3–2% make OCD up to twice as frequent as panic disorder (without agoraphobia) (see Table 1.2).

It would be surprising and distressing indeed if these figures were found in their entirety to represent such severe cases as those described above. Fortunately, this does not seem to be true. We know with increasing certainty that obsessions and compulsions are on a continuum, as are most clinical features of anxiety disorders. Thus, much as there are nonclinical panickers, there seem to be nonclinical obsessionals and nonclinical compulsives.

Rachman and de Silva (1978) were the first to identify this phenomenon in a systematic and thorough study of obsessional thoughts in otherwise normal subjects. A questionnaire administered to 124 subjects inquired about the presence of intrusive, unacceptable thoughts and impulses.

1. Milne, A. A. Lines and squares. From *When we were very young* (pp. 14–15). New York: E. P. Dutton. Copyright 1924 by E. P. Dutton, renewed 1952 by E. P. Dutton. Reprinted by permission of the publisher, E. P. Dutton, a division of NAL Penguin Inc.

Additional questions addressed frequency of intrusive thoughts, as well as whether these thoughts or impulses could be easily dismissed. Fully 80% of the sample reported obsessional thoughts, with a somewhat greater percentage in women than men.

In a second stage of the study, the obsessional thoughts in a normal sample were compared to those experienced by a clinical sample with OCD. Typical obsessions from the patients included impulses to strangle children or to attack and harm someone; thoughts of disgusting sexual acts; and ruminations over whether someone had been poisoned or not. These obsessional thoughts or impulses are familiar to any clinician working with this population. Once again, normals reported almost identical thoughts and impulses in terms of content. Blind evaluation of the content by independent judges confirmed the similarities. Further detailed analyses revealed that normal and abnormal obsessions were also similar in form and bore the same relationship to mood. That is, both clinical and nonclinical subjects reported that obsessions were more frequent during periods of anxiety or depression. Obsessions were very meaningful to both groups; they were not simply senseless, random thoughts. Finally, both groups reported attempting to resist the thoughts because they provoked discomfort and considered them to be ego-alien. Clinical and non-clinical obsessionals also differed in several important respects. Clinical obsessions lasted longer and were judged to be more intense and frequent, thereby provoking more discomfort. They also were less acceptable and therefore more strongly resisted.

The investigators concluded that there are quantitative differences between groups, but not qualitative ones. That is, obsessions are similar in form and content for both clinical and nonclinical groups, but differ in frequency, intensity, and consequences, in that patients try harder to resist or neutralize the obsessions. Attempts to neutralize the behavior, both overt and covert, reduce discomfort in both clinical and nonclinical subjects. These results were essentially replicated by Salkovskis and Harrison (1984) with a larger sample. In fact, these investigators found a slightly higher percentage of their normal subjects reporting obsessions.

One group of investigators has specifically studied the characteristics of nonclinical compulsive checkers (Frost, Sher, & Geen, 1986; Sher, Frost, & Otto, 1983; Sher, Mann, & Frost, 1984). Administering the Maudsley Obsessional–Compulsive Inventory (see below), these investigators found that a very consistent 10–15% of a large population of college students scored above 5 on the Checking subscale of this inventory. (A score above 5 puts an individual well within the clinical range.) Between 40% and 50% of individuals in these samples were noncheckers, while the remaining 40% fell somewhere in between.

When "normal" checkers were compared to noncheckers, a number of differences emerged. For example, checkers had a poorer memory for prior actions then noncheckers. They also evidenced some difficulty distinguishing between real and imagined events—a process referred to as "reality monitoring." It is possible that such cognitive deficits are mediated by increased anxiety and somewhat poorer concentration. Supporting this interpretation was the finding that nonclinical checkers were generally more depressed and anxious than noncheckers (Frost *et al.*, 1986). Significantly, the investigators suggest that the checking behavior of nonclinical subjects "is a reaction to general distress and may represent attempts to reestablish control over the environment" (Frost *et al.*, 1986, p. 133). Like the phenomenon of nonclinical panic attacks, this information is important for the model of OCD presented below.

OCD AND PERSONALITY TRAITS

Chapter 10 has explored the evidence for the relationship between agoraphobic behavior and the passive, dependent personality traits so often observed in clinical practice. Despite the frequency of this clinical observation, the evidence that these traits are differentially associated with phobic behavior is weak. Furthermore, the retrospective correlational nature of these studies makes it difficult to determine for certain whether passive, dependent personality traits have preceded the onset of agoraphobia in those cases where these traits are noticed.

In a similar vein, many have assumed that OCD is related to obsessive–compulsive personality traits. But the evidence for this is even weaker. For example, comprehensive reviews by Black (1974) and Pollak (1979) reveal that approximately 35% of OCD patients have no evidence whatsoever of obsessive–compulsive personality traits that might predispose them to the disorder. Even clinical observations have not strongly supported this hypothetical connection. One of the acknowledged experts on OCD in his lifetime, Sir Aubrey Lewis (1936), concluded that obsessive or compulsive personality traits (e.g., excessive orderliness, conscienciousness, uncertainty, and cleanliness) are not found among OCD patients at a greater frequency than among other psychiatric patients. He also observed that these traits are common among healthy people and, conversely, are not present in a substantial proportion of the premorbid personalities of patients with severe OCD. Furthermore, he pointed out, in an observation later supported in a quantitative way by Pollak (1979), that these traits can be differentiated from symptoms of OCD, since they lack any immediate sense of subjective compulsion. In other words, there is little affect or emotion associated with these traits. Mavissakalian, Turner, and Michelson (1985) suggests that obsessive–compulsive personality traits may find their pathological expression in the curious but infrequent disorder that Rachman (1974) has termed "primary obsessional slowness."

This is a very interesting suggestion, because those rare individuals with primary obsessional slowness also seem devoid of distress or affect surrounding their pathologically excessive meticulousness.

OCD AND DEPRESSION

The puzzling relationship between anxiety and depression has been considered at some length in previous chapters (see Chapters 7 and 9). Nowhere is this relationship stronger than within OCD. Studies of comorbidity suggest that up to 80% of patients with OCD may be currently depressed. In a substantial proportion of these cases, a major depressive episode is present (Barlow, Di Nardo, et al., 1986; Insel, Zahn, & Murphy, 1985). This is not actually a diagnostic problem in DSM-III-R, since it is not difficult to ascertain whether depression accompanies OCD. In the majority of cases, patients are at least mildly depressed as well as anxious. The legitimate issue raised by some investigators is whether OCD is simply a variant of an affective disorder (e.g., Insel, Gillin, et al., 1982; Insel, Kalin, Guttmacher, Cohen, & Murphy, 1982; Insel et al., 1985). If so, then on a conceptual basis it would be more consistent to group OCD with the affective disorders than with the anxiety disorders. In addition to high rates of comorbidity among the disorders, Insel and colleagues cite several other factors to support this position. For example, not all obsessionals are anxious, those with primary obsessional slowness constituting one example. Of course, as noted above, primary obsessional slowness may not be part of OCD, but rather an extension of compulsive personality traits. Other factors noted by Insel's group are common biological findings between depression and OCD, such as nonsuppression on the dexamethasone suppression test and "depressed" sleep EEG findings (see Turner et al., 1985). Patients with OCD also seem to display a broader range of negative afect in addition to anxiety (e.g., low self-esteem, indecision, guilt, etc.).

But these findings are difficult to interpret, for the same reasons outlined in previous chapters in regard to the relationship between anxiety and depression. For example, Monteiro, Marks, Noshirvani, and Checkley (1986) found normal results on the dexamethasone suppression test in 50 patients with OCD who were not depressed. Until cases of "pure" OCD without depression are compared in sufficient numbers to cases of "pure" depression on biological, genetic, and psychological indices, it will be very hard to determine how much overlap exists. While there are few patients with OCD who are not also depressed, enough exist to make these comparisons possible. A much clearer conceptualization of the nature of anxiety and depression, as suggested in Chapters 2, 7, and 9, will also be required before we can shed some light on this issue. Answers to questions regarding the relationship of anxiety and depression will probably not come from OCD, but rather from disorders such as panic disorder and GAD, where the overlap is not quite so marked.

My own view, as elaborated in Chapters 7 and 9, is that anxiety and depression are variable psychological expressions of a common biological vulnerability activated by stress. Whether one becomes anxious or depressed depends on the extent of one's psychological vulnerability, the severity of the current stressor, and coping mechanisms at one's disposal. This issue is discussed further below in connection with the model of OCD. In the meantime, sufficient evidence exists that OCD is more validly conceptualized as an anxiety disorder. For example, most patients with OCD experience anxiety both subjectively and physiologically when confronted with "obsessional" cues, and avoid these cues whenever possible (Grayson et al., 1982; Rachman & Hodgson, 1980).

DELUSIONS AND OVERVALUED IDEAS

Obsessions, by definition, are most usually experienced as intrusive, senseless, and ego-dystonic ideas that are to be resisted or suppressed. And yet it is not uncommon for obsessions and compulsions to be so entirely bizarre that clinicians are sure a schizophrenic process is present. Clinical reports have accumulated over the years that would convince even the most jaded observer that there is no limit to the variety of unusual ideas and situations implicated in OCD. Therefore, bizarreness alone has few, if any, implications. Factors that are capable of differentiating schizophrenia from OCD are considered below. Another phenomenological issue recently appearing in the literature is whether some obsessional processes are truly delusional. If so, there may well be different treatment implications for these than for obsessional processes that are not delusional. Insel and Akiskal (1986) review a number of cases in which obsessional ideas seemed to become delusions; specifically, the patients seemed to lose altogether the sense that their obsessions were irrational, and ceased all resistance. If an idea is no longer considered irrational and is not resisted, then it is not experienced as intrusive. Insel and Akiskal do not suggest that such delusions signify a schizophrenic diagnosis, but point out that they may best be considered as signs of reactive psychosis or perhaps an obsessive–compulsive psychosis.

There is no question that these patients exist. Every clinician has seen them. On the fierce battleground of the rational and irrational that is anxiety, sometimes one is in ascendance, sometimes the other. Earlier chapters have suggested that this is a process ongoing in all anxiety disorders to some degree, and that it represents the basic struggle between cognitive (rational) and emotional (irrational) systems. As Rachman and de Silva

(1978) demonstrated, neither clinical nor nonclinical obsessionals consider their obsessions to be totally senseless. Even simple phobics who are not particularly anxious will admit that their phobia is irrational, only to turn around and verbalize in the same language system that there may be something real about the fear this time. When the irrational wins out, is this a delusion?

McKenna (1984) traces the development in psychopathology of the notion of the "overvalued idea." First described by Wernicke (1900), the term refers to a solitary abnormal belief that is neither delusional or obsessional in nature, but that is preoccupying to the extent of dominating the sufferer's life. Jaspers (1959/1963) has provided a formal distinction between overvalued ideas and delusions. He believes that delusions are qualitatively different and characterized by a conviction that is alien, far beyond normal, and incorrigible in a way quite unlike that of regular beliefs. An overvalued idea, on the other hand, is an isolated notion strongly toned by an affect with which the person identifies. Its quality is considered similar to that of passionate, political, religious, or ethical convictions. In other words, the belief may be more emotional than rational. DSM-III-R makes the practical observation that individuals with overvalued ideation eventually can be persuaded that their ideas may be unfounded, whereas this is not possible with true delusions. Of course, this remains to be seen.

Steketee and Foa (1985) have adopted the notion that patients with OCD occasionally present with overvalued ideas and that these have treatment implications. Specifically, if an obsession that is irrational, intrusive, and to be resisted becomes an overvalued idea, the individual is not amenable to behavioral approaches. The overvalued idea must first be attacked until the patient is once again able to develop a rational perspective on what is basically an irrational process.

Currently, these differing opinions on the phenomenology of some obsessions have not progressed beyond descriptive analysis. But it will be important to determine whether the minority of OCD patients who seem to have tentatively accepted the rationality of their obsessions are simply suffering from strongly held, emotionally based overvalued ideas or from true delusions.

PRESENTING CHARACTERISTICS

The preceding discussion has considered forms and types of obsessions and compulsions, as well as controversies regarding continuity or discontinuity with normal processes; the relationship to personality characteristics; and the relationship to depression and delusions. At this point, the presenting characteristics of well-defined OCDs can be reviewed briefly

(Rachman & Hodgson, 1980; Rasmussen & Tsuang, 1986; Steketee, Grayson, & Foa, 1987).

As with other anxiety disorders, age of onset is generally placed from late adolescence to the early 20s, but onset can be as late as age 50 (Rachman & Hodgson, 1980; Rasmussen & Tsuang, 1986). Unlike some other disorders, OCD can erupt full-blown in childhood and has appeared as early as age 5 or 6 (e.g., Jenike et al., 1986). More interesting from the present point of view is the sex ratio, which, as with other anxiety disorders, is weighted in favor of females (see Table 1.2) (Rasmussen & Tsuang, 1986; Steketee et al., 1987). For those individuals with washing rituals as their primary problem, the differences seems even greater, with females predominating by as much as 80%.

A MODEL OF THE ETIOLOGY OF OCD

Any model of OCD must consider one firmly established, if paradoxical, fact. Despite the bizarreness and the debilitating nature of OCD in its severe forms, intrusive thoughts and even neutralizing compulsions are very common in the normal population. Furthermore, we now have evidence regarding the conditions that prompt intrusive thoughts in normals. It will not be surprising, in the context of the conception of anxiety presented in this book, that the primary antecedent of intrusive thoughts is stress. Horowitz (e.g., 1975) conducted a number of early studies in which normal subjects watched stressful films. These subjects reported many more intrusive thoughts and images than controls who did not see the film. More recently, Parkinson and Rachman (1981a, 1981c) studied this process in mothers whose children were about to be admitted for surgery. These mothers were compared with a control group of mothers with children the same age. Once again, mothers who were stressed reported many more intrusive thoughts than mothers in the control group. Furthermore, these thoughts and images were not necessarily related to the upcoming surgery.

The link between depression and OCD has also been clearly established. Not surprisingly, intrusive thoughts are much more common in the context of depressed and anxious mood (Farid, 1986; Rachman & Hodgson, 1980). This could be related in part to evidence presented in Chapter 2 regarding increased accessibility of negatively valenced cognitions while experiencing negatively affective mood states (Teasdale, 1983). Thus, stress and associated negative affect seem to be antecedents to intrusive thoughts in both normals and patients with OCD. There is also some evidence that compulsions are also associated with stress. For example, the animal behavior literature suggests that performance of certain stereotyped and ritualistic behavior may be an innate response to stress (Mineka, 1985a).

What we are left with, then, as in other anxiety disorders, is the need to account for differences in severity of intrusive thoughts (and related rituals) between patients appearing at our clinics and normals who may be undergoing stress. Once again, I hypothesize that both biological and psychological vulnerabilities are important. Specifically, individuals who go on to develop OCD are succeptible to reacting with a strong, biologically based emotional response to stress. Intrusive thoughts then emerge in the context of this stress. This tendency is present in all individuals with anxiety disorders, as well as in persons with other emotional disorders and in normals. Based on psychological vulnerabilities, the negative life events and consequences of stress are quickly elaborated into anxiety and a sense that events are out of control. Earlier chapters (e.g., Chapters 10, 12, and 14) have reviewed evidence on a differential disposition to focus anxious apprehension on certain situations or events. For example, social phobics are exposed as children to parents who display significantly more concerns with social evaluation than parents of agoraphobics do (Bruch *et al.*, 1987). Patients with OCD may undergo an etiological process similar to that of these social phobics or of simple phobics, who experience repeated, exaggerated misinformation in the context of biological and psychological anxiety proneness. The example given in Chapter 12 of a snake phobic who had never encountered a snake in her life but had been repeatedly warned of the dangers of snakes by her mother may be relevant. This women ended up wearing high boots any time she had to stray off paved surfaces.

It is my colleagues' and my unsubstantiated but rather firm clinical impression that patients with OCD have learned that some thoughts are dangerous and unacceptable. They learn this through the same process of misinformation that convinced the snake phobic that snakes were dangerous. Patients with OCD, then, equate thoughts with the specific actions or activity represented by the thoughts. This is a characteristic of many individuals with fundamental religious beliefs. For example, the woman in the case illustration at the beginning of the chapter believed that having a thought concerning abortion was the moral equivalent of having an abortion. She then spent years attempting to prevent similar thoughts concerning actions that might harm others. The college student whose particularly tragic case is also presented above finally admitted strong homosexual impulses that were unacceptable to him and to his father, who was a minister. Many Catholic and Jewish patients present with similar attitudes.

Of course, the source of this sensitivity need not be religious experience. Conversely, the vast majority of individuals holding fundamental religious beliefs to not develop OCD. Thus, as in any emotional disorder, the combination of biological and psychological vulnerabilities (including a disposition to focus anxiety in at least some cases) must line up correctly in order for the etiological process to ensue. This speculation has some support from Parkinson and Rachman (1981b), who noted that intrusive thoughts rated high on unacceptability by their normal subjects were experienced as more distressing and "worse in all respects" than alternative intrusive thoughts. Salkovskis (1985) also concludes that intrusions will only produce distress when they have some idiosyncratic meaning or salience to the individual experiencing them. Like social phobics, patients with OCD may have learned that certain intrusive thoughts, which almost everyone eventually experiences under stress, are unacceptable.

Becoming anxious over internal cognitive stimuli, as opposed to somatic events (as in panic disorder) or external objects or situations (as in simple or social phobia), has other implications. Individuals with simple or social phobia have some control through avoidance over events signaling panic and anxiety. Many patients with panic disorder seem to develop a series of safety signals that provide them with some sense of control over their next panic attack. But patients with OCD are most often continually buffeted with aversive, out-of-control, unacceptable cognitive processes. This has two consequences. First, the patients strongly resist these cognitive processes and develop other cognitions or behavior in an attempt to neutralize them (compulsions). Second, the increasing anxiety sets the stage for false alarms, which inevitably become associated with the focus of anxiety—specific thoughts. That patients with OCD experience panic has been firmly established (see Chapter 3).

Since thoughts are inherently uncontrollable, this process represents the most extreme example of negative events proceeding in an uncontrollable, unpredictable fashion. It is no surprise that utter helplessness engendered by this process results in a high frequency of reactive depression. Sir Aubrey Lewis (1966) has observed that "obsessional patients are in most cases depressed; their illness is a depressing one" (p. 1200). In this way, depression associated with antecedent stressful life events can follow the development of a full OCD syndrome, but depression also precedes OCD, as it does other anxiety disorders. Rachman and Hodgson (1980) and Gittelson (1966a, 1966b) reports that varying percentages of large groups of patients showed depression either preceding or following OCD. Most of Rachman's patients developed OCD before becoming depressed; presumably the depression in these cases was reactive. On the other hand, more of Gittelson's patients exhibited prior depression, which, along with preceding stress, may have prompted intrusive thoughts in the first place. In any case, it seems likely that a vicious downward spiral of depression and OCD is likely to occur, with one feeding and maintaining the other. To complicate matters further, a small percentage of patients with OCD develop severe depression, which is then associated with a decrease in their obsessive–compulsive behavior. As Rachman and Hodgson (1980) point out, this may well be due to the generally inhibiting qualities of a very severe, retarded depression.

Finally, questions on the etiology of specific forms of compulsion remain. In the face of overwhelmingly aversive, uncontrollable events, the origins of cognitive compulsions such as prayer or requests for reassurance seem clear. When the content of the obsession concerns contamination, cleaning rituals are easily explained. But the origins of checking rituals are less clear when they are not tied closely to the source of danger (e.g., checking the gas stove). Steketee *et al.* (1985) closely examined differences in the parental backgrounds of washers and checkers, and came to the interesting conclusion that the mothers of checkers were significantly more meticulous and demanding than the mothers of washers. Since both groups, by definition, had OCD, these data suggest a specifically learned disposition not only for the obsession, but also for the compulsive behavior chosen to neutralize or control it. That is, checkers may have a learned tendency to react to stress or negative events by becoming meticulous. Interestingly, Hoover and Insel (1984) have also reported that the parents of OCD patients emphasized cleanliness and perfection. Obviously, these data are only preliminary and subject to retrospective distortion.

In summary, the present model of OCD combines features of previous models of phobic disorders and GAD. Specifically, intense stress-related negative affect and neurobiological reactions are triggered by negative life events. The resulting intrusive thoughts, which are commonly experienced in the normal population (and other anxiety disorders) during periods of stress, are judged unacceptable; attempts are made to avoid or suppress these thoughts. Recurrence of these thoughts causes intensification of anxiety, with accompanying negative affect and a sense that these thoughts are proceeding in an unpredictable and uncontrollable fashion. The vicious negative feedback loop of anxiety then develops, with attention narrowed onto the content of the unacceptable thoughts themselves. The specific content of the obsessions is determined by learned dispositions that certain thoughts or images are unacceptable. These thoughts become much like discrete phobic stimuli in their capacity to elicit panic attacks or learned alarms. The severity of this process in the extreme, relative to other anxiety disorders, makes it more likely that hopelessness and accompanying depression will be associated with the process. Either depression will occur in reaction to the severity of OCD or (as is more likely) a prior depression will be maintained because of this severity. A diagram of this process is presented in Figure 16.1.

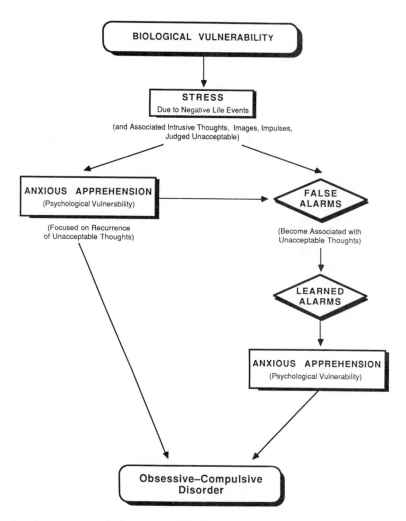

FIGURE 16.1. A model of the etiology of obsessive–compulsive disorder.

DIAGNOSIS AND ASSESSMENT

DIAGNOSIS

The distinctiveness of obsessive–compulsive phenomena would seem to make initial diagnosis of OCD a straightforward task. But, as with most disorders, several points of confusion arise. The confusion over the years in distinguishing OCD from a schizophrenic process has been alluded to above; more recently, clinicians are experiencing difficulty discriminating OCD from DSM-III-R definitions of GAD.

Recognizing the frequent misidentification of OCD as schizophrenia, Rachman and Hodgson (1980) constructed a table listing distinctive features of OCD as compared to closely related conditions. Specifically, obsessions and compulsions are distinguished from intrusive or repetitive cognitions that may be associated with schizophrenia, organic disorders, or "morbid preoccupations" as well as obsessional personality traits. These distinctive features are listed in Table 16.1. I have already discussed the issue of overvalued ideation sometimes present in OCD. Nevertheless, the prototypical obsession, no matter how bizarre, is clearly recognized to be one's own thought; by contrast, the schizophrenic delusion is attributed to external forces. Other prototypical distinctive features are listed in Table 16.1. In practice, if a clinician is not overwhelmed by the bizarreness of some obsessional content, this is not a difficult distinction to make.

The new definition of GAD, as described in Chapter 15, highlights apprehensive expectation. Specifically, arousal-driven "worry," accompanied by the requisite somatic symptoms of anxiety, becomes the defining feature of GAD. To make this disorder more easily discriminated, apprehension must be focused on at least two different life circumstances. One will note in Table 16.1 a heading Rachman and Hodgson refer to as "morbid preoccupations" (Rachman, 1973). These cognitions involve intrusive, repetitive ideas that differ from obsessions in that they are egosyntonic, rational but exaggerated, realistic and current in content, and seldom resisted. This is a good description of worry within GAD. Although the definitions are very clear and seemingly distinguishable, on occasion it proves difficult in practice to differentiate these cognitive phenomena. At present, my colleagues and I are developing a data base on the extent to which this difficulty occurs.

In this regard, recent data from Steketee *et al.* (1987), reviewed above, are interesting. Their comparison of a large group of OCD patients to groups of patients with other anxiety disorders on both demographic and clinical characteristics revealed clear distinctions on measures of obsessive–compulsive phenomena, with one exception: Patients with OCD did not score significantly higher than patients with GAD on the Checking subscale of the Maudsley Obsessional–Compulsive Inventory. In fact, patients with GAD scored higher than other anxiety disorder groups on both the total inventory and on the Checking subscale. In addition, GAD patients did not differ from OCD patients on the Obsessive–Compulsive scale of the Hopkins Symptoms Checklist. This seems to support the phenomenological similarity of these two disorders.

Nevertheless, in principle, the distinction is clear. The troublesome thoughts and ideas of patients with GAD may be intrusive and repetitive, but they are current in content (if exaggerated beyond all reason), and therefore are not resisted. There is no quality of a phobic reaction to these thoughts. In OCD, on the other hand, the thoughts are often bizarre and

TABLE 16.1. Distinctive Features of Obsessional–Compulsive Disorders and Their Relation to Schizophrenia, Organic Impairments, Morbid Preoccupations, and "Obsessional Personality"

Obsessions
    are unwanted
    have aggressive/sexual themes
    provoke internal resistance
    cause distress
    are recognized to be of internal origin
    are recognized to be senseless (insight)
    are ego-alien
    are associated with lack of confidence in memory or reality of memory
    are associated with depression
Compulsions are distinguished by repetitive, stereotyped behavior that
    is preceded or accompanied by a sense of compulsion that is recognized to be of internal origin
    provokes internal resistance
    is recognized to be senseless (insight)
    may cause embarrassment or distress
    is difficult to control over the long term
Schizophrenic conditions differ in that the intrusive ideas, images, or impulses are
    attributed to external forces
    not necessarily ego-alien
    not regarded as senseless (lack of insight)
    unlikely to provoke internal resistance
Organic impairments may involve repetitive ideas or acts that
    lack intellectual content
    lack intentionality
    have a mechanical and/or primitive quality
Morbid preoccupations (see Rachman, 1973) involve intrusive, repetitive ideas that are
    ego-syntonic
    rational (but exaggerated)
    realistic, and current in content
    seldom resisted
"Obsessional personality" traits
    show greater stability than obsessional disorders
    are ego-syntonic
    seldom cause distress
    are seldom accompanied by a sense of compulsion
    seldom provoke resistance

Note. From Rachman, S. J., & Hodgson, R. S. (1980). *Obsessions and compulsions* (p. 96). Englewood Cliffs, NJ: Prentice-Hall. Copyright 1980 by Prentice-Hall, Inc. Reprinted by permission.

alien to the individual. The thoughts themselves may produce a phobic or panic reaction and are most often avoided or resisted at all cost. In the prototypical example, then, OCD is another phobic reaction; the phobic object is cognition. This differs from panic disorder, where the phobic reaction is to a somatic event. Even when the ideas become overvalued and are not necessarily resisted ("I really believe I will contaminate my children with cancer if I touch them because medical science cannot rule it out"), the content seems distinguishable from the usual life circumstances that are the focus of GAD. The distinction is important because there are significantly different treatment implications within both pharmacological and cognitive–behavioral approaches.

Scattered cases continue to appear in the literature connecting OCD with neurological conditions (e.g., McKeon, McGuffin, & Robinson, 1984). Rachman and Hodgson (1980) and Kettl and Marks (1986) review the evidence on associations of OCD with organic conditions (including trauma, epilepsy, and other EEG abnormalities), as well as encephalitis and Parkinson disease. They conclude that neurological factors, while puzzling, are present in only a minority of cases, and that successful behavioral treatment (at least) is independent of such factors.

ASSESSMENT

A number of assessment tools have been developed over the years for OCD. These fall into the now familiar self-report, behavioral, and physiological categories, although physiological measures are seldom used in clinical practice with this disorder.

Questionnaires and Rating Scales

The most commonly used symptom checklist is the Maudsley Obsessional–Compulsive Inventory. This is a 30-item questionnaire developed by Hodgson and Rachman (1977). It provides a total score, as well as scores on four subscales referring to each of the following types of obsessional complaints: (1) Checking, (2) Washing, (3) Doubting, and (4) Slowness. The questionnaire possesses good test–retest reliability (Sanavio & Vidotto, 1985). More importantly, the inventory is short and easily administered. Unfortunately, the questionnaire does not address obsessional ruminations specifically.

Other questionnaires include the Leyton Obsessional Inventory, originated by Cooper (1970). This questionnaire is comprised of 69 items, 47 of which relate to obsessional symptoms and 27 to obsessive–compulsive personality traits. It does not cover horrific obsessional thoughts or compulsive hand washing. The emphasis on personality traits rather than symptoms of OCD is highlighted in the shorter version of the Leyton Obsessional Inventory, where only 10 or 20 items refer to OCD symptoms (Allen & Tune, 1975).

An additional instrument in wide use, particularly in clinical research centers, is a rating scale termed the Compulsive Activity Checklist. Originally described by Philpott (1975), this therapist rating scale has been modified several times. Freund, Steketee, and Foa (1987) developed satisfactory psychometric data on a 38-item version of the Compulsive Activity Checklist. They note that it has several advantages over the Maudsley Obsessional–Compulsive Inventory. It uses a 4-point scale rather than a dichotomous scale, and, with its exclusive focus on specific behaviors, it can be readily quantified. For example, the Compulsive Activity Checklist does not directly assess obsessional systems per se, but rather their interference with functioning and daily activities. Freund *et al.* (1987) recommend that this rating scale be used in conjunction with the Maudsley instrument and target symptom ratings.

Self-Monitoring Measures

Self-ratings in the form of SUDs are an important feature of the assessment of all anxiety disorders. However, for disorders such as panic disorder with agoraphobia, GAD, and OCD, where ongoing daily records of specific anxiety-related symptoms themselves constitute the targets for therapy, self-monitoring measures assume increased importance. In Chapters 10 and 15, these measures have been described in some detail. For OCD, these assessment strategies are no less important. Obviously, psychometric properties of these self-monitoring scales are less certain than those developed for questionnaires. Corroboration of the information by family members or other individuals close to the patient is desirable.

Important targets for self-monitoring are the frequency and duration of obsessive thoughts, as well as the distress and disturbance produced by the thought. One example of this type of form is presented in Figure 16.2. If possible, we attempt to get a frequency count. Sometimes a hand counter is used; however, this is often not feasible, since obsessional thoughts may be too numerous. If this is the case, we rely on daily estimates of duration of preoccupation with obsessional thoughts, as well as distress ratings.

We also attempt to establish self-monitoring of rituals or urges to engage in rituals. Once again, we decide on an individual basis whether to record total frequency of rituals or estimates of duration of rituals daily. A third alternative for patients with very frequent rituals is to time-sample whether rituals are occurring during specific periods of the day. For example, the individual may record every hour on the hour whether rituals have occurred during the past hour.

During behavioral treatment, monitoring of urges to perform rituals becomes an important measure, since the rituals themselves are often prevented in some way through monitoring. Treatment should continue

FIGURE 16.2. Daily record form for frequency, duration, and distress level of obsessive thoughts. From the Phobia and Anxiety Disorders Clinic, State University of New York at Albany.

DAILY RECORD

Name: _____

Date: _____

    Please provide the following information each day before bedtime:

1. Record the frequency of (primary) obsessional thoughts. _____
   (Record total number from counter before bedtime.)
2. Rate the degree of distress experienced today from (primary) obsessional thoughts.
   (Check appropriate number on scale below.)

0	--	1	--	2	--	3	--	4	--	5	--	6	--	7	--	8
No distress		Mildly disturbing/ distressing				Moderately disturbing/ distressing						Markedly disturbing/ distressing				Severely disturbing/ distressing

3. Estimate approximate time spent today preoccupied with (primary) obsessional thoughts (check appropriate number).

0 minutes	___	1–2 hours	___
Under 5 minutes	___	2–3 hours	___
5–15 minutes	___	3–4 hours	___
15–30 minutes	___	4–6 hours	___
30–60 minutes	___	Over 6 hours	___

COMMENTS:

---

until urges have diminished considerably or have been eliminated. We usually instruct the patients:

> In order for us to have some idea of how you feel during treatment, we will give you a card to fill out on a daily basis in which you are to indicate by a tally any urges you may have to engage in rituals. An urge is when you have the thought or desire to ritualize. You should carry this card with you at all times and keep an accurate record on any desires to engage in rituals.

Behavioral Measures

Short of direct behavioral observation or mechanical counting of rituals where possible (e.g., Mills, Agras, Barlow, & Mills, 1973; Turner, Hersen, Bellack, & Wells, 1979), most direct behavioral assessment of obsessive–compulsive behavior is conducted in the type of contrived situations used to assess phobic behavior. For example, patients with fears of contamination are asked to approach and touch rubbish, old newspapers, chemicals, or other items that provoke obsessional contamination fears and washing rituals. In this situation the behavior is assessed much as any simple phobia is assessed (i.e., on the basis of approach, as well as SUDs measures during the approach). Since this sort of activity often plays a prominent role in behavioral treatment, measures are easily collected. Similar contrived measures can be constructed for patients with checking rituals by arranging for the systematic presentation of internal or external stimuli that prompt checking. Obviously, this is much more difficult to do for pure obsessionals without overt behavioral rituals, but it is possible in some instances to present obsessional content in imagination. Subjective reports of distress, as well as of resistance and "urges" to neutralize the obsessional thoughts through counterthoughts or other cognitive processes, can then be assessed.

Physiological Measures

A number of investigators have demonstrated significant physiological responses during presentation of obsessional material and reduction of those responses during successful treatment (e.g., Boulougouris & Bassiakos, 1973; Boulougouris, Rabavilas, & Stefanis, 1977; Grayson, Nutter, & Mavissakalian, 1980). Rachman and his colleagues have made extensive use of psychophysiological measures for their studies on the psychopathology of OCD (Rachman & Hodgson, 1980). Nevertheless, pending further exploration of the additive value of this type of measure in predicting clinical outcome, there does not seem to be any reason to recommend routine clinical administration at the present time.

TREATMENT

BEHAVIORAL TREATMENT

For most anxiety disorders, particularly phobic disorders, procedures involving exposure form the heart of psychosocial treatments. Although no one is quite sure why exposure is effective (see Chapter 8), the major procedural issue in treatment is arranging for sufficient exposure to occur. Even for social phobia and GAD, where the best evidence exists for the utility of adjunctive procedures, exposure is important. The role of exposure in the treatment of OCD is more complex. In fact, good evidence exists that exposure in isolation is relatively ineffective in the treatment of OCD. At the same time, exposure forms an important component of a more comprehensive treatment discovered over 20 years ago.

Early studies using treatments successful with phobic behavior, such as systematic desensitization, yielded generally disappointing results with OCD (e.g., Beech & Vaughn, 1978; Cooper, Gelder, & Marks, 1965). A commonality among these studies was that they often ignored compulsive behavior associated with obsessions. A variety of early case studies took the opposite tack by attempting to block compulsive behavior (Marks, Crowe, Drewe, Young, & Dewhurst, 1969; Walton, 1960). While a case would occasionally respond well, this strategy was also disappointing, and relapses occurred quickly. In 1966, Victor Meyer reported results from a more comprehensive program in which rituals were prevented while the patient was exposed to circumstances that normally provoked distress and compulsive behavior. Clinical results from these early trials were very encouraging (e.g., Meyer, 1966; Meyer & Levy, 1973). This approach, which came to be known by the descriptive if unimaginative name of "exposure and response prevention," generated a great deal of interest. Subsequent controlled studies demonstrated quite clearly the effectiveness of this treatment for OCD.

Over the years, this treatment was further developed and investigated, first at the Maudsley Hospital by Rachman, Marks, and their colleagues (e.g., Marks, Bird, & Lindley, 1978; Rachman & Hodgson, 1980), and later by Edna Foa and her colleagues in Philadelphia (e.g., Foa, Steketee, & Ozarow, 1985). Foa et al. (1983) summarized data collected from 50 patients treated with this approach. Ratings of clinical improvement were made by an independent assessor. Of the 50 patients, 29 (58%) were rated as "much improved." These ratings referred specifically to improvement of 70% or more on an independent assessor's rating scale. Another 19, or 38%, were classified as "improved," which referred to improvement between 30% and 70% on the rating scale. Two patients, or 4%, improved 30% or less and were classified as failures. At follow-ups ranging from 3 months to 3 years, 59% of the patients remained much improved and 17% remained improved, but 24% were classified as failures. Foa et al. (1983) comment that partial improvers were most likely to relapse and move into the failed category.

Summarizing results from 18 controlled studies over the past two decades, Foa et al. (1985) conclude that 51% of the patients treated by exposure and response prevention were either symptom-free or much improved at the end of treatment, and 39% were moderately improved. The remaining 10% failed to benefit from therapy. Some relapse was also evident at follow-up in this survey, particularly in the moderately improved group.

While exposure and response prevention provided the first hope for alleviating suffering from this debilitating disorder, it departs considerably from the usual office-based outpatient treatment of anxiety disorders. In severe cases, the treatment is rigorous, demanding, and trying for both therapist and patient. By actively blocking or preventing rituals that have come to be equated with everything that is safe and comfortable, the therapist is forcing the patient to confront his or her worst fears. But, unlike *in vivo* exposure treatments for agoraphobia, the sessions are not over in an hour or two. Since patients are unable to use rituals to escape the overwhelming feelings of doom and disaster or thoughts of impending catastrophe associated with contamination, exposure is in effect 24 hours a day for weeks at a time. In the most severe cases, 24-hour-a-day supervision is necessary to assist patients in refraining from the overwhelming temptations to ritualize their worst fears away. This process has been described in some detail elsewhere (Steketee & Foa, 1985), and is illustrated in the treatment of the two cases presented at the beginning of the chapter. Because of the clinical research nature of the treatment of these two cases, ongoing measures of a number of aspects of OCD were collected and provide an illustration of the process of treatment.

Case Study: Washing Rituals

The 32-year-old woman described above was admitted to an inpatient unit and placed in a special room across from the nurses' station. Other than one supervised daily shower, her only opportunity to wash was at a sink in her room. This sink was wired to provide a 24-hour daily record of her frequency of approaching the sink to perform the ritual. The patient was also asked to record the number of urges to wash that she did not act on. That the patient found the hospital room full of contaminants is evident in the first phase of Figure 16.3 (Mills *et al.*, 1973). During a baseline phase of 7 days, she was instructed to wash her hands as she wished. Her rate of hand washing steadily increased until it reached approximately 60 times per day. During the next phase, we tested the effects of instructions alone. Specifically, the patient was told that therapy had begun and she was to try to decrease her hand washing as much as possible. In fact, she was able to return to the level observed at the beginning of baseline. Response prevention was facilitated by her lack of access to other bathrooms where she might wash; in addition, simply removing the handles from the faucets in Phase 3 effectively prevented all washing, making her daily shower the only washing opportunity. Three days of response prevention reduced hand washing frequency by about half, to an average of 12.6 times per day. Urges to wash increased but returned to a relatively low level once the phase ended. A longer period of response prevention in Phase 5, lasting 7 days, had little further effect on frequency of hand washing, as reflected in the frequency when the phase ended. Nevertheless, at this point with continued effort and support, she was able to reduce hand washing further to approximately 4 times per day with instructions alone (Phase 7).

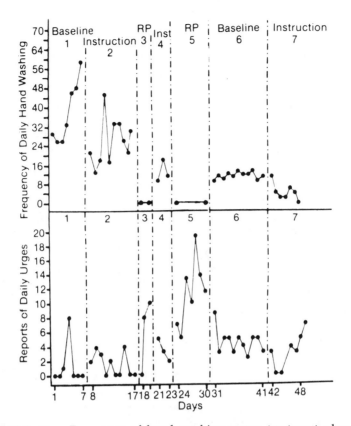

FIGURE 16.3. Top: Frequency of hand washing across treatment phases; each point represents one day. Bottom: Total number of urges upon which the patient did not act. RP, response prevention; Inst, instruction. From Mills, H. L., Agras, W. S., Barlow, D. H., & Mills, J. R. (1973). Compulsive rituals treated by response prevention. *Archives of General Psychiatry, 28,* 524–529. Copyright 1973 by the American Medical Association. Reprinted by permission.

Treatment did not stop upon release from the hospital. Although the patient learned in the hospital that she could function without extensive cleaning rituals, the locus of her problem as well as of all the contaminants she had confronted over the years was her home. Several months of continued response prevention with the assistance of her husband, friends, and pastor in her home environment facilitated a return to essentially normal functioning.

Despite the severity of this case, this patient was fortunate in becoming one of the 50% or so who improve substantially after exposure and response prevention. Results from the next case were not so encouraging, but illustrative nonetheless of the process of treatment.

Case Study: Severe Multiple Washing and Checking Rituals

The 19-year-old boy described earlier was also admitted to an inpatient unit where he received 24-hour-a-day supervision. One day's experience in the cafeteria convinced the staff that the other patients would not tolerate his grotesque eating patterns. Thus, he spent all of his time on the unit, where rituals associated with eating, cleaning, and checking were monitored.

Three sets of rituals were treated sequentially (Caldwell, McCrady, & Barlow, 1979). Since cleaning and washing rituals were the most severe, these were treated first. Prior to hospitalization, the patient had been spending up to 16 hours a day showering and engaging in other washing behavior. Several weeks before admission, he had begun avoiding the bathroom altogether and defecating and urinating in a corner of his closet, as noted at the beginning of the chapter. During baseline procedures in the hospital, the patient spent approximately 3 hours washing his hands. What followed was an elaborate 2-month-long exposure and response prevention program in which contingency management procedures were introduced. Throughout treatment the patient was exposed once each hour for 16 hours a day to a series of contaminating substances (e.g., ashes, dirt, urine, and butter) that ordinarily produced hand washing. The patient was instructed to rub each substance over his arms and hands and let it remain for at least 30 seconds before excess was wiped (but not washed) off. As indicated in Figure 16.4, a variety of additional steps were instituted during these 2 months. Since he spent long periods of time ritualizing while eating and showering, he was told (initially) that increased eating time would be contingent on decreased bathroom time. Specifically, he was given 30 minutes to shower, wash his hair, brush his teeth, and so on. He was further instructed (during Week 3) that response prevention would end when he could meet the 30-minute time limit, as well as refrain from defecating in his clothes for 7 days in a row (a practice he had taken up in the hospital to avoid bathroom rituals associated with bowel movements, since a convenient closet was no longer available). The third criterion involved sleeping in pajamas or other designated sleeping clothes, since he had begun wearing the same clothes 24 hours a day to avoid other rituals. During this phase the patient experienced the contingency of reduced eating time (as well as the loss of piano-playing privileges) only once. As treatment progressed, the staff was systematically faded out, and he took increasing responsibility for his own behavior.

After completion of exposure and response prevention for washing rituals, eating rituals were treated. Initially the patient ate only certain foods, as described earlier. While eating, he would engage in a variety of counting rituals with his utensils, attempt to expire all air from his lungs (which resulted in a variety of coughing and hissing sounds), and toss his head as if he were tossing his long hair out of his face before taking a bite. A baseline phase was followed by a short phase in which his hair

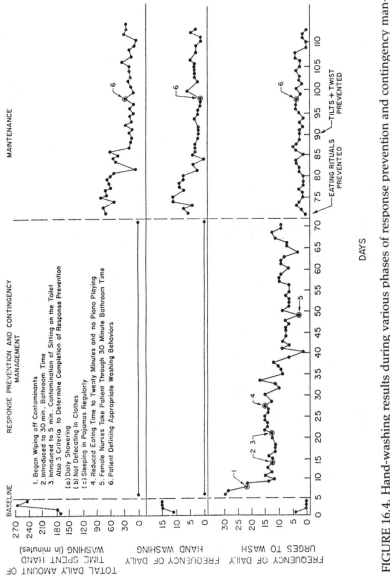

FIGURE 16.4. Hand-washing results during various phases of response prevention and contingency management treatment for a 19-year-old boy with severe OCD. From Caldwell, A. T., McCrady, B. S., & Barlow, D. H. (1979). *The effects of response prevention and contingency management in the treatment of obsessive–compulsive behavior.* Unpublished manuscript.

627

was tied in a ponytail. Monitoring of coughs, hisses, and head tosses demonstrated that his hair was not a factor in these rituals. During response prevention, the therapist stood directly behind him and gently held his head in place whenever head tossing was about to occur. He was also instructed not to cough or hiss at this time. Contingency management was also introduced, as indicated in Figure 16.4. As treatment progressed, staff members were faded out and the patient was gradually able to eat in the cafeteria, sitting with increasingly larger groups of people. Checking rituals associated with wastebasket, curtains, and so forth, which were least severe in terms of interfering with functioning, were successfully treated during the last week of the program.

After a hospitalization that lasted approximately 4 months, the patient returned home. Although he returned to school and maintained his gains on rituals treated in the hospital for some time, he re-established a variety of additional checking rituals that had been reported by his family but had not been present in the hospital. In addition, after several months in college, some ritualistic washing returned, although not at a frequency or intensity evident before hospitalization. He also began staring at his food during meals for long periods, although other eating rituals did not return.

Since this patient was one of the more severe cases we have encountered, Herculean efforts were required to attack the plethora of his obsessions and compulsions. Despite 4 months of 24-hour-a-day supervision and active treatment, the patient was only 50–60% improved, relapsing to 20–30% improved after 6 months. In view of this patient's enormous suffering, any therapeutic gain was worth the effort: however, for those clinicians and students unaware of the extent of incapacitation often present with this disorder, it may now be clear why thousands have been referred to psychosurgery (Ananth, 1985).

A variety of studies have attested to the importance of both exposure and response prevention procedures (e.g., Steketee, Foa, & Grayson, 1982). Treatment for the individual OCD patient (who, it may be hoped, is not as severely disordered as the case described above) involves ascertaining the best strategies to insure exposure and response prevention. As the functional classification of obsessions and compulsions presented earlier indicates, this can be more or less difficult, depending on the nature of the compulsion.

"Pure" Obsessions

While the process of response prevention is fairly clear for overt cleaning or checking rituals, it is more difficult when the compulsions are also cognitive, as is the case with "pure" obsessionals. In these cases, one must identify not only the obsessional thought, but also the cognitive ritual. In many cases they may be very similar. For example, we saw a case in which the obsession centered around thoughts or images of sei-

zures. Seeing the letter "E" (for epilepsy) or "S" (for seizure) would provoke the obsession. The compulsion associated with these obsessions involved imagining two numbers (6 and 7) juxtaposed in a certain way.

Traditional response prevention is more difficult to implement and
monitor in these cases. Early reports suggest that treatment of pure obsessionals, who comprise approximately 25% of OCD patients, has not
been as encouraging (e.g., Rachman & Hodgson, 1980), but more recent
reports are more optimistic (see below). A variety of procedures have been
used in an attempt to prevent cognitive compulsions. Among the more
popular, in addition to simple instructions not to think the thought, has
been thought stopping (e.g., Gullick & Blanchard, 1973; Stern, 1970). Other
methods used have been a mild aversive procedure, such as snapping a
rubber band against one's wrist whenever the compulsive thought occurs, or striving for a "blank mind."

At this time, the evidence is not sufficient to guide clinicians on the
appropriateness of one or more of these procedures. My colleagues and I
have often found instructions combined with practice in the office to be
helpful. That is, patients are instructed to experience their obsession without
shutting it off in any way through the use of a cognitive compulsion.
When they understand the rationale for this, they are usually reasonably
cooperative and successful. Systematic research on the effectiveness of
these procedures is required.

Failures and Extensions to Clinical Practice

Finally, Foa and her colleagues (Foa, 1979; Foa et al., 1985) have investigated factors associated with failure of these treatments. The difficulties
in treating patients with overvalued ideation have been mentioned above.
An additional finding, more widely noted, is the negative effect of initial
depression on treatment outcome. Foa and her colleagues have established some evidence suggesting that depressed patients habituate more
slowly and less effectively to obsessional cues (Foa et al., 1983); however,
this finding requires considerably more explication and replication before
we can ascertain factors associated with failures. For example, there is
little or no evidence that depression predicts failure in the treatment of
other anxiety disorders, where, presumably, similar mechanisms of action
are operative (see Chapter 8).

Cases such as that of the 19-year-old boy described above and many
of those summarized by Foa et al. (1985) are often failures from front-line
clinicians, who then refer these difficult patients to specialized treatment
centers. Thus, it is possible that implementing approximations of these
procedures in a standard everyday outpatient practice with, presumably,
less difficult patients may produce superior results. Now Kirk (1983) has
reported on such an effort with 36 consecutive patients with OCD. She
implemented a general, unsystematic behavioral treatment that relied more

TABLE 16.2. Outcome of Obsessive–Compulsive Problems after Treatment (Global Ratings)

			Outcome (global rating)		
	Worse	No change	Slightly improved	Moderately improved	Goal achieved
Compulsions					
Cleaning	—	1	1	1	1
Checking	—	—	1	2	5
Cleaning and checking	—	—	2	2	2
Slowness	—	—	1	—	1
All compulsions	—	1	5	5	9
Obsessions	—	—	1	1	12
Total ($n = 36$)[a]	—	1 (8%)	6 (17%)	6 (17%)	21 (58%)

Note. Adapted from Kirk, J. W. (1983). Behavioral treatment of obsessional–compulsive patients in routine clinical practice. *Behaviour Research and Therapy, 21,* 57–62. Copyright 1983 by Pergamon Journals, Ltd. Adapted by permission.

on task assignments at home and less on supervised *in vivo* practice. Including 4 dropouts, 75% evidenced moderate improvement or better. The results were even more favorable for pure obsessionals, where good progress was observed in 81% of the patients. The results are presented in Table 16.2. For 81% of the patients, no further treatment was required during a follow-up period extending to 5 years. Seven patients received additional treatment, including 5 who were referred back for more behavioral treatment. These results are encouraging to clinicians who wish to incorporate these procedures into outpatient practice. Nevertheless, overall results from behavioral procedures, according to the studies reviewed above, are somewhat less favorable than for phobic disorders or panic disorder. As the principles established in Chapter 8 indicate, the most important task will be discovering how best to instill a sense of control and to shift attention away from negative affect associated with runaway cognitive processes.

DRUG TREATMENT

Clomipramine

Pharmacological approaches to OCD, while greatly understudied, have been characterized by a unique development: The attention of both investigators and clinicians has focused on one specific drug, clomipramine. Ironically, this drug, which has generated such excitement in psychopharmacological circles, is not available for prescription in the United States. Nevertheless, word of its potential effectiveness has spread rapidly among clinicians confronted with OCD. For that reason, the airlines and highways to Canada carry an increasing number of travelers with one item on their business agenda: to bring back clomipramine in sufficient quantities to last until their next visit. While this may be a boom to the foreign exchange of Canada, the more important question revolves around whether the travel is worth it. Is clomipramine effective with OCD? If so, is clomipramine uniquely effective? Unfortunately, it is probably too early to answer either question definitively, although the majority of the evidence suggests that clomipramine can have a beneficial effect on OCD in some patients.

Early case reports and uncontrolled studies suggested the efficacy of clomipramine in treating obsessional symptoms (see Ananth, 1985). However, most of these early studies reported on patients with primary diagnoses of depression who also presented with some obsessional features. Since clomipramine is a tricyclic antidepressant, it is not surprising that depressed patients improved. Nevertheless, more carefully done open trials with well-selected, clearly defined OCD patients also suggest a beneficial effect of clomipramine (e.g., Ananth, Solyom, Bryntwick, & Krishnappa, 1979), as do preliminary placebo-controlled trials (e.g., Mavissakalian, Turner, Michelson, & Jacob, 1985). However, other case studies and controlled trials, although less numerous, report therapeutic effects from a variety of drugs. For example, Rao (1964) and Burrell, Culpan, and Newton (1974) both reported beneficial effects from benzodiazepines in uncontrolled trials with obsessive–compulsive patients. Similarly, several reports suggest that several different tricyclic antidepressants are useful (e.g., Freed, Kerr, & Roth, 1972; Mavissakalian & Michelson, 1983; Mavissakalian, Turner, Michelson, & Jacob, 1985). MAO inhibitors are also on the list of drugs reported to be successful with OCD (e.g., Jenike, 1981). Naturally, uncontrolled studies such as these do little more than suggest the potential usefulness of conducting more stringent evaluations of these drugs. Unfortunately, there are very few of these indeed that would satisfy any investigator in the area of psychopharmacology.

Comparisons of Clomipramine and Other Drugs

The contention that clomipramine is uniquely effective for obsessive compulsive disorder is questionable at this time. The conclusion rests on results from several very preliminary studies with small numbers of subjects and weak statistical outcomes. For example, Thorén Åsberg, Cronholm, Jörnestedt, and Träskman (1980) studied 24 patients who met the Research Diagnostic Criteria definition of OCD. Of these, 8 received clomipramine, 8 received nortriptyline, and 8 were administered a placebo in a 5-week randomized double-blind trial. There were no statistical differences on any measures between nortriptyline or clomipramine after

5 weeks; however, clomipramine was significantly different from placebo at this point on one measure, blind assessor ratings (but not on measures of functioning or on patient self-ratings). The fact that clomipramine, but not nortriptyline, was significantly different from placebo on this measure at 5 weeks is intriguing, but certainly not sufficient to support any conclusions about superior effect for clomipramine. Far more interesting would be an examination of differential drug effects at 3 or 6 months with a much larger sample.

Similarly, Ananth, Pecknold, Van Den Steen, and Engelsmann (1981) compared clomipramine with amitriptyline in 20 OCD patients. Once again, there were no significant differences between the two groups of 10 patients after the very short period of 4 weeks. However, as in the Thorén et al. (1980) study, only clomipramine produced statistically significant improvements from pre to posttreatment on ratings of obsessive symptoms. Once again, a greatly increased number of subjects studied over a longer period of time would be desirable.

Finally, Insel et al. (1983) compared clomipramine with clorgyline (an MAO inhibitor) in 10 patients completing a full crossover experimental design. Drugs were administered for only 6 weeks because of the plan of the crossover design, but clomipramine was superior to clorgyline on a number of measures at that time. Although the number of patients was small, this study provides good evidence for the effects of clomipramine, at least in comparison to clorgyline. Unfortunately, no placebo comparisons were possible with this design.

On the other hand, two studies have found no differences between the closely related tricyclics, clomipramine and imiprimine (Mavissakalian, Turner, Michelson, & Jacob, 1985; Volavka, Neziroglu, & Yaryura-Tobias, 1985). While larger studies are needed, these last two studies lend further support to the notion that a number of drugs may have some beneficial effects on OCD.

The most sophisticated examination of the effects of clomipramine on OCD occurred in a complex study where drug effects were examined in the context of behavioral therapy. A total of 40 well-defined OCD patients were divided into four groups receiving a variety of sequential treatments. All groups received behavioral treatment at some point during the course of the experiment. Two of the groups also received clomipramine, while the remaining two groups were administered placebo. This experiment yielded two reports emphasizing somewhat different aspects of the data analysis (Marks, Stern, Mawson, Cobb, & McDonald, 1980; Rachman et al., 1979).

The experimental design precluded a clean comparison of the separate and combined effect of these two approaches. Nevertheless, the data suggested that clomipramine had its primary effect on mood, particularly depressed mood, with weaker effects on obsessions and rituals. Behavioral treatments, on the other hand, manifested strong effects on compulsive behavior, but weaker effects on overall mood. No statistical interaction was observed. The treatments did not seem to potentiate each other. Consistent with observations made by Marks in the context of agoraphobia, Marks et al. (1980) attribute most of the drug effects to improvements in depression, since nondepressed patients with OCD improved very little in this study. On the other hand, neither Insel et al. (1983) nor Mavissakalian, Turner, Michelson, and Jacob (1985) found that level of depression was related to positive effect of clomipramine.

Mawson, Marks, and Ramm (1982) followed up these patients for 2 years. At follow-up, the sample as a whole was significantly improved on all measures. However, any effects of clomipramine when compared to placebo had disappeared entirely. In fact, these effects had begun to diminish shortly after treatment. This is not surprising, since the drug was discontinued shortly after treatment.

Interestingly, one of the strongest predictors of drug effects at posttreatment was level of anxiety or depression before treatment. The greater the initial anxiety or depression, the greater the superiority of clomipramine over placebo in the context of behavioral treatment. It is possible that if Insel et al. (1983) had looked at anxiety as well as depression, similar results would obtain. This would lend some support to the present contention that the primary effect of the drug is anxiolytic. However, along with all other drug–placebo differences, this effect had also disappeared by the time of the 2-year follow-up. That is, initial level of anxiety or depression no longer predicted degree of improvement.

One additional study with a more satisfactory number of subjects has now appeared, testing the effects of imipramine compared to placebo over the short term of 6 weeks (Foa, Steketee, Kozak, & Dugger, 1987). Nevertheless, OCD patients were somewhat more improved with imipramine than were 18 OCD patients who received placebo, but effects were due mostly to alleviation of depression in the more depressed patients.

Drug Treatment: Conclusions

The initial interest in clomipramine, as so often happens, was generated by some early case studies enthusiastically reporting positive results (e.g., Capstick, 1971). Other uncontrolled clinical series seemed to confirm the potential effectiveness of this drug. However, additional case studies and clinical series utilizing other drugs have also reported encouraging results on occasion. Studies comparing clomipramine with alternative tricyclics are far too preliminary to permit us to draw any conclusions at this point in time. Nor can we assume that clomipramine is effective specifically because of its serotonergic effects, as was hypothesized on the basis of recent data from Insel and Mueller (1984). As with most drug treatments for emotional disorders, mechanisms of action are not yet clear. As Ananth (1985) points out, most studies indicate that clomipramine does not eradicate obsessive–compulsive disorder or even the urge to perform the ritual. Rather, "the emotional force attached to the urge goes away" (p. 191). Relapse should also be expected when the drug is withdrawn (Mavissakalian, Turner, & Michelson, 1985).

Any potentially effective treatment with OCD deserves intensive investigation. In view of the evidence that clomipramine and probably other tricyclics may contribute to the treatment of these difficult patients, these drugs deserve additional investigation. Pharmacological treatment of OCD, relative to other anxiety disorders, is understudied. However, knowing what we know, we can reasonably assume that the evidence will demonstrate a pattern of pharmacological effects similar to that found in other anxiety disorders. Specifically, a variety of tricyclics will probably prove effective, although patients may be differentially responsive to one tricyclic or another. Similarly, MAO inhibitors and certain benzodiazepines may also prove effective when tested. If experience with panic disorder is any guide, the effects in OCD will not be limited to those who are depressed, although this will be more difficult to test because so many of these patients are depressed. More likely, the tricyclics and even the MAO inhibitors may prove to have an anxiolytic effect in OCDs, much as I have speculated they do in panic disorder. Recently, some strong evidence on the anxiolytic effect of clomipramine in OCD has appeared (Insel & Mueller, 1984).

To take this analysis one step further, one may also assume when proper studies are done that tricyclics will confer an advantage on exposure and response prevention treatments, as seems to be the case in panic disorder. The large study reported above (Marks et al., 1980; Rachman et al., 1979) suggests this, but the complexities of the experimental design do not permit a clear interpretation. Benzodiazepines, on the other hand, may interfere with the effects of more behavioral treatments. But all of these hypotheses are speculative in the absence of data.

In any case, until effective treatments or combinations of treatments are fully elucidated, we will continue to encounter tragic cases such as that of the 19-year-old boy described above. His extreme and constant suffering, along with severe behavioral debilitation, made many staff members wonder why he was not suicidal. But the patient himself, consumed as he was with anticipating the next dangerous unacceptable thought or impulse, had little time for philosophizing on the value of living; his only concern was coping, somehow, with the next minute of his life.

REFERENCES

Abel, G. G., Blanchard, E. B., & Barlow, D. H. (1981). The effects of stimulus modality, instructional set, and stimulus content on the objective measurement of sexual arousal in several paraphilias. *Behaviour Research and Therapy, 19,* 25–34.

Abrahamson, D. J., Barlow, D. H., & Abrahamson, L. S. (in press). Differential effects of performance demand and distraction on sexually functional and dysfunctional males. *Journal of Abnormal Psychology.*

Abrahamson, D. J., Barlow, D. H., Beck, J. G., Sakheim, D. K. & Kelly, J. P. (1985). The effects of attentional focus and partner responsiveness on sexual responding: Replication and extension. *Archives of Sexual Behavior, 14,* 361–371.

Abrahamson, D. J., Barlow, D. H., Sakheim, D. K., Beck, J. G., & Athanasiou, R. (1985). Effects of distraction on sexual responding in functional and dysfunctional men. *Behavior Therapy, 16,* 503–515.

Abramson, L. Y., Seligman, M. E. P., & Teasdale, J. D. (1978). Learned helplessness in humans: Critique and reformulation. *Journal of Abnormal Psychology, 87,* 49–74.

Achenbach, T. M., & Edelbrock, C. S. (1983). *Manual for the Child Behavior Checklist and Revised Child Behavior Profile.* Burlington: Department of Psychiatry, University of Vermont.

Ackerman, S., & Sachar, E. (1974). The lactate theory of anxiety: A review and reevaluation. *Psychosomatic Medicine, 36,* 69–81.

Aden, G. C., & Thein, S. G. (1980). Alprazolam compared to diazepam and placebo in the treatment of anxiety. *Journal of Clinical Psychiatry, 41,* 245–248.

Adler, C. M., Craske, M. G., & Barlow, D. H. (1987a, November). *The use of modified relaxation in the experimental induction of anxiety and panic.* Paper presented at the annual meeting of the Association for Advancement of Behavior Therapy, Boston.

Adler, C. M., Craske, M. G., & Barlow, D. H. (1987b). Relaxation-induced panic (RIP): When resting isn't peaceful. *Integrative Psychiatry, 5,* 94–112.

Agras, W. S., Chapin, H. N., & Oliveau, D. C. (1972). The natural history of phobia. *Archives of General Psychiatry, 26,* 315–317.

Agras, W. S., & Jacob, R. G. (1981). Phobia: Nature and measurement. In M. Mavissakalian & D. H. Barlow (Eds.), *Phobia: Psychological and pharmacological treatment.* New York: Guilford Press.

Agras, W. S., Leitenberg, H., & Barlow, D. H. (1968). Social reinforcement in the modification of agoraphobia. *Archives of General Psychiatry, 19,* 423–427.

Agras, W. S., Sylvester, D., & Oliveau, D. (1969). The epidemiology of common fears and phobia. *Comprehensive Psychiatry, 10,* 151–156.

Agulnik, P. L. (1970). The spouse of the phobic patient. *British Journal of Psychiatry, 117,* 59–67.

Akhtar, S., Wig, N. N., Verma, V. K., Pershad, D., & Verma, S. K. (1975). A phenomenological analysis of symptoms in obsessive–compulsive neurosis. *British Journal of Psychiatry, 127,* 342–348.

Alexander, P., & Alexander, D. (1986). Alprazolam treatment for panic disorders. *Journal of Clinical Psychiatry, 47,* 301–304.

Alho, H., Costa, E., Ferrero, P., Fujimoto, M., Cosenza-Murphy, D., & Guidotti, A. (1985). Diazepam-binding inhibitor: A neuropeptide located in selected neuronal populations of rat brain. *Science, 229,* 179–182.

Allen, J. J., & Tune, G. S. (1975). The Lynfield Obsessional/Compulsive Questionnaire. *Scottish Medical Journal, 201,* 21–26.

Alloy, L. B., Abramson, L. Y., & Viscusi, D. (1981). Induced mood and the illusion of control. *Journal of Personality and Social Psychology, 41,* 1129–1140.

American Psychiatric Association. (1980). *Diagnostic and statistical manual of mental disorders* (3rd ed.). Washington, DC: Author.

American Psychiatric Association. (1987). *Diagnostic and statistical manual of mental disorders* (3rd ed., rev.). Washington, DC: Author.

Amies, B. L., Gelder, M. G., & Shaw, P. M. (1983). Social phobia: A comparative clinical study. *British Journal of Psychiatry, 142,* 174–179.

Ananth, J. (1985). Pharmaco-therapy of obsessive–compulsive disorder. In M. Mavissakalian, S. M. Turner, & L. Michelson (Eds.), *Obsessive–compulsive disorder: Psychological and pharmacological treatment.* New York: Plenum Press.

Ananth, J., Pecknold, J., Van Den Steen, N., & Engelsmann, F. C. (1981). Double-blind comparative study of clomipramine and amitriptyline in obsessive neurosis. *Progress in Neuro-Psychopharmacology, 5,* 257–262.

Ananth, J., Solyom, L., Bryntwick, S., & Krishnappa, U. (1979). Clomipramine therapy for obsessive–compulsive neurosis. *American Journal of Psychiatry, 135,* 700–701.

Anderson, D. J., Noyes, R., Jr., & Crowe, R. R. (1984). A comparison of panic disorder and generalized anxiety disorder. *American Journal of Psychiatry, 141,* 572–575.

Andrasik, F., & Holroyd, K. A. (1980). A test of specific and nonspecific effects in the biofeedback treatment of tension headache. *Journal of Consulting and Clinical Psychology, 48,* 575–586.

Andrews, G. (1982). A treatment outline for agoraphobia: The Quality Assurance Project. *Australian and New Zealand Journal of Psychiatry, 16,* 25, 33.

Andrews, J. D. W. (1966). Psychotherapy of phobias. *Psychological Bulletin, 66,* 455–480.

Anisman, H. (1984). Vulnerability to depression: Contribution of stress. In R. Post & J. Ballenger (Eds.), *Neurobiology of mood disorders.* Baltimore: Williams & Wilkins.

Arena, J. G., Blanchard, E. B., Andrasik, F., Cotch, B. A., & Myers, P. E. (1983). Reliability of psychophysiological assessment. *Behaviour Research and Therapy, 21,* 447–460.

Arkowitz, H., Lichtenstein, K., McGovern, K., & Hines, P. (1975). Behavioral assessment of social competence in males. *Behavior Therapy, 6,* 3–13.

Arnow, B. A., Taylor, C. B., Agras, W. S., & Telch, M. J. (1985). Enhancing agoraphobia treatment outcome by changing couple communication patterns. *Behavior Therapy, 16,* 452–467.

Aronson, T. A., & Craig, T. J. (1986). Cocaine precipitation of panic disorder. *American Journal of Psychiatry, 143,* 643–645.

Arrindell, W. A. (1980). Dimensional structure and psychopathology correlates of the Fear Survey Schedule (FSS-III) in a phobic population: A factorial definition of agoraphobia. *Behaviour Research and Therapy, 18,* 229–242.

Arrindell, W. A., & Emmelkamp, M. G. (1986). Marital adjustment, intimacy and needs in female agoraphobics and their partners: A controlled study. *British Journal of Psychiatry, 149,* 592–602.

Ascher, L. M. (1980). Paradoxical intention. In A. Goldstein & E. B. Foa (Eds.), *Handbook of behavioral interventions: A clinical guide.* New York: Wiley.

Ascher, L. M. (1981). Employing paradoxical intention in the treatment of agoraphobia. *Behaviour Research and Therapy, 19,* 533–542.

Ax, A. F. (1953). The physiological differentiation between fear and anger in humans. *Psychosomatic Medicine, 15,* 433–442.

Ballenger, J. C. (1986). Biological aspects of panic disorder. *American Journal of Psychiatry,* ✳✳ *143,* 516–518.

Ballenger, J. C., Burrows, G., DuPont, R., Lesser, I., Noyes, R., Pecknold, J., Riskin, A., & Swinson, R. (in press). Alprazolam in panic disorder and agoraphobia; results from a multi center trial: I. Efficacy in short term treatment. *Archives of General Psychiatry.*

Ballenger, J. C., Peterson, G. A., Laraia, M., Hucek, A., Lake, C. R., Jimerson, D., Cox, D. J., Trockman, C., Shipe, J. R., & Wilkinson, C. (1984). A study of plasma catecholamines in agoraphobia and the relationship of serum, tricyclic levels to treatment response. In J. C. Ballenger (Ed.), *Biology of agoraphobia.* Washington, DC: American Psychiatric Press.

Bandura, A. (1969). *Principles of behavior modification.* New York: Holt, Rinehart & Winston.

Bandura, A. (1977a). Self-efficacy: Toward a unifying theory of behavioral change. *Psychological Review, 84,* 191–215.

Bandura, A. (1977b). *Social learning theory.* Englewood Cliffs, NJ: Prentice-Hall.

Bandura, A. (1983). Self-efficacy determinants of anticipated fears and calamities. *Journal of Personality and Social Psychology, 45,* 464–469.

Bandura, A. (1984). Recycling misconceptions of perceived self-efficacy. *Cognitive Therapy and Research, 8,* 231–255.

Bandura, A. (1986). *Social foundations of thought and action: A social cognitive theory.* Englewood Cliffs, NJ: Prentice-Hall.

Bandura, A., Adams, N. E., Hardy, A. B., & Howells, G. N. (1980). Tests of the generality of self-efficacy theory. *Cognitive Therapy and Research, 4,* 39–66.

Bandura, A., & Rosenthal, T. (1966). Vicarious classical conditioning as a function of arousal level. *Journal of Personality and Social Psychology, 3,* 54–62.

Bandura, A., Taylor, C. B., Williams, S. L., Mefford, I. N., & Barchas, J. D. (1985). Catecholamine secretion as a function of perceived coping self-efficacy. *Journal of Consulting and Clinical Psychology, 53,* 406–414.

Barfield, R., & Sachs, B. (1968). Sexual behavior: Stimulation by painful electric shock to skin in male rats. *Science, 161,* 392–395.

Barlow, D. H. (1978). Aversive procedures. In W. S. Agras (Ed.), *Behavior modification: Principles and clinical applications* (2nd ed.). Boston: Little, Brown.

Barlow, D. H. (Ed.). (1981). *Behavioral assessment of adult disorders.* New York: Guilford Press.

Barlow, D. H. (1983, October). *The classification of anxiety disorders.* Paper presented at the conference DSM-III: An Interim Appraisal, sponsored by the American Psychiatric Association, Washington, DC.

Barlow, D. H. (1985). The dimensions of anxiety disorders. In A. H. Tuma & J. D. Maser (Eds.), *Anxiety and the anxiety disorders.* Hillsdale, NJ: Erlbaum.

Barlow, D. H. (1986a). New perspectives on panic. Review of R. H. Hallam, *Anxiety: Psychological perspectives on panic and agoraphobia. Behaviour Research and Therapy, 24,* 693–696.

Barlow, D. H. (1986b). Behavioral conception and treatment of panic. *Psychopharmacology Bulletin, 22,* 802–806.

Barlow, D. H. (1986c). Causes of sexual dysfunction: The role of anxiety and cognitive interference. *Journal of Consulting and Clinical Psychology, 54,* 140–148.

Barlow, D. H. (1986d). In defense of panic disorder with extensive avoidance and the behavioral treatment of panic: A comment on Kleiner. *the Behavior Therapist, 9,* 99–100.

Barlow, D. H. (1987). The classification of anxiety disorders. In G. L. Tischler (Ed.), *Diagnosis and classification in psychiatry: A critical appraisal of DSM-III*. Cambridge, England: Cambridge University Press.

Barlow, D. H., & Beck, J. G. (1984). The psychosocial treatment of anxiety disorders: Current status, future directions. In J. B. W. Williams & R. L. Spitzer (Eds.), *Psychotherapy research: Where are we and where should we go?* New York: Guilford Press.

Barlow, D. H., Blanchard, E. B., Vermilyea, J. A., Vermilyea, B. B., & Di Nardo, P. A. (1986). Generalized anxiety and generalized anxiety disorder: Description and reconceptualization. *American Journal of Psychiatry, 143*, 40–44.

Barlow, D. H., & Cerny, J. A. (1988). *Psychological treatment of panic*. New York: Guilford Press.

Barlow, D. H., Cohen, A. S., Waddell, M., Vermilyea, J. A., Klosko, J. S., Blanchard, E. B., & Di Nardo, P. A. (1984). Panic and generalized anxiety disorders: Nature and treatment. *Behavior Therapy, 15*, 431–449.

Barlow, D. H., & Craske, M. G. (1988). The phenomenology of panic. In S. Rachman & J. D. Maser (Eds.), *Panic: Psychological perspectives*. Hillsdale, NJ: Erlbaum.

Barlow, D. H., Di Nardo, P. A., Vermilyea, B. B., Vermilyea, J. A., & Blanchard, E. B. (1986). Co-morbidity and depression among the anxiety disorders: Issues in diagnosis and classification. *Journal of Nervous and Mental Disease, 174*, 63–72.

Barlow, D. H., Hayes, S. C., & Nelson, R. O. (1984). *The scientist–practitioner: Research and accountability in clinical and educational settings*. New York: Pergamon Press.

Barlow, D. H., & Hersen, M. (1984). *Single case experimental designs: Strategies for studying behavior change* (2nd ed.). New York: Pergamon Press.

Barlow, D. H., Leitenberg, H., Agras, W. S., & Wincze, J. P. (1969). The transfer gap in systematic desensitization: An analog study. *Behavior Research and Therapy, 7*, 191–196.

Barlow, D. H., & Maser, J. D. (1984). Psychopathology in anxiety disorders. *Journal of Behavioral Assessment, 6*, 301–329.

Barlow, D. H., & Mavissakalian, M. (1981). Directions in the assessment and treatment of phobia: The next decade. In M. Mavissakalian & D. H. Barlow (Eds.), *Phobia: Psychological and pharmacological treatment*. New York: Guilford Press.

Barlow, D. H., Mavissakalian, M. & Hay, L. R. (1981). Couples treatment of agoraphobia: Changes in marital satisfaction. *Behaviour Research and Therapy, 19*, 245–255.

Barlow, D. H., Mavissakalian, M., & Schofield, L. D. (1980). Patterns of desynchrony in agoraphobia: A preliminary report. *Behaviour Research and Therapy, 18*, 441–448.

Barlow, D. H., O'Brien, G. T., & Last, C. G. (1984). Couples treatment of agoraphobia. *Behavior Therapy, 15*, 41–58.

Barlow, D. H., O'Brien, G. T., Last, C. G., & Holden, A. E. (1983). Couples treatment of agoraphobia: Initial outcome. In K. D. Craig & R. J. McMahon (Eds.), *Advances in clinical behavior therapy*. New York: Brunner/Mazel.

Barlow, D. H., Sakheim, D. K., & Beck, J. G. (1983). Anxiety increases sexual arousal. *Journal of Abnormal Psychology, 92*, 49–54.

Barlow, D. H., & Seidner, A. L. (1983). Treatment of adolescent agoraphobics: Effects on parent–adolescent relations. *Behaviour Research and Therapy, 21*, 519–527.

Barlow, D. H., Vermilyea, J. A., Blanchard, E. B., Vermilyea, B. B., Di Nardo, P. A., & Cerny, J. A. (1985). The phenomenon of panic. *Journal of Abnormal Psychology, 94*, 320–328.

Barlow, D. H., & Waddell, M. T. (1985). Agoraphobia. In D. H. Barlow (Ed.), *Clinical handbook of psychological disorders: A step-by-step treatment manual*. New York: Guilford Press.

Barlow, D. H., & Wolfe, B. E. (1981). Behavioral approaches to anxiety disorders: A report on the NIMH–SUNY Albany research conference. *Journal of Consulting and Clinical Psychology, 49*, 448–454.

Barrett, J. (1981). Psychiatric diagnoses (research diagnostic criteria) in symptomatic volunteers. *Archives of General Psychiatry, 38*, 153–154.

REFERENCES

Bartol, C. R. (1975). Extraversion and neuroticism and nicotine, caffeine, and drug intake. *Psychological Reports, 36*, 1007–1010.

Baum, A., Gatchel, R. J., & Schaeffer, M. A. (1983). Emotional, behavioral, and physiological effects of chronic stress at Three Mile Island. *Journal of Consulting and Clinical Psychology, 51*, 565–572.

Beaumont, G., (1977). A large open multicentre trial of clomipramine (Anafranil) in the management of phobic disorders. *Journal of International Medical Research, 5*, 116–123.

Beck, A. T. (1985). Theoretical perspectives on clinical anxiety. In A. H. Tuma & J. D. Maser (Eds.), *Anxiety and the anxiety disorders*. Hillsdale, NJ: Erlbaum.

Beck, A. T. (1988). Cognitive approaches to panic disorder: Theory and therapy. In S. Rachman & J. D. Maser (Eds.), *Panic: Psychological perspectives*. Hillsdale, NJ: Erlbaum.

Beck, A. T., & Emery, G. (1985). *Anxiety disorders and phobias: A cognitive perspective*. New York: Basic Books.

Beck, A. T., Laude, R., & Bohnert, M. (1974). Ideational components of anxiety neurosis. *Archives of General Psychiatry, 31*, 319–325.

Beck, A. T., Rush, A. J., Shaw, B. F., & Emery, G. (1979). *Cognitive therapy of depression*. New York: Guilford Press.

Beck, A. T., Ward, C. H., Mendelson, M., Mock, J., & Erbaugh, J. (1961). An inventory for measuring depression. Archives of General Psychiatry, 41, 561–571.

Beck, J. G., & Barlow, D. H. (1984). Current conceptualizations of sexual dysfunction: A review and an alternative perspective. *Clinical Psychology Review, 4*, 363–378.

Beck, J. G., & Barlow, D. H. (1986a). The effects of anxiety and attentional focus on sexual responding: I. Physiological patterns in erectile dysfunction. *Behaviour Research and Therapy, 24*, 9–17.

Beck, J. G., & Barlow, D. H. (1986b). The effects of anxiety and attentional focus on sexual responding: II. Cognitive and affective patterns in erectile dysfunction. *Behaviour Research and Therapy, 24*, 9–26.

Beck, J. G., Barlow, D. H., & Sakheim, D. K. (1983). The effects of attentional focus and partner arousal on sexual responding in functional and dysfunctional men. *Behaviour Research and Therapy, 21*, 1–8.

Beck, J. G., Barlow, D. H., Sakheim, D. K., & Abrahamson, D. J. (1984). *A cognitive processing account of anxiety and sexual arousal: The role of selective attention, thought content, and affective states*. Paper presented at the annual convention of the American Psychological Association, Toronto.

Beck, J. G., Barlow, D. H., Sakheim, D. K., & Abrahamson, D. J. (1987). Shock threat and sexual arousal: The role of selective attention, thought content, and affective states. *Psychophysiology, 24*, 165–172.

Beech, H. R., & Vaughn, M. (1978). *Behavioral treatment of obsessional states*. New York: Wiley.

Beidel, D. C., & Turner, S. M. (1986). A critique of the theoretical basis of cognitive–behavioral theories and therapy. *Clinical Psychology Review, 6*, 1977–197.

Beidel, D. C., Turner, S. M., & Dancu, C. V. (1985). Physiological, cognitive and behavioral aspects of social anxiety. *Behaviour Research and Therapy, 23*, 109–118.

Beiman, I., Israel, E., & Johnson, S. A. (1978). During training and post-training effects of live and taped extended progressive relaxation, self-relaxation, and electromyogram biofeedback. *Journal of Consulting and Clinical Psychology, 46*, 314–321.

Beitman, B. D., Basha, I., Flaker, G., DeRosear, L., Mukerji, V., & Lamberti, J. (1987). Nonfearful panic disorder: Panic attacks without fear. *Behaviour Research and Therapy, 25*, 487–492.

Beitman, B. D., DeRosear, L., Basha, I., Flaker, G., & Corcoran, C. (1987). Panic disorder in cardiology patients with atypical or non-anginal chest pain: A pilot study. *Journal of Anxiety Disorders, 1*, 277–282.

Beitman, B. D., Lamberti, J. W., Mukerji, V., DeRosear, L., Basha, I., & Schmid, L. (1987). Panic disorder in chest pain patients with angiographically normal coronary arteries: A pilot study. *Psychosomatics, 28*, 480–484.

Benedikt, V. (1870). Über platzschwindel. *Allgemeine Wiener Medizinische Zeitung, 15,* 488.

Bennett-Levy, J., & Marteau, T. (1984). Fear of animals: What is prepared? *British Journal of Psychology, 75,* 37–42.

Benshoof, B. G. (1987). *A comparison of anxiety and depressive symptomatology in the anxiety and affective disorders.* Unpublished doctoral dissertation, State University of New York at Albany.

Berg, I. (1976). School phobia in the children of agoraphobic women. *British Journal of Psychiatry, 128,* 86–89.

Bernadt, M. W., Silverstone, T., & Singleton, W. (1980). Behavioral and subjective effects of beta-adrenergic blockage in phobic subjects. *British Journal of Psychiatry, 137,* 452–457.

Bernstein, D. A., & Borkovec, T. D. (1973). *Progressive relaxation training.* Champaign, IL: Research Press.

Berscheid, E., & Walster, E. (1974). A little bit about love. In T. Huston (Ed.) *Foundations of interpersonal attraction.* New York: Academic Press.

Bibb, J., & Chambless, D. L. (1986). Alcohol use and abuse among diagnosed agoraphobics. *Behaviour Research and Therapy, 24,* 49–58.

Bignami, G. (1965). Selection for high and low rates of conditioning in the rat. *Animal Behavior, 13,* 221–227.

Bilsbury, C., & Morley, S. (1979). Obsessional slowness: A meticulous replication. *Behaviour Research and Therapy, 17,* 405–408.

Biran, M., Augusto, F., & Wilson, G. T. (1981). In vivo exposure vs. cognitive restructuring in the treatment of scriptophobia. *Behaviour Research and Therapy, 19,* 525–532.

Biran, M., & Wilson, G. T. (1981). Treatment of phobic disorders using cognitive and exposure methods: A self-efficacy analysis. *Journal of Consulting and Clinical Psychology, 49,* 886–899.

Bjertnaes, A., Block, J. M., Hafstead, L., Holte, M., Ottemo, I., Larsen, T., Pinder, R., & Steffensen, K. (1982). A multicentere placebo-controlled trial comparing the efficacy of nianserin and chloradiazepoxide in general practice patients with primary anxiety. *Acta Psychiatrica Scandanavica,66,* 199–207.

Black, A. (1974). The natural history of obsessional patterns. In H. R. Beech (Ed.). *Obsessional states.* London: Methuen.

Blanchard, E. B., & Epstein, L. H. (1977). *A biofeedback primer.* Reading, MA: Addison-Wesley.

Blanchard, E. B., Gerardi, R. J., Kolb, L. C., & Barlow, D. H. (1986). The utility of the Anxiety Disorders Interview Schedule (ADIS) in the diagnosis of post-traumatic stress disorder (PTSD) in Vietnam veterans. *Behaviour Research and Therapy, 24,* 577–581.

Blanchard, E. B., Kolb, L. C., Gerardi, R., Ryan, P., & Pallmeyer, T. P. (1986). Cardiac response to relevant stimuli as an adjunctive tool for diagnosing post-traumatic stress disorder in Vietnam veterans. *Behavior Therapy, 17,* 592–606.

Blanchard, E. B., Kolb, L. C., Pallmeyer, T. D., & Gerardi, R. J. (1982). The development of a psychophysiological assessment procedure for PTSD in Vietnam veterans. *Psychiatric Quarterly, 54,* 220–228.

Bland, K., & Hallam, R. S. (1981). Relationship between response to exposure and marital satisfaction in agoraphobics. *Behaviour Research and Therapy, 19,* 335–338.

Bleich, A., Siegel, B., Garb, R., & Lerer, B. (1986). Post-traumatic stress disorder following combat exposure: Clinical features and psychopharmacological treatment. *British Journal of Psychiatry, 149,* 365–369.

Bliss, E. L., Migeon, C. J., Branch, C. H. H., & Samuels, L. T. (1956). Reaction of the andrenocortex to emotional stress. *Psychosomatic Medicine, 18,* 56–76.

Bloom, L. J., Houston, B. K., & Burish, T. G. (1976). An evaluation of finger pulse volume as a psychophysiological measure of anxiety. *Psychophysiology, 13,* 40–42.

Blumberg, S. H., & Izard, C. E. (1986). Discriminating patterns of emotions in 10- and 11-year-old children's anxiety and depression. *Journal of Personality and Social Psychology, 51,* 1–6.

REFERENCES

Bond, A., & Lader, M. L. (1979). Benzodiazepines and aggression. In M. Sandler (Ed.), *Psychopharmacology of aggression.* New York: Raven Press.

Bonn, J. A., Harrison, J., & Rees, W. (1971). Lactate-induced anxiety: Therapeutic application. *British Journal of Psychiatry, 119,* 468–470.

Bonn, J. A., Readhead, C. P. A., & Timmons, B. H. (1984). Enhanced adaptive behavioral response in agoraphobic patients pretreated with breathing retraining. *Lancet, ii,* 665–669.

Boren, J. L., Gallup, G. G., Suarez, S. D., Wallnau, L. B. & Gagliardi, G. J. (1979). Pargyline and tryptophan enhancement of tonic immobility: Paradoxical attenuation with combined administration. *Pharmacology, Biochemistry and Behavior, 11,* 17–22.

Borkovec, T. D. (1978). Self-efficacy: Cause or reflection of behavioural change? *Advances in Behaviour Research and Therapy, 1,* 177–193.

Borkovec, T. D. (1979). Pseudo (experimental) insomnia and idiopathic (objective) insomnia: Theoretical and therapeutic issues. *Advances in Behaviour Research and Therapy, 2,* 27–55.

Borkovec, T. D. (1985). The role of cognitive and somatic cues in anxiety and anxiety disorders: Worry and relaxation-induced anxiety. In A. H. Tuma & J. S. Maser (Eds.), *Anxiety and the anxiety disorders.* Hillsdale, NJ: Erlbaum.

Borkovec, T. D. (in press). Worry: Physiological and cognitive processes. In P. Eelen (Ed.), *Advances in clinical research.* Hillsdale, NJ: Erlbaum.

Borkovec, T. D., Grayson, J. B., & Cooper, K. M. (1978). Treatment of general tension: Subjective and physiological effects of progressive relaxation. *Journal of Consulting and Clinical Psychology, 46,* 518–528.

Borkovec, T. D., & Hennings, B. L. (1978). The role of physiological attention focusing in the relaxation treatment of sleep disturbance, general tension, and specific stress reaction. *Behaviour Research and Therapy, 16,* 7–19.

Borkovec, T. D., Robinson, E., Pruzinsky, T., & DePree, J. A. (1983). Preliminary exploration of worry: Some characteristics and processes. *Behaviour Research and Therapy, 21,* 9–16.

Boulenger, J. P., Uhde, T. W., Wolff, E. A., & Post, R. M. (1984). Increased sensitivity to caffeine in patients with panic disorders. *Archives of General Psychiatry, 41,* 1067–1071.

Boulougouris, J. C., & Bassiakos, L. (1973). Prolonged flooding in cases with obsessive–compulsive neurosis. *Behaviour Research and Therapy, 11,* 227–231.

Boulougouris, J. C., Rabavilas, A. O., & Stefanis, C. (1977). Psychophysiological responses in obsessive–compulsive patients. *Behaviour Research and Therapy, 15,* 221–230.

Bourque, P., & Ladouceur, R. (1980). An investigation of various performance-based treatments with agoraphobics. *Behaviour Research and Therapy, 18,* 161–170.

Bowen, R. C., Cipywnyk, D., D'Arcy, C., & Keegan, D. (1984). Alcoholism, anxiety disorders and agoraphobia. *Alcoholism: Clinical and Experimental Research, 8,* 48–50.

Bower, G. H. (1981). Mood and memory. *American Psychologist, 36,* 129–148.

Bowlby, J. (1973). *Attachment and loss: Vol. 2. Separation: Anxiety and anger.* New York: Basic Books.

Boyd, J. H. (1986). Use of mental health services for the treatment of panic disorder. *American Journal of Psychiatry, 143,* 1569–1574.

Boyd, J. H., Burke, J. D., Gruenberg, E., Holzer, C. E. III, Rae, D. S., George, L. K., Karno, M., Stoltzman, R., McEvoy, L., & Nestadt, G. (1984). Exclusion criteria of DSM III: A study of co-occurrence of hierarchy-free syndromes. *Archives of General Psychiatry, 41,* 983–989.

Bradley, B., & Mathews, A. (1983). Negative self-schemata in clinical depression. *British Journal of Clinical Psychology, 22,* 173–181.

Brady, J. P. (1984a). Social skills training for psychiatric patients: I. Concepts, methods and clinical results. *American Journal of Psychiatry, 141,* 333–340.

Brady, J. P. (1984b). Social skills training for psychiatric patients: II. Clinical outcome studies. *American Journal of Psychiatry, 141,* 491–498.

641

Braestrup, C., & Nielsen, M. (1981). Modulation of benzodiazepine receptors. In B. Angrist, G. D. Burrows, M. Lader, O. Lingjaerde, G. C. Sedvall, & D. Wheatley (Eds.), *Recent advances in neuropsychopharmacology*. New York: Pergamon Press.

Braestrup, C., Nielsen, M., Honore, J., Jensen, L. M., & Petersen, E. N. (1983). Benzodiazepine receptor ligands with positive and negative efficacy. *Neuropharmacology, 22,* 1451–1457.

Brantigan, C. O., Brantigan, T. A., & Joseph, N. (1982). Effect of beta blockade and beta stimulation on stage fright. *American Journal of Medicine, 72,* 88–94.

Breggin, P. R. (1964). The psychophysiology of anxiety with a review of the literature concerning adrenaline. *Journal of Nervous and Mental Disease, 139,* 558–568.

Brehm, J., Gatz, M., Goethals, G., McCrimmon, W., & Ward, L. (1978). Physiological arousal and interpersonal attraction. *JSAS Catalog of Selected Documents in Psychology, 8,* 63.

Breier, A., Charney, D. S., & Heninger, G. R. (1984). Major depression in patients with agoraphobia and panic disorder. *Archives of General Psychiatry, 41,* 1129–1135.

Breier, A., Charney, D. S., & Heninger, G. R. (1985). The diagnostic validity of anxiety disorders and their relationship to depressive illness. *American Journal of Psychiatry, 142,* 787–797.

Breier, A., Charney, D. S., & Heninger, G. R. (1986). Agoraphobia with panic attacks. *Archives of General Psychiatry, 43,* 1029–1036.

Breslau, N. (1985). Depressive symptoms, major depression and generalized anxiety: A comparison of self-reports on CES-D and results from diagnostic interviews. *Psychiatry Research, 15,* 219–229.

Breslau, N., & Davis, G. C. (1985). DSM III generalized anxiety disorder: An empirical investigation of more stringent criteria. *Psychiatry Research, 14,* 231–238.

Breslau, N., & Davis, G. C. (1986). Chronic stress and major depression. *Archives of General Psychiatry, 43,* 309–314.

Breslau, N., & Davis, G. C. (1987). Posttraumatic stress disorder: The etiologic specificity of wartime stressors. *American Journal of Psychiatry, 144,* 578–583.

Briddell, D. W., Rimm, D. C., Caddy, G. R., Krawitz, G., Shalis, D., & Wunderlin, R. J. (1978). The effects of alcohol and cognitive set on sexual arousal to deviant stimuli. *Journal of Abnormal Psychology, 87,* 418–430.

Broadhurst, P. L. (1975). The Maudsley reactive and nonreactive strains of rats: A survey. *Behavior Genetics, 5,* 299–320.

Brown, F. W. (1942). Heredity in the psychoneurosis (summary). *Proceedings of the Royal Society of Medicine, 35,* 785–790.

Brownell, K. D., Heckerman, C. L., Westlake, R. J., Hayes, S. C., & Monti, P. M. (1978). The effects of couples training and partner cooperativeness in the behavioral treatment of obesity. *Behaviour Research and Therapy, 16,* 323–333.

Bruch, M. A., Heimberg, H. G., Berger, P., & Collins, T. M. (1987). *Parental and personal origins of social evaluative threat: Differences between social phobics and agoraphobics.* Unpublished manuscript.

Buglass, P., Clarke, J., Henderson, A. S., Kreitman, D. N., & Presley, A. S. (1977). A study of agoraphobic housewives. *Psychological Medicine, 7,* 73–86.

Buigues, J., & Vallejo, J. (1987). Therapeutic response to phenelzine in patients with panic disorder and agoraphobia with panic attacks. *Journal of Clinical Psychiatry, 48,* 55–59.

Bull, N. (1951). The attitude theory of emotion. *Nervous and Mental Disease Monographs, No. 81.*

Burdick, J. A. (1978). A review of heart rate variability and evaluation. *Perceptual and Motor Skills, 47,* 95–105.

Burgess, A. W., & Holmstrom, L. L. (1976). Coping behavior of the rape victim. *American Journal of Psychiatry, 133,* 413–417.

Burgess, I. S., Jones, L. W., Robertson, S. A., Radcliffe, W. N., Emerson, E., Lawler, P., & Crowe, T. J. (1981). The degree of control exerted by phobic and non-phobic verbal stimuli over the recognition behaviour of phobic and non-phobic subjects. *Behaviour Research and Therapy, 19,* 233–234.

Burish, T. G., & Carey, M. P. (1986). Conditioned aversive responses in cancer chemotherapy patients: Theoretical and developmental analysis. *Journal of Consulting and Clinical Psychology, 54,* 593–600.

Burns, L. E., & Thorpe, G. L. (1977). Fears and clinical phobias: Epidemiological aspects and the national survey of agoraphobics. *Journal of International Medical Research, 5,* 132–139.

Burns, L. E., Thorpe, G. L., & Cavallaro, L. A. (1986). Agoraphobia eight years after behavioral treatment: A follow-up study with interview, self-report, and behavioral data. *Behavioral Therapy, 17,* 580–591.

Burrell, R. H., Culpan, R. H., & Newton, K. J. (1974). Use of bromazepam in obsessional, phobic and related states. *Current Medical Research Opinion, 2,* 430–436.

Burnstein, A. (1984). Treatment of post-traumatic stress disorder with imipramine. *Psychosomatics, 25,* 681–682.

Butler, G. (1985). Exposure as a treatment for social phobia: Some instructive difficulties. *Behaviour Research and Therapy, 23,* 651–657.

Butler, G., Cullington, A., Hibbert, G., Klimes, I., & Gelder, M. (1987). Anxiety management for persistent generalized anxiety. *British Journal of Psychiatry, 151,* 535–542.

Butler, G., Cullington, A., Munby, M., Amies, P., & Gelder, M. (1984). Exposure and anxiety management in the treatment of social phobia. *Journal of Consulting and Clinical Psychology, 52,* 642–650.

Butler, G., & Mathews, A. (1983). Cognitive processes in anxiety. *Advances in Behaviour Research and Therapy, 5,* 51–62.

Byrne, D. (1977). Social psychology and the study of sexual behavior. *Journal of Personality and Social Psychology, 3,* 3–30.

Byrne, D. (1983a). The antecedents, correlates and consequences of erotophobia–erotophilia. In C. M. Davis (Ed.), *Challenges in sexual science.* Philadelphia: Society for the Scientific Study of Sex.

Byrne, D. (1983b). Sex without contraception. In D. Byrne & W. A. Fisher (Eds.), *Adolescents, sex, and contraception.* Hillsdale, NJ: Erlbaum.

Cacioppo, J. T., & Petty, R. E. (1981). Social psychological procedures for cognitive response assessment: The thought-listing technique. In T. V. Merluzzi, C. R. Glass, & M. Genest (Eds.), *Cognitive assessment.* New York: Guilford Press.

Caldwell, A. T., McCrady, B. S., & Barlow, D. H. (1979). *The effects of response prevention and contingency management in the treatment of obsessive–compulsive behavior.* Unpublished manuscript.

Callaway, E., & Stone, G. (1960). Re-evaluating the focus of attention. In L. Uhr & J. G. Miller (Eds.), *Drugs and behavior.* New York: Wiley.

Cameron, O. G., Thyer, B. A., Nesse, R. M., & Curtis, G. C. (1986). Symptom profiles of patients with DSM III anxiety disorders. *American Journal of Psychiatry, 143,* 1132–1137.

Campbell, D., Sanderson, R., & Laverty, S. G. (1964). Characteristics of a conditioned response in human subjects during extinction trials following a single traumatic conditioning trial. *Journal of Abnormal and Social Psychology, 66,* 627–639.

Campbell, S. B. (1986). Developmental issues in childhood anxiety. In R. Gittelman (Ed.), *Anxiety disorders of childhood.* New York: Guilford Press.

Campos, P. E., Solyom, L., & Koelink, A. (1984). The effects of timolol maleate on subjective and physiological components of air travel phobia. *Canadian Journal of Psychiatry, 29,* 570–574.

Cannon, W. B. (1927). *Bodily changes in pain, hunger, fear and rage.* New York: Appleton-Century-Crofts.

Cannon, W. B. (1929). *Bodily changes in pain, hunger, fear and rage* (2nd ed.). New York: Appleton-Century-Crofts.

Cannon, W. B. (1942). Voodoo death. *American Anthropologist, 44,* 169–181.

Canter, A., Kondo, C. Y., & Knott, J. R. (1975). A comparison of EMG feedback and progressive muscle relaxation training in anxiety neurosis. *British Journal of Psychiatry, 127,* 470–477.

Capstick, N. (1971). Clomipiamine in obsessional states. *Psychosomatics, 12,* 332–335.

Carey, G. (1982). Genetic influences on anxiety neurosis and agoraphobia. In R. J. Mathew (Ed.), *The biology of anxiety.* New York: Brunner/Mazel.

Carey, G. (1985). Epidemiology and cross-cultural aspects of anxiety disorders: A commentary. In A. H. Tuma & H. D. Maser (Eds.), *Anxiety and the anxiety disorders.* Hillsdale, NJ: Erlbaum.

Carey, G., & Gottesman, I. I. (1981). Twin and family studies of anxiety, phobic, and obsessive disorders. In D. F. Klein & J. G. Rabkin (Eds.). *Anxiety: New research and changing concepts.* New York: Raven Press.

Carey, G., Gottesman, I. I., & Robins, E. (1980). Prevalence rates for the neuroses: Pitfalls in the evaluation of familiarity. *Psycholigical Medicine, 10,* 437–443.

Carr, D. B., & Sheehan, D. V. (1984). Evidence that panic disorder has a metabolic cause. In J. C. Ballenger (Ed.), *Biology of agoraphobia.* Washington, DC: American Psychiatric Press.

Carr, D. B., Sheehan, D. V., Surman, O. S., Coleman, J. H., Greenblatt, D. J., Heninger, G. R., Jones, K. J., Levine, P. H., & Watkins, W. D. (1986). Neuroendocrine correlates of lactate-induced anxiety and their response to chronic alprazolam therapy. *Journal of Psychiatry, 143,* 483–494.

Carroll, E. M., Rueger, D. B., Foy, D. W., & Donahoe, C. P. (1985). Vietnam combat veterans with posttraumatic stress disorder: Analysis of marital and cohabitating adjustment. *Journal of Abnormal Psychology, 94,* 329–337.

Carver, C. S., Blaney, P. H., & Scheier, M. F. (1979). Focus of attention, chronic expectancy, and responses to a feared stimulus. *Journal of Personality and Social Psychology, 37,* 1186–1195.

Carver, C. S., Peterson, L. M., Folansbee, D. J., & Scheier, M. F. (1983). Effects of self-directed attention on performance and persistence among persons high and low in test anxiety. *Cognitive Therapy and Research, 7,* 333–354.

Carver, C. S., & Scheier, M. F. (1981). *Attention and self-regulation: A control theory approach to human behavior.* New York: Springer-Verlag.

Cassens, G., Roffman, M., Kuruc, A., Orsulak, P., & Schildkraut, J. (1980). Norepinephrine metabolism induced by environmental stimuli previously paired with inescapable shock. *Science, 209,* 1138–1140.

Cella, D. F., Pratt, A., & Holland, J. C. (1986). Persistent anticipatory nausea, vomiting and anxiety in cured Hodgkin's disease patients after completion of chemotherapy. *American Journal of Psychiatry, 143,* 641–643.

Cerny, J. A., Barlow, D. H., Craske, M., & Himadi, W. G. (1987). Couples treatment of agoraphobia: A two-year follow-up. *Behavior Therapy, 18,* 401–415.

Chambless, D. L., Caputo, G. C., Bright, P., & Gallagher, R. (1984). Assessment of fear in agoraphobics: The Body Sensations Questionnaire and the Agoraphobic Cognitions Questionnaire. *Journal of Consulting and Clinical Psychology, 52,* 1090–1097.

Chambless, D. L., Caputo, G. C., Jasin, S. E., Gracely, E. J., & Williams, C. (1985). The Mobility Inventory for Agoraphobia. *Behaviour Research and Therapy, 23,* 35–44.

Chambless, D. L., Cherney, J., Caputo, G. C., & Rheinstein, B. J. G. (1987). Anxiety disorders and alcoholism: A study with inpatient alcoholics. *Journal of Anxiety Disorders, 1,* 29–40.

Chambless, D. L., Goldstein, A. A., Gallagher, R., & Bright, P. (1986). Integrating behavior therapy and psychotherapy in the treatment of agoraphobia. *Psychotherapy: Theory, Research, and Practice, 23,* 150–159.

Chambless, D. L., & Mason, J. (1986). Sex, sex role stereotyping, and agoraphobia. *Behaviour Research and Therapy, 24,* 231–235.

Chaplin, E. W., & Levine, B. A. (1981). The effects of total exposure duration and inter-rupted versus continued exposure in flooding therapy. *Behavior Therapy, 12*, 360–368.

Charney, D. S., & Heninger, G. R. (1985). Noradrenergic function and the mechanism of action of antianxiety treatment. *Archives of General Psychiatry, 42*, 458–467.

Charney, D. S., & Heninger, G. R. (1986a). Abnormal regulation of noradrenergic function in panic disorders. *Archives of General Psychiatry, 43*, 1042–1054.

Charney, D. S., & Heninger, G. R. (1986b). Serotonin function in panic disorders: The effect of intravenous tryptophan in healthy subjects and patients with panic disorder before and during alprazolam treatment. *Archives of General Psychiatry, 43*, 1059–1065.

Charney, D. S., Heninger, G. R., & Breier, A. (1984). Noradrenergic function in pain at-tacks. *Archives of General Psychiatry, 41*, 751–763.

Charney, D. S., Heninger, G. R., & Jatlow, P. I. (1985). Increased anxiogenic effects of caffeine in panic disorders. *Archives of General Psychiatry, 42*, 223–243.

Chesney, M. A. (1985). Anger and hostility: Future implications for behavioral medicine. In M. A. Chesney & R. H. Rosenman (Eds.), *Anger and hostility in cardiovascular and behavioral disorders*. Washington, DC: Hemisphere.

Chesney, M. A. (1986, November). *Type A behavior: The biobehavioral interface*. Keynote ad-dress presented at the annual meeting of the Association for Advancement of Behav-ior Therapy, Chicago.

Chesney, M. A., & Black, G. W. (1986). Hypertension: Biobehavioral influences and their implications for treatment. In T. H. Schmidt, T. M. Dembroski, & G. Blumchen (Eds.), *Biological and psychological factors in cardiovascular disease*. Berlin: Springer-Verlag.

Chesney, M. A., & Rosenman, R. H. (Eds.). *Anger and hostility in cardiovascular and behavioral disorders*. Washington, DC: Hemisphere.

Chouinard, G., Annable, L., Fontaine, R., & Solyom, L. (1982). Alprazolam in the treatment of generalized anxiety and panic disorders: A double-blind placebo-controlled study. *Psychopharmacology, 77*, 229–233.

Clark, D. M. (1988). A cognitive model of panic attacks. In S. Rachman & J. D. Maser (Eds.), *Panic: Psychological perspectives*. Hillsdale, NJ: Erlbaum.

Clark, D. M., Salkovskis, P. M., & Chalkley, A. J. (1985). Respiratory control as a treatment for panic attacks. *Journal of Behavior Therapy and Experimental Psychiatry, 16*, 23–30.

Clark, D. M., & Teasdale, J. D. (in press). Constraints on the effects of mood on memory. *Journal of Personality and Social Psychology*.

Cloninger, C. R. (1986). A unified biosocial theory of personality and its role in the devel-opment of anxiety states. *Psychiatric Developments, 5*, 167–226.

Cloninger, C. R. (1987). Neurogenetic adaptive mechanisms in alcoholism. *Science, 236*, 410–416.

Cloninger, C. R., Martin, R. L., Clayton, P., & Guze, J. B. (1981). A blind follow-up and family study of anxiety neurosis: Preliminary analysis of the St. Louis 500. In D. F. Klein & J. Rabkin (Eds.), *Anxiety: New research and changing concepts*. New York: Raven Press.

Cobb, J. P., Mathews, A. M., Childs-Clarke, A., & Blowers, C. M. (1984). The spouse as co-therapist in the treatment of agoraphobia. *British Journal of Psychiatry, 144*, 282–287.

Cobb, J. P., McDonald, R., Marks, I. M., & Stern, R. S. (1980). Marital versus exposure therapy: Psychological treatments of co-existing marital and phobic–obsessive prob-lems. *European Journal of Behavioural Analysis and Modification, 4*, 3–17.

Cohen, A. S., Barlow, D. H., & Blanchard, E. B. (1985). The psychophysiology of relaxation-associated panic attacks. *Journal of Abnormal Psychology, 94*, 96–101.

Cohen, M. E., Badal, D. W., Kilpatrick, A., Reed, E. W., & White, P. D. (1951). The high familial prevalence of neurocirculatory asthenia (anxiety neurosis, effort syndrome). *American Journal of Human Genetics, 3*, 126–158.

Cohen, M. E., & White, P. D. (1947). Studies of breathing pulminary ventilation and sub-jective awareness of shortness of breath (dyspnea) in neurocirculatory asthenia, effort syndrome, anxiety neurosis. *Journal of Clinical Investigation, 26*, 520.

REFERENCES

Cohen, M. E., & White, P. D. (1950). Life situations, emotions and neurocirculatory asthenia (anxiety neurosis, neurasthenia, effort syndrome). In H. G. Wolff (Ed.), *Life stress and bodily disease* (Nervous and Mental Disease, Research Publication No. 29). Baltimore: Williams & Wilkins.

Cohen, S. D., Monteiro, W., & Marks, I. M. (1984). Two-year follow-up of agoraphobics after exposure and imipramine. *British Journal of Psychiatry, 144*, 276–281.

Connolly, J., Hallam, R. S., & Marks, I. M. (1976). Selective association of fainting with blood–injury–illness fear. *Behavior Therapy, 7*, 8–13.

Cook, E. W., III, Hodes, R. L., & Lang, P. J. (1986). Preparedness and phobia: Effects of stimulus content on human visceral conditioning. *Journal of Abnormal Psychology, 95*, 195–207.

Cook, M., Mineka, S., Wolkenstein, B., & Laitsch, K. (1985). Observational conditioning of snake fears in unrelated rhesus monkeys. *Journal of Abnormal Psychology, 94*, 591–610.

Cooper, J. (1970). The Leyton Obsessional Inventory. *Psychological Medicine, 1*, 48–64.

Cooper, J. E., Gelder, M. G., & Marks, I. M. (1965). Results of behavior therapy in 77 psychiatric patients. *British Medical Journal, i*, 1222–1225.

Coryell, W., Noyes, R., & Clancy, J. (1982). Excess mortality in panic disorder: A comparison with primary unipolar depression. *Archives of General Psychiatry, 39*, 701–703.

Coryell, W., Noyes, R., & House, J. D. (1986). Mortality among outpatients with anxiety disorders. *American Journal of Psychiatry, 143*, 508–510.

Costa, E. (1985). Benzodiazepine–GABA interactions: A model to investigate the neurobiology of anxiety. In A. H. Tuma & J. D. Maser (Eds.), *Anxiety and the anxiety disorders*. Hillsdale, NJ: Erlbaum.

Costello, C. G. (1982). Fears and phobias in women: A community study. *Journal of Abnormal Psychology, 91*, 280–286.

Cox, B. J., Norton, G. R., Dorward, J., & Fergusson, P. A. (in press). The relationship between panic attacks and chemical dependencies. *Addictive Behaviors*.

Cox, D., Hallam, R., O'Connor, K., & Rachman, S. (1983). An experimental analyses of fearlessness and courage. *British Journal of Psychiatry, 74*, 107–117.

Craske, M. G., & Craig, K. D. (1984). Musical performance anxiety: The three-system model and self-efficacy theory. *Behaviour Research and Therapy, 22*, 267–280.

Craske, M. G., & Rachman, S. J. (1987). Return of fear: Perceived skill and heart rate responsivity. *British Journal of Clinical Psychology, 26*, 187–199.

Craske, M. G., Rachman, S. J., & Tallman, K. (1986). Mobility, cognitions and panic. *Journal of Psychopathology and Behavioral Assessment, 8*, 199–210.

Craske, M. G., Sanderson, W. C., & Barlow, D. H. (1987a). How do desynchronous response systems relate to the treatment of agoraphobia: A follow-up evaluation. *Behaviour Research and Therapy, 25*, 117–122.

Craske, M. G., Sanderson, W. C., & Barlow, D. H. (1987b). The relationships among panic, fear, and avoidance. *Journal of Anxiety Disorders, 1*, 153–160.

Crowe, R. R., Noyes, R., Pauls, D. L., & Slymen, D. J. (1983). A family study of panic disorder. *Archives of General Psychiatry, 40*, 1065–1069.

Crowe, R. R., Pauls, D. L., Slymen, D. J., & Noyes, R. (1980). A family study of anxiety neurosis: Morbidity risk in families of patients with and without mitral valve prolapse. *Archives of General Psychiatry, 37*, 77–79.

Crowe, R. R., Pauls, D. L., Venkatesh, A., VanValkenberg, C., Noyes, R., Martins, J. B., & Kerber, R. E. (1979). Exercise and anxiety neurosis: Comparison of patients with and without mitral valve prolapse. *Archives of General Psychiatry, 36*, 652–653.

Curtis, G. C., Buxton, M., Lippman, D., Nesse, R., & Wright, J. (1976). "Flooding in vivo" during the circadian phase of minimal cortisol secretion: Anxiety and therapeutic success without adrenal cortical activation. *Biological Psychiatry, 11*, 101–107.

Curtis, G. C., Nesse, R. M., Buxton, M., & Lippman, D. (1978). Anxiety and plasma cortisol at the crest of the circadian cycle: Reappraisal of a classical hypothesis. *Psychosomatic Medicine, 40,* 368–378.

Curtis, G. C., Nesse, R. M., Buxton, M., & Lippman, D. (1979). Plasma growth hormone: Effect of anxiety during flooding in vivo. *American Journal of Psychiatry, 136,* 410–414.

Curtis, G. C., Nesse, R. M., Buxton, M., Wright, J., & Lippman, D. (1976). Flooding in vivo as research tool and treatment method for phobias: A preliminary report. *Comprehensive Psychiatry, 17,* 153–160.

Curtis, G. C., & Thyer, B. (1983). Fainting on exposure to phobic stimuli. *American Journal of Psychiatry, 140,* 771–774.

DaCosta, J. M. (1871). On irritable heart; a clinical study of a form of functional cardiac disorder and its consequences. *American Journal of Medical Science, 61,* 17–52.

Dager, S. R., Comess, K. A., Saal, A. K., & Dunner, D. L. (1986). Mitral valve prolapse in a psychiatric setting: Diagnostic assessment, research and clinical implications. *Integrative Psychiatry, 4,* 211–223.

Daly, R. J. (1983). Samuel Pepys and post traumatic stress disorder. *British Journal of Psychiatry, 143,* 64–68.

Darwin, C. R. (1872). *The expression of emotions in man and animals.* London: John Murray.

Davidson, R. J., & Schwartz, G. E. (1976). The psychobiology of relaxation and related states: A multi-process theory. In D. I. Mostofsky (Ed.), *Behavioral control and modification of physiological activity.* Englewood Cliffs, NJ: Prentice-Hall.

Davidson, J., Swartz, M., Storck, M., Krishnan, R. R., & Hammett, E. (1985). A diagnostic and family study of post traumatic stress disorder. *American Journal of Psychiatry, 142,* 90–93.

Davis, M., Parisi, T., Gendelman, D. S., Tischler, M., & Kehne, J. H. (1982). Habituation and sensitization of startle reflexes elicited electrically from the brainstem. *Science, 218,* 688–690.

Deffenbacher, J. L., Demm, P. M., & Brandon, A. D. (1986). High general anger: Correlates and treatment. *Behaviour Research and Therapy, 24,* 481–489.

Denny, M. R. (1975). Post-aversive relief and relaxation and their implications for behavior therapy. *Journal of Behavior Therapy and Experimental Psychiatry, 7,* 315–321.

Depue, R. A. (Ed.). (1979). *The psychobiology of the depressive disorders: Implications for the effects of stress.* New York: Academic Press.

Depue, R. A., & Monroe, S. M. (1986). Conceptualization and measurement of human disorder in life stress research: The problem of chronic disturbance. *Psychological Bulletin, 99,* 36–51.

Derogatis, L. R., Lipman, R. S., & Covi, L. (1973). SCL-90: An outpatient psychiatric rating scale. Preliminary report. *Psychopharmacological Bulletin, 9,* 13–25.

Derryberry, D., & Rothbart, M. K. (1984). Emotion, attention, and temperament. In C. E. Izard, J. Kagan, R. B. Zajonc (Eds.), *Emotions, cognition, and behavior.* New York: Cambridge University Press.

de Silva, P. (1986). Obsessional–compulsive imagery. *Behaviour Research and Therapy, 24,* 333–350.

de Silva, P., & Rachman, S. (1981). Is exposure a necessary condition for fear reduction? *Behaviour Research and Therapy, 19,* 227–232.

de Silva, P., & Rachman, S. (1984). Does escape behaviour strengthen agoraphobic avoidance? A preliminary study. *Behaviour Research and Therapy, 22,* 87–91.

Devereux, R. B., Kramer-Fox, R., Brown, W. T., Shear, M. K., Hartman, N., Kligfield, P., Lutas, E. M., Spitzer, M. C., & Litwin, S. D. (1986). Relation between clinical features of the "mitral prolapse syndrome" and echocardiographically documented mitral valve prolapse. *Journal of the American College of Cardiology, 8,* 763–772.

Devereux, R. B., Kramer-Fox, R., Shear, M. K., Spitzer, M. C., Kligfield, P., & Brown, W. T. (1988). *Clinical over-diagnosis of mitral valve prolapse: Relation to panic attacks and midsystolic murmurs.* Manuscript submitted for publication.

Dimberg, U., & Öhman, A. (1983). The effects of directional facial cues on electrodermal conditioning to facial stimuli. *Psychophysiology, 20,* 160–167.

Dimsdale, J. E., & Moss, J. (1980). Plasma catecholamines and stress and exercise. *Journal of the American Medical Association, 243,* 340–342.

Di Nardo, P. A., Barlow, D. H., Cerny, J., Vermilyea, B. B., Vermilyea, J. A., Himadi, W., & Waddell, M. (1985). *Anxiety Disorders Interview Schedule—Revised (ADIS-R).* Albany, NY: Phobia and Anxiety Disorders Clinic, State University of New York at Albany.

Di Nardo, P. A., O'Brien, G. T., Barlow, D. H., Waddell, M. T., & Blanchard, E. B. (1983). Reliability of DSM-III anxiety disorder categories using a new structured interview. *Archives of General Psychiatry, 40,* 1070–1074.

Dobbs, D., & Wilson, W. P. (1960). Observations on persistence of war neurosis. *Diseases of the Nervous System, 21,* 686–691.

Dobson, K. S. (1985). The relationship between anxiety and depression. *Clinical Psychology Review, 5,* 307–324.

Doctor, R. M. (1982). Major results of a large-scale pretreatment survey of agoraphobics. In R. L. DuPont (Ed.), *Phobia: A comprehensive summary of modern treatments.* New York: Brunner/Mazel.

Doongaji, D., Sheth, A., Apte, J., Lakdowal, P., Khare, C., & Thatte, S. (1978). Clobozam versus diazepam—a double-blind study in anxiety neurosis. *Journal of Clinical Pharmacology, 18,* 358–364.

Drury, A. N. (1919). The percentage of carbon dioxide in the alveolar air and the tolerance to accumulating carbon dioxide in cases of so-called "irritable heart" of soldiers. *Heart (London), 7,* 165–173.

Dunn, G. (1983). Longitudinal records of anxiety and depression in general practice: The Second National Morbidity Survey. *Psychological Medicine, 13,* 897–906.

Dutton, D. G., & Aron, A. P. (1974). Some evidence for heightened sexual attraction under conditions of high anxiety. *Journal of Personality and Social Psychology, 30,* 510–517.

Duval, S., & Wicklund, R. A. (1972). *A theory of objective self-awareness.* New York: Academic Press.

Easterbrook, J. A. (1959). The effect of emotion on cue utilization and the organization of behavior. *Psychological Review, 66,* 183–201.

Easton, J. D., & Sherman, D. G. (1976). Somatic anxiety attacks and propranolol. *Archives of Neurology, 33,* 689–691.

Eaves, L., & Eysenck, H. J. (1976). Genetic and environmental components of inconsistency and unrepeatability in twins' responses to a neuroticism questionnaire. *Behavior Genetics, 6,* 145–160.

✳ Egeland, J. A., Gerhard, D. S., Pauls, D. L., Sussex, J. N., Kidd, K. K., Allen, C. R., Hostetler, A. M., & Houseman, D. E. (1987). Bipolar affective disorders linked to DNA markers on chromosome 11. *Nature, 325,* 783–787.

Egendorf, A., Kadushin, C., Laufer, R. S., Rothbart, G., & Sloan, L. (1981). *Legacies of Vietnam: Comparative adjustment of veterans and their peers* (Publication No. V101 134P-630). Washington, DC: U.S. Government Printing Office.

Ehlers, A., Margraf, J., & Roth, W. T. (1986). Experimental induction of panic attacks. In I. Hand & H. U. Wittchen (Eds.), *Panic and phobias: Empirical evidence of theoretical models and longterm effects of behavioral treatments.* Berlin: Springer-Verlag.

Ehlers, A., Margraf, J., & Roth, W. T. (1987). Interaction of expectancy and physiological stressors in a laboratory model of panic. In D. Hellhammer & I. Florin (Eds.), *Neuronal control of bodily function—basic and clinical aspects: Vol II. Psychological and biological approaches to the understanding of human disease.* Göttingen: Hogrefe.

Ehlers, A., Margraf, J., Roth, W. T., Taylor, C. B., & Birbaumer, N. (1988). Anxiety induced by false heart rate feedback in patients with panic disorder. *Behaviour Research and Therapy, 26,* 1–11.

Ehlers, A., Margraf, J., Roth, W. T., Taylor, C. B., Maddock, R. J., Sheikh, J., Kobell, M. L., McClenahan, K. L., Gossard, D., Blowers, G. H., Agras, W. S., & Kopell, B. S.

(1986). Lactate infusions and panic attacks: Do patients and controls respond differently? *Psychiatry Research, 17,* 295–308.

Eison, A., & Temple, D. (1986). Buspirone: Review of its pharmacology and current perspectives on its mechanism of action. *American Journal of Medicine, 80* (Suppl. 3B), 1–9.

Ekman, P., Levenson, R., & Friesen, W. (1983). Autonomic nervous system activity distinguishes among emotions. *Science, 221,* 1208–1210.

Elam, M., Yoa, T., Thoren, P., & Svensson, T. H. (1981). Hypercapnia and hypoxia: Chemoreceptor-mediated control of locus ceruleus neurons and splanchnic, sympathetic nerves. *Brain Research, 222,* 373–381.

Ellis, A. (1979). A note on the treatment of agoraphobics with prolonged exposure in vivo. *Behaviour Research and Therapy, 17,* 162–164.

Emde, R. N. (1980). Levels of meaning for infant emotions: A biosocial view. In W. A. Collins (Ed.), *Minnesota Symposia on Child Psychology: Vol 13. Development of cognition, affect and social relations.* Hillsdale, NJ: Erlbaum.

Emde, R. N., Gaensbauer, T. J., & Harmon, R. J. (1976). *Emotional expressions in infancy.* New York: International Universities Press.

Emde, R. N., Kligman, D. H., Reich, J. H., & Wade, T. D. (1978). Emotional expression in infancy: Initial studies of social signaling and an emergent model. In M. Lewis & L. Rosenblum (Eds.), *The development of affect.* New York: Plenum Press.

Emmelkamp, P. M. G. (1974). Self-observation versus flooding in the treatment of agoraphobia. *Behaviour Research and Therapy, 22,* 87–91.

Emmelkamp, P. M. G. (1980). Agoraphobics' interpersonal problems: Their role in the effects of exposure in vivo therapy. *Archives of General Psychiatry, 37,* 1303–1306.

Emmelkamp, P. M. G. (1982). *Phobic and obsessive–compulsive disorders: Theory, research, and practice.* New York: Plenum Press.

Emmelkamp, P. M. G., Brilman, E., Kuiper, H., & Mersch, P. P. (1986). The treatment of agoraphobia: A comparison of self-instructional training, rational emotive therapy, and exposure in vivo. *Behavior Modification, 10,* 37–53.

Emmelkamp, P. M. G., & Kuipers, A. C. M. (1979). Agoraphobia: A follow-up study four years after treatment. *British Journal of Psychiatry, 128,* 86–89.

Emmelkamp, P. M. G., Kuipers, A. C. M., & Eggeraat, J. G. (1978). Cognitive modification versus prolonged exposure in vivo: A comparison with agoraphobics as subjects. *Behaviour Research and Therapy, 16,* 33–41.

Emmelkamp, P. M. G., & Mersch, P. P. (1982). Cognition and exposure in vivo in the treatment of agoraphobia: Short term and delayed effects. *Cognitive Therapy and Research, 6,* 77–88.

Emmelkamp, P. M. G., Mersch, P. P., Vissia, E., & van der Helm, M. (1985). Case histories and shorter communications–social phobia: A comparative evaluation of cognitive and behavioural interventions. *Behaviour Research and Therapy, 23,* 365–369.

Emmelkamp, P. M. G., & Ultee, K. A. (1974). A comparison of "successive approximation" and "self-observation" in the treatment of agoraphobia. *Behavior Therapy, 5,* 606–613.

Emmelkamp, P. M. G., van der Hout, A., & de Vries, K. (1983). Assertive training for agoraphobics. *Behaviour Research and Therapy, 21,* 63–68.

Emmelkamp, P. M. G., & Wessels, H. (1975). Flooding in imagination vs. flooding in vivo: A comparison with agoraphobics. *Behaviour Research and Therapy, 13,* 7–15.

Endicott, J., & Spitzer, R. L. (1978). The Schedule for Affective Disorders and Schizophrenia. *Archives of General Psychiatry, 35,* 837–844.

Endicott, J., & Spitzer, R. L. (1979). Use of the Research Diagnostic Criteria and the Schedule for Affective Disorders and Schizophrenia to study affective disorders. *American Journal of Psychiatry, 136,* 52–56.

Engel, G. E. (1962). *Fainting: Physiological and psychological considerations.* Springfield, IL: Charles C. Thomas.

Evans, L., Schneider, P., Ross-Lee, L., Wiltshire, B., Eadie, M., Kenaidy, J., Hoey, H. (1986). Plasma serotonin levels in agoraphobia. *American Journal of Psychiatry, 142,* 267.

Eysenck, H. J. (Ed.). (1960). *Behavior therapy and the neuroses.* Oxford: Pergamon Press.

Eysenck, H. J. (1961). *The handbook of abnormal psychology.* New York: Basic Books.

Eysenck, H. J. (Ed.). (1967). *The biological basis of personality.* Springfield, IL: Charles C. Thomas.

Eysenck, H. J. (1970). *The structure of human personality.* London: Methuen.

Eysenck, H. J. (1976). The learning theory model of neurosis: A new approach. *Behaviour Research and Therapy, 14,* 251–267.

Eysenck, H. J. (1979). The conditioning model of neurosis. *The Behavioral and Brain Sciences, 2,* 155–199.

Eysenck, H. J. (1980). Psychological theories of anxiety. In G. D. Burrows & B. Davies (Eds.), *Handbook of studies on anxiety.* Amsterdam: Elsevier/North-Holland.

Eysenck, H. J. (Ed.). (1981). *A model for personality.* New York: Springer-Verlag.

Eysenck, H. J. (1982). Neobehavioristic (S-R) theory. In G. T. Wilson & C. M. Franks (Eds.), *Contemporary behavior therapy: Conceptual and empirical foundations.* New York: Guilford Press.

Fairbank, J. A., & Brown, T. A. (1987). Current behavioral approaches to the treatment of posttraumatic stress disorder. *the Behavior Therapist, 10,* 57–64.

Fairbank, J. A., Gross, R. T., & Keane, T. M. (1983). Treatment of posttraumatic stress disorder: Evaluating outcome with a behavioral code. *Behavior Modification, 7,* 557–568.

Fairbank, J. A., & Keane, T. M. (1982). Flooding for combat-related stress disorders: Assessment of anxiety reduction across traumatic memories. *Behavior Therapy, 13,* 499–510.

Fairbank, J. A., McCaffrey, R., & Keane, T. M. (1985). Psychometric detection of fabricated symptoms of PTSD. *American Journal of Psychiatry, 142,* 501–503.

Falcon, S., Ryan, C., Chamberlain, K., & Curtis, G. (1985). Tricyclics: Possible treatment for posttraumatic stress disorder. *Journal of Clinical Psychiatry, 46,* 385–388.

Falconer, D. S. (1965). The inheritance of liability to certain diseases, estimated from the incidence among relatives. *Annals of Human Genetics, 29,* 51–76.

Falloon, I. R. H., Boyd, J. L., McGill, C. W., Williamson, M., Razani, J., Moss, H. B., Gilderman, A. M., & Simpson, G. M. (1985). Family management in the prevention of morbidity of schizophrenia. *Archives of General Psychiatry, 42,* 887–895.

Falloon, I. R. H., Lindley, P., McDonald, R., & Marks, I. (1977). Social skills training of outpatient groups: A controlled study of rehearsal and homework. *British Journal of Psychiatry, 131,* 610–615.

Falloon, I. R. H., Lloyd, G. G., & Harpin, R. E. (1981). The treatment of social phobia: Real-life rehearsal with nonprofessional therapists. *Journal of Nervous and Mental Disease, 169,* 180–184.

Faravelli, C. (1985). Life events preceding the onset of panic disorder. *Journal of Affective Disorders, 9,* 103–105.

Farid, B. T. (1986). Obsessional symptomatology and adverse mood states. *British Journal of Psychiatry, 149,* 108–112.

Farrell, A. D., Curran, J. P., Zwick, W. R., & Monti, P. M. (1983). Generalizability and discriminant validity of anxiety and social skills ratings in two populations. *Behavioral Assessment, 6,* 1–14.

Feighner, J. D., Meredith, C. H., & Hendrickson, G. A. (1982). A double blind comparison of buspirone and diazepam in outpatients with generalized anxiety disorder. *Journal of Clinical Psychiatry, 43,* 103–107.

Feighner, J. P., Robins, E., Guze, S. B., Woodruff, R. A., Winokur, G., & Munoz, R. (1972). Diagnostic criteria for use in psychiatric research. *Archives of General Psychiatry, 26,* 57–63.

Feltz, D. (1982). Path analysis of the causal elements in Bandura's theory of self-efficacy and an anxiety-based model of avoidance behavior. *Journal of Personality and Social Psychology, 42,* 764–781.

Fenichel, O. (1945). *The psychoanalytic theory of neurosis.* New York: Norton.

Fenigstein, A., & Carver, C. S. (1978). Self-focusing effects of heartbeat feedback. *Journal of Personality and Social Psychology, 36,* 1241–1250.

Fewtrell, W. D. (1984). Relaxation and depersonalization. *British Journal of Psychiatry, 145,* 217.

Figley, C. R. (Ed.). (1978). *Stress disorders among Vietnam veterans: Theory, research, and treatment.* New York: Brunner/Mazel.

Fink, M., Taylor, M. A., & Volavka, J. (1970). Anxiety produced by lactate. *New England Journal of Medicine, 281,* 1429–1440.

Finlay-Jones, R., & Brown, G. W. (1981). Types of stressful life event and the onset of anxiety and depressive disorders. *Psychological Medicine, 11,* 801–815.

Fisher, M. F. K. (1978). The wind chill factor or, a problem of mind and matter. In S. Cahill (Ed.), *Women and fiction 2: Short stories by and about women.* New York: New American Library.

Flor, H., Turk, D. C., & Birbaumer, N. (1985). Assessment of stress-related psychophysiological reactions in chronic back pain patients. *Journal of Consulting and Clinical Psychology, 53,* 354–364.

Foa, E. B. (1979). Failure in treating obsessive–compulsives. *Behaviour Research and Therapy, 17,* 169–176.

Foa, E. B., & Foa, U. G. (1982). Differentiating depression and anxiety: Is it possible? Is it useful? *Psychopharmacology Bulletin, 18,* 62–68.

Foa, E. B., Grayson, J. B., Steketee, G., Doppelt, H. G., Turner, R. M., & Latimer, P. L. (1983). Success and failure in the behavioral treatment of obsessive–compulsives. *Journal of Consulting and Clinical Psychology, 15,* 287–297.

Foa, E. B., Jameson, J. S., Turner, R. M., & Payne, L. L. (1980). Massed vs. spaced exposure sessions in the treatment of agoraphobia. *Behaviour Research and Therapy, 18,* 333–338.

Foa, E. B., & Kozak, M. S. (1985). Treatment of anxiety disorders: Implications for psychopathology. In A. H. Tuma & J. D. Maser (Eds.), *Anxiety and the anxiety disorders.* Hillsdale, NJ: Erlbaum.

Foa, E. B., & Kozak, M. S. (1986). Emotional processing of fear: Exposure to corrective information. *Psychological Bulletin, 99,* 20–35.

Foa, E. B., Steketee, G., Kozak, M. J., & Dugger, D. (1987). Imipramine and placebo in the treatment of obsessive–compulsives: Their effect on depression and on obsessional symptoms. *Psychopharmacology Bulletin, 23,* 8–11.

Foa, E. B., Steketee, G. S., & Ozarow, B. J. (1985). Behavior therapy with obsessive–compulsives: From theory to treatment. In M. Mavissakalian, S. M. Turner, & L. Michelson (Eds.), *Obsessive–compulsive disorders: Psychological and pharmacological treatment.* New York: Plenum Press.

Fontaine, R., Chouinard, G., & Annable, L. (1984). Rebound anxiety in anxious patients after abrupt withdrawal of benzodiazepine treatment. *American Journal of Psychology, 141,* 848–852.

Foote, S. L., Ashton-Jones, G., & Bloom, F. E. (1980). Impulsive activity of locus coeruleus in awake rats and squirrel monkeys is a function of sensory stimulation and arousal. *Proceedings of the National Academy of Sciences, USA, 77,* 3033–3037.

Fowles, D. C. (1986). The psychophysiology of anxiety and hedonic affect: Motivational specificity. In B. F. Shaw, Z. V. Segal, T. M. Vallis, & F. E. Cashman (Eds.), *Anxiety disorders: Psychological and biological perspectives.* New York: Plenum Press.

Foy, D. W., Carroll, E. M., & Donahoe, C. P. Jr. (1987). Etiological factors in the development of P. T. S. D. in clinical samples of Vietnam combat veterans. *Journal of Clinical Psychology, 43,* 17–27.

Foy, D. W., Resnick, H. S., Sipprelle, R. C., & Carroll, E. M. (1987). Premilitary military and postmilitary factors in the development of combat related posttraumatic stress disorder. *the Behavior Therapist, 10,* 3–9.

Foy, D. W., Sipprelle, R. C., Rueger, D. B., & Carroll, E. M. (1984). Etiology of posttraumatic stress disorder in Vietnam veterans: Analysis of premilitary, military, and combat exposure influences. *Journal of Consulting and Clinical Psychology, 52,* 79–87.

Frankl, V. E. (1960). Paradoxical intention: A logotherapeutic technique. *American Journal of Psychotherapy, 14,* 520–535.

Freed, A., Kerr, T. A., & Roth, M. (1972). The treatment of obsessional neurosis. *British Journal of Psychiatry, 120,* 590–591.

Freedman, M. D., Leary, T. F., Ossorio, A. G., & Coffey, H. S. (1951). The interpersonal dimension of personality. *Journal of Personality, 20,* 143–161.

Freedman, R. R., Ianni, P., Ettedgui, E., & Puthezhath, N. (1985). Ambulatory monitoring of panic disorder. *Archives of General Psychiatry, 42,* 244–250.

Freud, S. (1940). The justification for detaching from neurasthenia a particular syndrome: The anxiety-neurosis (J. Rickman, Trans.). In *Collected papers* (Vol. 1). New York: Basic Books. (Original work published 1895)

Freud, S. (1959). Turnings in the ways of psycho-analytic therapy (J. Riviere, Trans.). In *Collected papers* (Vol. 2). New York: Basic Books. (Original work published 1919)

Freud, S. (1959). Inhibitions, symptoms and anxiety. In J. Strachey (Ed. and Trans.), *The standard edition of the complete psychological works of Sigmund Freud* (Vol. 20). London: Hogarth Press. (Original work published 1926)

Freud, S. (1962). Obsessions and phobias: Their psychical mechanism and their aetiology. In J. Strachey (Ed. and Trans.), *The standard edition of the complete psychological works of Sigmund Freud* (Vol. 3). London: Hogarth Press. (Original work published 1895)

Freud, S. (1963). Introductory lectures on psycho-analysis: Lecture 25. Anxiety. In J. Strachey (Ed. and Trans.), *The standard edition of the complete psychological works of Sigmund Freud* (Vol. 16). London: Hogarth Press. (Original work published 1917)

Freund, B., Steketee, G. S., & Foa, E. B. (1987). Compulsive Activity Checklist (CAC): Psychometric analysis with obsessive–compulsive disorder. *Behavioral Assessment, 9,* 67–79.

Fridlund, A. J., & Gilbert, A. N. (1985). Emotions and facial expression. *Science, 230,* 207–208.

Fridlund, A. J., Hatfield, M. E., Cottam, G. L., & Fowler, J. C. (1986). Anxiety and striate-muscle activation: Evidence from electromyographic pattern analysis. *Journal of Abnormal Psychology, 95,* 228–236.

Friedman, M. J., Schneiderman, C. K., West, A. N., & Corson, J. A. (1986). Measurement of combat exposure, posttraumatic stress disorder, and life stress among Vietnam combat veterans. *American Journal of Psychiatry, 143,* 537–539.

Friedman, S., Paully, G. S., & Rosenblum, L. A. (in press). A non-human primate model of panic disorder. *Psychiatry Research.*

Frohlich, E. D., Tarazi, R. C., & Duston, H. P. (1969). Hyperdynamic beta-adrenergic circulatory state. *Archives of Internal Medicine, 123,* 1–7.

Frost, R. O., Sher, K. J., & Geen, T. (1986). Psychotherapy and personality characteristics of non-clinical compulsive checkers. *Behaviour Research and Therapy, 24,* 133–143.

Fry, W. F. (1962). The marital context of an anxiety syndrome. *Family Process, 1,* 245–252.

Frye, J. S., & Stockton, R. A. (1982). Discriminant analysis of post-traumatic stress disorder among a group of Vietnam veterans. *American Journal of Psychiatry, 139,* 52–56.

Fuller, J. L., & Thompson, W. R. (1978). *Foundations of behavior genetics.* St. Louis: C. V. Mosby.

Fyer, A., Liebowitz, M., Gorman, J., Compeas, R., Levin, A., Davies, S., Goetz, D., & Klein, D. (1987). Discontinuation of alprazolam treatment in panic patients. *American Journal of Psychiatry, 144,* 303–308.

Fyer, A., Liebowitz, M. R., Gorman, J., Davies, S. O., & Klein, D. F. (1983). Sodium lactate reinfusion of recovered lactate-vulnerable panic-disorder patients. *Psychopharmacology Bulletin, 19,* 576–577.

Fyer, M. R., Uy, J., Martinez, J., Goetz, R., Klein, D. F., Liebowitz, M. R., Fyer, A. J., & Gorman, J. (1986, May). *Carbon dioxide challenge of patients with panic disorder.* Paper presented at the annual convention of the American Psychiatric Association, Washington, DC.

Gallers, J., Foy, D. W., Donahoe, C. P., & Goldfarb, J. (in press). Combat-related posttraumatic stress disorder: An empirical investigation of traumatic violence exposure. *Journal of Traumatic Stress Disorder.*

Gallup, G. G., Jr. (1974). Animal hypnosis: Factual status of a fictional concept. *Psychological Bulletin, 81,* 836–853.

Garakani, H., Zitrin, C. M., & Klein, D. F. (1984). Treatment of panic disorder with imipramine alone. *American Journal of Psychiatry, 141,* 446–448.

Garcia, J., McGowan, B. K., & Green, K. F. (1972). Biological constraints on conditioning. In A. H. Black & W. F. Prokasy (Eds.), *Classical conditioning II: Current research and theory.* New York: Appleton-Century-Crofts.

Garfield, S. L., Gershon, S., Sletten, I., Sundland, D. W., & Ballows, S. (1967). Chemically induced anxiety. *International Journal of Neuropsychiatry, 3,* 426–433.

Garssen, B., vanVeenendaal, W., & Bloemink, R. (1983). Agoraphobia and the hyperventilation syndrome. *Behaviour Research and Therapy, 21,* 643–649.

Geer, J. H., Davison, G. C., & Gatchel, R. I. (1970). Reduction of stress in humans through nonveridical perceived control of averse stimulation. *Journal of Personality and Social Psychology, 16,* 731–738.

Geer, J. H., & Fuhr, R. (1976). Cognitive factors in sexual arousal: The role of distraction. *Journal of Consulting and Clinical Psychology, 44,* 238–243.

Gelder, M. G. (1986). Panic attacks: New approaches to an old problem. *British Journal of Psychiatry, 149,* 346–352.

Gelder, M. G., & Marks, I. M. (1966). Severe agoraphobia: A controlled prospective trial of behaviour therapy. *British Journal of Psychiatry, 112,* 309–319.

Gelder, M. G., & Marks, I. M. (1968). Desensitization and phobias: A crossover study. *British Journal of Psychiatry, 114,* 323–328.

Gelder, M. G., Marks, I. M., & Wolff, H. H. (1967). Desensitization and psychotherapy in the treatment of phobic states: A controlled inquiry. *British Journal of Psychiatry, 113,* 53–73.

Geller, I., & Seifter, J. (1960). The effects of meprobamate, barbituates, d-amphetamine and promazine on experimentally induced conflict in the rat. *Psychopharmacologia, 1,* 482–492.

Gentil, M. L. F., & Lader, M. (1978). Dream content and daytime attitudes in anxious and calm women. *Psychological Bulletin, 8,* 297–304.

Gershon, E. S., Targum, S. D., Matthysse, S., & Bunney, W. E. (1983). Current status of genetic research in affective disorders. In J. Angst (Ed.), *The origins of depression: Current concepts and approaches.* Berlin: Springer-Verlag.

Ghosh, A., & Marks, I. M. (1987). Self-treatment of agoraphobia by exposure. *Behavior Therapy, 18,* 3–16.

Ghosh, A., Marks, I. M., & Carr, A. C. (1984). Self-exposure treatment for phobias: A controlled study. *Journal of the Royal Society of Medicine, 77,* 483–487.

Gillian, P., & Rachman, S. (1974). An experimental investigation of desensitization in phobic patients. *British Journal of Psychiatry, 124,* 392–401.

Gilligan, S. G., & Bower, G. H. (1984). Cognitive consequences of emotional arousal. In C. E. Izard, J. Kagan, & R. B. Zajonc (Eds.), *Emotions, cognition, and behavior.* New York: Cambridge University Press.

Gitlan, B., Martin, M., Shear, K., Frances, A., Ball, G., & Josephson, S. (1985). Behavior therapy for panic disorder. *Journal of Nervous and Mental Disease, 173,* 742–743.

Gittelman, R., & Klein, D. F. (1985). Childhood separation anxiety and adult agoraphobia. In A. H. Tuma & J. D. Maser (Eds.), *Anxiety and the anxiety disorders.* Hillsdale, NJ: Erlbaum.

Gittelman, R., Shatin, L., Birenbaum, M., Fleischman, A. I., & Hayton, T. (1968). Effects of quantified stressful stimuli on blood lipids in man. *Journal of Nervous and Mental Disease, 147,* 196–201.

Gittelman-Klein, R. (1975). Psychiatric characteristics of the relatives of school phobic children. In D. Siv-Sankar (Ed.), *Mental health in children* (Vol. 1). New York: P. J. D.

Gittelman-Klein, R., & Klein, D. F. (1973). School phobia: Diagnostic considerations in the light of imipramine effects. *Journal of Nervous and Mental Disease, 156,* 199–215.

Gittelson, N. (1966a). The effect of obsessions on depressive psychosis. *British Journal of Psychiatry, 112,* 253–259.

Gittelson, N. (1966b). The fate of obsessions in depressive psychosis. *British Journal of Psychiatry, 112,* 705–708.

Glass, C. R., Merluzzi, T. V., Biever, J. L., & Larsen, K. H. (1982). Cognitive assessment of social anxiety: Development and validation of a self-statement questionnaire. *Cognitive Therapy and Research, 6,* 37–55.

Goldberg, H. L., & Finnerty, R. (1982). Comparison of buspirone in two separate studies. *Journal of Clinical Psychiatry, 43,* 87–91.

Goldfried, M. R. (1986). Self-control skills for the treatment of anxiety disorders. In B. F. Shaw, Z. V. Segal, T. M. Vallis, & F. E. Cashman (Eds.), *Anxiety disorders: Psychological and biological perspectives.* New York: Plenum Press.

Goldfried, M. R., Decenteceo, E. T., & Weinberg, L. (1974). Systematic rational restructuring as a self-control technique. *Behavior Therapy, 5,* 247–254.

Goldstein, A. J. (1970). Case conference: Some aspects of agoraphobia. *Journal of Behavior Therapy and Experimental Psychiatry, 1,* 305–313.

Goldstein, A. J., & Chambless, D. L. (1978). A reanalysis of agoraphobia. *Behavior Therapy, 9,* 47–59.

Goldstein, I. B. (1964). Physiological responses in anxious women patients: A study of autonomic activity and muscle tension. *Archives of General Psychiatry, 10,* 382–388.

Good, B. J., & Kleinman, A. M. (1985). Culture and anxiety: Cross-cultural evidence for the patterning of anxiety disorders. In A. H. Tuma & J. D. Maser (Eds.), *Anxiety and the anxiety disorders.* Hillsdale, NJ: Erlbaum.

Gorman, J. M., Askanazi, J., Liebowitz, M. R., Fyer, A. J., Stein, J., Kinney, J. M., & Klein, D. F. (1984). Response to hyperventilation in a group of patients with panic disorder. *American Journal of Psychiatry, 141,* 857–861.

Gorman, J. M., Cohen, B. S., Liebowitz, M. R., Fyer, A. J., Ross, D., Davies S. D., & Klein, D. F. (1986). Blood gas changes and hypophosphatemia in lactate-induced panic. *Archives of General Psychiatry, 43,* 1067–1071.

Gorman, J. M., Fyer, A. F., Gliklich, J., King, D., & Klein, D. F. (1981). Effect of imipramine on prolapsed mitral valves of patients with panic disorder. *American Journal of Psychiatry, 138,* 977–978.

Gorman, J. M., & Klein, D. F. (1985). In reply to effect of acute β-adrenergic blockade on lactate-induced panic. *Archives of General Psychiatry, 42,* 104–105.

Gorman, J. M., Levy, G. F., Liebowitz, M. R., McGrath, P., Appleby, I. L., Dillon, D. J., Davies, J. O., & Klein, D. F. (1983). Effect of acute β-adrenergic blockade on lactate-induced panic. *Archives of General Psychiatry, 40,* 1079–1082.

Gorman, J. M., Liebowitz, M. R., Fyer, A. J., Dillon, D., Davies, S. O., Stein, J. & Klein, D. F. (1985). Lactate infusions in obsessive–compulsive disorder. *American Journal of Psychiatry, 142,* 864–860.

Gorman, M. R., Liebowitz, J. M., Gorman, J. M., Fyer, A., Dillon, D., Levitt, M., & Klein, D. F. (1986). Possible mechanisms for lactate's induction of panic. *American Journal of Psychiatry, 143,* 495–502.

Graham, D. J., Kabler, J. D., & Lunsford, L. (1961). Vasovagal fainting: a diphasic response. *Psychosomatic Medicine, 23,* 493–507.

Gray, J. A. (1971). *The psychology of fear and stress.* London: Weidenfeld & Nicholson.

Gray, J. A. (1977). Drug effects on fear and frustration: Possible limbic site of action of minor tranquilizers. In L. L. Iversen, S. D. Iversen, & S. H. Snyder (Eds.), *Handbook of psychopharmacology 8: Drugs, neurotransmitters and behavior*. New York: Plenum.

Gray, J. A. (1982). *The neuropsychology of anxiety*. New York: Oxford University Press.

Gray, J. A. (1985). Issues in the neuropsychology of anxiety. In A. H. Tuma & J. D. Maser (Eds.), *Anxiety and the anxiety disorders*. Hillsdale, NJ: Erlbaum.

Grayson, J. B., Foa, E. B., & Steketee, G. (1982). Habituation during exposure treatment: Distraction versus attention-focusing. *Behaviour Research and Therapy, 20*, 323–328.

Grayson, J. B., Nutter, P., & Mavissakalian, M. (1980). Psychophysiological assessment of imagery in obsessive–compulsives: A pilot study. *Behaviour Research and Therapy, 18*, 590–593.

Green, B. L., Grace, M. C., Lindy, J. D., Titchener, J. L., & Lindy, J. G. (1983). Levels of functional impairment following a civilian disaster: The Beverly Hills Supper Club fire. *Journal of Consulting and Clinical Psychology, 51*, 573–580.

Green, B. L., Lindy, J. D., & Grace, M. C. (1985). Posttraumatic stress disorder—toward DSM-IV. *Journal of Nervous and Mental Disease, 173*, 406–411.

Greenberg, L. S., & Safran, J. D. (1987). *Emotion in psychotherapy*. New York: Guilford Press.

Greenblatt, D. J., & Shader, R. I. (1978). Pharmacotherapy of anxiety with benzodiazepines and beta-adrenergic blockers. In M. Lipton, A. DiMascio, & F. Killiam (Eds.), *Psychopharmacology: A generation of progress*. New York: Raven Press.

Greist, J. H., Marks, I. M., Berlin, F., Gourney, K., & Noshirvani, H. (1980). Avoidance versus confrontation of fear. *Behavior Therapy, 11*, 1–14.

Grey, S., Rachman, S., & Sartory, G. (1981). Return of fear: The role of inhibition. *Behaviour Research and Therapy, 19*, 135–143.

Grey, S., Sartory, G., & Rachman, S. (1979). Synchronous and desynchronous changes during fear reduction. *Behaviour Research and Therapy, 10*, 124–133.

Griez, E., & van den Hout, M. A. (1983). Treatment of phobophobia by exposure to CO_2 induced symptoms. *Journal of Nervous and Mental Disease, 171*, 506–508.

Griez, E., & van den Hout, M. A. (1986). CO_2 inhalation in the treatment of panic attacks. *Behaviour Research and Therapy, 24*, 145–150.

Grinker, R. R., & Spiegel, J. P. (1943). *War neurosis in North Africa, the Tunisian campaign, January to May 1943*. New York: Josiah Macy Foundation.

Grinker, R. R., & Spiegel, J. P. (1945). *Men under stress*. Philadelphia: Blackston.

Grosz, H. J., & Farmer, B. B. (1969). Blood lactate in the development of anxiety symptoms: A critical examination of Pitts and McClure's hypothesis and experimental study. *Archives of General Psychiatry, 21*, 611–619.

Grosz, H. J., & Farmer, B. B. (1972). Pitts and McClure's lactate anxiety study revised. *British Journal of Psychiatry, 120*, 415–418.

Groves, P. M., & Lynch, G. S. (1972). Mechanisms of habituation in the brain stem. *Psychological Review, 79*, 237–244.

Groves, P. M., & Thompson, R. F. (1970). Habituation: A dual process theory. *Psychological Review, 77*, 429–450.

Grunhaus, L., Gloger, S., Rein, A., & Lewis, B. S. (1982). Mitral valve prolapse and panic attacks. *Israel Journal of Medical Sciences, 18*, 221–223.

Gullick, E. L., & Blanchard, E. B. (1973). The use of psychotherapy and behavior therapy in the treatment of an obsessional patient by reciprocal inhibition. *Journal of Nervous and Mental Disease, 156*, 427–431.

Guttmacher, L. B., & Nelles, C. (1984). In vivo desensitization alteration of lactate-induced panic: A case study. *Behavior Therapy, 15*, 369–372.

Hafner, R. J. (1976). Fresh symptom emergence after intensive behavior therapy. *British Journal of Psychiatry, 129*, 378–383.

Hafner, R. J. (1977). The husbands of agoraphobic women: Assortative mating or pathogenic interaction? *British Journal of Psychiatry, 130*, 233–239.

Hafner, R. J. (1979). Agoraphobic women married to abnormally jealous men. *British Journal of Medical Psychology, 52*, 99–104.

Hafner, R. J. (1983). Behaviour therapy for agoraphobic men. *Behaviour Research and Therapy, 21*, 51–56.

Hafner, R. J., & Marks, I. M. (1976). Exposure in vivo of agoraphobics: Contributions of diazepam, group exposure and anxiety evocation. *Psychological Medicine, 6*, 71–88.

Hafner, R. J., & Milton, F. (1977). The influence of propranolol on the exposure in vivo of agoraphobics. *Psychological Medicine, 7*, 419–425.

Hafner, R. J., & Ross, M. M. (1983). Predicting the outcome of behaviour therapy for agoraphobia. *Behaviour Research and Therapy, 21*, 375–382.

Haggard, E. (1943). Some conditions determining adjustment during and readjustment following experimentally induced stress. In S. Tomkins (Ed.), *Contemporary psychopathology*. Cambridge, MA: Harvard University Press.

Hall, R. C. W. (Ed.). (1980). *Anxiety in psychiatric presentation of medical illness: Somato-psychic disorders*. New York: SP Medical & Scientific Books.

Hallam, R. S. (1978). Agoraphobia: A critical review of the concept. *British Journal of Psychiatry, 133*, 314–319.

Hallam, R. S. (1985). *Anxiety: Psychological perspectives on panic and agoraphobia*. New York: Academic Press.

Hallstrom, C., Treasaden, I., Edwards, J., & Lader, M. (1981). Diazepam, propranolol, and their combination in the management of chronic anxiety. *Archives of General Psychiatry, 41*, 741–750.

Hamilton, M. (1959). The assessment of anxiety states by rating. *British Journal of Medical Psychology, 32*, 50–55.

Hamilton, M. (1960). A rating scale for depression. *Journal of Neurology, Neurosurgery and Psychiatry, 23*, 56–62.

Hammen, C., Mayol, A., deMayo, R., & Marks, I. (1986). Initial symptom levels and the life-event–depression relationship. *Journal of Abornmal Psychology, 95*, 114–122.

Hand, I., & Lamontagne, Y. (1976). The exacerbation of interpersonal problems after rapid phobia-removal. *Psychotherapy: Theory, Research, and Practice, 13*, 405–411.

Hand, I., Lamontagne, Y., & Marks, J. M. (1974). Group exposure (flooding) in vivo for agoraphobics. *British Journal of Psychiatry, 124*, 588–602.

Harris, E. L., Noyes, R., Crowe, R. R., & Chaudhry, D. R. (1983). Family study of agoraphobia. *Archives of General Psychiatry, 40*, 1061–1064.

Harrison, B. J. (1985). *Anxiety provoked ideation in phobic and nonphobic panickers*. Unpublished bachelor of arts (honors) thesis, University of Winnipeg.

Hartmann, N., Kramer, R., Brown, W. T., & Devereux, R. B. (1982). Panic disorder in patients with mitral valve prolapse. *American Journal of Psychiatry, 139*, 669–670.

Haslam, M. T. (1974). The relationship between the effect of lactate infusion on anxiety states and their amelioration by carbon dioxide inhalation. *British Journal of Psychiatry, 125*, 88–90.

Hauri, P., Friedman, M., Ravaris, R., & Fisher, J. (1985). Sleep in agoraphobia with panic attacks. In M. H. Chafe, D. J. McGinty, & R. Wilder-Jones (Eds.), *Sleep research*. Los Angeles: BIS/BRS.

Heide, F. J., & Borkovec, T. D. (1983). Relaxation-induced anxiety: Paradoxical anxiety enhancement due to relaxation training. *Journal of Consulting and Clinical Psychology, 51*, 171–182.

Heide, F. J. & Borkovec, T. D. (1984). Relaxation-induced anxiety: Mechanisms and theoretical implications. *Behaviour Research and Therapy, 22*, 1–12.

Heimberg, R. G., Becker, R. E., Goldfinger, K., & Vermilyea, J. A. (1985). Treatment of social phobia by exposure, cognitive restructuring and homework assignments. *Journal of Nervous and Mental Disease, 173*, 236–245.

Heimberg, R. G., Dodge, C. S., & Becker, R. E. (1987). Social phobia. In L. Michelson & M.

Ascher (Eds.), *Cognitive behavioral assessment and treatment of anxiety disorders.* New York: Plenum Press.

Heimberg, R. G., Dodge, C. S., Hope, D. A., Kennedy, C. R., Zollo, L., & Becker, R. E. (1988). *Cognitive behavioral group treatment for social phobia: Comparison to a credible placebo control.* Manuscript submitted for publication.

Heimberg, R. G., Hope, D. A., Dodge, C. S., & Becker, R. E. (1987). *DSM-III-R subtypes of social phobia: Comparison of generalized social phobics and public speaking phobics.* Unpublished manuscript.

Heimberg, R. G., Vermilyea, J. A., Dodge, C. S., Becker, R. E., & Barlow, D. H. (1987). Attributional style, depression, and anxiety: An evaluation of the specificity of depressive attributions. *Cognitive Therapy and Research, 11,* 537–550.

Helzer, J. E., Robins, L. N., & McEvoy, L. (1987). Posttraumatic stress disorder in the general population: Findings from the Epidemiologic Catchment Area survey. *New England Journal of Medicine, 317,* 1630–1634.

Hershberg. S., Carlson, G. A., Cantwell, D., & Strober, M. (1982). Anxiety and depressive disorders in psychiatrically disturbed children. *Journal of Clinical Psychiatry, 43,* 358–361.

Hibbert, G. A. (1984). Ideational components of anxiety: Their origin and content. *British Journal of Psychiatry, 144,* 618–624.

Himadi, W. G., Boice, R., & Barlow, D. H. (1986). Assessment of agoraphobia II: Measurement of clinical change. *Behaviour Research and Therapy, 24,* 321–332.

Himadi, W. G., Cerny, J. A., Barlow, D. H., Cohen, S. L., & O'Brien, G. T. (1986). The relationship of marital adjustment to agoraphobia treatment outcome. *Behaviour Research and Therapy, 24,* 107–115.

Hodgson, R. J., & Rachman, S. (1977). Obsessional–compulsive complaints. *Behaviour Research and Therapy, 15,* 389–395.

Hoehn-Saric, R. (1981). Characteristics of chronic anxiety patients. In D. F. Klein & J.G. Rabkin (Eds.), *Anxiety: New research and changing concepts.* New York: Raven Press.

Hoehn-Saric, R. (1982). Neurotransmitters in anxiety. *Archives of General Psychiatry, 39,* 735–742.

Hoehn-Saric, R., Merchant, A., Keyser, M., & Smith, V. (1981). Effects of clonidine on anxiety disorder. *Archives of General Psychiatry, 38,* 1278–1282.

Hogben, G. L., & Cornfield, R. B. (1981). Treatment of traumatic war neurosis with phenelzine. *Archives of General Psychiatry, 38,* 440–445.

Holden, A. E., & Barlow, D. H. (1986). Heart rate and heart rate variability recorded in vivo in agoraphobics and nonphobics. *Behavior Therapy, 17,* 26–42.

Holden, A. E., O'Brien, G. T., Barlow, D. H., Stetson, D., & Infantino, A. (1983). Self-help manual for agoraphobia: A preliminary report of effectiveness. *Behavior Therapy, 14,* 545–556.

Hollandsworth, J. G., Jr. (1986). *Physiology and behavior therapy: Conceptual guidelines for the clinician.* New York: Plenum Press.

Holmberg, G., & Gershon, S. (1961). Autonomic and psychiatric effects of yohimbine hydrochloride. *Psychopharmacologia, 2,* 93–106.

Holmes, M.R., & St. Lawrence, J. S. (1983). Treatment of rape-induced trauma: Proposed behavioral concepualization and review of the literature. *Clinical Psychology Review, 3,* 417–433.

Holmgren, A., & Strom, G. (1959). Blood lactate concentration in relation to absolute and relative work load in normal men, and in mitral stenosis, atrial septal defect and vasoregulatory asthenia. *Acta Medica Scandinavica, 163,* 185–193.

Holroyd, K. A., Penzien, D. B., Hursey, K. G., Tobin, D. L., Rogers, L., Holm, J. E., Marcille, P. J., Hall, J. R., & Chila, A. G. (1984). Change mechanisms in EMG biofeedback training: Cognitive changes underlying improvements in tension headache. *Journal of Consulting and Clinical Psychology, 52,* 1039–1053.

REFERENCES

Holt, L., & Gray, J. A. (1983). Septal driving of the hippocampal theta rhythm produces a long term, proactive and nonassociative increase in resistance to extinction. *Quarterly Journal of Experimental Psychology, 35B,* 97–118.

Hoon, P., Wincze, J., & Hoone, E. (1977). A test of reciprocal inhibition: Are anxiety and sexual arousal in women mutually inhibitory? *Journal of Abnormal Psychology, 86,* 65–74.

Hoover, C. F., & Insel, T. R. (1984). Families of origin in obsessive–compulsive disorder. *Journal of Nervous and Mental Disease, 172,* 207–215.

Horowitz, M. (1975). Intrusive and repetitive thoughts after experimental stress. *Archives of General Psychiatry, 32,* 1457–1463.

Horowitz, M. (1986). *Stress response syndromes* (2nd ed.) New York: Jason Aronson.

Horowitz, M., Krupnick, J., Kaltreider, N., Wilner, N., Leong, A., & Marmar, C. (1981). Initial psychological response to parental death. *Archives of General Psychiatry, 38,* 316–323.

Hudson, B. (1974). The families of agoraphobics treated by behaviour therapy. *British Journal of Social Work, 4,* 51–59.

Hudson, C. J. (1981). Agoraphobia in Alaskan Eskimos. *New York State Journal of Medicine, 81,* 224–225.

Huey, S. R., & West, S. G. (1983). Hyperventilation: Its relation to symptom experience and to anxiety. *Journal of Abnormal Psychology, 92,* 422–432.

Hull, J. G., & Young, R. D. (1983). Self-consciousness, self-esteem, and success–failure as determinants of alcohol consumption in male social drinkers. *Journal of Personality and Social Psychology, 44,* 1097–1109.

Hulse, S. H., Fowler, H., & Honig, W. K. (1978). *Cognitive processes in animal behavior.* Hillsdale, NJ: Erlbaum.

Hume, W. I. (1973). Physiological measures in twins. In G. Claridge, S. Canter, & W. I. Hume (Eds.), *Personality differences and biological variations: A study of twins.* Oxford: Pergamon Press.

Hutchings, D. F., Denney, D. R., Basgall, J., & Houston, B. K. (1980). Anxiety management and applied relaxation in reducing general anxiety. *Behaviour Research and Therapy, 18,* 181–190.

Ingram, R. E. (1986). *Vulnerability to dysfunctional cognition in chronic self-consciousness.* Manuscript submitted for publication.

Ingram, R. E., & Smith, T. W. (1984). Depression and internal versus external focus of attention. *Cognitive Therapy and Research, 8,* 139–152.

Inkeles, A. (1983). *Exploring individual modernity.* New York: Columbia University Press.

⚹ Insel, T. R. (Ed.). (1984). *New findings in obsessive–compulsive disorder.* Washington, DC: American Psychiatric Press.

⚹ Insel, T. R. (1986). The neurobiology of anxiety: A tale of two systems. In B. F. Shaw, Z. V. Segal, T. M. Vallis, & F. E. Cashman (Eds.), *Anxiety disorders: Psychological and biological perspectives.* New York: Plenum Press.

⚹ Insel, T. R., & Akiskal, H. S. (1986). Obsessive–compulsive disorder with psychotic features: A phenomenology analysis. *American Journal of Psychiatry, 143,* 1527–1533.

Insel, T. R., Champoux, M., Scanlan, J. M., & Suomi, S. J. (1986, May). *Rearing condition and response to anxiogenic drug.* Paper presented at the annual meeting of the American Psychiatric Association, Washington, DC.

Insel, T. R., Gillin, J. C., Moore, A., Mendelson, W. B., Loewenstein, R. J., & Murphy, D. L. (1982). Sleep in obsessive–compulsive disorder. *Archives of General Psychiatry, 39,* 1372–1377.

Insel, T. R., Kalin, N. H., Guttmacher, L. B., Cohen, R. M., & Murphy, D. L. (1982). The dexamethasone suppression test in patients with primary obsessive–compulsive disorder. *Psychiatry Research, 6,* 153–160.

Insel, T. R., & Mueller, E. A. (1984). The psychopharmacologic treatment of obsessive–

compulsive disorder. In T. R. Insel (Ed.), *New findings in obsessive–compulsive disorder.* Washington, DC: American Psychiatric Press.

Insel, T. R., Murphy, D. L., Cohen, R. M., Alterman, I., Kilts, C., & Linnoila, M. (1983). Obsessive–compulsive disorder: A double blind trial of clomipramine and clorgyline. *Archives of General Psychiatry, 40,* 605–612.

Insel, T. R., Ninan, P., Aloi, J., Jimerson, D., Skolnick, P., & Paul, S. M. (1984). A benzodiazepine receptor mediated model of anxiety: Studies in nonhuman primates and clinical implications. *Archives of General Psychiatry, 41,* 741–750.

Insel, T. R., Zahn, T., & Murphy, D. L. (1985). Obsessive–compulsive disorder: An anxiety disorder? In A. H. Tuma & J. D. Maser (Eds.), *Anxiety and the anxiety disorders.* Hillsdale, NJ: Erlbaum.

Izard, C. E. (Ed.). (1971). *The face of emotion.* New York: Appleton-Century-Crofts.

Izard, C. E. (Ed.). (1972). *Patterns of emotion: A new analysis of anxiety and depression.* New York: Academic Press.

Izard, C. E. (Ed.). (1977). *Human emotions.* New York: Plenum Press.

Izard, C. E., & Blumberg, M. A. (1985). Emotion theory and the role of emotions in anxiety in children and adults. In A. H. Tuma & J. D. Maser (Eds.), *Anxiety and the anxiety disorders.* Hillsdale, NJ: Erlbaum.

Izard, C. E., Kagan, J., & Zajonc, R. B. (Eds.). (1984). *Emotions, cognition, and behavior.* New York: Cambridge University Press.

Jablensky, A. (1985). Approaches to the definition and classification of anxiety and related disorders in European psychiatry. In A. H. Tuma & J. D. Maser (Eds.), *Anxiety and the anxiety disorders.* Hillsdale, NJ: Erlbaum.

Jacob, R. G., Moller, M. B., Turner, S. M., & Wall, C. L. O., III. (1985). Otoneurological examination in panic disorder and agoraphobia with panic attacks: A pilot study. *American Journal of Psychiatry, 142,* 715–720.

Jacobson, R., & Edinger, J. D. (1982). Side effects of relaxation treatment. *American Journal of Psychiatry, 139,* 952–953.

James, I. M., Burgoyne, W., & Savage, I. T. (1983). Effect of pindilol on stress-related disturbances of musical performance: Preliminary communication. *Journal of the Royal Society of Medicine, 76,* 194–196.

James, I. M., Griffith, D. N. W., Pearson, R. M., & Newby, P. (1977). Effect of oxprenolol on stage-fright in musicians. *Lancet, ii,* 952–954.

James, W. (1890). *The principles of psychology.* New York: Holt.

Jannoun, L., Munby, M., Catalan, J., & Gelder, M. (1980). A home-based treatment program for agoraphobia: Replication and controlled evaluation. *Behavior Therapy, 11,* 294–305.

Jannoun, L., Oppenheimer, C., & Gelder, M. (1982). A self-help treatment program for anxiety state patients. *Behavior Therapy, 13,* 103–111.

Jansson, L., Jerremalm, A., & Öst, L. G. (1986). Follow-up of agoraphobic patients treated with exposure in-vivo or applied relaxation. *British Journal of Psychiatry, 149,* 486–490.

Jansson, L., & Öst, L. G. (1982). Behavioral treatments for agoraphobia: An evaluative review. *Clinical Psychology Review, 2,* 311–336.

Jansson, L., Öst, L. G., & Jerremalm, A. (1987). Prognostic factors in the behavioural treatment of agoraphobia. *Behavioural Psychotherapy, 15,* 31–44.

Jaspers, K. (1963). *General psychopathology* (J. Hoenig & M. W. Hamilton, Trans.). Manchester, England: Manchester University Press. (Original work published 1959)

Jenike, M. A. (1981). Rapid response of severe obsessive compulsive disorder to tranylcypromine. *American Journal of Psychiatry, 138,* 1249–1251.

Jenike, M. A., Baer, L., & Minichiello, W. E. (Eds.). (1986). *Obsessive–compulsive disorders: Theory and management.* Littleton, MA: PSG.

Jerremalm, A., Jansson, L., & Öst, L. G. (1986). Individual response patterns and the effects

659

of different behavioural methods in the treatment of dental phobia. *Behaviour Research and Therapy, 24,* 587–596.

Johnson, J. H., & Sarason, I. G. (1978). Life stress, depression and anxiety: Internal–external control as a moderator variable. *Journal of Psychosomatic Research, 22,* 205–208.

Johnston, D., & Gath, D. (1973). Arousal levels and attribution effects in diazepam-assisted flooding. *British Journal of Psychiatry, 123,* 463–466.

Johnstone, E. C., Bourne, R. C., Crow, T. J., Frith, C. D., Gamble, S., Lofthouse, R., Owen, F., Owens, D. G. C., Robinson, J., & Stevens, M. (1981). The relationship between clinical response, psychophysiological variables and plasma levels of amitriptyline and diazepam in neurotic outpatients. *Psychopharmacology, 72,* 233–240.

Jones, J. C., Bruce, T. J., & Barlow, D. H. (1986, November). *The effects of four levels of "anxiety" on sexual arousal in sexually functional and dysfunctional men.* Poster presented at the annual convention of the Association for Advancement of Behavior Therapy, Chicago.

Jones, M., & Mellersh, V. (1946). Comparison of exercise response in anxiety states and normal controls. *Psychosomatic Medicine, 8,* 180–187.

Kahn, J. P., Stevenson, E., Topol, P., & Klein, D. (1986). Agitated depression, alprazolam, and panic anxiety. *American Journal of Psychiatry, 143,* 1172–1173.

Kahn, R. J., McNair, D. M., Lipman, R. S., Covi, L., Rickels, K., Downing, R., Fisher, S., & Frankenthaler, L. M. (1986). Imipramine and clordiazepoxide in depressive and anxiety disorders. *Archives of General Psychiatry, 43,* 79–85.

Kahneman, D. (1973). *Attention and effort.* Englewood Cliffs, NJ: Prentice-Hall.

Kandel, E. R. (1983). From metapsychology to molecular biology: Explorations into the nature of anxiety. *American Journal of Psychiatry, 140,* 1277–1293.

Kantor, J. S., Zitrin, C. M., & Zeldis, S. M. (1980). Mitral valve prolapse syndrome in agoraphobia patients. *American Journal of Psychiatry, 137,* 467–469.

Kaplan, H. S. (1974). *The new sex therapy.* New York: Brunner/Mazel.

Katon, W., Vitaliano, P. P., Russo, J., Jones, M., & Anderson, K. (1987). Panic disorder: Spectrum of severity and somatization. *Journal of Nervous and Mental Disease, 175,* 12–19.

Keane, T. M., Caddell, J. M., & Taylor, K. L. (1986). *The Mississippi scale for combat-related PTSD: Studies in reliability and validity.* Unpublished manuscript.

Keane, T. M., Fairbank, J. A., Caddell, J. M., Zimering, R. T., & Bender, M. E. (1985). A behavioral approach to assessing and treating post-traumatic stress disorder in Vietnam veterans. In C. R. Figley (Ed.), *Trauma and its wake.* New York: Brunner/Mazel.

Keane, T. M., & Kaloupek, D. G. (1982). Imaginal flooding in the treatment of posttraumatic stress disorder. *Journal of Consulting and Clinical Psychology, 50,* 138–140.

Keane, T. M., Malloy, P. F., & Fairbank, J. A. (1984). Empirical development of MMPI subscale for the assessment of combat-related posttraumatic stress disorder in Vietnam veterans. *Journal of Consulting and Clinical Psychology, 51,* 488–494.

Keller, M. B., & Shapiro, R. W. (1982). "Double depression": Superimposition of acute depressive episodes on chronic depressive disorders. *American Journal of Psychiatry, 139,* 438–442.

Kelly, D. H. W. (1966). Measurement of anxiety by forearm blood flow. *British Journal of Psychiatry, 112,* 789–798.

Kelly, P., Mitchel-Heggs, N., & Sherman, D. (1971). Anxiety in the effects of sodium lactate assessed clinically and physiologically. *British Journal of Psychiatry, 119,* 468–470.

Kemali, D., Del Vecchio, M., & Maj, M. (1982). Increased noradrenaline levels in CSF and plasma of schizophrenic patients. *Biological Psychiatry, 17,* 711–717.

Kendall, P. C., & Butcher, J. N. (1982). *Handbook of research methods in clinical psychiatry.* New York: Wiley.

Kendall, R. E. (1975). *The role of diagnosis in psychiatry.* Oxford: Blackwell.

Kendler, K. S., Heath, A. C., Martin, N. G., & Eaves, L. J. (1986). Symptoms of anxiety and depression in a volunteer twin population. *Archives of General Psychiatry, 43,* 213–221.

Kendler, K. S., Heath, A. C., Martin, N. G., & Eaves, L. J. (1987). Symptoms of anxiety and symptoms of depression: Same genes, different environments? *Archives of General Psychiatry, 44,* 451–457.

Kendrick, M. (1979). *Reduction of musical performance anxiety by attentional training and behavioral rehearsal: An exploration of cognitive mediational processes.* Unpublished doctoral dissertation, University of British Columbia.

Kendrick, M., Craig, K. D., Lawson, D., & Davidson, P. (1982). Cognitive and behavioral therapy for music performance anxiety. *Journal of Consulting and Clinical Psychology, 50,* 333–362.

Kennedy, R. (1976). Self-induced depersonalization syndrome. *American Journal of Psychiatry, 133,* 1326–1328.

Kettl, P. A., & Marks, I. M. (1986). Neurological factors in obsessive–compulsive disorder: Two case reports and a review of the literature. *British Journal of Psychiatry, 149,* 315–319.

Kettner, B. (1972). Combat strain and subsequent mental health. *Acta Psychiatrica Scandinavica, 22,* 5–107.

Kety, S. S. (1950). Cerebral circulation and metabolism in health and disease. *American Journal of Medicine, 8,* 205–217.

Kierkegaard, S. (1944). *The concept of dread* (W. Lowrie, Trans.). Princeton, NJ: Princeton University Press. (Original work published 1844)

Kilpatrick, D. G., Best, C. L., Veronen, L. J., Amick, A. E., Villeponteaux, L. A., & Ruff, G. A. (1985). Mental health correlates of criminal victimization: A random community survey. *Journal of Consulting and Clinical Psychology, 53,* 866–873.

Kilpatrick, D. G., Veronen, L. J., & Best, C. L. (1985). Factors predicting psychological distress among rape victims. In C. R. Figley (Ed.), *Trauma and its wake.* New York: Brunner/Mazel.

King, R., Margraf, J., Ehlers, A., & Maddock, R. (1986). Panic disorder—overlap with symptoms of somatization disorder. In I. Hand & H. U. Wittchen (Eds.), *Panic and phobias: Empirical evidence of theoretical models and longterm effects of behavioral treatments..* Berlin: Springer-Verlag.

Kirk, J. W. (1983). Behavioural treatment of obsessive–compulsive patients in routine clinical practice. *Behaviour Research and Therapy, 21,* 57–62.

Klein, D. F. (1964). Delineation of two drug responsive anxiety syndromes. *Psychopharmacologia, 5,* 397–408.

Klein, D. F. (1967). Importance of psychiatric diagnosis in prediction of clinical drug effects. *Archives of General Psychiatry, 16,* 118–126.

Klein, D. F. (1981). Anxiety reconceptualized. In D. F. Klein & J. Rabkin (Eds.), *Anxiety: New research and changing concepts.* New York: Raven Press.

Klein, D. F. (1983). Reply to panic attacks in phobia treatment studies. *Archives of General Psychiatry, 40,* 1151–1152.

Klein, D. F., & Fink, M. (1962). Psychiatric reaction patterns to imipramine. *American Journal of Psychiatry, 119,* 438.

Klein, D. F., Rabkin, J. G., & Gorman, J. M. (1985). Etiological and pathophysiological inferences from the pharmacological treatment of anxiety. In A. H. Tuma & J. D. Maser (Eds.), *Anxiety and the anxiety disorders.* Hillsdale, NJ: Erlbaum.

Klein, D. F., Zitrin, C. M., Woerner, M. G., & Ross, D. C., II. (1983). Behavior therapy and supportive psychotherapy: Are there any specific ingredients? *Archives of General Psychiatry, 40,* 139–153.

Kleiner, L., & Marshall, W. L. (1985). Relationship difficulties and agoraphobia. *Clinical Psychology Review, 5,* 581–595.

Kleiner, L., Marshall, W. L., & Spevak, M. (1987). Training in problem solving and exposure treatment for agoraphobics with panic attacks. *Journal of Anxiety Disorders, 1,* 219–238.

Klerman, G. L. (1980). Anxiety and depression. In G. D. Burrows & B. Davies (Eds.), *Handbook of studies on anxiety*. Amsterdam: North-Holland.

Klerman, G. L., & Weissman, M. M. (1982). Interpersonal psychotherapy: Theory and research. In A. J. Rush (Ed.), *Short-term psychotherapies for depression*. New York: Guilford Press.

Klonoff, E. A., Polefrone, J. M., Dambrocia, J. P., & Nochomovitz, M. L. (1986). *Treatment of panic attacks associated with chronic obstructive pulmonary disease (COPD)*. Paper presented at the annual meeting of the Association for Advancement of Behavior Therapy, Chicago.

Klorman, R. (1974). Habituation of fear: Effects of intensity and stimulus order. *Psychophysiology, 11*, 15–26.

Klosko, J. S. (1987). *A comparison of alprazolam and cognitive behavior therapy in the treatment of panic disorder*. Unpublished doctoral dissertation, State University of New York at Albany.

Klosko, J. S., & Barlow, D. H. (1987). *The treatment of panic in panic disorder and agoraphobia: A clinical replication*. Unpublished manuscript.

Klosko, J. S., & Barlow, D. H., Tassinari, R. B., & Cerny, J. A. (1988). Comparison of alprazolam and cognitive behavior therapy in the treatment of panic disorder: A preliminary report. In I. Hand & H. U. Wittchen (Eds.), *Treatments of panic and phobias: Modes of application and variables affecting outcome*. Berlin: Springer-Verlag.

Kluznick, J. C., Speed, N., VanValkenberg, C., & Magraw, R. (1986). Forty-year follow-up of United States prisoners of war. *American Journal of Psychiatry, 143*, 1443–1446.

Ko, G. N., Elsworth, J. D., Roth, R. H., Rifkin, B. G., Leigh, H., & Redmond, E. (1983). Panic induced elevation of plasma MHPG levels in phobic-anxious patients: Effects of clonidine and imipramine. *Archives of General Psychiatry, 40*, 424–430.

Koenigsberg, H. W., Kaplan, R. D., Gilmore, M. M., & Cooper, A. M. (1985). The relationship between syndrome and personality disorder in DSM III: Experience with 2,462 patients. *American Journal of Psychiatry, 142*, 207–212.

Kolb, L. C. (1987). Neuropsychological hypothesis explaining posttraumatic stress disorder. *American Journal of Psychiatry, 144*, 989–995.

Kolb, L. C., Burris, B. C., & Griffiths, S. (1984). Propranolol and clonidine in treatment of the chronic posttraumatic stress disorders of war. In B. A. VanderKolk (Ed.), *Posttraumatic stress disorder: Psychological and biological sequence*. Washington, DC: American Psychiatric Press.

Kopin, I. (1984). Avenues of investigation for the role of catecholamines in anxiety. *Psychopathology, 17*, 83–97.

Korchin, S. (1964). Anxiety and cognition. In C. Scheerer (Ed.), *Cognition: Theory, research, and practice*. New York: Harper & Row.

Koshland, D. E., Jr. (1987). Nature, nurture, and behavior. *Science, 235*, 1445.

Kozak, M. J., & Montgomery, G. K. (1981). Multimodel behavioural treatment of recurrent injury-scene elicited fainting (vasodepressor syncope). *Behavioural Psychotherapy, 9*, 316–321.

Kraepelin, E. (1896). *Psychiatrie: Vol. 5. Auflage*. Leipzig: Barth.

Kraft, A. R., & Hooguin, C. A. L. (1984). The hyperventilation syndrome: A pilot study of the effectiveness of treatment. *British Journal of Psychiatry, 145*, 538–542.

Kuch, K., Swinson, R. P., & Kirby, M. (1985). Posttraumatic stress disorder after car accidents. *Canadian Journal of Psychiatry, 30*, 426–427.

Lader, M. H. (1967). Plamar skin conductance measures in anxiety and phobic states. *Journal of Psychosomatic Research, 11*, 271–281.

Lader, M. H. (1975). *The psychophysiology of mental illness*. London: Routledge & Kegan Paul.

Lader, M. H. (1980a). Psychophysiological studies in anxiety. In G. D. Burrows & D. Davies (Eds.), *Handbook of studies on anxiety*. Amsterdam: Elsevier/North-Holland.

Lader, M. H. (1980b). The psychophysiology of anxiety. In H. van Praag, M. H. Lader, O.

Rafaelsen, & E. Sachar (Eds.), *Handbook of biological psychiatry*. New York: Marcel Dekker.

Lader, M. H. (1985). Benzodiazepines, anxiety, and catecholamines: A commentary. In A. ⚥ H. Tuma & J. D. Maser (Eds.), *Anxiety and the anxiety disorders*. Hillsdale, NJ: Erlbaum.

Lader, M. H., & Mathews, A. (1970). Physiological changes during spontaneous panic attacks. *Journal of Psychosomatic Research, 14,* 377–382.

Lader, M. H., & Wing, L. (1964). Habituation of the psycho-galvanic reflex in patients with anxiety states and in normal subjects. *Journal of Neurology, Neurosurgery, and Psychiatry, 27,* 210–218.

Lader, M. H., & Wing, L. (1966). *Physiological measures, sedative drugs, and morbid anxiety*. London: Oxford University Press.

Ladouceur, R. (1983). Participant modeling with or without cognitive treatment for phobias. *Journal of Consulting and Clinical Psychology, 51,* 942–944.

Lake, C. R., Pickar, D., Ziegler, M. G., Lipper, S., Slater, S., & Murphy, D. L. (1982). High plasma norepinephrine levels in patients with major affective disorder. *American Journal of Psychiatry, 132,* 1315–1318.

Lang, P. J. (1968). Fear reduction and fear behavior: Problems in treating a construct. In J. M. Shlien (Ed.), *Research in psychotherapy* (Vol. 3). Washington, DC: American Psychological Association.

Lang, P. J. (1977a). Imagery in therapy: An information processing analysis of fear. *Behavior Therapy, 8,* 862–886.

Lang, P. J. (1977b). Physiological assessment of anxiety and fear. In J. D. Cone & R. A. Hawkins (Eds.), *Behavioral assessment: New directions in clinical psychology*. New York: Brunner/Mazel.

Lang, P. J. (1978). Anxiety: Toward a psychophysiological definition. In H. S. Akiskal & W. L. Webb (Eds.), *Psychiatric diagnosis: Exploration of biological predictors*. New York: Spectrum.

Lang, P. J. (1979). A bio-informational theory of emotional imagery. *Psychophysiology, 16,* 495–512.

Lang, P. J. (1984). Cognition in emotion: Concept and action. In C. Izard, J. Kagan, & ✳ R. Zajonc (Eds.), *Emotions, cognition, and behavior*. New York: Cambridge University Press.

Lang, P. J. (1985). The cognitive psychophysiology of emotion: Fear and anxiety. In A. H. ✳ Tuma & J. D. Maser (Eds.), *Anxiety and the anxiety disorders*. Hillsdale, NJ: Erlbaum.

Lang, P. J., Levin, D. N., Miller, G. A., & Kozak, M. J. (1983). Fear, behavior, fear imagery, and the psychophysiology of emotion: The problem of affective response integration. *Journal of Abnormal Psychology, 92,* 276–306.

Lansky, D., & Wilson, G. T. (1981). Alcohol, expectations, and sexual arousal in males: An information processing analysis. *Journal of Abnormal Psychology, 90*(1), 35–45.

Last, C. G., Barlow, D. H. & O'Brien, G. T. (1984a). Cognitive changes during in vivo exposure in an agoraphobic. *Behavior Modification, 8,* 93–113.

Last, C. G., Barlow, D. H. & O'Brien, G. T. (1984b). Cognitive change during treatment of agoraphobia: Behavioral and cognitive behavioral approaches. *Behavior Modification, 8,* 181–210.

Last, C. G., Barlow, D. H., & O'Brien, G. T. (1984c). Precipitants of agoraphobia: Role of stressful life events. *Psychological Reports, 54,* 567–570.

Last, C. G., & Blanchard, E. B. (1982). Classification of phobics versus fearful nonphobics: Procedural and theoretical issues. *Behavioral Assessment, 4,* 195–210.

Latimer, L. (1977). Carbon dioxide as a reciprocal inhibitor in the treatment of neurosis. *Journal of Behavior Therapy and Experimental Psychiatry, 8,* 83–85.

Laufer, R. S., Brett, E., & Gallops, M. S. (1985). Dimensions of posttraumatic stress disorder among Vietnam veterans. *Journal of Nervous and Mental Disease, 173,* 538–545.

Laufer, R. S., & Gallops, G. (1982). *A model of war stress and post-war trauma: The Vietnam*

663

experience. Paper presented at the convention of the American Sociological Association, San Francisco.

Laughren, T. P., Battey, Y., & Greenblatt, D. J. (1982). A controlled trial of diazepam withdrawal in chronically anxious outpatients. *Acta Psychiatrica Scandinavica, 65,* 171–179.

Lavallée, Y. J., Lamontagne, Y., Pinard, G., Annable, L., & Tétreault, L. (1977). Effects of EMG-feedback, diazepam and their combination on chronic anxiety. *Journal of Psychosomatic Research, 21,* 65–71.

Lazarus, R. S. (1966). Behaviour rehearsal vs. non-directive therapy vs. advice in effecting behaviour change. *Behaviour Research and Therapy, 4,* 209–212.

Lazarus, R. S. (1968). Emotions and adaptation: Conceptual and empirical relations. In W. J. Arnold (Ed.), *Nebraska Symposium on Motivation* (Vol. 16). Lincoln: University of Nebraska Press.

Lazarus, R. S. (1984). On the primacy of cognition. *American Psychologist, 39,* 124–129.

Lazarus, R. S., Averill, J. R., & Opton, E. M., Jr. (1970). Towards a cognitive theory of emotion. In M. Arnold (Ed.), *Feelings and emotion.* New York: Academic Press.

Leary, T. F. (1957). *Interpersonal diagnosis of personality: A functional theory and methodology for personality evaluation.* New York: Ronald Press.

LeBoeuf, A., & Lodge, J. (1980). A comparison of frontalis EMG feedback training and progressive relaxation in the treatment of chronic anxiety. *British Journal of Psychiatry, 137,* 279–284.

Leckman, J. F., Merikangas, K. R., Pauls, D. L., Prusoff, B. A., & Weissman, M. M., (1983). Anxiety disorders associated with episodes of depression: Family study data contradict DSM-III convention. *American Journal of Psychiatry, 140,* 880–882.

Leckman, J. F., Weissman, M. M., Merikangas, K. R., Pauls, D. L., & Prusoff, B. A. (1983). Panic disorder and major depression. *Archives of General Psychiatry, 40,* 1055–1060.

Lee, C. (1984). Efficacy expectations and outcome expectations as predictors of performance in a snake-handling task. *Cognitive Therapy and Research, 8,* 37–48.

Lee, M. A., & Cameron, O. G. (1986). Anxiety disorders, type A behavior, and cardiovascular disease. *International Journal of Psychiatry in Medicine, 16,* 123–129.

Lee, M. A., Cameron, O. G., & Greden, J. F. (1985). Anxiety and caffeine consumption in people with anxiety disorders. *Psychiatry Research, 15,* 211–217.

Leelarthaepin, B., Gray, W., & Chesworth, E. (1980). Exersentry: An evaluation of its cardiac frequency monitoring accuracy. *Australian Journal of Sports Science,* 1–11.

Leitenberg, H., Agras, W. S., Butz, R., & Wincze, J. (1971). Relationship between heart rate and behavioral change during the treatment of phobias. *Journal of Abnormal Psychology, 78,* 59–68.

Leitenberg, H., Agras, W. S., Edwards, J. A., Thompson, L. E., & Wincze, J. P. (1970). Practice as a psychotherapeutic variable: An experimental analysis within single cases. *Journal of Psychiatric Research, 7,* 215–225.

Leo, J. (1983, August 15). Take me out to the ballgame. *Time,* p. 72.

Leventhal, H., Brown, D., Shachan, S., & Engquist, G. (1979). Effect of preparatory information about sensations, threat of pain and attention on cold pressor distress. *Journal of Personality and Social Psychology, 37,* 688–714.

Levin, A., Liebowitz, M., Fyer, A., Gorman, J., & Klein, D. F. (1984). Lactate induction of panic: Hypothesized mechanisms and recent findings. In J. C. Ballenger (Ed.), *Biology of agoraphobia.* Washington, DC: American Psychiatric Press.

Lewinsohn, P. M. (1974). Clinical and theoretical aspects of depression. In K. S. Calhoun, H. E. Adams, & K. M. Mitchell (Eds.), *Innovative treatment methods on psychopathology.* New York: Wiley.

Lewinsohn, P. M., Hoberman, H. M., & Rosenbaum, M. (in press). A prospective study of risk factors for unipolar depression. *Journal of Abnormal Psychology.*

Lewinsohn, P. M., & Lee, W. M. L. (1981). Assessment of affective disorders. In D. H. Barlow (Ed.), *Behavioral assessment of adult disorders.* New York: Guilford Press.

Lewis, A. (1936). Problems of obsessional illness. *Proceedings of the Royal Society of Medicine, 29,* 325–336.

Lewis, A. (1966). Obsessional disorder. In R. Scott (Ed.), *Price's textbook of the practice of medicine* (10th ed.). London: Oxford University Press.

Lewis, A. J. (1980). Problems presented by the ambiguous word "anxiety" as used in psychopathology. In G. D. Burrows & B. Davies (Eds.), *Handbook of studies on anxiety.* Amsterdam: Elsevier/North-Holland. ✳ ✳

Lewis, C. E., Biglan, A., & Steinblock, E. (1978). Self-administered relaxation training and the money deposits in the treatment of recurrent anxiety. *Journal of Consulting and Clinical Psychology, 46,* 1274–1283.

Lewis, T. (1917). *Medical research committee: Report upon soldiers returned as cases of "disordered action of the heart" (D. A. H.) or "valvular disease of the heart" (V.D.H.).* London: His Majesty's Stationery Office.

Ley, R. (1985a). Agoraphobia, the panic attack and the hyperventilation syndrome. *Behaviour Research and Therapy, 23,* 79–81.

Ley, R. (1985b). Blood, breath, and fears: A hyperventilation theory of panic attacks and agoraphobia. *Clinical Psychology Review, 5,* 271–285.

Ley, R., & Walker, H. (1973). Effects of carbon dioxide–oxygen inhalation on heart rate, blood pressure, and subjective anxiety. *Journal of Behavior Therapy and Experimental Psychiatry, 4,* 223–228.

Liddell, H. S. (1949). The role of vigilance in the development of animal neurosis. In P. Hoch & J. Zubin (Eds.), *Anxiety.* New York: Grune & Stratton.

Liden, S., & Gottfries, C. G. (1974). Beta-blocking agents in the treatment of catecholamine-induced symptoms in musicians. *Lancet, ii,* 529.

Liebowitz, M. R. (1986). *Pharmacological treatment of social phobia.* Paper presented at the annual meeting of the American Psychiatric Association, Washington, D.C.

Liebowitz, M. R., Fyer, A., Gorman, J., Campas, R., Levin, A., Davies, S., Goetz, D., & Klein, D. (1986). Alprazolam in the treatment of panic disorders. *Journal of Clinical Psychopharmacology, 6,* 13–20.

Liebowitz, Mr. R., Fyer, A. J., Gorman, J. M., Dillon, D., Appleby, I. L., Levy, G., Anderson, S., Levitt, M., Palij, M., Davies, S. O., & Klein, D. F. (1984). Lactate provocation of panic. *Archives of General Psychiatry, 41,* 764–770.

Liebowitz, M. R., Fyer, A., McGrath, P., & Klein, D. (1981). Clonidine treatment of panic disorder. *Psychopharmacology Bulletin, 17,* 122–123.

Liebowitz, M. R., Gorman, J. M., Fyer, A., Dillon, D., Levitt, M. M., & Klein, D. F. (1986). Possible mechanisms for lactate's induction of panic. *American Journal of Psychiatry, 143,* 495–502.

Liebowitz, M. R., Gorman, J. M., Fyer, A. J., & Klein, D. F. (1985). Social phobia: Review of a neglected anxiety disorder. *Archives of General Psychiatry, 42,* 729–736.

Liebowitz, M. R., Gorman, J. M., Fyer, A. J., Levitt, M., Dillon, D., Levy, P., Appleby, I. L., Anderson, S., Palij, M., Davies, S. O., & Klein, D. F. (1985). Lactate provocation of panic attacks: II. Biochemical and physiological findings. *Archives of General Psychiatry, 42,* 709–719.

Liebowitz, M. R., & Klein, D. F. (1979). Clinical psychiatric conferences: Assessment and treatment of phobic anxiety. *Journal of Clinical Psychology, 40,* 486–492.

Lindemann, E. (1944). Symptomatology and management of acute grief. *American Journal of Psychiatry, 101,* 141–148.

Lindemann, E., & Finesinger, J. E. (1938). The effect of adrenaline and mecholyl in states of anxiety in psychoneurotic patients. *American Journal of Psychiatry, 95,* 353–370.

Linden, W. (1981). Exposure treatments for focal phobias. *Archives of General Psychiatry, 38,* 769–775.

Lindsley, D. B. (1951). Emotion. In S. S. Stevens (Ed.), *Handbook of experimental psychology.* New York: Wiley.

REFERENCES

Linko, E. (1950). Lactate acid response to muscular exercise in neurocirculatory asthenia. *Annales Medicinae Internue Fenniae, 39*, 161–176.

Lipman, R. S. (1982). Differentiating anxiety and depression in anxiety disorders: Use of rating scales. *Psychopharmacology Bulletin, 18*, 69–77.

Lipsedge, M. S., Hajioff, P., Napier, L., Pearce, J., Pike, D. J., & Rich, M. (1973). The management of severe agoraphobia: A comparison of iproniazid and systematic desensitization. *Psychopharmacologia, 32*, 67–80.

Lloyd, C. (1980). Life events and depressive disorder review: II. Events as precipitating factors. *Archives of General Psychiatry, 37*, 542–548.

Lukas, S. E., & Griffiths, R. R. (1982). Precipitated withdrawal by a benzodiazepine receptor antagonist (RO 15-1788) after 7 days of diazepam. *Science, 217*, 1161–1163.

Lum, L. C. (1975). Hyperventilation: The tip of the iceberg. *Journal of Psychosomatic Research, 19*, 375–383.

Lum, L. C. (1976). The syndrome of habitual chronic hyperventilation. In O. W. Hill (Ed.), *Modern trends in psychosomatic medicine* (Vol. 3). London: Butterworths.

Maas, J., Hattox, S., Greene, N., & Landis, D. (1979). 3-Methoxy-4-hydroxyphenylethylene glycol production by human brain in vivo. *Science, 205*, 1025.

MacDougall, J. M., Dembroski, T. M., Dimsdale, J. E., & Hackett, T. P. (1985). Components of Type A, hostility and anger-in: Further relationships to angiographic findings. *Health Psychology, 4*, 137–152.

Mackenzie, T. B., & Popkin, M. K. (1983). Organic anxiety syndrome. *American Journal of Psychiatry, 140*, 342–344.

MacLean, P. D. (1963). Phylogenesis. In P. H. Knapp (Ed.), *Expression of the emotions in man.* New York: International Universities Press.

MacLeod, C., Mathews, A., & Tata, P. (1986). Attentional bias in emotional disorders. *Journal of Abnormal Psychology, 95*, 15–20.

Mahoney, M. J. (1974). *Cognition and behavior modification.* Cambridge, MA: Ballinger.

Maier, N. R. F. (1949). *Frustration: The study of behavior without a goal.* New York: McGraw-Hill.

Maller, R. G., & Reiss, S. (1987). A behavioral validation of the Anxiety Sensitivity Index. *Journal of Anxiety Disorders, 1*, 265–272.

Malloy, P. F., Fairbank, J. A., & Keane, T. M. (1983). Validation of a multimethod assessment of posttraumatic stress disorders in Vietnam veterans. *Journal of Consulting and Clinical Psychology, 51*, 488–494.

Malmo, R. B., Shagass, C., David, J. F., Cleghorn, R. A., Graham, B. F., & Goodman, A. J. (1948). Standardized pain stimulation as controlled stress in physiological studies of psychoneurosis. *Science, 108*, 509–511.

Malmo, R. B., Shagass, C., & Heslam, R. M. (1951). Blood pressure response to repeated brief stress in psychoneurosis: A study of adaptation. *Canadian Journal of Psychology, 5*, 167–179.

Mandler, G. (1966). Anxiety. In D. L. Sills (Ed.), *International encyclopedia of the social sciences.* New York: Macmillan.

Mandler, G. (1975). *Mind and emotion.* New York: Wiley.

Maple, S., Bradshaw, C. M., & Szabadi, E. (1981). Pharmacological responsiveness of sweat glands in anxious patients and healthy volunteers. *British Journal of Psychiatry, 141*, 154–161.

Margraf, J., Ehlers, A., & Roth, W. T. (1986a). Biological models of panic disorder and agoraphobia: A review. *Behaviour Research and Therapy, 24*, 553–567.

Margraf, J., Ehlers, A., & Roth, W. T. (1986b). Sodium lactate infusions and panic attacks: A review and critique. *Psychosomatic Medicine, 48*, 23–51.

Margraf, J., Taylor, C. B., Ehlers, A., Roth, W. T., & Agras, W. T. (1987). Panic attacks in the natural environment. *Journal of Nervous and Mental Disease, 175*, 558–565.

Marks, I. M. (1969). *Fears and phobias.* London: Heinemann.

Marks, I. M. (1970). The classification of phobic disorders. *British Journal of Psychiatry, 116,* 377–386.

Marks, I. M. (1971). Phobic disorders four years after treatment: A prospective follow-up. *British Journal of Psychiatry, 118,* 683–686.

Marks, I. M. (1981a). *Cure and care of neurosis: Theory and practice of behavioral psychotherapy.* New York: Wiley.

Marks, I. M. (1981b). Space "phobia": A pseudo-agoraphobic syndrome. *Journal of Neurology and Neurosurgery, 44,* 387–391.

Marks, I. M. (1983). Comparative studies on benzodiazepines and psychotherapies. *L'Encephale, 9,* 23–30.

Marks, I. M. (1985). Behavioural treatment of social phobia. *Psychopharmacology Bulletin, 21,* 615–618.

Marks, I. M. (1986). Genetics of fear and anxiety disorders. *British Journal of Psychiatry, 149,* 406–418.

Marks, I. M., & Bebbington, P. (1976). Space phobia: Syndrome or agoraphobic variant? *British Medical Journal, ii,* 345–347.

Marks, I. M., Bird, J., & Lindley, P. (1978). Behavioural nurse therapists 1978—developments and implications. *Behavioural Psychotherapy, 6,* 25–36.

Marks, I. M., Birley, J. L. T., & Gelder, M. G. (1966). Modified leucotomy in severe agoraphobia: A controlled serial inquiry. *British Journal of Psychiatry, 112,* 757–769.

Marks, I. M., Crowe, E., Drewe, E., Young, J., & Dewhurst, W. G. (1969). Obsessive–compulsive neurosis in identical twins. *British Journal of Psychiatry, 15,* 991–998.

Marks, I. M., & Gelder, M. G. (1965). A controlled retrospective study of behaviour therapy in phobic patients. *British Journal of Psychiatry, 111,* 561–573.

Marks, I. M., & Gelder, M. G. (1966). Different ages of onset in varieties of phobias. *American Journal of Psychiatry, 123,* 218–221.

Marks, I. M., Grey, S., Cohen, S. D., Hill, R., Mawson, D., Ramm, E. M., & Stern, R. S. (1983). Imipramine and brief therapist-aided exposure in agoraphobics having self exposure homework: A controlled trial. *Archives of General Psychiatry, 40,* 153–162.

Marks, I. M., & Lader, M. (1973). Anxiety states (anxiety neurosis): A review. *Journal of Nervous and Mental Disease, 156,* 3–18.

Marks, I. M., & Mathews, A. M. (1979). Brief standard self-rating for phobic patients. *Behaviour Research and Therapy, 17,* 263–267.

Marks, I. M. Stern, R. S., Mawson, D., Cobb, J., & McDonald, R. (1980). Clomipramine and exposure for obsessive compulsive rituals. *British Journal of Psychiatry, 136,* 1–25.

Marks, I. M., Viswanathan, R., & Lipsedge, M. S. (1972). Enhanced extinction of fear by flooding during waning diazepam effect. *British Journal of Psychiatry, 121,* 493–505.

Marshall, G. (1976). *The affective consequences of "inadequately explained" physiological arousal.* Unpublished doctoral dissertation, Stanford University.

Marshall, G., & Zimbardo, P. G. (1979). Affective consequences of inadequately explained physiological arousal. *Journal of Personality and Social Psychology, 37,* 970–998.

Marshall, W. L. (1985). The effects of variable exposure in flooding therapy. *Behavior Therapy, 16,* 117–135.

Marsland, D. W., Wood, M., & Mayo, F. (1976). Content of family practice: A data bank for patient care, curriculum, and research in family practice—526,196 patient problems. *Journal of Family Practice, 3,* 25–68.

Martin, I. (1983). Human classical conditioning. In A. Gale & J. A. Edward (Eds.), *Physiological correlates of human behavior: Vol. 2. Attention and performance.* London: Academic Press.

Martin, I., & Levey, A. B. (1985). Conditioning, evaluations and cognitions: An axis of integration. *Behaviour Research and Therapy, 23,* 167–175.

Maser, J. D. (1985). List of phobias. In A. H. Tuma & J. D. Maser (Eds.), *Anxiety and the anxiety disorders.* Hillsdale, NJ: Erlbaum.

Maser, J. D., & Gallup, G. G. (1974). Tonic immobility in the chicken: Calalepsy potentiation by uncontrollable shock and alleviation by imipramine. *Psychosomatic Medicine, 36,* 199–205.

Maslach, C. (1979a). The emotional consequences of arousal without reason. In C. E. Izard (Ed.), *Emotions in personality and psychopathology.* New York: Plenum Press.

Maslach, C. (1979b). Negative emotional biasing of unexplained emotional arousal. *Journal of Personality and Social Psychology, 37,* 953–969.

Masserman, J. H., & Carmichael, H. T. (1938). Diagnosis and prognosis in psychiatry. *Journal of Mental Science, 84,* 893–946.

Masters, W. H., & Johnson, V. E. (1970). *Human sexual inadequacy.* Boston: Little, Brown.

Mathew, R. J., Ho, B. T., Francis, D. J., Taylor, D. L., & Weinman, M. L. (1982). Catecholamines and anxiety. *Acta Psychiatrica Scandinavica, 65,* 142–147.

Mathew, R. J., Ho, B. T., Kralik, P., Taylor, D. L., & Claghorn, J. L. (1981). Catecholamines and monoamine oxidase activity in anxiety. *Acta Psychiatrica Scandinavica, 63,* 245–252.

Mathew, R. J., Ho, B. T., Kralik, P., Weinman, M., & Claghorn, J. L. (1981). Anxiety and platelet MAO levels after relaxation training. *American Journal of Psychiatry, 138,* 371–373.

Mathew, R. J., Weinman, M. L., & Claghorn, J. L. (1982). Anxiety and cerebral blood flow. In R. J. Mathew (Ed.), *The biology of anxiety.* New York: Brunner/Mazel.

Mathews, A. M. (1978). Fear-reduction research and clinical phobias. *Psychological Bulletin, 85,* 390–404.

Mathews, A. M., Gelder, M. G., & Johnston, D. W. (1981). *Agoraphobia: Nature and treatment.* New York: Guilford Press.

Mathews, A. M., Johnston, D. W., Lancashire, M., Munby, M., Shaw, P. N., & Gelder, M. G. (1976). Imaginal flooding and exposure to real phobic situations: Treatment outcome with agoraphobic patients. *British Journal of Psychiatry, 129,* 362–371.

Mathews, A. M., & MacLeod, C. (1986). Discrimination of threat cues without awareness in anxiety states. *Journal of Abnormal Psychology, 95,* 131–138.

Mathews, A. M., Teasdale, J., Munby, M., Johnston, D., & Shaw, P. (1977). A home-based treatment program for agoraphobia. *Behavior Therapy, 8,* 915–924.

Mavissakalian, M. (1979). Functional classification of obsessive–compulsive phenomena. *Journal of Behavioral Assessment, 1,* 271–279.

Mavissakalian, M. (1983). Antidepressants in the treatment of agoraphobia and obsessive–compulsive disorder. *Comprehensive Psychiatry, 24,* 278–284.

Mavissakalian, M. (1985). Male and female agoraphobia: Are they different? *Behaviour Research and Therapy, 23,* 469–471.

Mavissakalian, M. (1986a). The Fear Questionnaire: A validity study. *Behaviour Research and Therapy, 24,* 83–85.

Mavissakalian, M. (1986b). Clinically significant improvement in agoraphobia research. *Behaviour Research and Therapy, 24,* 369–370.

Mavissakalian, M. (1987). Initial depression and response to imipramine in agoraphobia. *Journal of Nervous and Mental Disease, 175,* 358–361.

Mavissakalian, M. R., & Barlow, D. H. (1981a). Assessment of obsessive–compulsive disorders. In D. H. Barlow (Ed.), *Behavioral assessment of adult disorders.* New York: Guilford Press.

Mavissakalian, M., & Barlow, D. H. (Eds.). (1981b). *Phobia: Psychological and pharmacological treatment.* New York: Guilford Press.

Mavissakalian, M., & Hamann, M. S. (1986a). Assessment and significance of behavioral avoidance in agoraphobia. *Journal of Psychopathology and Behavioral Assessment, 8,* 317–327.

Mavissakalian, M., & Hamann, M. S. (1986b). DSM-III personality disorder in agoraphobia. *Comprehensive Psychiatry, 27,* 471–479.

Mavissakalian, M., & Michelson, L. (1983). Self-directed in vivo exposure practice in behavioral and pharmacological treatments of agoraphobia. *Behavior Therapy, 14,* 506–519.

Mavissakalian, M., & Michelson, L. (1986a). Agoraphobia: Relative and combined effectiveness of therapist-assisted in vivo exposure and imipramine. *Journal of Clinical Psychiatry, 47,* 117–122.

Mavissakalian, M., & Michelson, L. (1986b). Two-year follow-up of exposure and imipramine treatment of agoraphobia. *American Journal of Psychiatry, 143,* 1106–1112.

Mavissakalian, M., Michelson, L., & Dealy, R. S. (1983). Pharmacological treatment of agoraphobia: Imipramine versus imipramine with programmed practice. *British Journal of Psychiatry, 143,* 348–355.

Mavissakalian, M., Michelson, L., Greenwald, D., Kornblith, S., & Greenwald, M. (1983). Cognitive–behavioural treatment of agoraphobia: Paradoxical intention versus self–statement training. *Behaviour Research and Therapy, 21,* 75–86.

Mavissakalian, M., & Perel, J. M. (1985). Imipramine in the treatment of agoraphobia: Dose–response relationships. *American Journal of Psychiatry, 142,* 1032–1036.

Mavissakalian, M., Perel, J. M., Bowler, K., & Dealy, R. (1987). Trazodone in the treatment of panic/agoraphobia. *American Journal of Psychiatry, 144,* 785–787.

Mavissakalian, M., Perel, J. M., & Michelson, L. (1984). The relationship of plasma/imipramine and N-desmethylimipramine to improvement in agoraphobia. *Journal of Clinical Psychopharmacology, 4,* 36–40.

Mavissakalian, M., Salerni, R., Thompson, M. E., & Michelson, L. (1983). Mitral valve prolapse and agoraphobia. *American Journal of Psychiatry, 140,* 1612–1614.

Mavissakalian, M., Turner, S. M., & Michelson, L. (1985). Future directions in the assessment and treatment of obsessive–compulsive disorder. In M. Mavissakalian, S. M. Turner, & L. Michelson (Eds.), *Psychological and pharmacological treatment of obsessive–compulsive disorder.* New York: Plenum Press.

Mavissakalian, M., Turner, S. M., Michelson, L., & Jacob, R. (1985). Tricyclic antidepressants in obsessive–compulsive disorder: Anti-obsessional or antidepressant agents? *American Journal of Psychiatry, 142,* 572–576.

Mawson, D., Marks, I. M., & Ramm, L. (1982). Clomipramine and exposure for chronic obsessive–compulsive rituals: III. Two year follow-up and further readings. *British Journal of Psychiatry, 140,* 11–18.

May, J. R. (1977a). A psychophysiology of self-regulated phobic thoughts. *Behavior Therapy, 8,* 150–159.

May, J. R. (1977b). A psychophysiological study of self and externally regulated phobic thoughts. *Behavior Therapy, 8,* 849–861.

May, R. (1979). *The meaning of anxiety.* New York: Washington Square Press.

Mazza, D. L., Martin, D., Spacavento, L., Jacobsen, J., & Gibbs, H. (1986). Prevalence of anxiety disorders in patients with mitral valve prolapse. *American Journal of Psychiatry, 143,* 349–352.

McCaffrey, R. J., Rapee, R. M., Gansler, D. A., & Barlow, D. H. (1987, October). *A neuropsychological anslysis of two cases of "space" phobia.* Poster presented at the annual meeting of the National Academy of Neuropsychologists, Chicago.

McCallum, W. C., & Walter, W. G. (1968). The effects of attention and distraction on the cintingent negative variation in normal and neurotic subjects. *Electroencephalography and Clinical Neurophysiology, 25,* 319–329.

McCauley, P. A., Di Nardo, P. A., & Barlow, D. H. (1987, November). *Differentiating anxiety and depression using a modified scoring system for the Hamilton scales.* Poster presented at the annual meeting of the Association for Advancement of Behavior Therapy, Boston.

McCrady, B. S. (1985). Alcoholism. In D. H. Barlow (Ed.), *Clinical handbook of psychological disorders: A step-by-step treatment manual.* New York: Guilford Press.

McCue, E. C., & McCue, P. A. (1984). Organic and hyperventilatory causes of anxiety-type symptoms. *Behavioural Psychotherapy, 12,* 308–317.

McCullough, J. P. (1984). The need for new single-case design structure in applied cognitive psychology. *Psychotherapy: Theory, Research, and Practice, 21,* 389–400.

McGuffin, P., & Reich, T. (1984). Psychopathology and genetics. In H. E. Adams & P. B. Sutker (Eds.), *Comprehensive handbook of psychopathology.* New York: Plenum Press.

McKeon, J., Roa, B., & Mann, A. (1984). Life events and personality traits in obsessive-compulsive neurosis. *British Journal of Psychiatry, 144,* 185–189.

McKenna, P. J. (1984). Disorders with overvalued ideas. *British Journal of Psychiatry, 145,* 579–585.

McKeon, J., McGuffin, P., & Robinson, P. (1984). Obsessive–compulsive neurosis following head injury. *British Journal of Psychiatry, 144,* 190–192.

McNair, D. M., Lorr, M., & Droppleman, L. F. (1971). *Manual: Profile of Mood States.* San Diego, CA: Educational and Industrial Testing Services.

McNally, R. J. (1987). Preparedness and phobias: A review *Psychological Bulletin, 101,* 283–303.

McNally, R. J., & Steketee, G. S. (1985). The etiology and maintenance of severe animal phobias. *Behaviour Research and Therapy, 23,* 431–435.

McNamara, H., & Fisch, R. (1964). Effect of high and low motivation on two aspects of attention. *Perceptual and Motor Skills, 19,* 571–578.

McPherson, F. M., Brougham, L., & McLaren, S. (1980). Maintenance of improvement in agoraphobic patients treated by behavioral methods—four-year follow-up. *Behaviour Research and Therapy, 18,* 150–152.

Meichenbaum, D. H. (1974). *Therapist manual for cognitive behavior modification.* Unpublished manuscript, University of Waterloo, Ontario, Canada.

Mellman, T. A., & Davis, G. C. (1985). Combat related flashbacks in posttraumatic stress disorder: Phenomenology and similarity to panic attacks. *Journal of Clinical Psychiatry, 46,* 379–382.

Mellman, T. A., & Uhde, T. W. (1986). Withdrawal syndrome with gradual tapering of alprazolam. *American Journal of Psychiatry, 143,* 1464–1466.

Mendel, J. G. C., & Klein, D. F. (1969). Anxiety attacks with subsequent agoraphobia. *Comprehensive Psychiatry, 10,* 190–195.

Meyer, V. (1966). Modification of expectations in cases with obsessional rituals. *Behaviour Research and Therapy, 4,* 273–280.

Meyer, V., & Gelder, M. G. (1963). Behaviour therapy and phobic disorders. *British Journal of Psychiatry, 109,* 19–28.

Meyer, V., & Levy, R. (1973). Modification of behavior in obsessive–compulsive disorders. In H. E. Adams & P. Unikel (Eds.), *Issues and trends in behavior therapy.* Springfield, IL: Charles C Thomas.

Michels, R., Frances, A., & Shear, M. K. (1985). Psychodynamic models of anxiety In A. H. Tuma & J. D. Maser (Eds.), *Anxiety and the anxiety disorders.* Hillsdale, NJ: Erlbaum.

Michelson, L. (1986). Treatment consonance and response profiles in agoraphobia: The role of individual differences in cognitive behavioural and physiological treatments. *Behaviour Research and Therapy, 24,* 263–275.

Michelson, L. (1988). Cognitive, behavioral and psychophysiological treatments and correlates of panic. In S. Rachman & J. D. Maser (Eds.), *Panic: Psychological perspectives.* Hillsdale, NJ: Erlbaum.

Michelson, L., & Mavissakalian, M. (1985). Psychophysiological outcome of behavioral and pharmacological treatments of agoraphobia. *Journal of Consulting and Clinical Psychology, 53,* 229–236.

Michelson, L., Mavissakalian, M., & Marchione, K. (1985). Cognitive and behavioral treatments of agoraphobia: Clinical, behavioral and psychophysiological outcomes. *Journal of Consulting and Clinical Psychology, 53,* 913–925.

Michelson, L., Mavissakalian, M., Marchione, K., Dancu, C., & Greenwald, M. (1986). The role of self-directed in vivo exposure practice in cognitive, behavioral, and psycho-physiological treatments of agoraphobia. *Behavior Therapy, 17,* 91–108.

Miller, S. M. (1979). Controllability and human stress: Method, evidence and theory. *Behaviour Research and Therapy, 17,* 287–304.

Mills, H. L., Agras, W. S., Barlow, D. H., & Mills, J. R. (1973). Compulsive rituals treated by response prevention. *Archives of General Psychiatry, 28,* 524–529.

Milne, A. A. (1952). Lines and squares. In A. A. Milne, *When we were very young.* New York: E. P. Dutton. (Original work published 1924)

Milton, F., & Hafner, J. (1979). The outcome of behavior therapy for agorphobia in relation to marital adjustment. *Archives of General Psychiatry, 36,* 807–811.

Mineka, S. (1985a). Animal models of anxiety based disorders: Their usefulness and limitations. In A. H. Tuma & J. D. Maser (Eds.), *Anxiety and the anxiety disorders.* Hillsdale, NJ: Erlbaum.

Mineka, S. (1985b). The frightful complexity of the origins of fears. In F. R. Bruch & J. B. Overmier (Eds.), *Affect, conditioning, and cognition: Essays on the determinants of behavior.* Hillsdale, NJ: Erlbaum.

Mineka, S. (1987). A primate model of phobic fears. In H. Eysenck & I. Martin (Eds.), *Theoretical foundations of behavior therapy.* New York: Plenum Press.

Mineka, S., Cook, M., & Miller, S. (1984). Fear conditioned with escapable and inescapable shock: The effects of a feedback stimulus. *Journal of Experimental Psychology: Animal Behavior Processes, 10,* 307–323.

Mineka, S., Davidson, M., Cook, M., & Keir, R. (1984). Observational conditioning of snake fear in rhesus monkeys. *Journal of Abnormal Psychology, 93,* 355–372.

Mineka, S., Gunnar, M., & Champoux, M. (1986). Control and early socioemotional development: Infant rhesus monkeys reared in controllable versus uncontrollable environments. *Child Development, 57,* 1241–1256.

Mineka, S., & Kihlstrom, J. (1978). Unpredictable and uncontrollable aversive events. *Journal of Abnormal Psychology, 87,* 256–271.

Mischel, W., & Peake, P. K. (1982). Beyond deja vu in the search for cross situational consistency. *Psychological Review, 89,* 730–735.

Mizes, J. S., & Crawford, J. (1986). Normative values on the Marks and Mathews fear questionnaire: A comparison as a function of age and sex. *Journal of Psychopathology and Behavioral Assessment, 8,* 253–262.

Mogg, K., Mathews, A., & Weinman, J (1987). Memory bias in clinical anxiety. *Journal of Abnormal Psychology, 96,* 94–98.

Mohler, H., & Okada, T. (1977). Benzodiazepine receptor: Demonstration in the central nervous system. *Science, 198,* 849.

Monroe, S. M. (1983). Social support and disorder: Toward an untangling of cause and effect. *American Journal of Community Psychology, 11,* 81–97.

Monroe, S. M., Bromet, E. J., Connell, M. M., & Steiner, S. C. (1986). Social support, life events, and depressive symptoms: A one-year prospective study. *Journal of Consulting and Clinical Psychology, 54,* 424–431.

Monteiro, W., Marks, I. M., Noshirvani, H., & Checkley, S. (1986). Normal dexamethasone suppression test in obsessive–compulsive disorder. *British Journal of Psychiatry, 148,* 326–329.

Monteiro, W., Marks, I. M., & Ramm, E. (1985). Marital adjustment and treatment outcome in agoraphobia. *British Journal of Psychiatry, 146,* 383–390.

Moore, R. Y. (1973). Retinohypothalamic projection in mammals: A comparative study. *Brain Research, 49,* 403–409.

Moran, C., & Andrews, G. (1985). The familial occurrence of agoraphobia. *British Journal of Psychiatry, 146,* 262–267.

Morokoff, P. J., & Heiman, J. R. (1980). Effects of erotic stimuli on sexually functional and dysfunctional women: Multiple measures before and after therapy. *Behaviour Research and Therapy, 18,* 127–137.

Mountjoy, C. Q., Roth, M., Garside, R. F., & Leitch, I. M. (1977). A clinical trial of phenelzine in anxiety, depression and phobic neurosis. *British Journal of Psychiatry, 131,* 486–492.

Mowrer, O. H. (1939). Stimulus response theory of anxiety. *Psychological Review, 46,* 553–565.

Mowrer, O. H. (1947). On the dual nature of learning: A reinterpretation of "conditioning" and "problem solving." *Harvard Educational Review, 17,* 102–148.

Mowrer, O. H. (1950). *Learning theory and the personality dynamics.* New York: Arnold Press.

Mowrer, O. H., & Viek, P. (1948). An experimental analogue of fear from a sense of helplessness. *Journal of Abnormal Social Psychology, 83,* 193–200.

Mullan, M. J., Gurling, H. M. D., Oppenheim, B. E., & Murray, R. M. (1986). The relationship between alcoholism and neurosis: Evidence from a twin study. *British Journal of Psychiatry, 148,* 435–441.

Mullaney, J. A., & Trippett, C. J. (1979). Alcohol dependence and phobias: Clinical description and relevance. *British Journal of Psychiatry, 135,* 565–573.

Munby, J., & Johnston, D. W. (1980). Agoraphobia: The long-term follow-up of behavioural treatment. *British Journal of Psychiatry, 137,* 418–427.

Munjack, D. J. (1984). The onset of driving phobias. *Journal of Behavior Therapy and Experimental Psychiatry, 15,* 305–308.

Murray, E. J., & Foote, F. (1979). The origins of fear and snakes. *Behaviour Research and Therapy, 17,* 489–493.

Myers, J. K., Weissman, M. M., Tischler, C. E., Holzer, C. E., III, Orvaschel, H., Anthony, J. C., Boyd, J. H., Burke, J. D., Jr., Kramer, M., & Stoltzman, R. (1984). Six-month prevalence of psychiatric disorders in three communities *Archives of General Psychiatry, 41,* 959–967.

Nace, E. P., O'Brien, C. P., Mintz, J., Ream, N., & Meyers, A. L. (1978). Adjustment among Vietnam veteran drug users two years post-service. In C. R. Figley (Ed.), *Stress disorders among Vietnam veterans: Theory, research, and treatment.* New York: Brunner/Mazel.

Nathan, P. E. (Ed.). (1967). *Cues, decisions and diagnosis.* New York: Academic Press.

Neale, J. M., & Katahn, M. (1968). Anxiety, choice and stimulus uncertainty. *Journal of Personality, 36,* 238–245.

Neff, D. F., & Blanchard, E. B. (1987). A multi-component treatment for irritable bowel syndrome. *Behavior Therapy, 18,* 70–83.

Nelles, W. B., & Barlow, D. H. (1987). *Do children panic?* Unpublished manuscript.

Nelson, R. O., & Barlow, D. H. (1981). Behavioral assessment: Basic strategies and initial procedures. In D. H. Barlow (Ed.), *Behavioral assessment of adult disorders.* New York: Guilford Press.

Ness, R. M., Cameron, O. G., Curtis, G. C., & Lee, M. (1986). How antipanic drugs might work. *American Journal of Psychiatry, 143,* 945.

Nesse, R. M., Cameron, O. G., Curtis, G. C., McCann, D. S., & Huber-Smith, M. J. (1984). Adrenergic function in patients with panic anxiety. *Archives of General Psychiatry, 41,* 771–776.

Nesse, R. M., Curtis, G. C., & Brown, G. M. (1982). Phobic anxiety does not affect plasma levels of thyroid stimulating hormone in man. *Psychoendocrinology, 7,* 69–74.

Nesse, R. M., Curtis, G. C., Brown, G. M., & Rubin, R. T. (1980). Anxiety induced by flooding therapy for phobias does not elicit prolactin secretory response. *Psychosomatic Medicine, 42,* 25–31.

Nesse, R. M., Curtis, G. C., Thyer, B. A., McCann, D. S., Huber-Smith, M. J., & Knopf, R. F. (1985). Endocrine and cardiovascular responses during phobic anxiety. *Psychosomatic Medicine, 47,* 320–332.

REFERENCES

Newman, C. J. (1976). Children of disaster: Clinical observations at Buffalo Creek. *American Journal of Psychiatry, 133*, 306–312.

Ngui, P. W. (1969). The *koro* epidemic in Singapore. *Australian and New Zealand Journal of Psychiatry, 3*, 263–266.

Nichols, K. A. (1974). Severe social anxiety. *British Journal of Medical Psychology, 47*, 301–306.

Nolen-Hoeksema, S. (1987). Sex differences in unipolar depression: Evidence and theory. *Psychological Bulletin, 101*, 259–282.

Norton, G. R., Allen, G. E., & Hilton, J. (1983). The social validity of treatments for agoraphobia. *Behaviour Research and Therapy, 21*, 393–399.

Norton, G. R., Allen, G. E., & Walker, J. R. (1985). Predicting treatment preferences for agoraphobia. *Behaviour Research and Therapy, 23*, 699–701.

Norton, G. R., Dorward, J., & Cox, B. J. (1986). Factors associated with panic attacks in nonclinical subjects. *Behavior Therapy, 17*, 239–252.

Norton, G. R., Harrison, B., Hauch, J., & Rhodes, L. (1985). Characteristics of people with ✳ infrequent panic attacks. *Journal of Abnormal Psychology, 94*, 216–221.

Norton, G. R., & Johnson, W. E. (1983). A comparison of two relaxation procedures for reducing cognitive and somatic anxiety. *Journal of Behavior Therapy and Experimental Psychiatry, 14*, 209–214.

Norton, G. R., Rhodes, L., Hauch, J., & Kaprowy, E. A. (1985). Characteristics of subjects experiencing relaxation and relaxation-induced anxiety. *Journal of Behavior Therapy and Experimental Psychiatry, 16*, 211–216.

Novaco, R. W. (1975). *Anger control.* Lexington, MA: D. C. Heath.

Nowlis, V., & Nowlis, H. (1956). The description and analysis of mood. *Annals of the New York Academy of Sciences, 65*, 345–355.

Noyes, R., Jr., Anderson, D. J., Clancy, J., Crowe, R. R., Slymen, D. J., Ghoneim, M. M., & Hinrichs, J. V. (1984). Diazepam and propranolol in panic disorder and agoraphobia. *Archives of General Psychiatry, 41*, 287–292.

Noyes, R., Jr., & Clancy, J. (1976). Anxiety neurosis: A 5 year follow-up. *Journal of Nervous and Mental Disease, 162*, 200–205.

Noyes, R., Jr., Clancy, J., Coryell, W. H., Crowe, R. R., Chaudhry, D. R., & Domingo, D. V. (1985). A withdrawal syndrome after abrupt discontinuation of alprazolam. *American Journal of Psychiatry, 142*, 114–116.

Noyes, R., Jr., Clancy, J., Hoenk, P. R., & Slymen, D. J. (1980). The prognosis of anxiety neurosis. *Archives of General Psychiatry, 37*, 173–178.

Noyes, R., Jr., Crowe, R. R., Harris, E. L., Hamra, B. J., McChesney, C. M., & Chaudhry, D. R. (1986). Relationship between panic disorder and agoraphobia: A family study. *Archives of General Psychiatry,* 227–232.

Nutt, D. J. (1986). Increased central alpha adrenoceptor sensitivity in panic disorder. *Psychopharmacology, 90*, 268–269.

Nyman, D., & Heimberg, R. G. (1985). *Heterosocial anxiety among college students: A reasonable analogue to social phobia?* Paper presented at the annual meeting of the Association for Advancement of Behavior Therapy, Houston, TX.

Oatley, K., & Hodgson, D. (1987). Influence of husbands on the outcome of their agoraphobic wives' therapy. *British Journal of Psychiatry, 150*, 380–386.

O'Brien, G. T., & Barlow, D. H. (1984). Agoraphobia. In S. M. Turner (Ed.), *Behavioral treatment of anxiety disorders.* New York: Plenum Press.

O'Brien, G. T., Barlow, D. H., & Last, C. G. (1982). Changing marriage patterns of agoraphobics as a result of treatment. In R. DuPont (Ed.), *Phobia: A comprehensive summary of modern treatments.* New York: Brunner/Mazel.

O'Brien, G. T., & Borkovec, T. D. (1977). The role of relaxation in systematic desensitization: Revisiting an unresolved issue. *Journal of Behavior Therapy and Experimental Psychiatry, 8*, 359–364.

Oei, T. P. S. (1986). The roles of positive and negative self-statements in socially anxious females. *Behaviour Change, 3,* 142–149.

O'Hanlon, J. F., Haak, J. W., Blaauw, G. J., & Riemersma, J. B. J. (1982). Diazepam impairs lateral position control in highway driving. *Science, 27,* 79–81.

Öhman, A. (1986). Face the beast and fear the face: Animal and social fears as prototypes for evolutionary analyses of emotion. *Psychophysiology, 23,* 123–145.

Öhman, A., & Dimberg, U. (1984). An evolutionary perspective on human social behavior. In W. M. Waid (Ed.), *Sociophysiology.* New York: Springer-Verlag.

Öhman, A., Dimberg, U., & Öst, L. G. (1985). Animal and social phobias: A laboratory model. In P. O. Sjoden & S. Bates (Eds.), *Trends in behavior therapy.* New York: Academic Press.

Öhman, A., Erixon, G., & Lofburg, I. (1975). Phobias and preparedness: Phobic versus neutral pictures as conditional stimuli for human autonomic responses. *Journal of Abnormal Psychology, 84,* 41–45.

Oppenheim, B. S. (1918). Report on neurocirculatory asthenia and its management. *Military Surgeon, 42,* 711–744.

Orenstein, H., & Carr, J. (1975). Implosion therapy by tape-recording. *Behaviour Research and Therapy, 13,* 177–182.

Orwin, A. (1973). The running treatment: A preliminary communication on a new use for an old therapy (physical activity) in the agoraphobic syndrome. *British Journal of Psychiatry, 122,* 175–179.

Öst, L. G. (1978). Fading vs. Systematic desensitization in the treatment of snake and spider phobia. *Behaviour Research and Therapy, 16,* 379–389.

Öst, L. G. (1985). Mode of acquisition of phobias. *Acta Universitatis Uppsaliensis (Abstracts of Uppsala Dissertations from the Faculty of Medicine, 529,* 1–45.

Öst, L. G. (1987). Age at onset in different phobias. *Journal of Abnormal Psychology, 96,* 223–229.

Öst, L. G., & Hugdahl, K. (1981). Acquisition of phobias and anxiety response patterns in clinical patients. *Behaviour Research and Therapy, 19,* 439–447.

Öst, L. G. & Hugdahl, K. (1983). Acquisition of agoraphobia, mode of onset and anxiety response patterns. *Behaviour Research and Therapy, 21,* 623–631.

Öst, L. G., Jerremalm, A., & Johansson, J. (1981). Individual response patterns and the effects of different behavioral methods in the treatment of social phobia. *Behaviour Research and Therapy, 19,* 1–16.

Öst, L. G., Johansson, J., & Jerremalm, A. (1982). Individual response patterns and the effects of different behavioural methods in the treatment of claustrophobia. *Behaviour Research and Therapy, 20,* 445–460.

Öst, L. G., Lindahl, I. L., Sterner, U., & Jerremalm, A. (1984). Exposure in vivo vs. applied relaxation in the treatment of blood phobia. *Behaviour Research and Therapy, 22,* 205–216.

Öst, L. G., & Sterner, U. (1987). Applied tension: A specific behavioural method for treatment of blood phobia. *Behaviour Research and Therapy, 25,* 25–30.

Öst, L. G., Sterner, U., S. Lindahl, I. L. (1984). Physiological responses in blood phobics. *Behaviour Research and Therapy, 22,* 109–117.

Overton, D. A. (1977). Drug state-dependent learning. In M. E. Jarvik (Ed.), *Psychopharmacology in the practice of medicine.* New York: Appleton-Century-Crofts.

Pallmeyer, T. P., Blanchard, E. B., & Kolb, L. C. (1986). The psychophysiology of combat-induced post-traumatic stress disorder in Vietnam veterans. *Behaviour Research and Therapy, 24,* 645–652.

Panksepp, J. (1982). Toward a general psychobiological theory of emotions. *The Behavioral and Brain Sciences, 5,* 407–422.

Paolino, T. J., & McCrady, B. S. (1977). *The alcoholic marriage: Alternative perspectives.* New York: Grune & Stratton.

Papez, J. W. (1937). A proposed mechanism of emotion. *Archives of Neurology and Psychiatry*, *38*, 725–743.

Pariser, S. F., Jones, B. A., Pinta, E. R., Young, E. A., & Fontana, M. E. (1979). Panic attacks: Diagnostic evaluations of 17 patients. *American Journal of Psychiatry*, *136*, 105–106.

Parker, G. (1979). Reported parental characteristics of agoraphobics and social phobics. *British Journal of Psychiatry*, *135*, 555–560.

Parkes, C. (1970). The first year of bereavement: A longitudinal study of reaction of London widows to the death of their husbands. *Psychiatry*, *33*, 444–467.

Parkinson, L., & Rachman, S. (1981a). Intrusive thoughts: The effects of an uncontrived stress. *Advances in Behaviour Research and Therapy*, *3*, 111–118.

Parkinson, L., & Rachman, S. (1981b). The nature of intrusive thoughts. *Advances in Behaviour Research and Therapy*, *3*, 101–110.

Parkinson, L., & Rachman, S. (1981c). Speed of recovery from an uncontrived stress. *Advances in Behaviour Research and Therapy*, *3*, 119–123.

Paul, G. L. (1966). *Insight versus desensitization in psychotherapy*. Stanford, CA: Stanford University Press.

Paul, S. M., & Skolnick, P. (1978). Rapid changes in brain benzodiazepine receptors after experimental seizures. *Science*, *202*, 892–894.

Paul, S. M., & Skolnick, P. (1981). Benzodiazepine receptors and psychopathological states: Towards a neurobiology of anxiety. In D. F. Klein & J. Rabkin (Eds.), *Anxiety: New research and changing concepts*. New York: Raven Press.

Pavlov, I. P. (1927). *Conditional reflexes* (G. Anrep, Trans.). New York: Oxford University Press.

Paykel, E. S. (1978). Contribution of psychiatric illness. *Psychological Medicine*, *8*, 245–253.

Paykel, E. S. (1979). Causal relationships between clinical depression and life events. In J. E. Barrett (Ed.), *Stress and mental disorder*. New York: Raven Press.

Pearce, J., LeBow, M., & Orchard, J. (1981). The role of spouse involvement in the behavioral treatment of overweight women. *Journal of Consulting and Clinical Psychology*, *49*, 236–244.

Pearce, K. A., Schauer, A. H., Garfield, N. J., Ohlde, C. O., & Patterson, T. W. (1985). A study of post-traumatic stress disorder in Vietnam veterans. *Journal of Clinical Psychiatry*, *41*, 9–15.

Penk, W. E., Robinowitz, R., Roberts, W. R., Patterson, E. T., Dolan, M. P., & Atkins, H. G. (1981). Adjustment differences among male substance abusers varying in degree of combat experience in Vietnam. *Journal of Consulting and Clinical Psychology*, *49*, 426–437.

Perley, M. H., & Guze, S. B. (1962). Hysteria—the stability and usefulness of clinical criteria: A quantitative study based on a follow-up period of 6–8 years in 39 patients. *New England Journal of Medicine*, *266*, 421–426.

Pervin, L. A. (1963). The need to predict and control under conditions of threat. *Journal of Personality*, *31*, 570–585.

Peterson, C. Semmel, A., von Baeyer, C., Abramson, L. Y., Metalsky, G. I., & Seligman, M. E. P. (1982). The Attributional Style Questionnaire. *Cognitive Therapy and Research*, *6*, 287–299.

Petursson, H., & Lader, M. H. (1981). Withdrawal from long-term benzodiazepine treatment. *British Medical Journal*, *283*, 643–645.

Philpott, R. (1975). Recent advances in the behavioral measurement of obsessional illness: Difficulties common to these and other instruments. *Scottish Medical Journal*, *201*, 33–40.

Pilkonis, P. A., & Zimbardo, P. G. (1979). The personal and social dynamics of shyness. In C. E. Izard (Ed.), *Emotions in personality and psychopathology*. New York: Plenum Press.

Pitman, R. K., & Orr, S. P. (1986). Test of the conditioning model of neurosis. Differential aversive conditioning of angry and neutral facial expressions in anxiety disorder patients. *Journal of Abnormal Psychology, 95*, 208–213.

Pitts, F. N., & Alan R. (1979). Beta-adrenergic receptor blocking drugs in psychiatry. In W. E. Fann, I. Karacan, A. D. Pokorny, & R. L. Williams (Eds.), *Phenomenology and treatment of anxiety.* New York: Spectrum.

Pitts, F. N., & McClure, J. N. (1967). Lactate metabolism in anxiety neurosis. *New England Journal of Medicine, 277*, 1329–1336.

Plomin, R., & Daniels, D. (1985). Genetics and shyness. In W. H. Jones, J. M. Cheek, & S. R. Briggs (Eds.), *Shyness: Perspectives on research and treatment.* New York: Plenum Press.

Plutchik, R. (1980). *Emotion: A psychoevolutionary synthesis.* New York: Harper & Row.

Pollak, J. M. (1979). Obsessive–compulsive personality: A review. *Psychological Bulletin, 86*, 225–241.

Post, R. M., Rubinow, D. R., & Ballenger, J. C. (1986). Conditioning and sensitization in the longitudinal course of affective illness. *British Journal of Psychiatry, 149*, 191–201.

Powell, B. J., Penick, E. C., Othmer, E., Bingham, S. F., & Rice, A. S. (1982). Prevalence of additional psychiatric syndromes among male alcoholics. *Journal of Clinical Psychiatry, 43*, 404–407.

Powell, G. E. (1979). *Brain and personality.* London: Saxon House.

Prinz, R. J., Foster, S., Kent, R. N., & O'Leary, K. D. (1979). Multivariate assessment of conflict in distressed and non-distressed mother–adolescent dyads. *Journal of Applied Behavior Analysis, 12*, 691–700.

Prusoff, B., & Klerman, G. L. (1974). Differentiating depressed from anxious neurotic outpatients. *Archives of General Psychiatry, 30*, 302–309.

Pruzinsky, T., & Borkovec, T. D. (1983, December). *Cognitive characteristics of chronic worriers.* Paper presented at the annual meeting of the Association for Advancement of Behavior Therapy, Washington, DC.

Puig-Antich, J., & Rabinovich, H. (1986). Relationship between affective and anxiety disorders in childhood. In R. Gittelman (Ed.), *Anxiety disorders of childhood.* New York: Guilford Press.

Pylyshyn, Z. W. (1973). What the mind's eye tells the mind's brain: A critique of mental imagery. *Psychological Bulletin, 80*, 1–22.

Quarantelli, E. L. (1985). An assessment of conflicting views on mental health: The consequences of traumatic events. In C. R. Figley (Ed.), *Trauma and its wake.* New York: Brunner/Mazel.

Quitkin, F. M., Rifkin, A., Kaplan, J., & Klein, D. F. (1972). Phobic anxiety syndrome complicated by drug dependence and addiction. *Archives of General Psychiatry, 27*, 159–162.

Rachman, S. J. (1973). Some similarities and differences between obsessional ruminations and morbid preoccupations. *Canadian Psychiatric Association Journal, 18*, 71–74.

Rachman, S. J. (1974). Primary obsessional slowness. *Behaviour Research and Therapy, 12*, 9–18.

Rachman, S. J. (1976). Obsessional–compulsive checking. *Behaviour Research and Therapy, 14*, 269–277.

Rachman, S. J. (1977). The conditioning theory of fear acquisition: A critical examination. *Behaviour Research and Therapy, 15*, 375–387.

Rachman, S. J. (1978). *Fear and courage.* San Francisco: W. H. Freeman.

Rachman, S. J. (1980). Emotional processing. *Behaviour Research and Therapy, 18*, 51–60.

Rachman, S. J. (1981). The primacy of affect: Some theoretical implications. *Behaviour Research and Therapy, 19*, 279–290.

Rachman, S. J. (1983a). Fear and courage among military bomb disposal operators. *Advances in Behaviour Research and Therapy, 4*, 99–165.

Rachman, S. J. (1983b). The modification of agoraphobic avoidance behaviour. *Behaviour Research and Therapy, 21,* 567–574.

Rachman, S. J. (1984). Agoraphobia: A safety-signal perspective. *Behaviour Research and Therapy, 22,* 59–70.

Rachman, S. J. (1985). The treatment of anxiety disorders: A critique of the implications for psychopathology. In A. H. Tuma & J. D. Maser (Eds.), *Anxiety and the anxiety disorders.* Hillsdale, NJ: Erlbaum.

Rachman, S. J., Cobb, J., Grey, S., McDonald, B., Mawson, D., Sartory, G., & Stern, R. (1979). The behavioural treatment of obsessional–compulsive disorders, with and without clomipramine. *Behaviour Research and Therapy, 17,* 467–478.

Rachman, S. J., Craske, M., Tallman, K., & Solyom, C. (1986). Does escape behavior strengthen agoraphobic avoidance? A replication. *Behaviour Therapy, 17,* 366–384.

Rachman, S. J., & de Silva, P. (1978). Abnormal and normal obsessions. *Behaviour Research and Therapy, 16,* 233–248.

Rachman, S. J., & Hodgson, R. S. (1974). Synchrony and desynchrony in fear and avoidance. *Behaviour Research and Therapy, 12,* 311–318.

Rachman, S. J., & Hodgson, R. S. (1980). *Obsessions and compulsions.* Englewood Cliffs, NJ: Prentice-Hall.

Rachman, S. J., & Levitt, K. (1985). Panics and their consequences. *Behaviour Research and Therapy, 23,* 585–600.

Radouco-Thomas, S., Garcin, F., Murthy, M. R. V., Faure, N., Leman, A., Forest, J. C., & Radouco-Thomas, C. (1984). Biological markers in major psychosis and alcoholism: Phenotypic and genotypic markers. *Journal of Psychiatric Research, 18,* 513–539.

Rainey, J. M., Ettedgui, E., Pohl, R. B., & Bridges, M. (1985). Effect of acute β-adrenergic blockade on lactate-induced panic. *Archives of General Psychiatry, 42,* 104–105.

Rainey, J. M., Pohl, R. B., Williams, M., Kritter, E., Freedman, R. R., & Ettedugi, E. (1984). A comparison of lactate and isoproterenol anxiety states. *Psychopathology, 17,* 74–82.

Ramm, E., Marks, I. M., Yuksel, S., & Stern, R. S. (1981). Anxiety management training for anxiety states: Positive compared with negative self–statements. *British Journal of Psychiatry, 140,* 367–373.

Ramsey, R. (1979). Bereavement: A behavioral treatment of pathological grief. In P. O. Sjoden, S. Bates, & W. S. Dockens (Eds.), *Trends in behavior therapy.* New York: Academic Press.

Ramsey, G. (1943). The sexual development of boys. *American Journal of Psychology, 56,* 217.

Rao, A. V. A. (1964). A controlled trial with "Valium" in obsessive–compulsive state. *Journal of the Indian Medical Association, 42,* 564–567.

Rapee, R. M. (1985a). A case of panic disorder treated with breathing retraining. *Journal of Behavior Therapy and Experimental Psychiatry, 16,* 63–65.

Rapee, R. M. (1985b). A distinction between panic disorder and generalized anxiety disorder: Clinical presentation. *Australian and New Zealand Journal of Psychiatry, 19,* 227–232.

Rapee, R. M. (1986). Differential response to hyperventilation in panic disorder and generalized anxiety disorder. *Journal of Abnormal Psychology, 95,* 24–28.

Rapee, R. M. (1987). The psychological treatment of spontaneous panic attacks: Theoretical conceptualization and review of evidence. *Clinical Psychology Review, 7,* 427–438.

Rapee, R. M., Ancis, J., & Barlow, D. H. (in press). Emotional reactions to physiological sensations: Comparison of panic disorder and nonclinical subjects. *Behaviour Research and Therapy.*

Rapee, R. M., Mattick, R., & Murrell, E. (1986). Cognitive mediation in the affective component of spontaneous panic attacks. *Journal of Behavior Therapy and Experimental Psychiatry, 17,* 245–253.

Rapee, R. M., Sanderson, W. C., & Barlow, D. H. (1987, November). *Social phobia symptoms across the DSM-III anxiety disorders categories.* Paper presented at the annual meeting of the Association for Advancement of Behavior Therapy, Boston.

Raskin, A., Marks, J. M., & Sheehan, D. V. (1983). [The influence of depressed mood of the antipanic effects of antidepressant drugs]. Unpublished raw data.

Raskin, M. (1975). Decreased skin conductance response habituation in chronically anxious patients. *Biological Psychology, 2,* 309–319.

Raskin, M., Bali, L. R., & Peeke, H. V. (1980). Muscle biofeedback and transcendental meditation. *Archives of General Psychiatry, 37,* 93–97.

Raskin, M., Peeke, H. V. S., Dickman, W., & Pinkster, H. (1982). Panic and generalized anxiety disorders: Developmental antecedents and precipitants. *Archives of General Psychiatry, 39,* 687–689.

Rasmussen, S. A., & Tsuang, M. T. (1986). Clinical characteristics and family history in DSM-III obsessive–compulsive disorder. *American Journal of Psychiatry, 143,* 317–322.

Razran, G. (1961). The observable unconscious and the inferable conscious in current Soviet psychophysiology: Interoceptive conditioning, semantic conditioning, and the orienting reflex. *Psychological Review, 68,* 81–150.

Redd, W. H., & Andrykowski, M. A. (1982). Behavioral interventions in cancer treatment: Controlling aversion reactions to chemotherapy. *Journal of Consulting and Clinical Psychology, 50,* 1018–1029.

Redmond, D. E., Jr. (1977). Alterations in the function of the nucleus locus coeruleus: A possible model for studies of anxiety. In I. Hanin & E. Usdin (Eds.), *Animal models in psychiatry and neurology.* New York: Pergamon Press.

Redmond, D. E., Jr. (1979). New and old evidence for the involvement of a brain norepinephrine system in anxiety. In W. E. Fann, I. Karacan, A. D. Pokorny, & R. L. Williams (Eds.), *Phenomenology and treatment of anxiety.* New York: Spectrum.

Redmond, D. E., Jr. (1985). Neurochemical basis for anxiety and anxiety disorders: Evidence from drugs which decrease human fear of anxiety. In A. H. Tuma & J. D. Maser (Eds.), *Anxiety and the anxiety disorders.* Hillsdale, NJ: Erlbaum.

Redmond, D. E., Jr., & Huang, V. H. (1979). Current concepts: II. New evidence for a locus coeruleus–norepinephrone connection with anxiety. *Life Sciences, 25,* 2149–2162.

Reed, G. F. (1985). *Obsessional experience and compulsive behavior: A cognitive-structured approach.* New York: Academic Press.

Regier, D. A., Myers, J. K., Kramer, L. N., Robins, L. N., Blazer, D. G., Hough, R. L., Eaton, W. W., & Locke, B. Z. (1984). The NIMH Epidemiologic Catchment Area program. *Archives of General Psychiatry, 41,* 934–941.

Reich, J., Noyes, R., Jr., Hirshfeld, R., Coryell, W., & O'Gorman, T. (1987). State and personality in depressed and panic patients. *American Journal of Psychiatry, 144,* 181–187.

Reich, J., Noyes, R., Jr., & Troughton, E. (1987). Dependent personality disorder associated with phobic avoidance in patients with panic disorder. *American Journal of Psychiatry, 144,* 323–326.

Reiman, E. M., Raichle, M. E., Butler, F. K., Herscovitch, P., & Robins, E. (1984). A focal brain abnormality in panic disorder, a severe form of anxiety. *Nature, 310,* 683–685.

Reiman, E. M., Raichle, M. E., Robins, E., Butler, F. K., Herscovitch, P., Fox, P., & Perlmutter, J. (1986). The application of positron emission tomography to the study of panic disorder. *American Journal of Psychiatry, 143,* 469–476.

Reisenzein, R. (1983). The Schachter theory of emotion: Two decades later. *Psychological Bulletin, 94,* 239–264.

Reiss, S. (1980). Pavlovian conditioning and human fear: An expectancy model. *Behavior Therapy, 11,* 380–396.

Reiss, S., Peterson, R. A., Gursky, D. M., & McNally, R. J. (1986). Anxiety sensitivity, anxiety frequency, and the prediction of fearfulness. *Behaviour Research and Therapy, 24,* 1–8.

Rescorla, R. A. (1979). Conditioned inhibituation and extinction. In A. Dickenson & R. A. Boakes (Eds.), *Mechanisms of learning and motivation*. Hillsdale, NJ: Erlbaum.

Resick, P. A., Veronen, L. J., Kilpatrick, D. G., Calhoun, K. S., & Atkinson, B. M. (1986). Assessment of fear reactions in sexual assault victims: A factor analytic study of the Veronen–Kilpatrick modified fear survey. *Behavioral Assessment, 8*, 271–283.

Reynolds, D. (1976). *Morita psychotherapy*. Berkeley: University of California Press.

Rice, K. M., & Blanchard, E. B. (1982). Biofeedback in the treatment of anxiety disorders. *Clinical Psychological Review, 2*, 557–577.

Rickels, K., Csanalosi, I., Greisman, P., Cohen, D., Werblowsky, J., Ross, H., & Harris, H. (1983). A controlled clinical trial of alprazolam for the treatment of anxiety. *American Journal of Psychiatry, 140*, 82–85.

Rickels, K., Csanalosi, I., Greisman, P., Mirman, M., Morris, R., & Weise, C. (1980). Ketazolam and diazepam in anxiety: A controlled study. *Journal of Clinical Pharmacology, 20*, 134–143.

Rickels, K., Weisman, K., Norstad, N., Singer, M., Stoltz, D., Brown, A., & Danton, J. (1982). Buspirone and diazepam in anxiety: A controlled study. *Journal of Clinical Psychiatry, 43*, 81–86.

Rifkin, A., Klein, D. F., Dillon, D., & Levitt, M. (1981). Blockade by imipramine or desipramine of panic induced by sodium lactate. *American Journal of Psychiatry, , 138*, 676–677.

Rimm, D. C., Janda, L. H., Lancaster, D. W., Nahl, M., & Dittmar, K. (1977). An exploratory investigation of the origin and maintenance of phobias. *Behaviour Research and Therapy, 15*, 231–238.

Riordan, C. (1979). *Interpersonal attraction in aversive situations*. Unpublished doctoral dissertation, State University of New York at Albany.

Riskind, J. H., & Beck, A. T. (1983, December). *Phenomenology of "emotional" disorder: Symptoms that differentiate between generalized anxiety disorder, major depressive disorder, and "mixed" disorder-II*. Paper presented at the World Congress on Behavior Therapy, Washington, DC.

Riskind, J. H., Beck, A. T., Brown, G. B., & Steer, R. A. (1987). Taking the measure of anxiety and depression: Validity of reconstructed Hamilton Scales. *Journal of Nervous and Mental Disease, 175*, 474–479.

Roberts, W. R., Penk, W. E., Gearing, M. L., Robinowitz, R., Dolan, M. P., & Patterson, E. T. (1982). Interpersonal problems of Vietnam combat veterans with symptoms of posttraumatic stress disorder. *Journal of Abnormal Psychology, 91*, 444–450.

Robertson, H. A., Martin, I. L., & Candy, J. M. (1978). Differences in benzodiazepines mediated by a GABA-ergic mechanism in the amygdala. *European Journal of Pharmacology, 82*, 115.

Robins, L. N., Helzer, J. E., Croughan, J., & Ratcliff, K. S. (1981). National Institute of Mental Health Diagnostic Interview Schedule: Its history, characteristics, and validity. *Archives of General Psychiatry, 38*, 381–389.

Robins, L. N., Helzer, J. E., Weissman, M. M., Orvaschel, H., Gruenberg, E., Burke, J. D., & Regier, D. A. (1984). Prevalence of specific psychiatric disorders in three sites. *Archives of General Psychiatry, 41*, 949–958.

Robinson, A., & Reading, C. (1985). Imagery in phobic subjects: A psychophysiological study. *Behaviour Research and Therapy, 23*, 247–253.

Rodin, J., & Langer, E. J. (1977). Long-term effects of a control-relevant intervention with the institutionalized aged. *Journal of Personality and Social Psychology, 35*, 897–902.

Rolls, E. T., Burton, M. J., & Mora, F. (1980). Neurophysiological analysis of brain stimulation reward in the monkey. *Brain Research, 194*, 339–357.

Rose, R. J., & Chesney, M. A. (1986). Cardiovascular stress reactivity: A behavior–genetic perspective. *Behavior Therapy, 17*, 314–323.

Rose, R. J., & Ditto, W. B. (1983). A developmental– genetic analysis of common fears from early adolescence to early adulthood. *Child Development, 54,* 361–368.

Rosenthal, T. L., & Bandura, A. (1978). Psychological modeling: Theory and practice. In S. L. Garfield & A. E. Bergin (Eds.), *Handbook of psychotherapy and behavior change: An empirical analysis* (2nd ed.). New York: Wiley.

Rosellini, R. A., Warren, D. A., & DeCola, J. P. (1987). Predictability and uncontrollability: Differential effects upon contextual fear. *Learning and Motivation, 18,* 392–420.

Roth, M. (1959). The phobic anxiety–depersonalization syndrome. *Proceedings of the Royal Society of Medicine, 52,* 587–596.

Roth, M. (1960). The phobic anxiety–depersonalization syndrome and some general aetiological problems in psychiatry. *Journal of Neuropsychiatry, 306,* 293–306.

Roth, M., & Mountjoy, C. Q. (1982). The distinction between anxiety states and depressive disorders. In E. S. Paykel (Ed.), *Handbook of affective disorders.* Edinburgh: Churchill Livingstone.

Rounsaville, B. J., Weissman, M. M., Prusoff, B. A., & Herceg-Baron, R. L. (1979). Marital disputes and treatment outcome in depressed women. *Comprehensive Psychiatry, 20,* 483–490.

Roy-Byrne, P. P., Geraci, M., & Uhde, T. W. (1986). Life events and the onset of panic disorder. *American Journal of Psychiatry, , 143,* 1424–1427.

Rupert, P. A., Dobbins, K., & Mathew, R. J. (1981). EMG biofeedback and relaxation instructions in the treatment of chronic anxiety. *American Journal of Clinical Biofeedback, 4,* 52–61.

Rusalova, M. N., Izard, C. E., & Simonov, P. V. (1975, September). Comparative analysis of mimical and autonomic components of man's emotional state. *Aviation, Space, and Environmental Medicine,* pp. 1132–1134.

Russell, J. A. (1980). A circumplex model of affect. *Journal of Personality and Social Psychology, 39,* 1161–1178.

Russell, J. A., & Mehrabian, A. (1977). Evidence for a three-factor theory of emotions. *Journal of Research in Personality, 11,* 273–294.

Rychtarik, R. G., Silverman, W. K., Van Landingham, W. P., & Prue, D. M. (1984). Treatment of an incest victim with implosive therapy: A case study. *Behavior Therapy, 15,* 410–420.

Rygh, J. L., & Barlow, D. H. (1986, November). *Treatment of simple phobias with panic management techniques.* Paper presented at the annual meeting of the Association for Advancement of Behavior Therapy, Chicago.

Saigh, P. A. (1984a). Pre- and post-invasion anxiety in Lebanon. *Behavior Therapy, 15,* 185–190.

Saigh, P. (1984b). An experimental analysis of delayed posttraumatic stress. *Behaviour Research and Therapy, 22,* 679–682.

Saigh, P. A. (1987). In vitro flooding of childhood post-traumatic stress disorders: A systematic replication. *Professional School Psychology, 2,* 133–144.

Saigh, P. A. (in press-a) Anxiety, depression, and assertion across alternating intervals of stress. *Journal of Abnormal Psychology.*

Saigh, P. A. (in press-b). The validity of the DSM-III posttraumatic stress disorder classification as applied to adolescents. *Professional School Psychology.*

Sakheim, D. K., Barlow, D. H., Abrahamson, D. J., & Beck, J. G. (in press). Waking assessment of erectile dysfunction and the role of erectile potential exams in differentiating organogenic and psychogenic erectile dysfunction. *Behaviour Research and Therapy.*

Salkovskis, P. M. (1985). Obsessional–compulsive problems: A cognitive behavioral analysis. *Behaviour Research and Therapy, 23,* 571–583.

Salkovskis, P. M., & Harrison, J. (1984). Abnormal and normal obsessions: A replication. *Behaviour Research and Therapy, 22,* 549–552.

Salkovskis, P. M., Jones, D. R. O., & Clark, D. M. (1984). Treatment of panic attacks by respiratory control: Covariation of clinical state and carbon dioxide. *Bulletin of European Physiology and Pathology of Respiration, 20,* 91.

Salkovskis, P. M., Jones, D. R. O., & Clark, D. M. (1986). Respiratory control in the treatment of panic attacks: Replication and extension with concurrent measurement of behaviour and pCO^2. *British Journal of Psychiatry, 148,* 526–532.

Salkovskis, P. M., Warwick, H. M. C., Clark, D. M., & Wessels, D. J. (1986). A demonstration of acute hyperventilation during naturally occurring panic attacks. *Behaviour Research and Therapy, 24,* 91–94.

Sanavio, E., & Vidotto, G. (1985). The components of the Maudsley Obsessional–Compulsive Questionnaire. *Behaviour Research and Therapy, 23,* 659–662.

Sanderson, W. C., & Barlow, D. H. (1986, November). *Domains of worry within the DSM-III-R generalized anxiety disorder category: Reliability and description.* Paper presented at the annual meeting of the Association for Advancement of Behavior Therapy, Chicago.

Sanderson, W. C., Rapee, R. M., & Barlow, D. H. (1987b, November). *The DSM-III—Revised anxiety disorder categories: Description and patterns of co-morbidity.* Paper presented at the annual meeting of the Association for Advancement of Behavior Therapy, Boston.

Sanderson, W. C., Rapee, R. M., & Barlow, D. H. (1987b, November). *Panic induction via inhalation of 5% CO_2 enriched air: A single subject analysis of psychological and pysiological effects.* Paper presented at the annual meeting of the Association for Advancement of Behavior Therapy, Boston.

Sanderson, W. C., Rapee, R. M., & Barlow, D. H. (1988). *The influence an illusion of control on panic attacks induced via inhalation of 5.5% CO_2 enriched air.* Manuscript submitted for publication.

Sarason, I. G. (1982). *Stress, anxiety and cognitive interference: Reactions to tests.* Arlington, VA: Office of Naval Research.

Sarason, I. G. (1984). Stress, anxiety, and cognitive interference: Reactions to tests. *Journal of Personality and Social Psychology, 46,* 929–938.

Sarason, I. G. (1985). Cognitive processes, anxiety, and the treatment of anxiety disorders. In A. H. Tuma & J. D. Maser (Eds.), *Anxiety and the anxiety disorders.* Hillsdale, NJ: Erlbaum.

Sarason, I. G., Johnson, J. H., & Seigel, J. M. (1978). Assessing the impact of life changes: Development of the Life Experiences Survey. *Journal of Consulting and Clinical Psychology, 46,* 932–946.

Sarason, I. G., & Sarason, B. R. (1981). Teaching cognitive and social skills to high school students. *Journal of Consulting and Clinical Psychology, 49,* 908–919.

Sarbin, T. R. (1964). Anxiety: Reification of a metaphor. *Archives of General Psychiatry, 10,* 630–638.

Sarrel, D. M., & Masters, W. H. (1982). Sexual molestation of men by women. *Archives of Sexual Behavior, 11,* 117–131.

Sartory, G. (1983). Benzodiazepines and behavioural treatment of phobic anxiety. *Behavioural Psychotherapy, 11,* 204–217.

Sartory, G. (1986). Effect of phobic anxiety on the orienting response. *Behaviour Research and Therapy, 24,* 251–261.

Sartory, G., Rachman, S., & Grey, S. J. (1982). Return of fear: The role of rehearsal. *Behaviour Research and Therapy, 20,* 123–133.

Schachter, S. (1964). The interaction of cognitive and physiological determinants of emotional state. In L. Berkowitz (Ed.), *Advances in experimental social psychology* (Vol. 1). New York: Academic Press.

Schachter, S., & Singer, J. (1962). Cognitive, social and physiological determinants of emotional state. *Psychological Review, 69,* 379–397.

Scheier, M. F., & Carver, C. (1983). Two sides of the self: One for you and one for me. In J. Suls & A. G. Greenwald (Eds.), *Psychological perspectives on the self* (Vol. 2). Hillsdale, NJ: Erlbaum.

Scheier, M. F., Carver, C. S., & Gibbons, F. X. (1981). Self-focused attention and reactions to fear. *Journal of Research in Personality, 15,* 1–15.

Scheier, M. F., Carver, C. S., & Matthews, K. A. (1983). Attentional factors in the perception of bodily states. In J. T. Cacioppo & R. E. Petty (Eds.), *Social psychophysiology: A sourcebook.* New York: Guilford Press.

Schildkraut, J. J. (1965). The catecholamine hypothesis of affective disorders: A review of supporting evidence. *American Journal of Psychiatry, , 122,* 509–522.

Schinder, F. E. (1980). Treatment by systematic desensitization of a recurring nightmare of a real life trauma. *Journal of Behavior Therapy and Experimental Psychiatry, 11,* 53–54.

Schroeder, H. E., & Rich, A. R. (1976). The process of fear reduction through systematic desensitization. *Journal of Consulting and Clinical Psychology, 44,* 191–199.

Schwartz, G. E. (1976). Self-regulation of response patterning: Implications for psychophysiological research and therapy. *Biofeedback and Self-Regulation, 1,* 7–30.

Schwartz, G. E. (1978). Psychobiological foundations of psychotherapy and behavior change. In S. L. Garfield & A. E. Bergin (Eds.), *Handbook of psychotherapy and behavior change: An empirical analysis* (2nd ed.). New York: Wiley.

Schwartz, G. E., Davidson, R. J., & Goleman, D. J. (1978). Patterning of cognitive and somatic processes in the self-regulation of anxiety: Effects of meditation versus exercise. *Psychosomatic Medicine, 40,* 321–328.

Schwartz, G. E., Fair, P. L., Salt, P., Mandel, M. R., & Klerman, G. L. (1976). Facial muscle patterning to affective imagery in depressed and nondepressed subjects. *Science, 192,* 489–491.

Schwartz, G. E., Weinberger, D. A., & Singer, B. A. (1981). Cardiovascular differentiation of happiness, sadness, anger, and fear following imagery and exercise. *Psychosomatic Medicine, 43,* 343–364.

Schweizer, E. E., Swenson, C. M., Winokur, A., Rickels, K., & Maislin, G. (1986). The dexamethasone suppression test in generalized anxiety disorder. *British Journal of Psychiatry, 149,* 320–322.

Schweizer, E. E., Winokur, A., & Rickels, K. (1986). Insulin-induced hypoglycemia and panic attacks. *American Journal of Psychiatry, 143,* 654–655.

Segal, M., & Bloom, F. (1976). The action of norepinephrine in the rat hippocampus: III. Hippocampal cellular responses to locus coeruleus stimulation in the awake rate. *Brain Research, 107,* 499–501.

Seligman, M. E. P. (1968). Chronic fear produced by unpredictable electric shock. *Journal of Comparative and Physiological Psychology, 66,* 402–411.

Seligman, M. E. P. (1971). Phobias and preparedness. *Behavior Therapy, 2,* 307–320.

Seligman, M. E. P. (1975). *Helplessness: On depression, development and death.* San Francisco: W. H. Freeman.

Seligman, M. E. P., & Johnston, J. (1973). A cognitive theory of avoidance learning. In J. McGuigan & B. Lumsden (Eds.), *Contemporary approaches to conditioning and learning.* New York: Wiley.

Selye, H. (1956). *The stress of life.* New York: McGraw-Hill.

Selye, H. (1976). *The stress of life* (rev. ed.). New York: McGraw-Hill.

Senior, N., Gladstone, T., & Nurcombe, B. (1982). Child snatching: A case report. *Journal of the American Academy of Child Psychiatry, 21,* 579–583.

Sewitch, T. S., & Kirsch, I. (1984). The cognitive content of anxiety: Naturalistic evidence for the predominance of threat-related thoughts. *Cognitive Therapy and Research, 8,* 49–58.

Shafar, S. (1976). Aspects of phobic illness: A study of 90 personal cases. *British Journal of Medical Psychology, 49,* 221–236.

Shagass, C. (1955). Differentiation between anxiety and depression by the photically activated electroencephalogram. *American Journal of Psychiatry, 112,* 41–46.

Shapiro, A. K., Streuning, E. L., Shapiro, E., & Milearek, J. (1983). Diazepam: How much better than placebo? *Journal of Psychiatric Research, 17,* 51–73.

Shapiro, D. (1974). Operant-feedback control of human blood pressure: Some clinical issues. In P. A. Obrist, A. H. Black, J. Brener, & L. V. DiCara (Eds.), *Cardiovascular psychophysiology: Current issues in response mechanisms, biofeedback, and methodology.* Chicago: Aldine.

Shaw, P. (1979). A comparison of three behaviour therapies in the treatment of social phobia. *British Journal of Psychiatry, 134,* 620–623.

Shear, M. K. (1986). Pathophysiology of panic: A review of pharmacologic provocative tests and naturalistic monitoring data. *Journal of Clinical Psychiatry, 47,* 18–26.

Shear, M. K., Devereux, R. B., Kramer-Fox, M. S., Mann, J. J., & Frances, A. (1984). Low prevalence of mitral valve prolapse in patients with panic disorder. *American Journal of Psychiatry, 141,* 302–303.

Sheehan, D. V., Ballenger, J. C., & Jacobson, G. (1980). Treatment of endogenous anxiety with phobic, hysterical, and hypochondriacal symptoms. *Archives of General Psychiatry, 37,* 51–59.

Sheehan, D. V., Sheehan, K. E., & Minichiello, W. E. (1981). Age of onset of phobic disorders: A reevaluation. *Comprehensive Psychiatry, 22,* 544–553.

Sheehan, D. V., & Sheehan, M. S. (1982). The classification of anxiety and hysterical states: Part I. Historical review and empirical delineation. *Journal of Clinical Psychopathology, 2,* 235–243.

Sheki, M., & Patterson, M. (1984). Treatment of panic attacks with alprazolam and propranolol. *American Journal of Psychiatry, 141,* 900–901.

Shepherd, M., Cooper, B., Brown, A. C., & Kalton, C. W. (1966). *Psychiatric illness in general practice.* London: Oxford University Press.

Sher, K. J., Frost, R. O., & Otto, R. (1983). Cognitive deficits in compulsive checks: An exploratory study. *Behaviour Research and Therapy, 21,* 357–363.

Sher, K. J., Mann, B., & Frost, R. O. (1984). Cognitive dysfunction in compulsive checkers: Further explorations. *Behaviour Research and Therapy, 22,* 493–502.

Sherman, A. R., & Plummer, I. L. (1973). Training in relaxation as a behavioral self-management skill: An exploratory investigation. *Behavior Therapy, 4,* 543–550.

Shields, J. (1962). *Monozygotic twins brought up apart and together.* London: Oxford University Press.

Shiller, V. M., Izard, C. E., & Hembree, E. A. (1986). Patterns of emotion expression during separation in the strange-situation procedure. *Developmental Psychology, 22,* 378–382.

Siever, L. J., & Uhde, T. W. (1984). New studies and perspectives on the nonadrenergic receptor system in depression: Effects of the alpha-2-adrenergic agonist clonidine. *Biological Psychiatry, 19,* 131.

Silverman, W. K., Cerny, J. A., & Nelles, W. B. (in press). Psychopathology in children with anxiety disorders. In B. B. Lahey & A. Kazdin (Eds.), *Advances in clinical child psychology* (Vol. 11). New York: Plenum Press.

Singer, J. L., & Antrobus, J. S. (1972). Daydreaming, imaginal processes, and personality: A normative study. In P. Sheehan (Ed.), *The function and nature of imagery.* New York: Academic Press.

Sinnott, A., Jones, R. B., Scott-Fordham, A., & Woodward, R. (1981). Augmentation of in vivo exposure treatment for agoraphobia by the formation of neighborhood self-help groups. *Behaviour Research and Therapy, 19,* 339–347.

Skolnick, P., & Paul, S. M. (1982). Molecular pharmacology of the benzodiazepines. *International Review of Neurobiology, 23,* 103.

Slater, E. (1943). The neurotic constitution: A statistical study of two thousand soldiers. *Journal of Neurology and Psychiatry, 6,* 1–16.

Slater, E., & Shields, J. (1969). Genetical aspects of anxiety. *British Journal of Psychiatry, 3,* 62–71.

Smail, P., Stockwell, T., Canter, S., & Hodgson, R. (1984). Alcohol dependence and phobic anxiety states: I. A prevalence study. *British Journal of Psychiatry, 144*, 53–57.

Smith, J. S., & Kiloh, L. G. (1980). The psychosurgical treatment of anxiety. In G. D. Burrows & B. Davies (Eds.), *Handbook of studies on anxiety*. Amsterdam: Elsevier/North-Holland.

Snaith, R. P. (1968). A clinical investigation of phobia. *British Journal of Psychiatry, 114*, 673–697.

Solomon, K., & Hart, R. (1978). Pitfalls and prospects in clinical research on antianxiety drugs: Benzodiazepines and placebos. *Journal of Clinical Psychiatry, 39*, 823–831.

Solomon, Z., & Benbenishty, R. (1986). The role of proximity, immediacy, and expectancy in frontline treatment of combat stress reaction among Israelis in the Lebanon war. *American Journal of Psychiatry, 143*, 613–617.

Solyom, C., Solyom, L., LaPierre, Y., Pecknold, J. C., & Morton, L. (1981). Phenelzine and exposure in the treatment of phobias. *Journal of Biological Psychiatry, 16*, 239–248.

Solyom, L., Beck, P., Solyom, C., & Hugel, R. (1974). Some etiological factors in phobic neurosis. *Canadian Journal of Psychiatry, 19*, 69–78.

Solyom, L., Heseltine, G. F., McClure, P. J., Solyom, C., Ledwidge, B., & Steinberg, G. (1973). Behaviour therapy versus drug therapy in the treatment of phobic neurosis. *Canadian Psychiatric Association Journal, 18*, 25–31.

Solyom, L., Ledwidge, B., & Solyom, C. (1986). Delineating social phobia. *British Journal of Psychiatry, 149*, 464–470.

Solyom, L., Silberfeld, M., & Solyom, C. (1976). Maternal overprotection in the etiology of agoraphobia. *Canadian Psychiatric Association Journal, 21*, 109–113.

Sperry, R. (1982). Some effects of disconnecting the cerebral hemispheres *Science, 217*, 1223–1226.

Spielberger, C. D. (1966). Theory and research on anxiety. In C. D. Spielberger (Ed.), *Anxiety and behavior*. New York: Academic Press.

Spielberger, C. D. (1972). Anxiety as an emotional state. In C. D. Spielberger (Ed.), *Anxiety: Current trends in theory and research* (Vol. 1). New York: Academic Press.

Spielberger, C. D. (1979). *Understanding stress and anxiety*. New York: Harper & Row.

Spielberger, C. D. (1983). *Manual for the State–Trait Anxiety Inventory* (STAI Form Y). Palo Alto, CA: Consulting Psychologists Press.

Spielberger, C. D. (1985). Anxiety, cognition, and affect: A state–trait perspective. In A. H. Tuma & J. D. Maser (Eds.), *Anxiety and the anxiety disorders*. Hillsdale, NJ: Erlbaum.

Spielberger, C. D., Gorsuch, R. L., & Lushene, R. E. (1970). *Manual for the State–Trait Anxiety Inventory*. Palo Alto, CA: Consulting Psychologists Press.

Spielberger, C. D., & Sarason, J. G. (1978). *Stress and anxiety* (Vol. 5). Washington, DC: Hemisphere.

Spier, S., Tesar, G., Rosenbaum, L., & Woods, S. (1986). Treatment of panic disorders with clonazepam. *Journal of Clinical Psychiatry, 47*, 238–242.

Spitzer, R. L., & Williams, J. B. W. (1985). Proposed revisions in the DSM III classification of anxiety disorders based on research and clinical experience. In A. H. Tuma & J. D. Maser (Eds.), *Anxiety and the anxiety disorders*. Hillsdale, NJ: Erlbaum.

Spitzer, R. L., Williams, J. B. W., & Gibbon, M. (1985). *Instruction manual for the Structured Clinical Interview for DSM-III* (SCID, 7/1/85 revision). New York: Biometrics Research Department, New York State Psychiatric Institute.

Squires, R. F., & Braestrup, C. (1970). Benzodiazepine receptors in rat brain. *Nature* (London), *266*, 732–734.

Sroufe, L. A. (1977). Wariness of strangers and the study of infant development. *Child Development, 48*, 731–746.

Stampfl, T. G., & Lewis, D. J. (1967). Essentials of implosive therapy: A learning theory based psychodynamic behavioral therapy. *Journal of Abnormal Psychology, 72*, 496–503.

Staub, E., Tursky, B., & Schwartz, G. E. (1971). Self-control and predictability: Their effects on reactions to aversive stimulation. *Journal of Personality and Social Psychology, 18*, 157–162.

Steketee, G., & Foa, E. B. (1985). Obsessive–compulsive disorder. In D. H. Barlow (Ed.), *Clinical handbook of psychological disorders: A step-by-step treatment manual.* New York: Guilford Press.

Steketee, G. S., Foa, E. B., & Grayson, J. B. (1982). Recent advances in the behavioral treatment of obsessive–compulsives. *Archives of General Psychiatry, 39*, 1365–1371.

Steketee, G. S., Grayson, J. B., & Foa, E. B. (1985). Obsessive–compulsive disorder: Differences between washers and checkers. *Behaviour Research and Therapy, 23*, 197–201.

Steketee, G. S., Grayson, J. B., & Foa, E. B. (1987). A comparison of characteristics of obsessive–compulsive disorder and other anxiety disorders. *Journal of Anxiety Disorders, 1*, 325–335.

Stern, R. S. (1970). Treatment of a case of obsessional neurosis using thought stopping technique. *British Journal of Psychiatry, 117*, 441–442.

Stern, R. S., & Cobb, J. P. (1978). Phenomenology of obsessive–compulsive neurosis. *British Journal of Psychiatry, 132*, 233–239.

Stern, R. S., & Marks, I. (1973). Brief and prolonged flooding: A comparison of agoraphobic patients. *Archives of General Psychiatry, 28*, 270–276.

Stockwell, R., Smail, P., Hodgson, R., & Canter, S. (1984). Alcohol dependence and phobic anxiety states: II. A retrospective study. *British Journal of Psychiatry, 144*, 58–63.

Stokes, P. (1985). The neuroendocrinology of anxiety. In A. H. Tuma & J. D. Maser (Eds.), *Anxiety and the anxiety disorders.* Hillsdale, NJ: Erlbaum.

Storms, M. D., & Nisbett, R. E. (1970). Insomnia and the attribution process. *Journal of Personality and Social Psychology, 16*, 319–328.

Stravynski, A., Marks, I., & Yule, W. (1982). Social skills problems in neurotic outpatients: Social skills training with and without cognitive modification. *Archives of General Psychiatry, 39*, 1378–1385.

Street, L. L., Craske, M. G., & Barlow, D. H. (1987, November). *Sensations, cognitions and antecedents associated with expected and unexpected panic attacks.* Paper presented at the annual meeting of the Association for Advancement of Behavior Therapy, Boston.

Sturgis, E. T. (1980, November). *Physiological lability and reactivity in headache activity.* Paper presented at the annual meeting of the Association for Advancement of Behavior Therapy, New York.

Sturgis, E. T., & Arena, J. G. (1984). Psychophysiology assessment. *Progressive Behavior Modification, 17*, 1–30.

Sturt, E. (1981). Hierarchical patterns in the distribution of psychiatric symptoms. *Psychological Medicine, 11*, 783–794.

Suarez, S. D., & Gallup, G. G., Jr. (1979). Tonic immobility as a response to rape in humans: A theoretical note. *Psychological Record, 29*, 315–320.

Suinn, R. M., & Richardson, R. (1971). Anxiety management training: A nonspecific behavior therapy program for anxiety control. *Behavior Therapy, 2*, 498–510.

Suls, J., & Fletcher, B. (1985a). The relative efficacy of avoidant and nonavoidant coping strategies: A meta-analysis. *Health Psychology, 4*, 249–288.

Suls, J., & Fletcher, B. (1985b). Self-attention, life stress, and illness: A prospective study. *Psychosomatic Medicine, 47*, 469–481.

Suomi, S. J. (1986). Anxiety-like disorders in young nonhuman primates. In R. Gittelman (Ed.), *Anxiety disorders of childhood.* New York: Guilford Press.

Suomi, S. J., Kraemer, G. W., Baysinger, C. M., & DeLizio, R. D. (1981). Inherited and experimental factors associated with individual differences in anxious behavior displayed by rhesus monkeys. In D. F. Klein & J. Rabkin (Eds.), *Anxiety: New research and changing concepts.* New York: Raven Press.

Surtees, P. G., & Kendall, R. E. (1979). The hierarchy model of psychiatric symptomatology:

An investigation based on Present State Examination ratings. *British Journal of Psychiatry, 135,* 438–443.

Swinson, R. P. (1986). Reply to Kleiner. *the Behavior Therapist, 9*(6), 110–128.

Swinson, R. P., & Kirby, M. (1986). The differentiation of anxiety and depressive syndromes. In B. F. Shaw, F. Cashman, Z. V. Segal, & T. M. Vallis (Eds.), *Anxiety disorder: Theory, diagnosis and treatment.* New York: Plenum Press.

Tan, E. S. (1969). The symptomatology of anxiety in West Malaysia. *Australian and New Zealand Journal of Psychiatry, 3,* 271–276.

Tan, E. S. (1980). Transcultural aspects of anxiety. In G. D. Burrows & B. Davies (Eds.), *Handbook of studies on anxiety.* Amsterdam: Elsevier/North-Holland.

Taylor, C. B., Sheikh, J., Agras, W. S., Roth, W. T., Margraf, J., Ehlers, A., Maddock, R. J., & Gossard, D. (1986). Self-report of panic attacks: Agreement with heart rate changes. *American Journal of Psychiatry, 143,* 478–482.

Taylor, C. B., Telch, M. J., & Haavik, D. (1983). Ambulatory heart rate changes during panic attacks. *Journal of Psychosomatic Research, 17,* 1–6.

Taylor, M. A. (1987). DSM-III organic metal disorders. In G. L. Tischler (Ed.), *Diagnosis and classification in psychiatry: A critical appraisal of DSM-III.* Cambridge, England: Cambridge University Press.

Tearnan, B. H., Telch, M. J., & Keefe, P. (1984). Etiology and onset of agoraphobia: A critical review. *Comprehensive Psychiatry, 25,* 51–62.

Teasdale, J. D. (1978). Self-efficacy: Toward a unifying theory of behavioral change? *Advances in Behaviour Research and Therapy, 1,* 211–215.

Teasdale, J. D. (1983). Negative thinking in depression: Cause, effect, or reciprocal relationship. *Advances in Behaviour Research and Therapy, 5,* 3–25.

Teasdale, J. D. (1985). Psychological treatments for depression: How do they work? *Behaviour Research and Therapy, 23,* 157–165.

Teasdale, J. D., & Fogarty, S. J. (1979). Differential effects of induced mood on retrieval of pleasant and unpleasant events from episodic memory. *Journal of Abnormal Psychology, 88,* 248–257.

Telch, M. J. (1988). Combined pharmacologic and psychological treatments for panic sufferers. In S. Rachman & J. D. Maser (Eds.), *Panic: Psychological perspectives.* Hillsdale, NJ: Erlbaum.

Telch, M. J., Agras, W. S., Taylor, C. B., Roth, W. T., & Gallen, C. (1985). Combined pharmacological and behavioural treatment for agoraphobia. *Behaviour Research and Therapy, 23,* 325–335.

Telch, M. J., Tearnan, B. H., & Taylor, C. B. (1983). Anti-depressant medication in the treatment of agoraphobia: A critical review. *Behaviour Research and Therapy, 21,* 505–527.

Tellegen, A. (1985). Structures of mood and personality and their relevance to assessing anxiety, with an emphasis on self-report. In A. H. Tuma & J. D. Maser (Eds.), *Anxiety and the anxiety disorders.* Hillsdale, NJ: Erlbaum.

Tennant, C., Hurry, J., & Bebbington, P. (1982). The relation of childhood separation experiences to adult depressive and anxiety states. *British Journal of Psychiatry, 141,* 475–482.

Terhune, W. B. (1949). The phobic syndrome. *Archives of Neurology and Psychiatry, 62,* 162–172.

Thompson, R. F., & Spencer, W. A. (1966). Habituation: A model phenomenon for the study of neuronal substrates of behavior. *Psychological Review, 73,* 16–43.

Thorén, P., Åsberg, M., Cronholm, B., Jörnestedt, L., & Träskman, L. (1980). Clomipramine treatment of obsessive–compulsive disorder: A controlled clinical trial. *Archives of General Psychiatry, 37,* 1281–1289.

Thorpe, G. L., & Burns, L. E. (1983). *The agoraphobic syndrome.* New York: Wiley.

Thyer, B. A., & Curtis, G. C. (1983). The repeated pretest–posttest single-subject experiment: A new design for empirical clinical practice. *Journal of Behavior Therapy and Experimental Psychiatry, 14,* 311–315.

Thyer, B. A., & Curtis, G. C. (1984). The effects of ethanol intoxication on phobic anxiety. *Behaviour Research and Therapy, 22,* 559–610.

Thyer, B. A., & Himle, J. (1985). Temporal relationships between panic attack onset and phobic avoidance in agoraphobia. *Behaviour Research and Therapy, 23,* 607–608.

Thyer, B. A., Himle, J., Curtis, G. C., Cameron, O. G., & Nesse, R. M. (1985). A comparison of panic disorder and agoraphobia with panic attacks. *Comprehensive Psychiatry, 26,* 208–214.

Thyer, B. A., Nesse, R. M., Cameron, O. G., & Curtis, G. C. (1985). Agoraphobia: A test of the separation anxiety hypotheses. *Behaviour Research and Therapy, 23,* 75–78.

Thyer, B. A., Nesse, R. M., Curtis, G. C., & Cameron, O. G. (1986). Panic disorder: A test of the separation anxiety hypothesis. *Behaviour Research and Therapy, 24,* 209–211.

Thyer, B. A., Papsdorf, J. D., & Wright, P. (1984). Physiological and psychological effects of acute intentional hyperventilation. *Behaviour Research and Therapy, 22,* 587–590.

Thyer, B. A., Parrish, R., Curtis, G. C., Nesse, R. M., & Cameron, O. G. (1985). Ages of onset of DSM-III anxiety disorders. *Comprehensive Psychiatry, 26,* 113–122.

Thyer, B. A., Parrish, R. T., Himle, J., Cameron, O. G., Curtis, G. C., & Nesse, R. M. (1986). Alcohol abuse among clinically anxious patients. *Behaviour Research and Therapy, 24, 357–359.*

Tompkins, S. S. (1981). *The quest for primary motives: Biography and audiobiography of an idea. Journal of Personality and Social Psychology, 41,* 306–329.

Torgersen, S. (1979). The nature and origin of common phobic fears. *British Journal of Psychiatry, 134,* 343–351.

Torgersen, S. (1983a). Genetic factors in anxiety disorders. *Archives of General Psychiatry, 40,* 1085–1089.

Torgersen, S. (1983b). Genetics of neurosis—the effects of sampling variation upon the twin concordance ratio. *British Journal of Psychiatry, 142,* 126–132.

Trower, P., Yardley, K., Bryant, B., & Shaw, P. (1978). The treatment of social failure: A comparison of anxiety-reduction and skills acquisition procedures on two social problems. *Behavior Modification, 2,* 41–60.

Tsuang, M. T., & Vandermey, R. (1980). *Genes and the mind: Inheritance of mental illness.* New York: Oxford University Press.

Turner, S. M., Beidel, D. C., & Costello, A. (1987). Psychopathology in the offspring of anxiety disorders patients. *Journal of Consulting and Clinical Psychology, 55,* 229–235.

Turner, S. M., Beidel, D. C., Dancu, C. V., & Keys, D. J. (1986). Psychopathology of social phobia and comparison to avoidant personality disorder. *Journal of Abnormal Psychology, 95,* 389–394.

Turner, S. M., Beidel, D. C., & Jacob, R. G. (1988). Assessment of panic. In S. Rachman & J. D. Maser (Eds.), *Panic: Psychological perspectives.* Hillsdale, NJ: Erlbaum.

Turner, S. M., Beidel, D. C., & Nathan, R. S. (1985). Biological factors in obsessive–compulsive disorders. *Psychological Bulletin, 97,* 451–461.

Turner, S. M., Hersen, M., Bellack, A. S., & Wells, K. C. (1979). Behavioural treatment of obsessive–compulsive neurosis. *Behaviour Research and Therapy, 17,* 95–106.

Turner, S. M., McCann, B. S., Beidel, D. C., & Mezzich, J. E. (1986). DSM-III classification of the anxiety disorders: A psychometric study. *Journal of Abnormal Psychology, 95,* 168–172.

Turner, S. M., Williams, S. L., Beidel, D. C., & Mezzich, J. E. (1986). Panic disorder and agoraphobia with panic attacks: Covariation along the dimensions of panic and agoraphobic fear. *Journal of Abnormal Psychology, 95,* 384–388.

Twentyman, C. T., & McFall, R. M. (1975). Behavioral training of social skills in shy males. *Journal of Consulting and Clinical Psychology, 43,* 384–395.

Tyrer, P. J. (1976). *The role of bodily feelings in anxiety.* London: Oxford University Press.

Tyrer, P. J. (1980). Comments: Dependence on benzodiazepines. *British Journal of Psychiatry, 137*, 576–577.

Tyrer, P. J. (1984). Classification of anxiety. *British Journal of Psychiatry, 144*, 78–93.

Tyrer, P. J., Candy, J., & Kelly, D. A. (1973). A study of the clinical effects of phenelzine and placebo in the treatment of phobic anxiety. *Psychopharmacologia, 32*, 237–254.

Tyrer, P. J., Casey, P., & Gall, J. (1983). Relationship between neurosis and personality disorder. *British Journal of Psychiatry, 142*, 404–408.

Tyrer, P. J., & Lader, M. H. (1974). Response to propranolol and diazepam in somatic anxiety. *British Medical Journal, ii*, 14–16.

Tyrer, P. J., & Owen, R. (1984). Anxiety in primary care: Is short-term drug treatment appropriate? *Journal of Psychiatric Research, 18*, 73–79.

Tyrer, P. J., Rutherford, D., & Huggett, T. (1981). Benzodiazepine withdrawal symptoms and propranolol. *Lancet, i*, 520.

Uhde, T. W., Boulenger, J. P., Post, R. M., Siever, L. J., Vittone, B. J., Jimerson, D. C., & Roy-Byrne, P. P. (1984). Fear and anxiety: Relationship to noradrenergic function. *Psychopathology, 17*, 8–23.

Uhde, T. W., Boulenger, J. P., Roy-Byrne, P. P., Geraci, M. P., Vittone, B. J., & Post, R. M. (1985). Longitudinal course of panic disorder: Clinical and biological considerations. *Progressive Neuro-Psychopharmacology and Biological Psychiatry, 9*, 39–51.

Uhde, T. W., Boulenger, J. P., Vittone, B., Siever, L., & Post, R. M. (1985). Human anxiety and nonadrenergic function: Preliminary studies with caffeine, clonidine and yohimbine. In *Proceedings of the Seventh World Congress of Psychiatry*. New York: Plenum Press.

Uhde, T. W., Roy-Byrne, P. P., Vittone, B. J., Boulenger, J. P., & Post, R. M. (1985). Phenomenology and neurobiology of panic disorder. In A. H. Tuma & J. D. Maser (Eds.), *Anxiety and the anxiety disorders*. Hillsdale, NJ: Erlbaum.

Uhde, T., Siever, L., & Post, R. M. (1984). Clonidine: Acute challenge and clinical trial paradigms for the investigation and treatment of anxiety disorders, affective illness, and pain syndromes. In R. M. Post & J. C. Ballenger (Eds.), *Neurobiology of mood disorders*. Baltimore: Williams & Wilkins.

Uhde, T., Siever, L., Post, R. M., Jimerson, D., Boulenger, J. P., & Buchsbaum, M. (1982). The relationship of plasma-free MHPG to anxiety and psychophysical pain in normal volunteers. *Psychopharmacological Bulletin, 18*, 129–132.

Uhde, T. W., Vittone, B. M., & Post, R. M. (1984). Glucose tolerance listing in panic disorder. *American Journal of Psychiatry, 14*, 1461–1463.

Uhlenhuth, E. H., Baltzer, M. B., Mellinger, G. E., Cisin, I. H., & Clinthorne, J. (1983). Symptom checklist syndromes in the general population. *Archives of General Psychiatry, 40*, 1167–1173.

Ulett, G. A., Gleser, G., Winokur, G., & Lawler, A. (1953). The EEG and reaction to phobic stimulation as an index of anxiety-proneness. *Electronencephalography and Clinical Neurophysiology, 5*, 23–32.

van den Hout, M. A. (1988). Metabolism, reflexes and cognitions in experimental panic. In S. Rachman & J. D. Maser (Eds.), *Panic: Psychological perspectives*. Hillsdale, NJ: Erlbaum.

van den Hout, M. A., & Griez, E. (1982). Cardiovascular and subjective responses to inhalation of carbon dioxide. *Psychotherapy and Psychosomatics, 37*, 75–82.

van den Hout, M. A., van der Molen, G. M., Griez, E., & Lousberg, H. (1987). Specificity of interoceptive fear to panic disorders. *Journal of Psychopathology and Behavioral Assessment, 9*, 99–106.

Van der Kolk, B. A., Greenberg, M., Boyd, H., & Krystal, J. (1985). Inescapable shock, neurotransmitters, and addition to trauma: Toward a psychobiology of post-traumatic stress. *Biological Psychiatry, 20*, 314–325.

van der Molen, van den Hout, M. A., Vroemen, J., Lousberg, H., & Griez, E. (1986). Cognitive determinants of lactate-induced anxiety. *Behaviour Research and Therapy, 24,* 677–680.

Van Oot, P. H., Lane, T. W., & Borkovec, T. D. (1984). Sleep disturbances. In H. E. Adams & P. B. Sutker (Eds.), *Comprehensive handbook of psychopathology.* New York: Plenum Press.

Vermilyea, B. B., Barlow, D. H., & O'Brien, G. T. (1984). The importance of assessing treatment integrity: An example in the anxiety disorders. *Journal of Behavioral Assessment, 6,* 1–11.

Vermilyea, J. A., Boice, R., & Barlow, D. H. (1984). Rachman and Hodgson (1974) a decade later: How do desynchronous response systems relate to the treatment of agoraphobia? *Behaviour Research and Therapy, 22,* 615–621.

Volavka, J., Neziroglu, F., & Yaryura-Tobias, J. A. (1985). Clomipramine and imipramine in obsessive–compulsive disorder. *Psychiatry Research, 14,* 85–93.

Von Korff, M. R., Eaton, W. W., & Keyl, P. (1985). The epidemiology of panic attacks and panic disorders: Results of three community surveys. *American Journal of Epidemiology, 122,* 970–981.

Waddell, M. T., Barlow, D. H., & O'Brien, G. T. (1984). A preliminary investigation of cognitive and relaxation treatment of panic disorder: Effects on intense anxiety vs. "background" anxiety. *Behaviour Research and Therapy, 22,* 393–402.

Wade, T. C., Malloy, T. E., & Proctor, S. (1977). Imaginal correlates of self-reported fear and avoidance behavior. *Behaviour Research and Therapy, 15,* 17–22.

Wallnau, L. B., & Gallup, G. G., Jr. (1977). A serotonergic, midbrain–raphe model of tonic immobility. *Biobehavioral Reviews, 1,* 35–43.

Walter, W. G. (1964). Slow potential waves in the human brain associated with expectancy, attention and decision. *Archives für Psychiatrie und Nervenkrankheiten, 206,* 309–322.

Walton, D. (1960). The relevance of learning theory to the treatment of an obsessive–compulsive state. In H. J. Eysenck (Ed.), *Behaviour therapy and neuroses.* Oxford: Pergamon Press.

Wamboldt, M. Z., & Insel, T. R. (1988). Pharmacologic models of anxiety. In C. Last & M. Hersen (Eds.), *Handbook of anxiety disorders.* New York: Pergamon Press.

Washington Diarist (pseudonym). (1985, October). Strung out. *New Republic,* p. 59.

Watson, D., & Friend, R. (1969). Measurement of social-evaluative anxiety. *Journal of Consulting and Clinical Psychology, 33,* 448–457.

Watson, J., & Raynor, R. (1920). Conditioned emotional reactions. *Journal of Genetic Psychology, 37,* 394–419.

Watson, J. P., & Marks, I. M. (1971). Relevant and irrelevant fear in flooding—a crossover study of phobic patients. *Behavior Therapy, 2,* 275–293.

Watts, F. N. (1979). Habituation model of systematic desensitization. *Psychological Bulletin, 86,* 627–637.

Waynbaum, I. (1907). *La physionomie humaine: Son mécanisme et son rôle social.* Paris: Alcan.

Wearn, J. T., & Sturgis, C. C. (1919). Studies on epinephrine: I. Effects of the injection of epinephrine in soldiers with "irritable heart." *Archives of Internal Medicine, 24,* 247–268.

Webster, A. S. (1953). The development of phobias in married women. *Psychological Monographs, 67,* 367.

Weekes, C. (1968). *Hope and help for your nerves.* New York: Hawthorne.

Weekes, C. (1972). *Peace from nervous suffering.* New York: Hawthorne.

Weekes, C. (1973). A practical treatment of agoraphobia. *British Medical Journal, ii,* 469–471.

Weekes, C. (1976). *Simple, effective treatment of agoraphobia.* New York: Hawthorne.

Wegner, D. M., & Giuliano, T. (1980). Arousal-induced attention to the self. *Journal of Personality and Social Psychology, 38,* 719–726.

Weiner, H. (1985). The psychobiology and pathophysiology of anxiety and fear. In A. H. Tuma & J. D. Maser (Eds.), *Anxiety and the anxiety disorders.* Hillsdale, NJ: Erlbaum.

REFERENCES

Weiss, J. M. (1971a). Effects of coping behavior with and without a feedback signal on stress pathology in rats. *Journal of Comparative and Physiological Psychology, 77*, 1–13.

Weiss, J. M. (1971b). Effects of coping behavior in different warning signal conditions on stress pathology in the rat. *Journal of Comparative and Physiological Psychology, 77*, 14–21.

Weiss, J. M., Bailey, W. H., Goodman, P. A., Hoffman, L. J., Ambrose, M. J., Salman, S., & Charry, J. M. (1982). A model for neurochemical study of depression. In M. Y. Spiegelstein & A. Levy (Eds.), *Behavioral models and the analysis of drug action.* Amsterdam: Elsevier.

Weiss, J. M., Glazer, H. I., & Poherecky, L. A. (1976). Coping behavior and neurochemical changes: An alternative explanation for the original "learned helplessness" experiments. In A. Serban & A. Kling (Eds.), *Animal models in human psychobiology.* New York: Plenum Press.

Weiss, K. J., & Rosenberg, D. J. (1985). Prevalence of anxiety disorders among alcoholics. *Journal of Clinical Psychiatry, 46*, 3–5.

Weissman, M. M. (1985). The epidemiology of anxiety disorders: Rates, risks and familial patterns. In A. H. Tuma & J. D. Maser (Eds.), *Anxiety and the anxiety disorders.* Hillsdale, NJ: Erlbaum.

Weissman, M. M., Leaf, P. J., Blazer, D. G., Boyd, J. H., & Florio, L. (1986). The relationship between panic disorder and agoraphobia: An epidemiologic perspective. *Psychopharmacology Bulletin, 43*, 787–791.

Weissman, M. M., Leckman, J. F., Merikangas, K. R., Gammon, G. D., & Prusoff, B. A. (1984). Depression and anxiety disorders in parents and children. *Archives of General Psychiatry, 41*, 845–852.

Wernicke, C. (1900). *Grundriss der Psychiatrie.* Leipzig: Verlag von Georg Thieme.

Westphal, C. (1871). Die agoraphobia: Eine neuropathische Eischeinung. *Archives für Psychiatrie und Nervenkrankheiten, 3*, 384–412.

Wheeler, E. O., White, P. D., Reed, E., & Cohen, M. E. (1948). Familial incidence of neurocirculatory asthenia ("anxiety neurosis," "effort syndrome"). *Journal of Clinical Investigation, 27*, 562.

White, B. V., & Gildea, E. F. (1937). "Cold pressor test" in tension and anxiety: A cardiochronographic study. *Archives of Neurology of Psychiatry, 38*, 964–984.

Whitehead, W. E., Robinson, A., Blackwell, B., & Stutz, R. (1978). Flooding treatment of phobias: Does chronic diazepam increase effectiveness? *Journal of Behavior Therapy and Experimental Psychiatry, 9*, 219–225.

Williams, S. L. (1985). On the nature and measurement of agoraphobia. *Progress in Behavior Modification, 19*, 109–144.

Williams, S. L., Dooseman, G., & Kleifield, E. (1984). Comparative effectiveness of guided mastery and exposure treatments for intractable phobias. *Journal of Consulting and Clinical Psychology, 52*, 505–518.

Williams, S. L., & Rappoport, J. A. (1983). Cognitive treatment in the natural environment for agoraphobics. *Behavior Therapy, 14*, 299–313.

Williams, S. L., Turner, S. M., & Peer, D. F. (1985). Guided mastery and performance desensitization treatments for severe acrophobia. *Journal of Consulting and Clinical Psychology, 53*, 237–247.

Wilson, G. T. (1982). Psychotherapy process and procedure: The behavioral mandate. *Behavior Therapy, 13*, 291–312.

Wilson, G. T. (1984). Clinical issues and strategies in the practice of behavior therapy. In C. M. Franks, G. T. Wilson, P. C. Kendall, & K. D. Brownell, *Annual review of behavior therapy: Theory and practice* (Vol. 10). New York: Guilford Press.

Wing, J. K., Cooper, J. E., & Sartobrius, N. (1974). *The measurement and classification of psychiatric symptoms.* Cambridge, England: Cambridge University Press.

REFERENCES

Wirtz, P. W., & Harrell, A. V. (1987). Effects of postassault exposure to attack-similar stimuli on long-term recovery victims. *Journal of Consulting and Clinical Psychology, 55,* 10–16.

Wittchen, H. U. (1986). Epidemiology of panic attacks and panic disorders. In I. Hand & H. U. Wittchen (Eds.), *Panic and phobias: Empirical evidence of theoretical models and longterm effects of behavioral treatments.* Berlin: Springer-Verlag.

Wolpe, J. (1952). Experimental neurosis as learned behavior. *British Journal of Psychology, 43,* 243–268.

Wolpe, J. (1954). Reciprocal inhibition as the main basis of psychotherapeutic effects. *Archives of Neurology and Psychiatry, 72,* 205.

Wolpe, J. (1958). *Psychotherapy by reciprocal inhibition.* Stanford, CA: Stanford University Press.

Wolpe, J. (1970). Identifying the antecedents of an agoraphobic reaction: A transcript. *Journal of Behavior Therapy and Experimental Psychiatry, 1,* 299–304.

Wolpe, J. (1973). *The practice of behavior therapy* (2nd ed.). New York: Pergamon Press.

Wolpe, J. (1976). Behavior therapy and its malcontents: II. Multimodal electicism, cognitive exclusivism and "exposure" empiricism. *Journal of Behavior Therapy and Experimental Psychiatry, 7,* 109–116.

Wolpe, J. (1981). The dichotomy between classical conditioned and cognitively learned anxiety. *Journal of Behavior Therapy and Experimental Psychiatry, 12,* 35–42.

Wolpe, J., & Lang, P. J. (1969). *Fear Survey Schedule.* San Diego, CA: Educational and Industrial Testing Service.

Woodruff, M. L., & Lippincott, W. I. (1976). Hyperemotionality and enhanced tonic immobility after septal lesions in the rabbit. *Brain, Behavior and Evolution, 13,* 22–33.

Woodruff, R. H., Guze, S. B., & Clayton, P. J. (1972). Anxiety neurosis among psychiatric outpatients. *Comprehensive Psychiatry, 13,* 165–170.

Woods, S. W., Charney, D. S., Goodman, W. K., & Heninger, G. R. (1987). Carbon dioxide-induced anxiety: Behavioral, physiologic, and biochemical effects of 5% CO_2 in panic disorder patients and 5 and 7.5% CO_2 in healthy subjects. *Archives of General Psychiatry, 44,* 365–375.

Woods, S. W., Charney, D. S., Loke, J., Goodman, W. K., Redmond, D. E., & Heninger, G. R. (1986). Carbon dioxide sensitivity in panic anxiety. *Archives of General Psychiatry, 43,* 900–909.

Woods, S. W., Charney, D. S., McPherson, C. A., Gradman, A. H., & Heninger, G. R. (1987). Situational panic attacks: Behavioral, physiological, and biochemical characterization. *Archives of General Psychiatry, 44,* 365–375.

Woodward, R., & Jones, R. B. (1980). Cognitive restructuring treatment: A controlled trial with anxious patients. *Behaviour Research and Therapy, 22,* 393–402.

Worthington, E. R. (1977). Post-service adjustment and Vietnam era veterans. *Military Medicine, 142,* 865–866.

Worthington, E. R. (1978). Demographic and pre-service variables as predictors of post-military service adjustment. In C. R. Figley (Ed.), *Stress disorders among Vietnam veterans: Theory, research, and treatment.* New York: Brunner/Mazel.

Wundt, W. (1896). *Grundriss der psychologie.* Leipzig: Engelman.

Yerkes, R. M., & Dodson, J. D. (1908). The relation of strength of stimulus to rapidity of habit-formation. *Journal of Comparative Neurology and Psychology, 18,* 459–482.

Young, J. P. R., Fenton, G. W., & Lader, M. H. (1971). Inheritance of neurotic traits: A twin study of the Middlesex Hospital Questionnaire. *British Journal of Psychiatry, 119,* 393–398.

Yuksel, S., Marks, I., Ramm, E., & Ghosh, A. (1984). Slow versus rapid exposure in vivo of phobics. *Behavioural Psychotherapy, 12,* 249–256.

Yule, W., & Fernando, P. (1980). Blood phobia—beware. *Behaviour Research and Therapy, 18,* 587–590.

REFERENCES

Zajonc, R. B. (1980). Feeling and thinking: Preferences need no inferences. *American Psychologist, 35,* 151–175.

Zajonc, R. B. (1984). On the primacy of affect. *American Psychologist,* 117–123.

Zajonc, R. B. (1985). Emotion and facial efference: A theory reclaimed. *Science, 228,* 15–21.

Zevon, M. A., & Tellegen, A. (1982). The structure of mood change: Anidrographic/nomothetic analysis. *Journal of Personality and Social Psychology, 43,* 111–122.

Zillman, D. (1983a). Arousal and aggression. In R. G. Geen & E. Donnerstein (Eds.), *Aggression: Theoretical and empirical reviews* (Vol. 1). New York: Academic Press.

Zillmann, D. (1983b). Transfer of excitation in emotional behavior. In J. T. Cacioppo & R. E. Petty (Eds.), *Social psychophysiology: A sourcebook.* New York: Guilford Press.

Zitrin, C. M. (1981). Combined pharmacological and psychological treatment of phobias. In M. Mavissakalian & D. H. Barlow (Eds.), *Phobia: Psychological and pharmacological treatment.* New York: Guilford Press.

Zitrin, C. M., Klein, D. F., & Woerner, M. G. (1978). Behavior therapy, supportive psychotherapy, imipramine, and phobias. *Archives of General Psychiatry, 37,* 63–72.

Zitrin, C. M., Klein, D. F., & Woerner, M. G. (1980). Treatment of agoraphobia with group exposure in vivo and imipramine. *Archives of General Psychiatry, 37,* 63–72.

Zitrin, C. M., Klein, D. F., Woerner, M. G., & Ross, D. C. (1983). Treatment of phobias: I. Comparison of imipramine hydrochloride and placebo. *Archives of General Psychiatry, 40,* 125–138.

Zuckerman, M., & Lubin, B. (1965). *Manual for the Multiple Affect Adjective Checklist.* San Diego, CA: Educational and Industrial Testing Service.

Zung, W. W. (1965). A self-rating depression scale. *Archives of General Psychiatry, 12,* 63–70.

INDEX

693